THE
RENAISSANCE
READER

David (Donatello), in the Bargello, Florence

THE RENAISSANCE READER

EDITED BY

Kenneth J. Atchity

ASSISTANT EDITOR, ROSEMARY MCKENNA

HarperCollins*Publishers*

FIRST EDITION

Designed by Irving Perkins Associates

Library of Congress Cataloging-in-Publication Data

The Renaissance reader / Kenneth J. Atchity, editor. — 1st ed.
　　　p.　cm.
　　Includes bibliographical references.
　　ISBN 0-06-270129-0
　　1. Renaissance.　2. European literature—Renaissance, 1450–1600—
History and criticism.　3. European literature—Renaissance,
1450–1600.　I. Atchity, Kenneth John.
　　PN721.R45　1996
　　809'.894—dc20　　　　　　　　　　　　　　　　　　　　95-26153

96 97 98 99 00 ❖/RRD 10 9 8 7 6 5 4 3 2 1

Lowry Nelson, Jr.
1926–1994
in memoriam boni amici, praeceptoris optimi

CONTENTS

PART 3
SEVENTEENTH CENTURY 279

PREFACE

This book seeks to present the widest possible perspective on the period known as "The Renaissance," beginning with its precursors Dante Alighieri and Francesco Petrarca and concluding with those who looked back in awe upon its exhausting splendors like Miguel de Cervantes, Oliver Cromwell, and Diego Velásquez. The selection is admittedly biased, especially in favor of the positive. Though bankruptcy, plague, prejudice, genocide, and witchcraft characterize this age, as they do the medieval period that preceded and the modern era that followed, the Renaissance still and rightly resonates in the modern mind for its idealism, energy, and exploration. My purpose is to introduce by being provocative and tantalizing, not by being scholarly or definitive. For the same reason I have not tried to present a "feminist revision" of the times, although included here are the strongest representative women's voices. On the subject of Renaissance women, I acknowledge in particular Margaret L. King and Albert Rabil, Jr.'s *Her Immaculate Hand: Selected Works By and About The Women Humanists of Quattrocento Italy,* Katharina M. Wilson's *Women Writers of the Renaissance and Reformation,* and Julia O'Faolain and Lauro Martines' *Not in God's Image.* During the Renaissance a remarkable number of strong and learned women came into power—from Elizabeth of England and Mary of Scotland, to Catherine dei Medici, Isabella d'Este, Marguerite de Navarre, and Isabella of Spain—all of them exhibiting the new humanism and the excitement of rediscovered human values. Nonetheless, despite the emergence of eloquent and learned female contributions, women by and large weren't encouraged to participate in the rebirth, and, when they did, managed to escape equal recognition. The Renaissance was, in the final analysis, male-dominated, and its magnificent achievements as such merit its being presented in its own image. Chronical arrangement allows the reader to set out on a journey from the earliest inklings on the Italian peninsula to the final convolutions in Spain. Since this was a period of unprecedented travel and communication, the interdependence of dreamers and doers is best seen in order as they appeared on the screen of history. The dates given are dates of publication or dates when the work entered into the human dialogue. Because each of these encounters with Renaissance expression is set in perspective by its own introduction, anyone unfamiliar with the Renaissance can just as easily dip in and out of this anthology serendipitously, following the paradoxical weave of Roman practicality and Greek idealism, folly and fortune, madness and method, optimism and cynicism, nationalism and individualism in any direction.

Students of the Renaissance—literature, art history, political science, philosophy, history, history of religion—will find here my favorite texts from Comp. Lit. 102, without the frustration of having their selection limited by a ten-week academic term. The selections can be used as stepping-stones to lead into deeper investigations. The themes, images, and characteristics discussed in the General Introduction can be used to map individual routes through the texts here reprinted.

A generous budget provided by HarperCollins for obtaining copyright permissions has allowed the consistent use of good translations. I have sometimes selected contemporary translations, both because of their excellence and to give today's reader tangible access to the flavor of the time itself.

I am grateful to Robert A. Kaplan, my editor, for the suggestion that I undertake this anthology; and to my Renaissance mentors at Georgetown and Yale, Thomas Bergin, A. Bartlett Giamatti, Thomas M. Greene, Davis Harding, Raymond Reno, Dante della Terza, Bernard Wagner, and Franklin Williams who filled me with love and admiration for this remarkable time in history. This book's advisory board—Michael J. B. Allen, Margaret Ferguson, Walter Kaiser, and Giuseppe Mazzotta—have been invaluable sources of general perspective and particular suggestions. Yale's Lowry Nelson, Jr., one of the truly learned "Renaissance men" whom I've been privileged to encounter in real life, has been a constant inspiration and close adviser not just on this book but in personal and professional matters throughout our long friendship, until his death in November, 1994. This collection, reflecting his diversity, is dedicated to Lowry's memory.

I also wish to thank the following:

Rosemary McKenna, for her research, suggestions, and commentary.

Sara van den Berg and Terry Stanfill, for feedback and encouragement along the way.

My reference agent, Sandra Watt.

John P. Ricco, who did the picture research under my direction.

Chi-Li Wong, for her assistance in putting the manuscript together.

My students at Occidental College.

Art Resources and *The Frick Collection* which allowed reproduction of the images from their excellent collections.

GENERAL INTRODUCTION

I will never forget my first live encounter with the Renaissance: my arrival by train in Florence. My nostrils filled with the city's unique fusion of pine, brick, and espresso as I made my first pilgrimage from the train station to the Uffizi Galleries. Along the way I was infused with admiration of:

- Ghirlandaio's frescoes in the church of Santa Maria Novella;
- Michelangelo's *David* in the Accademia,
- Donatello's pulpit and
- Michelangelo's library staircase in the Church of San Lorenzo and
- Michelangelo's princely tombs there in the *capella de' Medici*;
- Brunelleschi's majestic *duomo* of the cathedral of Santa Maria de' Fiori
- and its slender striped-marble *campanile,* by Giotto, looking down on
- Ghiberti's massive bronze doors of the Baptistery of San Giovanni;
- the Piazza della Signoria where Savonarola bonfired the "vanities," and was himself burned at the stake; and
- where Cellini's *Perseus with the Gorgon's Head* stands watch over
- the Medici *Palazzo Vecchio*;
- the church of Santa Croce, which holds
- the tombs of Michelangelo and Ghiberti, among those of many other great Florentines.

I found myself walking in awe through the *portici* of the Uffizi, sentineled by statues of the city's greatest citizens: Dante, Petrarca, Alberti, Boccaccio, Pico della Mirandola, Bruni, Machiavelli, Cellini, Galileo, Leonardo da Vinci, Lorenzo de' Medici, Vespucci, and many, many more. Awe gave way to exuberant reverence as I surveyed the towers, palaces, and churches of Florence, this Disneyland of the cultivated mind and spirit, from the hillside across the Arno River where the monument to her greatest son, Michelangelo, quotes these words in Latin: "If you seek my monument, look around you."

What had gone on in this tiny city so many years ago to account for such an explosion of cultural change?

The Renaissance, "the rebirth of western civilization," began here.

In creating this collection I seek to introduce you to the excitement and intrigue of the Renaissance I felt encountering Florence for that first time. The biggest obstacle to the reading public's access to Renaissance expression is bulk. The output of the Renaissance is prodigious, filling entire libraries from the Villa I Tatti on the slopes above Florence to the Huntington Library in California's San Marino. Thoughtful selection is required on behalf of the lay reader and the college student to provide the widest possible and most useful perspective without it being a mere "survey."

The Renaissance Reader is intended to be that useful selection by identifying the Renaissance's inspiriting origins in the idealistic thought of the exiled Florentines Dante Alighieri and Francesco Petrarca, and its nostalgic echoes in the mannered disillusionment of the Spaniards Miguel de Cervantes, Francisco Quevedo, and Diego Velásquez. The span represented in these pages is over three hundred fifty years—from 1300, the year Dante claimed he traveled through hell to see "our own image" in the face of God, to 1656 when Velásquez painted *The Royal Family*. By the time of John Milton's *Paradise Lost,* 1667, we are already clearly looking back on an age that was fast receding into memory. But during that time Europe saw the rise of the middle class, international banking, the city-states, and the modern universities; the multiplication of national and religious viewpoints; the emergence of scores of individual geniuses who brought a new way of seeing to the world; and the dawn of modern science, with its techniques of active, measured observation. A number of scholars today feel that the term "Renaissance" has, because of difficulties of precise definition, lost much of its usefulness to historians and literary critics. This volume is addressed, not to them, but to the general reader for whom the traditional word Renaissance remains intriguing and inspiring.

French historian Jules Michelet, writing in the mid-nineteenth century, was the first to use the term Renaissance to describe "the discovery by man of himself and of the world" in that seminal epoch of European history that followed the Middle Ages and preceded the Modern Era. Yet the Renaissance did not die, as some say, in England or in baroque Spain; its influence remains undiminished today, in nearly every realm of human experience, as the source of how we in the West interact with the world and think about ourselves. In its most sweeping sense, the Renaissance was a rediscovery of the natural world, its actual characteristics and physical boundaries; and even more importantly a redefinition, through self-definition, of humanity. Men could control their own destinies and master nature. Into the medieval system that had become static, the Renaissance introduced a dynamic new way of thinking, a new way of seeing. Because of the Renaissance revolution we still say, "I want to take a look at this for myself," or "I've got to see this with my own eyes" before we accept a reported "fact."

Rediscovery of the Greek classics of literature, mathematics, political science, and philosophy led to the encounter with Plato's master Socrates, whose life was an embodiment of the admonition inscribed on the portals of the oracle at Delphi: "Know thyself." Renaissance artists, scholars, writers, and rulers knew that they were living in a watershed time, and daringly and exuberantly reopened all the doors—brilliant and sordid, magnanimous and avaricious, sane and insane—to the almighty self that remains the focal reality of Western civilization to this day. Socrates' "god inside" (the Greek word was *daemon*) set him against the gods on Olympus and his fellow Athenians. In the Renaissance Socrates' *daemon* is reconceived of as "the self." The Roman Virgil had opened his imperial epic *The Aeneid* with "arms and the man, I sing." The Florentine Dante, at the fading of the Middle Ages, on the threshold of the

Renaissance, opened his *Commedia:* "In the middle of the journey of my life, in a dark wood, I found *myself.*" The exiled Dante turns his personal mid-life crisis into an all-encompassing statement about the workings of the universe! Reality in this new Socratic Athens will henceforth be defined as it is perceived by a thinking individual, not as it has been dictated by a divinely inspired organization. Question. Review. Rethink. Reevaluate. Redefine. From newfound freedom of thought comes rebirth.

Jacob Burckhardt, in his *The Civilization of the Renaissance in Italy* (1860), rightly claimed that the period's distinguishing characteristics included a sharp break with the Middle Ages, a rejection of its divine-centered values in favor of human-centered ones focused on the individual. Naturally the Renaissance preserved and transformed much of the Middle Ages. But by the fourteenth and fifteenth centuries, medieval thought had reached the apex of its social and artistic evolution. The result was a static model of reality that would be blown apart, partly in reaction to the imperfections of its own rigidity, in an atmosphere permeated with new economics and new politics. During Dante's lifetime, at the high point of the Middle Ages, the structure of the cosmos was seen as a series of concentric circles. The innermost, stationary circle was that of Earth, the outermost, that of God—whose center, by St. Thomas Aquinas' definition, was everywhere and whose circumference was nowhere. Hell, presided over by Satan, lay within the depths of the earth. Above the earth was the sphere of the moon, followed by Mercury, Venus, the Sun, Mars, Jupiter, and Saturn—in ever-widening circles. A circle of fixed stars surrounded Saturn, and beyond was a "crystalline circle" from which "the Empyrean" stretched out indefinitely. From the Greek Pythagoreans the Middle Ages had inherited the belief that ascension toward the Empyrean was ascension toward order and the Good; and that descent toward Earth was a movement toward chaos and Evil. Below the sphere of the moon—on Earth—all was disorderly, random, chaos—the domain of the capricious Lady Fortune.

The Renaissance, partly by the acceleration of scientific discoveries that made the medieval cosmography less and less tenable, reversed all this. Earth, though no longer the "center" of the cosmos, was because of its newfound planetary equality seen to be the proper center of human endeavor. Human beings, during their lifetimes on earth, were the creators of order, using their free will to counter the chaos of Fortune. "Men at some time are masters of their fates," says Cassius in Shakespeare's *Julius Caesar:* "The fault, dear Brutus, is not in our stars, but in ourselves, that we are underlings." Or, in the words of Pico della Mirandola's argument against astrology: "The stars are bodies and we are spirits; it cannot be allowed that a bodily, and therefore inferior, being should effect our higher self and limit our freedom." Instead of seeing Earth as the sink of the universe, a vale of sorrow, into which Evil sank toward its natural level, the Renaissance saw Earth as a launching pad, a petri dish, a vale of opportunity for self-definition. For all the glorious self-expression this revolutionary attitude gave rise to, an increasingly dear price would be paid. Without the certainty of divine authority in the governance of human behavior, humans faced the endless task of defining themselves through challenge. Challenge leads to success, but also to failure. By giving themselves the right to fail, men and women of the Renaissance understood that they were risking not only their sanity but also their immortal souls.

Although the Renaissance evolved as it commenced in one country after another, and although its diversity beggars any final simplification, its distinguishing characteristics, themes, and images—and the paradoxes each reflected—are easily identified.

Humanism This term is given to describe the first philosopher-scholars of early Renaissance Florence, underwritten by the Medici family, who reintroduced Plato, Aristotle, Plotinus, and other classical Greek thinkers by importing translators from Byzantium. For the first time since the fall of the Roman Empire Europeans had direct access to the full scope of Aristotelian and Platonic thought, which had been carefully contained throughout the Middle Ages by expurgated "authorized versions" in the hands of Latin monks. At the same time that the writings of the Greeks were rediscovered by western thinkers, archaeologists were digging up original Greek art and its Roman imitations in the neglected ruins of Italy, providing a powerful impetus for a new *naturalism and secularism*.

Naturalism and secularism Although the sacred is never far from consideration in the Renaissance, if only as a stylistic model, reviewing nature with open eyes led to increasing secularism. Abandoning the flat and stylized iconography of the Middle Ages—by which ecclesiastical doctrine so dominated artistic expression that the greatest artworks of medieval times, the cathedrals, are by and large anonymous—artists, following Greek models, celebrated the natural lines of the human body and stamped their private vision, from the sublime to the tortured, on their paintings, drawings, architecture, and sculptures. Because time had erased the color from Greek statuary, serendipitously a paradigm of sublimity and purity was conveyed to the Renaissance discoverers. The vibrant white marble figures of gods and goddesses, men and women, fed into the Renaissance penchant for *idealism*.

Idealism The grace achieved by the Middle Ages at its most harmonious is transformed by the Renaissance into humanistic idealism. Propelled by Marsilio Ficino's 1482 translation of Plato's dialogues into Latin, the belief in human perfectibility dominates major expressions, from Pico della Mirandola's "On the Dignity of Man" and Baldassare Castiglione's *Courtier* to Sir Thomas Elyot's *Governour* and Sir Thomas More's *Utopia*. Man is capable of defining his own nature, and of fulfilling that nature's noblest potential. The primary tenets of Renaissance idealism included:

- the immortality of the human spirit against the corruptibility of the flesh;
- a vision of the ideal commonwealth presided over by the ideal ruler;
- the concept of intellectual, asexual "Platonic love" as the highest form of bonding between two individuals.

Renaissance idealism often took expression in a literary genre that is the ancestor of motivational how-to books: the "institute" or "curriculum," a dialogue or treatise devoted to laying out the rules for an ideal prince, courtier, governor, teacher, housewife—or accountant (Frater Lucas Pacioli's *Treatise on Double-entry Bookkeeping),* or archer (Roger Ascham's *Toxophilus,* "The School of Shooting," the great-grandfather of this century's *Zen and the Art of Archery* and *The Inner Game of Tennis).* Like the self-help books of today, the Renaissance institutes pursued a "better life," the golden age, a utopia, "getting centered," and "getting our heads straight."

Individualism The breakdown of the Church's authority, accelerated by the decadence into which the papacy had fallen, left a vacuum in behavioral standards that was immediately occupied by individual genius as the fulcrum for human definition. Beginning with Dante's autobiographical epic quest and Petrarca's self-defining "Letter to Posterity," Renaissance thought is characterized by the thinker's awareness, and celebration, of his own importance—until we reach the ultimate philosophical extension of this trend in René Descartes' "I think; therefore, I am." Michelangelo, when told that someone was laying claim to the *Pietà,* rushed into St. Peter's and carved his name in the marble. But individualism, multiplied, leads to anarchy. The "downside" of the phenomenon is seen in the self-defeating imagination of Cervantes' Don Quixote, and the machiavellian cynicism of Shakespeare's Iago, who remarks, while his playacting is destroying his overly trustful master Othello: "I am not what I am" (on a bad day, because we inherited the "modular self" from the Renaissance, we might say: "I can relate to that!"). The rise of the middle class, of merchants and shopkeepers and artisans, is the economic manifestation of this tidal wave of individualism.

Exploration and discovery Especially during the late fifteenth and early sixteenth centuries, geographical explorations, beginning with Christopher Columbus' voyages to "the new world," literally redefined the world. No wonder Ludovico Ariosto's epic hero takes a trip to the moon, Christopher Marlowe's Faustus makes a pact with the devil, or François Rabelais' comic narrator descends into the mouth of a giant. Literature was reflecting psychologically the geographical and scientific explorations that threw all values into question. From mathematics to sexual politics, from mechanics to music and art, from astronomy to political governance, anatomy to melancholy, men and women in the Renaissance more than at any previous time in western history—with the possible exception of classical Athens—threw their energy into exploring themselves and the world around them by direct observation instead of through a lens inherited from tradition.

Scientific method Rediscovery of classical thought led naturally to a refusal to accept the monolithic medieval orthodoxy, with its insistence on philosophical grounding consistent with Catholic moral teachings. The question "Am I right?" asked by a pious medieval scholar of his hierarchical superior before accepting the results of his private investigations, became a rhetorical statement in the Renaissance. As an expression of individualism, observation became the primary method in astronomy, where Nicolaus Copernicus' thesis that the earth moves around the sun, and Tycho Brahe and Galileo Galilei's telescopes, refuted the Ptolemaic theory that the earth was the center of the universe; geography, where the navigators, freed to follow their eyes instead of the dictates of superstition, sailed over the horizon to explore "the ends of the earth"; and anatomy, where the dissections of Vesalius, Leonardo da Vinci, and William Harvey revolutionized our view of the workings of the human body.

Fragmentation and nationalism As the Emperors sought to hold the Holy Roman Empire together, pride in local heritage, and in the vernacular languages and dialects that heritage spawned, accelerated the forces of individualism onto large plateaus of expression. The wars of religion between England and France, and between England and Spain, were as much over national self-interest as over their alleged spiritual causes.

All these general characteristics of the Renaissance had their impact on every realm of human endeavor. Music, primarily under French impetus, moved from the monotony of the Middle Ages to polyphony and harmonic experimentation, faster and more complicated tempos and rhythms, and a more modern chordal structure; music was considered part of a good humanistic education. Art progressed from stylized and iconic stiffness of depiction, alienating man from his own vital nature, to stunningly sensual naturalism, *chiaroscuro,* a return to Greco-Roman roots, precise though idealized characterization, and heroic representations of Massaccio ("The Expulsion of Adam and Eve from Paradise," "Peter Baptising," "The Cure of Petronilla"), whose Eve in "Adam and Eve before the Fall" is the first beautiful nude female figure of modern art; Paolo Uccello; Sandro Botticelli; Leonardo da Vinci; Michelangelo Buonarroti; Raphael; Fra Filippo Lippi; Titian. Founders of the "Flemish school," Hubert and Jan van Eyck ("The Adoration of the Lamb") represent the Renaissance in the Netherlands; Pieter Brueghel ("The Sack of Rome"), Albrecht Dürer ("The Adoration of the Trinity") and portraitist Hans Holbein ("More," "Erasmus," "Cromwell") in Germany; painter ("Charles VII") and illustrator Jean Fouquet in France; Rincon and El Greco ("The Adoration of the Shepherds") in Spain. Education moved from the traditionalism of the medieval universities stressing indoctrination by the authoritative wisdom of the Church Fathers, to the Renaissance ideal of the authoritative individual—the self-educated man of genius who, albeit aided by the rediscovery of movable type, learns what he needs as much from the book of life, and the scope of whose intellectual curiosity is infinite. In economics, things moved from the feudal European system based on divine-right monarchs, land grants, and tribute levied from those inferior on the hierarchical feeding chain, to an interdependent system based on individual effort enhanced by mercantile enterprise and military inventiveness.

All this diversification was embodied in the concept of "the Renaissance man," to whom nothing human is alien, who at most is a magnificently polymathic visionary like Leonardo da Vinci or Sir Philip Sidney employing artistry and words to ennoble the spirit; and, at least, a delightfully hedonistic dilettante like Pietro Aretino, or Calderón de la Barca, employing words to create dreamlike illusion. The first men to whom the epithet "Renaissance man" might arguably be applied are Dante Alighieri and Francesco Petrarca.

Dante's life is one of political turmoil amidst the Guelf-Ghibelline wars that tortured his beloved Florence. His literary ambitions were encyclopedic. He interrupted his *Convivio,* aimed at presenting all knowledge in a single work, to pursue the vision that inspired the *Divine Comedy,* which may well be in its scope of vision the most universal of all human poems. The Latin *Convivio* was medieval in concept and form. The Tuscan *Commedia* contained elements that must be identified with the great cultural rebirth. The author himself is the hero of this epic, which has been called "Dante's novel of the self." He boldly sets out from earth to explore the supernatural worlds of time and eternity. Along the way Dante's pilgrim redefines the nature of vision itself, and finally recognizes the form of human nature in the face of its creator.

Francesco Petrarca, who was so envious of his fellow Florentine that he refused to refer to Dante directly by name, expressed this new sense of the pivotal importance of the self by following his instincts into a multiplicity of careers. Insisting that the only important subject of human thought is man himself, he wrote and thought endlessly, leaving behind, in addition to his vast formal writing, letters to friends, family, classical authors, and even one "to posterity." In his letters, which since Roman times he was the first to collect, we find a mind that resembles less the Middle Ages into which he was born, than the Renaissance that he both personified and inspired. He was the first man to retire—from the hubbub of the worldly papal court at Avignon—for intellectual reasons. Like Montaigne's retirement, Petrarca's was dedicated to study, to improving and refining his own mind and spirit. He saw himself as a man of many parts, playing the roles of:

- Christian, seeking to tame his natural arrogance;
- student, whose role is to listen carefully to authority and to *question* everything;
- scholar, who relentlessly searched for ancient manuscripts and provided for their proper care and analysis;
- linguist, who imported a monk from Constantinople to teach him Greek so that he could read Homer in the original;
- traveler, who enjoyed both leaving and returning home, and writing about them, and who became the first man to climb a mountain for the sake of climbing it;
- commentator, whose scope of interests was boundless;
- courtly lover, whose Italian sonnets to "Laura" remain his greatest works;
- poet laureate, who had himself crowned as such by the king.

Yet he also enjoyed the role of "the humble man," disclaiming his own studied accomplishments, in a letter to Francesco Bruni:

You make an orator of me, a historian, philosopher, and poet, and finally even a theologian. You would certainly not do so if you were not persuaded by one whom it is hard to disbelieve: I mean Love. Perhaps you might be excused if you did not extol me with titles so overwhelmingly great: I do not deserve to have them heaped on me. But let me tell you, my friend, how far I fall short of your estimation. It is not my opinion only; it is a fact: I am nothing of what you attribute to me. What am I then? I am a fellow who never quits school, and not even that, but a backwoodsman who is roaming around through the lofty beech trees all alone, humming to himself some silly little tune, and—the very peak of presumption and assurance—dipping his shaky pen into his inkstand while sitting under a bitter laurel tree. I am not so fortunate in what I achieve as passionate in my work, being much more a lover of learning than a man who has got much of it. I am not so very eager to belong to a definite school of thought; I am striving for truth. Truth is difficult to discover, and, being the most humble and feeble of all those who try to find it, I lose confidence in myself often enough. So much do I fear to become entangled in errors that I throw myself into the embrace of doubt instead of truth. Thus I have gradually become a proselyte of the Academy as one of the big crowd, as the very last of this humble flock; I do not believe in my faculties, do not affirm anything, and doubt every single thing, with the single exception of what I believe is a sacrilege to doubt.

Obviously Petrarca's aim, like Socrates', was not to "find his niche," as medieval advisers might have insisted, but to "follow his bliss" in whatever quixotic directions his "inner god" dictated.

The gap between the Renaissance and Middle Ages may best be seen in major themes and images of this period.

The Great Chain of Being The medieval world demanded "a place for everything, and everything in its place" in the infinite order and ultimate unity of God's great creation. As A. E. Lovejoy eloquently argues, the metaphor of the "chain of being," dating back to Homer's *Iliad* and Plato's *Timaeus,* had been given focal importance: At the top of the chain is God himself. Below Him, the whole creation is arrayed in hierarchical order from angels (themselves arranged in hierarchies) to the lowliest of beasts and plants. Human beings, somewhere in the middle of the chain, occupied links of "higher" or "lower" status depending on whether they were popes and emperors or serfs. Where the medieval "great chain" disallowed *vertical* movement (a serf does not act like a pope), the Renaissance shook the chain metaphor in every direction. The Renaissance individual could play many roles, profess multiple careers; he was free to move up and down the chain, aspiring to nobility, sinking to venality. The Renaissance transported us from the linear interpretation of human behavior to a modular, relative way of conceiving man's role in the cosmos and as determiner of his own lifestyle. The self becomes not an "obedient servant" of the feudal lord, but an explorer of "undiscover'd countries" psychological, moral, and geographical. With the breakdown of a static concept of the "great chain of being," a Michelangelo can dare to refuse the Pope's invitation, and a Henry VIII can be "Defender of the Faith," refined musician, glutton at the table, and promiscuous in bed. Exploration was both from one side of the brain to another (the brain that Vesalius dared to dissect) and from one side of the earth to the other (that Columbus, Magellan, Vasco da Gama, Vespucci, and Sir Francis Drake transected).

Proteus Renaissance man was "protean," changing shapes and masks like the slippery god faced by Menelaos in Homer's *Odyssey.* If you hold him fast through the shape-changing you might obtain the truth from him, but holding him fast is not an easy task. He is "a man for all seasons," "all things to all men." The truth of character, in Renaissance thought, becomes hidden beneath appearances. If words could create, imitate, and ennoble, they could also falsify, deceive, and project dangerous illusions. At one end of the spectrum from divine to demonic, Proteus is the energetic flexibility of lightning; at the other, the dark magic of Faust. Machiavelli advises his ideal prince to master the art of dissimulation, and Rabelais compares his satirical novel to the *sileni,* ugly little apothecary boxes that contain precious drugs.

Dream, Vision, Insight Medieval vision aspired to be harmonious and unanimous, looking to churchly authorities for common interpretations within the accepted boundaries of orthodox doctrine. Although a few mystics like St. Teresa of Avila and St. John of the Cross continued to receive visions from above, the Renaissance was dominated by the dreams of the individual, their claims for universal power culminating with Calderón de la Barca's statement, "Life is a dream. Even dreams are dreams." Human imagination began to replace divine inspiration. Leonardo imagined that the air was filled with images and that the artist's challenge was to seek them out, just as Michelangelo believed that he could "see" the statue hidden within the block of marble. The Renaissance replaced the monolith of communal myth with the multiplicity of individual dreams and visions. If the individual could focus his dream and execute it successfully, no dream was impossible— whether it was a trip to the moon, a voyage over the edge of the earth, or a descent into the unexplored caverns of the self. The daring dreamer could shape a new myth, in the sense of Joseph Campbell's, "Dream is private myth; myth is public dream." The private myths of Hieronymus Bosch and El Greco, successfully executed in their compellingly idiosyncratic paintings, have become part of Western humanity's common myth. Against the medieval question, "Does my vision comply with the divine will?" the Renaissance artist posed the question: "Does my vision express my dream powerfully enough to move others to share it?" The seriousness of medieval "dream vision" is forever overturned in Shakespeare's *Midsummer Night's Dream,* as Bottom the Weaver awakens from a drugged sleep to find he has the ears of an ass, his commentary turning his name into a metaphor for the unconscious itself:

> I have had a most rare vision. I have had a dream, past the wit of man to say what dream it was. . . . The eye of man hath not heard, the ear of man hath not seen, man's hand is not able to taste, his tongue to conceive, nor his heart to report, what my dream was; I will get Peter Quince to write a ballad of this dream: it shall be called Bottom's Dream; because it hath no bottom. . . .

When the dreamy Don Quixote descends into the "bottomless" cave of the Montesinos, Cervantes, like his British contemporary, is exploring the same awareness of the central role of dreams in human life. As for Shakespeare, for Cervantes the source of dreams is not divine influence, but man's own unconscious ("that obscure region below" to which there is no "certain or determined path"). But the excitement of "all-licens'd" dreaming has its downside: the veracity of anyone's visualization is essentially unquestionable, and consequently all values are up for grabs.

Homo faber Because Renaissance thinkers had the courage of their inner visions, the Greco-Roman concept of "man, the maker" became, for them, the highest justification for freedom and experimentation. The Greek Sophist Protagoras had said, "Man is the measure of all things; of things that are, that they are, and of things that are not, that they are not." Though he had spoken metaphorically, the Renaissance took him literally and set out to measure everything. The Renaissance maker makes by dissecting, analyzing, *measure for measure,* until by knowing intimately his materials he recreates them into the dreamed image of his private myth. He is measuring time and eternity, the human body and the terrestrial globe, the distance between planets and the distance between shoelaces. When he descends into the bottomless cave, Don Quixote laments not having brought a cattle bell to measure the distance of his descent; and when Pantagruel's army is caught in a rainstorm, the giant sticks out his arm to shelter them "as a hen shelters her chicks," but there is no room for Alcofribas, the storyteller, "because a foot is a foot and not fourteen inches." And, of course, Renaissance man is measuring himself, his own limits; heroically he has given himself permission to fail by going beyond those limits because he knows there is no other sure way to measure them: "May your reach always exceed your grasp." Whether it be Leonardo da Vinci's endless sketches of inventions, Thomas Deloney's rowdy clothiers, Pietro Aretino's stinging pasquinades, or Marguerite de Navarre's stately storytellers, the sheer delight in measured making—artifacts, feasts, arguments, and identities—resounds from one end of the Renaissance to the other.

The Golden Age Where the ancient Greeks believed that the golden age was in the remote past, and the medieval Church preached that the golden age lay after death when man achieves perfection in the world beyond the earth, the Renaissance recovered the Augustan Roman belief that the golden age was *here* and *now*. How could a Florentine living in the *quattrocento* not think his own time was golden? With new discoveries in optics, navigation, and archaeology the subject of daily news reports, the time was indeed "a marvel to behold"—and in this sense is perhaps most like our own. Columbus, in his logbook, repeatedly wonders if he's found the legendary "earthly paradise." What is the "golden age," but a dream? Shakespeare creates a dreamlike and magical "brave new world" in *The Tempest*. From this belief in the living dream of the golden age comes the Renaissance adherence to the hedonistic philosophy of *carpe diem*. If you are living in a dream, then you must play the part. Prince Hal scolds the bon vivant Falstaff for showing a coward's reluctance on the battlefield:

HAL.   Thou owest God a death.
Falstaff.   'Tis not due yet. I would be loathe to pay him before his day.

For Renaissance hedonists like Falstaff, life is too exciting to risk for questionable values like "honor." There's too much left to do, too many games left to play:

Homo ludens   The beneficiary of the Renaissance cornucopia of novelty is "man, the player" for whom the world is a sandbox and whose life is a game. In the works of Boccaccio, Rabelais, Castiglione, and especially of Cervantes, the childlike nature of Renaissance man is at its most serious when it comes to games. Playing games is recognized as an effective metaphor for managing one's own life and taking charge of it; seeing life as a game board provides the perspective required for precise action under pressure. Gamesmanship and "spin control," after all, is what Machiavelli is proposing to the ideal prince, who must make his judgments based not on abstract moral or social concepts but purely on the basis of efficacy: What does it take to win?

Life as a stage and man as the actor   In the human-centered Renaissance perspective, the world, seen from its furthest boundaries, becomes a stage. All this action led to a stress on style, a newfound appreciation of the stimulating, involving dramatic. The eloquent con man (Machiavelli's prince, Shakespeare's Falstaff, or Tirso de Molina's playboy of Seville), as well as the crafty rogue (Giovanni Boccaccio's Friar Onion, François Rabelais' Panurge, or Thomas Nashe's Jack Wilton) are admired equally. The player, with his "modular self," takes on characters: knaves, fools, drunkards, lovers, courtiers, questing knights, god/men, giants, directors, seekers, utopians, commentators, counselors, explorers, confidants, gossips. Multiple role-playing as the Renaissance ideal for the self-fulfilled individual is, at its most sublime, expressed most eloquently by Juan Luis Vives' *A Fable About Man*; and by Shakespeare's *As You Like It* (Act 2, scene 3), when Jaques explains to the banished Duke:

All the world's a stage,
And all the men and women, merely players;
They have their exits and their entrances,
And one man in his time plays many parts

Prometheus   The Greek hero who stole fire from heaven is another constant Renaissance model. In his most heroic moment, he is the patron saint of the

Renaissance, stealing fire from the gods to enlighten humanity—as Pico della Mirandola's oration on human dignity frees men to aspire to divinity. But Prometheus is punished for his heroism by the gods themselves, by having his liver plucked out for all eternity. At his most demonic, Prometheus is the devil that possesses the overreaching individual. Robert Burton's *The Anatomy of Melancholy*, at the waning of the Renaissance, seeks to explain the horrors of excessive visionary ambition that Marlowe depicts in *Doctor Faustus* and Shakespeare in *Macbeth*.

Self-confidence and self-doubt These are modern terms that may trace their conceptual origins to the Renaissance. Confidence in the power of the self leads to exploration, to unimagined successes but also to nightmarish failures that, in turn, plant the seeds of modern *angst*. Self-doubt comes only in a worldview that honors the self above all, and is a determining characteristic that the Western psyche has inherited from its rebirth.

Folly The character of the "wise fool," as Walter Kaiser has traced it in *Praisers of Folly*, goes back to Plato's account of his master Socrates in *The Apology*. Socrates, though he knew nothing by his own account, discovered he was wiser than all others because, as he interviewed his Athenian contemporaries, he found they *thought* they knew something when in fact they did not. From Thomas à Kempis' *Imitation of Christ* to Cervantes' *Don Quixote*, with stops along the way for Erasmus' Folly, Skelton's *Collyn Clout*, Rabelais' Panurge, and Shakespeare's Falstaff and Lear's Fool, the Renaissance yearns for the childlike innocence it has forever left behind with the dawning of ingenious self-consciousness. Beyond the Fool's loving and instinctual wisdom is this character's usefulness as a mask for the satirist's reforming purpose. If Folly is the source, how can the reporter be blamed for the truth of what Folly says? Falstaff's speeches to Prince Hal about "counterfeit man" and Panurge's observations about the uselessness of Pantagruel's education can be ignored by the ego, because they issue from "all-licens'd" fools, at the same time that they are assimilated by the superego which recognizes the truth in the fool's observation. The fool's lack of responsibility to any power but that of truth is yet another aspect of rebirth.

Insanity The movement from monolith to multiplicity, from unity to fragmentation eventually led to awareness that self-definition must ultimately throw the very notion of sanity into question. And indeed insanity is the other side of the coin from "brilliant inspiration," the natural outcome of rejecting the institutionalized sanity of the Middle Ages. An era bursting with dreams is flirting with madness; and, in its intrepid search for self-determined method, Renaissance man constantly courted insanity. The faces of Renaissance madness are as diverse as humanity itself.

The *Renaissance Reader* allows the men and women of this turbulent time of change to speak in their own voices, sane and insane, brilliant and mundane, inspired and possessed, oblivious and incisive—to today's reader who will recognize in their contradictions, pretensions, and self-analysis his own. Such flaws as this anthology may have I hope may be seen as those of the Renaissance itself, and eloquently hath the Renaissance answered them in Prospero's announcement, from Shakespeare's *The Tempest* Act 4, scene 1:

Our revels now are ended. These our actors,
As I foretold you, were all spirits, and
Are melted into air, into thin air;

And like the baseless fabric of this vision,
The cloud-capp'd towers, the gorgeous palaces,
The solemn temples, the great globe itself,
Yes, all which it inherit, shall dissolve;
And like this insubstantial pageant faded,
Leave not a rack behind: we are such stuff
As dreams are made on; and our little life
Is rounded with a sleep. . . .

It is the final irony of the Renaissance that a period that began with the breakdown of the established medieval order should wind down with the self-conscious breakdown of the human mind. Infinite expansiveness may lead to infinite chaos. Unlimited freedom brings unlimited joy, but also unlimited pain. Encountering the Renaissance directly, as this book allows, may then be a cautionary tale. We are living in a world where the bombardment of dreams, visions, and images is perhaps the most threatening, and most challenging, aspect of human life. Our ability to cope with that bombardment, the key to our capacity to survive and progress as a species, may be enhanced by understanding where men and women of the Renaissance succeeded, and where they failed, in withstanding the images unleashed by the new freedom. Echoing its explosive initial energy, the Renaissance draws to a close with exuberance intact, even in the face of diminution. The sleep of life Macbeth "does murder" with his overactive ambitions. But the "sleep of death" is accepted freely as the ultimate "consummation, devoutly to be wished" after a fully experienced life of exhausting explorations. Medieval man may have lived a life of equal misery and equal joy, but he lived it in servitude to an infinitely superior God. Renaissance man made the agony and the ecstasy his own. The Spanish philosopher José Ortega y Gasset wrote, "I think the only immoral thing is for a being not to spend every instant of its life with the utmost intensity." Surely the Renaissance bequeathed to us that standard of noble behavior, that "impossible ideal," as its most challenging legacy. And though we may not be more content, we are essentially richer for it. The Renaissance was a time of joy and terror, elation and anxiety, and in our own time where anxiety has thrown joy into its millennial shadow, reacquainting ourselves with our rebirth may renew our joie de vivre.

PART 1

FOURTEENTH CENTURY

Portrait of Dante (Giotto), in the Bargello, Florence

DANTE ALIGHIERI (1265–1321)

COMMEDIA

The Divine Comedy (1307?–20)

Perhaps the most lyrical and precise sustained poem ever written, Dante's *Commedia* traces its origins to the ancient epic tradition and its influence to the modern "novel of the self." Its heroic quest moves the hero from earth to hell, from purgatory to paradise, then back to earth again where the hero, returned, becomes the storyteller who leads the reader on the same quest for understanding both the cosmos and the self. Dante's break with the epic tradition was to make the hero *himself*, Dante Alighieri: "In the middle of the journey of our life, *I found myself. . .* " Because of this brilliant, even arrogant, innovation, Dante's *Commedia* transcends the medieval character of its orthodox allegorical and religious dimensions to foreshadow the Renaissance. Dante chose to write his masterpiece not in the traditional Latin of his earlier works, but in the Tuscan vernacular because, as he explains in his letter to Can Grande della Scala, the *Inferno* treats of coarse and vulgar things; and because, despite the roughness of this first cantica (the *Commedia* is divided into three *cantiche: Inferno, Purgatorio,* and *Paradiso*), it is ultimately, by Greco-Roman definition, a "comedy" since its ending is happy, revealing that free will, guided by grace, can lead the questing pilgrim to the ultimate source of his quest: identification with the creator of the cosmos. Yet the pilgrim-hero of the story would never have succeeded in his pilgrimage from time to eternity were it not for the guidance of his pagan master, the epic poet Virgil (whom Dante meets in this first canto). Dante has embodied Christian grace as the single sufficient source of redemption with a pagan master! At journey's end (in *Paradiso* 33), the pilgrim Dante stands face to face with God and discovers reflected in the divine countenance, as though in a mirror, "our own image." As arrogantly iconoclastic as it may have seemed to Dante's contemporaries to identify the face of God with the visage of humanity, the identification has both past and future validity. On the one hand, it harks back to the words of the Bible's *Genesis:* "In His own image and likeness He created them"; on the other, the identification is a harbinger of Renaissance expressions like Pico della Mirandola's oration, "On the Dignity of Man" and Michelangelo's ceiling of the Sistine Chapel. Louis Biancolli's graceful and accurate translation allows us to appreciate the modernity of Dante's epic midlife crisis.

INFERNO
Canto 1

Halfway along the journey of our life,
Having strayed from the right path and lost it,
I awoke to find myself in a dark wood.
O how hard it is to tell what it was like,
That wild and mighty and unfriendly forest,
The very thought of which renews my fear!
So bitter was it that death could be no worse.
But, to reveal what benefit it brought me,
I shall tell of the other things I found.
How I came to be there, I can scarcely say,
I was so overwhelmed with sleep
When I began to wander off the road.
I soon came to the bottom of a hill
Where the valley that had impaled my heart
With terror came to an end.
I looked high up the hill and could see its back
Already clad in the rays of that star
Which guides other men along the proper way.
And then I felt a lessening of the terror
Which had lingered in the lake of my heart
That entire night, which was so cruelly long.
And just as a man, panting from exhaustion,
Emerges from the sea and feels the shore,
Then turns to glance back at the perilous deep,
So my mind, that had not yet stopped running,
Turned round to contemplate the vale again
That not one person had ever left alive.
My tired body having had some rest,
I resumed my way along that bare incline,
Keeping my lower foot at all times firmer.

Suddenly, just where the ground began to rise,
I saw in front of me an agile beast
Whose body was all covered with a dappled fur.
Never moving out of sight, it stood there
And so completely blocked the way
That several times I started to go back.
The time was just about the start of day.
The sun was moving up with all those stars
That were with him when the Love of God
First set in motion all those lovely things.
Both the sweet season and the time of day
Gave me cause to hope that some good still
    would come

Of having met that beast with the spotted skin.
But that did not make me less terrified
When in a flash a lion sprang into view
Who seemed to be advancing towards me
With his head high and in such a famished rage
That even the air itself appeared to fear him;
And a she-wolf, too, who seemed to have loaded
Every known craving into her leanness
And blighted many lives already:
The terror emanating from her look
Laid on my spirit such a heavy gloom
That I gave up hope of climbing to the top.
As is he who happily amasses wealth,
Until the day comes that he loses it,
And then, each time he thinks, cries and grows
    sad,
Such was I when that unsatiated beast,
Who step by step was slowly drawing close,
Kept pushing me to where the sun is silent.
While I was hastening down the slope,
There suddenly appeared before my eyes
A man whose voice seemed weak from long
    disuse.
When I caught sight of him in that bleak place,
I cried out to him: "Have pity on me,
Whatever you are, living man or ghost!"
"No man am I," he said, "though at one time I
    was.
Both my parents came from Lombardy, and
    both
Were Mantuans as well.

I was born while Caesar was alive, though late,
And I lived in Rome while good Augustus ruled
And in a day of false and lying gods.
I was a poet, and sang of that just son
Of Anchises who had come from Troy
When all proud Ilium went up in flames.
But why are you going back to such distress?
Why not climb the delightful mountain, which
Is the reason and beginning of all joy?"
"So you are that Virgil, and that fountain,
Which spreads so broad a river of discourse,"
I answered him with shamed and humble brow.
"O light and honor of all other poets,
May I now profit from the study and great love
I long applied to fathoming your book.

You are my author, and my teacher, too;
You are the only one from whom I took
That style of beauty which has won me
    praise.
Look there, at that beast who forced me to turn
    back;
Help me to escape her, O noted sage!
She makes my pulses throb, and all my veins."
"You must take a different direction now,
If you want to get out of this wild place,"
He answered, when he saw that I was crying.
"This animal who makes you scream with fear
Never lets anyone at all get past her.
She blocks his way and finally she slays him.
And she is so evil and malevolent,
She never satisfies her gluttonous wants,
But after a full meal is hungrier still.
Many are the animals with whom she mates,
And there shall be many more, until the day
A greyhound comes to bring her painful death
That nourishes itself on neither land nor wealth,
But feeds instead on wisdom, love, and virtue.
The place of its birth between two Feltros lies.
May he be the Saviour of humble Italy,
For which the maid Camilla gave her life, as did
The wounded Nisus, Turnus, Euryalus.
The hound shall chase the wolf through every
    town,
Until at last he puts her back in Hell,

Where jealousy and hate first turned her loose.
For your own welfare, I believe, therefore,
That you should follow me, and I shall guide
    you
Out of this place into the timeless dwelling
Where you shall hear the cries of desperation
And see the tortured souls of ancient men
Who scream out loud for second death.
Others you will see there who are content
To live in fire, because they hope one day—
Come when it may—to join the blessed ranks.
If you wish to ascend to where those are,
A soul shall come far worthier than I
To whom I shall entrust you when I leave.
The truth is that the Emperor who rules up
    there,
Because I was a rebel to his law,
Will not admit me into his city.
Everywhere else he commands; there he is
    King.
That is his city, and that his high throne, too.
Happy the man he chooses to let come!"
And I said to him: "Poet, I implore you,
By that very God whom you did not know,
To help me flee this evil thing and worse,
By conducting me to the place you speak of,
That I may behold St. Peter's gate
And those whom you make out to be so sad."
Then he set off, and I went on behind.

FRANCESCO PETRARCA (PETRARCH) (1304–74)

Letter to Posterity (1351)

Petrarch is the first to whom the title "a Renaissance man" may arguably be attributed. His egoism, according to Thomas Greene, "was so monumental and so acute that it was an event in European intellectual history"; yet his articulate introspection heralded a new era in which the psychology of the self joined philosophy as a major human preoccupation. Priding himself on being a recluse, lover, scholar-philologist, poet laureate, public voice, Christian, friend, and wanderer, Petrarch refused to be limited to existing on any single link of the great chain of being. His restlessness of body, mind, and soul was a hallmark of the dawning era—defining the very concept of "the Renaissance man" as that now-familiar paradigm would be exemplified in Leonardo da Vinci, Marguerite de Navarre, and Sir Thomas More. Petrarch established the new paradigm as *anthropocentric.* Where Dante had turned with spiritual and intellectual longing to the outermost spheres, Petrarch was introspectively expanding human potential by exploring his own mind and abilities.

Petrarch's new paradigm had its roots in classical Greco-Roman civilization, in which human achievement gradually eroded a belief in the power of primitive gods. Petrarch's disaffection with his own times made him look to the imagined grandeur of the classical past, without discarding his loyalties to the Roman Catholic church. "Christ is my God," he wrote. "Cicero, on the other hand, is the prince of the language I use." In his *Familiar Letters* Petrarch rewords St. Augustine and Seneca: "Nothing except the spirit is admirable," foreshadowing Ficino, Pico, and other Renaissance thinkers who redefine humanity's place in the universal hierarchy in terms of freedom and uniqueness. Petrarch was a prolific writer of letters (to his contemporaries, as well as to classical authors), as well as an inveterate traveler and professional guest gladly patronized by the most powerful families of his time. His letters reveal intense self-awareness, a mind almost compulsively greedy for experience, exemplifying American poet Wallace Stevens' observation, "It is never satisfied, the mind, never." Petrarch wrote to Matteo Longo: "I read, write, and think; this is my life, my joy."

Characteristic of his lack of false modesty, in 1341, Petrarch, imitating his classical Roman idols, arranged for himself to be crowned poet laureate in Rome by King Robert of Naples; then he tells us that he was amazed at the event. Petrarch renounced the study of law for the study of literature and "moral philosophy" because he felt the latter would lead to a more honest way of life. His ambivalence about cities, and the solution he found in the solitude of Vaucluse, harks back to the Roman Horace's love for his country place, and looks forward to Sir Philip Sidney's *Arcadia*. The "overwhelming love affair" Petrarch speaks of was that involving Laura (possibly Laure de Noves, the wife of Hugues de Sade), whom Petrarch met in the church of St. Claire in 1327; and for whom he composed his *Canzoniere*, the lyric poems which are his strongest claim to literary fame. His "epistle to posterity" reinvokes the classical belief in the immortality of the written word, but at the same time places writing in the service of personality. The voice of the writer of this letter, purportedly speaking to us rather than to his contemporaries, is immediately accessible at the same time that it is engaged in reshaping the reputation of the author to his own image and likeness. As such it may be properly called satirical, employing honesty as an ironic mask for self-justification.

You may perhaps have heard something about me—although it is doubtful that my poor little name may travel far in space and time. Still, you may by chance want to know what sort of man I was or what was the fate of my works, especially of those whose reputation may have persisted, or whose name you may have vaguely heard. There will be various opinions on this score, for most people's words are prompted not by truth but by whim. There is no measure for praise or blame. But I was one of your own flock, a little mortal man, neither of high nor base origin, of an old family—as Augustus Caesar says of himself—and by nature not evil or brazen, except as contagious custom infected me. Youth led me astray, young manhood corrupted me, but maturer age corrected me and taught me by experience the truth of what I had read long before: that youth and pleasure are vain. This is the lesson of that Author of all times and ages, who permits wretched mortals, puffed with vain wind, to stray for a time until, though late in life, they become mindful of their sins.

In my youth I was blessed with an active, agile body, though not particularly strong. I can't boast of being handsome, but in my greener years I made a good impression. I had a fine complexion, between light and dark, ardent eyes, and a vision that was for many years very sharp. (But it failed me unexpectedly when I was over sixty, so that I was forced reluctantly to the use of spectacles. Old age suddenly took possession of my body, which had always been perfectly healthy, and assailed me with its usual train of illnesses.)

I have always been a great scorner of money—not that I shouldn't like to be rich, but because I hated the labors and cares that are the inseparable companions of wealth. I escaped the trouble of giving sumptuous feasts; but I led a happier life with a simple diet and common foods than all the successors of Apicius with their gourmet dinners. I never liked so-called banquets, which are mere festivals of gluttony, hostile to sobriety and good manners. I have always thought it tiresome and useless to invite others formally, and no less so to be invited by others. But I have always been happy to take a meal with friends, so that I have never found anything pleasanter than their unannounced appearance; and I have never willingly sat down without a friend. Nothing annoyed me more than display, not only because it is bad in itself and the enemy of humility, but because it is troublesome and disturbing.

When I was young I was racked by an overwhelming love affair—but it was pure and it was my only one. I should still be racked by it, had not death, bitter but providential for me, extinguished the flames when they were already cooling. Certainly I wish I could say that I have been free from lusts of the flesh, but if I should say so I should be lying. But this I can surely say, that when I was drawn to them by the ardor of my age and by my temperament, I always inwardly detested their vileness. When in fact I was nearing forty and my vigor and impulses were still strong, I renounced not only that obscene act but the very recollection of it, as if I had never looked at a woman. I number that among my highest blessings, and I thank God, who freed me when still sound and vigorous from that vile servitude, always odious to me.

But let me change the subject. Pride I recognized in others, not in myself; and though I was a person of small account, I was of even less account in my own esteem. As for wrath, it often did harm to me, never to others. I may frankly say, since I know I am telling the truth, that though I have a touchy spirit, I readily forget offenses and well remember benefits received. I have been very desirous of honorable friendships and have faithfully cherished them. It is the torture of the elderly that they must so often mourn the death of those dear to them. I was lucky enough to be intimate with kings and princes and to hold the friendship of nobles, to the point of arousing envy. But I held aloof from many of whom I was very fond; my love of freedom was so deeply implanted in me that I carefully shunned those whose high standing seemed to threaten my freedom. Some of the greatest kings of our time have loved me and cultivated my friendship. Why I don't know; that is their affair. When I was their guest it was more as if they were mine. I was never made uncomfortable by their eminence; I derived from it many advantages.

My mind was rather well balanced than keen, adept for every good and wholesome study, but especially inclined to moral philosophy and poetry. I neglected poetry in the course of time, finding my pleasure in sacred literature, wherein I discovered a hidden sweet-ness which I had previously despised, and I came to regard poetry as merely decorative. I devoted myself, though not exclusively, to the study of ancient times, since I always disliked our own period; so that, if it hadn't been for the love of those dear to me, I should have preferred being born in any other age, forgetting this one; and I always tried to transport myself mentally to other times. Thus I have delighted in the historians, though troubled by their disagreements. In case of doubt I decided either according to verisimilitude or the authority of the writer.

People have said that my utterance is clear and compelling, but it seems to me weak and obscure. In fact in my ordinary speech with friends and familiars I have never worried about fine language; I am amazed that Caesar Augustus took such care about it. When, however, the subject matter or the circumstances of the hearer seemed to demand something else, I have taken some pains with style, I don't know if effectively or not. Those to whom I spoke must decide. If only I have lived well, I make small account of how I have spoken. To seek reputation by mere elegance of language is only vainglory.

My parents were worthy people, of Florentine origin, middling well-off, indeed, to confess the truth, on the edge of poverty. As they were expelled from their home city, I was born in exile in Arezzo, in the 1304th year of Christ's era, at dawn on a Monday, the 20th of July.

Either circumstances or my own choices have thus disposed my life up to now. Most of my first year was spent in Arezzo, where Nature had brought me to birth; the six years following in Incisa, the home of my paternal ancestors, fourteen miles from Florence. (My mother had had her exile remitted.) The eighth year was spent in Pisa, the ninth and later years in Transalpine Gaul, on the left bank of the Rhone. The city's name is Avignon, where the Roman Pontiff kept, and still keeps, the Church of Christ in shameful exile—though a few years ago Urban V seemed to have reestablished it in its proper place. But obviously his attempt came to nothing, since—and this is very grievous to me—while still living he seemed to repent of his good deed. If he had lived a little longer he would certainly have learned what I thought about his return. I had already taken pen in hand, when he suddenly renounced both his glorious purpose and his life. Unhappy man! How joyfully he could have died before Peter's altar and in his own proper home! For either his successors would have remained in their seat, and he would have been the author of that boon, or they would have departed thence, and his merit would have shone the brighter as their fault would have been the more evident. But my lamentations here would be all too long and out of place.

So there on the banks of that windy river I spent my boyhood under the care of my parents, and my youth under the direction only of my own vanities. There were, however, considerable breaks, for at that time I spent a full four years in Carpentras, a small city not far to the eastward. In both these places I learned a little grammar, dialectic, and rhetoric, fitted to my age. And how much one commonly learns in the schools, or how little, you know well, dear reader. Then I went to study law at Montpellier for four years, and then to Bologna, where I took a three-year course and heard lectures on the whole body of civil law. Many asserted that I would have done very well if I had persisted in my course. But I dropped that study entirely as soon as my parents' supervision was removed. Not because I disliked the power and authority of the law, which are undoubtedly very great, or the law's saturation with Roman antiquity, which I love; but because law practice is befouled by its practitioners. I had no taste for learning a trade which I would not practice dishonestly and could not honestly. If I had been willing to practice, my principles would have been ascribed to incompetence.

Thus at twenty-two I came home. Since custom has nearly the force of nature, I call "home" that Avignon exile, where I had lived since childhood. I was already beginning to be known there, and my acquaintance was sought out by important people. Why, I now admit I don't know, and I wonder at it; but then I did not wonder at all, because, in the manner of young men, I thought I was most worthy of every honor. I was especially welcomed by the eminent and noble Colonna family, which then attended, or better, adorned the Roman Curia. I was received by them, and honored in a way that might possibly be justified now, but certainly was not so then. I was taken to Gascony by the illustrious, the incomparable Giacomo Colonna, then Bishop of Lombez, whose like I doubt if I have ever seen or ever shall see. In the shadow of the Pyrenees I passed an almost celestial summer, with host and companions in a common mood of high spirits. Returning, I was attached to his brother, Cardinal Giovanni Colonna, for many years, not as if to an employer but as to a father, or rather as to a very affectionate brother. I was practically independent, in my own home.

At that time my youthful curiosity tempted me to visit France and Germany. And although other reasons were alleged to gain the approval of my superiors for this journey, the real reason was my ardent desire to see something new. In that excursion I first saw Paris, and I took pleasure in finding out what was true and what fabulous in the tales of that city. After my return I made a trip to Rome, which I had longed to see from childhood on. There I paid my court to the great-spirited father of the family, Stefano Colonna, a man cast in the antique mold, and I was so warmly welcomed by him that one would say he made no distinction between me and one of his own sons. This excellent man's affectionate good will persisted until the end of his life, and it is still vivid in my spirit, and will not fade until I cease to be.

Back again, I could not bear the congenital irritation and disgust I feel for all cities, but most of all for that abhorrent Avignon. Seeking some haven, I discovered a very narrow valley, but solitary and delightful, called Vaucluse [Closed Valley], fifteen miles from Avignon, where the Sorgue, king of all fountains, has its source.

Captured by the charm of the place, I transported my books and myself thither when I had passed my thirty-fourth birthday. It would make a long story if I should tell what I did there, through many a year. In a nutshell: almost all my little works were either completed or begun or conceived there; they were so abundant that even to the present they keep me busy and worn out. My mind was like my body, marked more by agility than strength; thus I easily conceived many projects which I dropped because of the difficulty of execution. The very aspect of my retreat suggested my undertaking my *Bucolicum carmen,* a book about life in the woods, and two books of my *De vita solitaria,* dedicated to my friend Philippe [de Cabassoles]. He was always a great man, but then he was the insignificant Bishop of Cavaillon. Now he is a cardinal and the great Bishop of Sabina, and the last survivor of all my old friends. He loved me, and still loves me, not episcopally, as Ambrose did Augustine, but as a brother.

One Good Friday, as I was wandering in the hills, a compelling inspiration came to me to write an epic poem about that first Scipio Africanus, whose glorious name had been dear to me since boyhood. I called it *Africa,* after its hero. By some good fate, whether the book's or my own, it was acclaimed even before publication. I began it with a great burst of enthusiasm, but soon, distracted by various concerns, I put it aside.

While I was leading my retired life there, in a single day—*mirabile dictu!*—arrived letters from the Roman Senate and from the Chancellor of the University of Paris. They summoned me, as if in competition, to receive the laurel crown of poetry in Rome and in Paris. With youthful exultation I thought myself worthy of the honor that men of such standing proposed. I measured my own merit by the testimony of others. But I hesitated a little as to which invitation I should heed. So I wrote to the aforementioned Giovanni Colonna, asking his advice. He was nearby; I wrote to him late in the day, and I had his answer by nine the next morning. I followed his advice, and decided that

the prestige of Rome was to be preferred to all else. (I still have the two letters containing my query and his approval.) So I went to Rome. And although, as is the way of youth, I was a very kindly judge of my own affairs, I was uneasy about accepting my own estimation of myself and that of my proposers. But they surely would not have made the offer if they hadn't thought me worthy of the honor.

I decided therefore to visit Naples first. I presented myself there to that noblest of kings and philosophers, Robert, illustrious in his government and in literature. He is the only king of our times who has been a friend of learning and of virtue. I asked him to examine me according to his own lights. Today I wonder— and I think you too, reader, will wonder, if you are well informed—at the warmth of his judgments and of his reception. When he learned the reason for my coming, he was delighted and amused at my youthful self-confidence. And perhaps he reflected that the honor I sought redounded to his own credit, since I had chosen him from all mortal men to be my only qualified critic. To be brief, after endless conversations on all sorts of subjects I showed him my *Africa,* which pleased him so much that he asked me to dedicate it to him. Naturally I could not and would not refuse. He then set a day to deal with my examination, and he kept me at it from noon to evening. And since the time was too short, with one thing leading to another, he did the same on the two following days. Thus, after sounding my ignorance for three days, he decided on the third day that I was worthy of the laurel. He wanted me to receive it in Naples and he begged me earnestly to agree; but my love for Rome was more mighty than the honorific instances of even so great a king. Finding that my purpose was inflexible, he gave me letters and escorts to the Roman Senate, whereby he benevolently stated his recommendation.

This royal judgment was echoed by many others and especially, in those days, by myself. But today I can't accept the unanimous verdict. There was more affection and encouragement to youth in it than conscientiousness.

Anyway, I went to Rome; and, unworthy as I was, bolstered by the royal judgment, I, who had been merely a raw student, received the poet's laurel crown, to the great joy of the Romans who could attend the ceremony. There are some letters of mine about this also, both in prose and in verse. The laurel did not increase my knowledge, though it did evoke a great deal of envy. But that is a longer tale than I can tell here.

From Rome I went to Parma, and spent some little time with the Correggi, very worthy men and very generous to me, but much at odds with each other. They gave their city such a good government as it had never had within man's memory, and such as it is not likely to have again. I was very conscious of the honor I had just received and worried for fear that I should seem unworthy of it. Then one day I was climbing in the high hills beyond the Enza River in the Reggio region, and I came to a wood called Selvapiana. Suddenly struck by the beauty of the site, I was moved to pick up my interrupted *Africa*. My creative fervor roused from its torpor, and I wrote a little that very day, and somewhat more every day thereafter. Returning to Parma and finding there a secluded, quiet house (which I later bought and still own), I completed the work in a short time with so much ardor that today I am still amazed at it.

I then returned to the fountain of the Sorgue and to my transalpine solitude.

Long after, my growing reputation attracted the kind interest of Giacomo da Carrara the Younger, the best of men—I doubt if any ruler in our times could match him. I doubt? No, I know he was unique. He sent agents and letters across the Alps when I was in France, and wherever I happened to be in Italy. Beaten down through the years by his appeals and proposals of friendship, I decided at last, though I hope little from the fortunate men of earth, to visit him and see what the instances of a great man, unknown to me, might mean. Therefore after a long delay and a stay in Parma and Verona, where I was acclaimed, thank God, much more than I deserved, I went to Padua. There I was welcomed by that man of illustrious memory not as a mere mortal, but as the blessed souls are received in heaven, with such joy, indescribable affection and respect that I must draw a veil over it, since I can't hope to find words to describe it. Just one thing—knowing that I had been a cleric from my youth, he had me appointed a canon of Padua, to bind me closer to himself and to his city. In short, if his life had been longer, that would have been the end of all my vagabond wanderings. But alas, nothing mortal is enduring, and if some sweetness falls to our lot it ends soon in bitterness. When he had not yet given two years to me, to his city, to the world, God reft him away. Blame not my love for him; I know that neither I nor his city nor the world were worthy of him. He was succeeded by his son, a very sensible and distinguished man and like his father very cordial and respectful toward me. But when he to whom I was so closely linked, even by our common age, was gone, I could stay no longer, and I returned to France, not so much from a desire to see again what I had already seen a thousand times as, like a sick man, to be rid of distress by shifting position. . . .

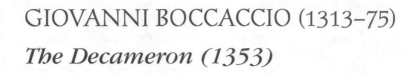

GIOVANNI BOCCACCIO (1313–75)

The Decameron (1353)

The third of Florence's "three crowns" (with Dante and Petrarch), Giovanni Boccaccio, illegitimate child of a Florentine merchant and a Parisian woman, was to become a friend of Petrarch, and an admirer and biographer of Dante. Like Petrarch, Boccaccio was associated with King Robert's court in Naples, where he turned from the study of commerce and canon law under the Bardis to follow in the poet laureate's wake. His first works were forays into allegorical poetry in the style of Dante, including the courtly *Filostrato,* heavily borrowed from by Chaucer for his *Troilus and Criseyde,* and by Shakespeare for *Troilus and Cressida.* But Boccaccio's most impressive earlier work was his *Elegia di Madonna Fiametta,* a predecessor of the modern novel in its psychological sensitivities. His beloved Fiametta may have been the daughter of King Robert; like Dante's Beatrice and Petrarch's Laura, her historical identity is clouded with uncertainty. Boccaccio's later works include Latin treatises *On the Fall of Illustrious Men* and *Concerning Famous Women* (inspired by Petrarch's *On Famous Men*) as well as the misogynistic *Corbaccio,* his last work in Italian. Leonzio Pilato, whose translations of Greek into Latin provided Petrarch and the early humanists with their only knowledge of Homer's poems, was Boccaccio's houseguest for years. Despite holding a series of ambassadorial positions for the city-state of Florence, Boccaccio experienced money problems throughout his productive life. His claim to a secure place in history was a collection of one hundred stories in vibrant vernacular prose celebrating love in all its aspects from profane to sacred, romantic to farcical, erotic to courtly, folkloric to mythic, comic to tragic. The *Decameron*, with *The Thousand and One Arabian Nights* and the Indian *Panchatantra* as models and Chaucer's *Canterbury Tales* as a descendant, is unique in its audacity, its explicit subject matter, its comprehensiveness—and its completion. More than perhaps any other work of its century, the *Decameron* is a kaleidoscopic reflection of the daily life, conversation, and concerns of its times, showing an exuberant attention to detail that truly foreshadows the Renaissance. Although characterization in these tales is more or less static, in that the characters don't progress in the fashion of the later novel, the personages of Boccaccio, drawn from every walk of life from the lowliest peasant to the most spiritual abbot and most worldly merchant, represent the entire human comedy. The themes their stories illustrate, like their unabashedly secular subject matter and their international pedigrees, are no longer purely medieval. An energetic individualism, pitting a variety of men and women against fortune, creates a spirit that Castiglione would later identify in *The Courtier* as *sprezzatura*—in which the brash and intrepid energy of the willful, self-confident individual makes fate itself seem no longer inevitable. Boccaccio has replaced scholastic didacticism with comic satire that will be the hallmark of so many Renaissance masterpieces to come. In his "Preface," Boccaccio sets up a narrative framework for the stories that is as ingenious as it is revealing of the darkness of the social environment. In the year of the plague, 1348, over a period of two weeks, seven young women, with three young men as companions, travel to a pastoral setting away from the epic horrors of the city with the express intention of "escapism." Sometimes, as in García Márquez's *One Hundred Years of Solitude,* reality can be withstood only through the gamelike rituals of storytelling. Replacing urban chaos with idealistic harmony, the young people agree to tell ten stories each on each of ten days, with weekends set aside for refreshment and dance. Boccaccio's description of the cureless plague haunts the modern reader: "The calamity had instilled such horror into the ears of men and women that brother abandoned brother, uncles, sisters and wives left their dear ones to perish and. . . parents avoided visiting or nursing their very children. . . ." Boccaccio, in an unprecedented reach for popularity and perhaps to counter his well-deserved reputation for misogynism, dedicates his Preface "to the Ladies, because they suffer so much for love." Yet at the same time that he recognizes women as the true civilizers and priestesses of life and arbiters of love, his later misogynism, manifest in his ladies' acknowledgment of their subordination to men, reveals that Boccaccio shared the darker medieval view of the capricious female, *semper mutabile.* In the preface to his *Concerning Famous Women,* we read:

> If men should be praised whenever they perform great deeds (with strength which Nature has given them), how much more should women be extolled (almost all of whom are endowed with tenderness, frail bodies, and sluggish minds by Nature), if they have acquired a manly spirit and if with keen intelligence and remarkable fortitude they have dared undertake and have accomplished even the most difficult deeds?

Generalization about their nature tears women from their pedestal of chivalric perfection. Courtly in its framework, the *Decameron* at the same time signals the end of the era of courtly love. "The Second Story" of the "First Day," of the Parisian Jehannot de Chevigny and his Jewish friend Abraham the merchant's visit to the Papal See in Rome, reveals the paradox of awareness of the Roman church's corruption and continued acceptance of its authority that will later be embodied in the tragic careers of Erasmus and Thomas More.

Portrait of Giovanni Boccaccio in the Convent of Sant'Apollonia

Preface, "To the Ladies"

. . . In the year of Our Lord 1348 the deadly plague broke out in the great city of Florence, most beautiful of Italian cities. Whether through the operation of the heavenly bodies or because of our own iniquities which the just wrath of God sought to correct, the plague had arisen in the East some years before, causing the death of countless human beings. It spread without stop from one place to another, until, unfortunately, it swept over the West. Neither knowledge nor human foresight availed against it, though the city was cleansed of much filth by chosen officers in charge and sick persons were forbidden to enter it, while advice was broadcast for the preservation of health. Nor did humble supplications serve. Not once but many times they were

ordained in the form of processions and other ways for the propitiation of God by the faithful, but, in spite of everything, toward the spring of the year the plague began to show its ravages in a way short of miraculous.

It did not manifest itself as in the East, where if a man bled at the nose he had certain warning of inevitable death. At the onset of the disease both men and women were afflicted by a sort of swelling in the groin or under the armpits which sometimes attained the size of a common apple or egg. Some of these swellings were larger and some smaller, and all were commonly called boils. From these two starting points the boils began in a little while to spread and appear generally all over the body. Afterwards, the manifestation of the disease changed into black or livid spots on the arms, thighs and the whole person. In many these blotches were large and far apart, in others small and closely clustered. Like the boils, which had been and continued to be a certain indication of coming death, these blotches had the same meaning for everyone on whom they appeared.

Neither the advice of physicians nor the virtue of any medicine seemed to help or avail in the cure of these diseases. Indeed, whether the nature of the malady did not suffer it, or whether the ignorance of the physicians could not determine the source and therefore could take no preventive measures against it, the fact was that not only did few recover, but on the contrary almost everyone died within three days of the appearance of the signs—some sooner, some later, and the majority without fever or other ill. Moreover, besides the qualified medical men, a vast number of quacks, both men and women, who had never studied medicine, joined the ranks and practiced cures. The virulence of the plague was all the greater in that it was communicated by the sick to the well by contact, not unlike fire when dry or fatty things are brought near it. But the evil was still worse. Not only did conversation and familiarity with the diseased spread the malady and even cause death, but the mere touch of the clothes or any other object the sick had touched or used, seemed to spread the pestilence.

What I am going to relate is indeed a strange thing to hear—a thing that I should hardly have dared believe and much less write about, though I had heard it from a trustworthy witness, had I not seen it with my own eyes, and in the presence of many others. So active, I say, was the virulence of the plague in communicating itself from one person to another, that not only did it affect human beings, but, what is more strange, it very often proceeded in an extraordinary way. If an article belonging to one sick of the plague or who had died of it was touched by an animal outside of the human species, the creature was not only infected, but in a very short time it died of the disease—a fact which among others I observed one day with my own eyes, as I said before. The rags of a poor fellow who had died of the plague, had been thrown into the public street. Two hogs came across them and, according to their habit, first they went for them with their snouts and then, taking them in their teeth, began shaking them about their jaws. A little while later, after rolling round and round as though they had swallowed poison, both of them fell down dead upon the rags they had found to their misfortune.

Because of such happenings and many others of a like sort, various fears and superstitions arose among the survivors, almost all of which tended toward one end—to flee from the sick and whatever had belonged to them. In this way each man thought to be safeguarding his own health. Some among them were of the opinion that by living temperately and guarding against excess of all kinds, they could do much toward avoiding the danger; and forming a band they lived away from the rest of the world. Gathering in those houses where no one had been ill and living was more comfortable, they shut themselves in. They ate moderately of the best that could be had and drank excellent wines, avoiding all luxuriousness. With music and whatever other delights they could have, they lived together in this fashion, allowing no one to speak to them and avoiding news either of death or sickness from the outer world.

Others, arriving at a contrary conclusion, held that plenty of drinking and enjoyment, singing and free living and the gratification of the appetite in every possible way, letting the devil take the hindmost, was the best preventative of such a malady; and as far as they could, they suited the action to the word. Day and night they went from one tavern to another drinking and carousing unrestrainedly. At the least inkling of something that suited them, they ran wild in other people's houses, and there was no one to prevent them, for everyone had abandoned all responsibility for his belongings as well as for himself, considering his days numbered. Consequently most of the houses had become common property and strangers would make use of them at will whenever they came upon them even as the rightful owners might have done. Following this uncharitable way of thinking, they did their best to run away from the infected.

Meanwhile, in the midst of the affliction and misery that had befallen the city, even the reverend authority of divine and human law had almost crumbled and fallen into decay, for its ministers and executors, like other men, had either died or sickened, or had been left so entirely without assistants that they were unable to attend to their duties. As a result everyone had leave to do as he saw fit.

Many others followed a middle course, neither restricting themselves in their diet like the first, nor giving themselves free rein in lewdness and debauchery like the second, but using everything to sufficience, according to their appetites. They did not shut themselves in, but went about, some carrying flowers in their hands, some fragrant herbs, and others divers kinds of spices which they frequently smelled, thinking it good to comfort the brain with such odors, especially since the air was oppressive and full of the stench of corruption, sickness and medicines.

Still others, of a pitiless though perhaps

more prudent frame of mind, maintained that no remedy against plagues was better than to leave them miles behind. Men and women without number, encouraged by this way of thinking and caring for nobody but themselves, abandoned the city, their houses and estates, their own flesh and blood even, and their effects, in search of a country place—it made no difference whether it were their own or their neighbor's. It was as if God's wrath in seeking to punish the iniquity of men by means of the plague could not find them out wherever they were, but limited itself to doom only those who happened to be found within the walls of the city. They reasoned as though its last hour had struck, and therefore no one ought to be there. . . .

But I am weary of dwelling on such miseries. . . . Let me pass over as many of them as I can. Now, while our city was in the throes of this tragedy, and nearly empty of inhabitants, it chanced that seven young women were gathered in the venerable church of Santa Maria Novella, as I have been informed by trustworthy persons. It was on a Tuesday morning, when there was hardly anyone else present. They were attending the divine service in deep mourning, the proper garb for such unfortunate times, and one could see they were bound by ties of friendship, acquaintance and blood. Not one of them had passed her twenty-eighth year, and the youngest was hardly less than eighteen years old. Each was of noble birth, and wise, lovely of body, well-mannered and of honest charm. . . .

Now these young women, who had met rather by chance than by appointment in a corner of the church, sat down in a circle and, heaving frequent sighs, ceased their devotions and began discussing the times in which they lived. After a while, when the others were silent, Pampinea spoke.

"Dear girls," she said, "you must have heard often enough, as well as I, that a person who uses his just rights legitimately injures nobody. It is the natural right of everyone born to help, preserve and defend his life as best he can. In fact, this is taken so much for granted that it is sometimes done at the expense of another's innocent blood. Now if this is conceded by laws that are supposed to look to the welfare and safety of every mortal, how much more justified we ought to be, or others like us, in taking every possible means to preserve our lives—of course, without harming others! Whenever I consider what we did this morning, and many mornings past, and call to mind the things that form the subject of our conversation, I am convinced that each one of us is in mortal terror for herself. I'm sure all of you feel the same way. And it's no great wonder! But I certainly do wonder that, clever though we are, we take no measures to prevent what we have so much reason to dread.

"We all look, for all I know, as though we were waiting to see just how many bodies are brought in for burial. Or are we keeping tab on these poor friars whose chapter has almost dwindled to nothing? Or listening to find out whether they chant their offices at the proper hours? Are we perhaps making a show of our multiple afflictions by the clothes we wear, for the benefit of the chance passer-by? Whenever we leave this place we see nothing but corpses or the bodies of sick persons being dragged about. Or we see evil-doers whom the law has banished, swarming the place, indulging in crime as if they laughed at authority—for do you suppose they do not realize that those who enforced the laws are either sick or dead? Then there are the dregs of the city population, those creatures who call themselves *sextons*. Battening on our blood they mock our sorrows, ramp everywhere and overrun the streets, throwing up our griefs to us with indecent song. We hear nothing but *So-and-So is dead* and *So-and-So is about to die*. If there were any left to weep, we'd hear nothing but wailing everywhere.

"When we return to our homes—I don't know whether it is the same with you as with me—what do we see? Of my large household I, for one, find not a soul at home, only my servant, and I am terrified! I feel every hair of my body standing on end! No matter where I go, wherever I may be about the house, the shades of the dead are always before my eyes, not with the same faces they once had, but ghastly, horrible! God only knows how they came to look that way. . . and I am scared out of my wits!

"Consequently, whether at home or not, I am uneasy, for I do not think there is a single person left besides us, who has strength enough to go about. Yet even if there are others remaining, for there must be, as I have been told, they have lost all sense of right and wrong. Let their appetites prick them and they give in to them, whether alone or in company, by day or night, it makes no difference. And it's not only of the common run of folk that this holds true. Even monks and nuns shut up in monasteries break the laws of obedience, thinking what's sauce for the goose is also sauce for the gander, and give themselves up to all kinds of debauchery like the worst of them, fancying the while they're escaping from peril!

"Now if things are as they are—and you can surely see for yourselves—what are we doing here? What are we waiting for? Why are we moping? Why are we less solicitous for our welfare than the rest of the people? Do we hold ourselves more cheap than everybody else? Or do we imagine our lives are linked to our bodies by a stronger chain, so that we don't have to worry that anything will hurt them? We are mistaken. We deceive ourselves. What fools we are if we believe all that! If we'd only take the trouble to think of the many young men and women who have been carried off by this cruel plague, we'd need no other proof!

"I don't know whether you're of the same opinion, but for my part I think it would be a mighty good thing if we all left this town, that through stubbornness or nonchalance we may not fall into a mess we could avoid if we cared. Of course we'd shun the bad example of others like death itself. We would go quietly to our own country places, which all of us have a-plenty and there, without in the least overstepping reasonable restraint, we would take what innocent pleasure and enjoyment we could find.

"There we'll hear the little birds sing, and see the green of the hills and the plains, and watch the fields full of wheat rising and falling like the waves of the sea. A thousand kinds of trees will rustle there, and the sky will reveal itself more open overhead. Even if it should frown it could not deny us its eternal beauty, far more pleasing to the eye than the desolate walls of our city! Besides, the air is more refreshing, and we would have plenty of everything we needed, with fewer worries to trouble us. It's true the peasants die there, as the townspeople do here, but the sorrows are less, for the houses and dwellers are fewer.

"On the other hand, here we abandon nobody, unless I'm mistaken. I might more truly say we are the forsaken ones, for our folks, whether dying or fleeing from death, have left us alone in this great suffering as if we were nothing to them. What could we be blamed for if we followed my advice? Nothing. But sorrow and trouble and even death, perhaps, might come upon us if we did not.

"So then, let's take our servants whenever you please, and let them follow us with whatever we need. We'll stay here to-day and there to-morrow, and get as much fun and enjoyment out of it as these evil times allow. Surely, I think it would be the best thing to do. Besides we'll be able to see what end heaven has in view in all this—unless death should intervene. To begin with, I want you to bear in mind that it is no more forbidden us to go away honorably, than it is to many other women to remain in dishonor."

When the rest of the ladies had heard Pampinea they not only approved of her advice but, eager to follow it, they had already entered into the details of carrying it through, as though the moment they got up they were to set out on their way. But Filomena, who was a very prudent young lady, said: "My friends, although Pampinea was right in all she said, it does not mean you should rush into things, as you seem to desire. Remember, we are all women, and none of us is so young that she doesn't know what foolish things we would do without the help of some man. By nature fickle, we are all stubborn, suspicious, cowardly and timorous, which fine qualities, I am sure, would cause us to break up our company sooner than we expected, and with little honor to ourselves, unless we had someone else to guide us. It wouldn't be a bad idea to provide ourselves before we begin."

"As a matter of fact," Elisa rejoined, "men are the betters of women, and seldom does anything we undertake succeed well without their help. But how can we get these men? We all know that most of our men-folk are dead, and those that have been spared are scattered far and wide with various groups, goodness only knows where, running away from the very thing we're trying to escape. It wouldn't be proper, on the other hand, to invite strangers. The only way to avoid trouble and scandal, then, if we want to look out for ourselves, is to decide upon some rule to follow, wherever we may wander, for rest or pleasure."

While the women were debating among themselves three young men entered the church, the youngest of whom was about twenty-five. They were brisk lads, the fire of whose love neither evil times, the loss of friends and kin nor fear for themselves had been able to quench, much less to cool. The first of them was called Pamfilo, the second Filostrato, and the last Dioneo—all three very agreeable and well-bred gentlemen. As it was, they had come to look for their mistresses, their only source of cheer in these troublous times. It happened that the three women they were seeking were among the seven gathered there, and of the others some were related to either one or another of them.

No sooner had they espied the ladies than they themselves were seen, and Pampinea began, smiling: "Fortune certainly is favorable to our undertaking, for here she has sent us these fine young gentlemen, who would gladly serve and guide us if we only took the trouble to ask them."

But Neifile exclaimed, blushing, for she was the mistress of one of the youths: "For good-ness' sake, Pampinea, guard your tongue! I know nothing but good could be said of any one of them, and I think them capable of undertaking a far greater responsibility than this. Not only that, but they could certainly be trusted in the company of far lovelier gentlewomen than we, and still retain their honor. But you see, they're in love with some of us here, and I'm afraid that, without any fault of ours or theirs, for that matter, we might stir up scandal if we took them with us."

"That doesn't mean a thing," said Filomena. "If I live in honesty and there's nothing to bother my conscience, let people say what they will. God and truth will take up arms for me. If only those young men were willing to join us we might really say with Pampinea that Fortune favors us."

Hearing the decisiveness of her tone the other women not only did not protest, but agreed to call the youths and inform them of what was required of them in the proposed expedition. Pampinea, who was related to one of them, got up and walked toward the three gentlemen, who were standing there observing the women. Cheerfully she greeted them, told them her errand and entreated them on behalf of her friends to keep them company in pure fraternal friendship. At first the men thought she was making fun of them, but when they saw she was in earnest they answered gaily that they were ready, and gave orders then and there for the necessary preparations.

Their servants they dispatched in advance to the place they intended visiting and bade them make everything ready for their arrival. Toward daybreak the following morning, that is, Wednesday, they left the city and started on their way, the women with a number of their servants and the three men with three of their domestics. They had hardly left the city two short miles behind when they came to the place they had set out for.

It was a charming spot on a little hill, removed on every side from the roads, full of different shrubs and plants, and lush with green foliage that was a delight to the eye. On the summit there rose a palace with a lovely spacious court in its midst, and halls, parlors and chambers, each perfect in itself and decorated with gay and costly paintings. Lawns surrounded it, and marvelous gardens; there were wells of cool water and vaults of rare wines, more suitable to carousers than to sober and virtuous ladies. The whole place had been swept clean; the beds were made in the chambers, and everywhere, to their delight, the happy group found the season's wealth of flowers and green rushes strewn about.

They sat down at the first opportunity and Dioneo, who was the handsomest youth of the three, and full of fun, began: "Ladies, it was your cleverness rather than our prevision that led us here. I don't know what you intend doing with your worries. . . . I, for one, left them inside the city gate the moment I quit it to follow you. Now either you make up your minds to have a good time and laugh and sing with me—of course, in all propriety—or you give me leave to go back to my cares and remain in the city of sorrow."

Pampinea, as carefree as though she herself had checked all her troubles, lightly answered him: "Very well said, Dioneo! We're here to have a jolly good time, for no other reason prompted us to flee our sorrows. But, since extremes can't last very long, I who started the argument which brought this fine band together, should like to have us continue in our joy. Therefore I think it necessary for us to choose someone whom we must honor and obey as leader, and whose every thought must be to keep us entertained. But that all of us may feel the weight of responsibility as well as the fun of leadership, I propose that each should be granted the burden and the honor for a day. And that there may be no jealousy and nobody be overlooked, the leader must be chosen in turn from among the men and the women. Let the first be elected by us all, and as for the others, let them be chosen toward evening by whichever one has had the leadership for the day, when he may select this man or that woman as he pleases. Then each new ruler will dictate where or how we are to

pass our time, according to his pleasure, all through the period of his sovereignty."

Pampinea's words met with great favor, and unanimously she was elected queen for the first day. Filomena, running to a laurel tree whose leaves she had often heard spoken of as worthy of honor and as conferring honor upon anyone wearing them, broke off some branches and twined a beautiful wreath. This she placed upon Pampinea's head, and from that day on while their band lasted, it became the symbol of royal office and leadership.

Pampinea, now queen, requested them all to be silent and, calling together the servants of the three youths and the maids, who were four in number, she said: "To set you the first example by which our group may ever prosper and continue happy, orderly and virtuous as long as we see fit, I appoint first of all Parmeno, Dioneo's servant, to be my steward. To him I commit the care and management of our family in everything that concerns the house and banquet-hall. Sirisco, Pamfilo's servant, I choose to be our treasurer and purveyor, under the direction of Parmeno. Tindaro will be in Filostrato's and the other two gentlemen's employ, taking care of their rooms whenever the others are prevented by different business. My maid Misia, and Licisca, Filomena's, will remain in the kitchen and diligently prepare whatever meals Parmeno orders. Lauretta's Chimera and Fiammetta's maid Stratilia I delegate to the care of the women's rooms and the keeping of the places where we shall be. I further request and command each and every one of you, at the cost of my friendship, to beware of bringing any but good news from the outside world, no matter where you roam, or what you may hear and see."

These orders summarily given and approved, she rose briskly to her feet. "Here are gardens," she said. "Here are lawns and many other pleasant places where you may go wandering to your hearts' content. By three o'clock I want you all back here, that we may dine when the day is cooler."

The gay company was now at liberty, whereupon the young men and women went walking easily in the garden, chatting of pleasant things, weaving themselves garlands of different leaves and singing love-ditties. When they had whiled away the time the queen had designated, they returned to the palace, where they found that Parmeno had made a skilful beginning at his office. The tables in one of the lower halls were laid with snow-white cloths and glasses that shone like silver, and blossoms of the broom were scattered everywhere. At the queen's pleasure they washed their hands and then took their places according to Parmeno's arrangement.

Dishes exquisitely concocted were brought, and delicate wines, and the three serving men waited quietly at the tables. Cheer rose high, inspired by meat and drink and the merry-making and pleasant talk that seasoned them. Finally the tables were cleared. All of them, both men and women, were graceful dancers, and some excelled in playing and singing. Knowing this, the queen commanded the instruments to be brought and at her bidding Dioneo took a lute and Fiammetta a viol. Softly, and in unison, they struck up a dance-measure. Meanwhile the servants were sent away to their meal in the kitchen, and the queen, with the rest of the women and the two youths, commenced a round. With slow, graceful steps the dancing was begun, and no sooner did it come to a close than charming, lightsome ditties were gaily sung. So for a long time they amused themselves, until the queen decided it was time to retire and dismissed them all. The three young men withdrew to their chambers, removed from those of the women. The beds were beautifully decked, and many flowers were strewn about as in the hall. Undressing, they went to sleep; and the women in their apartments followed suit.

The morning hour had hardly struck when the queen rose and bade the rest follow her example, the three men as well as the women, for she maintained it was injurious to the health to sleep late into the day. They went to a meadow, full of tall, green grass. There the sun could not penetrate, and a delicious little breeze stirred. Following the queen's wish they sat down in a circle upon the green, and she addressed them.

"As you see," she said, "the sun is high, and the heat intense, and we hear nothing but the cricket in the olive-trees. It would be utter foolishness to go anywhere at this time. Here it is cool and pleasant, and see, we are provided with tables and chess-boards for our amusement if we should be so minded. But if you want my opinion, I'd rather we did not play— for in chess the mind of one of the players must necessarily be uneasy about the moves, which is no fun, either for the other player or for those who look on. Let us rather tell stories to while away these sultry hours of the day, for when one tells a story the whole company derives pleasure listening. You'll hardly have finished telling your stories when the sun will have gone down and the hottest part of the day be over. Then we'll be free to go wherever we choose for our diversion. If you're pleased with my idea—for mind, I'm here to follow your pleasure—let's begin. If not—well, let each one do as he pleases until evening."

Everyone, however, acclaimed the idea of telling stories.

"Well, then," said the queen, "since this suits you, I'll leave each one free this first day to choose whatever subject he pleases."

She turned to Pamfilo, who was seated on her right, and cheerfully asked him to begin the story-telling with some tale of his. They listened to him, as he readily complied with the queen's bidding.

THE SECOND STORY

Abraham the Jew, Urged by Jehannot de Chevigny, Visits the Court of Rome, and Witnessing the Loose Life of the Clergy becomes a Christian.

Pamfilo's story roused laughter in part and won the undivided approval of the women, who had listened to it attentively to the end. Then the queen asked Neifile who was sitting beside Pamfilo to take up the thread of the diversion by telling a story of her own. Neifile, as charming and courteous as she was beautiful, willingly acquiesced and began:

Pamfilo has shown us in his story how the lovingkindness of God overlooks our faults when they proceed from causes of which we have no knowledge. In mine I intend to show how this same lovingkindness—suffering patiently the faults of those who should bear true witness of it both by word and deed, yet practice the contrary—gives us a veritable proof of itself, to help us pursue our belief with even firmer strength of mind.

I have heard tell, gracious ladies, of a wealthy merchant who lived in Paris—a fine fellow, loyal and upright, whose name was Jehannot de Chevigny. He carried on an extensive business in cloth and stuffs, and he was a friend, strangely enough, of a very rich Jew called Abraham, a merchant, like himself, and like him, too, an honest and upright man. Observing Abraham's fine qualities, Jehannot began to be very much concerned that the soul of such a splendid fellow should be damned for his mistaken faith, so out of friendship he constantly urged him to forsake the errors of the Jewish creed and embrace Christian verity, which, he argued, Abraham could see prospering and growing for its holiness and good, while his own, on the contrary, was ever waning and coming to nothing. At that the Jew would reply he believed no faith but the Jewish to be either good or holy. Besides, he argued, he had been born into it, and in it he wanted to live and die. There was nothing that could ever move him from his resolve.

Nevertheless Jehannot was not deterred from returning to the argument a few days later with similar words, trying to prove to Abraham in his blunt, simple, business-like way why his religion was better than the Jewish. Now the Jew was a learned master in the Hebraic law, but whether Jehannot's whole-hearted friendship touched him, or whether the words which the Holy Ghost put into the uncultured fellow's mouth worked the miracle, the Jew soon began to take pleasure in Jehannot's arguments. Still, holding firmly to his faith, he would not allow himself to be shaken. The more obdurate he remained, the more insistent grew Jehannot's importunities. Finally, conquered by so continued an attack, the Jew said:

"Now, listen, Jehannot. You insist that I become a Christian. I am willing to do so, but first I want to go to Rome and see the man who, you say, is God's vicar on earth, that I may consider his ways and habits and those of his brother cardinals. If they seem to me such that between them and your arguments I can convince myself your faith is better than mine, as you have gone out of your way to show me,— why, I'll do what I said. If not, I'll keep on being the Jew I am."

Jehannot was exceedingly troubled to hear this, and said to himself: "I've wasted my efforts, which I thought so well-employed, when I imagined I was converting Abraham. If he should go to the court of Rome and see the filthy life of the clergy, far from being converted from Jew to Christian, he would most assuredly turn Jew again were he the most devout Christian in the world!" But turning to Abraham he said: "Now look, my friend, why should you want to go to the trouble and expense of traveling from here to Rome, especially when you consider that for a man of your wealth a trip by land or sea is full of danger? Are you afraid you'll not find the man here to baptize you? If you should still have some doubts concerning the faith I've preached to you—where could you find greater teachers and more learned men than here, to explain whatever questions you'd like to ask? In my opinion your trip is unnecessary, taking all in all. Just realize that the prelates there are no different from ours here— they're only better for being nearer the chief Shepherd. So follow my advice and reserve this trouble for some other occasion when you may wish to attend a jubilee. Perhaps then I'll even keep you company."

"I am sure, Jehannot," answered the Jew, "that everything is as you say. But to make a long story short, if you want me to do what you've asked me so often, I insist upon going on my trip. If not, I wash my hands of the whole matter."

Jehannot saw Abraham was determined. "Well, go and good luck to you," he said, though he was certain Abraham would never become a Christian when he saw the court of Rome. But then, reflecting that he himself was losing nothing, he refrained from further action.

The Jew took horse and without losing time went to the court of Rome, where he was welcomed with all due honor by his fellow Jews on his arrival. Then, remaining in Rome without telling anyone the purpose of his visit, he began prudently studying the habits of the Pope, the cardinals and other prelates, as well as all the members of the papal court. Between what he himself gathered, for he was a very perceptive man, and what he heard from others, he found that all, from the highest of rank, to the meanest, were shamefully guilty of the sin of lechery. Not only did they indulge in normal lust, but without the least restraint of remorse or shame, even in sodomy, and to such an extent that the influence of whores and minions was of no little importance in currying favor. Various other attributes he found them to possess besides lechery. They were gluttons, swillers, guzzlers in general, and devoted to their bellies like brute beasts. Investigating further he saw they were all avaricious and greedy for money. Human blood, indeed, Christian and sacred things pertaining to the sacrifice, they used to barter for money, making a bigger business of them and employing more agents than the people of Paris had for their stuffs and merchandise. Blatant simony they called *procuration* and gluttony *sustentation,* as if God did not know either the meaning of the words or the intention of those evil minds, and allowed Himself to be gulled like His creatures by the mere names of things.

These, and many other enormities that were better passed over in silence, offended the Jew, who was a sober and humble man, and thinking he had witnessed enough, he decided to go back to Paris.

When Jehannot heard of his return the last thing he hoped for was that Abraham should have become a Christian. He went to see him, nevertheless, and they greeted each other joyfully. Then, when Abraham had rested a day or so, Jehannot asked him what he thought of the Holy Father, the cardinals and others of the papal court.

"I think they are rotten," the Jew readily replied. "God punish the whole brood of them! I tell you—unless I did not see things straight— I found no holiness, no devotion, no good work or example or anything else in a single man of the clergy. On the contrary, lust, gluttony, avarice and worse things, if there could be anything worse—all were in such high favor, I would have taken it all for a mill of devilish works, not holy! For all I can judge it seems to me your Shepherd and consequently everyone else with him do their utmost, exercise every care, wit and art at their disposal to ruin the Christian faith entirely and ban it altogether from the world, instead of striving to be its foundation and mainstay. Yet when I notice their aim is not fulfilled, but that your religion continually grows and becomes more bright and clear, it seems to me very evident that the Holy Spirit is its foundation and support, so it must be the truest and holiest of all faiths. Therefore in spite of my obduracy in rejecting your pleas for my conversion, I tell you frankly that nothing in the world could deter me from becoming a Christian. Come, let's go to the church, then, where I may be baptized according to the proper custom of your holy faith."

Jehannot, who had expected quite the contrary conclusion, was the happiest man alive when he heard his friend express himself in this fashion. He went with him to the church of Notre-Dame in Paris, and asked the clergy to baptize Abraham. When they heard Abraham himself make the request, they granted it readily. Jehannot then raised him from the sacred font and named him Jean. In after-days Jean had himself duly instructed by famous men in all matters pertaining to our faith, which he learned without trouble, and he became a much respected man, renowned for holy living.

PART 2

FIFTEENTH AND SIXTEENTH CENTURIES

CHRISTINE DE PIZAN (1365–C.1431)

LA CITÉ DES DAMES

The Book of the City of Ladies (1404–5)

The clear-sighted insight of a Venetian-born French patriot presages the twentieth century's Renaissance of woman's consciousness in the autobiographical energy and insights she weaves into her poetry and prose. Christine de Pizan celebrated the victory of Joan of Arc at the battle of Agincourt, and attacked the misogynism of Jean de Meung's *Romance of the Rose.* Provoked by Boccaccio's patriarchal and condescending *De mulieribus claris* ("concerning famous women"), Christine, in her pedagogical treatise *The Book of the City of Ladies,* envisions a female utopia, in which the term "lady" is redefined to distinguish nobility of spirit rather than of birth. By exploring her feminine potential, every woman can be enrolled as a citizen in this ideal commonwealth. When her husband Étienne du Castel left her a widow at 24, she determined to support her three children with her prolific pen. Rewriting the history of women, Christine invites ladies of the past, present, and future to her society in which women are judged, not by reference to male accomplishments, but only by the degree to which they fulfill their own dreams and capabilities. The *City* is written, like so many Renaissance institutes, in the dialogue form. The characters of the dialogue are Reason, Rectitude, Justice—and Christine herself. The subjects treated in its pages include the criminality of rape, the affinity of women for learning, and the talent of women for government.

Here Christine Tells How, Under Reason's Command and Assistance, She Began to Excavate the Earth and Lay the Foundation.

Then Lady Reason responded and said, "Get up, daughter! Without waiting any longer, let us go to the Field of Letters. There the City of Ladies will be founded on a flat and fertile plain, where all fruits and freshwater rivers are found and where the earth abounds in all good things. Take the pick of your understanding and dig and clear out a great ditch wherever you see the marks of my ruler, and I will help you carry away the earth on my own shoulders."

I immediately stood up to obey her commands and, thanks to these three ladies, I felt stronger and lighter than before. She went ahead, and I followed behind, and after we had arrived at this field I began to excavate and dig, following her marks with the pick of cross-examination. And this was my first work:

"Lady, I remember well what you told me before, dealing with the subject of how so many men have attacked and continue to attack the behavior of women, that gold becomes more refined the longer it stays in the furnace, which means the more women have been wrongfully attacked, the greater waxes the merit of their glory. But please tell me why and for what reason different authors have spoken against women in their books, since I already know from you that this is wrong; tell me if Nature makes man so inclined or whether they do it out of hatred and where does this behavior come from?"

Then she replied, "Daughter, to give you a way of entering into the question more deeply, I will carry away this first basketful of dirt. This behavior most certainly does not come from Nature, but rather is contrary to Nature, for no connection in the world is as great or as strong as the great love which, through the will of God, Nature places between a man and a woman. The causes which have moved and which still move men to attack women, even those authors in those books, are diverse and varied, just as you have discovered. For some have attacked women with good intentions, that is, in order to draw men who have gone astray away from the company of vicious and dissolute women, with whom they might be infatuated, or in order to keep these men from going mad on account of such women, and also so that every man might avoid an obscene and lustful life. They have attacked all women in general because they believe that women are made up of every abomination."

"My lady," I said then, "excuse me for interrupting you here, but have such authors acted well, since they were prompted by a laudable intention? For intention, the saying goes, judges the man."

"That is a misleading position, my good daughter," she said, "for such sweeping ignorance never provides an excuse. If someone killed you with good intention but out of foolishness, would this then be justified? Rather, those who did this, whoever they might be, would have invoked the wrong law; causing any damage or harm to one party in order to help another party is not justice, and likewise attacking all feminine conduct is contrary to the truth, just as I will show you with a hypothetical case. Let us suppose they did this intending to draw fools away from foolishness. It would be as if I attacked fire—a very good and necessary element nevertheless—because some people burnt themselves, or water because someone drowned. The same can be said of all good things which can be used well or used badly. But one must not attack them if fools abuse them, and you have yourself touched on this point quite well elsewhere in your writings. But those who have spoken like this so abundantly—whatever their intentions might be—have formulated their arguments rather loosely only to make their point. Just like someone who has a long and wide robe cut from a very large piece of cloth when the material costs him nothing and when no one opposes him, they exploit the rights of others. But just as you have said elsewhere, if these writers had only looked for the ways in which men can be led away from foolishness and could have been kept from tiring themselves in attacking the life and behavior of immoral and dissolute women—for to tell the straight truth, there is nothing which should be avoided more than an evil, dissolute, and perverted woman, who is like a monster in nature, a counterfeit estranged from her natural condition, which must be simple, tranquil, and upright—then I would grant you that they would have built a supremely excellent work. But I can assure you that these attacks on all women—when in fact there are so many excellent women—have never originated with me, Reason, and that all who subscribe to them have failed totally and will continue to fail. So now throw aside these black, dirty, and uneven stones from your work, for they will never be fitted into the fair edifice of your City.

"Other men have attacked women for other reasons: such reproach has occurred to some men because of their own vices and others have been moved by the defects of their own bodies, others through pure jealousy, still others by the pleasure they derive in their own personalities from slander. Others, in order to show they have read many authors, base their own writings on what they have found in books and repeat what other writers have said and cite different authors.

"Those who attack women because of their own vices are men who spent their youths in dissolution and enjoyed the love of many different women, used deception in many of their encounters, and have grown old in their sins without repenting, and now regret their past follies and the dissolute life they led. But Nature, which allows the will of the heart to put into effect what the powerful appetite desires, has grown cold in them. Therefore they are pained when they see that their 'good times' have now passed them by, and it seems to them that the young, who are now what they once were, are on top of the world. They do not know how to overcome their sadness except by attacking women, hoping to make women less attractive to other men. Everywhere one sees such old men speak obscenely and dishonestly, just as you can fully see with Matheolus, who himself confesses that he was an impotent old man filled with desire. You can thereby convincingly prove, with this one example, how what I tell you is true, and you can assuredly believe that it is the same with many others.

"But these corrupt old men, like an incurable leprosy, are not the upstanding men of old whom I made perfect in virtue and wisdom—for not all men share in such corrupt desire, and it would be a real shame if it were so. The mouths of these good men, following their hearts, are all filled with exemplary, honest, and discreet words. These same men detest misdeeds and slander, and neither attack nor defame men and women, and they counsel the avoidance of evil and the pursuit of virtue and the straight path.

"Those men who are moved by the defect of their own bodies have impotent and deformed limbs but sharp and malicious minds. They have found no other way to avenge the pain of their impotence except by attacking women who bring joy to many. Thus they have thought to divert others away from the pleasure which they cannot personally enjoy.

"Those men who have attacked women out of jealousy are those wicked ones who have seen and realized that many women have greater understanding and are more noble in conduct than they themselves, and thus they are pained and disdainful. Because of this, their overweening jealousy has prompted them to attack all women, intending to demean and diminish the glory and praise of such women, just like the man—I cannot remember which one—who tries to prove in his work, *De philosophia,* that it is not fitting that some men have revered women and says that those men who have made so much of women pervert the title of his book: they transform 'philosophy,' the love of wisdom, into 'philofolly,' the love of folly. But I promise and swear to you that he himself, all throughout the lie-filled deductions of his argument, transformed the content of his book into a true philofolly.

"As for those men who are naturally given to slander, it is not surprising that they slander women since they attack everyone anyway. Nevertheless, I assure you that any man who freely slanders does so out of a great wickedness of heart, for he is acting contrary to reason and contrary to Nature: contrary to reason insofar as he is most ungrateful and fails to recognize the good deeds which women have done for him, so great that he could never make up for them, no matter how much he try, and which he continuously needs women to perform for him; and contrary to Nature in that there is no naked beast anywhere, nor bird, which does not naturally love its female counterpart. It is thus quite unnatural when a reasonable man does the contrary.

"And just as there has never been any work so worthy, so skilled is the craftsman who made it, that there were not people who wanted, and want, to counterfeit it, there are many who wish to get involved in writing poetry. They believe they cannot go wrong, since others have written in books what they take the situation to be, or rather, *mis*-take the situation—as I well know! Some of them undertake to express themselves by writing poems of water without salt, such as these, or ballads without feeling, discussing the behavior of women or of princes or of other people, while they themselves do not know how to recognize or to correct their own servile conduct and inclinations. But simple people, as ignorant as they are, declare that such writing is the best in the world.". . .

She Begins to Discuss Several Ladies who were Enlightened With Great Learning, and First Speaks About the Noble Maiden Cornificia.

"Cornificia, the noble maiden, was sent to school by her parents along with her brother Cornificius when they were both children, thanks to deception and trickery. This little girl so devoted herself to study and with such marvelous intelligence that she began to savor the sweet taste of knowledge acquired through study. Nor was it easy to take her away from this joy to which she more and more applied herself, neglecting all other feminine activities. She occupied herself with this for such a long period of time that she became a consummate poet, and she was not only extremely brilliant and expert in the learnedness and craft of poetry but also seemed to have been nourished with the very milk and teaching of perfect philosophy, for she wanted to hear and know about every branch of learning, which she then mastered so thoroughly that she surpassed her brother, who was also a very great poet, and excelled in every field of learning. Knowledge was not enough for her unless she could put her mind to work and her pen to paper in the compilation of several very famous books. These works, as well as her poems, were much prized during the time of Saint Gregory and he himself mentions them. The Italian, Boccaccio, who was a great poet, discusses this fact in his work and at the same time praises this woman: 'O most great honor for a woman who abandoned all feminine activities and applied and devoted her mind to the study of the greatest scholars!' As further proof of what I am telling you, Boccaccio also talks about the attitude of women who despise themselves and their own minds, and who, as though they were born in the mountains totally ignorant of virtue and honor, turn disconsolate and say that they are good and useful only for embracing men and carrying and feeding children. God has given them such beautiful minds to apply themselves, if they want to, in any of the fields where glorious and excellent men are active, which are neither more nor less accessible to them as compared to men if they wished to study them, and they can thereby acquire a lasting name, whose possession is fitting for most excellent men. My dear daughter, you can see how this author Boccaccio testifies to what I have told you and how he praises and approves learning in women."....

Here She Speaks of Sappho, That Most Subtle Woman, Poet, and Philosopher.

"The wise Sappho, who was from the city of Mytilene, was no less learned than Proba. This Sappho had a beautiful body and face and was agreeable and pleasant in appearance, conduct, and speech. But the charm of her profound understanding surpassed all the other charms with which she was endowed, for she was expert and learned in several arts and sciences, and she was not only well-educated in the works and writings composed by others but also discovered many new things herself and wrote many books and poems. Concerning her, Boccaccio has offered these fair words couched in the sweetness of poetic language: 'Sappho, possessed of sharp wit and burning desire for constant study in the midst of bestial and ignorant men, frequented the heights of Mount Parnassus, that is, of perfect study. Thanks to her fortunate boldness and daring, she kept company with the Muses, that is, the arts and sciences, without being turned away. She entered the forest of laurel trees filled with may boughs, greenery, and different colored flowers, soft fragrances and various aromatic spices, where Grammar, Logic, noble Rhetoric, Geometry, and Arithmetic live and take their leisure. She went on her way until she came to the deep grotto of Apollo, god of learning, and found the brook and conduit of the fountain of Castalia, and took up the plectrum and quill of the harp and played sweet melodies, with the nymphs all the while leading the dance, that is, following the rules of harmony and musical accord.' From what Boccaccio says about her, it should be inferred that the profundity of both her understanding and of her learned books can only be known and understood by men of great perception and learning, according to the testimony of the ancients. Her writings and poems have survived to this day, most remarkably constructed and composed, and they serve as illumination and models of consummate poetic craft and composition to those who have come afterward. She invented different genres of lyric and poetry, short narratives, tearful laments and strange lamentations about love and other emotions, and these were so well made and so well ordered that they were named 'Sapphic' after her. Horace recounts, concerning her poems, that when Plato, the great philosopher who was Aristotle's teacher, died, a book of Sappho's poems was found under his pillow.

"In brief this lady was so outstanding in learning that in the city where she resided a statue of bronze in her image was dedicated in her name and erected in a prominent place so that she would be honored by all and be remembered forever. This lady was placed and counted among the greatest and most famous poets, and, according to Boccaccio, the honors of the diadems and crowns of kings and the miters of bishops are not any greater, nor are the crowns of laurel and victor's palm.

"I could tell you a great deal about women of great learning. Leontium was a Greek woman and also such a great philosopher that she dared, for impartial and serious reasons, to correct and attack the philosopher Theophrastus, who was quite famous in her time."

LEONARDO BRUNI (1370–1444)

Laudatio florentinae urbis

Praise of the City of Florence (1403–4)

Bruni was one of the first European humanists to master the Greek language, under the tutelage of the transplanted Byzantine scholar Manuel Chrysoloras, who arrived in Italy in 1396, and to Latinize works by Aristotle and Plato, making them more widely and accurately accessible than ever before. Author of the *Historiae florentini populi,* he said of the Florentine republic: "One of the democratic characteristics of our constitution is that we worship freedom more than anything else, as the end and goal of our commonwealth." Following Dante's lead, Bruni was among the strongest proponents of the vernacular, writing an early *Life of Dante* in Italian. While pursuing his historical studies and writings, Bruni served as an officer both in the papal court and for the city of Florence. His numerous letters reflect the impact of humanism on everyday life. One in particular, known as "On the Study of Literature" and written to the Lady Battista Malatesta, outlines the principles for a literary education:

- Read the authorities.
- Read analytically.
- Read aloud.
- Excellence comes from the width and diversity of knowledge.
- The ideal is to appear eloquent, well-rounded, refined, and widely cultivated.

But as this city is to be admired for its foreign policy, so it is for its internal organization and institutions. Nowhere else is there such order, such elegance, such symmetry. For just as there is a proportion among strings which, when they have been tightened, produces a harmony from the different pitches, than which there is nothing sweeter or more agreeable to the ear; so all the parts of this prudent city are so tempered that the resulting whole commonwealth fits together in a way that brings pleasure to the mind and eyes of men for its harmony. There is nothing in it that is out of order, nothing that is ill-proportioned, nothing that is out of tune, nothing that is uncertain. Everything has its place, and this is not only fixed, but correct in relation to the others. Offices, magistracies, courts and ranks are all separate. But they are separated in such a way that they are in harmony with the whole commonwealth, as tribunes were with respect to the general.

First, every consideration is given to providing that justice shall be held sacred in the city, for without that, no city can exist or deserve the name; secondly, that there be liberty, without which this people never thought life was worth living. Toward these two ideals together, as toward a kind of ensign and haven, all the institutions and legislative acts of this republic are directed.

It is for the sake of justice that the magistracies were established, and endowed with sovereign authority and the power to punish criminals, and above all so that they may see to it that no one's power in the city will be above the law. Accordingly all private citizens, as persons of lesser rank, are enjoined to obey the magistrates

and to honor their symbols of office. But lest these defenders of the law, who have been put into positions of the highest authority, should get the idea that what had been offered them was an opportunity to tyrannize over the citizens rather than to protect them, and lest a measure of freedom should be lost as a result of their persecution of others, many precautions have been taken.

In the first place, the supreme magistracy, which once was perceived to possess something like royal power, has been tempered by the following safeguard: that it is not conferred on one, but on nine persons at once, and not for a whole year but for a two-month term. In this way the city believes that the commonwealth would be well-governed, as expression of more than one opinion would counter erroneous advice, and the shortness of the term would serve as a check on ambition. The city is divided into four quarters, and two men are elected from each, so that none of them will ever lack the honor of being represented. Not just anyone is elected, but only those who have already been subjected to the scrutiny and judged to be worthy of such an honor. For the government of the commonwealth, besides these eight citizens, one man of outstanding virtue and authority is added. He is chosen from the various quarters of the city in turn. His role is to preside over the college of magistrates, and to bear a standard as a symbol of his duty to execute justice against seditious persons. These nine men, on whom the government of the commonwealth is conferred, are not supposed to reside outside the city hall where they may be the better prepared to conduct public affairs. They are not supposed to venture forth un-

Il Duomo, general view (Filippo Brunelleschi; belltower by Giotto), Florence

less preceded by lictors to enhance their dignity.

Because it sometimes happens that there seems need of wider counsel, twelve good men are added to offer their advice together with the nine priors for the benefit of the commonwealth. Also added are the standard-bearers, to whom, when it is necessary to defend liberty by force of arms, the whole people rallies. They too assist in council, and, like the magistrates above, are elected from the quarters, but they hold office for four months.

The three colleges do not have the power of decision in all matters. Many, after being approved by them, are referred to the Councils of the People and of the Commune. For it is believed by this city that what affects the many it was not fitting in law or reason to decide except by the will of the many. In this way liberty flourishes and justice is devotedly served in this city, since nothing can be carried out in response to the desire of one or another man against the will of so many. Instead, men like these offer their advice to the commonwealth, ratify and repeal laws and determine what is equitable.

For the actual pronunciation of sentences on the basis of these laws, however, and for the execution of sentences, there are lesser magistracies; and for this purpose foreigners from far away are called into the city to serve in the place of citizens, not because the citizens would not know how to do it (for they do do it in foreign cities every day), but so that carrying out the judicial function should not become a cause of mutual hatred and enmity among the citizens. For there are many who, deceived by excessive love of self, claim more authority for themselves than the laws permit; who, even if the judgment has been right, pursue complaints against the magistracy. It was seen to be an especially serious matter for a citizen in a free city to impose a capital sentence upon another citizen; for if he did so, however justly, he would be viewed by the other citizens as polluted and obnoxious. It is for this reason that the judges are recruited from a long distance, and that laws governing their conduct are prescribed from which they may not depart in any way. For they must agree to them under oath, and when they leave office, they must, like brokers, submit an account of their performance in office to the people. Thus in every sphere the people and liberty rule.

In order, however, for everyone in such a large city to secure his rights the more easily, and to be sure that some citizens would not be left unprotected by justice and the laws while magistracies were preoccupied with other citizens' affairs, certain guilds have been given cognizance and power of judgment over their own members, for example, merchants, bankers, and certain others, some of whom even have the right of coercion over their own men. There are other magistracies, established for either public or pious purposes, among which are the tax masters and the directors of the treasury, and the guardians of orphans and of orphan property—a magistracy which serves both a public and a private purpose, and was conceived by a generous city in a spirit that was both pious and beneficial.

But of all the many and distinguished magistracies in this city, none is more illustrious nor does any have a more splendid origin or purpose than the captains of the good party (*optimarum partium duces*), about whose origin it will perhaps not be irrelevant to say something, so that their position of distinction may be better understood. It will, however, be a very brief digression, and one that I think will contain useful and valuable knowledge.

Once the scale of the catastrophe on the Arbia was appreciated, when as a result of that great wound to the commonwealth there seemed to be no way to defend the city, all the citizens of a high-minded and noble spirit who did not want to see those who had so openly betrayed their country in control of the city, left their hearths and betook themselves with their wives and children to Lucca, imitating the noble and praiseworthy example of the Athenians who left their city during the second Persian War in order that they might some day live in it again as free men. It was in this spirit that the outstanding citizens who had survived the great disaster left the city, thinking that in this way they would have a better chance for revenge than if they were to wait within the city walls for starvation or the city's destruction. After moving to Lucca and calling together all those who had been scattered by the fortune of war, they equipped themselves so well with arms, horses, and every instrument of war that men everywhere began to marvel at their superior courage and readiness.

After many deeds of valor performed in Italy in which they often contributed their assistance to friends and exhibited their courage and bravery against the men of the enemy faction and were victorious wherever they fought, believing then that the time had come for which they had been hoping to wipe out the stain and blot on their country, they set out against Manfred, king of Sicily (since he was the head of the opposing party in Italy and had sent his soldiers to the Arbia), following the outstanding and excellent leader whom the pope had summoned from Gaul to counter the arrogance of Manfred. I should be happy to describe the courage they showed in various encounters after they got to Apulia if this were the place to recount such a story. But to put it briefly, they distinguished themselves in such a fashion that even the bitterest enemy was forced to praise their prowess and honor.

Apulia was conquered, the enemy destroyed, and then they returned to Tuscany, proudly bearing the king's decorations and gifts. They drove out of the city the men who had been misgoverning the commonwealth and took splendid vengeance upon neighboring enemies, and then established an institution for themselves and set over it their leaders to be the captains of the good party and the heads of this lawful and distinguished association.

Coming as it does from such an origin, this magistracy possesses enormous authority in the city. For it has been given the position of a sentinel and guardian, as it were, to see to it that the commonwealth shall not deviate from the course followed by our ancestors, and that the government of the commonwealth should not fall into the hands of men of opposing sentiments. Thus the function performed by the censors in Rome, by the council of the Areopagus in Athens and by the ephors in Sparta, is performed in Florence by the captains of the party. In other words, it is from among these citizens who love the republic that the leaders are chosen to serve as guardians of the republic.

So excellent and caring is the government of this city under these magistracies that one may say that there never was a household with better discipline under a watchful *paterfamilias*. Accordingly no one here can suffer injury, nor does anyone lose his property involuntarily. The courts and magistracies are always ready to hear cases; the courtroom and the supreme court are open. There is the freest opportunity in this city to file a complaint against persons of any rank, but under laws that are prudent and salutary and always accessible to afford relief. There is no place on earth in which justice is fairer for all. For nowhere does such liberty flourish, nor such a balanced relationship between greater and lesser. For here, too, this city's prudence—greater perhaps than that of any other—is noteworthy. For when the powerful, relying on their wealth, were seen to be injuring and disdaining the weak, the republic itself undertook the defense of the powerless and secured their persons and property by the establishment of higher penalties upon the former. In accordance with reason the city decided that it was fitting that different penalties should be imposed on different ranks of men; and that it should provide those in need with greater help out of its resources of skill and justice. Thus a certain balance among the various ranks was created, since the great can rely on their power, the small on the commonwealth, and both on the fear of punishment to deter transgressors. From this the saying was born, which we hear most frequently hurled against the powerful, for when they threaten something, the cry goes up at once: "I, too, am a Florentine citizen!" By this saying they seem to be attesting and publicly warning that no one should despise anybody on account of his weakness, nor continue to threaten injury by exploiting his own power; that the situation of everyone is the same, since those with less power will be avenged by the commonwealth itself.

Not only citizens, but aliens as well are protected by this commonwealth. It suffers injury to be done to no man, and endeavors to see that everyone, citizen or alien, shall receive the justice that is owing to him. This same justice and equity, while fostering good human relations among citizens, since nobody can be too puffed up or hold the rest in contempt, at the same time really encourages courtesy to all men. As for the rectitude of their lives and the high level of their morality, who could do them justice in the time remaining?

There are in this city the most talented men, who easily surpass the limits of other men in whatever they do. Whether they follow the military profession, or devote themselves to the task of governing the commonwealth, or to certain studies or to the pursuit of knowledge, or to commerce—in everything they undertake and in every activity they far surpass all other mortals, nor do they yield first place in any field to any other nation. They are patient in their labor, ready to meet danger, ambitious for glory, strong in counsel, industrious, generous, elegant, pleasant, affable, and above all, urbane. . . .

LEON BATTISTA ALBERTI (1404–72)

DELLA FAMIGLIA

On the Family (1434–43)

The wisdom and formality of the classics mingles with the streetwise practicality of the Florentine *borghese* in a remarkable dialogue by Leon Battista Alberti, one of the first humanists. Accomplished not only as a man of letters, he was also a scholar, musician, painter, art theorist, mathematician, mechanic, and architect; his best known work in Latin was the *De re aedifacatoria* (*On Building*), stressing that artwork must be based upon sound theory, and that beauty must be wed to accuracy of representation. The Renaissance ideal of the universal man was derived from his insistence that the artist be versed in all realms of knowledge, both philosophical and scientific, to achieve his accuracy. Alberti was a crusader in the use of the vernacular in place of Latin. Though he wrote in both languages, his most popular work, *On the Family,* was written in Tuscan in the form of a dialogue following Xenophon's *Oeconomicus*. The dialogue's purpose is to present the relationship between a well-governed family and a well-governed state, dealing with family management, finances, marriages, do-

Bed chamber, in the Palazzo Davanzati, Florence

After my wife had been settled in my house a few days, and after her first pangs of longing for her mother and family had begun to fade, I took her by the hand and showed her around the whole house. I explained that the loft was the place for grain and that the stores of wine and wood were kept in the cellar. I showed her where things needed for the table were kept, and so on, through the whole house. At the end there were no house-hold goods of which my wife had not learned both the place and the purpose. Then we returned to my room, and, having locked the door, I showed her my treasures, silver, tapestry, garments, jewels, and where each thing had its place. . . .

Only my books and records and those of my ancestors did I determine to keep well sealed. . . . These my wife not only could not read, she could not even lay hands on them. I kept my records at all times. . . locked up and arranged in order in my study, almost like sacred and religious objects. I never gave my wife permission to enter that place, with me or alone. I also ordered her, if she ever came across any writing of mine, to give it over to my keeping at once. To take away any taste she might have for looking at my notes or prying into my private affairs, I often used to express my disapproval of bold and forward females who try too hard to know about things outside the house and about the concerns of their husband and of men in general. . . .

[Husbands] who take counsel with their wives. . . are madmen if they think true prudence or good counsel lies in the female brain. . . . For this very reason I have always tried carefully not to let any secret of mine be known to a woman. I did not doubt that my wife was

most loving, and more discreet and modest in her ways than any, but I still considered it safer to have her unable, and not merely unwilling, to harm me. . . . Furthermore, I made it a rule never to speak with her of anything but household matters or questions of conduct, or of the children. Of these matters I spoke a good deal to her. . . .

When my wife had seen and understood the place of everything in the house, I said to her, 'My dear wife. . . you have seen our treasures now, and thanks be to God they are such that we ought to be contented with them. If we know how to preserve them, these things will serve you and me and our children. It is up to you, therefore, my dear wife, to keep no less careful watch over them than I.'

. . . She said she would be happy to do conscientiously whatever she knew how to do and had the skill to do, hoping it might please me. To this I said, 'Dear wife, listen to me. I shall be most pleased if you do just three things: first, my wife, see that you never want another man to share this bed but me. You understand.' She blushed and cast down her eyes. Still I repeated that she should never receive anyone into that room but myself. That was the first point. The second, I said, was that she should take care of the household, preside over it with modesty, serenity, tranquility, and peace. That was the second point. The third thing, I said, was that she should see that nothing went wrong in the house.

[Addressing the other interlocutors]. . . I could not describe to you how reverently she replied to me. She said her mother had taught her only how to spin and sew, and how to be virtuous and obedient. Now she would gladly learn from me how to rule the family and whatever I might wish to teach her.

. . . Then she and I knelt down and prayed to God to give us the power to make good use of those possessions which he, in his mercy and kindness, had allowed us to enjoy. We also prayed. . . that he might grant us the grace to live together in peace and harmony for many happy years, and with many male children, and that he might grant to me riches, friendship, and honor, and to her, integrity, purity, and the character of a perfect mistress of the household. Then, when we had stood up, I said to her: 'My dear wife, to have prayed God for these things is not enough. . . . I shall seek with all my powers to gain what we have asked of God. You, too, must set your whole will, all your mind, and all your modesty to work to make yourself a person whom God has heard. . . . You should realize that in this regard nothing is so important for your-self, so acceptable to God, so pleasing to me, and precious in the sight of your children as your chastity. The woman's character is the jewel of her family; the mother's purity has always been a part of the dowry she passes on to her daughters; her purity has always far out-weighed her beauty. . . . Shun every sort of dishonor, my dear wife. Use every means to appear to all people as a highly respectable woman. To seem less would be to offend God, me, our children, and yourself.'

[Finally, turning to the interlocutors again]. . . Never, at any moment, did I choose to show in word or action even the least bit of self-surrender in front of my wife. I did not imagine for a moment that I could hope to win obedience from one to whom I had confessed myself a slave. Always, therefore, I showed myself virile and a real man.

THE MEDICI

Letters (1443–92)

The cultural landscape of Florence today is unimaginable without the monuments erected under the patronage of the princely banking family whose progeny included popes Leo X, Clement VII, Pius IV, and Leo XI, and queens of France, Marie and Catherine; and whose protégés included Fra Angelico, Botticelli, Brunelleschi, Cellini, Donatello, Ficino, Ghiberti, Leonardo da Vinci, Poliziano, Pico della Mirandola, and Michelangelo. Michelangelo's breathtaking design for the *Cappella dei Principi,* the family burial chapel, in the Church of San Lorenzo celebrates the splendor of this hereditary principality—which was born with Cosimo the Elder's return from Venetian exile in 1434. The "Laurentian" library, in the same building, is a monument to Cosimo's voracious appetite for acquiring ancient manuscripts. His worldwide search led him to a fascination with the Greek language and to founding, at the Villa Careggi, a recreation of Plato's academy that became, under Marsilio Ficino, a seminal force in the development of Neoplatonic philosophy. Where others used force of arms to win power, the Medici used the persuasion of gold. When they needed troops, they bought them from the Sforzas of Milan. The Medici feted the middle class with circuses, winning their support against the Albizzi and other would-be enemies even while they were transforming Florence's beloved republic into a constitutional despotism. Their alliance with the city's artisans lay at the roots of their banking success, and eventually led them to become history's most dedicated patrons of the arts—from Lorenzo *Il Magnifico*, who died in 1492, to his seventeenth-century descendants.

Medici coat of arms, Via dei Pucci e dei Servi, Florence

MARSILIO FICINO TO THE NOBLE LORENZO DE' MEDICI

Even as harmony delights us more at the moment it strikes our ears than when we remember tunes we have heard, and the actual sight of war moves us more than any recital thereof, thus the great deeds of noble and illustrious men animate our courage far more than the words of orators and philosophers who dispute about valour. For it is ordered by nature that things themselves should be more potent than their names, and that real events should move the soul with greater force than what is either false or may have happened. Therefore by imitating the deeds of Socrates we are taught better how to attain courage than by the art displayed by Aristotle in his writings on morality. And Christ solely by His example has done more to make us adopt a holy and virtuous way of life than all the orators and philosophers that ever existed. Therefore, my Lorenzo, whilst I applaud you for not despising the writings which teach morals, I beg you to prefer learning from reality instead of from description, as you would prefer a living thing from a dead. Particularly as you have decided to emulate that aged man on whom our Senate bestowed the title of Father of His Country. I mean the great Cosimo, your grandfather and my lord. A man prudent above all men, pious towards God, just and most charitable towards men, temperate in living, diligent in his care for his family,

Medals of Giuliano Medici (Lucia della Robbia), in the Bargello, Florence

and still more so in the affairs of the Republic; a most honourable man who lived not only for himself, but for the good of his country and his God; whose soul was as humble as any man's, and yet great and exalted. I, my Lorenzo, for more than twelve years gave myself up to philosophy with him. He was as acute in reasoning as he was prudent and strong in governing. Certainly I owe much to Plato, but must confess that I owe no less to Cosimo. Inasmuch as Plato only once showed me the Idea of courage, Cosimo showed it me every day. For the moment I will not mention his other qualities. Cosimo was as avaricious and careful of time as Midas of money; he spent his days parsimoniously, carefully counting every hour and avariciously saving every second; he often lamented the loss of hours. Finally, having like Solon the philosophor (even when occupied in most serious business) diligently studied philosophy, yet even till the last day when he departed from this world of shadows to go to light he devoted himself to the acquisition of knowledge. For when we had read together Plato's book dealing with the *Origin of the Universe* and the *Summum Bonum* he, as you who were present well know, soon after quitted this life as though he was really going to enjoy that happiness which he had tasted during our conversations. Farewell, and as God fashioned Cosimo according to the Idea of the world, do you continue as you have begun to fashion yourself according to the Idea of Cosimo.

Marsilio Ficino

Pope Pius II. to Piero de' Medici

Beloved Son,

—Greeting and apostolic blessing. We have just heard that Cosimo, your father, has departed this life. This is indeed bitter and mournful news, and most grievous to us. For we loved him with sincere affection as a man whom we always found devoted to ourselves and to the Apostolic See, whom we knew to be gifted with unusual insight and kindness. Yet, my son, though many besides yourself will mourn his death, you must bear with a brave heart this fate which divine law has ordained for mortals. Accept this expression of God's will patiently, and do not give way to grief. If you consider the course of human existence, Cosimo has had a long life; he has paid his debt to nature, and in his old age he has gone the way of all flesh. His life was full of honour; his glory extended beyond his own city to all Italy, nay, to the whole world; he has lived in the highest esteem and, what we must value more, in piety, and abiding in the fear of God. It is not right to mourn the death of a man who has lived righteously and justly, since we must believe that he has gone from this troubled human existence to one that is full of peace and tranquility. As for us, beloved son, we intend to preserve towards you the feelings we had for your father, and for him we had a singular paternal affection. We promise that we shall always do what in our judgment will be conducive to your honour and your interest, and to that of the house of Medici. This we wish you to understand.

> —*Given at Ancona under the seal of the Fisherman, the 8th day of August 1464, in the sixth year of our pontificate.*

Louis XI., King of France, to Piero de' Medici

Dilecto Filio Nobili Viro Petro de' Medicis.
Louis, by the grace of God King of France.

Most Dear and Great Friend,

—We have received by our beloved and faithful courier Francesco Nori your letters which you sent to us by him. From him and from your letters we have learned how kindly you have acted in our favour towards our dear and beloved uncle the Duke of Milan about the affair of the Marches of which we wrote, and we are much pleased and very grateful to you. We also heard of the death of the late Cosimo de' Medici, our great friend and your father, which has given and does give us much sorrow, both for the singular love we bore him and for the great and laudable services he rendered to us and to the French crown during his whole life. For the enduring memory thereof and of the friendship he showed to us and to the crown, and in order to honour him and you and all his relatives and family, and for the salvation of his soul, we beg you to dedicate to the service of your said dead father banners with our arms, of such number as seems best to you and is customary in such

cases. We have also, in order to show the confidence we place in you, in your wisdom, loyalty, goodness, and diligence, and for the preservation of the friendship and goodwill which always existed between your late father and ourselves, appointed you one of our privy councillors, and have ordered the letters patent to be made out, which we send by the bearer; and when you desire anything for yourself, for your family or for your Commune, we shall grant it in your favour if you signify it and let us know by the said Franceschino, for whom we have always felt and feel singular affection and esteem. . . .

Lorenzo de' Medici to Louis XI., King of France

Most Serene King and especially my Lord,

—The letter Your Majesty has designed to write about our unhappy case, replete with great love and paternal benevolence, shows me how keenly you felt our misfortune, and how kindly disposed you are towards me. Should I even attempt to return adequate thanks to Your Majesty I should deserve to be called utterly unfit to understand so great a benefit, because words so full of love and benevolence coming from Your Majesty to a humble servant cannot be repaid by any act or word. I can therefore only beg Your Majesty specially to accept my heartfelt declaration of loyalty as a token and a pledge of my gratitude, trusting that God will repay to Your Majesty the rest of my debt. As to Your Majesty's wise counsels to bear this calamity with fortitude, you may rest assured that I do not so much deplore what has happened to myself as the grave affront to the Christian name; because where I hoped, in such bitter trouble, to receive help, I found instead the fountain-head and instigator of all ill. For he, in the presence of many, dared to confess spontaneously that this crime was caused by him, and promulgated against me, my children, successors, intimates, and well-wishers, an iniquitous sentence of excommunication. Not satisfied with that, he is arming against this Republic, has instigated King Ferdinand against us, and has urged the King's eldest son to march against us with a formidable army in order with violence and arms to destroy him he could not succeed in utterly ruining by deceit and fraud. For I well know, and God is my witness, that I have committed no crime against the Pope, save that I am alive, and having been protected by the grace of Almighty God have not allowed myself to be murdered. This is my sin, for this alone have I been excommunicated and massacred. But I believe that God, scrutiniser of hearts and most just Judge, who knows my innocence, will not permit this and will defend me, whom He saved from those sacrilegious hands in front of His Body, from such unjust calumny. On our side we have Canon Law, on our side laws natural and political, on our side truth and innocence, on our side God and men. He has violated all these at once, and now desires to annihilate us. I write these things to Your Majesty as to a compassionate father, and from you, on account of your goodness, piety, and greatness of soul, I have no doubt I shall receive much help, favour, and military aid, if required. For we cannot believe that any good man can tolerate that he, who wilfully precipitates himself into such an abyss of crime, should drag with him the Christian name. May Your Majesty keep well, to whom I humbly commend myself.

—Florence, June 19, 1478. . . .

LORENZO DE' MEDICI TO THE KING OF SPAIN

Most Serene and Excellent Lord my King: after humble recommendation, &c.,—I have been informed during the last few days that your Majesty wrote me a letter full of affection and benevolence at that terrible time when my beloved brother Giuliano was so cruelly torn from me in the centre of the church, and when I was wounded. This letter, I know not why, never reached me; would to God it had, for the emotion evinced by so great a King would have been a great comfort to me when I was oppressed by such a terrible sorrow. Had I only known that the letter had been sent by your Majesty and delayed in the journey, it would have been no small comfort, and I should have at once thanked your Majesty for such a proof of kindly feeling towards me. Even now I send most heartfelt thanks and express my deep obligation. I desire nothing more than that an opportunity may arise for me to show my devotion to your Majesty. It is far beyond my power to repay not alone the letter, but even the slightest sign from so great a King, all I can do is to place myself entirely at your Majesty's orders. I commend myself ever to your Majesty O my Lord and King, and beg to be taken under the shadow of your wings. Your Majesty is I know fully acquainted with our affairs. We are preparing for war and working hard to be able to resist the forces of the enemy. Resist we shall, as I hope, because we shall not fail to ourselves, and I trust God will aid the good cause. Again I commend myself to your Majesty, whom may God preserve in happiness.

—Florence, April 3, 1479. Your Serene Majesty's most devoted servant, Lorenzo de' Medici. . . .

LOUIS XI., KING OF FRANCE, TO LORENZO DE' MEDICI

My Cousin,

—By your letter of January 30th I learn your wishes regarding your son Giovanni, if I had only known this before the death of the Cardinal de Rohan I should have done all in my power to please you. I will gladly do whatever I can when a benefice falls vacant. As to Ferrara, where you have promised to go, I should have advised you to abstain, and to be very careful about your personal safety, for I do not know the people or the place you will be in. I would gladly have sent an ambassador from here to excuse you. However as you have promised I leave it to you, to good fortune, and to God.

—Written at Plessis du Parc, February 17, 1482 (1483).

Luy. . . .

LORENZO DE' MEDICI TO POPE INNOCENT VIII. (1489)

My ambassador has written to tell me that at last by the kindness of Your Holiness the contract of the alum works has been awarded to me, for this I owe infinite thanks to Your Holiness who has thus added another to the many obligations I already owe, and hope to enjoy in the future from the liberality and kindness of Your Beatitude. I am exceedingly grateful for and pleased by the paternal charity shown to me every day by Your Holiness, and should be yet more happy did I not hear that Your Holiness has been suffering from gout and slight fever. Although the attack is not a severe one, still, depending as I do on Your Holiness, and Your Holiness' life being of such importance, I cannot but feel uneasy even at a small indisposition, particularly as these attacks come oftener than one could wish. Your Holiness can rest assured that even as S. Francis by reason of his stigmate felt the pain of the wounds of Jesus Christ, thus do I feel every pain and ill suffered by Your Holiness in my own person and am much molested thereby. Among other things the condition of our Ser Francesco touches me deeply, as well as that of other dependants of Your Holiness, who by reason of the uprightness and honesty of Your Beatitude may be said to be still fasting and to have had but a small share of the great good fortune which our Lord God has so worthily bestowed on Your Holiness. Should anything happen to Your Holiness, *quod absit,* the sepulchre will open also for them. Although I feel compassion for them all I am more moved by what ought to touch Your Holiness more nearly than myself, and that is the sad condition of poor Ser Francesco, who in the five years of the pontificate of Your Holiness has never yet had anything he can call his own. Your Holiness is the best judge of what support he enjoys in the Sacred College and what office, dignity or means, he has to enable him to live, even poorly. If Your Holiness studies the lives of other Popes you will see that there are but few who during five years of pontifical rule, and some in even less time, have not manifested their intention of acting as a Pope, and have not shown the respect for honesty and uprightness displayed by Your Holiness, which is justified before God and man. But speaking as a devoted servant, this honesty might now be imputed and attributed to another motive. Maybe I appear presumptuous, but zeal and the duty I owe to Your Holiness so touch my conscience that I must speak thus openly and remind Your Holiness that all men are mortal, and that a Pope is what he wills to be; he cannot leave the Papacy as a heritage and can only call his own the honours, the glory and the benefits, he gives to his family. The prudence, experience and long acquaintance Your Sanctity has of a court, will I am sure without words from me, recall to Your Holiness what always happens to the fortune and inheritance of popes, and seeing that Ser Francesco and the others of Your Holiness' family are as yet not to be envied but rather merit compassion, Your Sanctity ought to follow the example of Your Holiness' predecessors and place them in such a position that they should have no need of others, particularly as whatever is bestowed on them does not diminish the substance of Your Holiness and is not lost or thrown away. Briefly, with all humility, I entreat Your Sanctity at last to begin and act as a Pope with regard to the family of Your Holiness and not to trust so much in posterity and good health, which can only retard the fulfillment of what Your Holiness intends to do for them. Delay might perhaps prevent this being accomplished. Especially do I recommend Your and my Ser Francesco and the Lady Maddalena, who pray that God may grant Your Holiness a long life in order that their affairs may be properly adjusted, and when better arranged they will give thanks to God and to Your Holiness, and have reason to remember and to bless the day when Your Sanctity was called to the honours and dignity of the pontificate. It is time, Holy Father, to liberate these Holy Fathers from limbo, so that it may not happen to them as to the Jews who awaited the Messiah. I beg Your Holiness' pardon with all humility and reverence for this my presumption only caused by reasons which I am sure Your Holiness will appreciate, and I place myself humbly at Your most holy feet.

Humilis Servitor,
Laurentius de Medicis

LORENZO DE' MEDICI TO HIS SON, CARDINAL GIOVANNI, AT ROME, IN MARCH 1492

Messer Giovanni,

—You are much beholden to our Lord God, as we all are for your sake, as besides many benefits and honours our house has received from Him it has pleased Him to bestow on you the highest dignity our family has yet enjoyed. Great as this is it is much enhanced by circumstances, particularly your youth and our condition. Therefore my first recommendation is that you endeavour to be grateful to our Lord God, remembering every hour that it is not by your own merits or solicitude that you have attained the Cardinalate, but by the grace of God. Show your gratitude to Him by leading a saintly, exemplary, and honest life. You are the more bound to do this because during your youth you have shown a disposition which gives hope of good fruit. It would be indeed most shameful, contrary to your duty, and to my expectations if at a time when others generally acquire more reason and a better understanding of life, you should forget the good precepts learned as a boy. It is incumbent on you to try and lighten the burden of the dignity you have attained by leading a pure life and persvering in the studies suitable to your profession. I was greatly pleased last year to learn that without being reminded by any one you had been several times to confession and to communion, for I conceive there is no better way of obtaining the grace of God than by ha-

bituating oneself to persevere in these duties. This seems to me the best advice I can begin with. I know, as you are now going to Rome, that sink of all iniquities, that you will find some difficulty in following it, as bad examples are always catching, and inciters to vice will not be wanting. Your promotion to the Cardinalate, as you may imagine, at your age and for the other reasons already mentioned, will be viewed with great envy, and those who were not able to prevent your attaining this dignity will endeavour, little by little, to diminish it by lowering you in public estimation and causing you to slide into the same ditch into which they have themselves fallen, counting on success because of your youth. You must be all the firmer in your stand against these difficulties, as at present one sees such a lack of virtue in the College. I recollect however to have known a good many learned and good men in the College, leading exemplary lives. It will be well that you should follow their example, for by so doing you will be the more known and esteemed as being different from the others. It is imperative above all things that you should avoid as you would Scylla and Charybdis the reputation of being a hypocrite and of evil fame. Be not ostentatious, and have a care to avoid anything offensive in conduct and in conversation, without affecting austerity or severity. These are things you will in time understand and practise better, I conceive, than I can write them. You know how important is the position and the example of a Cardinal, and that the world would be far better if the Cardinals were what they ought to be, for then there would always be a good Pope, from whom emanates, one may say, peace for all Christians. Make every effort therefore to be this, if others had done so we might hope for universal good. Nothing is more difficult than to hold converse with men of various characters, and in this I can ill advise you; only recollect when with the Cardinals and other men of rank to try and be charitable and respectful in your conversation, weighing your reasons well without being influenced by the passions of others; for many desiring what they cannot attain turn reason into abuse. Satisfy your conscience therefore by taking care that your conversation with every man should be devoid of offence. This seems to me a general rule most applicable in your case, for should passion by chance make an enemy, as his enmity would have no reasonable cause he may sometimes return with more ease to the old friendship. It will be better I think on this, your first visit to Rome, to use your ears more than your tongue. To-day I have given you entirely to our Lord God and to Holy Church; it is therefore essential that you become a good ecclesiastic, cherishing the honour and the State of Holy Church and of the Apostolic See above aught else in this world, and devoting yourself entirely to their interests. While doing this it will not be difficult for you to aid the city and our house, for the city being united to the Church you will represent the solid chain, and our house is part of the city. Although it is impossible to foresee what may happen I think it is likely that a way will be found to save, as the proverb says, the goat and the cabbages, always keeping steadfastly to your above-mentioned duty of setting the interests of the Church above all else. You are the youngest Cardinal, not only of the College, but the youngest that has hitherto been made, it is therefore most necessary that where you have to compete with the others you should be the most eager and the humblest, and avoid making others wait for you in Chapel, in Consistory, or in Deputation. You will soon learn who has a good or an evil reputation. With the latter avoid any great intimacy, not only on your own account, but for the sake of public opinion; converse in a general way with all. I advise you on feast-days to be rather below than above moderation, and would rather see a well-appointed stable and a well-ordered and cleanly household than magnificence and pomp. Let your life be regular and reduce your expenses gradually in the future, for the retinue and the master being both new at first it will be difficult. Jewels and silken stuffs must be used sparingly by one in your position. Rather have a few good antiques and fine books, and well-bred and learned attendants, than many of them. Ask people to your own house oftener than you accept invitations to theirs, but do both sparingly. Eat plain food and take much exercise, for those who wear your habit, if not careful, easily contract maladies. The rank of Cardinal is as secure as it is great, men therefore often become negligent; they conceive they have done enough and that without exertion they can preserve their position. This is often prejudicial to character and to life, and a thing against which you must guard; rather trust too little than too much in others. One rule I recommend to you above all others, and that is to get up betimes; besides being good for health one can meditate over and arrange all the business of the following day, and in your position, having to say the office, to study, to give audiences &c. you will find it most useful. Another thing absolutely necessary to one in your station is to reflect, particularly at this, the commencement of your career, in the evening on all you have to do next day, so that an unforeseen event may not come upon you unawares. As to speaking in the Consistory, I think it would be more seemly and becoming if you refer all that comes before you to His Holiness, alleging that as you are young and inexperienced you consider it your duty to submit everything to the most learned judgment of His Holiness. You will probably be asked to intercede in various matters with our Holy Father. Be cautious however at the beginning to ask as few favours as possible and not to bother him; the disposition of the Pope is to be grateful to those who do not break his ears. Bear this in mind in order not to annoy him. When you see him, talk about amusing things, and if you have to beg, do it with all humility and modesty. This will please him and be in accordance with his nature.

Keep well. —Florence.

CARDINAL GIOVANNI DE' MEDICI TO HIS FATHER LORENZO MAGNIFICO VIRO LAURENTIO DE MEDICI PATER OPTIMO

Salvus sis,

—In case. . . (I) did not tell you of some things. On Friday morning I was given a public reception and went accompanied by all the Cardinals, nearly the whole court, and very heavy rain, from S.M. del

Popolo to the palace and from the palace to Campo di Fiore. Our Holy Father received me most graciously: I hardly spoke to him. The following day the ambassadors waited on our Holy Father; their audience was most satisfactory. The Pope desired to hear me the day after, which is to-day. I have been, and His Holiness spoke as lovingly as was possible to me, and reminded me, and advised me, to do something when I visited these Cardinals, and I have begun to do so with those to whom as yet I have paid visits. Another time I will tell you who they are. All professed the greatest good-will towards you. Of former things I know that you have been told. Of myself I have nought to say save that I will try hard to do you honour. *De me proloqui ulterius, nefas.* The news that you are so much better has been a great joy to me and I have no other wish than to hear this often. For this I send thanks to Ser Piero [Leoni, the doctor]. I commend myself to you. No more at present.

—*Rome, March 25, 1492.*

LORENZO VALLA (1407–57)

De falso credita et ementita Constantini donatione declamatio

On the Donation of Constantine (1440; first printed 1517)

A direct attack on Papal claims to temporal power was launched by a Roman literary critic, with a surprisingly modern methodology that combines psychological insight with textual analysis. Lorenzo Valla, after teaching rhetoric at the University of Pavia, became secretary to Alfonso of Aragon, King of Sicily and Naples, who at the time was at war with Pope Eugenius IV. Valla reexamined the anonymous late eighth-century Latin document known as *The Donation of Constantine,* and declared it to be a fraud. The "alleged donation" was the legal basis upon which the papacy claimed the city of Rome, the kingdom of Sicily and Naples, as well as France, Spain, Germany, Britain, and all of Italy as its own political territory in perpetuity. Presenting itself as a legal document, the *Donation* includes Constantine's account of his leprosy cured by Sylvester, the Bishop of Rome, and his subsequent baptism. The document establishes Sylvester as head of all the clergy and supreme over the other four patriarchates of the Catholic church, and, in addition to the territories themselves, bestows upon him a largesse of imperial property in various parts of the world, including the Lateran palace and the imperial diadem and tiara. The *Donation* gives Sylvester and his successors freedom to consecrate men as clerics, and tells how Constantine acknowledged his loyalty to the pope by holding the bridle of his horse. This document was considered almost universally as genuine until Valla subjected it to the scrutiny of diction and historical analysis and declared that its Latin could not possibly have been written in the time of Constantine. Valla also contributed to establishing classical authors like Cicero and Quintilian as models in the humanists' campaign to restore the Latin language to its eloquence and vigor. His *In novum testamentum,* subjecting the Bible to the same principles of textual criticism employed in the *Declamatio,* caused as much controversy then as Biblical textual analysis causes in our own century. It was, in fact, written in the service of the pope, though placed on the Index of Forbidden Books by the Counter-Reformation. His attack on the Apostles' Creed—Valla's analysis declared that it was not composed by the original twelve apostles—brought him trouble with the Inquisition, and only the intervention of King Alfonso saved him from execution. Like other humanists of the early Renaissance, Valla's aim was to reconcile the rediscovery of classical authorities with the Christian scheme of things. His iconoclastic contributions to the spirit of free inquiry produced revolutionary results in history, religion, politics, and philosophy that disturbed many of his more medieval contemporaries. Valla delighted, as Camille Paglia (author of *Sexual Personae* and *Vamps and Tramps*) now does, in disrupting fixed notions with scholarly insight.

. . . It is not my aim to inveigh against any one and write so-called Philippics against him—be that villainy far from me—but to root out error from men's minds, to free them from vices and crimes by either admonition or reproof. I would not dare to say [that my aim is] that others, taught by me, should prune with steel the papal see, which is Christ's vineyard, rank with overabundant shoots, and compel it to bear rich grapes instead of meager wildings. When I do that, is there any one who will want to close either my mouth or his own ears, much less propose punishment and death? If one should do so, even if it were the Pope, what should I call him, a good shepherd, or a deaf viper which would not choose to heed the voice of the charmer, but to strike his limbs with its poisonous bite?

I know that for a long time now men's ears are waiting to hear the offense with which I charge the Roman pontiffs. It is, indeed, an enormous one, due either to supine ignorance, or to gross avarice which is the slave of idols, or to pride of empire of which cruelty is ever the companion. For during some centuries now, either they have not known that the Donation of Constantine is spurious and forged, or else they themselves forged it, and their successors walking in the same way of deceit as their elders have

defended as true what they knew to be false, dishonoring the majesty of the pontificate, dishonoring the memory of ancient pontiffs, dishonoring the Christian religion, confounding everything with murders, disasters and crimes. They say the city of Rome is theirs, theirs the kingdom of Sicily and of Naples, the whole of Italy, the Gauls, the Spains, the Germans, the Britons, indeed the whole West; for all these are contained in the instrument of the Donation itself. So all these are yours, supreme pontiff? And it is your purpose to recover them all? To despoil all kings and princes of the West of their cities or compel them to pay you a yearly tribute, is that your plan?

I, on the contrary, think it fairer to let the princes despoil you of all the empire you hold. For, as I shall show, that Donation whence the supreme pontiffs will have their right derived was unknown equally to Sylvester and to Constantine.

But before I come to the refutation of the instrument of the Donation, which is their one defense, not only false but even stupid, the right order demands that I go further back. And first, I shall show that Constantine and Sylvester were not such men that the former would choose to give, would have the legal right to give, or would have it in his power to give those lands to another, or that the latter would be willing to accept them or could legally have done so. In the second place, if this were not so, though it is absolutely true and obvious, [I shall show that in fact] the latter did not receive nor the former give possession of what is said to have been granted, but that it always remained under the sway and empire of the Caesars. In the third place, [I shall show that] nothing was given to Sylvester by Constantine, but to an earlier Pope (and Constantine had received baptism even before that pontificate), and that the grants were inconsiderable, for the mere subsistence of the Pope. Fourth, that it is not true either that a copy of the Donation is found in the Decretum [of Gratian], or that it was taken from the History of Sylvester; for it is not found in it or in any history, and it is comprised of contradictions, impossibilities, stupidities, barbarisms and absurdities. Further, I shall speak of the pretended or mock donation of certain other Caesars. Then by way of redundance I shall add that even had Sylvester taken possession, nevertheless, he or some other pontiff having been dispossessed, possession could not be resumed after such a long interval under either divine or human law. Last [I shall show] that the possessions which are now held by the supreme pontiff could not, in any length of time, be validated by prescription.

And so to take up the first point, let us speak first of Constantine, then of Sylvester.

It would not do to argue a public and quasi imperial case without more dignity of utterance than is usual in private cases. And so speaking as in an assembly of kings and princes, as I assuredly do, for this oration of mine will come into their hands, I choose to address an audience, as it were, face to face. I call upon you, kings and princes, for it is difficult for a private person to form a picture of a royal mind; I seek your thought, I search your heart, I ask your testimony. Is there any one of you who, had he been in Constantine's place, would have thought that he must set about giving to another out of pure generosity the city of Rome, his fatherland, the head of the world, the queen of states, the most powerful, the noblest and the most opulent of peoples, the victor of the nations, whose very form is sacred, and betaking himself thence to an humble little town, Byzantium; giving with Rome Italy, not a province but the mistress of provinces; giving the three Gauls; giving the two Spains; the Germans; the Britons; the whole West; depriving himself of one of the two eyes of his empire? That any one in possession of his senses would do this, I cannot be brought to believe.

What ordinarily befalls you that is more looked forward to, more pleasing, more grateful, than for you to increase your empires and kingdoms, and to extend your authority as far and wide as possible? In this, as it seems to me, all your care, all your thought, all your labor, night and day is expended. From this comes your chief hope of glory, for this you renounce pleasures; for this you subject yourselves to a thousand dangers; for this your dearest pledges, for this your own flesh you sacrifice with serenity. Indeed, I have neither heard nor read of any of you having been deterred from an attempt to extend his empire by loss of an eye, a hand, a leg, or any other member. Nay, this very ardor and this thirst for wide dominion is such that whoever is most powerful, him it thus torments and stirs the most. Alexander, not content to have traversed on foot the deserts of Libya, to have conquered the Orient to the farthest ocean, to have mastered the North, amid so much bloodshed, so many perils, his soldiers already mutinous and crying out against such long, such hard campaigns, seemed to himself to have accomplished nothing unless either by force or by the power of his name he should have made the West also, and all nations, tributary to him. I put it too mildly; he had already determined to cross the ocean, and if there was any other world, to explore it and subject it to his will. He would have tried, I think, last of all to ascend the heavens. Some such wish all kings have, even though not all are so bold. I pass over the thought how many crimes, how many horrors have been committed to attain and extend power, for brothers do not restrain their wicked hands from the stain of brothers' blood, nor sons from the blood of parents, nor parents from the blood of sons. Indeed, nowhere is man's recklessness apt to run riot further nor more viciously. And to your astonishment, you see the minds of old men no less eager in this than the minds of young men, childless men no less eager than parents, kings than usurpers.

But if domination is usually sought with such great resolution, how much greater must be the resolution to preserve it! For it is by no means so discreditable not to increase an empire as to impair it, nor is it so shameful not to annex another's kingdom to your own as for your own to be annexed to another's. And when we read of men being put in charge of a kingdom or of cities by some king or by the people, this is not done in the case of the chief or the greatest portion of the empire, but in the case of the last and least, as it were, and that with the understanding that the recipient should always recognize the donor as his sovereign and himself as an agent.

Now I ask, do they not seem of a base and most ignoble mind who suppose that Constantine gave away the better part of his empire? I say nothing of Rome, Italy, and the rest, but the Gauls where he had waged war in person, where for a long time he had been sole master, where he had laid the foundations of his glory and his empire! A man who through thirst for dominion had waged war against nations, and attacking friends and relatives in civil strife had taken the government from them, who had to deal with remnants of an opposing faction not yet completely mastered and overthrown; who waged war with many nations not only by inclination and in the hope of fame and empire but by very necessity, for he was harassed every day by the barbarians; who had many sons, relatives and associates; who knew that the Senate and the Roman people would oppose this act; who had experienced the instability of conquered nations and their rebellions at nearly every change of ruler at Rome; who remembered that after the manner of other Caesars he had come into power, not by the choice of the Senate and the consent of the populace, but by armed warfare; what incentive could there be so strong and urgent that he would ignore all this and choose to display such prodigality? . . .

AENEAS SILVIUS (ENEA SILVIO DE' PICCOLOMINI) (PIUS II) (1405–64)

Letters to Sigismund of Austria (1443)

The worldliness of the Tuscan who was elected pope in 1458 appears in this letter of counsel to the young prince of Austria, Sigismund, written five years before his papal coronation. So committed was he to his secular hedonism as secretary and poet laureate to the Emperor Frederick III, that Silvius had not been ordained until 1445, when he was forty. The next year he was appointed Bishop of Trieste, quickly advancing to Bishop of Siena, then Cardinal. His impoverished childhood no doubt influenced his love for luxury. Like many of his time he fought a lifelong inner battle between his spiritual ambitions, fired by

San Bernardino of Siena, and his humanistic inclinations, refined by his master Mario Sozzini. When he was elected pope, he chose the name "Pius" to pay tribute to his classical master, Virgil, whose "*pius Aeneas*" follows duty rather than personal temptation. As famous for his humanistic studies and writing as he was for the achievements of his papacy, Silvius lived to see his native village Corsignano renamed Pienza in his honor. His Latin writings include a romantic novel, which brought him instant fame throughout Europe; a ribald Terentian comedy; poetry; orations; and prose. His geographical theories inspired Columbus. His wide-ranging autobiographical *Commentaries* offer an important perspective on the people and events of his life. Silvius' description of his own style may still serve today as a model:

> I speak directly and clearly since I reject purple prose. I do not strain to express myself because I do not handle matters beyond my reach. I know what I know and feel that the man who understands himself well can make others understand what he has to say. . . . I avoid a knotty style and long periodic sentences. If I use elegant words I try to make them fit in their context; in any case, I do not ransack my dictionary but use those that come to mind. My one goal is to be understood.

The following letter attends to the young prince's ideal education, balancing instruction with admonition and solicitousness.

TO SIGISMUND OF AUSTRIA, DECEMBER 5, 1443.

Aeneas Silvius, Poet and Royal Secretary, sends heartfelt greetings to his Lord, Sigismund of Austria, Illustrious Prince of Royal Blood, etc., Duke and Count of the Tyrol.

. . . Now I must return to my reason for undertaking the writing of this letter which resides in the fact that when I became part of the staff of the king, your uncle, everyone I met spoke of you as a virtuous and outstanding young man. One individual would praise your great kindness, another your admirable honesty and modesty; another man would state that you were wise beyond your years. I would hear too that you were generous, cherished justice, and that you were that unusual prince among princes who studied Latin keenly. All of these qualities elicited my admiration and I found it difficult to believe that one prince was the repository of so many good qualities. This lurking disbelief prompted me not

to lend credence to the first people I encountered; I sought out others and when I did I found that they confirmed the general opinion about you. But I still had to find out for myself so I managed to find opportunities to be close to you by taking a place in the crowds of nobles that surrounded you. You were unaware that I was there to examine you; I observed your gestures, your manner of speaking, the way you bore yourself—in short, I examined everything about you and was impressed with your modest bearing and your use of pure Latin.

The result of my inquiry is that I had to conclude that the truth about you exceeded even your reputation. I really could not believe this, but how was I to doubt my own eyes and ears which confirmed that you indeed did possess the qualities I was seeking in you. Please do not think that I am saying this to flatter you. I have a low opinion of flatterers and I urge you to avoid them all like a foul plague. You must avoid those who praise you within earshot of everyone, who agree with everything you do, who say no when you say no, and say yes when you say yes and are like Terence's Gnatho who states, "When they say yes, I say yes," or are like the character of whom Juvenal states, "If someone says, 'I'm hot,' he sweats." These really are the worst kind of men and princes do well in avoiding them and bringing them to ruin; they should be shunned by young and old alike. I must therefore now explain why I praised you openly and why I did not keep quiet about you. The reason is that I want you to preserve your shining qualities, not that you gloat over them. You must not let my praise go to your head but must take my remarks as words of advice to you that you should guard your good qualities, increase them, and not let them slip away. Your virtues thus guarded will grow as you grow and will prevent you from falling into that category of good youths who turned out to be wicked old men, or, as the proverb has it, grow into bad chickens from good chicks. My wish is for you to become the worthiest of men from the good youth you are now, a change which will be easier for your having been brought up correctly. Your admirable upbringing is owed to your father, a most illustrious prince, who taught you how to cultivate your spirit, who guided your growth and procured the best teachers for you. In educating you thus he has given you a better inheritance than a kingdom.

Riches and powers are marks of contemporary honor but are dependent on the whim of luck, can go from good to bad, change rapidly, and can as readily be taken from a person as given to him. Human beings are the toys of Fortune and in her scales she makes one man's luck sink as another's rises. It is in her power to make a potter a king and just as quickly cast him back into his former state. Juvenal expresses this thought when he states, "If Fortune wills, you will become a consul from a rhetor; if she wills it too, you can be turned back into a rhetor from a consul." To illustrate how much power he had, Alexander the Great elevated a certain farmer to the rank of governor. While Diocletian was the ruler of the world he put aside his robes and scepters in order to devote himself to irrigating his vegetable garden and planting trees. The things we consider the goods of the soul—continence, chastity, fortitude, justice, moderation, intellect, character, memory—all of these are fused inextricably onto a man and are so much a part of him that they perish only with his death. These qualities are real riches and make our lives valuable while we live among men and, after we die, are our hope for eternal bliss. Nature has blessed you with these gifts and your father has augmented them; my hope, therefore, is that you will continue to cherish the good which you have inherited.

Nothing can help you in guiding your life more than the study of literature, a study in which you have already been initiated. Yet it is my understanding that you have thrown off your studies like some yoke which obliges me to try to induce you to take them up again. Some people think that princes should study literature so that their knowledge of Latin may permit them to converse with foreigners. This certainly is an attractive feature of literary studies, but is far from being the most important one. We ought to study literature because it offers us models of behavior after which we can pattern our lives; knowing these will be helpful. And one must know literature deeply, not superficially, if real progress is to be made. Contemporary rulers are happy with a smattering of knowledge and leave detailed study to philosophers and jurisconsultants, just as if it were less important for them to know the principles of a good life. I entreat you not to fall into this pattern of thinking which will block your developing into a good man and a famous ruler. It is only when natural intelligence has been formed by study that a gifted ruler will appear, as the outstanding rulers found in previous centuries well illustrate, for all of these were eager students of literature.

Philip of Macedon rejoiced that Aristotle was his contemporary and that he could entrust the education of his son, Alexander, to him. At the age you are now Alexander did not cease his studies; even when he was advancing towards Asia he took Aristotle and Callisthenes with him and in the midst of his campaigns found time to study philosophy. It is a pity that he was intemperate in drinking wine, for his life would otherwise have been completely happy. Alcibiades and Themistocles, both famous Greeks, were very interested in philosophy. Epaminondas of Thebes, once the greatest general in Greece, gave as much of his time to literature as he did to arms.

Let me turn now to Roman examples. What can be found more elegantly and eloquently composed than the *Commentaries* Caesar wrote while on his campaigns in Gaul? Caesar spent his day-time hours campaigning, but his evenings were devoted to his literary pursuits. Caesar's heir, Augustus, spoke gracefully and could write poetry very well, as his extant verses in praise of the *Aeneid* illustrate. The same qualities existed in the Fabii, the Cornelii, and the Catos. I can also mention Pompey who was so devoted to literature that he interrupted his stay in Rhodes to visit the sick philosopher Posidonius, even though he was occupied with consular affairs. Cato had a chauvinistic pride in Latin learning and scorned Greek literature for many years. But later, repenting of his earlier views, he dedicated himself to the study of foreign literature, old as he was, and trained himself to speak Greek correctly. These figures I have mentioned—men who were princes and ruled whole nations—wanted to cultivate literature and knew well Plato's thought, echoed in Cicero and Boethius, that states would be run well if their rulers are eager to obtain wisdom. This wisdom, of course, comes about as a result of drinking deep from the streams of philosophy.

You may perhaps think that the reports about the ancients' wish to have leisure during business and to engage in business in leisure hours are mere stories. If this is the case, you may remove your doubts by the examples of living men who take part in affairs of state, who hold the most demanding government offices, and yet find time for intellectual pursuits. Consider, for example, Leonello, Margrave of Esthonia, who writes so well that his letters bear comparison with Cicero's. The Margrave of Saluzzo also writes Latin in the best style, and the sons of the Margrave of Mantua are equally adept in arms and in literature. Alphonse, King of Aragon, who

holds sway over Sicily and the southern part of Italy, once referred to as Magna Graecia, a man who tasted of adversity many times but who finally triumphed over adverse fortune, never engages in military exploits without bringing his personal library with him. It makes no difference whether he is indoors or out; wherever he is he reads or has others recite to him. . . .

Do you see then that our age does furnish examples of literate princes? Why don't you continue your studies and find a place among these princes? The standards for entering their company is high and your knowledge of Latin—admirable as it is—does not alone qualify you, because even crows and woodpeckers can be taught to speak. We hear that a crow learned Latin and said, "Hail, Augustus Caesar, General," to Octavian after he conquered Antony. Persius' question comes to mind, "Who taught the parrot to say 'hello' and who taught magpies how to speak?" Persius answers the question by saying, "It was the Belly, which is the master of arts and the dispenser of genius." Why then should you think it a fine thing that you can understand a Hungarian, an Italian, or a Frenchman speaking Latin, and that you can do this, young as you are, while older men stand dumbly by? I don't think you should esteem your accomplishments highly until you have attained such literacy as will permit you to read and study the orators, poetry, and philosophy, with ease and enjoyment. You may imagine such an accomplishment too hard for you and beyond your ability; this is not so. It is not that I want you to study night and day, for an hour devoted every day to the study of literature will bring about the desired level of literacy.

When you do begin such a program of studies you should be careful, moreover, that your instructor be erudite and wise, and that you are not influenced in your choice by empty titles. An instructor is not learned by virtue of the fact that he has degrees from Paris or Athens. You must search for that man who is naturally intelligent, who has had much experience teaching, who has read and studied widely. Such a man will have committed many books to memory and will be versed in, and imbued with, secular and sacred texts. Then too, your instructor must be willing to follow the schedule you set, that is, must talk when you indicate that this is your pleasure, must teach when you wish him to, and who will recite to you at the time you select. The setting of a schedule of studies must be wholly in your hands. If you adhere to such a program of studies for two years, I guarantee that you will have gained more profit by this reading and study than if you had fallen heir to a province. I do think it praiseworthy, however, that your palace is full of soldiers, for they protect your country and are a symbol of your pre-eminence in arms; yet, I am disturbed that you do not have learned men in your entourage. You should support scholars as well as soldiers, for they will instruct you in making correct choices between wrong and right and will further your development as a complete man in every respect. It does you no credit to fall into that wide category of rulers who cut back the salaries of teachers as an economic measure and then lavish money on their personal whims, such as the feeding of lions. You may recall the jibe of Juvenal:

> Poor Numitor has nothing to send his friend, but does have enough for his Quintilla and manages to find ways to pay for the great quantities of meat his pet lions consume.

Then he adds in a vein of irony:

> It costs less to keep an animal, for, you know, nothing is as capacious as a poet's belly!

Do not spare expenses, then, when it comes to selecting your instructor who will, I assure you, bestow great profit on you. Perhaps you are sceptical and want to know precisely what sort of profit. Well, I will tell you in a few words just what profit there is to be derived from literature and try to impress you why you should not neglect it.

When you have reached a man's estate you will see that your education will be to your honor and advantage, that your knowledge will lift you above other men, and that your words will be listened to eagerly by all in council. No man will be able to deceive you or urge a dishonest action since you in your wisdom will instantly detect the difference between just and unjust courses of action. Also, no one will dare to advance a program concealing base motives when he knows you will penetrate the façade and expose him. A knowledge of literature will equip you for speaking effectively to your nation and a mastery of Quintilian and Cicero will make you able to praise and vituperate as the occasion demands. Should you consider going to war, Vegetius will be your guide. Historians are also valuable instructors in the arts of war, men such as Livy, Quintus Curtius, Justinus, Lucius Florus, Suetonius, Sallustius Crispus; in short, all the historians will be helpful. In their works you will become acquainted with the fortitude of Alexander the Great, the cleverness of Hannibal, the inventiveness of Fabius, the cleverness of Scipio, the boldness of Marcellus, and the stratagems of Jugurtha. I can assure you that no amount of practical experience will ever supply you with the knowledge you will glean from books. If you want to acquire the principles of government and politics, read the works of Aristotle in this area which Leonardo of Arezzo has translated into Latin, but be sure to acquire a modern translation since the style of old versions is poor and makes for difficult reading. If you want practical knowledge in the management of your household, read Aristotle's economic works, and read his ethical works for an understanding of psychology. In this regard, read the *De Officiis* of Cicero and the *Letters* of Seneca and all the rest of his works. The Venetian Francesco Barbaro is a good author to read on how to live with a wife. Plutarch is a good guide on the raising of children. Cicero has good advice on how to approach old age and how to conduct yourself with friends. In the *Tusculan Disputations* Cicero takes up the question of the proper way of looking at death and other emotional questions. All of these authors just mentioned, with the addition of Macrobius who wrote later, are good guides towards the acquisition of moral virtue, and write eloquently as well. Vergil's *Georgics* are an excellent guide for agriculture; and if you are interested in world geography and the character and products of different lands, you should read Pliny's *Natural History* and the works of Ptolemy, Solinus, and Isodore of Seville. Aristotle, Seneca, and Vergil are useful in studying the various constellations, the motions of the planets, and meteorology. If you want to understand the psychology of princes, their likes and dislikes, read Seneca's tragedies. Plautus and Terence are guides to coping with boastful soldiers, with the wiles of procurers, and with the tricks of slaves; reading these you will know how to avoid the pitfalls all of these conceal. Horace, Juvenal, and Persius will teach you the proper terms with which to thunder at vices, and Vergil's *Georgics* will acquaint you with the shepherd's way of life. If you wish to know the myths of various nations, the trials miserable people undergo, the types of letters lovers write, or wish to know the remedies for love, Ovid is the author who will instruct you. Two very valuable poems which abound in profound observations are Statius' *Thebaid* and *Archilleid.* . . .

. . . I know you have been persuaded not by my eloquence, which is negligible, but by your own character and the love of knowledge which is innate in you. I have to bring this letter to a close because of the noisy talk and uproar here. I have to live among shouting which would break "the sleep of Drusus and the calves of the sea." All of us in the chancery have to work in one office and we also have to eat and drink in one room; ants are not so crowded in their quarters as we are. Bees are at least separated into individual cells; we crowd together like sheep in a corral so that no one can spit without dirtying someone else's clothes. Such quiet prevails here that you would think yourself in the company of magpies and crows in a forest, or frogs in a swamp; I really am surprised that I have been able to write so much to you. Perhaps I've written too much and you have thrown my letter off as you would a yoke and feel that you now are to be called and not dragged to studies. I regret very much that I have not been able to polish what I hoped you would read because I have had to write amidst confusion. Yet I hope you will understand the situation I'm in and make allowances for my lack of literary ability which makes it necessary that I have peace and quiet in order to revise what I have written. Farewell and cherish me as much as it meets with the approval of the king.

From Graz, December 5, 1443.

ISOTTA NOGAROLA (1418–66)

Of the Equal or Unequal Sin of Adam and Eve (1453)

This debate between a learned lady of the *quattrocento* and an earnest would-be mentor offers insight into the intellectual position of even the most respected women. The issue, fraught with ramifications of the ancient battle between men and women, is whether Eve or Adam committed the graver sin. If the answer is found to be Eve, of course, patriarchal misogynists can point to the Bible itself as the proper source of their attitude toward the "weaker sex." Even the arguments Nogarola employs to prove her case, however, indicate the extent to which she has accepted the inferiority of women. She uses that very inferiority against her opponent, to suggest that Eve can't be held as responsible as Adam. Though her rhetoric and logic are superior to Foscarini's, her built-in prejudice against her own sex ultimately defeats her.

Of the Equal or Unequal Sin of Adam and Eve: An honorable disputation between the illustrious lord Ludovico Foscarini, Venetian doctor of arts and both laws, and the noble and learned and divine lady Isotta Nogarola of Verona, regarding this judgment of Aurelius Augustine: They sinned unequally according to sex, but equally according to pride.

LUDOVICO BEGINS: If it is in any way possible to measure the gravity of human sinfulness, then we should see Eve's sin as more to be condemned than Adam's [for three reasons]. [First], she was assigned by a just judge to a harsher punishment than was Adam. [Second], she believed that she was made more like God, and that is in the category of unforgiveable sins against the Holy Spirit. [Third], she suggested and was the cause of Adam's sin—not he of hers; and although it is a poor excuse to sin because of a friend, nevertheless none was more tolerable than the one by which Adam was enticed.

ISOTTA: But I see things—since you move me to reply—from quite another and contrary viewpoint. For where there is less intellect and less constancy, there there is less sin; and Eve [lacked sense and constancy] and therefore sinned less. Knowing [her weakness] that crafty serpent began by tempting the woman, thinking the man perhaps invulnerable because of his constancy. [For it says in] *Sentences* 2: Standing in the woman's presence, the ancient foe did not boldly persuade, but approached her with a question: "Why did God bid you not to eat of the tree of paradise?" She responded: "Lest perhaps we die." But seeing that she doubted the words of the Lord, the devil said: "You shall not die," but "you will be like God, knowing good and evil."

[Adam must also be judged more guilty than Eve, secondly] because of his greater contempt for the command. For in Genesis 2 it appears that the Lord commanded Adam, not Eve, where it says: "The Lord God took the man and placed him in the paradise of Eden to till it and to keep it," (and it does not say, "that they might care for and protect it") ". . . and the Lord God commanded the man" (and not "them"): "From every tree of the garden you may eat" (and not "you" [in the plural sense]), and, [referring to the forbidden tree], "for the day you eat of it, you must die," [again, using the singular form of "you"]. [God directed his command to Adam alone] because he esteemed the man more highly than the woman.

Moreover, the woman did not [eat from the forbidden tree] because she believed that she was made more like God, but rather because she was weak and [inclined to indulge in] pleasure. Thus: "Now the woman saw that the tree was good for food, pleasing to the eyes, and desirable for the knowledge it would give. She took of its fruit and ate it, and also gave some to her husband and he ate," and it does not say [that she did so] in order to be like God. And if Adam had not eaten, her sin would have had no consequences. For it does not say: "If Eve had not sinned Christ would not have been made incarnate," but "If Adam had not sinned." Hence the woman, but only because she had been first deceived by the serpent's evil persuasion, did indulge in the delights of paradise; but she would have harmed only herself and in no way endangered human posterity if the consent of the first-born man had not been offered. Therefore Eve was no danger to posterity but [only] to herself; but the man Adam spread the infection of sin to himself and to all future generations. Thus Adam, being the author of all humans yet to be born, was also the first cause of their perdition. For this reason the healing of humankind was celebrated first in the man and then in the woman, just as [according to Jewish tradition], after an unclean spirit has been expelled from a man, as it springs forth from the synagogue, the woman is purged [as well].

Moreover, that Eve was condemned by a just judge to a harsher punishment is evidently false, for God said to the woman: "I will make great your distress in childbearing; in pain shall you bring forth children; for your husband shall be your longing, though he have dominion over you." But to Adam he said: "Because you have listened to your wife and have eaten of the tree of which I have commanded you not to eat" (notice that God appears to have admonished Adam alone [using the singular form of "you"] and not Eve) "Cursed be the ground because of you; in toil shall you eat of it all the days of your life; thorns and thistles shall it bring forth to you, and you shall eat the plants of the field. In the sweat of your brow you shall eat bread, till you return to the ground, since out of it you were taken; for dust you are and unto dust you shall return." Notice that Adam's punishment appears harsher than Eve's; for God said to Adam: "to dust you shall return," and not to Eve, and death is the most terrible punishment that could be assigned. Therefore it is established that Adam's punishment was greater than Eve's.

I have written this because you wished me to. Yet I have done so fearfully, since this is not a woman's task. But you are kind, and if you find any part of my writing clumsy you will correct it.

LUDOVICO: You defend the cause of Eve most subtly, and indeed defend it so [well] that, if I had not been born a man, you would have made me your champion. But sticking fast to the truth, which is attached by very strong roots, I have set out [here] to assault your fortress with your own weapons. I shall begin by attacking its foundations, which can be destroyed by the testimony of Sacred Scripture, so that there will be no lack of material for my refutation.

Eve sinned from ignorance and inconstancy, from which you conclude that she sinned less seriously. [But] ignorance—especially of those things which we are obligated to know—does not excuse us. For it is written: "If anyone ignores this, he shall be ignored." The eyes which guilt makes blind punishment opens. He who has been foolish in guilt will be wise in punishment, especially when the sinner's mistake occurs through negligence. For the woman's ignorance, born of arrogance, does not excuse her, in the same way that Aristotle and the [lawyers], who teach a true philosophy, find the drunk and ignorant deserving of a double punishment. Nor do I understand how in the world you, so many ages distant from Eve, fault her intellect, when her knowledge, divinely created by the highest craftsman of all things, daunted that clever serpent lurking in paradise. For, as you write, he was not bold enough to attempt to persuade her but approached her with a question.

But the acts due to inconstancy are even more blameworthy [than those due to ignorance]. For to the same degree that the acts issuing from a solid and constant mental attitude are more worthy and distinct from the preceding ones, so should those issuing from inconstancy be punished more severely, since inconstancy is an evil in itself and when paired with an evil sin makes the sin worse.

Nor is Adam's companion excused because Adam was appointed to protect her, [contrary to your contention that] thieves who have been trustingly employed by a householder are not punished with the most severe punishment like strangers or those in whom no confidence has been placed. Also, the woman's frailty was not the cause of sin, as you write, but her pride, since the demon promised her knowledge, which leads to arrogance and inflates [with pride], according to the apostle. For it says in Ecclesiasticus: "Pride was the beginning of every sin." And though the other women followed, yet she was the first since, when man existed in a state of innocence, the flesh was obedient to him and [did not struggle] against reason. The first impulse [of sin], therefore, was an inordinate appetite for seeking that which was not suited to its own nature, as Augustine wrote to Orosius: "Swollen by pride, man obeyed the serpent's persuasion and disdained God's commands." For the adversary said to Eve: "Your eyes will be opened and you will be like God, knowing good and evil." Nor would the woman have believed the demon's persuasive words, as Augustine says [in his commentary] on Genesis, unless a love of her own power had overcome her, which [love is] a stream sprung from the well of pride. [I shall continue to follow Augustine in his view that at the moment] when Eve desired to capture divinity, she lost happiness. And those words: "If Adam had not sinned, etc." confirm me in my view. For Eve sinned perhaps in such a way that, just as the demons did not merit redemption, neither perhaps did she. I speak only in jest, but Adam's sin was fortunate, since it warranted such a redeemer.

And lest I finally stray too far from what you have written, [I shall turn to your argument that Adam's punishment was more severe than Eve's and his sin, accordingly, greater. But] the woman suffers all the penalties [inflicted on] the man, and since her sorrows are greater than his, not only is she doomed to death, condemned to eat at the cost of sweat, denied by the cherubim and flaming swords entry to paradise, but in addition to all these things which are common [to both], she alone must give birth in pain and be subjected to her husband. [Her punishment is thus harsher than Adam's, as her sin is greater].

But because in such a matter it is not sufficient to have refuted your arguments without also putting forward my own, [I shall do so now]. Eve believed that she was made similar to God and, out of envy, desired that which wounds the Holy Spirit. Moreover, she must bear responsibility for every fault of Adam because, as Aristotle testifies, the cause of a cause is the cause of that which is caused. Indeed, every prior cause influences an outcome more than a secondary cause, and the principle of any genus, according to the same Aristotle, is seen as its greatest [component]. In fact, is considered to be more than half the whole. And in the *Posterior Analytics* he writes: "That on account of which any thing exists is that thing and more greatly so." Now [since] Adam sinned on account of Eve, it follows that Eve sinned much more than Adam. Similarly, just as it is better to treat others well than to be well-treated, so it is worse to persuade another to evil than to be persuaded to evil. For he sins less who sins by another's example, inasmuch as what is done by example can be said to be done according to a kind of law, [and thus justly]. For this reason it is commonly said that "the sins that many commit are [without fault]." [Thus Eve, who persuaded her husband to commit an evil act, sinned more greatly than Adam, who merely consented to her example]. And if Adam and Eve both had thought that they were worthy of the same glory, Eve, who was inferior [by nature], more greatly departed from the mean, and consequently sinned more greatly. Moreover, as a beloved companion she could deceive her husband [vulnerable to her persuasion because of his love for her] more easily than the shameful serpent could deceive the woman. And she persevered longer [in sin] than Adam, because she began first, and offenses are that much more serious (according to Gregory's decree) in relation to the length of time they hold the unhappy soul in bondage. Finally, to bring my discourse to a close, Eve was the cause and the example of sin, and Gregory greatly increases the guilt in the case of the example. And Christ, who could not err, condemned more severely the pretext of the ignorant Jews, because it came first, than he did the sentence of the learned Pilate, when he said: "They who have betrayed me to you have greater sin, etc." All who wish to be called Christians have always agreed with this judgment, and you, above all most Christian, will approve and defend it. Farewell, and do not fear, but dare to do much, because you have excellently understood so much and write so learnedly.

ISOTTA: I had decided that I would not enter further into a contest with you because, as you say, you assault my fortress with my own weapons. [The propositions] you have presented me were so perfectly and diligently defended that it would be difficult not merely for me, but for the most learned men, to oppose them. But since I recognize that this contest is useful for me, I have decided to obey your honest wish. Even though I know I struggle in vain, yet I will earn the highest praise if I am defeated by so mighty a man as you.

Eve sinned out of ignorance and inconstancy, and hence you contend that she sinned more gravely, because the ignorance of those things which we are obligated to know does not excuse us, since it is written: "He who does not know will not be known." I would concede your point if that ignorance were crude or affected. But Eve's ignorance was implanted by nature, of which nature God himself is the author and founder. In many people it is seen that he who knows less sins less, like a boy who sins less than an old man or a peasant less than a noble. Such a person does not need to know explicitly what is required for salvation, but implicitly, because [for him] faith alone suffices. The question of inconstancy proceeds similarly. For when it is said that the acts which proceed from inconstancy are more blameworthy, [that kind of] inconstancy is understood which is not innate but the product of character and sins.

The same is true of imperfection. For when gifts increase, greater responsibility is imposed. When God created man, from the beginning he created him perfect, and the powers of his soul perfect, and gave him a greater understanding and knowledge of truth as well as a greater depth of wisdom. Thus it was that the Lord led to Adam all the animals of the earth and the birds of heaven, so that Adam could call them by their names. For God said: "Let us make mankind in our image and likeness, and let them have dominion over the fish of the sea, and the birds of the air, the cattle, over all the wild animals and every creature that crawls on the earth," making clear his own perfection. But of the woman he said: "It is not good that the man is alone; I will make him a helper like himself." And since consolation and joy are required for happiness, and since no one can have solace and joy when alone, it appears that God created woman for man's consolation. For the good spreads itself, and the greater it is the more it shares itself. Therefore, it appears that Adam's sin was greater than Eve's. [As] Ambrose [says]: "In him to whom a more indulgent liberality has been shown is insolence more inexcusable."

"But Adam's companion," [you argue], "is not excused because Adam was appointed to protect her, because thieves who have been trustingly employed by a householder are not punished with the most severe punishment like strangers or those in whom the householder placed no confidence." This is true, however, in temporal law, but not in divine law, for divine justice proceeds differently from temporal justice in punishing [sin].

[You argue further that] "the fragility of the woman was not the cause of sin, but rather her inordinate appetite for seeking that which was not suited to her nature," which [appetite] is the product, as you write, of pride. Yet it is clearly less a sin to desire the knowledge of good and evil than to transgress against a divine commandment, since the desire for knowledge is a natural thing, and all men by nature desire to know. And even if the first impulse [of sin] were this inordinate appetite, which cannot be without sin, yet it is more tolerable than the sin of transgression, for the observance of the commandments is the road which leads to the country of salvation. [It is written]: "But if thou wilt enter into life, keep the commandments;" and likewise: "What shall I do to gain eternal life? Keep the commandments." And transgression is particularly born of pride, because pride is nothing other than rebellion against divine rule, exalting oneself above what is permitted according to divine rule, by disdaining the will of God and displacing it with one's own. Thus Augustine [writes] in *On Nature and Grace:* "Sin is the will to pursue or retain what justice forbids, that is, to deny what God wishes." Ambrose agrees with him in his *On Paradise:* "Sin is the transgression against divine law and disobedience to the heavenly commandments." Behold! See that the transgression against and disobedience to the heavenly commandments is the greatest sin, whereas you have thus defined sin: "Sin is the inordinate desire to know." Thus clearly the sin of transgression against a command is greater than [the sin of] desiring the knowledge of good and evil. So even if inordinate desire be a sin, as with Eve, yet she did not desire to be like God in power but only in the knowledge of good and evil, which by nature she was actually inclined to desire.

[Next, as to your statement] that those words, "if Adam had not sinned," confirm you in your view [of Eve's damnability], since Eve may have so sinned that, like the demons, she did not merit redemption, I reply that she also was redeemed with Adam, because [she was] "bone of my bone and flesh of my flesh." And if it seems that God did not redeem her, this was undoubtedly because God held her sin as negligible. For if man deserved redemption, the woman deserved it much more because of the slightness of the crime. For the angel cannot be excused by ignorance as can the woman. For the angel understands without investigation or discussion and has an intellect more in the likeness of God's—to which it seems Eve desired to be similar—than does man. Hence the angel is called intellectual and the man rational. Thus where the woman sinned from her desire for knowledge, the angel sinned from a desire for power. While knowledge of an appearance in some small way can be partaken of by the creature, in no way can it partake in the power of God and of the soul of Christ. Moreover, the woman in sinning thought she would receive mercy, believing certainly that she was committing a sin, but not one so great as to warrant God's inflicting such a sentence and punishment. But the angel did not think [of mercy]. Hence Gregory [says in the] fourth book of the *Moralia:* "The first parents were needed for this, that the sin which they committed by transgressing they might purge by confessing." But that persuasive serpent was never punished for his sin, for he was never to be recalled to grace. Thus, in sum, Eve clearly merited redemption more than the angels.

[As to your argument] that the woman also suffers all the penalties inflicted on the man, and beyond those which are common [to both] she alone gives birth in sorrow and has been subjected to man, this also reinforces my earlier point. As I said, the good spreads itself, and the greater it is the more it shares itself. So also evil, the greater it is the more it shares itself, and the more it shares itself the more harmful it is, and the more harmful it is the greater it is. Furthermore, the severity of the punishment is proportional to the gravity of the sin. Hence Christ chose to die on the cross, though this was the most shameful and horrible kind of death, and on the cross he endured in general every kind of suffering by type. Hence Isidore writes concerning the Trinity: "The only-born Son of God in executing the sacrament of his death, in himself bears witness that he consummated every kind of suffering when, with lowered head, he gave up his spirit." The reason was that the punishment had to correspond to the guilt. Adam took the fruit of the forbidden tree; Christ suffered on the tree and so made satisfaction [for Adam's sin]. [As] Augustine [writes]: "Adam disdained God's command" (and he does not say Eve) "accepting the fruit from the tree, but whatever Adam lost Christ restored." [For Christ paid the penalty for sin he had not committed, as it says in] Psalm 64: "For what I have not taken, then I atoned." Therefore, Adam's sin was the greatest [possible], because the punishment corresponding to his fault was the greatest [possible] and was general in all men. [As the] apostle [says]: "All sinned in Adam."

"Eve," [you say], "must bear responsibility for every fault of Adam because, as Aristotle shows, whatever is the cause of the cause is the cause of the thing caused." This is true in the case of things which are, as you know better [than I], in themselves the causes of other things, which is the case for the first cause, the first principle, and "that on account of which anything is what it is." But clearly this

Original sin (Titian), in the Prado, Madrid

was not the case with Eve, because Adam either had free will or he did not. If he did not have it, he did not sin; if he had it, then Eve forced the sin [upon him], which is impossible. For as Bernard says: "Free will, because of its inborn nobility, is forced by no necessity," not even by God, because if that were the case it would be to concede that two contradictories are true at the same time. God cannot do, therefore, what would cause an act proceeding from free will and remaining free to be not free but coerced. [As] Augustine [writes in his commentary] on Genesis: "God cannot act against that nature which he created with a good will." God could himself, however, remove that condition of liberty from any person and bestow some other condition on him. In the same way fire cannot, while it remains fire, not burn, unless its nature is changed and suspended for a time by divine force. No other creature, such as a good angel or devil can do this, since they are less than God; much less a woman, since she is less perfect and weaker than they. Augustine clarifies this principle [of God's supremacy] saying: "Above our mind is nothing besides God, nor is there anything intermediary between God and our mind." Yet only something which is superior to something else can coerce it; but Eve was inferior to Adam, therefore she was not herself the cause of sin. [In] Ecclesiasticus 15 [it says]: "God from the beginning created man and placed him in the palm of his counsel and made clear his commandments and precepts. If you wish to preserve the commandments, they will preserve you and create in you pleasing faith." Thus Adam appeared to accuse God rather than excuse himself when he said: "The woman you placed at my side gave me fruit from the tree and I ate it."

[Next you argue] that the beloved companion could have more easily deceived the man than the shameful serpent the woman. To this I reply that Eve, weak and ignorant by nature, sinned much less by assenting to that astute serpent, who was called "wise," than

Adam—created by God with perfect knowledge and understanding—in listening to the persuasive words and voice of the imperfect woman.

[Further, you say] that Eve persevered in her sin a longer time and therefore sinned more, because crimes are that much more serious according to the length of time they hold the unhappy soul in bondage. This is no doubt true, when two sins are equal, and in the same person or in two similar persons. But Adam and Eve were not equals, because Adam was a perfect animal and Eve imperfect and ignorant. [Therefore, their sins were not comparable, and Eve, who persevered longer in sin, was not on that account more guilty than Adam].

Finally, if I may quote you: "The woman was the example and the cause of sin, and Gregory emphatically extends the burden of guilt to [the person who provided] an example, and Christ condemned the cause of the ignorant Jews, because it was first, more than the learned Pilate's sentence when he said:

'Therefore he who betrayed me to you has greater sin.'" I reply that Christ did not condemn the cause of the ignorant Jews because it was first, but because it was vicious and devilish due to their native malice and obstinacy. For they did not sin from ignorance. The gentile Pilate was more ignorant about these things than the Jews, who had the law and the prophets and read them and daily saw signs concerning [Christ]. For John 15 says: "If I had not come and spoken to them, they would have no sin. But now they have no excuse for their sin." Thus they themselves said: "What are we doing? for this man is working signs." And: "Art thou the Christ, the Son of the Blessed One?" For the [Jewish] people was special to God, and Christ himself [said]: "I was not sent except to the lost sheep of the house of Israel. It is not fair to take the children's bread and cast it to the dogs." Therefore the Jews sinned more, because Jesus loved them more.

Let these words be enough from me, an unarmed and poor little woman.

IPPOLITA SFORZA (1445–88)

Oration, to Pope Pius II (1459)

The daughter of Bianca and Francesco Sforza, Duke of Milan, addressed the pope and his Consistory of Cardinals in Mantua at the age of fourteen. The pope reported that "all present were lost in wonder and admiration." Ippolita's straightforwardness, brevity, and pious subservience to the patriarchy epitomized by the Holy Father transports us back to her eloquent presence, giving insight into the power of Roman Catholicism in the *quattrocento*. Yet the future Duchess of Calabria's subtle message is clear: By building up the pope's image as a reformer she applies the pressure of his own saintly image to advance her desire for religious leaders worthy of her spiritual dedication.

Portrait of an old man and his son (Domenico Ghirlandaio), in the Louvre, Paris

Oration of the illustrious Duchess of Calabria, daughter of the glorious Francesco, Duke of Milan, delivered to the Highest Lord Pope Pius in the Consistory of Cardinals, Mantua, 1459, in the month of July

So great, I have often heard, is the authority and majesty of this holiest See, blessed [father], that no one, however intelligent, eloquent [or] worthy, has ever petitioned it who did not perform his task with trepidation. Certainly, then, I, who suffer shyness and timidity because of my age, sex and frailty of mind, am struck with fear, especially in the presence of such a judge as you, who are, by the consensus of all the worthiest men, most learned and wise. [Thus], blushing, I am silent not merely because of that blush, but because, indeed, I have not the courage to look upon your Holiness with unwavering eyes. But

since I am also aware that you are good-natured, extraordinarily humane, benevolent, and merciful, and because I know it is holy to obey one's parents' commands, I shall undertake, bashfully and fearfully, the duty of speaking imposed on me. In a brief oration, I shall first explain the cause for our presence here, and then our petition.

When we learned that your Holiness had been exalted to this splendid throne, my illustrious parents and our whole family were suddenly overcome by such deep pleasure that nothing, I thought, could ever occur more contributory to our happiness, partly because of our family's great hopes, and partly, or rather particularly, for the sake of the general well-being of the Christian religion. For, indeed, we believe you are a star sent down from heaven to govern the bark of St. Peter [which is today] imperilled and nearly submerged. It augurs well, they feel, that [in these times when] Christendom is so endangered, you were chosen as the supreme pastor of the Lord's flock, not because of favor or privilege, but because of your lofty virtue and saintliness. But to what end do I dare to praise you? Is it in order to use my crude and childish words to make filthy your golden and nearly divine virtues? When we heard, then, that your Holiness had decided to set out for this city, my parents decided likewise to come too, to revere, worship [and] adore you; and since, consequently, I, too, am able to kiss your blessed feet, I feel I have experienced not a small, but a tremendous happiness. For since you are on earth the vicar of our Savior, we earthly mortals owe you much reverence and show you much obedience. I pray that you believe this: no one more zealously obeys or more ardently desires your prosperity and welfare, or the prosperity and welfare of the holy Roman Church, than my parents. And I, indeed, though I have no fortune of my own, both devote and dedicate my will, which is free, to your sanctity. It remains to be said only that my illustrious parents, my brothers, myself, our whole condition, I commend to your Holiness.

FRANÇOIS VILLON (1431–63?)

The Testament and Ballad (1461–62)

François Villon, the first fresh air in fifteenth-century French poetry, was the nom de plume for François Montcorbier or François des Loges. At the age of twenty-four he murdered a priest, and wandered through France spending much of his life in and out of trouble with the law, condemned to death and also pardoned several times.

The date of his death is unknown. Villon, "the father of poetry," mysteriously disappeared at the age of thirty-two. Villon's verse, a tremendous departure from the allegorical romances of the thirteenth century, advances the language of what was becoming modern French by freeing it from its institutional and syntactic straightjacket. In contrast to a medieval work like *The Romance of the Rose*, where every detail of character, gesture, and description is determined by traditional emblematic dictates, in Villon's simple, direct, profane lines we sense new growth, audacity, and excitement rising from the ashes of an exhausted literary language. His poetry plants the seeds that will sprout in the bawdy prose exuberance of his countryman Rabelais and reach full bloom in the egalitarian pronouncements of the French Revolution. Villon's unruly passion extends equally to his lady loves, his enemies, his food and lack thereof, and the discomforts of his bowels. He was Henry Miller in rhyme, the forefather of twentieth-century rap. Like Boccaccio's *Decameron* and Nashe's *Unfortunate Traveler*, Villon's poetry exposes us to the slang of brothels and taverns, the lingo of marketplace and public house, the blasphemy of prison cell and highway as they depict the human circus parading past his all-seeing, participating eye: monks and working girls, cutpurses and pompous officials, unfortunate rogues and ladies blessed by fortune. His profanity and tenderness are displayed in these elegant translations by Galway Kinnell proving that confessional poetry based on the banalities of daily life is no exclusive property of the twentieth century. Villon's most famous poem is his "Ballade des pendus" ("Ballad of the Hanged Men"), also known as "Villon's Epitaph." It was written under sentence of death.

The Testament

Carthusians and Celestines
Mendicants and Devotes
Wool-gatherers and clack-pattens
Serving wenches and pretty girls
In jackets and tight-fitting skirts
Boyfriends of loves passed on
Happily fitted into tawny boots
I cry everyone's pardon.

Girls showing their breasts
To draw in a fatter clientele
Brawlers, starters of fights
Jugglers with monkeys at heel
Fools and clowns male and female
Who march whistling six by six
Puppets and marionettes
I cry everyone's pardon.

Except the sons-of-bitches
Who made me shit small and gnaw
Crusts many a dusk and dawn
Who don't scare me now three turds
I'd raise for them farts and belches
But as I'm sitting down I can't manage
Anyway to avoid starting a riot
I cry everyone's pardon.

Let their fifteen ribs be mauled
With big hammers heavy and strong
And lead weights and that kind of balls
I cry everyone's pardon.

Here ends and finishes
The testament of poor Villon
Come to his burial
When you hear the bell ringing
Dressed in red vermilion
For he died a martyr to love
This he swore on his testicle
As he made his way out of this world.

And I think it wasn't a lie
For he was chased like a scullion
By his loves so spitefully
From here to Roussillon

There isn't a bush or a shrub
That didn't get, he speaks truly
A shred from his back
As he made his way out of this world.

It was like this, so that
By the time he died he had only a rag
What's worse, as he died, sorely
The spur of love pricked into him
Sharper than the buckle-tongue
Of a baldric he could feel it
And this is what we marvel at
As he made his way out of this world.

Prince graceful as a merlin
Hear what he did as he left
He took a long swig of dead-black wine
As he made his way out of this world.

Ballad

Brother humans who live on after us
Don't let your hearts harden against us
For if you have pity on wretches like us
More likely God will show mercy to you
You see us five, six, hanging here
As for the flesh we loved too well
A while ago it was eaten and has rotted away
And we the bones turn to ashes and dust
Let no one make us the butt of jokes
But pray God that he absolve us all.

Don't be insulted that we call you
Brothers, even if it was by Justice
We were put to death, for you understand
Not every person has the same good sense
Speak up for us, since we can't ourselves
Before the son of the virgin Mary
That his mercy toward us shall keep flowing
Which is what keeps us from hellfire
We are dead, may no one taunt us
But pray God that he absolve us all.

The rain has rinsed and washed us
The sun dried us and turned us black
Magpies and ravens have pecked out our eyes

Interior, L'Hotel-Dieu (sixteenth-century "French school"), Paris

And plucked our beards and eyebrows
Never ever can we stand still
Now here, now there, as the wind shifts
At its whim it keeps swinging us
Pocked by birds worse than a sewing thimble
Therefore don't join in our brotherhood
But pray God that he absolve us all.

Prince Jesus, master over all
Don't let us fall into hell's dominion
We've nothing to do or settle down there
Men, there's nothing here to laugh at
But pray God that he absolve us all.

SIR THOMAS MALORY (1400?–71)

Le Morte Darthur (written 1469–70; published 1485)

Like many other great works of the age, Malory's *Le Morte Darthur* was written in prison. Almost nothing else is known about the author's life, and indeed the very identity of Malory remains the subject of great scholarly controversy. Was he the rapist Thomas Malory of Newbold Revel of Warwickshire, as G. L. Kittredge attests, or the Thomas Malory of Yorkshire, as admirers of his writing insist? The haunting chivalric cycle of mythic folklore associated with King Arthur, as Malory reweaves the thirteenth-century French tales and presents them to his contemporaries for the first time in English, became a reverse metaphor for the splendor of the Renaissance about to dawn in England. At the same time that Malory's version of the Arthurian saga replaces courtly themes with emphasis on male-centered Christian heroism, it underlines values that are receding rapidly from the realities of British political and social life. The vividness of Malory's English countryside, like the energy of his dialogue, reflects the embryonic enthusiastic nationalism that would soon change the face of England forever, displacing divinely sanctioned feudal rituals with Henry VIII's institutionalized egocentrism. With Malory's depiction of the death of Arthur, the tapestry of medieval feudalism at its most vibrant is unraveled with poignant nostalgia, revealing moods of individualism and greed as all that remain. The one ray of hope is the ambiguous promise of Arthur's return, which the narrator seems to have stitched on to the otherwise relentlessly pessimistic ending of Camelot. *Le Morte Darthur,* with its bittersweet *envoi* to the epoch of courtly love, stands as one "bookend" to the Renaissance—the other being Cervantes' poignantly satirical *Don Quixote,* in which a knight of "individualism" is finally defeated by his own exhaustion. Malory's retelling of the Arthurian saga is the most influential source and inspiration for Spenser's *The Faerie Queene,* Tennyson's *Idylls of the King,* T. H. White's twentieth-century bestseller, *The Once and Future King,* as well as the Broadway hit musical *Camelot* which inspired Jacqueline Kennedy to compare her husband's brief presidency to this lost golden age.

THE DEATH OF ARTHUR

When Sir Mordred heard King Arthur he ran toward him with his sword drawn in his hand. Then King Arthur smote Sir Mordred under the shield with a thrust of his spear on through the body more than a fathom. When Sir Mordred felt that he had his death-wound, he thrust himself with all his might up to the handguard of King Arthur's spear; and right so, holding his sword in both his hands, he smote his father King Arthur upon the side of the head so that the sword pierced the helmet and the brain-pan. Therewith Sir Mordred fell stark dead to the earth; and the noble King Arthur fell to the earth and there he swooned often, and Sir Lucan and Sir Bedivere lifted him up each time. So they led him, weak between them, to a little chapel not far from the sea, and when the king was there he seemed reasonably comfortable.

Then they heard people cry out in the field.

"Now go thou, Sir Lucan," said the king, "and let me know what that noise in the field betokens."

So Sir Lucan departed slowly, for he was grievously wounded in many places; as he went he saw and noticed by the moonlight how plunderers and robbers had come into the field to plunder and to rob many a full noble knight of brooches and beads, of many a good ring, and of many a rich jewel. And whoever was not fully dead, the robbers slew them for their armor and their riches. When Sir Lucan understood this work, he came back to the king as quickly as he could and told him all that he had heard and seen.

"Therefore, by my counsel," said Sir Lucan, "it is best that we bring you to some town."

"I would it could be so," said the king, "but I cannot stand, my head aches so. Ah, Sir Lancelot, this day have I sorely missed thee! And alas, that ever I was against thee! For now I have my death, whereof Sir Gawain warned me in my dream."

Then Sir Lucan took up the king on one side and Sir Bedivere did so on the other side, and in the lifting the king swooned. Also with the lifting, Sir Lucan fell into a swoon and part of his guts fell out of his body, and therewith the noble knight's heart burst. When the king awoke he beheld Sir Lucan, how he lay foaming at the mouth, and how part of his guts lay at his feet.

"Alas," said the king, "this is to me a full heavy sight to see this noble duke die so for my sake; for he wished to help me, he who had more need of help than I. Alas, he would not complain, his heart was so set upon helping me. Now Jesus have mercy upon his soul!"

Then Sir Bedivere wept for the death of his brother.

"Leave this mourning and weeping," said the king, "for all this will not avail me. For wit thou well, if I might live myself the death of Sir Lucan would grieve me evermore, but my time passeth on fast. Therefore take thou here Excalibur, my good sword, and go with it to yonder water's side; when thou comest there, I charge thee to throw my sword into that water and come again and tell me what thou saw there."

"My lord," said Sir Bedivere, "your command shall be done, and quickly I shall bring you word back."

So Sir Bedivere departed. And along the way he beheld that noble sword, that the pommel and the haft were all of precious stones. Then he said to himself, "If I throw this rich sword into the water, thereof shall never come good, but only harm and loss." Then Sir Bedivere hid Excalibur under a tree, and as soon as he might he came again unto the king and said that he had been at the water and had thrown the sword into the water.

"What saw thou there?" said the king.

"Sir," he said, "I saw nothing but waves and winds."

"That is untruly said by thee," said the king. "Therefore go thou quickly again and do my command. As thou art dear to me, spare not but throw it in."

Then Sir Bedivere returned again and took the sword in his hand, and again he thought it a sin and a shame to throw away that noble sword. So once more he hid the sword and returned again and told the king that he had been at the water and done his command.

"What saw thou there?" said the king.

"Sir," he said, "I saw nothing but waves and winds."

"Ah, traitor untrue," said King Arthur, "now hast thou betrayed me twice! Who would have thought that thou who hast been to me so lief and dear and thou who art called a noble knight would betray me for the richness of this sword?

But now go again quickly; thy long tarrying putteth me in great jeopardy of my life, for I have taken cold. And unless thou do now as I bid thee, if ever I may see thee again I shall slay thee with my own hands; for thou would for my rich sword see me dead."

Then Sir Bedivere departed and went to the sword and quickly took it up and went to the water's side, and there he bound the girdle about the hilt; then he threw the sword as far into the water as he might. And there came an arm and a hand above the water which caught it and shook and brandished it thrice and then vanished with the sword into the water. So Sir Bedivere came back to the king and told him what he saw.

"Alas," said the king, "help me hence, for I fear that I have tarried over-long."

Then Sir Bedivere took the king upon his back and so went with him to the water's side. When they reached there they saw a little barge which waited fast by the bank with many fair ladies in it. Among them all was a queen, and they all had black hoods; they all wept and shrieked when they saw King Arthur.

"Now put me into that barge," said the king.

Sir Bedivere did so gently, and three queens received him there with great mourning and put him down; in one of their laps King Arthur laid his head. Then that queen said, "Ah, dear brother, why have ye tarried so long from me? Alas, this wound on your head hath caught over-much cold."

So they rowed from the land and Sir Bedivere beheld all those ladies go from him. Then Sir Bedivere cried, "Ah, my lord Arthur, what shall become of me, now that ye go from me and leave me here alone among my enemies?"

"Comfort thyself," said the king, "and do as well as thou may, for in me is no more trust to trust in. I must go into the Vale of Avalon to heal me of my grievous wound. And if thou hear nevermore of me, pray for my soul!"

But ever the queens and ladies wept and shrieked, so that it was a pity to hear. As soon as Sir Bedivere had lost sight of the barge, he wept and wailed and then took to the forest and walked all night. And in the morning he was aware of a chapel and a hermitage between two ancient woods.

Then Sir Bedivere was glad, and thither he went. When he came into the chapel he saw where a hermit lay grovelling on all fours fast by a tomb that was newly made. When the hermit saw Sir Bedivere he knew him at once, for he was the Bishop of Canterbury whom Sir Mordred recently put to flight.

"Sir," said Sir Bedivere, "what man is interred there whom you pray so earnestly for?"

"Fair son," said the hermit, "I know not truly but by deeming. But this night at midnight a number of ladies came here and brought hither a dead corpse and prayed me to bury him. And here they offered a hundred tapers and they gave me a thousand besants."

"Alas," said Sir Bedivere, "that was my lord King Arthur who here lieth buried in this chapel." Then Sir Bedivere swooned and when he awoke he prayed the hermit that he might remain with him always, there to live with fasting and prayers. "For hence I will never go," said Sir Bedivere, "of my own will. But all the days of my life I will be here to pray for my lord Arthur."

"Ye are welcome to me here," said the hermit, "for I know you better than ye think I do. Ye are Sir Bedivere the Bold, and the full noble duke Sir Lucan le Butler was your brother."

Then Sir Bedivere told the hermit all, as ye have heard before, and he remained with the hermit who was earlier the Bishop of Canterbury. There he put on poor clothes and served the hermit full humbly in fasting and in prayers.

Thus, concerning Arthur I find no more written in books which are authorized. Nor did I ever hear or read more with true certainty concerning his death, except that he was thus led away in a ship wherein were three queens: one was King Arthur's sister, Queen Morgan le Fay; the second was the queen of North Wales; and the third was the queen of the Waste Lands. Also there was Dame Nymue, the chief Lady of the Lake, who had wedded Sir Pelleas, the good knight; and this lady had done much for King

Arthur. Also she would never allow Sir Pelleas to be in any place where he would be in danger of his life; so he lived with her to the last of his days in quiet peace.

More concerning the death of King Arthur could I never find, except that these ladies brought him to his grave. And such a man was buried there, as the hermit who was sometime Bishop of Canterbury bore witness. But still the hermit knew not with certainty that it was truly the body of King Arthur. This tale Sir Bedivere, a knight of the Round Table, caused to be written down.

Yet some men say in many parts of England that King Arthur is not dead, but was taken by the will of our Lord Jesus into another place. And men say that he shall come again and shall win the Holy Cross. Yet I will not say that it shall be so; rather, I would say that here in this world he changed his form of life. But many men say that there is written upon his tomb this line:

Here Lies Arthur, The Once And Future King.

Thus I here leave Sir Bedivere with the hermit who dwelled at that time in a chapel beside Glastonbury, and his hermitage was also there. So they lived in prayer and fasting and great abstinence.

When Queen Guenivere understood that King Arthur was slain with all the noble knights, Sir Mordred, and all the remnant, she then stole away with five ladies and went to Amesbury. There she had herself made a nun and wore white and black clothes, and as great penance she took upon herself as ever did a sinful woman in this land. No creature could ever make her merry, but ever she lived in fasting, prayer, and alms-deeds, so that all manner of people marvelled how virtuously she was changed.

MARSILIO FICINO (1433–99)

DE VITA

On Life (c.1490)

Founder in 1462, under the patronage of Cosimo de' Medici, of the Florentine Platonic Academy at Villa Careggi, Marsilio Ficino coined the term "platonic love" to describe the purest and ideal affection that inspires the noblest souls. He was the first humanist to translate Plato's complete works into Latin, and as scholar and tutor to the young Medici princes, dedicated himself to reconciling Platonism with Christianity. Ficino believed that the highest activity of humanity is its own self-reflexive contemplation, which would naturally lead it to a vision of God. Paradise for him is ultimate and total self-consciousness, where all human beings are enlightened and in communion with their own nature, and the divine nature human nature reflects. Ficino's belief in the "cosmic love" that governs an intrinsically orderly universe attracted him to astrology, and he is supposed to have predicted that the young Giovanni de' Medici (later Leo X) would one day be Pope. The late twentieth-century popular psychology based on "finding your right livelihood" is foreshadowed in Ficino's essay "On Life," which its editors call "the first treatise on the health of the intellectual." Happiness and productivity on earth consist of identifying and following your own individual "star" or *ingenium* ("genius").

To Live Well and Prosper, First Know Your Natural Bent, Your Star, Your Genius, and the Place Suitable to These; Here Live. Follow Your Natural Profession.

Whoever is born possessed of a sound mind is naturally formed by the heavens for some honorable work and way of life. Whoever therefore wants to have the heavens propitious, let him undertake above all this work, this way of life; let him pursue it zealously, for the heavens favor his undertakings. Assuredly for this above all else you were made by nature—the activity which from tender years you do, speak, play-act, choose, dream, imitate; that activity which you try more frequently, which you perform more easily, in which you make the most progress, which you enjoy above all else, which you leave off unwillingly. That assuredly is the thing for which the heavens and the lord of your horoscope gave birth to you. Therefore they will promote your undertakings and will favor your life to the extent that you follow the auspices of the lord of your geniture, especially if that Platonic doctrine is true (with which all antiquity agrees) that every person has at birth one certain daemon, the guardian of his life, assigned by his own personal star, which helps him to that very task to which the celestials summoned him when he was born. Therefore anyone having thoroughly scrutinized his own natural bent [here he begins to use "ingenium" in its normal sense] by the aforesaid indicators will so discover his natural work as to discover at the same time his own star and daemon. Following the beginnings laid down by them, he will act successfully, he will live prosperously; if not, he will find fortune adverse and will sense that the heavens are his enemy.

Hence there are two kinds of people who are unfortunate beyond the rest: those who, having professed nothing, do nothing at all; others who subject themselves to a profession unsuited to their natural bent, contrary to their Genius. The do-nothings vegetate lazily when all the time the ever-moving heavens are continually inciting them to activity. The misfits, while they do things unsuited to their celestial patrons, labor in vain, and their supernal patrons desert them. The first sort confirms the ancient proverb: "The gods help those who are doing something; they are hostile to the lazy"; the second confirms another ancient proverb: "Do nothing with Minerva unwilling." I think it is for this reason that the Pythagorean verses beseech Jupiter either that he himself would relieve the human race of its many evils or that at least he would show us what daemon we should adopt as our leader.

Consequently it would be worthwhile to investigate exactly what region your star and your daemon initially designated you to dwell in and cultivate, because there they will favor you more. Assuredly, it is that region in which, as soon as you reach it, your spirit is somehow refreshed through and through, where your sense stays vigorous, where your physical health is stronger, where the majority favor you more, where your wishes come true. Learn about these things, therefore, by experience; select the region where you find them; inhabit it in good fortune. When you leave it, your fortune will be bad, unless you return and undertake similar activities. But while you are within this region, exercise by keeping constantly in motion and make various circular movements like those of the heavenly bodies [= Orphic dancing]. Since by their movings and circlings you were engendered, by making similar motions you will be preserved.

In addition, it will be useful for you to keep in mind what pertains to your dwelling-place. Just as the country supplies to the city the food necessary for life, but the city consumes it, so also you extend life itself by frequent residence in the country, where weariness will never begin for you; but in the city, you wear down your life as much by not working as by working. As far as pertains to dwelling and profession, that saying of the Oriental astrologers is by no means to be scorned, namely, that by change of name, profession, habits, manner of living, and place, the celestial influence can be changed in us as much for the better as for the worse. The Platonists will judge that daemons also are replaced or that we behave differently toward the same daemons in one place and in another. The astrologers agree with the Platonists that the guardian daemons of every individual whatsoever can be two, the one proper to his nativity, the other to his profession. As often as our profession agrees with our nature, we are attended by the same daemon for each, or at least a very similar one; and our life will thence be more internally harmonious and tranquil. But if our profession sits ill with our natural bent, the daemon acquired by art is discordant with the natural Genius and the life troublesome and full of care.

For those who want to find out what sort of daemon attended every individual from his very begetting, Porphyry searches for a rule from the planet that is lord of the geniture. Now the lord of the geniture, Julius Firmicus affirms, is either that planet who has the greater number of dignities at the time or else, on the basis of a sounder opinion, the one whose house the Moon will enter just after leaving the sign which she occupies when the man is born. But one's daemon, Julius Firmicus thinks, cannot be sought out from that same rule, but rather, according to the Chaldean opinion, from the Sun or the Moon. From the Sun to the Moon in a daytime nativity, conversely from the Moon to the Sun in a nighttime nativity: when you have computed the interval between these, you measure out an equal space descending from the degree of the Ascendant and you note in what term you stop. To whichever star that term belongs, they think your daemon belongs to it too. But in short, from the lord of the nativity together with the daemon, they usually assess your course of life and your fortune. I added "fortune" because some compute your Part of Fortune by nearly the same system.

The ancients wished that their daemon would have descended to them from some cardine of the heavens, namely from the East or from the West, or from the mid-heaven either above us or below us, or at least from the eleventh or the fifth place. The eleventh, indeed, is succeedent to the mid-heaven above our heads and is called "the good daemon," and is in a sextile aspect with that degree which is Ascendant from the East. But the fifth place is succeedent to the mid-heaven beneath our feet and is called "good fortune" and is in a trine aspect with the degree of the Ascendant. As a third choice, if a daemon came only from a cadent place, they wished him to have come at least from either the ninth or the third. For the ninth place is called "god," the third, "goddess." And the former is in a trine aspect with the degree of the Ascendant, the latter, in a sextile. But they had a horror of the cadent twelfth and sixth places, naming the former indeed "bad daemon," the latter, "bad fortune."

We, however, thinking it superfluous to wish for things that have already happened, advise observing the same places which they wanted observed for daemons and fortunes, for the purpose rather of accommodating planets and stars for the effecting of some work, whether they be in the cardines, or in the two succeedent places which we listed, or at the very least in the two cadent places which we previously named. For it is not irrelevant what they say, that the Sun rejoices in the ninth place, the Moon in the third, Jupiter in the eleventh, Venus in the fifth. For these places aspect the degree of the Ascendant.

But let us return to the subject with which we began. Therefore let us first of all search out the inclination of our nature and of our daemon—whether by that experiment and careful attention which we narrated above, or by the astrological art which I have just now recounted. We will judge a person to be unfortunate who has professed no respectable employment; for he who does not undertake respectable work does not in fact have a daemonic guide in his profession, and he scarcely has a daemonic guide for his natural self either, for it is the duty of the stars and daemons (or guiding angels divinely stationed on guard) to act always, excellently, and on a grand scale. Still less fortunate is the person who, as we said above, subjects himself, by a profession contrary to his nature, to a daemon unlike his Genius. Now remember that you receive daemons or, if you will, angels, more and more worthy by degrees in accordance with the dignity of the professions, and still worthier ones in public government; but even if you proceed to these more excellent [levels], you can receive from your Genius and natural bent an art and a course of life neither contrary to, nor very unlike, themselves.

Once more, remember to go in the company of those to whom the celestial "Graces" are propitious. You will assess what people have from the goods of soul, of body, and of fortune; for just as odor from musk, so something good exhales from the good man to his neighbor, and once infused, often persists. But a party of three fortunate ones would be wonderful, or of two, overflowing wonderfully into each other. And finally, remember to flee far away from the unbridled, the impudent, the malicious, and the unlucky. For these, being full of bad daemons or rays, are maleficent; and like lepers and people stricken with the plague, they harm not only by touch but even by proximity and by sight. Indeed, mere proximity of animate bodies is thought to constitute contact on account of the powerful exhalation of vapors emanating outward from bodily heat, from spirit, and from emotions. But most pestilent of all will be the company of the profligate and the cruel, if it is true that after the infusion of vegetable life in us in the month of Jupiter (that is, the second), next in the month of Mars (that is, the third) the sensual soul is infused, given over to agitation. For those who are carried away by agitation, being full of Mars, infect their neighbors with Martial contagion. By a contrary principle, however, the frequent company and close contact with the fortunate and the excellent, as we have said, usually does wonders for you. They say that Apollonius of Tyana apprehended an old man of Ephesus in whose shape lay hidden a daemon who by his presence alone was contaminating the whole city with a plague. Xenophon and Plato testify how much Socrates profited many by his presence alone.

CHRISTOPHER COLUMBUS (1451–1506)

The Log Book (1492)

ABSTRACTED BY FRAY BARTOLOMÉ DE LAS CASAS

Renaissance fantasies of brave new worlds, and the new wave of cosmographers who believed that the earth itself was a globe, reached the zenith of validation with the Italian-born Columbus' "discovery" of a small island in the Bahama group, off the coast of what would soon become known as "America." The Vikings, the Carthaginians, the Russians, and even the Romans, had possibly been here earlier, but their knowledge had been converted into saga or vague memories, never acted upon by navigators, merchants, or rulers. Columbus' first voyage, in 1492–93, under the patronage of Spain's Queen Isabella, led him to planting the Spanish flag first on a tiny island known to its

Stone-Age inhabitants as Guanahani, generally believed to be San Salvador (or Watling Island)—and then on the island of Cuba. Like many of his great contemporaries Columbus was a dreamer and soldier of fortune, more effective with daring and imagination than with pragmatic execution and consolidation of his findings. The romanticism with which Columbus' explorations were enshrined for centuries has, in the twentieth century, finally been displaced with a realistic view of the exploitative European consciousness represented in his comment about the natives who greeted him—"They should be good and intelligent servants, for I see that they say very quickly everything that is said to them. . ."— and by his eagerness to move on from this tiny island in search of gold and cotton. In Europe, reaction to the reports of his voyages was similar to the Apollo astronauts' descriptions of the moon, with every detail savored, deliberated, magnified, and, in the case of Rabelais' *Pantagruel,* satirized. Upon his first return to the court of Isabella, Columbus was met with the honors he'd dreamed of. But, true to the character of the era itself, as his voyages continued his fortune evaporated until he fell into disgrace because of his ineffectiveness as a governor and the excesses of his administration. He died in Valladolid, Spain, in near poverty.

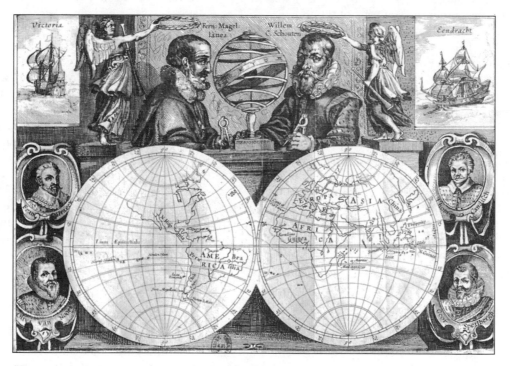

World map, with portraits of Magellan and Van Schouten, engraving in the Bibliothèque Nationale, Paris

The Diario of Christopher Columbus's First Voyage to America

Thursday 11 October

. . . [T]he Admiral entreated and admonished them to keep a good lookout on the forecastle and to watch carefully for land; and that to the man who first told him that he saw land he would later give a silk jacket in addition to the other rewards that the sovereigns had promised, which were ten thousand *maravedís* as an annuity to whoever should see it first. At two hours after midnight the land appeared, from which they were about two leagues distant. They hauled down all the sails and kept only the *treo*, which is the mainsail without bonnets, and jogged on and off, passing time until daylight Friday, when they reached an islet of the Lucayas, which was called Guanahani in the language of the Indians. Soon they saw naked people; and the Admiral went ashore in the armed launch, and Martín Alonso Pinzón and his brother Vicente Anes, who was captain of the *Niña*. The Admiral brought out the royal banner and the captains two flags with the green cross, which the Admiral carried on all the ships as a standard, with an F and a Y, and over each letter a crown, one on one side of the ✝ and the other on the other. Thus put ashore they saw very green trees and many ponds and fruits of various kinds. The Admiral called to the two captains and to the others who had jumped ashore and to Rodrigo Descobedo, the *escrivano* of the whole fleet, and to Rodrigo Sánchez de Segovia; and he said that they should be witnesses that, in the presence of all, he would take, as in fact he did take, possession of the said island for the king and for the queen his lords, making the declarations that were required, and which at more length are contained in the testimonials made there in writing. Soon many people of the island gathered there. What follows are the very words of the Admiral in his book about his first voyage to, and discovery of, these Indies. I, he says, in order that they would be friendly to us—because I recognized that they were people who would be

better freed [from error] and converted to our Holy Faith by love than by force—to some of them I gave red caps, and glass beads which they put on their chests, and many other things of small value, in which they took so much pleasure and became so much our friends that it was a marvel. Later they came swimming to the ships' launches where we were and brought us parrots and cotton thread in balls and javelins and many other things, and they traded them to us for other things which we gave them, such as small glass beads and bells. In sum, they took everything and gave of what they had very willingly. But it seemed to me that they were a people very poor in everything. All of them go around as naked as their mothers bore them; and the women also, although I did not see more than one quite young girl. And all those that I saw were young people, for none did I see of more than 30 years of age. They are very well formed, with handsome bodies and good faces. Their hair [is] coarse—almost like the tail of a horse—and short. They wear their hair down over their eyebrows except for a little in the back which they wear long and never cut. Some of them paint themselves with black, and they are of the color of the Canarians, neither black nor white; and some of them paint themselves with white, and some of them with red, and some of them with whatever they find. And some of them paint their faces, and some of them the whole body, and some of them only the eyes, and some of them only the nose. They do not carry arms nor are they acquainted with them, because I showed them swords and they took them by the edge and through ignorance cut themselves. They have no iron. Their javelins are shafts without iron and some of them have at the end a fish tooth and others of other things. All of them alike are of good-sized stature and carry themselves well. I saw some who had marks of wounds on their bodies and I made signs to them asking what they were; and they showed me how people from other islands nearby came there and tried to take them, and how they defended themselves; and I believed and believe that they come here from *tierra firme* to take them captive. They should be good and intelligent servants, for I see that they say very quickly everything that is said to them; and I believe that they would become Christians very easily, for it seemed to me that they had no religion. Our Lord pleasing, at the time of my departure I will take six of them from here to Your Highnesses in order that they may learn to speak. No animal of any kind did I see on this island except parrots. All are the Admiral's words.

SATURDAY 13 OCTOBER

As soon as it dawned, many of these people came to the beach—all young as I have said, and all of good stature—very handsome people, with hair not curly but straight and coarse, like horsehair; and all of them very wide in the forehead and head, more so than any other race that I have seen so far. And their eyes are very handsome and not small; and none of them are black, but of the color of the Canary Islanders. Nor should anything else be expected since this island is on an east-west line with the island of Hierro in the Canaries. All alike have very straight legs and no belly but are very well formed. They came to the ship with dugouts that are made from the trunk of one tree, like a long boat, and all of one piece, and worked marvelously in the fashion of the land, and so big that in some of them 40 and 45 men came. And others smaller, down to some in which came one man alone. They row with a paddle like that of a baker and go marvelously. And if it capsizes on them they then throw themselves in the water, and they right and empty it with calabashes that they carry. They brought balls of spun cotton and parrots and javelins and other little things that it would be tiresome to write down, and they gave everything for anything that was given to them. I was attentive and labored to find out if there was any gold; and I

saw that some of them wore a little piece hung in a hole that they have in their noses. And by signs I was able to understand that, going to the south or rounding the island to the south, there was there a king who had large vessels of it and had very much gold. I strove to get them to go there and later saw that they had no intention of going. I decided to wait until the afternoon of the morrow and then depart for the southwest, for, as many of them showed me, they said there was land to the south and to the southwest and to the northwest and that these people from the northwest came to fight them many times. And so I will go to the southwest to seek gold and precious stones. This island is quite big and very flat and with very green trees and much water and a very large lake in the middle and without any mountains; and all of it so green that it is a pleasure to look at it. And these people are very gentle, and because of their desire to have some of our things, and believing that nothing will be given to them without their giving something, and not having anything, they take what they can and then throw themselves into the water to swim. But everything they have they give for anything given to them, for they traded even for pieces of bowls and broken glass cups, and I even saw 16 balls of cotton given for three Portuguese *çeotis,* which is a Castilian *blanca.* And in them there was probably more than an *arroba* of spun cotton. This I had forbidden and I did not let anyone take any of it, except that I had ordered it all taken for Your Highnesses if it were in quantity. It grows here on this island, but because of the short time I could not declare this for sure. And also the gold that they wear hung in their noses originates here; but in order not to lose time I want to go to see if I can find the island of Cipango. Now, since night had come, all the Indians went ashore in their dugouts. . . .

GIROLAMO SAVONAROLA (1452–98)

Advent Sermon (1493)

Fortune's wheel linked the fate of this Dominican zealot with the princely family he served and despised. Girolamo Savonarola was imported to Florence's San Marco for his eloquence by Lorenzo de' Medici. Lorenzo would live to regret his hospitality, for Savonarola soon turned his rhetoric against his host and caught the ear of other Medici protégés, including Michelangelo Buonarroti. Attending Lorenzo's deathbed in 1492, Savonarola dared him to restore republican rule to the city whose artistic and humanistic splendors the monk associated with pagan decadence and Medici despotism. Lorenzo refused to grace the audacious demand with an answer, but history answered for him when Charles VIII's French invaded Italy in 1494 and the ineffective Piero de' Medici was forced into exile. Savonarola's earnest reformist message placed him in the limelight of the restored Republic. From his bully pulpit in San Marco, his confidence reached new peaks of daring. The "scourge of princes" arranged a bonfire of vanities that largely limited itself to the instruments of gambling and pornography. As Florence became an ideal Christian community, its ambitious Dominican directed his demands for reform to the Church at large, to Roman hierarchy in general, and to the licentious private life of the Borgia Pope Alexander VI in particular. Supporters of the exiled principality, now allied with the Borgia pope, took the occasion to silence Savonarola's inflexible dogmatism by reestablishing Medici rule. The monk was tortured, tried, found guilty of heresy, hanged, forgiven by the triumphant Pope, and burned in his own private bonfire amidst a carnival atmosphere in the Piazza della Signoria. The same crowds who had applauded his rise to power, and faithfully took down verbatim sermons like the following, were pleased to bear witness to his self-inflicted martyrdom. After his death Savonarola was canonized for his purity in the hearts of many Florentines, but never officially by the Roman Catholic Church.

When the devil sees that a man is weak, he strikes him with a hatchet in order to make him fall into sin; but if he sees that he is strong, he then strikes him with an axe. If a young girl be modest and well brought up, he throws some dissipated youth in her way, and causes her to yield to his flatteries and fall into sin. Thus the devil strikes her with his axe. Here is a citizen of good repute; he enters the courts of the great lords, and there is the axe so well sharpened that no virtue can resist its strokes. But we are now living in still more evil days; the devil has called his followers together, and they have dealt terrible blows on the very gates of the temple. It is by the gates that the house is entered, and it is the prelates who should lead the faithful into the Church of Christ.

Therefore the devil hath aimed his heaviest blows at them, and hath broken down these gates. Thus it is that no more good prelates are to be found in the Church. Seest thou not that they do all things amiss?. . . the cure of souls is no longer their concern; they are content with the receipt of revenue. . . . This is the new Church, no longer built of living rock, namely, of Christians steadfast in the living faith and in the mould of charity; but built of sticks, namely, of Christians dry as tinder for the fires of hell. . . . Go thou to Rome and throughout Christendom; in the mansions of the great prelates and great lords there is no concern save for poetry and the oratorical art. Go thither and see, thou shalt find them all with books of the humanities in their hands, and telling one another that they can guide men's souls by means of Vergil, Horace, and Cicero. Wouldst thou see how the Church is ruled by the hands of astrologers? And there is no prelate nor great lord that hath not intimate dealings with some astrologers, who fixeth the hour and the moment in which he is to ride out or undertake some piece of business. . . .

Piazza della Signoria, with the punishment of Savonarola and his followers (unknown sixteenth-century Florentine), in the Museo di San Marco, Florence

Thus our Church hath many fine outer ceremonies for the solemnization of ecclesiastical rites, grand vestments and numerous draperies, with gold and silver candlesticks, and so many chalices that it is a majestic sight to behold. There thou seest the great prelates with splendid mitres of gold and precious stones on their heads, and silver crosiers in hand; there they stand at the altar, decked with fine copes and stoles of brocade, chanting those beautiful vespers and masses, very slowly, and with so many grand ceremonies, so many organs and choristers, that thou art struck with amazement; and all these priests seem to thee grave and saintly men, thou canst not believe that they may be in error, but deem that all which they say and do should be obeyed even as the Gospel; and thus is our Church conducted. Men feed upon these vanities and rejoice in these pomps, and say that the Church of Christ was never so flourishing whereas our prelates, for the sake of obtaining chalices, will rob the poor of their sole means of support. But dost thou know what I would tell thee? In the primitive Church the chalices were of wood, the prelates of gold; in these days the Church hath chalices of gold and prelates of wood. These have introduced devilish games among us; they have no belief in God, and jeer at the mysteries of our faith! What doest Thou, O Lord? Why dost Thou slumber? Arise, and come to deliver Thy Church from the hands of the devils, from the hands of tyrants, the hands of iniquitous prelates. Hast Thou forsaken Thy Church? Dost Thou not love her? Is she not dear unto Thee? O Lord, we are become the despised of all nations; the Turks are masters of Constantinople; we have lost Asia, have lost Greece, we already pay tribute to the Infidel. O Lord God, Thou hast dealt with us as a wrathful father, Thou hast cast us out from Thy presence! Hasten then the chastisement and the scourge, that it may be quickly granted us to return to Thee. *Effunde iras tuas in gentes.* Be ye not scandalized, O my brethren, by these words; rather, when ye see that the righteous desire chastisement, know that it is because they seek to banish evil, so that the kingdom of our blessed Lord, Jesus Christ, may flourish in the world. The only hope that now remains to us, is that the sword of God may soon smite the earth.

FRATER LUCAS BARTOLOMEO PACIOLI (C.1445–1520?)

Treatise on Double-Entry Book-keeping (1494)

The age in which banking families were as powerful as princes gave us the methods of accounting still in use worldwide today. Ironically the double-entry method of "debit" and "credit" by which to keep track of "capital" and "cash" was memorialized by a Franciscan monk, whose respect and love for business is so strong he lists it first before reminding his ducal reader that God should also be invoked at each transaction. From the pen of this Tuscan-born itinerant professor of mathematics, counselor to the Sforzas, and friend of Leonardo da Vinci, we gain insight into the Renaissance emphasis on the primacy of order in successful commerce, a healthy respect for profits, and the single-mindedness of the merchant who must put business and money above all other considerations—as in Jack Benny's remark, "I never said money was the most important thing in life; it's just a long ways in front of whatever's in second place!" The good brother reminds the Duke of Urbino that three things are necessary in business: cash or "any other substantial power" (leverage); good accounting; and always having one's affairs in perfect order, for "where there is no order there is chaos" ("*Ubi non est ordo ibi est confusio*"). He would have been thrilled to see today's personal computer software, allowing the double-entry method to be employed by the ordinary citizen to pay his monthly bills.

Chapter XII. The manner of knowing how to enter and arrange in the Journal items of Debit and Credit—with many examples, and of the two other terms used in the Ledger, the one called "Cash" and the other "Capital," and What is to be understood by them.

Exterior, Palazzo Strozzi (B. de Maiano and Simone del Pollaiolo) in Florence

Therefore, in the name of God you shall begin to put in your Journal the first item of your Inventory; that is, the quantity of money you possess; and so as to know how to write up the Inventory into the Ledger and Journal, you must imagine two other terms, one called "Cash" and the other called "Capital." By "Cash" is meant your share or purse, by "Capital" is understood all you possess. Said "Capital" must always be placed as "Creditor" at the commencement of all your mercantile Ledgers and Journals, and said "Cash" must always be placed as "Debtor." Never may cash be creditor in any type of mercantile management; but only debtor unless it is balanced. He, who in the balance of his book found it Creditor, it would denote an error in the book, as in its place hereinafter I will give you summary reminders. Now in the Journal, said item of Cash must be put in this way. . . .

EXAMPLE OF POSTING IN JOURNAL

8th of November, MCCCCLXXXXIII. Venice.

1. *"Per"* Cash. *"A"* Capital of myself for so much cash etc., which I have in such and such place, in gold, coin, silver, and copper of various coinage as appears in the Inventory sheet posted in cash, in all so many ducats in gold, and in coins, so many ducats. In our Venetian money it is all valued in gold, that is, in *grossi* 24 per ducat, and in *picioli* 32 per *grosso*, so many gold *lire*.

Debitor 1

Line of debit.

Creditor 2

L. . . (lire) S. . . (soldi) G. . . (grossi)
P. . . (picioli).

2. "*Per*" set and unset Jewels of various kinds. "*A*" capital ditto for so many set "*balassi*," weighing so much; so many sapphires, rubies and diamonds, as appear in above said Inventory. These I value at current prices: the "*balassi*" so much—and thus you will state the current prices for each kind, amounting in all to so many ducats. Value.

For the 2nd Item you shall say thus:

L. . . . S. . . . G. . . . P. . . .

Having already named the day once, and again the debtor and creditor, you may say: On such and such a day, "*Per*" ditto, and "*A*" ditto; this for brevity, providing no other item is entered in between.

3. "*Per*" silverware. "*A*" ditto; by which is understood to Capital; per many kinds of silver in my possession at present; that is, basins, so many; coppers, so many; cups so many; "*pironi*" so many; "*cosileri*" so many; they weigh all together so much; Value. . . . L. . . . S. . . . G. . . . P. . . .

Thus you will describe these first items well in detail, everything as you described in the Inventory, giving to each entry an average price for your own personal knowledge, rather higher than low; that is, should they appear to you as worth 20, put them down at 24. By this means you will obtain better profit. You will thus enter, one by one, all the other things, with their respective weights, numbers and values, etc.

4. "*Per*" woollen clothes. "*A*" ditto for so many clothes of such and such colour and style, lined, used or new, for myself, my wife or for my children. These I value by current estimate all together at so many ducats; for cloaks, so many of such and such colour, etc., as you stated for all the other clothes and everything else:

L. . . . S. . . . G. . . . P. . . .

5. "*Per*" "*pannelini*" (linen). "*A*" ditto, for so many bed-sheets; put down everything as entered in the Inventory, their number and value:

L. . . . S. . . . G. . . . P. . . .

6. "*Per*" feather beds. "*A*" ditto, for feathers so much; here put down as entered in the Inventory—their number; value.

L. . . . S. . . . G. . . . P. . . .

7. "*Per*" "*mechini*" ginger. "*A*" ditto for so many packages; say what is contained as in the Inventory, their number, etc. Valued at current estimate at so many ducats.

L. . . . S. . . . G. . . . P. . . .

and by yourself thus you will continue to enter all the other items concerning all other things, putting down for each item a separate entry as we have done for the ginger, giving the current prices as said above, their numbers, marks, weights, just as they appear on said Inventory sheet, indicating what kinds of money you want for each item; but when summing up, these monies should be stated under one kind as it would not be nice to totalise them under different kinds.

All the said Journal entries you will close one by one by drawing a line from the end of your written narrative to the figures obtained. You will do the same with the entries in the Memorandum; and as you transfer from the Memorandum to the Journal you will draw a single line across each item thus / , which will denote that said item has been posted in the Journal. Should you not want to draw this line through the entry, you shall mark off the first letter at the commencement of said entry, or else the last letter as we have done at the head of this one, or else make use of some other sign recognisable to you as showing that the item had been transferred to the Journal. Should you make use of various terms and signs, you must nevertheless always try to make use of those common to other Merchants in the country you find yourself in, so that you do not appear deficient in the use of the usual mercantile ways.

PIETRO PERUGINO

Contract of Pietro Perugino with the Benedictine Monks of S. Pietro at Perugia (1495)

Lest anyone wonder, after reading of the Sforzas, d'Estes, and Medici, whether artists' relationships with patrons were universally more magnanimous in the Renaissance than they are today, a look at this contract between Perugino and St. Peter's in Perugia over the commissioning of an altarpiece makes it clear that, as Dwight Eisenhower once said, "things are more like they are today than they ever were before." The stipulations, pledge of collateral, and indemnifications are typical of such contracts from the time. Another such contract, between the painter Enguerrand Quarton and Dominus Jean de Montagne, reads, in part:

> Item. The vestments should be very rich; those of Our Lady should be white figured damask according to the judgement of said Master Enguerrand; and surrounding the Holy Trinity should be cherubim and seraphim. . . .
> Item. Said altarpiece shall be made in fine oil colors and the blue should be fine blue of Acre, except that which will be put on the frame, that should be fine German blue, and the gold that will be used on the frame as well as around the altarpiece should be fine gold and burnished. . . .

Perugino actually began the altarpiece described below in 1496, completing it in 1500. The central panel, thanks to Napoleon, must now be seen in the cathedral in Lyons.

In the name of the Lord, amen. In the year of our Lord 1495, in the thirteenth Indiction, at the time of the most Holy Father in Christ, Pope Alexander VI, ruling by Divine Providence, the eighth day of March. Drawn up in Perugia in the monastery of St. Peter in the presence of the following witnesses: Eusebio di Jacopo of Porta Santa Susanna of Perugia, Gianfrancisco Ciambello of Porta Sole of Perugia. The most Reverend Father in Christ, D. Lucianus of Florence, Abbot of the monastery of St. Peter of the Benedictine Order and of the congregation of Santa Giustina at Perugia, and D. Benedetto of Siena, and D. Daniele of Perugia, as the syndics of the order and procurators of the named monastery, with the permission, consent and desire of the above-mentioned Abbot, who is present and consenting. . . . have ordered and commissioned the most honorable man, master Pietro Cristoforo of Castel della Pieve, a most accomplished painter, who is present and has accepted the commission, to paint and ornament the picture for the main altar of the church of St. Peter. The picture must be painted in the following way:

In the rectangular panel, the Ascension of our Lord, Jesus Christ, with the figure of the glorious Virgin Mary, the Twelve Apostles and some angels and other ornaments, as may seem suitable to the painter.

In the semicircle above, supported by two angels, should be painted the figure of God the Almighty Father.

The predella below is to be painted and adorned with stories according to the desire of the present Abbot. The columns, however, and the mouldings and all other ornamentation of the panel should be embellished with fine gold and other fine colors, as will be most fitting, so that the panel will be beautifully and diligently painted, embellished and gilded from top to bottom as stated above and as it befits a good, experienced, honorable, and accomplished master. It will be executed within the space of the coming two and a half years, all at the cost and expense of the said master Pietro himself. The said master Pietro has promised the Reverend Abbot. . . to carry out this agreement in general and in particular under the penalties herein specified. The painter pledges all his goods, real and movable property, present and future.

This the said master Pietro consented to because the Reverend Father, the Abbot, has promised and agreed with him on the pledge of the monastery and his possessions to the said master Pietro, who is present and is executing this contract: namely, to give to him or to his heirs and actually to pay him for his painting, for paints, gold and other things necessary and suitable for the execution of the said painting, as well as for ornaments of the said panel, 500 gold ducats, payable within four years, counting from the day on which the painting shall be begun, at the rate of one quarter of the sum each year.

In said account, however, the frame which surrounds the panel is not to be included, nor the ornaments placed at the top of said frame, but only the panel itself with its ornaments. . . .

GIOVANNI PICO DELLA MIRANDOLA (1463–94)

ORATIO DE HOMINIS DIGNITATE

Oration, on the Dignity of Man (1486; 1496)

Neoplatonic mysticism reached its most eloquent high point with this oration "On the dignity of man" by this Florentine humanistic scholar and protégé of Lorenzo de' Medici. Versed in Arabic and Hebrew as well as Latin and Greek, Pico draws from all available sources to propound his view of humanity's place in the grand scheme of things. Although much of what it contains was preceded by Gianozzo Manetti's treatise *On the Dignity and Excellence of Man* (1452), Pico's ardent description of human nature's uniqueness expresses, more directly perhaps than any other document of the Renaissance, the characteristic spirit of the new age. Pico's oration is to Renaissance humanism what Charles Darwin's *Origin of Species* is to the theory of evolution. In classical Greek and Roman thought, reflecting a statement by Zeus to Hera in Homer's *Iliad*, the living universe is conceived of as a "great chain of being," with the father of gods and men at the top of the chain and all the other gods, humans, and animals at the other end trying in vain to pull him from Olympus. By the end of the Middle Ages, the image of the great chain expressed the perfection of Christian, feudal hierarchy. At the top rung was God, the creator of the chain. Then, link by link, came angels, popes, and emperors (the last two on the same link or different links depending on what school of thought you belonged to); then lords and bishops, knights and priests, down to the merchants, soldiers, serfs, and, finally, animals. The medieval worldview held that you were born into your position on the chain and could not move up without God's specific intervention (by that reasoning, it was believed that God Himself spoke when the cardinals voted for a new pope; kings and emperors were born, by divine right, to their crowns). Vertical movement on the chain was virtually unheard of. All that changed with Renaissance thinking, as expressed here by Pico. Human beings, through their free will and ability to play many roles, choose what rung on the ladder of being they wish to occupy. They are free to move up toward their higher nature and imitate the angels, or down toward their lower, more bestial desires. Moreover, as Petrarch's life and aspirations were the first of many to exemplify, man in the Renaissance is free to move horizontally on the chain as well. While the medieval scholastic proposition was, *operari sequitur esse,* "function follows form," in the Renaissance humans began to believe that form followed function. "We are," as Kurt Vonnegut, Jr., would put it in a twentieth-century echo of the Renaissance, "what we pretend to be, so we should be careful of what we pretend to be." Pico's is a view of human life both exhilarating for its challenge and opportunity, and exhausting for the endlessness of the roles it allows us to play and the quests it challenges us to undertake. Reflecting the Greek sophist Protagoras' view that "man is the measure of all things," Pico, always on the brink of heresy without intending to cross the line, argues that, "Nothing greater on earth than man, nothing greater in man than mind and spirit." In any order of being, man possesses only the position he assigns himself. Humans are more fortunate even than angels because their free will was created by God to appreciate His creation. While angels live in unearned bliss, man's bliss lies in the very struggle required by earthly life. This dynamic view of human nature remains with us to this day, when we still revere the Horatio Alger myth expressed in films like *Rocky* and books like Anthony Robbins' *Awaken the Giant Within* based on the premise that no one is an underdog except by his own choice.

ORATION ON THE DIGNITY OF MAN

I have read in the records of the Arabians, reverend Fathers, that Abdala the Saracen, when questioned as to what on this stage of the world, as it were, could be seen most worthy of wonder, replied: "There is nothing to be seen more wonderful than man." In agreement with this opinion is the saying of Hermes Trismegistus: "A great miracle, Asclepius, is man." But when I weighed the reason for these maxims, the many grounds for the excellence of human nature reported by many men failed to satisfy me—that man is the intermediary between creatures, the intimate of the gods, the king of the lower beings, by the acuteness of his senses, by the discernment of his reason, and by the light of his intelligence the interpreter of nature, the interval between fixed eternity and fleeting time, and (as the Persians say) the bond, nay, rather, the marriage song of the world, on David's testimony but little lower than the angels. Admittedly great though these reasons be, they are not the principal grounds, that is, those which may rightfully claim for themselves the privilege of the highest admiration. For why should we not admire more the angels themselves and the blessed choirs of heaven? At last it seems to me I have come to understand why man is the most fortunate of creatures and consequently worthy of all admiration and what precisely is that rank which is his lot in the universal chain of Being—a rank to be envied not only by brutes but even by the stars and by minds beyond this world. It is a matter past faith and a wondrous one. Why should it not be? For it is on this very account that man is rightly called and judged a great miracle and a wonderful creature indeed.

2. But hear, Fathers, exactly what this rank is and, as friendly auditors, conformably to your kindness, do me this favor. God the Father, the supreme Architect, had already built this cosmic home we behold, the most sacred temple of His godhead, by the laws of His mysterious wisdom. The region above the heavens He had adorned with Intelligences, the heavenly spheres He had quickened with eternal souls, and the excrementary and filthy parts of the lower world He had filled with a multitude of animals of every kind. But, when the work was finished, the Craftsman kept wishing that there were someone to ponder the plan of so great a work, to love its beauty, and to wonder at its vastness. Therefore, when everything was done (as Moses and Timaeus bear witness), He finally took thought concerning the creation of man. But there was not among His archetypes that from which He could fashion a new offspring, nor was there in His treasure-houses anything which He might bestow on His new son as an inheritance, nor was there in the seats of all the world a place where the latter might sit to contemplate the universe. All was now complete; all things had been assigned to the highest, the middle, and the lowest orders. But in its final creation it was not the part of the Father's power to fail as though exhausted. It was not

Door of the Uffizi and view of the Palazzo Vecchio during a flower show in Florence

the part of His wisdom to waver in a needful matter through poverty of counsel. It was not the part of His kindly love that he who was to praise God's divine generosity in regard to others should be compelled to condemn it in regard to himself.

3. At last the best of artisans ordained that that creature to whom He had been able to give nothing proper to himself should have joint possession of whatever had been peculiar to each of the different kinds of being. He therefore took man as a creature of indeterminate nature and, assigning him a place in the middle of the world, addressed him thus: "Neither a fixed abode nor a form that is thine alone nor any function peculiar to thyself have we given thee, Adam, to the end that according to thy longing and according to thy judgment thou mayest have and possess what abode, what form, and what functions thou thyself shalt desire. The nature of all other beings is limited and constrained within the bounds of laws prescribed by Us. Thou, constrained by no limits, in accordance with thine own free will, in whose hand We have placed thee, shalt ordain for thyself the limits of thy nature. We have set thee at the world's center that thou mayest from thence more easily observe whatever is in the world. We have made thee neither of heaven nor of earth, neither mortal nor immortal, so that with freedom of choice and with honor, as though the maker and molder of thyself, thou mayest fashion thyself in whatever shape thou shalt prefer. Thou shalt have the power to degenerate into the lower forms of life, which are brutish. Thou shalt have the power, out of thy soul's judgment, to be reborn into the higher forms, which are divine."

4. O supreme generosity of God the Father, O highest and most marvelous felicity of man! To him it is granted to have whatever he chooses, to be whatever he wills. Beasts as soon as they are born (so says Lucilius) bring with them from their mother's womb all they will ever possess. Spiritual beings, either from the beginning or soon thereafter, become what they are to be for ever and ever. On man when

he came into life the Father conferred the seeds of all kinds and the germs of every way of life. Whatever seeds each man cultivates will grow to maturity and bear in him their own fruit. If they be vegetative, he will be like a plant. If sensitive, he will become brutish. If rational, he will grow into a heavenly being. If intellectual, he will be an angel and the son of God. And if, happy in the lot of no created thing, he withdraws into the center of his own unity, his spirit, made one with God, in the solitary darkness of God, who is set above all things, shall surpass them all. Who would not admire this our chameleon? Or who could more greatly admire aught else whatever? It is man who Asclepius of Athens, arguing from his mutability of character and from his self-transforming nature, on just grounds says was symbolized by Proteus in the mysteries. Hence those metamorphoses renowned among the Hebrews and the Pythagoreans.

5. For the occult theology of the Hebrews sometimes transforms the holy Enoch into an angel of divinity whom they call "Mal'akh Adonay Shebaoth," and sometimes transforms others into other divinities. The Pythagoreans degrade impious men into brutes and, if one is to believe Empedocles, even into plants. Mohammed, in imitation, often had this saying on his tongue: "They who have deviated from divine law become beasts," and surely he spoke justly. For it is not the bark that makes the plant but its senseless and insentient nature; neither is it the hide that makes the beast of burden but its irrational, sensitive soul; neither is it the orbed form that makes the heavens but its undeviating order; nor is it the sundering from body but his spiritual intelligence that makes the angel. For if you see one abandoned to his appetites crawling on the ground, it is a plant and not a man you see; if you see one blinded by the vain illusions of imagery, as it were of Calypso, and, softened by their gnawing allurement, delivered over to his senses, it is a beast and not a man you see. If you see a philosopher determining all things by means of right reason, him you shall reverence: he is a heavenly being

and not of this earth. If you see a pure contemplator, one unaware of the body and confined to the inner reaches of the mind, he is neither an earthly nor a heavenly being; he is a more reverend divinity vested with human flesh.

6. Are there any who would not admire man, who is, in the sacred writings of Moses and the Christians, not without reason described sometimes by the name of "all flesh," sometimes by that of "every creature," inasmuch as he himself molds, fashions, and changes himself into the form of all flesh and into the character of every creature? For this reason the Persian Euanthes, in describing the Chaldaean theology, writes that man has no semblance that is inborn and his very own but many that are external and foreign to him; whence this saying of the Chaldaeans: "Hanorish tharah sharinas," that is, "Man is a being of varied, manifold, and inconstant nature." But why do we emphasize this? To the end that after we have been born to this condition—that we can become what we will—we should understand that we ought to have especial care to this, that it should never be said against us that, although born to a privileged position, we failed to recognize it and became like unto wild animals and senseless beasts of burden but that rather the saying of Asaph the prophet should apply: "Ye are all angels and sons of the Most High," and that we may not, by abusing the most indulgent generosity of the Father, make for ourselves that freedom of choice. He has given into something harmful instead of salutary. Let a certain holy ambition invade our souls, so that, not content with the mediocre, we shall pant after the highest and (since we may if we wish) toil with all our strength to obtain it.

7. Let us disdain earthly things, despite heavenly things, and, finally, esteeming less whatever is of the world, hasten to that court which is beyond the world and nearest to the Godhead. There, as the sacred mysteries relate, Seraphim, Cherubim, and Thrones hold the first places; let us, incapable of yielding to them, and intolerant of a lower place, emulate their dignity and their glory. If we have willed it, we shall be second to them in nothing.

8. But how shall we go about it, and what in the end shall we do? Let us consider what they do, what sort of life they lead. If we also come to lead that life (for we have the power), we shall then equal their good fortune. The Seraph burns with the fire of love. The Cherub glows with the splendor of intelligence. The Throne stands by the steadfastness of judgment. Therefore if, in giving ourselves over to the active life, we have after due consideration undertaken the care of the lower beings, we shall be strengthened with the firm stability of Thrones. If, unoccupied by deeds, we pass our time in the leisure of contemplation, considering the Creator in the creature and the creature in the Creator, we shall be all ablaze with Cherubic light. If we long with love for the Creator himself alone, we shall speedily flame up with His consuming fire into a Seraphic likeness. Above the Throne, that is, above the just judge, God sits as Judge of the ages. Above the Cherub, that is, above him who contemplates, God flies, and cherishes him, as it were, in watching over him. For the spirit of the Lord moves upon the waters, the waters, I say, which are above the firmament and which in Job praise the Lord with hymns before dawn. Whoso is a Seraph, that is, a lover, is in God and God in him, nay, rather, God and himself are one. Great is the power of Thrones, which we attain in using judgment, and most high the exaltation of Seraphs, which we attain in loving.

9. But by what means is one able either to judge or to love things unknown? Moses loved a God whom he saw and, as judge, administered among the people what he had first beheld in contemplation upon the mountain. Therefore, the Cherub as intermediary by his own light makes us ready for the Seraphic fire and equally lights the way to the judgment of the Thrones. This is the bond of the first minds, the Palladian order, the chief of contemplative philosophy. This is the one for us first to emulate, to court, and to understand; the one from whence we

may be rapt to the heights of love and descend, well taught and well prepared, to the functions of active life. But truly it is worth while, if our life is to be modeled on the example of the Cherubic life, to have before our eyes and clearly understood both its nature and its quality and those things which are the deeds and the labor of Cherubs. But since it is not permitted us to attain this through our own efforts, we who are but flesh and know of the things of earth, let us go to the ancient fathers who, inasmuch as they were familiar and conversant with these matters, can give sure and altogether trustworthy testimony. Let us consult the Apostle Paul, the chosen vessel, as to what he saw the hosts of Cherubim doing when he was himself exalted to the third heaven. He will answer, according to the interpretation of Dionysius, that he saw them being purified, then being illuminated, and at last being made perfect. Let us also, therefore, by emulating the Cherubic way of life on earth, by taming the impulses of our passions with moral science, by dispelling the darkness of reason with dialectic, and by, so to speak, washing away the filth of ignorance and vice, cleanse our soul, so that her passions may not rave at random or her reason through heedlessness ever be deranged.

10. Then let us fill our well-prepared and purified soul with the light of natural philosophy, so that we may at last perfect her in the knowledge of things divine. And lest we be satisfied with those of our faith, let us consult the patriarch Jacob, whose form gleams carved on the throne of glory. Sleeping in the lower world but keeping watch in the upper, the wisest of fathers will advise us. But he will advise us through a figure (in this way everything was wont to come to those men) that there is a ladder extending from the lowest earth to the highest heaven, divided in a series of many steps, with the Lord seated at the top, and angels in contemplation ascending and descending over them alternately by turns.

11. If this is what we must practice in our aspiration to the angelic way of life, I ask: "Who will touch the ladder of the Lord either with fouled foot or with unclean hands?" As the sacred mysteries have it, it is impious for the impure to touch the pure. But what are these feet? What these hands? Surely the foot of the soul is that most contemptible part by which the soul rests on matter as on the soil of the earth, I mean the nourishing and feeding power, the tinder of lust, and the teacher of pleasurable weakness. Why should we not call the hands of the soul its irascible power, which struggles on its behalf as the champion of desire and as plunderer seizes in the dust and sun what desire will devour slumbering in the shade? These hands, these feet, that is, all the sentient part whereon resides the attraction of the body which, as they say, by wrenching the neck holds the soul in check, lest we be hurled down from the ladder as impious and unclean, let us bathe in moral philosophy as if in a living river. Yet this will not be enough if we wish to be companions of the angels going up and down on Jacob's ladder, unless we have first been well fitted and instructed to be promoted duly from step to step, to stray nowhere from the stairway, and to engage in the alternate comings and goings. Once we have achieved this by the art of discourse or reasoning, then, inspired by the Cherubic spirit, using philosophy through the steps of the ladder, that is, of nature, and penetrating all things from center to center, we shall sometime descend, with titanic force rending the unity like Osiris into many parts, and we shall sometimes ascend, with the force of Phoebus collecting the parts like the limbs of Osiris into a unity, until, resting at last in the bosom of the Father who is above the ladder, we shall be made perfect with the felicity of theology. . . .

AMERIGO VESPUCCI (1454–1512)

Letter to Lorenzo Pietro Francesco de' Medici (1503)

Until recently historians have generally given Vespucci a bad rap compared to Columbus, denigrating him for having an entire new hemisphere named for him when the "actual" discoverer has no namesake to show for his discovery. Now that it's widely accepted that Columbus was hardly the first European to find America, the man for whom the "new world" was named, and who "discovered" the South American continent in 1501–2, bears reexamining. If nothing else, Vespucci, well financed by his Medici patron, was more articulate and self-possessed than his predecessor. In his three voyages to America, the first one in 1499, not only did he discover and explore the mouths of the Amazon, he also recognized South America as a continent, not part of Asia. As a result, the map of the world took on new dimensions in 1507, when cartographer Martin Waldseemüller published *Cosmographiae introductio (Introduction to cosmography)*, inscribing the name "America" across the area of Brazil, so naming the new continent in honor of the man who described it so eloquently. Though the Spanish tried to avoid using the term, it soon caught on universally. Vespucci's description of the land is so resonant of Sir Thomas More's *Utopia* that there can be little doubt that More had read this letter.

Letter on his Third Voyage from Amerigo Vespucci to Lorenzo Pietro Francesco di Medici.

MARCH (OR APRIL) 1503

Alberico Vesputio to Lorenzo Pietro di Medici, salutation. In passed days I wrote very fully to you of my return from the new countries, which have been found and explored with the ships, at the cost, and by the command, of this Most Serene King of Portugal; and it is lawful to call it a new world, because none of these countries were known to our ancestors, and to all who hear about them they will be entirely new. For the opinion of the ancients was, that the greater part of the world beyond the equinoctial line to the south was not land, but only sea, which they have called the Atlantic; and if they have affirmed that any continent is there, they have given many reasons for denying that it is inhabited. But this their opinion is false, and entirely opposed to the truth. My last voyage has proved it, for I have found a continent in that southern part; more populous and more full of animals than our Europe, or Asia, or Africa, and even more temperate and pleasant than any other region known to us, as will be explained further on. I shall write succinctly of

Incense burner in the shape of a ship

the principal things only, and the things most worthy of notice and of being remembered, which I either saw or heard of in this new world, as presently will become manifest.

We set out, on a prosperous voyage, on the 14th of May 1501, sailing from Lisbon, by order of the aforesaid King, with three ships, to discover new countries towards the west; and we sailed towards the south continuously for twenty months. Of this navigation the order is as follows: Our course was for the Fortunate Islands, so called formerly, but now we call them the Grand Canary Islands, which are in the third climate, and on the confines of the inhabited west. Thence we sailed rapidly over the ocean along the coast of Africa and part of Ethiopia to the Ethiopic Promontory, so called by Ptolemy, which is now called Cape Verde, and by the Ethiopians *Biseghier,* and that country *Mandraga,* 13° within the Torrid Zone, on the north side of the equinoctial line. The country is inhabited by a black race. Having taken on board what we required, we weighed our anchors and made sail, taking our way across the vast ocean towards the Antarctic Pole, with some westing. From the day when we left the before-mentioned promontory, we sailed for the space of two months and three days. Hitherto no land had appeared to us in that vast sea. In truth, how much we had suffered, what dangers of shipwreck, I leave to the judgment of those to whom the experience of such things is very well known. What a thing it is to seek unknown lands, and how difficult, being ignorant, to narrate briefly what happened. It should be known that, of the sixty-seven days of our voyage, we were navigating continuously forty-four. We had copious thunderstorms and perturbations, and it was so dark that we never could see either the sun in the day or the moon at night. This caused us great fear, so that we lost all hope of life. In these most terrible dangers of the sea it pleased the Most High to show us the continent and the new countries, being another unknown world. These things being in sight, we were as much rejoiced as anyone may imagine who, after calamity and ill-fortune, has obtained safety.

It was on the 7th of August 1501, that we reached those countries, thanking our Lord God with solemn prayers, and celebrating a choral Mass. We knew that land to be a continent, and not an island, from its long beaches extending without trending round, the infinite number of inhabitants, the numerous tribes and peoples, the numerous kinds of wild animals unknown in our country, and many others never seen before by us, touching which it would take long to make reference. The clemency of God was shown forth to us by being brought to these regions; for the ships were in a leaking state, and in a few days our lives might have been lost in the sea. To Him be the honour and glory, and the grace of the action.

We took counsel, and resolved to navigate along the coast of this continent towards the east, and never to lose sight of the land. We sailed along until we came to a point where the coast turned to the south. The distance from the landfall to this point was nearly 300 leagues. In this stretch of coast we often landed, and had friendly relations with the natives, as I shall presently relate. I had forgotten to tell you that from Cape Verde to the first land of this continent the distance is nearly 700 leagues; although I estimate that we went over more than 1,800, partly owing to ignorance of the route, and partly owing to the tempests and foul winds which drove us off our course, and sent us in various directions. If my companions had not trusted in me, to whom cosmography was known, no one, not the leader of our navigation, would have known where we were after running 500 leagues. We were wandering and full of errors, and only the instruments for taking the altitudes of heavenly bodies showed us our position. These were the quadrant and astrolabe, as known to all. These have been much used by me with much honour; for I showed them that a knowledge of the marine chart, and the rules taught by it, are more worth than all the pilots in the world. For these pilots have no knowledge beyond those places to which they have often sailed. Where the said point of land showed us the trend of the coast to the south, we agreed to continue our voyage, and to ascertain what there might be in those regions. We sailed along the coast for nearly 500 leagues, often going on shore and having intercourse with the natives, who received us in a brotherly manner. We sometimes stayed with them for fifteen or twenty days continuously, as friends and guests, as I shall relate presently. Part of this continent is in the Torrid Zone, beyond the equinoctial line towards the South Pole. But it begins at 8° beyond the equinoctial. We sailed along the coast so far that we crossed the Tropic of Capricorn, and found ourselves where the Antarctic Pole was 50° above our horizon. We went towards the Antarctic Circle until we were 17° 30' from it; all which I have

seen, and I have known the nature of those people, their customs, the resources and fertility of the land, the salubrity of the air, the positions of the celestial bodies in the heavens, and, above all, the fixed stars, over an eighth of the sphere, never seen by our ancestors, as I shall explain below.

As regards the people: we have found such a multitude in those countries that no one could enumerate them, as we read in the Apocalypse. They are people gentle and tractable, and all of both sexes go naked, not covering any part of their bodies, just as they came from their mothers' wombs, and so they go until their deaths. They have large, square-built bodies, and well proportioned. Their colour reddish, which I think is caused by their going naked and exposed to the sun. Their hair is plentiful and black. They are agile in walking, and of quick sight. They are of a free and good-looking expression of countenance, which they themselves destroy by boring the nostrils and lips, the nose and ears: nor must you believe that the borings are small, nor that they only have one, for I have seen those who had no less than seven borings in the face, each one the size of a plum. They stop up these perforations with blue stones, bits of marble, of crystal, or very fine alabaster, also with very white bones and other things artificially prepared according to their customs; which, if you could see, it would appear a strange and monstrous thing. One had in the nostrils and lips alone seven stones, of which some were half a palm in length. It will astonish you to hear that I considered that the weight of seven such stones was as much as sixteen ounces. In each ear they had three perforations bored, whence they had other stones and rings suspended. This custom is only for the men, as the women do not perforate their faces, but only their ears. Another custom among them is sufficiently shameful, and beyond all human credibility. Their women, being very libidinous, make the penis of their husbands swell to such a size as to appear deformed; and this is accomplished by a certain artifice, being the bite of some poisonous animal, and by reason of this many lose their virile organ and remain eunuchs.

They have no cloth, either of wool, flax, or cotton, because they have no need of it; nor have they any private property, everything being in common. They live amongst themselves without a king or ruler, each man being his own master, and having as many wives as they please. The children cohabit with the mothers, the brothers with the sisters, the male cousins with the female, and each one with the first he meets. They have no temples and no laws, nor are they idolaters. What more can I say! They live according to nature, and are more inclined to be Epicurean than Stoic. They have no commerce among each other, and they wage war without art or order. The old men make the youths do what they please, and incite them to fights, in which they mutually kill with great cruelty. They slaughter those who are captured, and the victors eat the vanquished; for human flesh is an ordinary article of food among them. You may be the more certain of this, because I have seen a man eat his children and wife; and I knew a man who was popularly credited to have eaten 300 human bodies. I was once in a certain city for twenty-seven days, where human flesh was hung up near the houses, in the same way as we expose butcher's meat. I say further that they were surprised that we did not eat our enemies, and use their flesh as food, for they say it is excellent. Their arms are bows and arrows, and when they go to war they cover no part of their bodies, being in this like beasts. We did all we could to persuade them to desist from their evil habits, and they promised us to leave off. The women, as I have said, go naked, and are very libidinous, yet their bodies are comely; but they are as wild as can be imagined.

They live for 150 years, and are rarely sick. If they are attacked by a disease they cure themselves with the roots of some herbs. These are the most noteworthy things I know about them.

The air in this country is temperate and good, as we were able to learn from their accounts that there are never any pestilences or epidemics caused by bad air. Unless they meet with violent deaths, their lives are long.

DESIDERIUS ERASMUS (1466–1536)

MORIAE ENCOMIUM

Folly's Eulogy (1511)

The Dutch humanist Erasmus (1466–1536), like many satirists of the Renaissance, explored the boundaries of secular thought from the relative safety of an ecclesiastical life. He was ordained an Augustinian priest in 1492, studied in Paris, taught in Cambridge, edited the Greek New Testament and translated it into classical Latin, and traveled throughout Europe to consort with the great minds and powers of the time. He thought of himself as a cosmopolitan, a Christian European. His *Handbook of the Christian Soldier* was an earnest plea for a return to the simplicity of the primitive church. Unhappy with and confused by the Church's inability to reform itself, Erasmus hid his attacks behind the mask of satire without having the courage to take the drastic steps of Protestant separation. Yet his correspondents and friends included Martin Luther, who called him a "Proteus," and Thomas More. Scholars define true tragedy as the conflict, not between right and wrong, but between right and right. Truly in this regard Erasmus, who determined to remain loyal to a church he recognized as corrupt, is one of the tragic figures of the Renaissance. His letters to influential contemporaries number in the thousands, and reveal the anguished frustration of a man who fits Matthew Arnold's definition, "wandering between two worlds, one dead, the other powerless to be born." It was More to whom Erasmus dedicated his most characteristic work, familiarly known as *The Praise of Folly* (in Latinized Greek, *Moriae Encomium*). "Folly's Eulogy" is presented as a parody of the classical oration as described by Aristotle and Quintillian, with the characteristically Renaissance twist that the orator, Folly, is eulogizing herself (since no one else will praise her). As we listen to her describe her virtues and power over the doings of mortals, we recognize her as one of the great exemplars of "the fool" whose origins can be traced back to the ironic simplicity of Plato's Socrates and whose contemporary relatives include Shakespeare's Falstaff and Cordelia, Rabelais' Panurge, and Cervantes' Don Quixote de la Mancha. Folly's underlying message is anything but frivolous. Under the safely satirical mask of foolishness, Erasmus uses her persona to express his reformer's heart, castigating the hypocrisy of his time: the Church which in its corruption had fallen away from the divine innocence of its founder (who said, "Suffer the children to come unto me, for theirs is the kingdom of heaven"), monks whose heads were more filled with trivial puns and worldly lusts than with spiritual exaltation, and political leaders whose self-important vanities and frivolities led regularly to economic and physical catastrophe for lesser men and women. Highlights of Folly's message include:

- The further a person departs from folly, the less life he has in him.
- Lovers' blindness is an old joke, but it binds the human race together, perpetuates the species, and leads to a great deal of happiness.
- A fool is in a better position than a wise person.
- All kings and rulers are fools.
- While wisdom begets a timid, grubby, hungry wretch, your unwise man rolls in money, is called to the helm of state, and prospers in every way.
- The Church is more foolish than wise.

Should one of his hosts accuse the peripatetic monk of political incorrectness in this exuberant *tour de force*, Erasmus could respond: "But all is being said here by Folly, and only a fool would take the words of Folly seriously." Nonetheless it's clear, as Kent says to Lear, that "this is not altogether fool, my lord." Like the political black humor of Art Buchwald, Erasmus' brilliant oration is anything but foolish. And like black humor, underlying it is a universal plea for tolerance and recognition of the frailties of human nature. If in all our

> **ambitious intellectual undertakings we are to remain sane we must laugh at ourselves. Holbein painted Folly as a young woman in a scholar's gown, a fool's cap covering her ass' ears.**

Stultitia loquitur

However mortal folk may commonly speak of me (for I am not ignorant how ill the name of Folly sounds, even to the greatest fools), I am she—the only she, I may say—whose divine influence makes gods and men rejoice. One great and sufficient proof of this is that the instant I stepped up to speak to this crowded assembly, all faces at once brightened with a fresh and unwonted cheerfulness, all of you suddenly unbent your brows, and with frolic and affectionate smiles you applauded; so that as I look upon all present about me, you seem flushed with nectar, like gods in Homer, not without some nepenthe, also; whereas a moment ago you were sitting moody and depressed, as if you had come out of the cave of Trophonius. Just as it commonly happens, when the sun first shows his splendid golden face to the earth or when, after a bitter winter, young spring breathes mild west winds, that a new face comes over everything, new color and a sort of youthfulness appear; so at the mere sight of me, you straightway take on another aspect. And thus what great orators elsewhere can hardly bring about in a long, carefully planned speech, I have done in a moment, with nothing but my looks.

As to why I appear today in this unaccustomed garb, you shall now hear, if only you will not begrudge lending your ears to my discourse—not those ears, to be sure, which you carry to sermons, but those which you are accustomed to prick up for mountebanks in the marketplace, for clowns and jesters, the ears which, in the old days, our friend Midas inclined to the god Pan. It is my pleasure for a little while to play the rhetorician before you, yet not one of the tribe of those who nowadays cram certain pedantic trifles into the heads of school-boys, and teach a more than womanish obstinacy in disputing; no, I emulate those ancients who, to avoid the unpopular name of philosophers, preferred to be called Sophists. Their study was to celebrate in eulogies the virtues of gods and of heroic men. Such a eulogy, therefore, you shall hear, but not of Hercules or Solon; rather of my own self—to wit, Folly. . . .

Now let anyone that will compare this boon of mine with the metamorphoses produced by other gods. Those which they worked when angry it is not well to mention; but take the stories of people toward whom they were especially friendly. They would transform somebody into a tree, or a bird, or a cicada, or even into a

Erasmus of Rotterdam (Quentin Metsys), in Galleria Nazionale d'Arte Antica, Palazzo Barberini, Rome

snake; as if this were not to perish indeed—to be made into something else! But I restore the very same man to the best and happiest part of his life. And if mortals would abstain utterly from any contact with wisdom, and live out their span continuously in my company, there would not be any such thing as old age, but in happiness they would enjoy perpetual youth. For do you not see that the austere fellows who are buried in the study of philosophy, or condemned to difficult and wracking business, grow old even before they have been young—and this because by cares and continual hard driving of their brains they insensibly exhaust their spirits and dry up their radical moisture? On the contrary, my morons are as plump and sleek as the hogs of Acarnania (as the saying is), with complexions well cared for, never feeling the touch of old age; unless, as rarely happens, they catch something by contagion from the wise—so true is it that the life of man is not destined to be in every respect happy.

These arguments have the strong support of a proverb current among the folk; as they often say, "Folly is the one thing that makes fleeting youth linger and keeps ugly old age away.". . .

Go, foolish mortals, and vainly seek for your Medeas and Circes and Venuses and Auroras, and the unknown fountain in which you may restore your youth! When all the time I alone have that power; I alone use it. In my shop is that miraculous juice with which the daughter of Memnon lengthened the days of her grandfather Tithonus. I am that Venus by whose favor Phaon grew young again so that he might be loved so much by Sappho. Mine are those herbs (if they exist), mine that fountain, mine the spells which not only bring back departed youth but, still better, preserve it in perpetuity. If, then, all of you subscribe to this sentiment, that nothing is better than adolescence or more undesirable than age, I think you must see how much you owe to me, who conserve so great a good and fend off so great an evil.

But what am I doing, talking about mortal men? Survey the universal sky, and you may cast my name in my teeth if you can find anyone at all among the gods who is not foul and despicable except so far as he is graced by my divine power. For why is Bacchus always young and curly-haired? Simply because, frantic and giddy, he passes his life in feasts, routs, dances, and games, and has no title of converse with Pallas. So far is he from wanting to be accounted wise, in brief, that it tickles him to be worshipped in gambols and sport; nor is he offended by the proverb which gave him the nickname of fool, as thus: "More foolish than Morychus." For as time went on they changed his name to Morychus, because the wanton countryfolk used to smear his statue, placed before the gates of his temple, with new wine and fresh figs. And then what scoffs the Old Comedy throws at him! "O stupid god," they say, "and worthy to be born from a thigh!" But who would not choose to be stupid and foolish Bacchus, always festive, always downy of cheek, always bringing gaiety and delight to all, rather than to be "deep-counselled" Jove, who frightens everybody, or Pan in his peevishness, infecting all things with his disorders, or Vulcan, full of cinders and foul from the labors of his shop, or even Pallas herself, "always peering grimly," with her Gorgon's head and fearful spear? Why is Cupid forever a boy? Why, but because he is a trifler, and cannot do or even consider anything at all sane. Why does the beauty of the aureate Venus keep an eternal spring? Surely because she is related to me; whence also she bears in her face my father's color, and for that reason in Homer she is "golden Aphrodite." Lastly, she laughs perpetually, if we can in anything believe the poets or their rivals, the sculptors. What divinity did the Romans ever worship more devoutly than Flora, that breeder of all delights? Nay, if one faithfully seeks in Homer to learn the story of the austere gods, he will find it replete with folly. But why stop to record the doings of the others, when you know so well the loves and pastimes of Jove the Thunderer himself? When the chaste Diana, forgetting her sex, does nothing but hunt, being all the time desperately in love with Endymion?. . .

May I not affirm, indeed, that you will find

no great exploit undertaken, no important arts invented, except at my prompting? As, for instance, is not war the seed-plot and fountain of renowned actions? Yet what is more foolish than to enter upon a conflict for I know not what causes, wherein each side reaps more of loss than of gain? As for those who fall, as was said of the Megarians, "no particulars." And when armored ranks engage each other and bugles bray with harsh accord, of what use are those wise men, who, exhausted by studies, scarce maintain any life in their thin, cold blood? The day belongs to stout, gross fellows; the littler wit they have, the bolder they are—unless, forsooth, you prefer a soldier like Demosthenes, who, since he agreed with the poetic sentiment of Archilochus, dropped his shield and ran, as cowardly in warfare as he was consummate in eloquence. But wise planning, they say, is of most importance in war. Yes, on the part of a general, I grant; yet is it military, not philosophical, wisdom. Far otherwise: this famous game of war is played by parasites, panders, bandits, assassins, peasants, sots, bankrupts, and such other dregs of mankind; never by philosophers, with their candles of wisdom.

How ineffective these philosophers are for the work of real life, the one and only Socrates himself, who was judged wisest by (not the wisest) oracle of Apollo, will serve for proof. When he tried to urge something, I know not what, in public, he hastily withdrew to the accompaniment of loud laughter from all quarters. Yet Socrates was not altogether foolish in this one respect, that he repudiated the epithet "wise," and gave it over to God; he also cherished the opinion that a wise man should abstain from meddling in the public business of the commonwealth. To be sure, he ought rather to have admonished us that one who wishes to have a place in the ranks of men should abstain from wisdom itself. And then, what but his wisdom drove him, once he had been impeached, to drink the hemlock? For while he disputed and reasoned of clouds and ideas, while he measured the feet of a flea, and marvelled at the voice of a gnat, he did not fathom the common-

est concerns of life. But with this teacher standing in peril of death, comes now his scholar Plato, that remarkable (shall we say?) advocate, who was so abashed by the murmur of the audience that he could scarcely deliver the well-known half of his first sentence. And what shall I say of Theophrastus? When he was starting to make a speech, he was suddenly struck dumb, as if he had caught sight of a wolf. Could he have heartened a soldier going into battle? Thanks to the timorousness of his nature, Isocrates never dared open his mouth in public. Marcus Tullius Cicero, father of Roman eloquence, used always to begin to speak with an unseemly peril, which he never pauses to weigh? The wise man runs to books of the ancients and learns from them a merely verbal shrewdness. The fool arrives at true prudence, if I am not deceived, by addressing himself at once to the business and taking his chances. Homer seems to have seen this, for all that he was blind, when he said, "Even a fool is wise after a thing is done." There are two great obstacles to developing a knowledge of affairs—shame, which throws a smoke over the understanding, and fear, which, once danger has been sighted, dissuades from going through with an exploit. Folly, with a grand gesture, frees us from both. Never to feel shame, to dare anything—few mortals know to what further blessings these will carry us!

Yet if they prefer to have that prudence which consists in the mere discernment of things, then hear, I adjure you, how far they are from it who still vaunt themselves upon the name. For first of all, the fact is that all human affairs, like the Sileni of Alcibiades, have two aspects, each quite different from the other; even to the point that what at first blush (as the phrase goes) seems to be death may prove, if you look further into it, to be life. What at first sight is beautiful may really be ugly; the apparently wealthy may be poorest of all; the disgraceful, glorious; the learned, ignorant; the robust, feeble; the noble, base; the joyous, sad; the favorable, adverse; what is friendly, an enemy; and what is wholesome, poisonous. In brief, you find all things suddenly reversed, when you open up the Silenus. Perhaps this seems too philosophical a saying; but come, with the help of a somewhat fat Minerva (to use an old expression), I shall make it more clear. Who would not avow that the king is a rich and great lord? Yet let the king be unfurnished in goods of the spirit, let him find satisfaction in nothing, and you see in a trice that he is the poorest of men. Suppose that his soul is given over to vices; now he is a vile slave. In like manner one might philosophize concerning others also, but let this one serve as an example.

But where, one asks, does it all lead? Have patience, and let us carry it further. If a person were to try stripping the disguises from actors while they play a scene upon the stage, showing to the audience their real looks and the faces they were born with, would not such a one spoil the whole play? And would not the spectators think he deserved to be driven out of the theater with brickbats, as a drunken disturber? For at once a new order of things would be apparent. The actor who played a woman would now be seen a man; he who a moment ago appeared young, is old; he who but now was a king, is suddenly an hostler; and he who played the god is a sorry little scrub. Destroy the illusion and any play is ruined. It is the paint and trappings that take the eyes of spectators. Now what else is the whole life of mortals but a sort of comedy, in which the various actors, disguised by various costumes and masks, walk on and play each one his part, until the manager waves them off the stage? Moreover, this manager frequently bids the same actor go back in a different costume, so that he who has but lately played the king in scarlet now acts the flunkey in patched clothes. Thus all things are presented by shadows; yet this play is put on in no other way.

But suppose, right here, some wise man who has dropped down from the sky should suddenly confront me and cry out that the person whom the world has accepted as a god and a master is not even a man, because he is driven sheeplike by his passions; that he is the lowest slave, because he willingly serves so many and such base masters. Or again, suppose the visitor should command some one mourning his father's death to laugh, because now his father has really begun to live—for in a sense our earthly life is but a kind of death. Suppose him to address another who is glorying in his ancestry, and to call him low and base-born because he is so far from virtue, the only true fount of nobility. Suppose him to speak of others in like vein. I ask you, what would he get by it, except to be considered by everyone as insane and raving? As nothing is more foolish than wisdom out of place, so nothing is more imprudent than unseasonable prudence. And he is unseasonable who does not accommodate himself to things as they are, who is "unwilling to follow the market," who does not keep in mind at least that rule of conviviality, "Either drink or get out"; who demands, in short, that the play should no longer be a play. The part of a truly prudent man, on the contrary, is (since we are mortal) not to aspire to wisdom beyond his station, and either, along with the rest of the crowd, pretend not to notice anything, or affably and companionably be deceived. But that, they tell us, is folly. Indeed, I shall not deny it; only let them, on their side, allow that it is also to play out the comedy of life.

As for the next, O ye immortal gods! Shall I speak or be silent? But why should I be silent, when it is more true than truth? Yet haply for such an undertaking it might be well to send up to Helicon and fetch the Muses, whom the poets are wont to invoke, quite often on most trivial occasions. Therefore, be present for a brief season, daughters of Jove, while I show to the world that one never attains to that renowned wisdom, which the wise themselves call the citadel of happiness, except by taking Folly as guide. And first, it is beyond dispute that all emotions belong to folly. Indeed, we distinguish a wise man from a fool by this, that reason governs the one, and passion the other. Thus the Stoics take away from the wise man all perturbations of the soul, as so many diseases. Yet these passions not only discharge the office of mentor and guide to such as are pressing toward the gate of wisdom, but they also assist in every exercise of virtue as spurs and goads—persuaders, as it were—to well doing. Although that double-strength Stoic, Seneca, stoutly denies this, subtracting from the wise man any and every emotion, yet in doing so he leaves him no man at all but rather a new kind of god, or demiurgos, who never existed and will never emerge. Nay, to speak more plainly, he creates a marble simulacrum of a man, a senseless block, completely alien to every human feeling.

Well, if they want it so, I give them joy of this wise man of theirs. They may love him with no fear of a rival, and may live with him in Plato's republic, or, if they prefer, in the world of ideas, or in the gardens of Tantalus. For who would not startle at such a man, as at an apparition or ghost, and shun him? He would be insensible to any natural sympathy, no more moved by feelings of love or pity than as if he were solid flint or Marpesian stone. Nothing gets by him; he never makes a mistake; as if another Lynceus, there is no thing he does not see; he measures everything with a standard rule; he forgives nothing; he alone is satisfied with himself alone, uniquely rich, uniquely sane, uniquely a king, uniquely a free man. . . .

But it is a sad thing, they say, to be deceived. No; the saddest thing is not to be deceived. For they are quite beside the mark who think that the happiness of a man is to be found in things, as such; it resides in opinion. For such is the obscurity and variety of human affairs that nothing can be clearly known, as has been correctly said by my Academics, the least impudent of the philosophers. Or if something can be known, usually it is something that makes against the enjoyment of life. Finally, the mind of man is so constructed that it is taken far more with disguises than with realities. If anyone wants to make a convincing and easy test of this, let him go to church and listen to sermons. If something solid is being said, every-

body sleeps, or yawns, or is ill at ease. But if the bawler—I made a slip, I meant to say prater—as they so often do, begins some old wives' tale, everybody awakens, straightens up, and gapes for it. Also if there is a somewhat fabulous or poetical saint (and if you want an example, imagine George or Christopher or Barbara to belong to this class), you will see him honored much more religiously than Peter or Paul or even Christ himself. But these things do not belong here.

Yet how little this addition to happiness costs! whereas it is necessary to lay out a much greater price for almost any of the solid things, even for the poorest of them—grammar, for instance. But opinion is picked up very easily, and yet for all that, it conduces far more to happiness. Suppose a man is eating some rotten kippers, and the man beside him cannot abide the smell of them; but to the eater they taste and smell like ambrosia. I ask you, what is the consequence, as regards happiness? On the other hand, if the best sturgeon turns your stomach, what can it contribute to the blessedness of existence? If a man has a wife who is notoriously ugly, yet who seems to her husband fit to enter a competition with Venus herself, is it not the same as if she were truly beautiful? If one was to behold a canvas daubed with red lead and mud, and to admire it under the persuasion that it was a picture by Apelles or Zeuxis, would he not be happier than another who buys the work of such masters at a high price, but feels less of pleasure, perhaps, in viewing it? I know a man of my name who gave his young wife some imitation jewels as a present, persuading her—for he is a plausible joker—that they were not only genuine and natural but also of unique and inestimable value. Pray tell me, what difference did it make to the girl, so long as she joyously delighted her eyes and heart with glass, and carefully kept these trinkets in a safe place never far from her person? In the meantime, her husband had avoided expense, he had enjoyed his wife's delusion, and he had bound her to himself no less than as if he had given greater purchases. In your judgment, what difference is there between those who in Plato's cave look admiringly at the shadows and simulacra of various things, desiring nothing, quite well satisfied with themselves, as against the wise man who emerges from the cave and sees realities? If Micyllus, in Lucian, had been allowed always to go on dreaming that rich and golden dream, there would have been no reason for him to choose any other happiness.

Hence there either is no difference or, if there is difference, the state of fools is to be preferred. First, their happiness costs least. It costs only a bit of illusion. And second, they enjoy it in the company of so many others. The possession of no good thing is welcome without a companion. And who has not heard of the paucity of wise men—if indeed any is to be found. Out of several centuries the Greeks counted seven altogether; yet, so help me, if one were to canvass them with care and accuracy, may I be shot if he would find so much as one half-wise man—nay, so much as one-third of one wise man! . . .

ALBRECHT DÜRER (1471–1528)

Writings (1512–13)

As prolific as he was as a painter, designer, inventor, and etcher, the Lutheran Albrecht Dürer, the "artist-prince" of Nuremberg, was no less prolific with his pen. Melanchthon said of him, "although he excelled at the art of painting, it was the least of his attainments." Following in the footsteps of the great Italian masters, he was the first German to move his art from that of a craftsman to that of a public figure, hobnobbing with the aristocracy of his day, eventually achieving the patronage of the Emperor Charles V (Emperor of Spain, the Lowlands, the Holy Roman Empire, and the Two Sicilies). Always aware of the importance of his personal vision, "for the sight is the noblest sense of man," he signed and dated each of his works. He considered his dreams significant enough to record and comment on. Yet he was truly humble in the lifelong pursuit of knowledge and self-awareness.

At the same time that Dürer brought German art to a universal plane, he wrote voluminously, planning an encyclopedic work that would offer the results of his observations and investigations to other artists, including a definitive "canon of the human figure." The charisma that led him to recognition within his own lifetime stemmed from his confidence in his own genius. Throughout his writing we hear the Renaissance insistence on the importance of reflection and of sharing one's thoughts with the world. He bitterly laments the absence of writing from the great artists of antiquity. In the following passage, Dürer presents his views of ideal beauty in a unique transformation of Platonic philosophy. Only God is privileged to see perfectly. Humanity, by *observing the opinions of the world regarding beauty, can and must strive for perfect vision. In his belief that great art comes only from the interaction between theory and practice he paved the way for today's academic artist.*

ITEM. The sight of a fine human figure is above all things pleasing to us, wherefore I will first construct the right proportions of a man. Thereafter, as God giveth me time, I will write of and put together other matters. I am well assured that the envious will not keep their venom to themselves; but nothing shall in any wise hinder me, for some of the greatest men have had to undergo the like. Though we see human figures of many kinds arising from the four temperaments, yet if we desire to make a figure, and if it lieth within our power, we ought to make it as beautiful as we can so far as the subject itself admits. No little art, however, is needed to make many various kinds of figures of men, for Deformity will continually of its own accord intwine itself into our work. No single man can be taken as a model of a perfect figure, for no man liveth on earth who uniteth in himself all manner of beauties; (how beautiful soever he be) he might still be much more beautiful. There liveth also no man upon earth who could give a final judgment upon what the perfect figure of a man is; God only knoweth that. How is beauty to be judged?—upon that we have to deliberate. A man by skill may bring it into every single thing, for in some things we recognise that as beautiful which elsewhere would lack beauty. 'Good' and 'better' in respect of beauty are not easy to discern, for it would be quite possible to make two different figures, one stout the other thin, which should differ one from the other in every proportion, and yet we scarce might be able to judge which of the two excelled in beauty. What Beauty is I know not, though it dependeth upon many things.

Hunt in honor of Charles V at the Chateau of Torgan (Lucas Cranach, the Elder), in the Prado, Madrid

When we wish to bring it into our work we find it very hard. We must gather it together from far and wide, and especially in the case of the human figure—we must study all its limbs seen from before and behind. One may often search through two or three hundred men without finding amongst them more than one or two points of beauty which can be made use of. Thou therefore, if thou desirest to compose a fine figure, art forced to choose the head from one man and the chest, arm, leg, hand, and foot from others. Seek diligently, therefore, through all members of every kind, for out of many beautiful things something good may be gathered, even as honey is gathered from many flowers. The true mean lieth between too much and too little. Strive to attain unto it in all thy works. I shall here apply to what is to be called beautiful the same touchstone as that by which we decide what is right. For as what all the world prizeth as right we hold to be right, so what all the world esteemeth beautiful that will we also hold for beautiful and ourselves strive to produce the like.

Item. I do not highly extol the proportions which I here set down, albeit I do not believe them to be the worst. Moreover I do not lay them down as beyond improvement, but that thou mayest search out and discover some better method by their help, for everyone should strive to better himself in his work. Howbeit let him accept this as good until he be sure of some better teaching; for one cometh nearer the truth than another according as his understanding is stronger, and the models from which he draweth excel in beauty.

Many fall into error because they follow their own taste alone; therefore let each look to it that his inclination blind not his judgment. For every mother is well pleased with her own child, and thus also it ariseth that many painters paint figures resembling themselves.

There are many causes and varieties of beauty; he that can prove them is so much the more to be trusted.

The more imperfection is excluded so much the more doth beauty abide in the work.

Let no man put too much confidence in himself, for many see more than one. Though it is possible for one man to comprehend more than a thousand, still that cometh but seldom to pass.

Use is a part of beauty; whatever therefore is useless unto men is without beauty.

Guard thyself from superfluity.

The accord of one thing with another is beautiful, therefore want of harmony is not beautiful. A real harmony linketh together things unlike.

Much will hereafter be written about subjects and refinements of painting. Sure am I that many notable men will arise, all of whom will write both well and better about this art and will teach it better than I. For I myself hold my art at a very mean value, for I know what my faults are. Let every man therefore strive to better these my errors according to his powers. Would to God it were possible for me to see the work and art of the mighty masters to come, who are yet unborn, for I know that I might be improved. Ah! how often in my sleep do I behold great works of art and beautiful things, the like whereof never appear to me awake, but so soon as I awake even the remembrance of them leaveth me. Let none be ashamed to learn, for a good work requireth good counsel. Nevertheless whosoever taketh counsel in the arts let him take it from one thoroughly versed in those matters, who can prove what he saith with his hand. Howbeit anyone *may* give thee counsel; and when thou hast done a work pleasing to thyself, it is good for thee to show it to dull men of little judgment that they may give their opinion of it. As a rule they pick out the most faulty points, whilst they entirely pass over the good. If thou findest something they say true, thou mayest thus better thy work.

Much remaineth that might be written on these matters, but for shortness sake I will make an end, and will enter upon the task of constructing the figures of man and woman. . . .

He that would be a painter must have a natural turn thereto.

Love and delight therein are better teachers of the Art of Painting than compulsion is.

If a man is to become a really great Painter he must be educated thereto from his very earliest years.

He must copy much of the work of good artists until he attain a free hand.

To paint is to be able to portray upon a flat surface any visible thing whatsoever that may be chosen.

It is well for anyone first to learn how to divide and reduce to measure the human figure, before learning anything else. . . .

In the night between Wednesday and Thursday after Whit-sunday (30, 31 May, 1525) I saw this appearance in my sleep—how many great waters fell from heaven. The first struck the earth about 4 miles away from me with terrific force and tremendous noise, and it broke up and drowned the whole land. I was so sore afraid that I awoke from it. Then the other waters fell and as they fell they were very powerful and there were many of them, some further away, some nearer. And they came down from so great a height that they all seemed to fall with an equal slowness. But when the first water that touched the earth had very nearly reached it, it fell with such swiftness, with wind and roaring, and I was so sore afraid that when I awoke my whole body trembled and for a long while I could not recover myself. So when I arose in the morning I painted it above here as I saw it. God turn all things to the best.

Albrecht Dürer. . .

Self-Portrait (Albrecht Dürer) in the Uffizi, Florence

NICCOLÒ MACHIAVELLI (1469–1527)

IL PRINCIPE

The Prince (1513; 1532)

The most famous document of Renaissance political science was written by an involuntarily "retired" Florentine republican to curry favor with the incoming Medici princes. Dedicated to Lorenzo, who promptly ignored it, *The Prince* went on to become an underground bestseller in its own time and, afterwards, the single most influential source of the *realpolitik* practiced by Napoleon, Richelieu, Bismarck, Mussolini, Lenin, and Stalin. Max Lerner called Machiavelli, "the first modern analyst of power," and *The Prince,* "a grammar of power." The word "machiavellian," broadcast by nearly all the playwrights of the British Renaissance, has become synonymous with justifying the means with the end. Machiavelli himself justified his wish to empower the Medici prince by reason of his lifelong vision of the unity of Italy. When the banking family not only took over Florence, but also raised one of their own to the papacy with the coronation of Giovanni de' Medici as Leo X, Machiavelli's vision suddenly

Big fish eat little fish (Pieter Brueghel, the Elder) in the Graphische Sammlung Albertina, Vienna

seemed possible. Machiavelli, from his exile, wrote *The Prince* to encourage Lorenzo to consolidate and expand his personal authority. What distinguishes this seminal treatise from its author's more ambitious and lengthier *Discourses, Art of War,* or *History of Italy* is the degree to which it abandons classical and idealistic sources and arguments, in favor of a practical, experiential, fully realistic vision of human nature. Machiavelli believed that humans will more quickly forgive the slaughter of a family member than the stealth of property, and that although the best would be for the prince to be simultaneously loved and feared, if only one could be chosen fear would be the safer choice. Unlike Renaissance essayists who seek to prescribe the ideal behavior of a courtier, a soldier, or a governor, Machiavelli's only intention is to make his princely reader more equipped for the jungle where effectiveness is determined by the brutal laws of necessity and not by an Aristotelian norm. Yet for all its cynicism, the earnest language of this remarkable document resounds with veracity. A prince who is too merciful will be ineffective. The commonwealth always requires some individuals to suffer pain. So decision-making always causes pain, and the prince must accustom himself to that harsh certainty or he will be judged to be ineffective by the very people he fears to harm. He must relish his power and find comfort in its natural repercussions. He must learn to dissemble, for the general good, and recognize that he is above the moral and social laws he must use to govern others. Shakespeare's Iago, in *Othello,* and Marlowe's Barabas, in *The Jew of Malta,* are two of the most powerful artistic embodiments of Machiavelli's political philosophy. At its most benign this philosophy feeds the fever of patriotism, becomes a handbook for nationalism and a guide to international strategy—used so effectively by Henry Kissinger. But, at the other end of the spectrum, when a sociopath, a man without conscience, steeped in *The Prince,* becomes himself a prince—we have the mesmerizing horrors of *Richard III,* or of Adolf Hitler, or of Richard Nixon.

Chapter XVII Of Cruelty and Clemency, and Whether it is Better to be Loved or Feared

Proceeding to the other qualities before named, I say that every prince must desire to be considered merciful and not cruel. He must, however, take care not to misuse this mercifulness. Cesare Borgia was considered cruel, but his cruelty had brought order to the Romagna, united it, and reduced it to peace and fealty. If this is considered well, it will be seen that he was really much more merciful than the Florentine people, who, to avoid the name of cruelty, allowed Pistoia to be destroyed. A prince, therefore, must not mind incurring the charge of cruelty for the purpose of keeping his subjects united and faithful; for, with a very few examples, he will be more merciful than those who, from excess of tenderness, allow disorders to arise, from whence spring bloodshed and rapine; for these as a rule injure the whole community, while the executions carried out by the prince injure only individuals. And of all princes, it is impossible for a new prince to escape the reputation of cruelty, new states being always full of dangers. Wherefore Virgil through the mouth of Dido says:

*Res dura, et regni novitas me talia cogunt
Moliri, et late fines custode tueri.*

Nevertheless, he must be cautious in believing and acting, and must not be afraid of his own shadow, and must proceed in a temperate manner with prudence and humanity, so that too much confidence does not render him incautious, and too much diffidence does not render him intolerant.

From this arises the question whether it is better to be loved more than feared, or feared more than loved. The reply is, that one ought to be both feared and loved, but as it is difficult for the two to go together, it is much safer to be feared than loved, if one of the two has to be wanting. For it may be said of men in general that they are ungrateful, voluble, dissemblers, anxious to avoid danger, and covetous of gain; as long as you benefit them, they are entirely yours; they offer you their blood, their goods, their life, and their children, as I have before said, when the necessity is remote; but when it approaches, they revolt. And the prince who has relied solely on their words, without making other preparations, is ruined; for the friendship which is gained by purchase and not through grandeur and nobility of spirit is bought but not secured, and at a pinch is not to be expended in your service. And men have less scruple in offending one who makes himself loved than one who makes himself feared; for love is held by a chain of obligation which, men being selfish, is broken whenever it serves their purpose; but fear is maintained by a dread of punishment which never fails.

Still, a prince should make himself feared in such a way that if he does not gain love, he at any rate avoids hatred; for fear and the absence of hatred may well go together, and will be always attained by one who abstains from interfering with the property of his citizens and subjects or with their women. And when he is obliged to take the life of any one, let him do so when there is a proper justification and manifest reason for it; but above all he must abstain from taking the property of others, for men forget more easily the death of their father than the loss of their patrimony. Then also pretexts for seizing property are never wanting, and one who begins to live by rapine will always find some reason for taking the goods of others, whereas causes for taking life are rarer and more fleeting.

But when the prince is with his army and has a large number of soldiers under his control, then it is extremely necessary that he should not mind being thought cruel; for without this reputation he could not keep an army united or disposed to any duty. Among the noteworthy actions of Hannibal is numbered this, that although he had an enormous army, composed of men of all nations and fighting in foreign countries, there never arose any dissension either among them or against the prince, either in good fortune or in bad. This could not be due to anything but his inhuman cruelty, which together with his infinite other virtues, made him always venerated and terrible in the sight of his soldiers, and without it his other virtues would not have sufficed to produce that effect. Thoughtless writers admire on the one hand his actions, and on the other blame the principal cause of them.

And that it is true that his other virtues would not have sufficed may be seen from the case of Scipio (famous not only in regard to his own times, but all times of which memory remains), whose armies rebelled against him in Spain, which arose from nothing but his excessive kindness, which allowed more license to the soldiers than was consonant with military discipline. He was reproached with this in the senate by Fabius Maximus, who called him a corrupter of the Roman militia. Locri having been destroyed by one of Scipio's officers was not revenged by him, nor was the insolence of that officer punished, simply by reason of his easy nature; so much so, that some one wishing to excuse him in the senate, said that there were many men who knew rather how not to err, than how to correct the errors of others. This disposition would in time have tarnished the fame and glory of Scipio had he persevered in it under the empire, but living under the rule of the senate this harmful quality was not only concealed but became a glory to him.

I conclude, therefore, with regard to being feared and loved, that men love at their own free will, but fear at the will of the prince, and that a wise prince must rely on what is in his power and not on what is in the power of others, and he must only contrive to avoid incurring hatred, as has been explained. . . .

Chapter XXI How a Prince Must Act in Order to Gain Reputation

Nothing causes a prince to be so much esteemed as great enterprises and giving proof of prowess. We have in our own day Ferdinand, King of Aragon, the present King of Spain. He may almost be termed a new prince, because from a weak king he has become for fame and glory the first king in Christendom, and if you regard his actions you will find them all very great and some of them extraordinary. At the beginning of his reign he assailed Granada, and that enterprise was the foundation of his state. At first he did it at his leisure and without fear of being interfered with; he kept the minds of the barons of Castile occupied in this enterprise, so that thinking only of that war they did not think of making innovations, and he thus acquired reputation and power over them without their being aware of it. He was able with the money of the Church and the people to maintain his armies, and by that long war to lay the foundations of his military power, which afterwards has made him famous. Besides this, to be able to undertake greater enterprises, and always under the pretext of religion, he had recourse to a pious cruelty, driving out the Moors from his kingdom and despoiling them. No more miserable or unusual example can be found. He also attacked Africa under the same pretext, undertook his Italian enterprise, and has lately attacked France; so that he has continually contrived great things, which have kept his subjects' minds uncertain and astonished, and occupied in watching their result. And these actions have arisen one out of the other, so that they have left no time for men to settle down and act against him.

It is also very profitable for a prince to give some outstanding example of his greatness in the internal administration, like those related of Messer Bernabò of Milan. When it happens that some one does something extraordinary, either good or evil, in civil life, he must find such means of rewarding or punishing him which will be much talked about. And above all a prince must endeavour in every action to obtain fame for being great and excellent.

A prince is further esteemed when he is a true friend or a true enemy, when, that is, he declares himself without reserve in favour of some one or against another. This policy is always more useful than remaining neutral. For if two neighbouring powers come to blows, they are either such that if one wins, you will have to fear the victor, or else not. In either of these two cases it will be better for you to declare yourself openly and make war, because in the first case if you do not declare yourself, you will fall a prey to the victor, to the pleasure and satisfaction of the one who has been defeated, and you will have no reason nor anything to defend you and nobody to receive you. For, whoever wins will not desire friends whom he suspects and who do not help him when in trouble, and whoever loses will not receive you as you did not take up arms to venture yourself in his cause.

Antiochus went to Greece, being sent by the Ætolians to expel the Romans. He sent orators to the Achaeians who were friends of the Romans to encourage them to remain neutral; on the other hand the Romans persuaded them to take up arms on their side. The matter was brought before the council of the Achaeians for deliberation, where the ambassador of Antiochus sought to persuade them to remain neutral, to which the Roman ambassador replied: 'As to what is said that it is best and most useful for your state not to meddle in our war, nothing is further from the truth: for if you do not meddle in it you will become, without any favour or any reputation, the prize of the victor.'

And it will always happen that the one who is not your friend will want you to remain neutral, and the one who is your friend will require you to declare yourself by taking arms. Irresolute princes, to avoid present dangers, usually follow the way of neutrality and are mostly ruined by it. But when the prince declares himself frankly in favour of one side, if the one to whom you adhere conquers, even if he is powerful and you remain at his discretion, he is under an obligation to you and friendship has been established and men are never so dishonest as to oppress you with such a patent ingratitude. Moreover, victories are never so prosperous that the victor does not need to have some scruples, especially as to justice. But if your ally loses, you are sheltered by him, and so long as he can, he will assist you; you become the companion of a fortune which may rise again. In the second case, when those who fight are such that you have nothing to fear from the victor, it is still more prudent on your part to adhere to one; for you go to the ruin of one with the help of him who ought to save him if he were wise, and if he conquers he rests at your discretion, and it is impossible that he should not conquer with your help.

And here it should be noted that a prince ought never to make common cause with one more powerful than himself to injure another, unless necessity forces him to it, as before said; for if he wins you rest in his power, and princes must avoid as much as possible being under the will and pleasure of others. The Venetians united with France against the Duke of Milan, although they could have avoided that alliance, and from it resulted their own ruin. But when one cannot avoid it, as happened in the case of the Florentines when the Pope and Spain went with their armies to attack Lombardy, then the prince ought to join for the above reasons. Let no state believe that it can always follow a safe policy, rather let it think that all are doubtful. This is found in the nature of things, that one never tries to avoid one difficulty without running into another, but prudence consists in being able to know the nature of the difficulties, and taking the least harmful as good.

A prince must also show himself a lover of merit, give preferment to the able, and honour those who excel in every art. Moreover he must encourage his citizens to follow their callings quietly, whether in commerce, or agriculture, or any other trade that men follow, so that this one shall not refrain from improving his possessions through fear that they may be taken from him, and that one from starting a trade for fear of taxes; but he should offer rewards to whoever does these things, and to whoever seeks in any way to improve his city or state. Besides this, he ought, at convenient seasons of the year, to keep the people occupied with festivals and shows; and as every city is divided either into guilds or into classes, he ought to pay attention to all these groups, mingle with them from time to time and give them an example of his humanity and munificence, always upholding, however, the majesty of his dignity, which must never be allowed to fail in anything whatever.

LUDOVICO ARIOSTO (1474–1533)

Orlando Furioso (1516)

Ludovico Ariosto retired from military and diplomatic service for Cardinal Ippolito d'Este and his brother the Duke Alfonso I to direct the Este theater in Ferrara. His masterpiece, the chivalric epic *Orlando Furioso* ("Mad Orlando"), reflects his dissatisfaction with the economically determined life of a court poet. But it also mirrors an ironic disillusionment that, from country to country

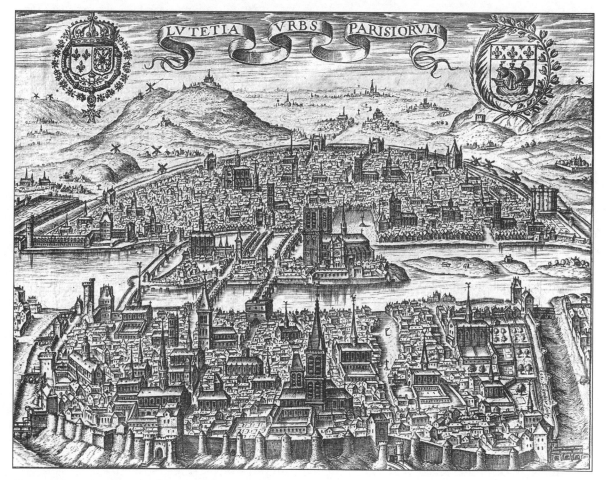

View of Paris (Leonard Gaultier)

across Europe, would become the telltale sign of fading Renaissance optimism—until its most magnificent embodiment in Cervantes' *Don Quixote*. Precisely because of the sadness that underlies the poem's emotional heroism and balanced comedy, *Orlando Furioso* is one of the greatest achievements of the period. Its mixture of fantasy and magic with history and realism makes it a predecessor of this century's Latin American magic realism. The epic's primary characters are derived from the French *Song of Roland*, its subject matter the eighth-century war between the Saracens and the Franks that moves from Spain to Africa to the gates of Paris. But Ariosto's Orlando, though he is Charlemagne's nephew, seems more like an Arthurian than a Carolingian hero, his romantic involvement with Angelica continuing the theme announced by Matteo Maria Boiardo's unfinished *Orlando Innamorato* ("Orlando in Love"). Ariosto glorifies his patron family by creating the story of the legendary ancestors of the Estes: Saracen Rogero's love for the strong-willed Christian warrior Bradamante is one of the high points of the epic.

THE FIRST BOOK

The Argument

Charles hath the foyle; Angelica flyes thence;
Renaldos horse holpe him his Love to finde;
Ferraw with him doth fight in her defence;
She flyes againe; they stay not long behind.
Argalias ghost reprooves Ferraws offence;
The Spaniard to new vow himselfe doth bind.
His mistres presence Sacrapant enjoyeth.
With Bradamant Renaldo him annoyeth.

1

Of Dames, of Knights, of armes, of loves delight,
Of curtesies, of high attempts I speake,
Then when the Moores transported all their
    might
On Affrick seas the force of France to breake,
Incited by the youthfull heate and spite
Of *Agramant* their king that vowd to wreake
The death of king *Trayano* (lately slayne)
Upon the Romane Emperour *Charlemaine.*

2

I will no lesse *Orlandos* acts declare
(A tale in prose ne verse yet song or sayd)
Who fell bestraught with love, a hap most rare
To one that erst was counted wise and stayd.
If my sweet Saint that causeth my like care
My slender muse afford some gracious ayd,
I make no doubt but I shall have the skill
As much as I have promist to fulfill.

3

Vouchsafe (O Prince of most renowmed race,
The ornament and hope of this our time)
T'accept this gift presented to your grace
By me your servant, rudely here in rime,
And though I paper pay and inke in place
Of deeper debt, yet take it for no cryme:
It may suffise a poore and humble debter
To say and if he could it should be better.

4

Here shall you finde among the worthie peers
Whose prayses I prepare to tell in verse
Rogero, him from whom of auncient yeers
Your Princely stemmes derived I reherse,
Whose noble minde by princely acts appeares,
Whose worthie fame even to the skye doth
    perse,
So you vouchsafe my lowlie stile and base
Among your high conceits a litle plase.

5

Orlando who long time had loved deare
Angelica the faire and for her sake
About the world in nations far and neare
Did high attempts performe and undertake
Returnd with her into the West that yeare
That *Charls* his power against the Turks did
    make
And with the force of Germanie and France
Neare Pyren Alpes his standard did advance

6

To make the Kings of Affrike and of Spayne
Repent their rash attempts and foolish vaunts,
One having brought from Affrike in his trayne
All able men to carry sword or launce;
The other mov'd the Spanyards now agayne
To overthrow the goodly Realme of Fraunce;
And hither (as I said) *Orlando* went,
But of his comming straight he did repent,

7

For here (behold how humane judgements arr
And how the wiser sort are oft mistaken)
His Ladie, whom he garded had so farr
Nor had in fights nor daungers great forsaken,
Without the dint of sword or open warr
Amid his friends away from him was taken,
For *Charls* the great, a valiant Prince and wise,
Did this to quench a broyle that did arise:

8

Betweene *Orlando* and *Renaldo* late
There fell about *Angelica* some brall,
And each of them began the tother hate,
This Ladies love had made them both so thrall,
But *Charls,* who much mislikes that such
    debate
Betweene such frends should rise on cause so
    small,

To *Namus* of Bavier in keeping gave her
And suffred neither of them both to have her

9

But promist he would presently bestow
The damsell faire on him that in that fight
The plainest proofe should of his prowesse
    show
And danger most the Pagans with his might,
But (ay the while) the Christens take the blow:
Their souldiers slaine, their Captains put to
    flight,
The Duke him selfe a prisner there was taken;
His tent was quite abandond and forsaken,

10

Where when the damsell faire a while had stayd
That for the victor pointed was a pray
She tooke her horse ne farther time delayd
But secretly convayd her selfe away,
For she foresaw and was full sore afrayd
That this to *Charls* would prove a dismall day,
And riding through a wood she hapt to meete
A knight that came against her on his feete,

11

His curats on, his helmet not undone,
His sword and target readie to the same,
And through the wood so swiftly he did runne
As they that go halfe naked for a game,
But never did a shepherds daughter shunne
More speedily a snake that on her came
Then faire *Angelica* did take her flight
When as she once had knowledge of the
    knight.

12

This valiant knight was Lord of Clarimount,
Duke *Ammons* sonne, as you shall understand,

Who having lost his horse of good account
That by mishap was slipt out of his hand,
He followd him in hope againe to mount,
Untill this Ladies sight did make him stand,
Whose face and shape proportiond were so
    well
They seeme the house where love it self did
    dwell,

13

But she that shuns *Renaldo* all she may
Upon her horses necke doth lay the raine;
Through thicke and thinne she gallopeth away,
Ne makes she choise of beaten way or plaine
But gives her palfrey leave to chuse the way,
And being mov'd with feare and with disdaine
Now up, now downe, she never leaves to ride
Till she arrived by a river side.

14

Fast by the streame *Ferraw* she sees anone
(Who noyd in part with dust and part with
    sweat)
Out of the battell hither came alone,
With drinke his thirst, with aire to swage his
    heat,
And minding backe againe to have bene gone
He was detained with an unlookt for let:
Into the streame by hap his helmet fell,
And how to get it out he cannot tell

15

And hearing now the noise and mournfull crie
Of one with piteous voice demaunding ayd,
Seeing the damsell eke approching nye
That nought but helpe against *Renaldo* prayd,
What wight it was he guessed by and by,
Though looking pale like one that had bene
    frayd,
And though she had not late bene in his sight,
He thought it was *Angelica* the bright,

16

And being both a stout and curteous knight
And love a little kindling in his breast,
He promist straight to ayd her all he might
And to performe what ever she request,
And though he want a helmet, yet to fight
With bold *Renaldo* he will do his best,
And both the one the other straight defied,
Oft having either others value tried.

17

Betweene them two a combat fierce began
With strokes that might have pierst the hardest
    rocks.
While they thus fight on foote and man to man
And give and take so hard and heavie knocks,
Away the damsell posteth all she can;
Their paine and travell she requites with
    mocks.
So hard she rode while they were at their fight
That she was cleane escaped out of sight.

18

When they long time contended had in vaine
Who should remaine the maister in the field
And that with force, with cunning, nor with
    paine
The tone of them could make the other yeeld,
Renaldo first did move the Knight of Spaine
(Although he usd such curtesie but seeld)
To make a truce, ne was he to be blamed,
For love his heart to other fight enflamed.

19

You thought (sayd he) to hinder me alone,
But you have hurt your selfe as much or more.
You se the faire *Angelica* is gone,
So soone we leese that earst we sought so sore.
Had you me tane or slaine your gaine were

Sith you were ner the neare your love therefore,
For while we two have made this little stay
She lets us both alone and go'th her way,

20

But if you love the Ladie as you say,
Then let us both agree to finde her out.
To have her first will be our wisest way,
And when of holding her there is no doubt,
Then by consent let her remaine his pray
That with his sword can prove himself most
    stout.
I see not else after our long debate
How either of us can amend his state

21

Ferraw (that felt small pleasure in the fight)
Agreed a sound and frendly league to make.
They lay aside all wrath and malice quight,
And at the parting from the running lake
The Pagan would not let the Christen knight
To follow him on foote for manners sake
But prays him mount behind his horses backe,
And so they seeke the damsell by the tracke.

22

O auncient knights of true and noble hart:
They rivals were, one faith they liv'd not under;
Beside they felt their bodies shrewdly smart
Of blowes late given, and yet (behold a won-
    der)
Through thicke and thin, suspition set apart,
Like frends they ride and parted not a sunder
Untill the horse with double spurring drived
Unto a way parted in two arrived,

23

And being neither able to descrie
Which way was gone *Angelica* the bright

Because the tracke of horses feete wherby
They seeke her out appeare alike in sight,
They part, and either will his fortune try;
The left hand one, the other takes the right.
The Spaniard when he wandred had a while
Came whence he went, the way did him
    beguile.

24

He was arriv'd but there with all his paine
Where in the foord he let his helmet fall,
And of his Ladie (whom he lov'd in vaine)
He now had litle hope or none at all.
His helmet now he thinks to get againe
And seeks it out, but seeke it while he shall,
It was so deeply sunken in the sand
He can not get it out at any hand.

25

Hard by the banke a tall young Pepler grew
Which he cut downe thereof a pole to make
With which each place in feeling and in vew
To find his scull he up and downe doth rake,
But lo, a hap unlookt for doth ensew:
While he such needlesse frutelesse paine doth
    take.
He saw a knight arise out of the brooke
Breast hye, with visage grim and angrie looke.

26

The knight was armd at all points save the
    hed,
And in his hand he held the helmet plaine,
That very helmet that such care had bred
In him that late had sought it with such
    paine,
And looking grimly on *Ferraw* he sed:
Ah faithlesse wretch, in promise false and
    vaine,
It greevs thee now this helmet so to misse
That should of right be rendered long er this.

27

Remember (cruell Pagan) when you killed
Me, brother to *Angelica* the bright,
You said you would (as I then dying willed)
Mine armour drowne when finisht were the
    fight.
Now if that fortune have the thing fulfilled
Which thou thy self sholdst have performd in
    right,
Greeve not thy selfe, or, if thou wilt be greeved,
Greeve that thy promise can not be beleeved;

28

But if to want an helmet thou repine,
Get one wherwith thine honor thou mayst
    save.
Such hath *Orlando,* Countie Paladine,
Renaldo such, or one perchance more brave;
That was from *Almont* tane, this from
    Mambrine.
Win one of these that thou with praise maist
    have,
And as for this, surcease to seeke it more,
But leave it as thou promisd me before.

29

Ferraw was much amazd to see the sprite
That made this straunge appearance unex-
pected.
His voice was gone, his haire did stand upright,
His sences all were so to feare subjected.
His hart did swell with anger and despite
To heare his breach of promise thus objected
And that *Argalia* (so the knight was named)
With just reproof could make him thus
    ashamed,

30

And wanting time the matter to excuse
And being guiltie of no litle blame
He rested mute and in a sencelesse muse,
So sore his hart was tainted with the shame,
And by *Lanfusas* life he vowd to use
No helmet till such time he gat the same
Which from the stout *Almont Orlando* wan
When as they two encountred man to man,

31

But he this vow to keepe more firmely ment
And kept it better then the first he had.
Away he parted hence a malcontent
And many dayes ensuing rested sad.
To seeke *Orlando* out is his intent
With whom to fight he would be very glad,
But now what haps unto *Renaldo* fell
That tooke the other way, tis time to tell.

SIR THOMAS MORE (1478–1535)
Utopia (1516)

The year 1516, which saw the publication of Desiderius Erasmus' translation of the New Testament as well as Thomas More's *Utopia,* may be looked upon as the high point of Christian humanism. With this modestly playful book from the pen of the lord chancellor of England, the words "utopia" and "utopian" entered the English language as badges of extreme idealism. Like his contemporary fellow countrymen John Colet, John Lyly, and Sir Thomas Elyot, and his close friend Erasmus (whom he encouraged to study Greek), More, who in 1529 succeeded Cardinal Wolsey as lord chancellor, was a humanist passionately committed to the revival of classical literature. He wrote *Utopia* in Latin. Yet his faith came before his humanism; More, like Erasmus, was a loyal Catholic, though favoring the reform of the Church. His Chelsea manor became a clearinghouse of wit and ideas. To dine at his family table was to take up company with the intellectual and political luminaries of his day. More's political loyalties and service to Henry VIII (who had married the sister of Charles V, Catherine of Aragon) ended in his execution at the Tower of London on July 6, 1535, and subsequent canonization as a saint of the Catholic Church. More seemed to have foreseen his death, as he told his son-in-law, William Roper: "I find his grace my very good lord indeed, and I believe he doth as singularly favor me as any subject within his realm. Howbeit, son Roper, I may tell thee I have no cause to be proud thereof, for if my head could win him a castle in France. . . it should not fail to go." He had resigned the Lord Chancellorship still in his friend Henry's good graces, but his refusal to attend Queen Anne's coronation led her to insist that he sign the Oath of Allegiance acknowledging the king's right to declare himself head of his own church. Even in the tower More hung on to his good humor, gentleness, and devotion to religion, there composing his *Dialogue of Comfort,* in the tradition of the philosopher Boethius' *The Consolation of Philosophy.* He asked his executioner if he could move his beard from the path of the ax since it was he, not his beard, that had committed "treason." Although his *Life of Richard III* was perhaps his most serious work, More remains most famous for *Utopia*—a dryly satirical account of a fictional journey to an island where the human race has perfected itself by institutionalizing its best instincts and common sense. Like many of his contemporaries More was fascinated by the explorations of the new world and may have been inspired to write his vision of an ideal commonwealth by his reading of Amerigo Vespucci's account of his four voyages (first published in Italy in 1507). He may also be writing to protest the progressive, relativistic morality of Machiavelli's *The Prince.* No portrait of More equals his friend Erasmus' description, in a letter to Ulrich Hutten, Antwerp, July 23, 1519:

> In human relations he looks for pleasure in everything he comes across, even in the gravest matters. If he has to do with intelligent and educated men, he takes pleasure in their brilliance; if with the ignorant and foolish, he enjoys their folly. He is not put out by perfect fools, and suits himself with marvelous dexterity to all men's feelings. For women generally, even for his wife, he has nothing but jests and merriment. You could say he was a second Democritus, or better, that Pythagorean philosopher who saunters through the marketplace with a tranquil mind gazing on the uproar of the buyers and sellers. None is less guided by the opinion of the herd, but again none is less remote from the common feelings of humanity.

Behind the satirical mask of his narrator "Raphael Hythloday," the voyager returned from Utopia, More found an indirectly forceful way of speaking out on contemporary paradoxes and abuses, including the high rent of land, the decay of husbandry, the cost of living, the greed of the rich, the number of vagrant retainers. Many of his complaints hauntingly echo our modern tribulations: "For if you suffer your people to be ill-educated, and their manners to be corrupted from their infancy, and then punish them for those crimes to which their first education disposed them, what else is to be concluded from this, but that you first make thieves and then punish them?" The utopians' conclusion that "property is the downfall of happiness" will find its echo in Ralph Waldo Emerson's observation, "Things are in the saddle and ride mankind." More's ideal society is primarily agricultural, holds property in common, insists on work for everyone on a foreshortened work week, has no currency and minimum laws, practices euthanasia, uses enslavement as punishment, has no lawyers, does not believe in alliances, offers universal public health, honors the aged, and is centered on improving the mind and spirit. It's not surprising that earlier in our century *Utopia* became a textbook of socialist propaganda. Translations into French, Italian, and Dutch were in circulation before the first English one, by Ralph Robinson, reached the public in 1551. The book's whimsical idealism can't disguise the primary flaw of Utopia, a flaw it shares equally with Rabelais' *Abbey of Thélème* and B. F. Skinner's *Walden Two:* Utopia is essentially an intellectual construct, an unrealizable, pure idea. Lacking in the frivolity caused by the caprices of free will, Utopia is a sterile and inhuman country in which More himself would not have found comfort. The very playfulness that characterizes the book's narration, and that makes its author a true hero of the Renaissance, finds no role in More's ideal society. *Utopia,* like Plato's *Republic,* may serve philosophers and social scientists as a point of reference, but cannot be accepted as the endpoint of human social evolution. George Orwell's *1984* and Aldous Huxley's *Brave New World* show us what might happen if utopians ruled the world. Unlike the England of More's lifetime, the Utopia he imagined practiced freedom of religion, as described in this excerpt from Book II. The Utopians' attitude toward investi-

gating nature, and toward finding an inherent divine principle, is too modern for More to have proclaimed openly. His description of Utopian priests is a casual indictment of contemporary clergy, switching ecclesiastic robes from those of one church to those of another as they jockeyed for position with the capricious monarch. The attitude of the Utopians toward death must have been More's premonition, as well as a standard he lived up to when he faced the ax.

. . . Actually, they count this principle among their most ancient institutions, that no one should suffer for his religion.

Utopus had heard that before his arrival the inhabitants had been continually quarreling among themselves. He had made the observation that the universal dissensions between the individual sects who were fighting for their country had given him the opportunity of overcoming them all. From the very beginning, therefore, after he had gained the victory, he especially ordained that it should be lawful for every man to follow the religion of his choice, that each might strive to bring others over to his own, provided that he quietly and modestly supported his own by reasons nor bitterly demolished all others if his persuasions were not successful nor used any violence and refrained from abuse. If a person contends too vehemently in expressing his views, he is punished with exile or enslavement.

Utopus laid down these regulations not merely from regard for peace, which he saw to be utterly destroyed by constant wrangling and implacable hatred, but because he thought that this method of settlement was in the interest of religion itself. On religion he did not venture rashly to dogmatize. He was uncertain whether God did not desire a varied and manifold worship and therefore did not inspire different people with different views. But he was certain in thinking it both insolence and folly to demand by violence and threats that all should think to be true what you believe to be true. Moreover, even if it should be the case that one single religion is true and all the rest are false, he foresaw that, provided the matter was handled reasonably and moderately, truth by its own natural

force would finally emerge sooner or later and stand forth conspicuously. But if the struggle were decided by arms and riots, since the worst men are always the most unyielding, the best and holiest religion would be overwhelmed because of the conflicting false religions, like grain choked by thorns and underbrush.

So he made the whole matter of religion an open question and left each one free to choose what he should believe. By way of exception, he conscientiously and strictly gave injunction that no one should fall so far below the dignity of human nature as to believe that souls likewise perish with the body or that the world is the mere sport of chance and not governed by any divine providence. After this life, accordingly, vices are ordained to be punished and virtue rewarded. Such is their belief, and if anyone thinks otherwise, they do not regard him even as a member of mankind, seeing that he has lowered the lofty nature of his soul to the level of a beast's miserable body—so far are they from classing him among their citizens whose laws and customs he would treat as worthless if it were not for fear. Who can doubt that he will strive either to evade by craft the public laws of his country or to break them by violence in order to serve his own private desires when he has nothing to fear but laws and no hope beyond the body?

Therefore an individual of this mind is tendered no honor, is entrusted with no office, and is put in charge of no function. He is universally regarded as of a sluggish and low disposition. But they do not punish him in any way, being convinced that it is in no man's power to believe what he chooses, nor do they compel him by threats to disguise his views, nor do they allow in the matter any deceptions or lies which they hate exceedingly as being next door to actual wrongdoing. They forbid him to argue in support of his opinion in the presence of the common people, but before the priests and important personages they not only permit but also encourage it, being sure that such madness will in the end give way to reason.

There are others, too, and these not a few, who are not interfered with because they do not altogether lack reason for their view and because they are not evil men. By a much different error, these believe that brute animals also have immortal souls, but not comparable to ours in dignity or destined to equal felicity. Almost all Utopians are absolutely certain and convinced that human bliss will be so immense that, while they lament every man's illness, they regret the death of no one but him whom they see torn from life anxiously and unwillingly. This behavior they take to be a very bad omen as though the soul, being without hope and having a guilty conscience, dreaded its departure through a secret premonition of impending punishment. Besides, they suppose that God will not be pleased with the coming of one who, when summoned, does not gladly hasten to obey but is reluctantly drawn against his will. Persons who behold this kind of death are filled with horror and therefore carry the dead out to burial in melancholy silence. Then, after praying God to be merciful to their shades and graciously to pardon their infirmities, they cover the corpse with earth.

On the other hand, when men have died cheerfully and full of good hope, no one mourns for them, but they accompany their funerals with song, with great affection commending their souls to God. Then, with reverence rather than with sorrow, they cremate the bodies. On the spot they erect a pillar on which are inscribed the good points of the deceased. On returning home they recount his character and his deeds. No part of his life is more frequently or more gladly spoken of than his cheerful death.

They judge that this remembrance of uprightness is not only a most efficacious means of stimulating the living to good deeds but also a most acceptable form of attention to the dead. The latter they think are present when they are talked about, though invisible to the dull sight of mortals. It would be inconsistent with the lot of the blessed not to be able to travel freely where they please, and it would be ungrateful of them to reject absolutely all desire of revisiting their friends to whom they were bound during their lives by mutual love and charity. Freedom, like all other good things, they conjecture to be increased after death rather than diminished in all good men. Consequently they believe that the dead move about among the living and are witnesses of their words and actions. Hence they go about their business with more confidence because of reliance on such protection. The belief, moreover, in the personal presence of their forefathers keeps men from any secret dishonorable deed.

They utterly despise and deride auguries and all other divinations of vain superstition, to which great attention is paid in other countries. But miracles, which occur without the assistance of nature, they venerate as operations and witnesses of the divine power at work. In their country, too, they say, miracles often occur. Sometimes in great and critical affairs they pray publicly for a miracle, which they very confidently look for and obtain.

They think that the investigation of nature, with the praise arising from it, is an act of worship acceptable to God. There are persons, however, and these not so very few, who for religious motives eschew learning and scientific pursuit and yet allow themselves no leisure. It is only by keeping busy and by all good offices that they are determined to merit the happiness coming after death. Some tend the sick. Others repair roads, clean out ditches, rebuild bridges, dig turf and sand and stone, fell and cut up trees, and transport wood, grain, and other things into the cities in carts. Not only for the public but also for private persons they behave as servants and as more than slaves.

If anywhere there is a task so rough, hard,

and filthy that most are deterred from it by the toil, disgust, and despair involved, they gladly and cheerfully claim it all for themselves. While perpetually engaged in hard work themselves, they secure leisure for the others and yet claim no credit for it. They neither belittle insultingly the life of others nor extol their own. The more that these men put themselves in the position of slaves the more are they honored by all.

Of these persons there are two schools. The one is composed of celibates who not only eschew all sexual activity but also abstain from eating flesh meat and in some cases from eating all animal food. They entirely reject the pleasures of this life as harmful. They long only for the future life by means of their watching and sweat. Hoping to obtain it very soon, they are cheerful and active in the meantime.

The other school is just as fond of hard labor, but regards matrimony as preferable, not despising the comfort which it brings and thinking that their duty to nature requires them to perform the marital act and their duty to the country to beget children. They avoid no pleasure unless it interferes with their labor. They like flesh meat just because they think that this fare makes them stronger for any work whatsoever. The Utopians regard these men as the sancr but the first named as the holier. If the latter based upon arguments from reason their preference of celibacy to matrimony and of a hard life to a comfortable one, they would laugh them to scorn. Now, however, since they say they are prompted by religion, they look up to and reverence them. For there is nothing about which they are more careful than not lightly to dogmatize on any point of religion. Such, then, are the men whom in their language they call by a special name of their own, Buthrescae, a word which may be translated as "religious par excellence."

They have priests of extraordinary holiness, and therefore very few. They have no more than thirteen in each city—with a like number of churches—except when they go to war. In that case, seven go forth with the army, and the same number of substitutes is appointed for the interval. When the regular priests come back, everyone returns to his former duties. Then those who are above the number of thirteen, until they succeed to the places of those who die, attend upon the high priest in the meantime. One, you see, is appointed to preside over the rest. They are elected by the people, just as all the other officials are, by secret ballot to avoid party spirit. When elected, they are ordained by their own group.

They preside over divine worship, order religious rites, and are censors of morals. It is counted a great disgrace for a man to be summoned or rebuked by them as not being of upright life. It is their function to give advice and admonition, but to check and punish offenders belongs to the governors and the other civil officials. The priests, however, do exclude from divine services persons whom they find to be unusually bad. There is almost no punishment which is more dreaded: they incur very great disgrace and are tortured by a secret fear of religion. Even their bodies will not long go scot-free. If they do not demonstrate to the priests their speedy repentance, they are seized and punished by the senate for their impiety.

To the priests is entrusted the education of children and youths. They regard concern for their morals and virtue as no less important than for their advancement in learning. They take the greatest pains from the very first to instill into children's minds, while still tender and pliable, good opinions, which are also useful for the preservation of their commonwealth. When once they are firmly implanted in children, they accompany them all through their adult lives and are of great help in watching over the condition of the commonwealth. The latter never decays except through vices which arise from wrong attitudes.

The feminine sex is not debarred from the priesthood, but only a widow advanced in years is ever chosen, and that rather rarely. Unless they are women, the priests have for their wives the very finest women of the country.

To no other office in Utopia is more honor

given, so much so that, even if they have committed any crime, they are subjected to no tribunal, but left only to God and to themselves. They judge it wrong to lay human hands upon one, however guilty, who has been consecrated to God in a singular manner as a holy offering. It is easier for them to observe this custom because their priests are very few and very carefully chosen.

Besides, it does not easily happen that one who is elevated to such dignity for being the very best among the good, nothing but virtue being taken into account, should fall into corruption and wickedness. Even if it does happen, human nature being ever prone to change, yet since they are but few and are invested with no power except the influence of honor, it need not be feared that they will cause any great harm to the state. In fact, the reason for having but few and exceptional priests is to prevent the dignity of the order, which they now reverence very highly, from being cheapened by communicating the honor to many. This is especially true since they think it hard to find many men so good as to be fit for so honorable a position for the filling of which it is not enough to be endowed with ordinary virtues.

They are not more esteemed among their own people than among foreign nations. This can easily be seen from a fact which, I think, is its cause. When the armies are fighting in battle, the priests are to be found separate but not very far off, settled on their knees, dressed in their sacred vestments. With hands outstretched to heaven, they pray first of all for peace, next for a victory to their own side—but without much bloodshed on either side. When their side is winning, they run among the combatants and restrain the fury of their own men against the routed enemy. Merely to see and to appeal to them suffices to save one's life; to touch their flowing garments protects one's remaining goods from every harm arising from war.

This conduct has brought them such veneration among all nations everywhere and has given them so real a majesty that they have saved their own citizens from the enemy as often as they have protected the enemy from their own men. The following is well known. Sometimes their own side had given way, their case had been desperate, they were taking to flight, and the enemy was rushing on to kill and to plunder. Then the carnage had been averted by the intervention of the priests. After the armies had been parted from each other, peace had been concluded and settled on just terms. Never had there been any nation so savage, cruel, and barbarous that it had not regarded their persons as sacred and inviolable.

They celebrate as holydays the first and the last day of each month and likewise of each year. The latter they divide into months, measured by the orbit of the moon just as the course of the sun rounds out the year. In their language they call the first days Cynemerni and

Map of Utopia (woodcut from the March, 1518, edition)

the last days Trapemerni. These names have the same meaning as if they were rendered "First-Feasts" and "Final-Feasts." Their temples are fine sights, not only elaborate in workmanship but also capable of holding a vast throng, and necessarily so, since only a very small number of the populace are priests. The temples are all rather dark. This feature is due not to an ignorance of architecture but to the deliberate intention of the priests. They think that excessive light makes the thoughts wander, whereas scantier and uncertain light concentrates the mind and conduces to devotion.

In Utopia, as has been seen, the religion of all is not the same, and yet all its manifestations, though varied and manifold, by different roads as it were, tend to the same end, the worship of the divine nature. Therefore nothing is seen or heard in the temples which does not seem to agree with all in common. If any sect has a rite of its own, it is performed within the walls of each man's home. Therefore no image of the gods is seen in the temple so that the individual may be free to conceive of God with the most ardent devotion in any form he pleases. They invoke God by no special name except that of Mithras. By this word they agree to represent the one nature of the divine majesty whatever it be. The prayers formulated are such as every man may utter without offense to his own belief.

On the evening of the Final-Feasts, they gather in the temple, still fasting. They thank God for the prosperity they have enjoyed in the month or year of which that holyday is the last day. Next day, which is the First-Feast, they flock to the temples in the morning. They pray for good luck and prosperity in the ensuing year or month, of which this holyday is the auspicious beginning.

On the Final-Feasts, before they go to the temple, wives fall down at the feet of their husbands, children at the feet of their parents. They confess that they have erred, either by committing some fault or by performing some duty carelessly, and beg pardon for their offense. Hence, if any cloud of quarrel in the family has arisen, it is dispelled by this satisfaction so that with pure and clear minds they may be present at the sacrifices, for it is sacrilegious to attend with a troubled conscience. If they are aware of hatred or anger against anyone they do not assist at the sacrifices until they have been reconciled and have cleansed their hearts, for fear of swift and great punishment. . . .

PIETRO ARETINO (1492–1556)

I RAGIONAMENTI

The Art of the Courtesan (1534–36)

Depending on which legend you take seriously, Pietro Aretino was the bastard son of a prostitute or the legitimate son of a village shoemaker. Taking the mild-mannered Petrarch's active self-definition to the extreme, Aretino grew up to be the first "bohemian," artistically versatile, prolifically self-promoting, and scandalously incorrigible. He was also the first modern critic of the arts, as well as the first modern "yellow" journalist, delighting in telling inside details of court and courtyard. He was a considerable dramatist and sonneteer. The caustic wit with which he pilloried those who annoyed him earned him the title "scourge of princes." His letters were libelous, his verses obscene, his lampoons the talk of the town as though David Letterman, Norman Mailer, and George Carlin had been rolled into one. His dialogues portray life in the papal courts of the Medici Leo X and Clement VII in Rome— a social milieu that included the Emperor Charles V, Henry VIII, Francis I, and Martin Luther—as well as Michelangelo Buonarotti, Titian, Raphael, but also Niccolò Machiavelli, the Borgias, Benvenuto Cellini, Torquato Tasso, and Ludovico Ariosto. The statue of Pasquino, to which Aretino affixed his lampoons (called "pasquinades"), still stands honored by passersby in Rome today. The *Ragionamenti*, focusing particularly on the lives of married women, of nuns, and of courtesans, provide a volatile perspective on these scandalously lusty times. Aretino concludes that courtesans, because of their freedom and the clearinghouse nature of their profession, have the best life of all. While fellow artists and writers might pretend to themselves that their patronage had lofty social status, Aretino freely admitted that he is a prostitute selling his wares. Though he was maligned for nearly everything imaginable, especially for compiling the lives of the saints, Aretino's letters and dialogues were never accused of being dull. His work brings us to the point in the Italian Renaissance where idealism begins to give way to the onrushing decadence. From the exhilaration of testing the boundaries of human potential comes the insanity and psychological amorphousness that occurs at and beyond these boundaries. In Aretino you will find no underlying moral, and no moral overlay; only the sensual, only the aesthetically pleasing or outrageous. His life was a monument to hedonism, seizing the day instant by intense instant. While his contemporaries continued to invoke the past, Aretino delighted in insulting it. His cynicism may be the most appropriate reaction to a time when, as Aristide Raimondi writes, "All is obscene and libidinous, everything is for sale, everything is false, nothing is sacred." Like François Villon's or Lenny Bruce's, Aretino's language reflects that of the street, marketplace, and brothel. Like Villon, too, he flirted with the gallows more than once, yet nearly became a Cardinal of the Roman Church! Profane and blasphemous to the last, he is supposed to have said on his deathbed, after receiving the holy oils of extreme unction, "Now that I'm all greased up, don't let the rats get me." Other accounts have it that he died of apoplexy from laughing too uproariously at a naughty joke. He died in Venice, the city archetypally associated with decadence. Legend also has it that he wrote his own epitaph:

> Here lies the Tuscan poet Aretino,
> Who spoke badly of everyone except God,
> For which he apologized by saying, "I don't know him."

Aretino has been called the Rabelais of the *cinquecento*, though his private life, complete with harems and stolen wealth, exemplifies the extreme of what can happen when Rabelais' "Do what you will" becomes an individual's *modus operandi*. His influence extended to Molière, Shakespeare, and Balzac. H. L. Mencken and Henry Miller pale by comparison. Howard Stern is his avatar. His writing is a precursor of literary realism; the powerful impact of his opinions looks forward to that of the all-dominating media of our times.

The Dialogues of Nanna and Antonia, held in Rome under a fig tree, composed by the divine Aretino for his pet monkey, Capricio, and for the correction of the three states of women. It has been given to the printer in this month of April, MDXXXIIII, in the illustrious city of Venice.

THE ART OF THE COURTESAN

NANNA: I can see a Florentine coming to your room with his chitter-chatter. Make love to him, for the Florentines outside of Florence are like those persons who, with a full bladder, are unwilling to go urinate out of respect for the place in which they find themselves, but when they get outside, they deluge a wide, wide space. I will tell you

Moor ringing the bell in the Clock Tower, Venice

that they are more generous abroad than they are at home; beyond this, they are virtuous, gentle, polished, sharp and pungent; and if they give you nothing else than their gallant words, do you not think you could be content with those?

PIPPA: Not I.

NANNA: That was merely a method of speaking on my part; they must spend as much as possible, give papal dinners and *feste* in quite a different manner from what the others do; and then, their tongue is pleasing to all.

PIPPA: And now let's speak a little of the Venetians.

NANNA: I do not want to tell you about them, for if my words are not equal to their merits, I shall be told that I am deceived in the love I have for them and certainly I am not deceived at all, for they are gods, and the patrons of everything, and the finest youths, the finest men and the finest old men that there are in the world; all the rest of the world will appear to you like wax-work soldiers by comparison, and although they are proud, having a right to be, they are the very image of kindness itself. And while they live the life of merchants, in accordance with our custom, they do it on a royal scale, and he who is on the right side of them is fortunate. Everything else is a joke, saving the grace of those old money bags who have piles and piles of ducats and who, no matter how much it thunders or rains, would not give you so much as a *bagattino*.

PIPPA: God keep them.

NANNA: He does it well enough. . . .And now to jump from Florence to Sienna. I will tell you that the Sienese madmen are gentle fools, although for a number of years they have been turned wicked, according to the chatter of some; and according to the experience I have had of men, the odds appear to me to be that they hold, in the matter of gentleness and virtue, to the Florentine, but they are not so crafty nor so dog-like, and he who knows how to deceive can flay and shear them alive. Moreover, they are big fellows down below, and their practices are pleasing and honorable.

PIPPA: They will do for me.

NANNA: Yes, certainly. And now let's on to Naples.

PIPPA: Don't talk to me of that town; it gives me the asthma to think of it.

NANNA: Listen, Signora, even though it be a death in life. The Neapolitans are made to drive away sleep and to provide you with a fine bellyful some day of the month when you have the whim in your head, alone or in the company of someone else, it does not matter whom. I can tell you that their fripperies rise to heaven: talk of horses—they have the first that came from Spain—of clothing—two or three wardrobes full—money in piles, and all the belles of the kingdom are dying for them directly; and if you drop your handkerchief or your glove, they will recover it for you with the most gallant parables that were ever heard in a Capuan chair, *si, Signora*.

PIPPA: What sport.

NANNA: I once wanted to get rid of a certain traitor by the name of Giovanni Agnesi, the very scum of all filth, if I am to force myself to counterfeit him in words, although the hangman could not counterfeit him in deeds; and at the sight of this, a certain Genoese burst into laughter, whereupon I turned on him and said: "My proud Genoa, proud because you know how to buy beef without bones, we others can teach you a thing or two." And it was true, because they are the subtlest of the subtle and the sharpest of the sharp, and they are altogether too good managers and cut the thing just as it should be cut and they will give you not the least bit too much. For the rest, I cannot tell you what glorious lovers they make, what gentle Neapolitan and unSpanish breeding they show, reverent, making what little they give you appear as sweet as sugar, and never failing to give you that little. You must always know how to get the better of them and measure your gifts as they measure theirs; and, without turning your stomach, with a pleasant speech in your throat, with your nose and with a sigh, take things as they come.

PIPPA: The Bergamasks have more grace than their speech.

NANNA: They also are gentle and dear, that is certain. But now, let us come to the Romanians. Daughter, if you delight in eating bread and buffalo cheese with sword points

Pietro Aretino (Titian)

and spear heads for a salad, pickled in the fine bravados which their great-grandfathers used to hurl at the town sheriffs, associate with them. The short of it is, on the day of the Sack, they defecated upon us (speaking with all reverence), and Pope Clement has no regard for them any more.

PIPPA: Don't forget Bologna, if for no other reason than for love of the count and of the *cavalier* who is of our house.

NANNA: Forget them, ah? What would the rooms of whores be without the shadow of those long-winded stocks? Born here solely for the purpose of making numbers and shade, says the *canzona;* I am speaking of love and not of arms, said Friar Mariano. A fine young chicken of twenty years told me that she had never seen madmen who were plumper or better clad. And so, do you, Pippa, make a feast for them as you would for courtiers, and take your pleasure in their thoughtless and foolish conversation; and such a practice as this is by no means without its use, and it will be more useful than any other, if they delight as much in she-goats as they do in kids. As for the rest of the Lombardians, who are snails and great dandies, treat them in the whorish manner, taking from them what you can get, giving to each of them a "*cavalier*," throwing in a "*Count*" for a moustache, with a "*Signor, sí*" and a "*Signor, no*"; for such deceits as these do not spoil the soup, and it is honest to indulge in them and even to boast of them; for they deceive the poor courtezans, and moreover, those houses in which such customs are to be found are praised above all others. . . .

ISABELLA D'ESTE (1474–1539)

Letters (1504–20)

Isabella was born in Ferrara, of Ercole and Leonora of Aragon, a year before her blonde younger sister Beatrice. The two sisters were famous rivals until Beatrice's dramatic death at the age of twenty-two. Isabella was named after the Queen of Naples, her grandmother Isabella of Aragon. At the age of six she was contracted to marry the Mantuan marquis Gianfrancesco Gonzaga. After studying music, dance, Greek, and Latin and becoming adept in translating both languages, Isabella was taken to her nuptials in Mantua in 1490, followed by thirteen chests carrying her trousseau. By Gonzaga she bore four daughters, Eleonora, Margherita, Ippolita, and Paola; and three sons, Federico, Ercole, and Ferrante. Her husband doted on her vivacity and graciousness, as well as on her considerable skills and sensitivity in diplomacy, statecraft, patronage, penchant for inventing her own perfumes, and sensitivity to the arts. One of the great beauties of the Renaissance, her portrait was painted by many, including Leonardo and Titian. Francesco went on to become a hero by vanquishing the forces of Charles VIII at Fornovo, but when Francesco's fortunes threw him into the hands of the Venetians Isabella protected Mantua with an iron will even at the risk of her husband's affections. When he spurned her, she took herself to the papal court in Rome, where the Medici Leo X received her with royal honors. Her stay in Rome turned her into a professional tourist, her avidity for antiquities reminiscent of Petrarch. When Gianfrancesco died, in 1519, she resumed her authority in Mantua during the regency of her adoring son Federico. When Federico acceded to power, she made her way to the Rome of the Medici Clement VII and maneuvered a cardinal's hat for her son Ercole. There she witnessed the "sack of Rome," May 6, 1527. More than anything else, says Maria Bellonci, Isabella was distinguished for her "individuality. . . the awareness of self that she sustained with all the force and conviction of a style. . . a style fashioned by the mind; it was the effective alliance of idea and action." Her letters reveal that she was indeed one of the great embodiments of the Renaissance spirit. They include:

- her directions to Leonardo da Vinci, as he was painting the "Battle of Anghiari."
- instructions to her French agent, refusing the promise of Louis XII to protect her son Federico from the Venetians, and insisting that he not be kept there as hostage for the freedom of his father.
- a letter to her friend the scholar and gambler Bernardo Bibbiena, expressing her ecstasy at the election of fellow epicure Giovanni Romolo Pomaso, Lorenzo the Magnificent's son, as Leo X.
- advice to Francesco della Rovere, not to make war on the Pope.
- to her husband, Gianfrancesco, apologizing for a misunderstanding concerning the naming of their son Ercole.
- to Cesare Borgia, in her campaign to have him spare Mantua in his sweep through northern Italy (her suit prevailed).

To Master Leonardo Vinci, the painter.

Hearing that you are settled at Florence, we have begun to hope that our cherished desire to obtain a work by your hand may be at length realized. When you were in this city, and drew our portrait in carbon, you promised us that you would some day paint it in colors. But because this would be almost impossible, since you are unable to come here, we beg you to keep your promise by converting our portrait into another figure, which would be still more acceptable to us; that is to say, a youthful Christ of about twelve years, which would be the age He had attained when He disputed with the doctors in the temple, executed with all that sweetness and charm of atmosphere which is the peculiar excellence of your art. If you will consent to gratify this our great desire, remember that apart from the payment, which you shall fix yourself, we shall remain so deeply obliged to you that our sole desire will be to do what you wish, and from this time forth we are ready to do your service and pleasure, hoping to receive an answer in the affirmative.

Mantua, May 14, 1504

To her French agent:

Tell His Christian Majesty that we do not deny that he [Federico] might be better off near his Majesty than in our care, insofar as the example of virtue and the acquisition of practical knowledge useful to men are concerned. Nor am I unmindful of the honor and benefits he would derive. Yet we feared—and now we are certain—that he might die, considering his tender age and his delicate constitution. He could not stand the voyage on horseback, nor the change of air, nor the different customs, being yet in the care and under the supervision of women. . . .

The father is not as linked to his children as the mother is. And Federico now is husband and son to me.

To Gianfrancesco:

My illustrious Lord: I am pained, though not surprised, that Your Excellency was dissatisfied with my explanation. I would feel even keener pain were I to think that your anger resulted from real guilt on my part. Considering, however, that I have not given in to Your Highness's wish solely because I acted in the interests of one of my brothers and to please my nephew, the Duke of Milan—and this with your knowledge and consent—it seems to me that you have no cause to feel aggrieved with me. I lament my unlucky fate, which always renders my deeds, however good they may be, repellent to you. I do not believe that either my behavior or any of my doings during this voyage to Milan are such as to "make people talk." I know that I have made a thousand new friends for you, as well as for myself. I know I have done my duty as always. God knows I have never needed an instructor to set down rules to teach me behavior or attitudes. Whatever my shortcomings may be, God has at least granted me this grace. Your Excellency owes me as much gratitude as any husband owes a wife. Even if you honored and loved me with a greater love than ever a human being loved another, you could never repay my fidelity. This, my loyalty, may be the reason why you sometimes claim that I am haughty, but it is only because I am cognizant of how much I deserve from you—and how little I receive. Yes, sometimes I fall into a dark humor and I appear other than what I really am.

Yet even if I were sure that I could expect from you nothing but bad treatment, I would not cease to try to do good. The more you show me that you love me with but a scant love, the more will I prove my love through deeds. In truth, I was born for this love. I was given to you at so early an age that I can no longer remember having lived without your love. It seems to me that through my love I ought to have earned the freedom to decide to postpone my return two or three weeks for reasons cited above—without incurring your ill will and your anger and without your jumping to the conclusion that I do not want to see you again. Read the signature of this letter! If you truly still longed for me, you would make it possible for me to see you in Mantua more often than I actually do. I commend myself to Your Excellency and hope you will read this overlong letter with forbearance.

She who loves you as well as herself
Isabella, Marchesa of Mantua

To Bernardo Bibbiena:

You will have already heard from Mario Equicola of the joy and delight with which this happy event has filled us, and really, since the day of our birth, we have never had any greater pleasure than this good news, which reached us immediately after we heard of the death of Pope Julius. For all of which we praise and thank our Lord God, hoping that, by the great goodness and wisdom of His Holiness, we may see the safety of the Duke our brother's state secured, that of our nephew the Duke of Milan established, as well as the honor and exaltation of our husband the Marchese and the peace of all Italy confirmed. On our own account we are satisfied that we shall enjoy the protection and perpetual favor of His Holiness, both because of the bond of our common sponsorship and of the love and regard we bore him as Cardinal dei Medici, not to speak of our intimate friendship with his brother, the Magnifico Giuliano. No less do we reckon on the favor and influence which you will retain with His Holiness, feeling no doubt that neither rank nor honors will change your nature, but that you will be as kind and affectionate to us as ever, even though we have made you lose 500 ducats!. . .

To Francesco della Rovere:

We are inclined to counsel you to try everything possible to avoid open warfare. All terms to avert conflict should be weighed by you, and such caution must be more praised than censured. To conserve the state is to conserve honor. Discuss the matter with the Marchese, with others of your relatives, with your friends. We could not help expressing our opinion, for the love we bear you and our daughter, though we know that you yourself are prudent. But in such a dilemma a man must turn to the advice of others. . . .

To Gianfrancesco:

Your letter apologizing for not having written before has filled me with confusion, for it is I who ought rather to have begged your pardon for my delay, not you, when I know you have hardly time to eat! But, since you are so kind as to make excuses to me, you will also be so good as to forgive my delays, which were caused by Federico's illness and my reluctance to give you any news which would make you anxious. Now, thank God, he is perfectly well, and I can the more gladly discharge my duty. The hat for which you ask shall be made as soon as the hat-maker arrives, and shall be as fine and gallant as possible. If you will say how soon you require it, I will try and have a coat made to match, if there is time; but please tell me this at once. Thank you for wishing me to see your entry into Bologna. It will no doubt be a magnificent sight. I am very well, and, if you desire it, will come gladly. I think even a bomb would have some trouble to make me miscarry. Your Highness must not say that it is my fault if I quarrel with you, because, as long as you show any love for me, no one else can make me believe the contrary. But no interpreter is needed to make me aware that Your Excellency has loved me little for some time past. Since this, however, is a disagreeable subject, I will cut it short, and say no more. . . .

I am sorry Your Highness objects to my calling our boy Ercole. I would not have done this if I had thought you would dislike it. But Your Highness knows that when you were at Sacchetta you said he was very like my father, of blessed memory; and I said that, this being the case, you were wrong not to call him Ercole. You laughed, and said no more; but if you had told me your opinion, I should not have made this mistake. Only let me have another boy, and you may call him Alvise, or whatever you like, and leave the other to be Ercole.

To Cesare:

Most illustrious Lord,—Your kind letter informing us of Your Excellency's fortunate progress has filled us with that joy and delight which is the natural result of that friendship and affection which exists between you and ourselves, and in our illustrious lord's name and our own we congratulate you on your safety and prosperity, and thank you for informing us of this, and also for your offer to keep us informed of your future successes. This we beg you of your courtesy to continue, since, loving you as we do, we are anxious to hear often of your movements, in order that we may rejoice in your welfare and share your triumphs. And because we think that you should take some rest and recreation after the fatigues and exertions of these glorious undertakings, we send you a hundred masks by our servant Giovanni, being well aware that so poor a gift is unworthy of your acceptance, but as a token that if in our land we could find an offering more worthy of your greatness, we would gladly send it to you. If these masks are not as fine as they should be, Your Excellency must blame the masters of Ferrara, since owing to the law against wearing masks in public, which has only lately been revoked, the art of making them has been in a great measure lost. We beg you to accept them as a token of our sincere good will and affection for Your Excellency. . . .

MICHELANGELO BUONARROTI (1475–1564)

On His Art

For most people the name Michelangelo Buonarroti is synonymous with the Renaissance. Michelangelo's sculptures, architecture, drawings, and paintings are the epitome of Renaissance art, earning him patronage from Lorenzo de' Medici, cardinals, kings, and popes. By his own definition he was first and foremost a painter and designer, whose lifelong mission was to express, in his representations of the transitory and always changing human body, the immortal and infinite human spirit. His sure mastery of classical composition, matched with the humanistic precision of his anatomical and geometrical compositions, is unique among his contemporaries and predecessors and, whether in the staircase of the Laurentian library, the chapel of the Medici, the dome of St. Peter's in Rome and the *Pietà* within it, the frescoes of the Vatican's Sistine Chapel, or the statue of the David, characteristic of his masterful vision and magnificent seriousness. The heroic seriousness was inspired by the reformer Girolamo Savonarola, whose voice, he said, he could "still hear ringing in his ears." According to legend, Michelangelo once was asked, "if it was difficult to carve the David," and is said to have replied: "Carving the David was not the difficult thing. The difficult thing was finding the block of marble in which David was. After that it was merely a matter of removing everything that was not David." This view of the artistic process as a "dreamwork" forming a continuum with the materials and vision from which it is drawn is suggested in the second poem that follows, "Not Has the Finest Artist." Ironically, Michelangelo carved the statue of David from a block of marble discarded by a previous sculptor. These first two translations of Michelangelo's poems are by Henry Wadsworth Longfellow, the third by Fanny Bunnett, the fourth (addressed to Vittoria Colonna) by John Addington Symonds.

Sun Purified with Passion (1532)

Not without fire can any workman mold
The iron to his preconceived design,
Nor can the artist without fire refine
And purify from all its dross the gold:
Nor can revive the phoenix, we are told,
Except by fire. Hence if such details be mine
I hope to rise again with the divine,
Whom death augments, and time cannot make
   old.
O sweet, sweet death! O fortunate fire that
   burns
Within me still to renovate my days,
Though I am almost numbered with the dead!

David (Michelangelo Buonarroti), in the Accademia, Florence

If by its nature unto heaven returns
This element, me, kindled by its blaze,
Will it bear upward when my life is dead.

Not Has the Finest Artist (1538–44)

Nothing the greatest artist can conceive
That every marble block doth not confine
Within itself; and only its design
The hand that follows intellect can achieve.

If Well Conceived (1545)

When godlike art has, with superior thought,
The limbs and motions in idea conceived,
A simple form, in humble clay achieved,
Is the first offering into being brought:
Then stroke on stroke from out the living rock
Its promised work the practised chisel brings,

And into life a form so graceful springs,
That none can fear for it time's rudest shock.

The Artist and His Work

How can that be, lady, which all men learn
By long experience? Shapes that seem alive,
Wrought in hard mountain marble, will survive
Their maker, whom the years to dust return!
Thus to effect cause yields. Art hath her turn,
And triumphs over Nature. I, who strive
With Sculpture, know this well; her wonders
    live
In spite of time and death, those tyrants stern.
So I can give long life to both of us
In either way, by color or by stone,
Making the semblance of thy face and mine.
Centuries hence when both are buried, thus
Thy beauty and my sadness shall be shown,
And men shall say, "For her 'twas wise to pine."

VITTORIA COLONNA (1492–1547)

Poems (1512-40)

The object of Michelangelo's platonic love sonnets, Vittoria Colonna was a distinguished Latin poet, of a famous Roman family. She was among the most influential political and intellectual leaders of the Renaissance, called by Joseph Gibaldi its "literary queen." The sonnet exchange between her and Michelangelo began when she met him in Rome in 1538, where she'd retired from Ferrara. Her father was Fabrizio Colonna, distinguished general and grand constable of Naples; and her maternal grandparents, Frederico duke of Urbino and Battista Sforza. In 1509, she married Ferdinando Francesco d'Avalos, marquis of Pescara, a knight in the army of Charles V. When he died in the battle of Pavia, in 1525, Vittoria's lonely life was turned upside down. Her crisis took the form of a religious experience, and she became involved with proponents of reform who, along with Ludovico Ariosto, Jacopo Sannazaro, and Pietro Bembo admired her intelligence, learning, ardor, and vivacity. She risked lifelong trouble with the Inquisition for being a staunch defender of the Capuchin order, lobbying with Paul III to stand behind these reformed Franciscans. Castiglione would not finalize *The Courtier* without getting her opinion, and she promoted the book's publication. Colonna's sonnets, in the mode of Petrarch but with a much more personal approach, express her piety and devotion and celebrate married love, against the backdrop of her own experience—from her longing for her soldier husband, celebration of his deeds, grief at his death, fidelity to his memory, and hope to rejoin him. Her correspondence was prolific, addressed to the great ones of her age including Marguerite of Navarre, Piero Aretino, Bernardo Tasso, and Matteo Ghiberti. A shining star in her century, Colonna expresses her sensitivity and eloquence in the sonnets which, along with her beauty and charisma, made her the universal object of adoration. Burckhardt called her "the most famous woman of Italy" during the Renaissance. Ariosto celebrated her genius in *Orlando Furioso,* calling her "embellished with trophies and with triumphs." Michelangelo said of her, "Nature, that never made so fair a face,/ Remained ashamed, and tears were in all eyes." The 1512 epistle to her husband, written after the battle of Ravenna, is a unique distillation of her personal emotion within the framework of classical form and the graceful and demanding *terza rima* used by Dante in the *Divine Comedy.*

Epistle to Ferrante Francesco d'Avalos, Her Husband, After the Battle of Ravenna (1512)

My most noble lord, I write you this
to recount to you how sadly—and amid so
    many
uncertain desires and harsh torments—I live.
I did not expect pain and sorrow from you.

I did not believe a marquis and a Fabrizio,
one a husband, the other a father, would be
the cruel, pitiless beginning of my suffering.
Love of my father and love of you,
like two famished and furious snakes,
have always lived, gnawing, in my heart.
I believed the fates had more kindness.

But now in this perilous assault,
in this horrible, pitiless battle
that has so hardened my mind and heart,
your great valor has shown you an equal
to Hector and Achilles. But what good is
this to me, sorrowful, abandoned?
My mind has always been uncertain:
those seeing me sad have thought
me hurt by absence and jealousy.
But I, alas, have always had in mind
your daring courage, your audacious soul,
with which wicked fortune ill accords.
Others called for war, I always for peace,
saying it is enough for me if my marquis
remains quietly at home with me.
Your uncertain enterprises do not hurt you;
but we who wait, mournfully grieving,
are wounded by doubt and by fear.
You men, driven by rage, considering nothing
but your honor, commonly go off, shouting,
with great fury, to confront danger.
We remain, with fear in our heart and
grief on our brow for you; sister longs for
brother, wife for husband, mother for son.

You live happily and know no sorrow;
thinking only of your newly acquired fame,
you carelessly keep me hungry for your love.
But I, with anger and sadness in my face,

lie in your bed, abandoned and alone,
feeling hope intermingled with pain,
and with your rejoicing I temper my grief.

LOVE POEMS

[1520s-early 1530s]

I

I write only to unbosom my inner sorrow,
on which my heart feeds, wishing nothing
    else,
and not to add light to my beautiful sun,
who left on earth a most glorious mark.

And I lament for good reason: just thinking
I might diminish his glory makes me grieve;
another pen and someone with far wiser words
must come to save his great name from dying.

Purest faith, fervor, and intense pain are
my excuse, for my sadness is so profound
that time and reason can never hope to curb it.

A bitter weeping, not a sweet song,
and melancholy sighs, not a clear voice,
make me vaunt not my style but my grief.

IV

You know, Love, that I never turned my foot
from your gentle prison, or freed my neck
from your sweet yoke, or tried to take back
all that my soul gave you from the first day.

Time has not changed my ancient faith;
the bond is still as tight as I tied it then;
nor has the bitter fruit that I ever gather
made the high cause less precious to my heart.

You have seen, in a burning, faithful heart,
how much your dear, sharp arrow can do—
against its strength even Death is powerless.

Make loose, at last, the bond yourself;
for liberty never really mattered to me,
and now, indeed, it seems late to regain it.

SACRED POEMS

I

Although my chaste love for a long time held
my soul desirous of fame, living like a serpent
in my breast, now, weeping, my soul languishes,
turned toward the Lord from whom comes its
    cure.

May those holy nails henceforth be my quills,
may the precious blood be my undiluted ink,
the sacred, bloodless body be my writing paper,
so that I may inscribe, within, what He suffered.

It is useless to invoke Parnassus or Delos here,
for I aspire to other water, to other mountains
tend, where human foot does not climb by
    itself.

That Sun Who illuminates the elements and sky,
I pray that, when He reveals His clear fountain,
He offers me drink equal to my great thirst.

VIII On Mary Magdalene

Seized in her sadness by that great desire
which banishes all fear, this beautiful woman,
all alone, by night, helpless, humble, pure,
and armed only with a living, burning hope.

Entered the sepulcher and wept and lamented;
ignoring the angels, caring nothing for herself,
she fell at the feet of the Lord, secure,
for her heart, aflame with love, feared nothing.

And the men, chosen to share so many graces,
though strong, were shut up together in fear;
the true Light seemed to them only a shadow.

If, then, the true is not a friend to the false,
we must give to women all due recognition
for having a more loving and more constant
    heart.

PHILIPP MELANCHTHON (1497–1560)

LOCI COMMUNES RERUM THEOLOGICARUM

Of Human Strength and Free Will (1521)

Although Philipp Melanchthon (born Schwartzwerd) was equally famous during his lifetime for his authorship of the *Confession of Augsburg of the Lutheran Church* (1530), his *Loci Communes* is now considered the first important and systematic Protestant treatise on evangelical dogmatic theology, giving its author status, with his colleague Martin Luther, as cofounder of *the Protestant Reformation. Queen Elizabeth is said to have memorized the book. Admired disciple of Erasmus, scholar, Biblical exegete, Greek grammarian, educator, reformer, and theologian, whose humanism balanced Luther's rigidity, Melanchthon spanned the spectrum from the exalted halls of academe to the public forums. Founding the German public school system on the twin bases of classical learning and Protestant theology, he earned the title Praeceptor Germaniae. Born in Bretten, Baden, he died as Professor of Greek in Wittenberg. In the face of Roman Catholic decadence, while troubled contemporaries remained ambivalently perched on a razor's edge, Melanchthon courageously brought to the moment of crisis an energetic breeze as refreshingly sweet and innocent as that expressed in Thomas à Kempis' Imitation of Christ.*

OF HUMAN STRENGTH AND FREE WILL

To speak about *free will* is simply to speak about man's strength or weakness, which everyone, as much as possible, should contemplate in his own nature. However, some people introduce extraneous questions: Do all the natural effects in the air, in the water, and on the earth, all the good deeds and all the evil, happen of necessity? Does God's knowing in advance force the human will to act in a certain way? As was said previously, we should not be sidetracked by these questions. The Stoics should not be judges and masters in the Christian Church. When we speak of free will, we are simply talking about the deterioration of human strength through sin, man's inability to free himself from sin and death, and about the works that man is able to do in such a state of weakness.

And first to be considered is how man was created and what his greatest strengths are. Of the latter there are five: First, he is able to digest food and drink and thus sustain his physical life. About this we need say nothing more.

Second, he has five external senses: sight, hearing, taste, smell, and touch, and three inner senses in his brain so that he can draw distinctions, find similarities, and remember.

Third, in his soul he has understanding and knowledge and can command some of his external members.

Fourth, he can have true desires in his heart and will without hypocrisy.

Fifth, he can stir and move his external members from one place to another; he can keep his hands, feet, tongue, and eyes still or move them here and there.

Originally man was thus created, to be God's image; that is, his understanding was endowed with a great light. He knew about number, he had knowledge of God and the divine laws, and he could distinguish virtue and vice. With this light his heart, his heart's desire, and his will were without hypocrisy. His heart was created full of the love of God, free of all evil desires. His will was free, so that he could choose to keep God's law, and his heart and external members could be fully obedient without any hindrance. It was also possible for his understanding and will to choose something else, as happened later.

Accordingly, when free will is mentioned, we mean understanding and will, heart and will; and they belong together, without hypocrisy.

Man was created wise and upright, and before the Fall he had a free, unimpeded will.

However, as Adam and Eve fell into sin and incurred God's wrath, God withdrew from them and man's natural powers became very weak. The light in his understanding became very dim, although some remained, for man can still use numbers and make distinctions between good and evil works and the teachings of the law. God wants all men to recognize sin; he wants to punish us by means of our own conscience; and he wants all men to maintain external discipline. For that reason knowledge remains in this corrupted nature, although it is dim and full of doubt and uncertainty about God, not knowing whether God wants to be man's judge or helper, or whether God wants to receive and listen to men—of which more will be said under law and gospel.

Further, all good virtues toward God in the heart and will were also lost—love of God, trust in God, and true fear of God. God is not received where the Holy Spirit has not first enlightened and kindled the understanding, will, and heart. Without the Holy Spirit man cannot of his own powers perform virtuous works, such as true faith, love of God, and true fear of God. And therefore the miserable human heart stands like a desolate, deserted, old and decaying house, God no longer dwelling within and winds blowing through. That is, all sorts of conflicting tendencies and lusts drive the heart to the manifold sins of uncontrolled love, hate, envy, and pride. The devils also spread their poisons.

When we speak about this great ruin of human powers, we are talking about free will, for man's will and heart are wretchedly imprisoned, impaired, and ruined, so that inwardly man's heart and will are unlike the divine law, offensive and hostile to it, and man cannot by his own inward natural powers be obedient. This is said about true inner obedience, without hypocrisy.

Now to speak of the movement and motion of external members of the body. Although the heart and the inner will, as we ourselves are aware, neither hear nor inwardly obey the law without hypocrisy, nevertheless God has left the understanding free to govern in that it can move and control the external members of the body. The understanding may say to one who is sick with a fever and very thirsty that he should hold his hand and not drink, and he restrains his hand from seizing the mug. Even in this cor-rupted nature God has allowed such freedom with regard to external motions of the body. He wants all men to have external morality, and thereby learn the distinction between powers that are free and powers that are bound; thus we can think in some degree that God acts freely and is not a prisoner or a bound Lord, as the Stoics have pictured him with regard to his created nature.

Whoever looks at himself and systematically considers the nature of the soul, the understanding, will, and heart, and the motion of external members of the body, can in large measure inform himself and others about free will; and it is very useful for virtue to learn as much as possible about how all the parts of the body operate and what such words as the following mean: *understanding,* the true will which is like the heart, and the *rationalizing* will which is not like the heart, but concerns itself with thinking and commanding the external members of the body to follow understanding, as in the case of the thirsty man with a fever whose hand is restrained from seizing a mug. The hypocrite has such a rationalizing will. Esau considered himself to be his brother's good friend.

In divine Scripture, the heart is often mentioned as the highest power in the soul. For this reason, if the heart is not in agreement with the will, then there is no true will, just thoughts and a rationalizing will which controls only the external forms.

Although with this much as a basis it is not difficult to answer questions about free will, I want nevertheless to mention a few additional items.

The First Answer

Let this be the first answer to the question about free will in this corrupted nature. Even though they are still not reborn and are not sanctified through the Holy Spirit, men have the power to move or to restrain external members of the body through thought and will. As far as external works are concerned, there remains in man a free will, as previously said about the thirsty man who restrains his hand. So also with Achilles; although his heart burned with rage so that he drew his sword, he checked himself, sheathed the sword, and departed from Agamemnon.

Honorable morality is to move or restrain the external members of the body in accordance with right reason and God's law.

Passages in St. Paul show that this freedom remains in man, for St. Paul often speaks of external righteousness, and calls it *justitiam carnis,* a righteousness of the physical nature which has not yet been reborn. To have such righteousness, man must also have the possibility of moving and using his external members—such as the tongue, hands, and feet—in the performance of commanded works and duties. Otherwise, no one could have such external righteousness. And if this freedom were not in men, then all worldly law and all education of children would be in vain. However, it is certainly true that through worldly law and the education of children God wants to force men into honorable customs, and such pain and work are not totally in vain.

For this reason St. Paul says to Timothy "that the law was given to the unrighteous that they might have curbs and prisons to keep them from becoming worse and doing other shameful deeds" [*cf.* 1 Tim. 1:8–11].

When young people hear that works do not merit remission of sins, they often become even wilder in their daily intemperance and immorality, and do even less praying, reading, and contemplating of Christian matters. In this way they open the door still wider for the devil. Contrary to such shameful indulgence, we should know that God earnestly desires all men to curb themselves with true morality, and the reasons for this are four in number.

The first is, on account of the divine commandments, for all angels and men are obliged to obey God.

The second is, to escape punishment in this and in the next life, for God truly punishes obvious external sins, like manslaughter, adultery, incest, robbery, fraud, perjury, Epicurean blasphemy, idolatry, and magic. He punishes these sins not only in the next life but in this present one, just as the text about manslaughter says, "Who takes the sword will by the sword perish." This clearly refers to physical punishment; and the same is said about stealing and fraud. "Woe to the robber, for he will be robbed"; and of immorality, Hebrews 13:4, "God will punish whores and adulterers"; and of contempt for parents, Deuteronomy 27:16, "Cursed be he who does not honor his father and mother." The Scriptures are full of such testimonies, and in our daily experience we can see the same right before our eyes, for manslaughter is not concealed and it does not go unpunished. . . .

The third reason is that God requires moral living so that other people may have peace. We were not created to use the world wantonly; our living should honor God and serve other men, for this is why we were created and redeemed. As God says, "You shall love God with your whole heart, and your neighbor as yourself" [Luke 10:27].

The fourth reason is, as St. Paul says, "The law is a schoolmaster to lead us to Christ" [Gal. 3:24]. That is, external morality is necessary, for in a life filled with dissolute, immoral, persistent adultery, gluttony, robbery, and murder there can be neither instruction in the gospel nor acquaintance with it. And in such foolish, mad people who continually and wantonly persist in sin against their own conscience there can be no effective work of the Holy Spirit. For this reason we are to preach about God's wrath and the punishment that he inflicts, as seen in the earth's great misery and wretchedness, war, evil government, tyranny, sickness, poverty, discord, shame, and all kinds of plagues. He wants worldly authorities to serve with genuine sincerity to further the maintenance of honorable morality.

All punishment through the authorities and others should remind us of God's wrath against our sin, and should warn us to amend our lives. We should carefully think about all this, so that those who are not yet reborn may learn that they are required to obey God and live in honorable morality. Those who have been reborn also need to know about this, for St. Paul warns, "Change with great care, not as fools do. . . " [*cf.* Eph. 5:3–20; Gal. 3:3].

In addition this should be noted. Although this capacity, or freedom, remains in man's corrupted nature, so that we can move or restrain our external members, the expression of this freedom has two obstacles—our own weakness and the devil's activity. Few people can resist evil tendencies. When we burn with love or anger, we often do a thing that we know is injurious to ourselves. We say, therefore, that one's own weakness conquers his freedom. But men, incited by the devil, fall even more dreadfully, for the devil drives men to murder, insurrection, adultery, and blasphemy, and in doing so the devil becomes ever more influential, so that he is like an invited guest, for men develop a lust and love of evil things and do not want to turn away from the source. Concerning this, the ancients say that if one does not want to fall into sin, he must turn away from the source. (*Vitare peccata est vitare occasiones peccatorum.*)

All this is related to assist us in contemplating our great weakness and miseries, for we are deeply mired in sin and death, and in our external works are easily overcome by our own weakness and by the devil's inflaming activity. And we should lament that we are so hardened and intractable that our wretchedness and danger do not touch our hearts. Not for a single moment of our lives are we without doubt; we err and often fall; we merit punishment and

God's wrath; the devil hunts us unceasingly; and there is no man on earth who associates with people who does not encounter all kinds of persecution and incitement. What great punishment many people behold in their own children! All fortune is unstable. How many great kings and princes are dislodged, exiled, confined, and imprisoned to die! This proverb is still true. "In an instant the mighty fall and are no more."

We should contemplate all this as a reminder to fear punishment and to live morally. On the other hand, we should also know how God, because of his great mercy and for the sake of his Son and through his Son, wants graciously to hear and assist his Church, those who rightly call upon him; and we should know what are the graces and gifts which the Son of God has obtained for us. About this we will speak later.

This also should be noted. Although it is certainly true that all men are obliged to live in external morality and that God earnestly punishes external depravity in this life, and in the next life will punish all those who do not become converted, we must also know that external morality *cannot merit* forgiveness of sins and eternal life. *It is not* a fulfillment of the law, and *neither is it the righteousness by which a man is justified and received before God.* Only the Son of God has merited forgiveness of sins for us, and for his sake we are received, *out of grace* and *mercy, by faith, without our deserving it.* Of this more will be said later.

LEONARDO DA VINCI (1452–1519)

Flying Machine (1519)

His multifaceted, wide-ranging mind, coupled with brilliant genius and ready wit, gave Leonardo da Vinci the title Renaissance man as soon as the word Renaissance came into use. He was an engineer who planned military machines for the Borgias, a sculptor for the Sforzas, a painter for Lorenzo de' Medici and Louis XII and Francis I of France, a musician for his own edification, an anatomist to satisfy his curiosity and demand for representational precision, an ornithologist, meteorologist, draftsman, mathematician, and hydraulic engineer. He was banished from Rome by the pope for his refusal to stop dissecting cadavers, and preferred to leave than to curtail his anatomical explorations. His best-known paintings include the *Mona Lisa, St. Jerome,* and *The Last Supper.* Born illegitimate, the young Leonardo studied painting under Andrea del Verrocchio in Florence; when he painted an angel, his master abandoned his brush never to paint again, horrified that he had been eclipsed by this child. Although he referred to himself as illiterate, Leonardo, in his *Notebooks,* recorded thousands of pages of luminously articulate observations on philosophy, anatomy, physiology, optics, acoustics, astronomy, botany, geography, topography, atmosphere, flight, movement and weight, mathematics, the nature of water, canalization, experiments, inventions, warfare, painting and the arts, landscape, light and shade, perspective, sculpture, casting, architecture, music, navigation, jests, fables, bestiaries, allegory, prophecy, letters, and books. The notebooks are a map of the human mind, and a tribute to the prodigious effort behind his seemingly effortless accomplishments. He knew that visualization was the first step in turning dreams to realities. His mere doodles read like a catalog of the future. His inventions recorded in them and in his scribble include the bicycle, the pedometer, the magnifying glass, the military tank (to take the place of elephants!), the gas mask, the alarm clock, the drilling machine, the life jacket, the harbor dredge, and the submarine—and how to turn white wine red by adding water. His observations on time make him a forerunner of Albert Einstein; on weight, of Sir Isaac Newton; on blood, of William Harvey; and on the sun's place in the universe, of Galileo Galilei. The calm self-confidence of his observational powers is unequaled. He insisted on the primacy of solitude as the source of all self-knowledge and creativity: "When you are alone, you are your own." If you must choose companionship, choose that of coworkers. He wrote backwards, fluently, so that his thoughts could be read only in a mirror. In the midst of it all, he records an astonishing sentiment: "I have wasted my hours." He felt that time expanded infinitely for those whose intensity shows them how to use it, and was a living embodiment of the classical Greek observation: "I am a man. I think nothing human is alien to me." It has taken humanity four hundred years to catch up with Leonardo's designs for a one-man helicopter, or "ornithopter." "If men were all virtuous," he said, "I should with great alacrity teach them all to fly. But what would be the security of the good, if the bad could at pleasure invade them from the sky?"

I find that if this instrument made with a screw be well made—that is to say, made of linen of which the pores are stopped up with starch—and be turned swiftly, the said screw will make its spiral in the air and it will rise high.

The man in the bird rests on an axis a little higher than his centre of gravity.

A bird is an instrument working according to mathematical law, which instrument it is

Madonna of the rocks (Leonardo da Vinci), in the National Gallery, London

within the capacity of man to reproduce with all its movements, but not with a corresponding degree of strength, though it is deficient only in the power of maintaining equilibrium. We may therefore say that such an instrument constructed by man is lacking in nothing except the life of the bird, and this life must needs be supplied from that of man.

The life which resides in the bird's members will without doubt better conform to their needs than will that of man which is separated from them, and especially in the almost imperceptible movements which preserve equilibrium. But since we see that the bird is equipped for many obvious varieties of movements, we are able from this experience to declare that the most rudimentary of these movements will be capable of being comprehended by man's understanding; and that he will to a great extent be able to provide against the destruction of that instrument of which he has himself become the living principle and the propeller.

[Diagrams of mechanism of flying machine]

I conclude that the upright position is more useful than face downwards, because the instrument cannot get overturned, and on the other hand the habit of long custom requires this.

And the raising and lowering movement will proceed from the lowering and raising of the two legs, and this is of great strength and the hands remain free; whereas if it were face downwards it would be very difficult for the legs to maintain themselves in the fastenings of the thighs.

And in resting the first impact comes upon the feet, and in rising they touch at *r S t;* and after these have been raised they support the

Study for a flying machine (Leonardo da Vinci), in the Institut de France, Paris

machine, and the feet moving up and down lift these feet from the ground.

Q is fastened to the girdle; the feet rest in the stirrups *K h; m n* come beneath the arms behind the shoulders; *o* represents the position of the head; the wing in order to rise and fall revolves and folds. . . the same.

[With drawings of parts of flying machine]

Spring of horn or of steel fastened upon wood of willow encased in reed.

The impetus maintains the birds in their flying course during such time as the wings do not press the air, and they even rise upwards.

If the man weighs two hundred pounds and is at *n* and raises the wing with his block, which is a hundred and fifty pounds, when he was above the instrument, with power amount-

ing to three hundred pounds he would raise himself with two wings.

[Drawing of wing of flying machine]

1 Let *a* be the first movement.
2 Undo one and remove. . . .
3 Double canes. . . soaped. . . .
4 . . . of rag or [skin] of flying fish.
5 Spring with lock *n o* is a wire that holds the spring, and it is not straight. Spring of wing.
6 The spring *b* should be strong, and the spring *a* feeble and bendable, so that it may easily be made to meet the spring *b,* and between *a b* let there be a small piece of leather, so that it is strong, and these springs should be of ox-horn, and to make the model you will make it with quills.
7 Take instead of the spring filings of thin and tempered steel, and these filings will be of uniform thickness and length between the ties, and you will have the springs equal in strength and power of resistance if the filings in each are equal in number.

[Drawing of wing of flying machine]

Net. Cane. Paper.
Try first with sheets from the Chancery.
Board of fir lashed in below.
Fustian. Taffeta. Thread. Paper. . .

[With drawings]

u b c causes the part *m n* to raise itself up quickly in the rising movement, *d e f* causes *m n* to descend rapidly in the falling movement, and so the wing performs its function.

r t lowers the wing by means of the foot, that is by stretching out the legs, *v s* raises the wing by the hand and turns it.

The way to cause the wing to turn just as it rises or descends.

Device which causes the wing as it rises to be all pierced through and as it falls to be united. And this is due to the fact that as it rises *b* separates from *a* and *d* from *c* and so the air gives place to the rising of the wing, and as it falls *b* returns to *a* and similarly *c* to *d;* and the net bound to the canes above makes a good protection, but take care that your direction be from *a* to *f* so that the landing does not find any obstacle. . . .

[With drawing of flying machine]

a twists the wing, *b* turns it with a lever, *c* lowers it, *d* raises it up, and the man who controls the machine has his feet at *f d;* the foot *f* lowers the wings, and the foot *d* raises them.

The pivot *M* should have its centre of gravity out of the perpendicular so that the wings as they fall down also fall towards the man's feet; for it is this that causes the bird to move forward.

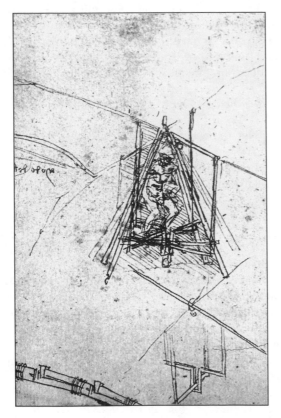

Man in an ornithopter (Leonardo da Vinci), in the Institut de France, Paris

This machine should be tried over a lake, and you should carry a long wineskin as a girdle so that in case you fall you will not be drowned.

It is also necessary that the action of lowering the wings should be done by the force of the two feet at the same time, so that you can regulate the movement and preserve your equilibrium by lowering one wing more rapidly than the other according to need, as you may see done by the kite and other birds. Also the downward movement of both the feet produces twice as much power as that of one: it is true that the movement is proportionately slower.

The raising is by the force of a spring or if you wish by the hand, or by drawing the feet towards you, and this is best for then you will have the hands more free.

[With drawing—figure of man lying face downwards working machine]

This can be made with one pair of wings and also with two.

If you should wish to make it with one, the arms will raise it by means of a windlass, and two vigorous kicks with the heels will lower it, and this will be useful.

And if you wish to make it with two pairs, when one leg is extended it will lower one pair of wings and at the same time the windlass worked by the hands will raise the others, helping also considerably those that fall, and by turning the hands first to the right and then to the left you will help first the one and then the other. This instrument resembles the large one on the opposite page except that in this the traction is twisted on the wheel *M* and goes to the feet.

In place of the feet you should make a ladder in three parts of three poles of fir, light and slender, as is represented here in front, and it should be ten braccia in length.

[With drawing—figure of man lying face downwards working machine]

Under the body between the pit and the fork of the throat should be a chamois skin and put it there with the head and the feet.

Hold a windlass with the hands and with feet and hands together you will exert a force equal to four hundred pounds, and it will be as rapid as the movement of the heels.

[With drawing—figure of man in vertical position working machine]

This man exerts with his head a force that is equal to two hundred pounds, and with his hands a force of two hundred pounds, and this is what the man weighs.

The movement of the wings will be cross-wise after the manner of the gait of the horse.

So for this reason I maintain that this method is better than any other.

Ladder for ascending and descending; let it be twelve braccia high, and let the span of the wings be forty braccia, and their elevation eight braccia, and the body from stern to prow twenty braccia and its height five braccia and let the outside cover be all of cane and cloth.

[With drawing of screw revolving round vertical axis]

Let the outer extremity of the screw be of steel wire as thick as a cord, and from the circumference to the centre let it be eight braccia.

I find that if this instrument made with a screw be well made—that is to say, made of linen of which the pores are stopped up with starch—and be turned swiftly, the said screw will make its spiral in the air and it will rise high.

Take the example of a wide and thin ruler whirled very rapidly in the air, you will see that your arm will be guided by the line of the edge of the said flat surface.

The framework of the above-mentioned linen should be of long stout cane. You may make a small model of pasteboard, of which the axis is formed of fine steel wire, bent by force, and as it is released it will turn the screw.

[With drawing]

If you wish to see a real test of the wings make them of pasteboard covered by net, and make the rods of cane, the wing being at least twenty braccia in length and breadth, and fix it over a plank of a weight of two hundred pounds, and make in the manner represented above a force that is rapid; and if the plank of two hundred pounds is raised up before the wing is lowered the test is satisfactory, but see that the force works rapidly, and if the aforesaid result does not follow do not lose any more time.

If by reason of its nature this wing ought to fall in four spaces of time and you by your mechanism cause it to fall in two the result will be that the plank of two hundred pounds will be raised up.

You know that if you find yourself standing in deep water holding your arms stretched out and then let them fall naturally the arms will proceed to fall as far as the thighs and the man will remain in the first position.

But if you make the arms which would naturally fall in four spaces of time fall in two then know that the man will quit his position and moving violently will take up a fresh position on the surface of the water.

And know that if the above-named plank weighs two hundred pounds a hundred of these will be borne by the man who holds the lever in his hand and a hundred will be carried upon the air by the medium of the wing.

Make the ladders curved to correspond with the body.

When the foot of the ladder *a* touches the ground it cannot give a blow to cause injury to the instrument because it is a cone which buries itself and does not find any obstacle at its point, and this is perfect.

Make trial of the actual machine over the water so that if you fall you do not do yourself any harm.

These hooks that are underneath the feet of the ladder act in the same way as when one jumps on the points of one's toes for then one is not stunned as is the person who jumps upon his heels.

This is the procedure when you wish to rise from an open plain: these ladders serve the same purpose as the legs and you can beat the wings while it is rising. Observe the swift, how when it has settled itself upon the ground it cannot rise flying because its legs are short. But when you have raised yourself, draw up the ladders as I show in the second figure above.

[Artificial wings]

In constructing wings one should make one cord to bear the strain and a looser one in the same position so that if the one breaks under the strain the other is in position to serve the same function.

[Artificial wings]

Shutters in Flying Machines

The smaller these shutters the more useful are they.

And they will be protected by a framework of cane upon which is drawn a piece of gauze and as it slants upward the movement of the whole is transversal, and such lines of shutters come to open by a slanting line and consequently the process of rising is not impeded.

Helm of Flying Machines

Here the head n is the mover of this helm, that is that when n goes towards b the helm becomes widened, and when it goes in the opposite direction the tail is contracted; and similarly when f is lowered the tail is lowered on this side, and so lowering itself on the opposite side it will do the same.

Of necessity in flight at uniform altitude the lowering of the wings will be as great as their elevation.

When the mover of the flying body has power divisible in four through its four chief ministering members, it will then be able to employ them equally and also unequally and also all equally and all unequally, according to the dictates of the various movements of the flying body.

If they are all moved equally the flying body will be of regular movement.

If they are used unequally, as it would be in continuous proportion, the flying body will be in circling movement.

Suppose that here there is a body suspended, which resembles that of a bird, and that its tail is twisted to an angle of various different degrees; you will be able by means of this to deduce a general rule as to the various twists and turns in the movements of birds occasioned by the bending of their tails.

In all the varieties of movements the heaviest part of the thing which moves becomes the guide of the movement.

JUAN LUIS (LUDOVICUS) VIVES (1492–1540)

FABULA DE HOMINE

A Fable About Man (1519)

One of the most important humanists of the sixteenth century, the Valencia-born Juan Luis Vives was an inveterate traveler who studied at Paris and spent most of his life away from Spain. He taught at Oxford and was a friend of Thomas More, Cardinal Wolsey, Catherine of Aragon, and tutor to Henry VIII's daughter Mary. When he opposed Henry's deposition of Catherine in favor of Anne Boleyn, he was forced to flee from his beloved England. As social reformer, Vives published *On the Help of the Poor* in 1526, outlining a proposal for a system of "workfare" still in discussion today. He argued that it was the responsibility of the secular authorities to come to the assistance of the underprivileged, where the Church had failed to do so. As humanistic educator he wrote an *Introduction to Wisdom*, which saw fifty reprints during his lifetime. His *Fable* on human greatness, influenced by Cicero and Pico della Mirandola and inspired by Erasmus, whom he'd met in Louvain, insists that a human being defines himself, not by birthright, but by his own activity. In the span of creation, humanity alone has no prescribed role except to exercise its unique gift of self-definition. Man as a wearer of masks, as actor, ultimately earns immortality by playing the highest role of all—the role of his own maker.

I should like to begin this essay of mine on man by some fables and plays, since man is himself a fable and a play. Once upon a time, after a certain lavish and sumptuous feast given by Juno on her birthday for all the gods, they, feeling carefree and elated by the nectar, asked whether she had prepared some plays which they might watch after the banquet. Thus nothing would be lacking to complete their happiness on this august occasion.

To gratify this wish of the immortal gods, Juno earnestly asked her brother and husband Jupiter, since he was all-powerful, to improvise an amphitheater and to bring forth new characters, after the manner of regular plays, lest in this respect a day which she wanted most distinguished seem deficient to the gods. Thereupon, all of a sudden, at a command of almighty Jupiter, by whom alone all things are done, this whole world appeared, so large, so elaborate, so diversified, and beautiful in places, just as you see it. This was the amphitheater: uppermost, to wit in the skies, were the stalls and seats of the divine spectators; nethermost—some say in the middle—the earth was placed as a stage for the appearance of the

View of the left wall of the Brancacci Chapel (Masaccio), in Santa Maria del Carmine, Florence

actors, along with all the animals and everything else.

When everything was ready and the banquet tables carried away, Mercurius Braubeta announced that the players were already on the stage. Joyfully the spectators went forth and were seated, each according to his rank. The great Jupiter was director of the plays, and when he saw that all were there, he gave the signal. Since he was the maker, he ordered everything and explained it to all that they might understand. Lest something be done differently from what he himself liked, he prescribed to the company of actors the entire arrangement and sequence of the plays, from which not even by the breadth of a finger, as they say, should they depart.

Indeed, as soon as the voice and signal of the great Jupiter reached the actors, each in their turn they came onto the stage, and there with such skill and poise, and so much in the manner of Roscius, did they perform tragedies, comedies, satires, mimes, farces, and other things of the sort that the gods swore that a more beautiful spectacle they had never beheld. Overjoyed at the delight and satisfaction of the gods, and quite elated herself, Juno kept asking them, one by one, how they liked the games. All agreed wholeheartedly that there had never been a more admirable spectacle, nothing worthier of Juno herself and of the birthday which they were celebrating.

This greatest spouse of the greatest god could not contain her excitement; briskly she would skip among the stalls of the immortal gods and, besides other things, repeatedly asked everyone which of the actors they considered the greatest. The wisest of the gods answered that none was more praiseworthy than man, and the father of the gods himself nodded his assent. Indeed, the more intently they watched the gestures, the words, and all the actions of this character, the greater was the astonishment that struck them. It pleased Jupiter to see so much admiration and praise given to man, his own offspring, by all the gods.

Those who sat at Jupiter's side, seeing how much pleasure he took in this human arch-mime, easily understood that he himself had made this personage; nay, looking more carefully, they recognized in man himself a great resemblance to Jupiter, so that even the dullest of gods might have known that man was born of Jupiter. Verily, man, peering oft through the mask which hides him, almost ready to burst forth and revealing himself distinctly in many things, is divine and Jupiter-like, participating in the immortality of Jupiter himself, in his wisdom, prudence, memory, sharing so many of his talents that it was easy to know that these great gifts had been bestowed upon him by Jupiter from out of his treasury and even from his own person.

Then, as he of gods the greatest, embracing all things in his might, is all things, they saw man, Jupiter's mime, be all things also. He would change himself so as to appear under the mask of a plant, acting a simple life without any power of sensation. Soon after, he withdrew and returned on the stage as a moral satirist, brought into the shapes of a thousand wild beasts: namely, the angry and raging lion, the rapacious and devouring wolf, the fierce and wild boar, the cunning little fox, the lustful and filthy sow, the timid hare, the envious dog, the stupid donkey. After doing this, he was out of sight for a short time; then the curtain was drawn back and he returned a man, prudent, just, faithful, human, kindly, and friendly, who went about the cities with the others, held the authority and obeyed in turn, cared for the public interest and welfare, and was finally in every way a political and social being.

The gods were not expecting to see him in more shapes when, behold, he was remade into one of their own race, surpassing the nature of man and relying entirely upon a very wise mind. O great Jupiter, what a spectacle for them! At first they were astonished that they,

too, should be brought to the stage and impersonated by such a convincing mime, whom they said to be that multiform Proteus, the son of the Ocean. Thereupon there was an unbelievable outburst of applause, and they prevented that great player from acting any longer. They begged Juno to let him into the stalls of the gods, unmasked, and to make of him a spectator rather than an actor. She was already eagerly going about obtaining this of her husband, when, at that very moment, man came out upholding the great Jupiter, the worthiest of gods, and with marvelous and indescribable gestures impersonating his father. He had transcended the characters of the lower gods and was piercing into that inaccessible light surrounded by darkness where Jupiter dwells, of kings and gods the king.

When the gods first saw him, they were roused and upset at the thought that their master and father had stooped to the stage. Soon, however, with composed minds, they glanced repeatedly at Jupiter's stall wondering whether he himself was sitting there or whether he had appeared masked to play a part. Seeing him there, they gazed back again at man and then at Jupiter. With such skill and propriety did he play Jupiter's part that, up and down, from Jupiter's stall to the stage, they kept glancing, lest they be misled by a likeness or the accurate mimic of an actor. Among the other players there were some who swore that this was not man but Jupiter himself, and they underwent severe punishment for their error.

Yet the gods, out of respect for this image of the father of all gods, and by their own suffrage, unanimously decreed that divine honors be granted to man. They prevailed upon Jupiter, through Juno's intercession, that man, who had so rightly played the parts of Jupiter and the gods, put off his mask and be seated among the gods. Jupiter complied with the gods, granting them what he himself, long before, had decided to bestow gratuitously upon man. Thus man was recalled from the stage, seated by Mercury among the gods, and proclaimed victor. There were no cheers to greet him but a silence of wonder. The whole man lay bare, showing the immortal gods his nature akin to theirs, this nature which, covered with mask and body, had made of him an animal so diverse, so desultory, so changing like a polypus and a chameleon, as they had seen him on the stage. Jupiter was then declared and proclaimed the father not only of the gods but also of men. With a gentle and mild countenance, he took delight in both, and was hailed and adored as a parent by both. With pleasure he received this august double name; and now, using also this favored title, we proclaim him of gods and men the father.

Now, when Mercury first came into the stalls of the gods, carrying in his arms the stage costumes, the gods looked at them with great interest; having examined them attentively, a long while, they praised Jupiter's wisdom and skill and adored him, for the costumes which he had made were no less appropriate than useful for all the acts. There was the lofty head, stronghold and court of the divine mind; in it the five senses arranged and placed ornately and usefully. The ears, accordingly, did not droop with soft skin, nor were they firmly fixed with a hard bone, but both were rounded by a sinuous cartilage. Thus they could receive sounds from all directions, and the dust, straw, fluff, gnats which might be flying around would not penetrate into the head but be caught in the folds. The eyes in equal number, two indeed, were high up so that they could observe all things and protected by a fine wall of lashes and eyelids against the same bits of straw and fluff, dust and tiny insects. They were the gauge of the soul and the noblest part of the human face. Then came the very attire of the mask or the mask itself, so handsomely shaped, divided into arms and legs which were long and ending with fingers, so good-looking and useful for all purposes. As there is no time to go through all that which others have related at great length, I shall add this conclusion. All is so well fitted and interrelated that if one were to withdraw or change or add something, all that harmony and beauty and the whole efficacy would be immediately lost. By no ingenuity could a more

appropriate mask be conceived for a man, unless someone perhaps wish for the impossible.

When the gods saw man and embraced their brother, they deemed it unworthy of him to appear on a stage and practice the disreputable art of the theater, and they could not find enough praise for their own likeness and that of their father. They investigated one by one and examined the many hidden secrets of man and derived more pleasure from this than from the spectacle of all the plays, "Nor having seen him once are they content; they wish to linger on." There indeed was a mind full of wisdom, prudence, knowledge, reason, so fertile that by itself it brought forth extraordinary things. Its inventions are: towns and houses, the use of herbs, stones and metals, the designations and names of all things, which foremost among his other inventions have especially caused wise men to wonder. Next and no less important, with a few letters he was able to comprise the immense variety of the sounds of the human voice. With these letters so many doctrines were fixed in writing and transmitted, including religion itself and the knowledge and cult of Jupiter the father and of the other brother-gods. This one thing, which is found in no other animal but man, shows his relationship to the gods. Of little good would all these inventions have been if there had not been added, as the treasury of all things and for the safe-keeping of these divine riches, a memory, the storehouse of all that we have enumerated. From religion and memory, fore-knowledge is almost obtained, with the prophecy of the future, evidently a spark of that divine and immense science which perceives all future events as if they were present.

The gods were gazing at these and other things, as yet sateless; just as those who contemplate their beautiful reflection in a mirror take delight in these things and willingly tarry on, so the gods, seeing themselves and Jupiter their father so well portrayed in man, wished to look more and more at what they had already beheld, inquiring about one thing after another.

How did he act plants, herbs, even wild animals, man, gods, the god king Jupiter, by what craft and gesture?

While man explained all this calmly and clearly, Jupiter ordered that ambrosia and nectar from the remains of the feast be placed before him. Cheerfully neglecting the plays, many of the gods had their afternoon refreshment with him. They were charmed by their brotherly guest or fellow-citizen, who, refreshed by heavenly victuals after the toil of the plays, wrapped like the other gods in the purple *praetexta* and bearing the crown, went forth to watch the spectacle. Many of the gods stood up for him, many gave up their seats. In different directions they pulled his cloak and retarded his progress that he might stay next to them, until the great Jupiter nodded to Mercury, who led him, that he was to be received in the orchestra among the gods of the first rank, who considered this a great honor. Far was it from those gods of the highest order to despise man, who had been an actor a short time before. He was received by

them with respect and invited to the front seats. He sat in their company and watched the games which proceeded without interruption, until Apollo himself reduced the light at Juno's request (for the masters of the feast and other servants, warned by the cooks, announced that supper was more than ready), and night fell upon them. Chandeliers, torches, wax tapers, candlesticks, and oil lamps brought by the stars were lighted, and they were entertained at supper with the same pomp as they had been at dinner. Juno also invited man, and Jupiter the father "assented and with a nod made all Olympus tremble."

Man, just as he had watched the plays with the highest gods, now reclined with them at the banquet. He put on his mask, which he had meanwhile laid aside, for this stage costume was so greatly honored. Since it had so well met the needs of man, it was deemed worthy of the most sumptuous feast and of the table of the gods. Thus it was given the power of perception and enjoyed the eternal bliss of the banquet.

MARTIN LUTHER (1483–1546)

On Christian Freedom (1520)

An Augustinian monk and biblical scholar at the University of Wittenberg made his first trip to Rome ten years after his ordination. As a result of the corruption Martin Luther observed there among the cardinals and the pope he shook the very foundations of Roman Catholicism in 1517 by nailing "95 Theses" indicting the corruption of the Church to the door of All Saints Church in Wittenberg. One of the theses, although like the others it was posed more as a question than as a declaration, was interpreted as a denial of the pope's authority. But Luther stressed that salvation comes from faith alone, and that each individual Christian, in the privacy of his inner life, has a direct relation with his maker. There is no need to deal with a decadent ecclesiastical hierarchy that financed its vices by the sale of indulgences (you could pay to have days deducted from your punishment in Purgatory!). Pope Leo X excommunicated Luther in 1520. Luther responded by burning the document of excommunication. When the Emperor Charles V banned him in the Holy Roman Empire, Luther sought the protection of Frederick, duke of Saxony. In the Castle of Wartburg he translated the New Testament into German. Eventually, having abandoned the concept of priesthood as unnecessary, he married the former nun Katherine von Bora. The founder of Lutheranism is generally regarded, along with Philipp Melanchthon, as the father of Protestantism. Certainly he was the initiator of the Protestant Reformation, which would tear Europe apart for nearly two centuries and finally bring about the Counter-Reformation of the Roman Catholic Church.

1. In order that we may have a true and proper understanding of what it is to be a Christian, or what is the freedom which Christ has won for us and given to us, and of which St. Paul often writes, I propose to begin with two propositions.

   A Christian is free and independent in every respect, a bondservant to none.

Martin Luther (Hans Holbein, the Younger), in the Galleria Corsini, Rome

A Christian is a dutiful servant in every respect, owing a duty to everyone.

These two axioms are clearly found in 1 Corinthians 9, where St. Paul says: "Though I am free from all men, I have made myself a servant to all." Again, Romans 13: "Owe no one anything, except to love one another. But love owes a duty, and is a bondservant of what she loves"; in the same way also in regard to Christ, Galatians 4: "God sent forth His Son, born of a woman, and made Him a bondservant of the law."

2. In order to understand these two antithetic assertions concerning freedom and bondage, we ought to remember that in every Christian there are two natures, a spiritual and a bodily. In as far as he possesses a soul, a Christian is a spiritual person, an inward, regenerate self; and in as far as he possesses flesh and blood, he is a sensual person, an outward, unregenerate self. Because of this difference, the Scriptures, in passages which directly contradict each other, speak of his freedom and bondage in the way I have just said.

3. When we consider the inner, spiritual man and see what belongs to him if he is to be a free and devout Christian, in fact and in name, it is evident that, whatever the name, no outer thing can make him either free or religious. For his religion and freedom, and, moreover, his sinfulness and servitude, are neither bodily nor outward. What avail is it

to the soul if the body is free, active, and healthy; or eats, drinks, and lives as it likes? Again, what harm does it do to the soul if the body is imprisoned, ill and weakly; or is hungry, thirsty, and in pain, even if one does not bear it gladly? This sort of thing never touches the soul a little bit, nor makes it free or captive, religious or sinful.

4. Thus it does not help the soul if the body puts on sacred vestments as the priests and clergy do. It does not help even when the body is in church or in holy places, or when busy with sacred affairs; nor when the body is offering prayers, keeping fasts, or making pilgrimages, and doing other good works, which are performed only in and through the body. It must surely be something quite different which brings religion and freedom to the soul. For even a sinful man, or a hypocrite and pretender, may have all the afore-named things, do these works, and follow these ways. Also, this is the way to make men nothing but sheer hypocrites. Further it does no harm to the soul if the body wears worldly clothes, tarries in worldly places, eats, drinks, does not go on pilgrimages, nor keep the appointed hours of prayer; and if it neglects all the works that hypocrites perform, as already said.

5. The only means, whether in heaven or on earth, whereby the soul can live, and be religious, free, and Christian, is the holy Gospel, the word of God preached by Christ. He Himself says in John 11, "I am the resurrection and the life. He that believeth in Me shall live eternally"; and John 14, "I am the way, the truth and the life"; and Matthew 4, "Man does not live by bread alone, but by every word that proceeds out of the mouth of God." Therefore, we can be certain that the soul can do without anything but the word of God; and apart from the word of God it has no means of help. When it has the word, however, it has no need of anything else. In short, it possesses food, joy, peace, light, ability, righteousness,

truth, wisdom, freedom, and sufficient to overflowing of everything good. Thus we read in the Psalms, especially in Psalm 119, that the prophet cries only for the word of God. And in the Scriptures, the worst calamity, the worst sign of God's wrath, is when He withdraws His word from man. On the other hand, it is held the greatest grace when He sends forth His word, as it is written in Psalm 107: "He sent His word and helped them thereby." Christ came for no other object than to preach the word of God. Moreover all apostles, bishops, priests, and the whole clergy, were called and instituted only for the sake of the word; although, unfortunately, things happen differently nowadays.

6. You may ask, however: "What then is that word which gives such signal grace, and how shall I use it?" The answer is: It is nothing else than the message proclaimed by Jesus, as contained in the gospel; and this should be, and, in fact, is, so presented that you hear your God speak to you. It shows how all your life and labour are as nothing in God's sight, and how you and all that is in you, must eternally perish. If you truly believe this, and that you are indeed guilty, you necessarily despair of yourself; you believe that Hosea was right when he said: "O Israel, there is nought in you except your corruption, but in Me is your help." In order that you may come out of yourself and flee from yourself, i.e., escape your corruption, He sets you face to face with His beloved Son, Jesus Christ, and says to you by means of His living and comforting word: "You should surrender yourself to Him with firm faith, and trust Him gladly." Then, for your faith's sake, all your sins shall be forgiven and all your wickedness overcome. You yourself will be righteous, upright, serene, and devout. You will fulfil all commands, and be free from all things, as St. Paul says in Romans 1: "A justified Christian lives only by his faith"; and in Romans 10: "Christ is the end and the fulfil-

ment of all commandments for them that believe in him."

7. Therefore it is reasonable to say that the only purpose for which all Christians should labour, is that they should build up both the divine word and Christ in themselves, by exercising and strengthening their faith continually. No other works can make a man a Christian. Thus Christ answered the Jews (John 6), when they asked Him what they should do in order to do works of a godly and Christian kind. He said: "That is the only divine work, that you believe in Him whom God has sent", whom God the Father has alone ordained to that end.

Therefore a right faith in Christ is, truly, superabundant wealth, for He brings with Himself all felicity, and takes away all infelicity. Thus Mark says, in the last chapter: "Therefore he who believes and is baptized is saved, and he who does not believe is condemned." The prophet Isaiah (Chapter 10) surveyed the wealth of the same faith, and said: "God will make a small remnant on earth, and into the remnant righteousness will flow like a flood", namely the faith, in which the fulfilling of all commands is quite briefly contained, will abundantly justify all who have it, till they need nothing more to become righteous and religious. Thus St. Paul says in Romans 10: "That which a man believes in his heart, makes him righteous and devout."

JOHN SKELTON (1464?–1529)

Collyn Clout (1522)

Court poet and tutor of Henry VIII, though more medieval than Renaissance, John Skelton tried to invent a new form of poetry which at one extreme is as scholastic as the *Romance of the Rose* but at the other is as vivid, bombastic, idiosyncratically personal, simplistic, and coarse as that of François Villon. A humanist who favored Latin over Greek, he was also a politically conservative parish priest. In a voice that resonates the stridency and power of the best of modern urban rap, *Collyn Clout* attacks the evils of the Church but not its doctrines. Skelton's invention of "Skeltonic meter" (short, irregular, consecutively rhymed verses in the rhyme-scheme aaabbbccc) accounts for the high energy of his satirical poetry that transports us into the world of his jester-fool storyteller with an endless stream of words, images, and witticisms at his disposal. The "innocent bumpkin" Collyn Clout, the shield from behind which the author securely aims his slings and arrow at ecclesiastical ("spiritualitie") and lay ("temporalitie") targets, is among the most convincing poetic personae of the early sixteenth century.

*Here after foloweth a lytell boke called
Collyn Clout compyled by Mayster Skelton,
Poete Laureate*

*Quis consurget mihi adversus malignantes,
aut quis stabit mecum adversus operantes
iniquitatem? Nemo, Domine!*

What can it avayle
To dryve forth a snayle,
Or to make a sayle
Of a herynges tayle?
To ryme or to rayle,
To wryte or to indyte,
Other for delyte
Or elles for despyte?
Or bokes to compyle
Of dyvers maner style,
Vyce to revyle
And synne to exyle?
To teche or to preche
As reason wyll reche?
Sey this and sey that:
'His heed is so fat
He wottyth never what
Ne whereof he speketh.'
'He cryeth and he creketh,
He pryeth and he preketh,
He chydeth and he chatters,
He prayeth and he patters;
He clyttreth and he clatters,
He medleth and he smatters,
He gloseth and he flatters.'
Or yf he speke playne,
Than he lacketh brayne:
'He is but a foole;
Let hym go to scole!
A thre-foted stole
That he may downe sytte,
For he lacketh wytte.'
And yf that he hytte
The nayle on the hede
It standeth in no stede:
'The devyll,' they say, 'is dede,
The devyll is dede.'
  It may well so be,
Or elles they wolde se

Otherwyse, and fle
From worldly vanyte
And foule covytousnesse
And other wretchednesse,
Fyckell falsenesse,
Varyablenesse,
With unstablenesse.
And yf ye stande in doute
Who brought this ryme aboute,
My name is Collyn Cloute.
I purpose to shake oute
All my connynge bagge,
Lyke a clerkely hagge.
For though my ryme be ragged,
Tattered and jagged,
Rudely rayne-beaten,
Rusty and mothe-eaten,
Yf ye take well therwith
It hath in it some pyth.
For, as farre as I can se,
It is wronge with eche degre;
For the temporalte
Accuseth the spirytualte;
The spirytualte agayne
Dothe grudge and complayne
Upon the temporall men.
Thus eche of other blother
The tone against the tother.
Alas, they make me shoder,
For in hoder-moder
The churche is put in faute.
The prelates ben so haute
They say, and loke so hye
As though they wolde flye
Aboute the sterry skye.
  Laye men say, in dede,
Howe they take no hede
Theyr sely shepe to fede,
But plucke away and pull
Theyr fleces of wull.
Unneth they leve a locke
Of wolle amongest theyr flocke.
And as for theyr connynge,
A glommynge and a mommynge,
And make therof a jape!
They gaspe and they gape
All to have promocyon:

There is theyr hole devocyon,
With money, yf it wyll happe
To catche the forked cappe.
For sothe, they are to lewde
To say so, all beshrewde!

What trowe ye they say more
Of the bysshoppes lore?
Howe in matters they ben rawe,
They lumber forth the lawe
To herken Jacke and Gyll
Whan they put up a byll;
And judge it as they wyll,
For other mens skyll,
Expoundynge out theyr clauses,
And leve theyr owne causes.
In theyr pryncypall cure
They make but lytell sure,
And meddels very lyght
In the churches ryght.
But *ire* and *venyre*,
And *sol fa* so *alamyre*
That the premenyre

Is lyke to be set afyre
In theyr jurysdictyons,
Through temporall afflictyons.
Men say they have prescrypcyons
Agaynst the spirytual contradictyons,
Accomptynge them as fictyons.
    And whyles the heedes do this,
The remenaunt is amys
Of the clergye all,
Bothe great and small.
I wote never howe they warke,
But thus the people carke,
And surely thus they sey:
'Bysshoppes, yf they may,
Small housholdes woll kepe,
But slombre forth and slepe,
And assay to crepe
Within the noble walles
Of the kynges halles,
To fatte theyr bodyes full,
Theyr soules lame and dull;
And have full lytell care
Howe evyll theyr shepe fare.'

ANNA BIJNS (1493–1575)

Poems (1528-48)

One of the strongest female voices of the Renaissance belonged to a Dutch schoolmistress, "the Germanic Sappho," who lived and died in Antwerp a burgher's daughter. Her hatred of Martin Luther and the Protestant Reformation inspired her to heights of vitriolic eloquence. Bijns, whose motto was, "Sour, not sweet," minces no words in castigating her enemies. Her rhetorical and energetic coarseness is comparable to that of François Villon; her tongue is as biting as Camille Paglia's. Yet she considered herself inspired by the Holy Spirit, and responsible for expressing her inspiration to defend the Church, threatened on all sides by Lutherans, Calvinists, and Anabaptists. Martin Rossom, to whom she compares Luther, was a soldier of fortune who had ravaged the Netherlands and slain two hundred thousand German peasants. She accused Luther of being a worse criminal than Rossom. Jacob van Lieshout was executed for printing the first collection of Bijns' work. "Unyoked Is Best! Happy the Woman Without a Man" is a feminist manifesto, urging women to support themselves, with all the joys and woes of living by work, in order to enjoy maximum independence. At the same time, she apologized for being a woman, fearing that her gender might interfere with her polemics being taken seriously. Bijns' rage against abusive males, and disdain for the traditional institution of marriage in which her sister had been miserably entrapped, is perhaps the most strikingly modern of all that was written by Renaissance women. Her passionate involvement in religion provides a rhetoric for today's controversies about the priesthood of women.

'Tis a Waste to Cast Pearls Before Swine

Crafty spirits, noble Mercurists,
Rhetoricians, subtle artists,
Economize on sterling words.
Hold in reserve ingenious conceits.
Men of letters: your cheap artistic claims
Apply Rhetoric where filthy dung belongs.
Noble Rhetoric, I weep for the affront
That you bear such verbal disrespects
From whomever and whenever. Shame!
Many a conceited fool you'll find
To whom Rhetoric seems naught but trite.
No need to perform our art soigné
Before vain windbags, tongue-tied themselves.
'Tis a waste to cast pearls before swine.

As the sweetest of fruits I sing your praise,
A gift directly from the Holy Ghost,
Respected by most, oh noble Rhetoric.
Joy with joyous occasion you join.
But where dense pigs convene in feast
Art is not invited at all.
Artist to philistine will yield
And shy away frustrated, for boors aplenty
Hold Grand Rhetoric and music sweet
No dearer than vile terrestrial mud.
Try to declaim—a play or pretty refrain,
Always one will chat or eat or quaff.
Nobody's giving a hoot! So, indeed,
'Tis a waste to cast pearls before swine.

If you're inclined to art beware,
Take care: avoid all spivvish churls
Who despise our refined ideas.
In hailing yokels of art unaware
Refuse your art—be grudging,
And don't spend it till they beg for it.
If they don't listen then be silent.
Where uncouth peasants have assembled
Art is held in low esteem,
And trod under foot, an artist demeaned,
Called a ranter, a fool, a goon—
His name acquired, and lost his honor.
Save your art for a more suitable cause.
'Tis a waste to cast pearls before swine.

Prince, I'm ill content with some confrères
Who quack their Art at any revel.
These fill their belly but don't pay off.
Famous artists cry out and rightly so:
The former shouldn't have been initiated at
     all
Or been given the lofty honor's name
Or been inscribed in nobler artists' lists.
Scratch them out, who like vulgar jinglers
Break down art and so forfeit their life.
My limbs tremble, my heart fails a beat
When Rhetoric I see on sale for money.
Like snow for sun my joy melts away,
And thus I repeat my initial remark:
'Tis a waste to cast pearls before swine.

[January 11, 1528]

Unyoked Is Best! Happy the Woman Without a Man

How good to be a woman, how much better to
    be a man!
Maidens and wenches, remember the lesson
    you're about to hear.
Don't hurtle yourself into marriage far too
    soon.
The saying goes: "Where's your spouse? Where's
    your honor?"
But one who earns her board and clothes
Shouldn't scurry to suffer a man's rod.
So much for my advice, because I suspect—
Nay, see it sadly proven day by day—
'T happens all the time!
However rich in goods a girl might be,
Her marriage ring will shackle her for life.
If however she stays single
With purity and spotlessness foremost,
Then she is lord as well as lady. Fantastic, not?
Though wedlock I do not decry:
Unyoked is best! Happy the woman without a
    man.

Fine girls turning into loathly hags—
'Tis true! Poor sluts! Poor tramps! Cruel mar-
    riage!
Which makes me deaf to wedding bells.
Huh! First they marry the guy, luckless dears,
Thinking their love just too hot to cool.
Well, they're sorry and sad within a single year.
Wedlock's burden is far too heavy.
They know best whom it harnessed.
So often is a wife distressed, afraid.
When after troubles hither and thither he goes
In search of dice and liquor, night and day,
She'll curse herself for that initial "yes."
So, beware ere you begin.
Just listen, don't get yourself into it.
Unyoked is best! Happy the woman without a
    man.

A man oft comes home all drunk and pissed
Just when his wife had worked her fingers to
    the bone
(So many chores to keep a decent house!),

But if she wants to get in a word or two,
She gets to taste his fist—no more.
And that besotted keg she is supposed to obey?
Why, yelling and scolding is all she gets,
Such are his ways—and hapless his victim.
And if the nymphs of Venus he chooses to fre-
    quent,
What hearty welcome will await him home.
Maidens, young ladies: learn from another's
    doom,
Ere you, too, end up in fetters and chains.
Please don't argue with me on this,
No matter who contradicts, I stick to it:
Unyoked is best! Happy the woman without a
    man.

A single lady has a single income,
But likewise, isn't bothered by another's whims.
And I think: that freedom is worth a lot.
Who'll scoff at her, regardless what she does,
And though every penny she makes herself,
Just think of how much less she spends!
An independent lady is an extraordinary
    prize—
All right, of a man's boon she is deprived,
But she's lord and lady of her very own hearth.
To do one's business and no explaining sure is
    lots of fun!
Go to bed when she list, rise when she list, all
    as she will,
And no one to comment! Grab tight your inde-
    pendence then.
Freedom is such a blessed thing.
To all girls: though the right Guy might come
    along:
Unyoked is best! Happy the woman without a
    man.

Prince,
Regardless of the fortune a woman might bring,
Many men consider her a slave, that's all.
Don't let a honeyed tongue catch you off guard,
Refrain from gulping it all down. Let them rave,
For, I guess, decent men resemble white ravens.
Abandon the airy castles they will build for you.
Once their tongue has limed a bird:
Bye bye love—and love just flies away.

To women marriage comes to mean betrayal
And the condemnation to a very awful fate.
All her own is spent, her lord impossible to
    bear.
It's *peine forte et dure* instead of fun and
    games.
Oft it was the money, and not the man
Which goaded so many into their fate.
Unyoked is best! Happy the woman without a
    man.

Yet, When Compared, Martin Rossom Comes Out Best

Lately, melancholy's weight was hard to bear,
Made sore my mind, chased phantoms throb-
    bing through my head,
Kept me brooding over oh so many things.
Just considering the world's present course,
What was there to brighten up my mood
With nothing but sorrow to spare—and I was
    sad.
And then my weary fancy in its rambling
Called forth a pair of men
With names the same but not much else.
One, Martin Luther, whose error spawns and
    spreads;
The other, Martin Rossom, whose cruel sword
Proved far too sharp for many far and near.
Rossom racks the body, Luther lays waste the
    soul,
So what's up! "Evil creature" fits them both.
To choose between these two? Waste of time.
Still, since Luther through his error kills your
    soul,
When compared, Martin Rossom comes out
    best.

Martin Rossom, nobleman by birth,
As Emperor's renegade also his honor forsook;
But Luther betrayed the Lord Supreme
To whom his allegiance he had pledged
And put a nun's coif above his own.
A nun who had promised God the same!
Why, Rossom spurns Emperor, but Luther's evil
    tongue

Wags at Pope and Emperor alike,
Teaches subjects' revolt against their betters,
Spreads defamatory libel of kings and princes,
Flings filth at church lords just the same.
Rossom wrought havoc fierce in Brabant's land
But his flaming fury did most often
Leave the Church alone, at least.
And blessed maidens he didn't even touch
(Though 'tis rumored that he did, here and
    there).
Martin Rossom: model of the tyrant harsh?
When compared, Martin Rossom comes out
    best.

Where Martin Rossom's crime was treason,
Martin Luther's was double so foul,
For many a Christian soul his evil kiss
Slammed heaven's gate forever shut. Thus,
The Desecrator of Our Lord must have sent
This double plague to infect the Christian
    world.
Rossom a killer? Luther through his actions
Sent two hundred thousand peasants to their
    graves.
Blood of men and women freely flowed, with
Water and fire curbing his heretic's views.
So, he has butchered both the soul and body.
Martin Rossom merely racked the latter.
Now, he's just as cruel to the meek and lowly,
But through his hand, if they're patient, they'll
    soon be placed in God's.
Not that this would make his guilt seem less—
I'm not excusing him, I'm not washing him
    white!
Yet, though both be venomous vipers,
When compared, Martin Rossom comes out
    best.

Martin Rossom and Martin Luther,
The best of both still a mutineer.
'Tis not strange that Rossom knows no fear,
For he's a soldier, a worldly cavalier.
But Martin Luther, that braggart, claims, he
    dares,
To comprehend Scripture down to its least
    detail,
With the Holy Ghost leading him on the way.

If supposedly he knows the way, his erring sure
    looks weird
But of course the ghostly spirit that guides him
    most
Has firmly wrapped its tail round Dymphna's
    painted feet.
Martin Rossom sacked Brabant for tons of loot,
A sad affair which many still deplore,
But Luther himself has hands none too clean.
Monasteries were emptied by apostates on his
    command
Of their treasure and holy vessels. God will find
    out
If he didn't get a share himself. How about that?
Satan clasps both Martins in a tight embrace,
Yet, when compared, Martin Rossom comes out
    best.

Martin Rossom, Freebooters' Prince,
Mastermind in stealing and plunder;
Luther, all false prophets' Prince,

If your histories I'd set out in full,
The reader would be much distressed, I guess—

'Twould also be a loss of time and paper.
Thus for now I hold my duty excellently done.
Allow me to defer the sequel to some other
    time.
Luther, Rossom, and Lucifer (for he fits in real
    well),
I wonder who's worthiest of the three.
Rossom piles much gruesome plunder in his
    lair,
Luther is conniving night and day,
Intent on poisoning our Christian lands.
So, this couple is wicked, very clearly so.
But Luther's venom most of all I fear,
For eternal damnation follows in its rear.
Even though the choice of either isn't worth a
    rotten fig,
When compared, Martin Rossom comes out
    best.

BALDASSARE CASTIGLIONE (1478–1529)

Il libro del cortegiano

The Book of the Courtier (1516; 1528)

The Mantua-born Baldassare Castiglione's *Courtier,* though no masterpiece of writing, was among the most influential and representative expressions of Renaissance moral and social idealism centered on the individual who, without regard to institutional or traditional restrictions, fully realizes his intellectual and spiritual potential. In the opening of his book, published in the same year as Ludovico Ariosto's *Orlando Furioso* and Thomas More's *Utopia,* the author makes it clear that what is most admirable about man is that he can posit the ideal in full knowledge of its impossibility. Because man alone can do this, because the limitations of his physical existence provide him with a dramatic stage upon which to act and reflect, Castiglione chooses the human over the superhuman ideal as the most truly admirable. He redefines the ideal in purely human terms, concerned not with the completed state of philosophical perfection but with the human courtier as the creature who comes nearest to it. Castiglione's ideal courtier is not imaginary, an inaccessible platonic ideal; he is only a man aspiring to discover his own limits by daring to surpass them. Presented as a dialogue among ladies and gentlemen of Duke Guidobaldo da Montefeltro's palace in the walled city of Urbino, the book is at once a portrait of manners and a celebration of the duke's achievement of a court, the atmosphere of which is perfectly conducive to the most beautiful and noble aspirations—following in the tradition of Plato's *Republic* and *Symposium*. Urbino, as Castiglione sees it, is a utopia of gentility. As presented here in Sir Thomas Hoby's 1561 translation, Castiglione's vision of human perfectibility—despite its male bias—is uplifting and contagious. It is the granddaddy of modern self-help books. Hoby's British rendition is a perfect reflection of the ideal gentleman's *sprezzatura*—a gracefully exuberant self-confidence, belief in self-improvement, and unshakable *élan vital*. Human nobility, we learn from this document, lies not in man's ability to ignore death, but in his willingness to confront it, and to derive from the confrontation the inspiration to live as if immortal.

The Courtier is the most comprehensive of the Renaissance curricula, the study of the gentleman's proper role in society as defined, not by tradition or law as in the Middle Ages, but by the gentleman himself. The result is a perfect amalgamation of medieval graces and Renaissance humanism. Castiglione's requirements for the perfect courtier, summarized by St. Ignatius Loyola (founder of the Society of Jesus, known familiarly as the "Jesuits") as *mens sana, in corpore sano* ("a sound man in a sound body"), include:

- nobility of birth (old blood brings stability);
- adept at the profession of arms;
- physical beauty, reflecting inner beauty;
- neat and elegant attire, preferably dark or black;
- versatile at sports fencing, wrestling, jousting, swimming, tennis as well as chess and card games, but all done in moderation. He is "the perfect horseman in every kind of saddle";
- well-spoken, a good conversationalist, preferring the vernacular to Latin;
- articulately literate, following classical models;
- at home with song, dance, and musical performance;
- virtues include honesty, prudence, and fortitude;
- guided always by reason in all things.

How well such a person would fare in today's personals ads! Moreover, Castiglione's perfect person wears his protean qualities lightly, concealing the effort he has undertaken to accomplish their perfection; this nonchalance is an essential characteristic. At his most successful he has made himself what we now call "a Renaissance man"; at his least, he may be disparaged as a dabbler. This excerpt from the fourth Book, highlighted by Bembo's eloquent monologue, illustrates a layman's understanding of the Neoplatonic doctrine of love and its place in human affairs. At the same time that Castiglione is influenced by Pico and Ficino, he assimilates their abstract doctrines into the immediate applications of the gentleman's everyday life. His courtier is not only an ontological dilettante but also a pragmatic opportunist, studiously befriending princes and patrons who can offer him a climate, like that of the ducal palace in Urbino, wherein he might thrive and shine. For it is the love of beauty and truth that inspires the courtier's arduous search for excellence. Here politeness raises flirtatious banter to new heights of seductive flourish, taking on the deliciousness that will become a familiar characteristic in works like *Dangerous Liaisons* and *School for Scandal.* Castiglione's gentleman is a person of masks and roles, at his best a charming rogue, at his worst an absolute cynic. His reality is not a state of being, but of ceaseless becoming. The characters engaged in Castiglione's dialogue concur that defining human nature is the finest game that could possibly be played. It's easy to see how Edmund Spenser, in his *Faerie Queene,* and William Shakespeare, in fashioning the character of Hamlet, made use of Hoby's Castiglione:

The courtier's, soldier's, scholar's eye, tongue, sword;
The expectancy and rose of the fair state,
The glass of fashion, and the mould of form,
The observ'd of all observers. . . (*Hamlet* Act 3 scene 1,155–59)

Castiglione served as papal legate to the court of the Emperor Charles V. According to legend, another of Castiglione's patrons, Francis I, encouraged him to write his handbook of manners and courtly conduct so that future generations could see "how we lived." The result was an unforgettable portrait of *homo ludens,* man "the player," that continues to influence how we think about our species to this day.

Then M. Peter Bembo: Beleave not (quoth he) but beautie is always good.

Here Count Lewis bicause he woulde retourn again to his former pourpose interrupted him and said: Sins M. Morello passeth not to understand that, which is so necessary for him, teache it me, and showe me howe olde men may come bye this hapinesse of love, for I will not care to be counted olde, so it may profit me.

M. Peter Bembo laughed and said: First will I take the errour out of these gentilmens minde: and afterwarde will I satisfie you also. So beeginning a fresh: My Lordes (quoth he) I would not that with speakynge ill of beawtie, which is a holy thinge, any of us as prophane and wicked shoulde purchase him the wrath of God. Therfore to give M. Morello and Sir Fridericke warninge, that they lose not their sight, as Stesichorus did, a peine most meete for who so

dispraiseth beawtie, I saye, that beawtie commeth of God, and is like a circle, the goodnesse wherof is the Centre. And therefore, as there can be no circle without a centre, no more can beawty be without goodnesse. Wherupon doeth verie sildome an ill soule dwell in a beawtifull bodye. And therefore is the outwarde beawtie a true signe of the inwarde goodnes, and in bodies thys comelynesse is imprynted more and lesse (as it were) for a marke of the soule, whereby she is outwardlye knowen: as in trees, in whiche the beawtye of the buddes giveth a testimonie of the goodnesse of the frute. . . .

It is not then to be spoken that Beawtie maketh women proude or cruel, although it seeme so to M. Morello. Neyther yet ought beawtifull women to beare the blame of that hatred, mortalytie, and destruction, which the unbridled appetites of men are the cause of. I will not nowe denye, but it is possible also to finde in the worlde beawtifull women unchast, yet not bicause beawtie inclineth them to unchast livinge, for it rather plucketh them from it, and leadeth them into the way of vertuous condicions, throughe the affinitie that beawtie hath with goodnesse: but otherwhile yll bringinge up, the continuall provocations of lovers, tokens, povertie, hope, deceites, feare, and a thousande other matters overcome the steadfastnesse, yea of beawtiful and good women: and for these and like causes may also beawtifull menn beccome wicked.

Then said the L. Cesar: In case the L. Gaspars sayinge be true of yesternight, there is no doubt but the faire women be more chast then the foule.

And what was my sayinge? quoth the L. Gaspar.

The L. Cesar answered: If I do well beare in minde, your saiynge was, that the women that are suide to, alwaies refuse of satisfie him that suith to them, but those that are not suide to, sue to others. There is no doubt but the beautiful women have alwaies more suyters, and be

Balthasar Castiglione (Raphael), in the Louvre, Paris

more instantlye laide at in love, then the foule. Therefore the beawtifull always deny, and consequentlye be more chast, then the foule, whiche not beeinge suied to, sue unto others.

M. Peter Bembo laughed and said: This argument can not be answered to.

Afterwarde he proceeded: It chaunseth also oftentimes, that as the other senses, so the sight is deceyved, and judgeth a face beawtyfull, which in deede is not beawtifull. And bicause in the eyes and in the wholl countenance of some women, a man behouldeth otherwhile a certein lavish wantonnes peincted with dishonest flickeringes, many, whom that maner deliteth bicause it promiseth them an easines to come by the thing, that they covet, cal it beawty: but in deed it is a cloked unshamefastnes, unworthy of so honorable and holy a name.

M. Peter Bembo held his peace, and those Lordes still were earnest upon him to speake somewhat more of this love and of the waye to enjoy beautye aright, and at the last: Me thinke (quoth he) I have showed plainly inough, that olde men may love more happelye then yonge, whiche was my drift, therfore it belongeth not me to entre anye farther.

Count Lewis answered: You have better declared the unluckinesse of yonge men, then the happynesse of olde menn, whom you have not as yet taught, what waye they must folow in this love of theirs: onelye you have saide, that they must suffre them selves to bee guided by reason, and the opinion of many is, that it is unpossible for love to stand with reason.

Bembo notwithstanding saught to make an ende of reasoning, but the Dutchesse desired him to say on, and he begane thus afreshe: Too unluckie were the nature of man, if oure soule (in the whiche this so fervent coveting may lightlie arrise) should be driven to nourish it with that onelye, whiche is commune to her with beastes, and coulde not tourn it to the other noble parte, whiche is propre to her. Therfore sins it is so your pleasure, I wil not refuse to reason upon this noble matter. And bicause I know my self unworthy to talke of the most holye mysteries of love, I beseche him to leade my thought and my tunge so, that I may show this excelent Courtier how to love contrarye to the wonted maner of the commune ignorant sort. And even as from my childhode I have dedicated all my wholl lief unto him, so also now that my wordes may be answerable to the same intent, and to the prayse of him: I say therfore, that sins the nature of man in youthfull age is so much inclined to sense, it may be graunted the Courtier, while he is yong, to love sensuallye. But in case afterwarde also in hys riper yeres, he chaunse to be set on fire with this coveting of love, he ought to be good and circumspect, and heedful that he beeguyle not him self, to be lead willfullye into the wretchednesse, that in yonge men deserveth more to be pitied then blamed: and contrarywise in olde men, more to be blamed then pitied. Therfore whan an amiable countenance of a beautiful woman commeth in his sight, that is accompanied with noble condicions and honest behaviours, so that as one practised in love, he wotteth well that his hewe hath an agreement with herres, assoone as he is a ware that his eyes snatch that image and carie it to the hart, and that the soule beeginneth to beehoulde it with pleasure, and feeleth within her self the influence that stirreth her and by litle and litle setteth her in heate, and that those livelye spirites, that twinkle out throughe the eyes, put continually freshe nourishment to the fire: he ought in this beginninge to seeke a speedye remedye and to raise up reason, and with her, to fense the fortresse of his hart, and to shutt in such wise the passages against sense and appetites, that they maye entre neyther with force nor subtill practise. Thus if the flame be quenched, the jeoperdye is also quenched. But in case it continue or encrease, then must the Courtier determine (when he perceiveth he is taken) to shonn throughlye all filthinesse of commune love, and so entre into the holye way of love with the guide of reason, and first consider that the body, where that beawtye shyneth, is not the fountaine frome whens beauty springeth, but rather bicause beautie is bodilesse and (as we have said) an heavenlie shyning beame, she loseth much of her honoure whan she is coopled with

that vile subject and full of corruption, bicause the lesse she is partner therof, the more perfect she is, and cleane sundred frome it, is most perfect. And as a mann heareth not with his mouth, nor smelleth with hys eares: no more can he also in anye maner wise enjoye beawtye, nor satisfye the desyre that shee stirrith up in oure myndes, with feelynge, but wyth the sense, unto whom beawtye is the verye butt to levell at: namelye, the vertue of seeinge. Let him laye aside therefore the blinde judgemente of the sense, and injoye wyth his eyes the bryghtnesse, the comelynesse, the lovynge sparkles, laughters, gestures and all the other pleasant fournitours of beawty: especially with hearinge the sweetenesse of her voice, the tunablenesse of her woordes, the melodie of her singinge and playinge on instrumentes (in case the woman beloved be a musitien) and so shall he with most deintie foode feede the soule through the meanes of these two senses, which have litle bodelye substance in them, and be the ministers of reason, without entringe farther towarde the bodye with covetinge unto anye longinge otherwise then honest. Afterward let him obey, please, and honoure with all reverence his woman, and recken her more deere to him then his owne lief, and prefarr all her commodites and pleasures beefore his owne, and love no lesse in her the beauty of the mind, then of the bodye: therfore let him have a care not to suffer her to renn into any errour, but with lessons and good exhortations seeke alwaies to frame her to modestie, to temperance, to true honestye, and so to woorke that there maye never take place in her other then pure thoughtes and farr wide from all filthinesse of vices. And thus in sowinge of vertue in the gardein of that mind, he shall also gather the frutes of most beautifull condicions, and savour them with a marveilous good relise. And this shall be the right engendringe and imprinting of beawtye in beawtie, the whiche some houlde opinion to be the ende of love. In this maner shall oure Courtier be most acceptable to his Lady, and she will always showe her self towarde him tractable, lowlye and sweete in language, and as willinge to please him, as to be beloved of him: and the willes of them both shall be most honest and agreeable, and they consequently shall be most happy.

Here M. Morello: The engendringe (quoth he) of beawtye in beawtye aright, were the engendringe of a beawtyfull chylde in a beautifull woman, and I woulde thinke it a more manifest token a great deale that she loved her lover, if she pleased him with this, then with the sweetenesse of language that you speake of.

M. Peter Bembo laughed and said: You must not (M. Morello) passe your boundes. I may tell you, it is not a small token that a woman loveth, whan she giveth unto her lover her beawtye, which is so precious a matter: and by the wayes that be a passage to the soule (that is to say, the sight and the hearinge) sendeth the lookes of her eyes, the image of her countenance, and the voice of her woordes, that perce into the lovers hart, and give a witnes of her love.

M. Morello said: Lookes and woordes may be, and oftentimes are, false witnesses. Therfore whoso hath not a better pledge of love (in my judgement) he is in an yll assurance. And surelye I looked still that you would have made this woman of yours somewhat more courteyous and free towarde the Courtier, then my L. Julian hath made his: but (me seemeth) ye be both of the proprietie of those judges, that (to appeere wise) give sentence against their owne.

Bembo said: I am well pleased to have this woman muche more courteyous towarde my Courtier not yonge, then the L. Julians is to the yong: and that with good reason, bicause mine coveteth but honest matters, and therfore may the woman graunt him them all without blame. But my L. Julians woman that is not so assured of the modestye of the yonge man, ought to graunt him the honest matters onlye, and denye him the dishonest. Therefore more happye is mine, that hath graunted him whatsoever he requireth, then the other, that hath parte graunted and parte denyed. And bicause you may moreover the better understande, that reasonable love is more happye then sensuall, I saye unto you, that self same thinges in sensuall ought to be denyed otherwhile, and in reason-

able, graunted: bicause in the one, they be honest, and in the other dishonest. Therfore the woman to please her good lover, beside the graunting him merie countenances, familiar and secret talke, jesting, dalying, hand in hand, may also lawfullye and without blame come to kissinge: whiche in sensuall love, according to the L. Julians rules, is not lefull. For sins a kisse is a knitting together both of body and soule, it is to be feared, least the sensuall lover will be more inclined to the part of the bodye, then of the soule: but the reasonable lover woteth well, that although the mouthe be a percell of the bodye, yet is it an issue for the wordes, that be the enterpreters of the soule, and for the inwarde breth, whiche is also called the soule: and therfore hath a delite to joigne hys mouth with the womans beloved with a kysse: not to stirr him to anye unhonest desire, but bicause he feeleth that, that bonde is the openynge of an entry to the soules, whiche drawen with a coveting the one of the other, power them selves by tourn, the one into the others bodye, and be so mingled together, that ech of them hath two soules, and one alone so framed of them both ruleth (in a maner) two bodyes. Wherupon a kisse may be said to be rather a cooplinge together of the soule, then of the bodye, bicause it hath suche force in her, that it draweth her unto it, and (as it were) seperateth her from the bodye. For this do all chast lovers covett a kisse, as a cooplinge of soules together. And therfore Plato the divine lover saith, that in kissing, his soule came as farr as his lippes to depart out of the body. And bicause the separatinge of the soule from the matters of the sense and the through coopling her with matters of understanding may be beetokened by a kisse, Salomon saith in his heavenlye boke of Balattes, Oh that he would kisse me with a kisse of his mouth, to expresse the desire he had, that hys soule might be ravished through heavenly love to the behouldinge of heavenly beawtie in such maner, that cooplyng her self inwardly with it, she might forsake the body.

They stoode all herkening heedfullie to Bembos reasoninge. . . .

HENRY VIII (1491–1547)

Pastime with good company (1520?)

As though he were a student of Castiglione, instead of John Skelton's as he was, the king of England who forever changed the history of Western religion with his drive for progeny also pursued the rounded education and self-expression of the Italian humanists. In addition to writing ballads and hymns that are still sung in England today, Henry VIII (king from 1509 to 1547) wrote theological tracts, letters, and poetry, and played three musical instruments. His treatise against the Lutherans led the Medici Pope Leo X to accord Henry the title "Defender of the Faith." His best friend, Sir Thomas More, he named lord chancellor to succeed Cardinal Wolsey, whom he'd branded as a traitor for protesting against Henry's taxation and suppression of the monasteries to raise funds for wars against the French and Spanish. When Henry's wife, Catherine of Aragon (sister of Spain's Emperor Charles V), proved barren, Henry determined to marry Anne Boleyn. The pope refused to accept Henry's characterization of the marriage with Catherine as invalid, so Henry himself declared it annulled—and declared himself head of the Church of England. When More would not sign the Act of Supremacy, acknowledging Henry in that role, the King had him executed. By the time Henry had worked his bloody way through four more wives (Jane Seymour, Anne of Cleves, Catherine Howard, and Catherine Parr) the Renaissance in England, invigorated by the versatile Henry's accession to the throne, had skidded to a halt—confounded by his hedonism and bloody Reformation. It was left to his daughter by the unfortunate Anne Boleyn, Elizabeth, to restart the engine of cultural expansion and experimentation.

Pastime with good company

Pastime with good company
I love, and shall until I die.
Grutch who lust, but none deny,
So God be pleased, thus live will I.
For my pastance,
Hunt, sing, and dance,
My heart is set;
All goodly sport

For my comfort,
Who shall me let?

Youth must have some dalliance,
Of good or ill some pastance;
Company methinks then best,
All thoughts and fancies to digest.
For idleness is chief mistress
Of vices all; then who can say
But mirth and play
Is best of all?

Sheet of music

Company with honesty
Is virtue, vices to flee;
Company is good and ill,
But every man hath his free will.
The best ensue,
The worst eschew;
My mind shall be,—
Virtue to use,
Vice to refuse,
Thus shall I use me.

FRANÇOIS RABELAIS (1483–1553?)

Gargantua

and

Pantagruel (1532-34)

Humanist satire received perhaps its most ribald and outrageous expression from a French Franciscan turned Benedictine doctor of medicine. Although much about his life remains uncertain, we know that François Rabelais studied medicine at Montpellier and received his doctorate in 1537. In the mock heroic chronicles of the giants Gargantua and Pantagruel, as much influenced by the comic epic tradition as by forces that would lead to development of the modern novel, earned its remarkable and irrepressible stylist patronage from Guillaume du Bellay, Marguerite de Navarre, and Cardinal de Chatillon. Like his contemporaries Erasmus and More, he chose to stand aloof from the wars of religion raging through France by steering a middle course between the purifying principles of incipient Protestantism and his own Roman church, creating a drunkard's mask behind which he could criticize the decaying institutions of feudal Europe. While they cajoled through nuances and subtleties of refined wit, the inebriated rabelaisian narrator lambastes and castigates behind a facade of inimitable verbosity and metaphorical nonsense that makes Erasmus' Folly seem in comparison a circumspect nun. Because he made exuberant fun of the scholasticism of the Paris theologians, the monasteries, royalty, manners, and the ascetic ideal, Rabelais was attacked with equal vigor by Scaliger, St. Francis de Sales, and Calvin. In a vein similar to Skelton's *Collyn Clout* and Nashe's *The Unfortunate Traveler,* Rabelais' preface is not to nobility, to the pages of the court, nor even to the ladies, but to readers who are willing to be categorized with him as "illustrious drunkards." He suggests that inebriation is a more conducive frame of mind for appreciating the pages to follow than academic sobriety. From the piety of churchgoing women, to the naiveté of Pantagruel who sets out to "know everything," to the entrancing ego of Panurge, Rabelais is a Monty Python wittily capturing the essential Renaissance spirit at its most profane, explosive, and disrespectful. His verbal pyrotechnics cry out for a contemporary rendition by Robin Williams. Rabelais brings into question the Renaissance search for universal knowledge, the value of irrational exploration of unknown lands on one hand and reason itself on the other, and any institution, belief, or political position that interferes for even a moment with the life force. More than by any other character this Dionysian life force is represented by Panurge, one of the greatest of Renaissance fools, presaging Shakespeare's Falstaff and Cervantes' Don Quixote. Against the plodding methodologies and banal beliefs of his giant master, Panurge is vital, mercurial, protean, iconoclastic, and a law unto himself alone. His chaotic, anarchic nature represents the author's awareness of the inevitable consequences of unbridled individualism, deadly precisely for its seductiveness. Chapter 32 of *Pantagruel,* "How Pantagruel Covered a Whole Army with His Tongue and What the Author Saw in His Mouth," is a magnificent spoof of both the traditional epic motif of the descent into hell and of the discovery of new worlds. One of the tragic ironies of revolution is that the revolutionaries must by default become authorities of a new system. Rabelais' is a vision of unending revolution, in which those who upturn the system turn the same rebellious energy upon themselves.

VI. How Pantagruel met a Limousin who spoke Spurious French

One evening after supper—I cannot say exactly when—Pantagruel was strolling with some friends near the north gate of Orléans, by the road to Paris. Here he met a neat young student walking down the road. After they had bowed to one another, Pantagruel asked:

"Well, friend, where are you coming from at this time of day?"

General view, Renaissance chateau

The scholar replied:

"From the alme, inclyte and celebrate academy which is vocitated Lucetia."

"What on earth does he mean?" Pantagruel asked one of his men.

"He means: 'From Paris!'"

"So you come from Paris, eh?" Pantagruel resumed. "And how do you gentlemen students spend your time in Paris?"

The scholar replied:

"We transfretate the Sequana at the dilucul and crepuscul; we deambulate by the compites and quadrives of the metropolis; we despume the Latin verbocination and, like verisimilary amorabonds, we captate the benevolence of the omnijugal, omniform and omnigeneous muliebrine sex. At certain diecules, we invisitate upon the lupanars and, amid a venerean ecstasis, we inculcate our virilia into the most antipodean recesses of the pudenda of these supremely amicable meretricules. Then we proceed to pabulate in the mercantile taberna of the *Fir Cone*, the *Castle*, the *Magdalen and the Mule*, upon rare vervicina spatula perforaminated with petrosil. If by misfortune, there be rarity or penury of numismatical in our marsupia, or if we be exhausted of ferrugine metal, to pay, we demit our codexes and we oppignerate our vestments while we prestolate the Tabellaries who are to come from our patriotic Lares and Penates."

"What the devil is this jargon?" cried Pantagruel. "By God, I think you must be some sort of heretic."

(There was no interpreter here to tell Pantagruel that what the fellow meant was this: "We cross the Seine at dawn and dusk; we walk through the thoroughfares and crossroads of the city; we rake up Latin to speak and, as true lusty fellows, we win the favors of women. Occasionally we go to brothels and, hot with love, push our cods into the depths of these friendly little harlots' cunnies. Then, in the taverns of the *Fir Cone*, the *Castle*, the *Magdalen and the Mule*, we eat shoulders of mutton garnished with parsley; should we have little money in our purses or be out of cash, we set-

tle the bill by pledging our books and pawning our clothes while awaiting remittances from home.")

So then, Pantagruel having taxed the Limousin student with heresy:

"Nay, my Lord," he replied, "for libentissimally as soon as it illucesces a minutule fragment of the day, I demigrate to some one of those so well architected ecclesiastical abodes. There, irrorigating myself with sweet lustral water, I rattle off little slices of some missic precation of our sacrificula. Submurmurating my horary precules, I elave and absterge my anima of its nocturnal inquinations; I revere the Olympicoles; I latrially venerate the supernal astripotent; I dilige and redame my proxims; I observe the Decalogical precepts and, according to the facultatule of my vires, I do not discede from them one unguicule. However it is veriform that since Mammona does not supergurgitate anything in my loculas, I am somewhat rare and tardigrade in supererogating the eleemosynaries to these indigents who hostially queritate their stipend."

(Poor Pantagruel! He could not know the fellow meant: "For when day breaks I withdraw to a well-built church, and there, sprinkling myself with holy water, I mumble a few words of the mass. While saying my prayers, I wash and cleanse my soul of the pollution of the night; I worship the high gods; I adore the master of the spheres; I love and cherish my neighbors; I follow the Ten Commandments and, within the measure of my power, I do not deviate a nail's breadth from these teachings. It is certain that because the Goddess of Wealth puts nothing in my purse, I very rarely give alms to the beggars who seek money from door to door.")

So, hearing the Limousin's mad flow of words:

"Midden and dung!" Pantagruel roared. "What does this lunatic mean? I think he is forging some diabolic tongue and laying a spell of witchcraft upon us."

To which one of his followers replied:

"Doubtless, My Lord, this rascal is trying to

imitate the language of the Parisians. But all he is doing is to flay the Latin tongue, under the impression that he is using the noble style of Pindar. He fancies himself no end of an orator in French because he disdains our usual mode of speech."

"Is that true?" Pantagruel asked the scholar.

"Ah, My Lord!" the scholar replied, "my genius is not natively adept to what this flagitious nebulon manifests, as he excoriates the cuticle of our vernacular Gallic. On the contrary, I applicate my scruples viceversally and with the auxiliary of both sails and oars—*veles et rames*—I effortize to locupletate it with Latinicome redundance."

(All of which simply meant: "My genius is not naturally apt to grasp what this worthless vagabond says as he accuses me of flaying the skin of our French vernacular. On the contrary, I devote all my attention and make every possible effort to endow it with a Latin richness.")

"By God," Pantagruel growled, "I'll teach you how to speak. But come here, first, and tell me where you hail from?"

"The primeval origin of my aves and ataves," said the scholar, "was indigenous to the Lemovican regions where requiesces the cadaver of the hagiotate St. Martial."

(Which being interpreted meant: "My ancestors were born in the Limousin where St. Martial is buried.")

"I understand you perfectly," Pantagruel roared. "It all boils itself down to the fact that you're a Limousin trying to play the Parisian. Come here, my lad, and I'll curry your hair for you."

Seizing him by the throat:

"You're a flayer of Latin, eh? By St. John, I'll make you flay the fox—or vomit, ay, since you don't understand French. Unless I flay you alive!"

The wretched Limousin at once changed his tune.

"Eh but lawd gen'leman! Ho, Sint Martiaw, ho, cum to me help! Ooh, ho, leave me but be, and do ye not tech me!"

To which Pantagruel answered:

"Now you are speaking naturally."

So he let him go, for the unhappy Limousin had completely befouled his breeches, which were cut like a codfish tail, with a slash and not full-bottomed. At which Pantagruel cried:

"By St. Alipentin, what a civet, what a stew! The devil take this turnip-fed bumpkin. Phew! he whiffs to high heaven!"

And Pantagruel fled. But the scholar was thoroughly impressed by Pantagruel's throat-squeezing influence. He declared ever after that Pantagruel held him by the gullet. And he repented throughout his life, until some years later he died the death of Roland—from thirst! Thus the law of divine vengeance vindicated the instructions of Favorinus, the philosopher, in Aulus Gellius' *Attic Nights* where we are warned to speak the common idiom and where Octavius Augustus urges us to steer clear of unusual words even as mariners avoid reefs at sea.

XXXII. How Pantagruel Covered a Whole Army with His Tongue and What the Author saw in his Mouth

Pantagruel's progress through Dipsody was one continuous triumph, the inhabitants greeting him joyfully and surrendering on the spot. Of their own accord, the citizens would come out to meet him bearing the keys of the city he was approaching. The Almyrodes or Dirtyones alone sought to resist, replying to his heralds that they would surrender only on the best terms.

"What better terms could we have been on than sitting together with my hand on the pot and their glasses in their fists?" Pantagruel grumbled. "Oh, well, come along, let us go sock them."

So he drew up his army in battle formation, and they proceeded against the enemy. As they were passing by extensive meadowlands, suddenly they were caught by a heavy rain, which made them shiver, worry, and crowd together. Pantagruel bade their captains assure them it was nothing serious. Could he not see over the top of the clouds? He could, he did and all he made out up there was a little dew. At all events, let them draw up in close order and he would shelter them. So they formed a serried line and Pantagruel, putting out his tongue, covered them as a hen covers her chicks.

Meanwhile, I, who am simply reporting cold fact, had sought cover under a burdock leaf almost as large as the arch of the Montrible Bridge. When I saw Pantagruel's men in their snug refuge, I decided to join them. But they were too numerous; there was no room for me. After all, a foot is a foot and not thirteen inches, as the saying goes. The best I could do, therefore, was to climb on to Pantagruel's tongue and make for his mouth, which I finally reached after a two leagues' journey.

But O gods and goddesses of high heaven, what did I behold? May Jupiter confound me with his three-pronged lightning if I lie!

I walked in there as people walk into the church of St. Sophia at Constantinople. And I saw tall rocks looming up like the mountains of Scandinavia (his teeth, I fancy). . . endless green fields. . . extensive forests. . . massive cities, fortified, and no less populous than Lyons or Poitiers. . . .

The first person I met was a goodman planting cabbages. Amazed, I asked:

"What are you doing here, friend?"

"Planting cabbages!"

"Why? How?"

"Faith, sir, we can't all sport ballocks as heavy as mortars and we can't all be rich. *I* earn *my* living planting cabbages *here* and selling them in market in the city yonder."

"Good Lord, is this a new world?"

"No, no, there's nothing new about this place. Though they do say there is a world beyond here somewhere—a new world too—with a sun and a moon in it and all sorts of fine jobs for a man. Maybe so, maybe not. At any rate, *this* is the *old* world!"

"Really?" I pondered the question a moment. Then: "This city where you sell your cabbages—what do they call it?"

"It's called Aspharage; the citizens are good Christians and friendly souls. They will give you

a rousing welcome."

On his recommendation, I decided to go. On my way, I came upon a man lying in wait for pigeons.

"Good morning, friend. Those pigeons you get—where do they come from?"

"From the other world."

I concluded that when Pantagruel yawned, the pigeons, believing his throat to be a dovecote, doubtless flew in in flocks. Presently I reached the city which I found to be picturesque, strongly fortified and prosperous in appearance. At the gate, the sentries stopped me for my pass. Amazed, I cried:

"What is the matter, gentlemen? Is there an epidemic of the plague?"

"My Lord!" they groaned. "We've had so many deaths hereabouts that the tumbrils drive through incessantly."

"Hereabouts, you say? Where?"

They told me the plague was raging in Larynx and Pharynx, large and bustling cities like Rouen and Nantes. It was due, apparently, to a noxious, malodorous and infectious exhalation which had been rising out of the abyss for some time now. Within seven days, more than twenty-two hundred and seventy-six thousand and sixteen people had perished. As I thought back, reckoning the dates, I realized that it was the unsavory breath emanating from Pantagruel's belly, since he had eaten the garlic-strewn stews that illustrated King Anarchus' wedding.

Leaving hastily, I passed among the rocks of his teeth and kept walking until I got to the top of one. Here I found the fairest pleasure resort in the world, with large tennis courts, spacious galleries, sweet meadows, plentiful vines and an infinity of pretty houses, built Italian-fashion in the midst of delightful verdure. Here I spent a good four months and never fared better in my life.

Then I went down by the back teeth towards the jaws, but I was robbed by footpads in a great forest near the ears. Coming down again, I stopped at a small village the name of which I have forgotten. Here I did even better than before; I actually managed to make a little money to live on. Do you know how? By sleeping.

I am not lying: in this extraordinary place, the inhabitants hire people to sleep and pay them five or six sous a day. Heavy snorers get as much as seven and a half.

I told the senators how I had been robbed in the valley. They explained that the folk in those parts were lowlifes and by nature inclined to brigandry. From which I concluded, just as we have countries Cisalpine and Transalpine, they have countries Cidentine and Tradentine. But it is better living on this side because the air is purer.

I began to appreciate the truth of the axiom *Not half the world knows how the other half lives.* Imagine: no one has yet described this country though it includes more than twenty-five populous kingdoms, vast stretches of desert and a great arm of the sea. But I have written a voluminous book upon the subject. The title is *History of the Gorgians.* I named them so because they live in the throat of my master Pantagruel.

At last I returned via the beard, cast myself on his shoulders and thence made my way to *terra firma.* I fell right in front of him. Seeing me:

"Where the devil have you been, Alcofribas?" he asked.

"In your throat, sir."

"How long, may I ask?"

"Ever since you set out against the Almyrodes."

"That was six months ago," he said. "And how did you live?"

"Handsomely, I thank you."

"What did you find to eat?"

"Plenty."

"To drink?"

"My Lord, I ate and drank just as you did, for I took my toll of the daintiest morsels and most toothsome wines that passed through your throat."

"Indeed, indeed. . . . But where did you cack?"

"Down your throat, My Lord."

"Ha, ha, what a wag you are!" he roared. "Well, since you left, with God's help we conquered all of Dipsody. I will give you the domain of Salmagundi for your part."

"I thank you, My Lord, you reward me beyond my deserts."

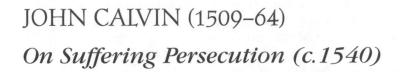

JOHN CALVIN (1509–64)

On Suffering Persecution (c.1540)

Known as "the Protestant Pope," reformer John Calvin used his legal education to compose and publish, first in Latin in 1536, then in French, an inspiring catechism he called *The Institutes of the Christian Religion.* Calvin's fundamental contribution to Protestantism was calmly and authoritatively to organize and conform increasingly chaotic doctrines and ecclesiastical disciplines—at the same time that he set new standards of precision and elegance for French prose. In Paris he had studied not only Latin, but also Greek and Hebrew; but he was banished from the city for his religious beliefs. The one-man theocracy he eventually established in Geneva in 1541 was reminiscent of Savonarola's rule in Florence. He was a harsh taskmaster, founding a religion of moral austerity that would become known as Puritanism. Calvinism today is still known for its severity and careful balancing of beliefs. His charismatic and visionary forcefulness made him enormously influential in spreading Reformed Protestantism throughout Europe. Geneva became known as "the Protestant Rome." Typically Calvin's sermons, like this one celebrating the proper Christian's ardor for suffering in the name of his religion, base their arguments on biblical texts.

The apostle says, "Let us go forth from the city after the Lord Jesus, bearing His reproach." In the first place he reminds us, altho the swords should not be drawn over us nor the fires kindled to burn us, that we can not be truly united to the Son of God while we are rooted in this world. Wherefore, a Christian, even in repose, must always have one foot lifted to march to battle, and not only so, but he must have his affections withdrawn from the world altho his body is dwelling in it. Grant that this at first sight seems to us hard, still we must be satisfied with the words of St. Paul, "We are called and appointed to suffer." As if he had said, Such is our condition as Christians; this is the road by which we must go if we would follow Christ.

Meanwhile, to solace our infirmity and mitigate the vexation and sorrow which persecution might cause us, a good reward is held forth: In suffering for the cause of God we are walking step by step after the Son of God and have Him for our guide. Were it simply said that to be Christians we must pass through all the insults of the world boldly, to meet death at all times and in whatever way God may be pleased to appoint, we might apparently have some pretext for replying, It is a strange road to go at a peradventure. But when we are commanded to follow the Lord Jesus, His guidance is too good and honorable to be refused.

Are we so delicate as to be unwilling to endure anything? Then we must renounce the grace of God by which He has called us to the hope of salvation. For there are two things which can not be separated—to be members of Christ, and to be tried by many afflictions. We certainly ought to prize such a conformity to the Son of God much more than we do. It is true that in the world's judgment there is disgrace in suffering for the Gospel. But since we know that unbelievers are blind, ought we not to have better eyes than they? It is ignominy to suffer from those who occupy the seat of justice, but St. Paul shows us by his example that we have to glory in scourgings for Jesus Christ, as marks by which God recognizes us and avows us for His own. And we know what St. Luke narrates of Peter and John; namely, that they rejoiced to have been "counted worthy to suffer infamy and reproach for the name of the Lord Jesus."

Ignominy and dignity are two opposites: so says the world which, being infatuated, judges against all reason, and in this way converts the glory of God into dishonor. But, on our part, let us not refuse to be vilified as concerns the world, in order to be honored before God and His angels. We see what pains the ambitious take to receive the commands of a king, and what a boast they make of it. The Son of God presents His commands to us, and every one stands back! Tell me, pray, whether in so doing are we worthy of having anything in common with Him? There is nothing here to attract our sensual nature, but such, notwithstanding, are the true escutcheons of nobility in the heavens. Imprisonment, exile, evil report, imply in men's imagination whatever is to be vituperated; but what hinders us from viewing things as God judges and declares them, save our unbelief? Wherefore let the name of the Son of God have all the weight with us which it deserves, that we may learn to count it honor when He stamps His marks upon us. If we act otherwise our ingratitude is insupportable.

Were God to deal with us according to our deserts, would He not have just cause to chastise us daily in a thousand ways? Nay, more, a hundred thousand deaths would not suffice for a small portion of our misdeeds! Now, if in His infinite goodness He puts all our faults under His foot and abolishes them, and, instead of punishing us according to our demerit, devises an admirable means to convert our afflictions into honor and a special privilege, inasmuch as through them we are taken into partnership with His Son, must it not be said, when we disdain such a happy state, that we have indeed made little progress in Christian doctrine?

It were easy indeed for God to crown us at once without requiring us to sustain any combats; but as it is His pleasure that until the end of the world Christ shall reign in the midst of His enemies, so it is also His pleasure that we, being placed in the midst of them, shall suffer their oppression and violence till He deliver us. I know, indeed, that the flesh kicks when it is to be brought to this point, but still the will of God must have the mastery. If we feel some repugnance in ourselves it need not surprise us; for it is only too natural for us to shun the cross. Still let us not fail to surmount it, knowing that God accepts our obedience, provided we bring all our feelings and wishes into captivity and make them subject to Him.

In ancient times vast numbers of people, to obtain a simple crown of leaves, refused no toil, no pain, no trouble; nay, it even cost them nothing to die, and yet every one of them fought for a peradventure, not knowing whether he was to gain or lose the prize. God holds forth to us the immortal crown by which we may become partakers of His glory. He does not mean us to fight a haphazard, but all of us have a promise of the prize for which we strive. Have we any cause, then, to decline the struggle? Do we think it has been said in vain, "If we die with Jesus Christ we shall also live with him?" Our triumph is prepared, and yet we do all we can to shun the combat. . . .

NICOLAUS COPERNICUS (1473–1543)

De revolutionibus orbium coelestium

On the Revolutions of the Heavenly Spheres (1536; 1543)

Although not as revolutionary as it was conservative, Nicolaus Copernicus' deathbed-published treatise was controversial in its own time for abandoning the traditionally accepted Ptolemaic astronomy and insisting that the sun, not the earth, is the center of the universe. And the earth is round! Like so many "new ideas" of the Renaissance, this one was a revival of a Greek source. Aristarchus of Samos had proposed the same system, but had been ignored by his fellow Alexandrians and repressed by the Roman Church. Retaining the Neoplatonic approach to reasoning based upon "ideals" rather than solely upon observed "realities," the Polish mathematician simply modernized Aristarchus and transferred Ptolemy's geocentric "epicycles and deferents" to the new heliocentric model. Yet the philosophical ramifications of Copernican theory were enormous. The earth was now one of several planets. Human beings, for all their unbounded energies and ambitions, may continue to be the measurers of all things; but they were no longer the center. At the same time that this humbled, it liberated. Needless to say, the fundamentalists of his time, both Protestants and Catholics, were unanimous in their condemnation of Copernicus. In his prefatory letter to Pope Paul III, the author writes: "I can well appreciate, Holy Father, that as soon as certain people realise that in these books which I have written about the Revolutions of the spheres of the universe I attribute certain motions to the globe of the Earth, they will at once clamour for me to be hooted off the stage with such an opinion." Copernicus left the stage before realizing that he had forever changed the theater of astronomy.

BOOK ONE

(Among the many and various pursuits in learning and the arts on which the genius of man is nourished, I believe that we should embrace especially and pursue with the great-est zeal those which are concerned with the most noble subjects and those which are best worth knowing. Such are those which deal with the divine revolutions of the universe, with the course of the stars, with their sizes, distances, rising and setting, and the causes of the other phenomena of the heaven, and lastly which display the whole pattern of them. What is nobler than the heaven, the heaven which contains all noble things? The very names proclaim the fact: Heaven, Universe. The latter suggests the undefiled and elegant, the former the exquisitely carved. Many philosophers on account of its great splendour have called it the visible god. Equally if the importance of the arts is reckoned by the subject matter with which they deal, the foremost among them by far is that which some call astronomy, others astrology, but many of the ancients call the consummation of mathematics. Chief of the liberal arts, the most fitting for a free man, it is supported by almost all the branches of mathematics. Arithmetic, geometry, optics, surveying, mechanics, and every other branch, all look towards it. While it is the function of all polite learning to turn away the mind of man from vice and direct it towards higher things, this art, besides an astonishing joy of the spirit, can perform that part more abundantly. For who while intent upon things which he sees to be established in the best possible arrangement and directed by divine ordinance would not by assiduous contemplation of them and a certain familiarity with them be impelled towards the best, and would not feel wonder for the Maker of all, in Whom is all happiness and every good thing? For would it not have been in vain for the divine psalmist to say that he delighted in the creations of God and in the works of His hands if we were not led by these means as if by some conveyance to the contemplation of the highest good? Further, how much usefulness and ornament it confers on the state [to pass over its innumerable benefits to private persons] is very well remarked by Plato who in the seventh book of the *Laws* considers that it should be cultivated most of all so that by the ordering of the days with its aid the assignment of the seasons for ceremonies and sacrifices to their proper months and years may make the state lively and vigilant; and if anyone, says he, were to deny that this art is essential for a man who is to understand any of the highest parts of learning, his thinking is very foolish. He believes that anyone is very far from being able to become or be called divine if he has not the essential knowledge of the Sun or the Moon or the other stars. Furthermore this science, divine rather than human, which enquires about the loftiest subjects, does not lack difficulties, especially since we see that many of those who have attempted to deal with them have disagreed about its principles and assumptions, which the Greeks call 'hypotheses', and accordingly have not based their work on the same systems. Moreover the courses of the planets and the revolutions of the stars could not be fixed by a reliable calculation and be brought fully within our understanding except with the lapse of time and with many past observations by which it was passed to posterity, so to speak, from hand to hand. For although Claudius Ptolemy of Alexandria, who far surpasses the others by his wonderful skill and accuracy, with observations over forty years and more almost perfected this art, so that there seemed to be nothing still lacking which he had not treated, yet we see that many points do not agree with what should follow from his teaching, certain other motions having been discovered which were not yet known to him. Hence Plutarch also, when he discusses the changing solar year, says 'so far the motion of the stars has defeated the skill of the mathematicians'. For to take the year itself as my example, I think it is evident how the opinions about it have always varied, to such an extent that many have despaired of being able to find a reliable system for it. Similarly I shall try in the cases of the other stars, with God's help, without which we can do nothing, to investigate these things more widely, since we have more aids to support our system in proportion to the greater interval of time by which the founders of this art have preceded us; and we may compare with what they found our own fresh findings. I confess that my account will differ from that of my predecessors in many other ways besides, though I depend on them, as they first opened the way to the investigation of these matters.)

CHAPTER I. THAT THE UNIVERSE IS SPHERICAL

First we must remark that the universe is globe-shaped, either because that is the most perfect shape of all, needing no joint, an integral whole; or because that is the most capacious of shapes, which is most fitting because it is to contain and preserve all things; or because the most finished parts of the universe, I mean the Sun, Moon and stars, are observed to have that shape, or because everything tends to take on this shape, which is evident in drops of water and other liquid bodies, when they take on their natural shape. There should therefore be no doubt that this shape is assigned to the heavenly bodies.

CHAPTER II. THAT THE EARTH ALSO IS SPHERICAL

The Earth also is globe-shaped, because every part of it tends towards its centre. Although it is not immediately apparent that it is a perfect sphere, because the mountains project so far and the valleys are so deep, they produce very little variation in the complete roundness of the Earth. That is evident from the fact that as one moves northward from any point that pole of the diurnal rotation rises little by little, while the other pole on the contrary sinks to the same extent, and several stars round the North Pole seem not to set, while some in the South no longer rise. Thus Italy does not see Canopus, which is visible in Egypt; and Egypt sees the last star of the River (Eridanus), which our region in a colder zone does not know. On the other hand to people going south the two former rise, while those which are high for us sink. Furthermore, the angles of inclination of the poles are always in the same ratio to the distances traversed on the Earth, which does not happen except on a spherical shape. Hence it is evident that the Earth also is bounded by the poles, and is therefore globe-shaped. In addition, the inhabitants of the Orient do not

observe evening eclipses of the Sun and Moon, nor people living in the west morning ones; but those in between are seen by eastern people later and by western people earlier. That the waters also tend to the same shape is realised by seafarers, because land which is not in view from a ship is often sighted from the top of the mast. But on the other hand if some bright light is put on top of the mast, as the vessel gets further from the land those who remain on shore see it sink little by little until finally it disappears as if it had set. Also it is known that the waters, being fluid by nature, always seek a lower level, exactly as Earth does, and do not tend to flow further in from the shore than the curvature of the land allows. It is accepted that this is why the land is so much higher, wherever it rises out of the Ocean.

CHAPTER III. HOW THE EARTH WITH ITS WATER MAKES UP A SINGLE GLOBE

Hence the Ocean which surrounds the Earth pours out its seas far and wide and fills the deeper hollows. Thus there had to be less water than Earth, so that the water should not wholly swallow up the land, as both of them by their weight strive towards the same centre, but should leave some parts of the Earth for the well-being of living creatures, as well as all the islands which are visible here and there. Indeed, what is a continent, or the whole land mass, but an island larger than the rest? We should not listen to certain of the Peripatetics who have declared that the total amount of water was ten times greater than the whole of the Earth. The reason they gave was that in the transmutation of the elements one part of Earth changed into ten of water, accepting a guess, and they say that the Earth projects to a certain extent, because its displacement is not everywhere in proportion to its weight, as it is full of cavities, and that the centre of gravity is not the same as the geometrical centre. But they are mistaken from ignorance of geometry, not knowing that the water cannot be even seven times more, and still allow some part of the Earth to be dry, unless the Earth were completely removed from the centre of gravity and made way for the water, as if the water were heavier than itself. For spheres are (in volume) as the third power of their own diameters. Therefore if for seven parts of water there were one of Earth, its diameter could not be greater than the distance from the centre to the circumference of the water: much less can the water be ten times more. It follows that there is no difference between the centre of gravity of the Earth and its geometrical centre. Hence we may conclude that the convexity of the Earth as it spreads out from the shore does not swell indefinitely with distance, otherwise it would keep the sea water out as far as possible, and would not in some way allow inland seas, and such vast inlets, to break in.

Further, from the shore of the ocean the depth of the abyss would increase continuously, and because of that no island, nor rock, nor anything of the nature of land would be encountered by seafarers as they voyaged onward. Yet it is known that between the Egyptian Sea and the Arabian Gulf there is a part not two miles wide in the middle of the land mass. On the other hand Ptolemy in his *Cosmography* extends the habitable Earth up to the middle circle (of longitude) of the Earth, leaving unknown territory in between, where recent discovery has added Cathay and extensive regions up to sixty degrees of longitude, so

that now the inhabited Earth is greater in longitude than the ocean which remains. This will be more evident if we add the islands discovered in our own time under the rulers of Spain and Portugal, and especially America, named after its discoverer the admiral, which because its size is still undiscovered is thought to be another land mass, besides many other previously unknown islands, making us less surprised at the existence of the Antipodes or Antichthones. For geometrical reasoning forces us to accept that America itself because of its situation is diametrically opposite to the India of the Ganges. All this seems to me to show that Earth and water both tend towards the same centre of gravity, which is no different from the geometrical centre of the Earth, the clefts in which, as it is heavier, are filled with water, and therefore the quantity of water is limited in comparison with the Earth, although on the surface there may appear to be more of the water. Indeed the Earth with the waters flowing round it must have the shape which its own shadow shows; for its perfectly circular outline produces the eclipses of the Moon. So the Earth is not flat, as Empedocles and Anaximenes believed; nor in the shape of a drum, as did Leucippus; nor in the shape of a bowl, as did Heraclitus; nor in any way hollow, as did Democritus. Nor again is it cylindrical, as Anaximander believed; nor does its under side go down in an indefinitely thick root, as did Xenophanes; but it is of perfect roundness, as the Philosophers are aware. . . .

ANDREAS VESALIUS (1514–64)

DE HUMANI CORPORIS FABRICA

On the workings of the human body (1543)

Biology can hardly be thought of as a science before the Flemish physician Vesalius, the first "modern" to rely almost entirely on direct observation and analysis, through dissection of human cadavers, and to describe fully the anatomy and physiology of the human body. The *Fabrica* presents "the organs and their action," and the nervous system that directs them, in a graphic and systematic way. What Leonardo da Vinci dared to undertake in the service of his art, and failed to publish, Vesalius' seven books brought to fruition and promulgated in the service of truth. At the same time that the *Fabrica* provides the foundation for modern comparative anatomy, the philosophical Latin of its language betrays its own deep roots in the neo-Aristotelian approach of medieval scholasticism. But Vesalius, ironically, employed this formal language to overturn the accepted wisdom of Galen, the classical imperial physician whose anatomical studies had until Vesalius been the unimpeachable authority. Vesalius' dissections proved that Galen had based his writing on the dissection not of human cadavers, but of animals. The woodcuts illustrating Vesalius' work were prepared by him personally in Titian's studio in Venice. The year after the publication of this revolutionary work, its author, at the age of twenty-eight, was appointed court physician to Emperor Charles V.

ON THE HUMAN BRAIN

Book VII, Chapter I . . . Short Enumeration of the Functions and the Parts of the Brain

The brain, like the senses, and also like volitional movement, is made for the Reigning Soul (*Princeps Anima*)

There is in the substance of the heart the power of the *vital spirit*. In the liver is the faculty of the *natural spirit*. The liver produces thick dark blood and from that the natural spirit; while the heart produces [thin light] blood which impetuously rushes through the body with the vital spirit, from which the inner organs draw their proper substances, by channels appropriate to all the bodily parts. So too the brain—containing a matter appropriate to its own function—produces, at the proper places and by those instruments which serve its function, the finest and subtlest of all [the three spirits, namely] the *animal spirit*. This it uses partly for the divine operations of the Reigning Soul, partly however it distributes it continuously to the organs of sense and motion through the nerves, as through little tubes. These organs are thus never without the spirit which is the chief author of their function, just as liver and heart supply all parts with their own proper substances (so long as man is in good health), though not always in identical amounts and quality.

We have shown in Book IV that the nerves originate in the brain. Nerves are to the brain as aorta [and its branches] to the heart, and vena cava [and its branches] to the liver. They deliver the spirit, which the brain has prepared, to those instruments to which it is to be conveyed. They are diligent servants and messengers of the brain. The vital spirit [from the aorta] supplies matter for the animal spirit [of the brain], for it inundates by numerous arteries the two membranes of the brain with things that it carries and further with that air which, as we have explained, is drawn to the brain by breathing.

[This air comes] through the little holes [= foramina of cribriform plate] pertaining to the organ of smell of the eighth cranial bone, and also through passages in the skull toward the palate [= imaginary passages from pituitary body]. Moreover, the air which we inhale is passed through very narrow, very curved, and very winding vessels in the membranes of the brain. It is refined by this arduous passage and, being so prepared, is sent up the brain where it finds entrance, penetrating into the right, left, and middle [= third] ventricles. Thus the vital spirit, which abounds in all the vessels or ducts of the cerebral membranes, is also very plentiful in the ventricles. [Thither it comes] from the main branches of the arteries, perforating the skull by a long and tortuous canal [= carotid canal] lateral to the pituitary—contrary to the opinion of Galen in his *De venarum arteriarumque dissectione.*

From these arteries—which Galen regarded as forming a plaited network—there go branches [= anterior chorioidal] of considerable size, supported by the tenuis, to the lowest parts of the ventricles, which pass along the whole expanse of those cavities. But apart from these arteries, and in the fourth sinus of the dura [= straight sinus], a vessel [= great cerebral = great vein of Galen] passes under the 'tortoisc' [= fornix] which is by us named the 'vault' (*cameratum*). This vessel goes on to the front of the brain through the cavity common to the right and left ventricles, that is the third ventricle. It there divides into two; one spreads out into the right ventricle, the other into the left [= internal cerebral veins]. Both mingle with the arteries of that region to form a plexus which takes its name from its resemblance to the outer coat of the foetus [= chorioid].

From the air which has entered the brain, and from that vital spirit which, by its devious course, becomes progressively more assimilated in the ventricles to the action of the brain, the animal spirit is elaborated by the cerebral power (*virtus*). We believe that this power depends on the opportune balancing of the elements of the brain substance.

Further, in the third ventricle a portion of this animal spirit is carried, through a contracted passage between the nates and testes, into that ventricle [= fourth ventricle] which is formed partly by the cavity of the cerebellum and partly by that of the dorsal marrow. From this a portion of the animal spirit is distributed to the dorsal marrow and thus to the nerves which spring therefrom. But from the other ventricles, so we believe, the spirit is distributed into the nerves which arise in their proximity [= cranial nerves] and so into the organs of sensation and voluntary motion.

We are not over-anxious to decide whether the power of the brain in this ultra-refined spirit is carried to the [peripheral] parts through passages in the nerves—as is the vital spirit through the arteries—or along the surface of the nerves, like [rays of] light along a column, or simply through the continuity of the nerves.

I can in some degree follow the brain's functions in dissections of living animals, with sufficient probability and truth, but I am unable to understand how the brain can perform its office of imagining, meditating, thinking, and remembering, or, following various doctrines, however, you may wish to divide or enumerate the powers of the Reigning Soul. . . .

How the Head is to be prepared for the Inspection of the Brain

. . . Heads of beheaded men are the most suitable since they can be obtained immediately after execution with the friendly help of judges and prefects. . . .

How the Skull has to be opened for Dissection of the Brain

Whatever way the head has fallen, its bone must be divided with the saw. Begin the dissection with the razor or knife in the orbital region, a thumb's breadth above the eyebrows; pass thence through the temples backward to the most prominent part of the occiput; return thence through the temples to the forehead again. This line having been drawn with a fine saw, such as is used for amputating gangrenous limbs, or by ivory-comb makers, divide the skull along that line, taking great care that the saw go no deeper than the bone. It will help here that the ears remain and the hair be not shorn, the better for you and your partner to steady the head with your hands. When you have thus cut round the skull, probe with a blunt knife along the section lest any of the bone remain undivided, and sever that also with the saw.

Lest you raise or lower the cut unduly, and if you distrust yourself without another's aid (though it is far easier [with such help] thus) you may tie a dyed cord tightly round the naked skull so that it leaves a line of colour to guide the saw, as do those who divide beams into laths. It is best to do this after you have made the circular cut in the skin, for that cannot guide your hand, though the head be firmly held, because the cut edges of skin gape apart from the line of incision.

After the skull has been thus divided, if you have the head free of neck and lower jaw, you can put it with its base on the table with a stone or the like on either side to prevent sliding. If the head be still attached to the body, then place square stones, or wood blocks, under the neck and occiput that the head rise up to you, being bent this way or that as though supported on a base. Insert the back of a strong knife into the cleft of the skull, near the forehead. When this has been eased by movement to and fro, separate the edges of the cut at one point. Do the same at the occiput and on the temples until you think the skull-cap freed from the dura. Then, seizing the hair on the top of the head, the bone will follow.

IGNATIUS OF LOYOLA (1491–1556)

Spiritual Exercises (1548)

Discipline of mind, body, and soul is the central rule of the Society of Jesus, founded by Ignatius of Loyola in 1534. This Spanish theologian and former soldier was one of most influential figures in the Catholic Counter-Reformation, which had begun in earnest when Pope Paul III opened the

Council of Trent in 1545. Ignatius was a perfectionist, an idealist, and also a realistic thinker who trained his Jesuits to emulate the rigors of his vision in their daily habits. His early life was quite worldly, filled with duels and romance. But after being wounded at Pampeluna, Ignatius occupied his convalescence with reading "holy lives," of Christ and the saints. In his characteristic chivalric fashion, he determined to make a pilgrimage to Jerusalem. En route, he was forced by various fortuitous circumstances to delay ten months at the town of Manresa (1522–23). There he conceived the basic outline of his "spiritual exercises." All was focused, from a military perspective, on the actualization of the Church's teachings, "for the greater glory of God," and on the defense of the "standard of Christ" against the "standard of Satan." His *Spiritual Exercises*, aimed at purifying the soul for apostolic missionary work, are still in use at Jesuit high schools throughout the world. His goal was to instill in the reader the pattern for creating a life of active engagement with the world from the perspective of contemplation, of sanctity supported by prayer. Ignatius lived in Rome for the last sixteen years of his life, establishing the first Jesuit College there in 1540. Loyalty to his insistence that the Jesuit aspirant arm himself with knowledge—of philosophy, many languages, mathematics, and music—makes the Society of Jesus the most persistent bastion of Renaissance humanistic education to this day. Ignatius was declared a saint in 1622.

PURPOSE OF THE EXERCISES

The purpose of these Exercises is to help the exercitant to conquer himself, and to regulate his life so that he will not be influenced in his decisions by any inordinate attachment.

PRESUPPOSITION

In order that the one who gives these Exercises and he who makes them may be of more assistance and profit to each other, they should begin with the presupposition that every good Christian ought to be more willing to give a good interpretation to the statement of another than to condemn it as false. If he cannot give a good interpretation to this statement, he should ask the other how he understands it, and if he is in error, he should correct him with charity. If this is not sufficient, he should seek every suit-able means of correcting his understanding so that he may be saved from error.

PRINCIPLE AND FOUNDATION

Man is created to praise, reverence, and serve God our Lord, and by this means to save his soul. All other things on the face of the earth are created for man to help him fulfill the end for which he is created. From this it follows that man is to use these things to the extent that they will help him to attain his end. Likewise, he must rid himself of them in so far as they prevent him from attaining it.

Therefore we must make ourselves indifferent to all created things, in so far as it is left to the choice of our free will and is not forbidden. Acting accordingly, for our part, we should not prefer health to sickness, riches to poverty, honor to dishonor, a long life to a short one, and so in all things we should desire and choose only those things which will best help us attain the end for which we are created.

PARTICULAR EXAMINATION OF CONSCIENCE TO BE MADE EVERY DAY

This Exercise is performed at three different times, and there are two examinations to be made.

The first time As soon as he arises in the morning the exercitant should resolve to guard himself carefully against the particular sin or defect which he wishes to correct or amend.

The second time After the noon meal he should ask God our Lord for what he desires, namely, the grace to remember how many times he has fallen into the particular sin or defect, and to correct himself in the future. Following this he should make the first examination demanding an account of his soul regarding that particular matter which he proposed for himself and which he desires to correct and amend. He should review each hour of the time elapsed from the moment of rising to the moment of this examination, and he should make note on the first line of the following diagram, a mark for each time that he has fallen into the particular sin or defect. He should then renew his resolution to improve himself until the time of the second examination that he will make.

The third time After the evening meal he will make a second examination, reviewing each hour from the first examination to this second one, and on to the second line of the same diagram he will again make a mark for each time that he has fallen into the particular sin or defect.

Four Additional Directions

The following directions will help to remove more quickly the particular sin or defect.

1. Each time that one falls into the particular sin or defect, he should place his hand on his breast, repenting that he has fallen. This can be done even in the presence of many people without their noticing it.
2. Since the first line of the diagram represents the first examination, and the second line, the second examination, at night the exercitant should observe whether there is an improvement from the first line to the second, that is, from the first examination to the second.
3. He should compare the second day with the first, that is to say, two examinations of the present day with the two examinations of the preceding day, and see if there is a daily improvement.
4. He should also compare one week with another and see if there is a greater improvement during the present week than in the past week. It may be noted that the first large G denotes Sunday. The second is smaller and stands for Monday, the third, for Tuesday, and so forth.

GENERAL EXAMINATION OF CONSCIENCE

To help the exercitant purify himself and make better confessions.

I presuppose that I have three kinds of thoughts in my mind. The first is a thought which is my own and which comes solely from my own liberty and will; the other two come from without, the one from the good spirit and the other from the evil one.

Thoughts There are two ways of gaining merit from an evil thought which comes from without:

1. The thought comes to me to commit a mortal sin. I resist the thought immediately and it is conquered.
2. When the same evil thought comes to me and I resist it, and it returns again and

again, but I continue to resist it until it is vanquished. This second way is much more meritorious than the first.

One is guilty of venial sin if the same thought of committing mortal sin comes to him and he gives it some attention or takes some sensual pleasure in it, or when there is some negligence in rejecting it.

There are two ways of sinning mortally
The first exists when one consents to an evil thought with the intention of carrying it out later, or with the intention of doing so if he could.

The second way of sinning mortally is to put the thought of the sin into action. This is a more grievous sin for three reasons:

1. Because of the greater length of time.
2. Because of the greater intensity.
3. Because of the greater injury done to both persons.

BARTOLOMÉ DE LAS CASAS (1474–1566)

In Defense of the Indians (1552)

This document, remarkable for its accusations of pillage and genocide in the "West Indies" and for its ineffectiveness in stemming the gold lust of the conquistadors, was written by the first priest to be ordained in the Americas. He takes up his pen against Emperor Charles' historian Ginés Sepúlveda's *On the Just Causes of War* (1542), which rationalized the Spanish expeditions. Prince Philip, to whom the *Defense* is addressed, convinced his father to convene a debate between Sepúlveda and de las Casas before the Council of the Indies. In 1551, after listening to both sides, the council of jurists and theologians voted that the *conquistas* were "evil, unlawful, and unjust," and should be outlawed. By that time, of course, most of the damage done was irreversible. At the same time that this Dominican missionary and bishop of Chiapa ardently put his efforts to converting native Americans to Catholicism, his record of their character and culture provides an invaluable anthropological perspective. His indictment of Spanish policy provoked, in turn, Bernal Díaz del Castillo's defense of Hernán Cortés, *The True History of the Conquest of Mexico*.

CHAPTER ONE

They who teach, either in word or in writing, that the natives of the New World, whom we commonly call Indians, ought to be conquered and subjugated by war before the gospel is proclaimed and preached to them so that, after they have finally been subjugated, they may be instructed and hear the word of God, make two disgraceful mistakes. First, in connection with divine and human law they abuse God's words

World map painted by order of Henry II. Detail: South America (Pierre Desceliers), in the Bibliotheque Nationale, Paris

and do violence to the Scriptures, to papal decrees, and to the teaching handed down from the holy fathers. And they go wrong again by quoting histories that are nothing but sheer fables and shameless nonsense. By means of these, men who are totally hostile to the poor Indians and who are their utterly deceitful enemies betray them. Second, they mistake the meaning of the decree or bull of the Supreme Pontiff Alexander VI, whose words they corrupt and twist in support of their opinions, as will be clear from all that follows.

Their error and ignorance are also convincingly substantiated by the fact that they draw conclusions on matters which concern a countless number of men and vast areas of extensive provinces. Since they do not fully understand all these things, it is the height of effrontery and rashness for them to attribute publicly to the Indians the gravest failings both of nature and conduct, condemning *en masse* so many thousands of people, while, as a matter of fact, the greater number of them are free from these faults. All this drags innumerable souls to ruin and blocks the service of spreading the Christian religion by closing the eyes of those who, crazed by blind ambition, bend all their energies of mind and body to the one purpose of gaining wealth, power, honors, and dignities. For the sake of these things they kill and destroy with inhuman cruelty people who are completely innocent, meek, harmless, temperate, and quite ready and willing to receive and embrace the word of God.

Who is there possessed of only a sound mind, not to say a little knowledge of theology, who has dared to pronounce a judgment and opinion so un-Christian that it spawns so many cruel wars, so many massacres, so many bereavements, and so many deplorable evils?

Do we not have Christ's words: "See that you never despise any of these little ones," "Alas for the man who provides obstacles," "He who is not with me is against me; and he who does not gather with me scatters," and "Each day has trouble enough of its own"? Who is so godless that he would want to incite men who are savage, ambitious, proud, greedy, uncontrolled, and everlastingly lazy to pillage their brothers and destroy their souls as well as their possessions, even though war is never lawful except when it is waged because of unavoidable necessity?

And so what man of sound mind will approve a war against men who are harmless, ignorant, gentle, temperate, unarmed, and destitute of every human defense? For the results of such a war are very surely the loss of the souls of that people who perish without knowing God and without the support of the sacraments, and, for the survivors, hatred and loathing of the Christian religion. Hence the purpose God intends, and for the attainment of which he suffered so much, may be frustrated by the evil and cruelty that our men wreak on them with inhuman barbarity. What will these people think of Christ, the true God of the Christians, when they see Christians venting their rage against them with so many massacres, so much bloodshed without any just cause, at any rate without any just cause that they know of (nor can one even be imagined), and without any fault committed on their [the Indians] part against the Christians?

What good can come from these military campaigns that would, in the eyes of God, who evaluates all things with unutterable love, compensate for so many evils, so many injuries, and so many unaccustomed misfortunes? Furthermore, how will that nation love us, how will they become our friends (which is necessary if they are to accept our religion), when children see themselves deprived of parents, wives of husbands, and fathers of children and friends? When they see those they love wounded, imprisoned, plundered, and reduced from an immense number to a few? When they see their rulers stripped of their authority, crushed, and afflicted with a wretched slavery? All these things flow necessarily from war. Who is there who would want the gospel preached to himself in such a fashion? Does not this negative precept apply to all men in general: "See that you do not do to another what you would not have done to you by another"? And the same for the affirmative command: "So always treat others as you would like them to treat you." This is something that every man knows, grasps, and understands by the natural light that has been imparted to our minds.

It is obvious from all this that they who teach that these gentlest of sheep must be tamed by ravening wolves in a savage war before they are to be fed with the word of God are wrong about matters that are totally clear and are opposed to the natural law. Moreover, they commit an ungodly error when they say that these wars are just if they are waged as they should be. They mean, I suppose, if they are waged with restraint, by killing only those who have to be killed in order to subjugate the rest. It is as if they held all the peoples of the New World shut up in cages or slave pens and would want to cut off as many human heads as are usually sold each day in the markets for the feeding and nourishment of the populace. (I suggest this as a comparison.) But if they would consider that war and the massacre of this timid race has lasted, not for one day or a hundred days, but for ten or twenty years, to the incredible harm of the natives; that, as they wander about, hidden and scattered through woods and forests, unarmed, naked, deprived of every human help, they are slaughtered by the Spaniards; that, stripped of their wealth and wretched, they are driven from their homes, stunned and frightened by the unbelievable terror with which their oppressors have filled them through the monstrous crimes they have committed. If those who say such things would only consider that the hearts of this unfortunate people are so shattered with fear that they want to hurl themselves headlong into the deepest caverns of the earth to escape the clutches of these plunderers, I have no doubt that they would say things that are more temperate and more wise.

To come to the point, then, this *Defense* will contain two main topics. First, I shall show that the Reverend Doctor Sepúlveda, together with his followers, is wrong in law in everything he alleges against the Indians. While doing this, I shall provide an answer to all his arguments and to the authorities he violently distorts. Second, I shall show how wrong they are in fact, with great harm to their own souls. For the Creator of every being has not so despised these peoples of the New World that he willed them to lack reason and made them like brute animals, so that they should be called barbarians, savages, wild men, and brutes, as they [Sepúlveda et al.] think or imagine. On the contrary, they [the Indians] are of such gentleness and decency that they are, more than the other nations of the entire world, supremely fitted and prepared to abandon the worship of idols and to accept, province by province and people by people, the word of God and the preaching of the truth.

As to the first point, which we have discussed elsewhere at greater length and in general against all those infected with errors of this kind about the question of unbelievers; for now, as a sort of assault on the first argument for Sepúlveda's position, we should recognize that there are four kinds of barbarians, according to the Philosopher in Books 1 and 3 of the *Politics* and in Book 7 of the *Ethics,* and according to Saint Thomas and other doctors in various places.

First, barbarian in the loose and broad sense of the word means any cruel, inhuman, wild, and merciless man acting against human reason out of anger or native disposition, so that, putting aside decency, meekness, and humane moderation, he becomes hard, severe, quarrelsome, unbearable, cruel, and plunges blindly into crimes that only the wildest beasts of the forest would commit. Speaking of this kind of barbarian, the Philosopher says in the *Politics* that just as the man who obeys right reason and excellent laws is superior to all the animals, so too, if he leaves the path of right reason and law, he is the wickedest, worst, and most inhuman of all animals.

Boethius also speaks of these when he refers to the courtiers of the tyrant Theodoric as barbarians because of their savage and insatiable greed. "How often," he asks, "have I protected, by putting my authority in danger, such poor wretches as the unpunished greed of the barbarians abused with uncounted false accusations?"

The Second Book of Maccabees also mentions this kind of barbarian. For when Nicanor, a ruthless and savage despot, wanted to join battle with Judas Maccabaeus in Samaria on the Sabbath, some of the Jews who were with him said to him: "You must not massacre them in such a savage, barbarous way," that is, savagely and inhumanly. Both the Greeks and the Latins, and any others who live even in the most highly developed states, can be called barbarians if, by the savagery of their behavior, they are anything like the Scythians, whose country was regarded as singularly barbaric, as Isidore notes, because of the savage and inhuman practices of this race.

Indeed, our Spaniards are not unacquainted with a number of these practices. On the contrary, in the absolutely inhuman things they have done to those nations they have surpassed all other barbarians.

To this class of barbarian belong all those who, aroused by anger, hatred, or some other strong feeling, violently defend something, completely forgetful of reason and virtue. Gregory speaks of this in his *Letters,* and Gratian, when speaking of the uprising that occurred at Milan over the election of one of the bishops, says: "Many of the Milanese, driven by barbaric fury, come together." In his *Ethics,* the Philosopher calls this type of barbarian brutish when he writes: "It is found chiefly among barbarians, but some brutish qualities are also produced by disease or deformity; and we also call by this evil name those men who go beyond all ordinary standards by reason of vice."

WILLIAM ROPER (1496–1578)

The Life of Sir Thomas More (1553)

No Renaissance biography gives greater access to the personality of its subject than William Roper's "life" of his beloved father-in-law. More's public and literary accomplishments are barely mentioned in this moving account of the man's generosity of spirit and nobility in the face of indictment, trial, and death. Roper himself progressed from employee of More, to husband of More's beloved daughter Margaret, to best friend and intimate confidant of the lord chancellor whose refusal to condone Henry VIII's divorce led him to the tower and the block. Roper waited nearly twenty years after More's death, until Queen Mary had restored England to Catholicism, before publishing his tribute. Roper's *Life* gives us the Thomas More later portrayed in Robert Bolt's *A Man for All Seasons,* the man whose conscience molds him into a moral hero who, reluctantly because of his joie de vivre and close friendship with Henry, would stand against the king himself trusting in the integrity of history to recognize the integrity of his individual decision.

Not long after came there to him the Lord Chancellor, the Dukes of Norfolk and Suffolk, with Master Secretary, and certain other of the privy council—at two several times—by all policies possible procuring him either precisely to confess the Supremacy or precisely to deny it. Whereunto as appeareth by his examinations in the said great book, they could never bring him.

Shortly hereupon, Master Rich (afterwards Lord Rich), then newly-made the King's Solicitor, Sir Richard Southwell, and one Master Palmer, servant to the Secretary, were sent to Sir Thomas More into the Tower to fetch away his books from him. And while Sir Richard Southwell and Master Palmer were busy in the trussing-up of his books, Master Rich, pretending friendly talk with him, among other things, of a set course as it seemed, said thus unto him:

"Forasmuch as it is well known, Master More, that you are a man both wise and well-learned, as well in the laws of the realm as otherwise, I pray you therefore, sir, let me be so bold as of good will to put unto you this case. Admit there were, sir," quoth he, "an act of Parliament that all the realm should take me for King. Would not you, Master More, take me for King?"

"Yes, sir," quoth Sir Thomas More, "that would I."

"I put case further," quoth Master Rich, "that there were an act of Parliament that all the realm should take me for Pope. Would not you, then, Master More, take me for Pope?"

"For answer, sir," quoth Sir Thomas More, "to your first case. The Parliament may well, Master Rich, meddle with the state of temporal princes. But to make answer to your other case, I will put you this case: Suppose the Parliament would make a law that God should not be God.

Sir Thomas More and Family (Rowland Lockey, after Holbein), in the Victoria & Albert Museum, London

Would you, then, Master Rich, say that God were not God?"

"No, sir," quoth he, "that would I not, since no Parliament may make any such law."

"No more," said Sir Thomas More, as Master Rich reported of him, "could the Parliament make the King supreme head of the Church."

Upon whose only report was Sir Thomas More indicted of treason upon the statute whereby it was made treason to deny the King to be supreme head of the Church. Into which indictment were put these heinous words— "Maliciously, traitorously, and diabolically."

When Sir Thomas More was brought from the Tower to Westminster Hall to answer the indictment, and at the King's Bench bar before the judges thereupon arraigned, he openly told them that he would upon that indictment have abidden in law, but that he thereby should have been driven to confess of himself the matter indeed, that was the denial of the King's Supremacy, which he protested was untrue. Wherefore he thereto pleaded not guilty; and so

reserved unto himself advantage to be taken of the body of the matter, after verdict, to avoid that indictment. And, moreover, added that if those only odious terms—"Maliciously, traitorously, and diabolically"—were put out of the indictment, he saw therein nothing justly to charge him.

And for proof to the jury that Sir Thomas More was guilty of this treason, Master Rich was called forth to give evidence unto them upon his oath, as he did. Against whom thus sworn, Sir Thomas More began in this wise to say:

"If I were a man, my lords, that did not regard an oath, I needed not, as it is well known, in this place at this time nor in this case, to stand here as an accused person. And if this oath of yours, Master Rich, be true, then pray I that I never see God in the face, which I would not say, were it otherwise, to win the whole world." Then recited he to the court the discourse of all their communication in the Tower according to the truth and said: "In good faith, Master Rich, I am sorrier for your perjury than for my own peril. And you shall understand that neither I, nor no man else to my knowledge, ever took you to be a man of such credit as in any matter of importance I or any other would at any time vouchsafe to communicate with you. And I, as you know, of no small while have been acquainted with you and your conversation, who have known you from your youth hitherto. For we long dwelled both in one parish together where, as yourself can tell (I am sorry you compel me to say) you were esteemed very light of your tongue, a great dicer and of no commendable fame. And so in your house at the Temple, where hath been your chief bringing-up, were you likewise accompted.

"Can it therefore seem likely unto your honorable lordships that I would, in so weighty a cause, so unadvisedly overshoot myself as to trust Master Rich, a man of me always reputed for one of so little truth as your lordships have heard, so far above my sovereign lord the King or any of his noble counsellors, that I would unto him utter the secrets of my conscience touching the King's Supremacy—the special point and only mark at my hands so long sought for? A thing which I never did, nor never would, after the statute thereof made, reveal either to the King's highness himself or to any of his honorable counsellors, as it is not unknown to your honors, at sundry several times sent from his grace's own person unto the Tower unto me for none other purpose. Can this, in your judgments, my lords, seem likely to be true?. . .

"Besides this the manifold goodness of the King's highness himself, that hath been so many ways my singular good lord and gracious sovereign, that hath so dearly loved and trusted me, even at my very first coming into his noble service with the dignity of his honorable privy council vouchsafing to admit me, and to offices of great credit and worship most liberally advanced me, and finally with that weighty room of his grace's High Chancellor (the like whereof he never did to temporal man before) next to his own royal person the highest officer in this noble realm, so far above my merits or qualities able and meet therefore, of his incomparable benignity honored and exalted me, by the space of twenty years and more showing his continual favor towards me. And, until at my own poor suit, it pleased his highness, giving me license with his majesty's favor, to bestow the residue of my life for the provision of my soul in the service of God—of his especial goodness thereof to discharge and unburthen me—most benignly heaped honors continually more and more upon me. All this his highness's goodness, I say, so long thus bountifully extended towards me, were in my mind, my lords, matter sufficient to convince this slanderous surmise by this man so wrongfully imagined against me.". . .

After this were there many other reasons, not now in my remembrance, by Sir Thomas More in his own defense alleged, to the discredit of Master Rich's aforesaid evidence and proof of the clearness of his own conscience. All which notwithstanding, the jury found him guilty.

And incontinent upon their verdict, the Lord Chancellor, for that matter chief commissioner, beginning to proceed in judgment against him, Sir Thomas More said to him: "My Lord, when I was toward the law, the manner in such case was to ask the prisoner before judgment, why judgment should not be given against him." Whereupon the Lord Chancellor, staying his judgment, wherein he had partly proceeded, demanded of him what he was able to say to the contrary. Who then in this sort most humbly made answer:

"Forasmuch as, my lord," quoth he, "this indictment is grounded upon an act of Parliament directly repugnant to the laws of God and His Holy Church, the supreme government of which, or of any part whereof, may no temporal prince presume by any law to take upon him, as rightfully belonging to the See of Rome, a spiritual pre-eminence by the mouth of Our Savior himself, personally present upon the earth, only to Saint Peter and his successors, Bishops of the same See, by special prerogative granted; it is therefore in law, amongst Christian men, insufficient to charge any Christian man."

And for proof thereof like as (among divers other reasons and authorities) he declared that this realm, being but one member and small part of the Church, might not make a particular law disagreeable with the general law of Christ's universal Catholic Church, no more than the City of London, being but one poor member in respect of the whole realm, might make a law against an act of Parliament to bind the whole realm. So farther showed he that it was contrary both to the laws and statutes of our own land yet unrepealed, as they might evidently perceive in Magna Charta: *Quod ecclesia Anglicana libera sit, et habeat omnia iura sua integra et libertates suas illaesas* ("That the English church may be free, and that it may exist with all its laws uncorrupted and its liberties unviolated."), and also contrary to that sacred oath which the King's highness and every Christian prince always with great solemnity received at their coronations. Alleging, moreover, that no more might this realm of England refuse obedience to the See of Rome than might the child refuse obedience to his own natural father.

For, as Saint Paul said of the Corinthians, "I have regenerated you my children in Christ," so might Saint Gregory, Pope of Rome, of whom by Saint Augustine, his messenger, we first received the Christian faith, of us Englishmen truly say: "You are my children because I have given to you everlasting salvation, a far higher and better inheritance than any carnal father can leave to his child, and by regeneration made you my spiritual children in Christ.". . .

Now when Sir Thomas More, for the avoiding of the indictment, had taken as many exceptions as he thought meet, and many more reasons than I can now remember alleged, the Lord Chancellor, loath to have the burthen of that judgment wholly to depend upon himself, there openly asked the advice of the Lord Fitz-James, then Lord Chief Justice of the King's Bench, and joined in commission with him, whether this indictment were sufficient or not.

Who, like a wise man, answered: "My lords all, by Saint Julian" (that was ever his oath), "I must needs confess that if the act of Parliament be not unlawful, then is not the indictment in my conscience insufficient."

Whereupon the Lord Chancellor said to the rest of the Lords: "Lo, my lords, lo, you hear what my Lord Chief Justice saith," and so immediately gave he judgment against him.

After which ended, the commissioners yet further courteously offered him, if he had anything else to allege for his defense, to grant him favorable audience. Who answered: "More have I not to say, my lords, but like as the blessed apostle Saint Paul, as we read in the Acts of the Apostles, was present and consented to the death of Saint Stephen, and kept their clothes that stoned him to death, and yet be they now both twain holy saints in heaven, and shall continue there friends forever, so I verily trust, and shall therefore right heartily pray, that though your lordships have now here in earth been judges to my condemnation, we may yet hereafter in heaven merrily all meet together, to our everlasting salvation.". . .

Now after this arraignment departed he from the bar to the Tower again, led by Sir William Kingston, a tall, strong, and comely knight, Constable of the Tower, and his very dear friend. Who, when he had brought him from Westminster to the Old Swan towards the Tower, there with an heavy heart, the tears running down by his cheeks, bade him farewell. Sir Thomas More, seeing him so sorrowful, comforted him with as good words as he could, saying: "Good Master Kingston, trouble not yourself but be of good cheer; for I will pray for you, and my good Lady, your wife, that we may meet in heaven together, where we shall be merry for ever and ever."

Soon after, Sir William Kingston, talking with me of Sir Thomas More, said: "In good faith, Master Roper, I was ashamed of myself that, at my departing from your father, I found my heart so feeble, and his so strong, that he was fain to comfort me which should rather have comforted him."

When Sir Thomas More came from Westminster to the Tower-ward again, his daughter—my wife—desirous to see her father, whom she thought she should never see in this world after, and also to have his final blessing, gave attendance about the Tower Wharf where she knew he should pass by before he could enter into the Tower—there tarrying for his coming home.

As soon as she saw him—after his blessing on her knees reverently received—she hasting towards him and, without consideration or care of herself, pressing in among the midst of the throng and company of the guard, that with halberds and bills went round about him, hastily ran to him and there openly, in the sight of them all, embraced him, took him about the neck, and kissed him. Who, well liking her most natural and dear daughterly affection towards him, gave her his fatherly blessing and many goodly words of comfort besides.

From whom after she was departed she, not satisfied with the former sight of him and like one that had forgotten herself, being all-ravished with the entire love of her dear father, having respect neither to herself nor to the press of the people and multitude that were there about him, suddenly turned back again, ran to him as before, took him about the neck, and divers times together most lovingly kissed him—and at last, with a full heavy heart, was fain to depart from him. The beholding whereof was to many of them that were present thereat so lamentable that it made them for very sorrow thereof to mourn and weep.

So remained Sir Thomas More in the Tower more than a seven-night after his judgment. From whence, the day before he suffered, he sent his shirt of hair—not willing to have it seen—to my wife, his dearly beloved daughter, and a letter written with a coal, contained in the foresaid book of his works, plainly expressing the fervent desire he had to suffer on the morrow, in these words following:

"I cumber you, good Margaret, much; but I would be sorry if it should be any longer than tomorrow. For tomorrow is Saint Thomas's Even and the Utas of Saint Peter; and therefore tomorrow long I to go to God. It were a day very meet and convenient for me, etc. I never liked your manner towards me better than when you kissed me last. For I like when daughterly love and dear charity hath no leisure to look to worldly courtesy."

And so upon the next morrow, being Tuesday, Saint Thomas's Even and the Utas of Saint Peter, in the year of our Lord one thousand five hundred thirty and five, according as he in his letter the day before had wished, early in the morning came to him Sir Thomas Pope, his singular friend, on message from the King and his council, that he should before nine of the clock the same morning suffer death. And that therefore forthwith he should prepare himself thereunto.

"Master Pope," quoth he, "for your good tidings I most heartily thank you. I have been always much bounden to the King's highness for the benefits and honors that he hath still from time to time most bountifully heaped upon me. And yet more bound am I to his grace for putting me into this place, where I have had convenient time and space to have remembrance of my end. And so help me God, most of all, Master Pope, am I bound to his highness that it pleaseth him so shortly to rid me out of the miseries of this wretched world. And therefore will I not fail earnestly to pray for his grace, both here and also in another world."

"The King's pleasure is further," quoth Master Pope, "that at your execution you shall not use many words."

"Master Pope," quoth he, "you do well to give me warning of his grace's pleasure, for otherwise I had purposed at that time somewhat to have spoken, but of no matter wherewith his grace, or any other, should have had cause to be offended. Nevertheless, whatsoever I intended, I am ready obediently to conform myself to his grace's commandments. And I beseech you, good Master Pope, to be a mean unto his highness that my daughter Margaret may be at my burial."

"The King is content already," quoth Master

Pope, "that your wife, children, and other your friends shall have liberty to be present thereat."

"O, how much beholden then," said Sir Thomas More, "am I to his grace that unto my poor burial vouchsafeth to have so gracious consideration."

Wherewithal Master Pope, taking his leave of him, could not refrain from weeping. Which Sir Thomas More perceiving, comforted him in this wise: "Quiet yourself, good Master Pope, and be not discomforted. For I trust that we shall, once in heaven, see each other full merrily, where we shall be sure to live and love together in joyful bliss eternally."

Upon whose departure, Sir Thomas More, as one that had been invited to some solemn feast, changed himself into his best apparel. Which Master Lieutenant espying, advised him to put it off, saying that he that should have it was but a javel.

"What, Master Lieutenant," quoth he, "shall I accompt him a javel that shall do me this day so singular a benefit? Nay, I assure you, were it cloth-of-gold, I would accompt it well bestowed on him, as Saint Cyprian did, who gave his executioner thirty pieces of gold." And albeit at length, through Master Lieutenant's importunate persuasion, he altered his apparel, yet after the example of that holy martyr, Saint Cyprian, did he of that little money that was left him send one angel of gold to his executioner.

And so was he by Master Lieutenant brought out of the Tower and from thence led towards the place of execution. Where, going up the scaffold, which was so weak that it was ready to fall, he said merrily to Master Lieutenant: "I pray you, Master Lieutenant, see me safe up and, for my coming down, let me shift for myself."

Then desired he all the people thereabout to pray for him, and to bear witness with him that he should now there suffer death in and for the faith of the Holy Catholic Church. Which done, he kneeled down and after his prayers said, turned to the executioner and with a cheerful countenance spake thus to him:

"Pluck up thy spirits, man, and be not afraid to do thine office. My neck is very short. Take heed therefore thou strike not awry, for saving of thine honesty."

So passed Sir Thomas More out of this world to God upon the very same day in which himself had most desired.

Soon after whose death came intelligence thereof to the Emperor Charles. Whereupon he sent for Sir Thomas Elyot, our English ambassador, and said unto him: "My Lord Ambassador, we understand that the King, your master, hath put his faithful servant and grave, wise counsellor, Sir Thomas More, to death." Whereunto Sir Thomas Elyot answered that he understood nothing thereof.

"Well," said the Emperor, "it is too true. And this will we say, that if we had been master of such a servant, of whose doings ourself have had these many years no small experience, we would rather have lost the best city of our dominions than have lost such a worthy counsellor."

Which matter was by the same Sir Thomas Elyot to myself, to my wife, to Master Clement and his wife to Master John Heywood and his wife, and unto divers other his friends accordingly reported.

Finis. Deo gratias

OGIER GHISELIN DE BUSBECQ (1522–92)

Letter (1555)

Ogier Ghiselin de Busbecq's letters to his school pal Nicolas Michault, ambassador to Portugal, provide a remarkably vivid eyewitness account of the Turkish government and military system that threatened Europe during the Renaissance. The Flemish diplomat's graceful and urbane report of his mission to Buda, and the trek there from Vienna at the command of the Habsburg Emperor Ferdinand I of Austria (King of the Romans, Sovereign of Hungary and Bohemia) is an invaluable source of historical information about contemporary Austro-Hungarian relations—at the same time that it is a compelling travelogue. In all the capitals of Europe, Busbecq's letters ran through twenty editions in his lifetime. He was at home in Latin, Italian, French, Spanish, German, and Slav, as well as his Flemish mother tongue. So cosmopolitan is Busbecq that no subtlety of diplomatic behavior is beyond him; so curious an observer, that no detail of hospitality omitted is beneath his notice. Through his gossipy account, as he describes the mysterious janizaries, we experience vicariously the inner recesses of the Muslim world that struck terror in the European heart. His description of the grandiosely rationalized drinking habits of his Turkish hosts, and his casual provision of the fuel for them, reads like a textbook case of codependency and a reminder that it was not only the native Americans who were plied with "fire water." The graceful casualness of Busbecq's style makes him sound like a newspaper correspondent rather than a successful emissary whose urbanity helped protect Renaissance Europe from threats of invasion.

At eleven, p.m., we reached Fiscagmund, a borough town of Hungary, four miles from Vienna, where we stopped for supper, for in our haste we had left Vienna supperless, and then pursued our way towards Komorn. One of the king's instructions was that I should get hold of one Paul Palyna at Komorn, who had great knowledge of the raids and robberies of the Turks, and take him with me to Buda; since, if he were at hand to prompt me, I should find it a great advantage when remonstrating with the Pasha concerning the outrages, and demanding satisfaction for the same. But that I should start

punctually appeared to Palyna the most unlikely thing in the world, and accordingly, when I arrived at Komorn, he had not yet left his home, and not a soul could give me any information as to when he was likely to arrive. I was intensely annoyed. I despatched a report of the matter to Ferdinand, and devoted the next day to waiting for this precious companion of mine at Komorn. All in vain; so on the third day I crossed the river Waag, and pursued my way towards Gran, the first fortress within the Turkish boundary line.

The officer in command at Komorn, John

Various Franciscan monks beheaded before the Sultan (Ambrogio Lorenzetti), in San Francesco, Siena

Pax, had given me an escort of sixteen hussars, as the Hungarians call these horsemen, with orders not to leave me until we came in sight of the Turkish outposts. The Turkish officer in command at Gran had given me to understand that his men would meet me midway between that town and Komorn. For three hours, more or less, we had advanced through a flat and open country, when four Turkish horsemen appeared in the distance; my Hungarians, however, continued to ride with me, until at last I advised them to retire, fearing that, if they came nearer, some troublesome breach of the peace might ensue. When the Turks saw me coming, they rode up, and, halting by my carriage, saluted me. In this manner we advanced a short distance, conversing with each other, for I had a lad who acted as interpreter.

I was not expecting any addition to my escort, when suddenly, as we came to a spot a little below the level of the rest of the country, I found myself surrounded by a troop of 150 horsemen, or thereabouts. I had never seen such a sight before, and I was delighted with the gay colours of their shields and spears, their jewelled scimitars, their many-coloured plumes, their turbans of the purest white, their robes of purple and dark green, their gallant steeds and superb accoutrements.

The officers ride up, give me a courteous welcome, congratulate me on my arrival, and ask whether I have had a pleasant journey. I reply in terms befitting the occasion, and so they escort me to Gran, which consists of a fort situated on a hill, at the foot of which flows the Danube, and a town hard by on the plain, where I take up my quarters. The archbishop of this place stands first among the nobles of Hungary both in rank and wealth. My lodging had more of the camp than the city. Instead of beds there were planks covered with coarse woollen rugs; there were no mattresses, no linen. And so my attendants had their first taste of Turkish luxury! As for myself, I had brought my bed with me.

Next day the Sanjak-bey in command of the place repeatedly urged me to visit him. This is the title which the Turks give to an officer in command; and the name comes from the sanjak, or standard, which is carried in front of his squadron of cavalry; it consists of a lance, on the top of which is a brass ball plated over with gold. I had no despatches or commission for this officer, but he was so persistent that I had to go. It turned out that all he wanted was to see me, to go through some civilities, ask my errand, urge me to promote a peace, and wish me a prosperous journey. On my way to his quarters I was surprised to hear the frogs croaking, although it was December and the weather was cold. The phenomenon was explained by the existence of some pools formed by hot sulphur springs.

I left Gran after a breakfast, which had to serve for a dinner as well, as there was no resting-place between it and Buda.

In spite of my entreaties that he would spare himself the trouble of paying me so great an attention, the Sanjak-bey must needs escort me with all his household, and the cavalry under his command. As the horsemen poured out of the gates they engaged in mimic warfare, and also performed several feats, one of which was to throw a ball on the ground, and to carry it off on the lance's point when at full gallop. Among the troopers was a Tartar with long thick hair, and I was told that he never wore any other covering on his head than that which nature afforded, either to protect him against

weather in a storm, or arrows in a battle. When the Sanjak-bey considered that he had gone far enough, we exchanged greetings, and he returned home, leaving an escort to conduct me to Buda.

As I drew near to the city I was met by a few Turks, who were by profession cavasses. These cavasses act as officials, and execute the orders of the Sultan and Pashas. The position of cavasse is considered by the Turks to be one of high honour.

I was conducted to the house of a Hungarian gentleman, where, I declare, my luggage, carriage, and horses were better treated than their owner. The first thing the Turks attend to is to get carriages, horses, and luggage into safe quarters; as for human beings they think they have done quite enough for them, if they are placed beyond the reach of wind and weather.

The Pasha, whose name was Touighoun (which, by the way, signifies a stork in Turkish), sent a person to wait on me and pay me his respects, and asked me to excuse him from giving me audience for several days, on account of a severe illness from which he was suffering, and assured me that he would attend to me as soon as his health permitted.

This circumstance prevented my business from suffering at all by Palyna's delay, and enabled him also to escape the charge of wilful negligence. For he used all diligence to reach me in time, and shortly afterwards made his appearance.

The illness of the Pasha detained me at Buda for a considerable time. The popular belief was that he had fallen sick from chagrin on receiving the news that a large hoard of his, which he had buried in some corner, had been stolen. He was generally supposed to be an arrant miser. Well, when he heard that I had with me William Quacquelben, a man of great learning and a most skilful physician, he earnestly desired me to send him to prescribe for his case. I made no objection to this proposal, but my consent was like to have cost me dear; for when the Pasha gradually got worse, and a fatal termination to his illness seemed probable, I was in great alarm lest, if he joined his Mahomet in Paradise, the Turks should accuse my physician of murdering him, to the danger of my excellent friend, and my own great disgrace as an accomplice. But, by God's mercy, the Pasha recovered, and my anxiety was set at rest.

At Buda I made my first acquaintance with the Janissaries; this is the name by which the Turks call the infantry of the royal guard. The Turkish state has 12,000 of these troops when the corps is at its full strength. They are scattered through every part of the empire, either to garrison the forts against the enemy, or to protect the Christians and Jews from the violence of the mob. There is no district with any considerable amount of population, no borough or city, which has not a detachment of Janissaries to protect the Christians, Jews, and other helpless people from outrage and wrong.

A garrison of Janissaries is always stationed in the citadel of Buda. The dress of these men consists of a robe reaching down to the ankles, while, to cover their heads, they employ a cowl which, by their account, was originally a cloak sleeve, part of which contains the head, while the remainder hangs down and flaps against the neck. On their forehead is placed a silvergilt cone of considerable height, studded with stones of no great value.

These Janissaries generally came to me in pairs. When they were admitted to my dining room they first made a bow, and then came quickly up to me, all but running, and touched my dress or hand, as if they intended to kiss it. After this they would thrust into my hand a nosegay of the hyacinth or narcissus; then they would run back to the door almost as quickly as they came, taking care not to turn their backs, for this, according to their code, would be a serious breach of etiquette. After reaching the door, they would stand respectfully with their arms crossed, and their eyes bent on the ground, looking more like monks than warriors. On receiving a few small coins (which was what they wanted) they bowed again, thanked me in loud tones, and went off blessing me for my kindness. To tell you the truth, if I had not been told beforehand that they were Janissaries, I should, without hesitation, have taken them for members of some order of Turkish monks, or brethren of some Moslem college. Yet these are the famous Janissaries, whose approach inspires terror everywhere.

During my stay at Buda a good many Turks were drawn to my table by the attractions of my wine, a luxury in which they have not many opportunities of indulging. The effect of this enforced abstinence is to make them so eager for drink, that they swill themselves with it whenever they get the chance. I asked them to make a night of it, but at last I got tired of the game, left the table, and retired to my bedroom. On this my Turkish guests made a move to go, and great was their grief as they reflected that they were not yet dead drunk, and could still use their legs. Presently they sent a servant to request that I would allow them access to my stock of wine and lend them some silver cups. 'With my permission,' they said, 'they would like to continue their drinking bout through the night; they were not particular where they sat; any odd corner would do for them.' Well, I ordered them to be furnished with as much wine as they could drink, and also with the cups they asked for. Being thus supplied, the fellows never left off drinking until they were one and all stretched on the floor in the last stage of intoxication.

To drink wine is considered a great sin among the Turks, especially in the case of persons advanced in life: when younger people indulge in it the offence is considered more venial. Inasmuch, however, as they think that they will have to pay the same penalty after death whether they drink much or little, if they taste one drop of wine they must needs indulge in a regular debauch; their notion being that, inasmuch as they have already incurred the penalty, appointed for such sin, in another world, it will be an advantage to them to have their sin out, and get dead drunk, since it will cost them as much in either case. These are their ideas about drinking, and they have some other notions which are still more ridiculous. I saw an old gentleman at Constantinople who, before taking up his cup, shouted as loud as he could. I asked my friends the reason, and they told me he was shouting to warn his soul to stow itself away in some odd corner of his body, or to leave it altogether, lest it should be defiled by the wine he was about to drink, and have hereafter to answer for the offence which the worthy man meant to indulge in. . . .

LOUISE LABÉ (C.1524–66)

Dedication (1555)

Legend has it that Louise Labé, of Lyon, known as "la Belle Cordière" because she was the wife of a ropemaker, dressed as a man and went off to war; and that she may have practiced the arts of a courtesan. She wrote love poems, elegies, and sonnets in the Italian style that were powerful in their elegant simplicity and evocation of her melancholy and passion. Without the circumlocutions and citations so familiar to others who write about the joys of learning, this "preface, to a friend," speaks so clearly and persuasively that it might have been written today.

Since a time has come, Mademoiselle, when the severe laws of men no longer prevent women from applying themselves to the sciences and other disciplines, it seems to me that those of us who can should use this long-craved freedom to study and to let men see how greatly they wronged us when depriving us of its honor and advantages. And if any woman becomes so proficient as to be able to write down her thoughts, let her do so and not despise the honor but rather flaunt it instead of fine clothes, necklaces, and rings. For these may be considered ours only by use, whereas the honor of being educated is ours entirely. . . . If the heavens had endowed me with sufficient wit to understand all I would have liked, I would serve in this as an example rather than an admonishment. But having devoted part of my youth to musical exercises, and finding the time left too short for the crudeness of my understanding, I am unable, in my own case, to achieve what I want for our sex, which is to see it outstrip men not only in beauty but in learning and virtue. All I can do is to beg our virtuous ladies to raise their minds somewhat above their distaffs and spindles and try to prove to the world that if we were not made to command, still we should not be disdained as companions in domestic and public matters by those who govern and command obedience. Apart from the good name that our sex will acquire thereby, we shall have caused men to devote more time and effort in the public good to virtuous studies for fear of seeing themselves left behind by those over whom they have always claimed superiority in practically everything. . . .

If there is anything to be recommended

after honor and glory, anything to incite us to study, it is the pleasure which study affords. Study differs in this from other recreations, of which all one can say, after enjoying them, is that one has passed the time. But study gives a more enduring sense of satisfaction. For the past delights us and serves more than the present. . . . When we write down our thoughts, no matter how much our mind runs on infinities of other matters. . . long afterward, on looking back at what we wrote, we return to the same point and humor as we were in before. Then our joy is doubled, for we revive the pleasure experienced in the past. . . .

From Lyon, this 24th of July, 1555.

CATHERINE ZELL (C.1497–C.1562)

Letters to Ludwig Rabus (1556–8)

Catherine Zell was the widow of a prominent Lutheran priest, Mathew, when she wrote her acerbic letter against intolerance to the anti-radical minister Ludwig Rabus of Memmingen. Rabus had accused her and her late husband of weakening the Strasbourg Church. Her letters are particularly notable for Zell's description of her conversion to the Lord by the eloquence of Martin Luther, of her good works as a convert and a dutiful Christian wife; and for her defense of the Anabaptists and of the separation of church and state: "Just because they cannot agree with us on lesser things, is this any reason to persecute them. . . ?" As throughout the history of humankind, so also in the Renaissance more wars were declared in the name of religion than for any other cause.

I, Catherine Zell, wife of the late lamented Mathew Zell, who served in Strasburg, where I was born and reared and still live, wish you peace and enhancement of God's grace. . . .

From my earliest years I turned to the Lord, who taught and guided me, and I have at all times, in accordance with my understanding and His grace, embraced the interests of His church and earnestly sought Jesus. Even in youth this brought me the regard and affection of clergymen and others much concerned with the church, which is why the pious Mathew Zell wanted me as a companion in marriage; and I, in turn, to serve the glory of Christ, gave devotion and help to my husband, both in his ministry and in keeping his house. . . .

Ever since I was ten years old I have been a student and a sort of church mother, much given to attending sermons. I have loved and frequented the company of learned men, and I conversed much with them, not about dancing, masquerades, and worldly pleasures but about the kingdom of God. . . .

Yet I resisted and struggled against that

Self portrait (Sofonisba Anguissola), in the Uffizi,

kingdom. Then, as no learned man could find a way of consoling me in my sins, prayers and physical suffering, and as none could make me sure of God's love and grace, I fell gravely ill in body and spirit. I became like that poor woman of the Gospel who, having spent all she had on doctors to no avail, heard speak of Christ, went to Him, and was healed. As I foundered, devoured by care and anxiety, vainly searching for serenity in the practices of the church, God took pity on me. From among our people He drew out and sent forth Martin Luther. This man so persuaded me of the ineffable goodness of our Lord Jesus Christ that I felt myself snatched from the depths of hell and transported to the kingdom of heaven. I remembered the Lord's words to Peter: 'Follow me and I shall make you a fisher of men'. Then did I labor day and night to cleave to the path of divine truth. . . .

While other women decorated their houses and ornamented themselves, going to dances, wedding parties, and giving themselves to plea-sure, I went into the houses of poor and rich alike, in all love, faith, and compassion, to care for the sick and the confined and to bury the dead. Was that to plant anxiety and turmoil in the church of Strasbourg?. . .

In 1524 a hundred-and-fifty burghers had to flee from the little town of Kenzingen, in Breisgau. That night they came to Strasbourg. I took eighty into our house. For the next four weeks there were never fewer than fifty or sixty people at table. Many nobles and burgesses helped us to take care of them. And what about the disorders we started in 1525 [at the time of the great peasant uprising], I and a lot of other devoted people? In the wake of the massacre of the poor peasants, many of those who got away, wretched and terrified, came to us in Strasbourg. The almoner Master Hackfurt, myself, and two widows lodged a great crowd of them in the [old] Franciscan cloister, and I got many other honorable men and women to help. A number of surviving noblemen in the town council know this, as do certain respectable rich women who also came to our aid. They could speak up. . . .

Consider the poor Anabaptists, who are so furiously and ferociously persecuted. Must the authorities everywhere be incited against them, as the hunter drives his dog against wild ani-mals? Against those who acknowledge Christ the Lord in very much the same way we do and over which we broke with the papacy? Just because they cannot agree with us on lesser things, is this any reason to persecute them and in them Christ, in whom they fervently believe and have often professed in misery, in prison, and under the torments of fire and water?

Governments may punish criminals, but they should not force and govern belief, which is a matter for the heart and conscience not for temporal authorities.

. . . When the authorities pursue one, they soon bring forth tears, and towns and villages are emptied. . . .

Strasbourg does not offer the example of an evil town but rather the contrary—charity, com-passion, and hospitality for the wretched and poor. Within its walls, God be thanked, there remains more than one poor Christian whom certain people would have liked to see cast out. Old Mathew Zell would not have approved of that: he would have gathered the sheep, not destroyed them. . . .

Whether they were Lutherans, Zwinglians, Schwenkfeldians, or poor Anabaptist brethren, rich or poor, wise or foolish, according to the word of St Paul, all came to us [to the Zells in Strasbourg]. We were not compelled to hold the same views and beliefs that they did, but we did owe to all a proof of love, service, and generosity: our teacher Christ has taught us that. . . .

[Hans Lenglin, a man with views like Rabus, had said:] Better to be a papist than an Anabaptist or a Schwenkfeldian. . . .[Catherine replies, addressing Rabus:] You think that people will let themselves be pushed into prejudgments and shackles. Not at all. Freedom and intellect have been taken and won.

MARGUERITE DE NAVARRE (1492–1549)

Heptameron (c.1540; 1559)

Marguerite of Angoulême and Valois, queen of Navarre, by her second marriage to Henri d'Albret (Henry II of Navarre), created around her the ideal court of culture and toleration envisioned by Baldassare Castiglione. Her interests and education were wide-ranging; her protégés included François Rabelais, Clément Marot, and, though she remained a loyal Catholic, Protestant reformers like John Calvin whom she defended by evoking the authority of her brother Francis I, king of France. Her patronage and inspired example showed nobility at its finest, earning her the title "beloved mother of the Renaissance." Although she also wrote *Le Miroir de l'âme pécheresse,* a pious mystical theological tract in verse later translated by England's Elizabeth I, and *Marguerites de la Marguerite des Princesses,* a collection of light verse, she is best noted for her cycle of love stories loosely modeled on Giovanni Boccaccio's *Decameron* and Geoffrey Chaucer's *Canterbury Tales.* The *Heptameron,* as it was named by its editor Claude Guget in 1559, is a collection of some seventy stories told by travelers seeking refuge from a deluge, for whom storytelling is a shield against the harshness of life. Although the characters and situations in Marie's tales resemble those in Boccaccio's and Chaucer's, ranging from the most ribald to the most sublime, the overall tone is more sensitive and restrained. Yet the underlying theme is a satirical attack on the licentious clerics. Through it all shine her self-confidence and exuberant joie de vivre.

PROLOGUE

On the first day in September, when as the springs of the Pyrenean mountains begin to put on their virtuousness, there came together at those of Cauterets much folk from France, Spain, and other countries; some to drink of the water, some to bathe therein, and others to take the mud-bath. And each and all of these are so marvellous in their operation that men given up by the doctors return from Cauterets whole and sound. Yet my aim is neither to show forth the place nor the virtuousness of these springs aforesaid, but only to relate that which appertaineth to the matter on which I am about to write. Now there tarried in this place for more than three weeks all the sick folk, until they discovered by the good case of their bodies that it was fit for them to return. But at the time appointed for their setting forth, there fell such great rains that it seemed as if God had forgotten the promise that He made to Noah, not again to destroy the world by water, since by it all the cottages of Cauterets were so filled that no one could dwell therein. And those who came from the land of Spain returned thither by the mountains, as best they could, and, trust me, they who had a good knowledge of the tracks were the ones to fare best. But the ladies and gentlemen of France, thinking to get them back to Therbes as easily as they came, found the rivulets so swollen that they were hardly to be crossed. And having come to the Gave Bearnois, which when they went was not more than two feet deep, they found it so mighty and rushing a stream that they turned aside to seek for bridges, but these being but of wood had been carried away by the strength of the torrent. Some indeed, believing that they could withstand its force by fording it in a body, were so quickly borne away that the rest, though they would fain cross, had small wish to do so; and so, as their inclination was, they separated and went in divers directions to seek for some new way. Some taking the mountain track, and passing through Aragon, came to the county of Roussillon and to Narbonne, and others fared straight to Barcelona, whence sailing they got to Marseilles and Aiguemorte.

But a certain widow, of much experience, named Oisille, determined to lay by all fear of the bad roads, and to journey to Our Lady of Serrance. Not that she was of so superstitious a mind as to think that the glorious Virgin would leave her session by the right hand of her Son, and dwell in that desert land, but only for her great desire of seeing that holy place of which so great a noise had come to her ears, and being assured likewise that if there were any way out of this peril, the monks would be advised thereof. And this she accomplished, yet traversing such a wild country and ways as hard to go up as to come down, that although she was old and slow in movement, she had to go the best part of the journey on foot. But of this the worst was that most of her folk and her horses died on the way, so she came to Serrance, having one man and one woman only, and was there taken in and kindly entreated by the monks.

Now there were among the French trav-ellers two gentlemen who had gone to the springs, rather that they might accompany their ladies than for any failing in their health. And seeing that the company was setting forth, and that the husbands of their ladies were likewise taking them away, they thought fit to follow them from afar, without making anyone privy to their design. But it came to pass that one evening when the married gentlemen were lodged with their wives at the house of one who was more a robber than a churl, that the lovers of these ladies, who were also lodged in a cottage hard by, heard at night a great tumult. Whereupon they and their servants arose, and inquired of their host what this noise might be. And he, much afraid, told them that it was some Roaring Boys, who had come to take their share of the booty that was at the house of the rob-ber, their comrade; at which the young gallants forthwith laid hold of their arms, and with their servants went to the succour of the ladies, death for whom they accounted far sweeter than life without them. And when they came to the place they found the outer gate broken in, and the two husbands with their servants defending themselves full bravely. But since the number of the robbers was great, and they were grievously wounded, having by this time lost the greater part of their servants, they were beginning to give way. The two gallants, seeing their ladies wailing and entreating at the win-dows, were worked by pity and love to such a point of courage that, after the fashion of two bears rushing down from the mountains, they burst upon the robbers and so handled them that many were killed, and those left alive would not stay for any more blows, but escaped to their hiding-place as best they could. The two gallants, having put these villains to flight, and killed the host among the rest, heard that the hostess was worse than her mate, where-upon they, with the thrust of a sword, sent her to join him. Next, entering into one of the lower rooms, they found therein one of the married gentlemen, who presently gave up the ghost. The other was scot-free of wounds, yet was all his vesture pierced with sword-thrusts, and his own sword broken in two. This poor man, beholding before him his rescue, prayed the young men, after both embracing and thanking them, by no means to leave him, which was to them a request mighty pleasant. And after they had buried the dead man, and comforted, after the best sort they could, his widow, they set forth again, not knowing which road to take but leaving it in God's hands. And if it be your pleasure to know the names of these three gentlemen, the one who was married was called Hircan, and his wife Parlamente, and the widow was Longarine. And the names of the two gallants were Dagoucin and Saffredent. And after that they had been all the day on horseback, toward evensong they made out a spire, whither, after much travail and labour, they arrived. Now this was the spire of the abbey of St. Savyn, and here they were taken in and well entreated by the abbot and his monks. And the abbot, who was of a noble house, gave them good lodging, and as he waited upon them to their rooms, inquired of them their hap. And having heard how bad it was, he told them that they were not alone in tasting of misfortune, for he had in one of his rooms two ladies who had escaped equal, if not greater peril, since they had had to do not with men but with beasts, in whom there is no pity. For these poor ladies, when half a league on this side of Peyrechitte, had met a bear coming down from the mountain, from before which they had fled at such a rate that at the gate of the abbey their horses dropped dead under them, and two of their maids, who came in a long while after, told them that the bear had killed all their menservants. Then did the two ladies and the three gentlemen go into the room where these unhappy ones were lodged, and found them weeping, and knew them for Nomerfide and Ennasuitte. So having embraced one another, they told what had befallen them, and in concert with the good abbot, comforted themselves for having again fallen into company. And in the morning they heard mass with much devotion, praising God for the perils which were overpast.

And while they were all at mass there came into the church a man clad only in his shirt, flying as if someone pursued him, and crying for help. Straightway did Hircan and the other gentlemen go forth to discover what the affair was; and there they beheld two men with drawn swords, who followed after him; and these seeing so great a number, would fain have fled; but Hircan and his company pursued them and put them to the sword. And when the aforesaid Hircan returned he found that the man clad in the shirt was Geburon, one of his comrades, who said that while he was in bed in a cottage near Peyrechitte there came upon him three men, and though he was in his shirt and armed only with a sword, he so shrewdly wounded one that he died upon the spot. And whilst the two others set themselves to succour their fellow, he, perceiving that he was naked and the robbers armed, thought he could scarcely win save by flight, being little impeded by his dress. And for the good event of this he gave thanks to God, and to those who had for him done vengeance.

After they had heard mass and dined, they went to see if it were possible to cross the Gave, and seeing that it was not they were in great affray, although the abbot many times entreated them to abide there until the waters were abated, and to this for the day they agreed. And in the evening, as they were going to bed, there came an old monk who, for many a year, had failed not to be present during September at Our Lady of Serrance. And on their asking him the news of his journey, he said that by reason of the floods he had come by the mountain tracks, and that they were the worst roads he had ever been on. But one most pitiful case he had to tell, and this was that he had found a young gentleman named Simontault, who, weary of the long time the floods took to abate, had determined to force the passage, trusting in the goodness of his horse, and having first placed all his servingmen around him, thereby to break the force of the water. But when they were in midstream, those who were badly mounted were borne headlong, men and horses, down-stream and were never rescued. The gentleman, finding himself alone, turned his horse to the bank whence he came, yet not so sharply as to avail anything. But God willed that he was so near to the shore as to be able, drawing himself on his hands and knees, and drinking a great deal of water, to reach the rough flintstones on the bank, so weak and feeble that he could not stand. But it chanced well for him that a shepherd, bringing his sheep home at evening, found him lying there among the stones, soaking wet, and sad at heart as well for himself as for his folk whom he had seen perishing before his eyes. The shepherd, who perceived his case more by his look than by his words, took him by the hand and led him to his cottage, where he dried him with a fire of broken sticks as well as might be. And, that night, God led thither this good monk, who showed him the way to Our Lady of Serrance, and told him he would be lodged there in better fashion than in any other place, and that he would find there an aged widow called Oisille, who was indeed his equal in misfortunes. And when all the company heard of the good lady Oisille, and the gentle knight Simontault, that they were safe, a great joy fell on them, and they praised the Creator that, deeming the serving-men and maids sufficient sacrifice, He had kept alive their master and mistress; and above all did Parlamente give thanks unto God from the bottom of her heart, since for a long while had Simontault been accepted by her as a devoted lover. And having made careful inquiry of the road to Serrance, although the good old man showed them how difficult it was, yet none the less did they determine to journey there; and on that very day did they set forth without lack of anything, for the abbot had given them of the best horses that were in Lavedan, and goodly cloaks of Bearn, and abundant provaunt, and an escort to guide them safely across the mountains. And so, faring more on foot than horseback, with great sweat and travail they came to Our Lady of Serrance, where the abbot, though he was an inhospitable man, durst not refuse them lodging, for

the fear he had of the Lord of Bearn, by whom he knew them to be well beloved; but he, being a well-taught hypocrite, put on for them his most obliging face, and led them to see the good lady Oisille and the gentle knight Simontault.

Now such delight was on the company, in such wondrous wise gathered together, that to them all the night seemed short, praising God in the church for the mercy He had showed toward them. And after that in the morning they had taken some short rest, they all went to hear mass and to receive the Holy Sacrament of concord, in which all Christians are united into one body, imploring Him who had gathered them together to perfect their journey to His glory. After dinner they sent to know if the floods were not yet abated, and finding that they were rather increased, they determined to make them a bridge, fixing it on two rocks which are very near to one another, and where there are still planks for those on foot, who, coming from Oleron, may wish to cross the Gave. In much delight was the abbot that they performed this at their own charges, to the end that the number of pilgrims and gifts should be increased for him, and so he furnished them with labourers, yet not one farthing did he give of his own, for he was too miserly. And since the labourers said that the bridge could not be finished before ten or twelve days, both the men and women of the company began to be very weary; but Parlamente, the wife of Hircan, who was never listless or melancholy, having asked of her husband leave to speak, spoke thus to the aged lady Oisille: "Good mistress, I am amazed that you, who have had so great experience, and who stand towards us women as a mother, do not think of some pastime wherewith to subdue this weariness of ours at the long delay; for if we do not get some pleasant and seemly pursuit, we shall be in danger of growing sick.". . .

The lady Oisille said she had had such toil to put out of mind all worldly vanities that she feared any choice of hers would be a bad one; but it was necessary to put the matter to the vote, and would have Hircan give his opinion first. "As for me," said Hircan, "if I conceived that the pastime I would fain choose were as agreeable to a certain one of this company as it is to me, my vote would soon be given, but as it is I am dumb, and wait to hear what others say." His wife Parlamente thereupon fell to blushing, thinking that his words were for her, and betwixt a frown and a smile spoke to him thus: "Peradventure, Hircan, that one whom you deem hard to be contented could find contentments enough if it was her humour; but let us leave those games at which only two can disport themselves, and think of some which all can play." Then said Hircan to all the ladies: "Since this wife of mine has understood so fairly what lay beneath my words, and since this privy play is not to her liking, I am assured that she, better than any other, can tell us of some pastime for all; and I do herewith profess myself of her mind, whatever it may be, and will in this matter be led entirely by her." And to this the whole company agreed. Whereupon Parlamente, seeing that the lot was fallen upon her, spoke as follows: "If I felt within me such parts as had the ancients, by whom were all arts invented, I would invent some game to discharge the duty that you have laid upon me; but knowing my wit and my power, how little it is, and scarce able so much as to call to mind how others have performed well this very thing, I shall esteem myself lucky if I can but follow in their steps. Among the rest I think that there is not one of you who has not read those Hundred Novels of Boccaccio, lately done from the Italian into French. These did King Francis, first of his name, his Highness the Dauphin, the Princess his wife, and my lady Margaret of Navarre, esteem at such a price that if old Boccaccio could have heard them from the place where he is, he would have been, through the praises of such mighty folk, well-nigh brought to life again. And I hear that these two illustrious ladies have determined to make likewise a Decameron, but yet in one thing they will have it different from Boccaccio's—namely, every history therein contained shall be the truth. And their intent was that they, and his

Highness with them, should each make ten stories, and afterwards should bring together ten persons whom they rated as most capable of telling them; but they would have no schoolmen or practised men of books, for his Highness must have nature and not art, and was in fear lest the truth of the histories might fare badly through odd-becoming tricks of rhetoric. But divers high affairs of state, as the peace between the King and the King of England, the bringing to bed of the Princess, and other matters of great consideration, have given all this scheme to forgetfulness at court; but by reason of the long delay we shall be able to accomplish it by the ten days in which the bridge is to be brought to a completion. And if it please you, every day from noon to four o'clock we will go to that pleasant meadow that is stretched along the Gave, where so thickly do the trees grow that the sun cannot pierce them through with his heat. There, seated at our ease, let each of us tell some story that he has either seen with his eyes or heard from the lips of a faithful witness. At the end of ten days we shall have summed up the hundred, and if God grants that our relations be pleasing to those lords and ladies aforesaid, we will lay them at their feet on our return from this journey in place of images or paternosters, to which I am assured they will be greatly preferred. Yet if any of you shall bring out a more pleasant pastime than this, to him I will give my vote." But all the company replied with one voice that than this there could be nothing better, and that they were weary for the morning to come, whereon to make a beginning of it.

So was this day joyously passed, one telling to another such notable things as he had seen in his life. But as soon as the morning was come, they went to the room of Oisille, whom they found at her prayers. And when for a full hour they had attended to her reading, and after this had devoutly heard mass, they went to dinner, it being now ten o'clock. And at noon they failed not, according to what had been determined, to go to the meadow, which was of such a sort that it would need Boccaccio himself to tell the pleasantness of it; but be you contented and know surely that never was there meadow to vie with it. And when all this company was seated in order on the grass, that was so fine and soft that no need was there of rugs or carpeting, Simontault began to say: "Who shall be the one to rule over us?" To whom Hircan: "Since you were the first to speak, it is fitting that you bear rule, for in the game we are all equal." "God knows," said Simontault, "that I would desire no bliss in the world so much as to bear rule over this company." This speech of his Parlamente understood so well that she was fain to cough that Hircan might not perceive the colour that came on to her cheeks; but she presently told Simontault to begin; and this he did.

JOHN FOXE (1516/17–87)

The Acts and Monuments (1563)

An Anglican priest and propagandist, intent on providing a passionate account of the Protestant martyrs under Queen ("Bloody") Mary, Oxford-educated John Foxe compiled a book that quickly became nearly as important as the King James Bible in forging British language and sensitivity. By the time of his death, nearly every church in England had enshrined copies for public use. Foxe had sought refuge, under Mary's reign, at first with John Knox at Frankfurt, then at Strasbourg where he began the book which became known popularly as *The Book of Martyrs*. Originally in Latin, Foxe himself expanded the work and translated it into English. He believed that everything that happens is caused by either God or the devil, that God in His righteousness punishes evil and rewards good, and that his chronicles would serve as cautionary tales to lead the faithful away from temptation. His account of Henry VIII's execution of his second wife, Anne Boleyn, gives poignant insight into the reverence with which she held her ruthlessly mercurial husband.

The Sum of the Condemnation of me Anne Askew at the Guildhall.

They said to me there, that I was a heretic, and condemned by the law, if I would stand in my opinion. I answered, that I was no heretic, neither yet deserved I any death by the law of God. But, as concerning the faith which I uttered and wrote to the council, I would not, I said, deny it, because I knew it true. Then would they needs know, if I would deny the sacrament to be Christ's body and blood. I said, 'Yea: for the same Son of God that was born of the Virgin Mary, is now glorious in heaven, and will come again from thence at the latter day like as he went up. And as for that ye call your God, it is a piece of bread. For a more proof thereof (mark it when you list,) let it but lie in the box three months, and it will be mouldy, and so turn to nothing that is good. Whereupon I am persuaded that it cannot be God.'

After that, they willed me to have a priest; and then I smiled. Then they asked me, if it were not good; I said, I would confess my faults unto God, for I was sure that he would hear me with favour. And so we were condemned without a quest.

My belief which I wrote to the council was this: That the sacramental bread was left us to be received with thanksgiving, in remembrance of Christ's death, the only remedy of our soul's recovery; and that thereby we also receive the whole benefits and fruits of his most glorious passion.

Then would they needs know, whether the bread in the box were God or no: I said, 'God is a Spirit, and will be worshipped in spirit and truth.' Then they demanded, 'Will you plainly deny Christ to be in the sacrament?' I answered, that I believe faithfully the eternal Son of God not to dwell there; in witness whereof I recited again the history of Bel, Dan. xix., Acts vii. and xvii., and Matt. xxiv., concluding thus: 'I neither wish death, nor yet fear his might; God have the praise thereof with thanks.'

MY LETTER SENT TO THE LORD CHANCELLOR.

The Lord God, by whom all creatures have their being, bless you with the light of his knowledge. Amen.

My duty to your lordship remembered, &c.: It might please you to accept this my bold suit, as the suit of one who, upon due consideration, is moved to the same, and hopeth to obtain. My request to your lordship is only that it may please the same to be a mean for me to the king's majesty, that his grace may be certified of these few lines which I have written concerning my belief, which when it shall be truly conferred with the hard judgment given me for the same, I think his grace shall well perceive me to

be weighed in an uneven pair of balances. But I remit my matter and cause to Almighty God, who rightly judgeth all secrets. And thus I commend your lordship to the governance of him, and fellowship of all saints, Amen.

By your handmaid, Anne Askew.

MY FAITH BRIEFLY WRITTEN TO THE KING'S GRACE.

I, Anne Askew, of good memory, although God hath given me the bread of adversity and the water of trouble, yet not so much as my sins have deserved, desire this to be known unto your grace, that, forasmuch as I am by the law condemned for an evil doer, here I take heaven and earth to record, that I shall die in my innocency: and, according to that I have said first, and will say last, I utterly abhor and detest all heresies. And as concerning the supper of the Lord, I believe so much as Christ hath said therein, which he confirmed with his most blessed blood. I believe also so much as he willed me to follow and believe, and so much as the catholic church of him doth teach: for I will not forsake the commandment of his holy lips. But look, what God hath charged me with his mouth, that have I shut up in my heart. And thus briefly I end, for lack of learning.

Anne Askew.

The Cruel Handling and Racking of Anne Askew After Her Condemnation.

The Effect of my Examination and Handling since my Departure from Newgate.

On Tuesday I was sent from Newgate to the sign of the Crown, where Master Rich, and the bishop of London, with all their power and flattering words went about to persuade me from God; but I did not esteem their glosing pretences.

Then came there to me Nicholas Shaxton, and counselled me to recant as he had done. I said to him, that it had been good for him never to have been born; with many other like words.

Then Master Rich sent me to the Tower, where I remained till three o'clock.

Then came Rich and one of the council, charging me upon my obedience, to show unto them, if I knew any man or woman of my sect. My answer was, that I knew none. Then they asked me of my lady of Suffolk, my lady of Sussex, my lady of Hertford, my lady Denny, and my lady Fitzwilliam. To whom I answered, if I should pronounce any thing against them, that I were not able to prove it. Then said they unto me, that the king was informed that I could name, if I would, a great number of my sect. I answered, that the king was as well deceived in that behalf, as dissembled with in other matters.

Then commanded they me to show how I was maintained in the compter, and who willed me to stick to my opinion. I said, that there was no creature that therein did strengthen me: and as for the help that I had in the compter, it was by means of my maid. For as she went abroad in the streets, she made moan to the prentices, and they, by her, did send me money; but who they were I never knew.

Then they said that there were divers gentlewomen that gave me money: but I knew not their names. Then they said that there were divers ladies that had sent me money. I answered, that there was a man in a blue coat who delivered me ten shillings, and said that my lady of Hertford sent it me; and another in a violet coat gave me eight shillings, and said my lady Denny sent it me: whether it were true or no, I cannot tell; for I am not sure who sent it me, but as the maid did say. Then they said, there were of the council that did maintain me: and I said, No.

Then they did put me on the rack, because I confessed no ladies or gentlewomen to be of my opinion, and thereon they kept me a long time; and because I lay still, and did not cry, my lord chancellor and Master Rich took pains to rack me with their own hands, till I was nigh dead.

Then the lieutenant caused me to be loosed from the rack. Incontinently I swooned, and then they recovered me again. After that I sat two long hours reasoning with my lord chancellor upon the bare floor; where he, with many flattering words, persuaded me to leave my opinion. But my Lord God (I thank his everlasting goodness) gave me grace to persevere, and will do, I hope, to the very end.

Then was I brought to a house, and laid in a bed, with as weary and painful bones as ever had patient Job; I thank my Lord God there-for. Then my lord chancellor sent me word, if I would leave my opinion, I should want nothing: if I would not, I should forthwith to Newgate, and so be burned. I sent him again word, that I would rather die, than break my faith.

Thus the Lord open the eyes of their blind hearts, that the truth may take place. Farewell, dear friend, and pray, pray, pray!

Touching the order of her racking in the Tower thus it was; first she was let down into a dungeon, where sir Anthony Knevet, the lieutenant, commanded his jailor to pinch her with the rack. Which being done as much as he thought sufficient, he went about to take her down, supposing that he had done enough. But Wriothesley, the chancellor, not contented that she was loosed so soon, confessing nothing, commanded the lieutenant to strain her on the rack again: which because he denied to do, tendering the weakness of the woman, he was threatened therefore grievously of the said Wriothesley, saying, that he would signify his disobedience unto the king. And so consequently upon the same, he and Master Rich, throwing off their gowns, would needs play the tormentors themselves; first asking her, if she were with child. To whom she answering again, said, "Ye shall not need to spare for that, but do your wills upon me." And so, quietly and patiently praying unto the Lord, she abode their tyranny, till her bones and joints were almost plucked asunder, in such sort as she was carried away in a chair. When the racking was past, Wriothesley and his fellow took their horse towards the court.

In the mean time, while they were making their way by land, the good lieutenant, eftsoons taking boat, sped him to the court in all haste to speak with the king before the others, and so did; who there making his humble suit to the king, desired his pardon, and showed him the whole matter as it stood, and of the racking of Mistress Askew, and how he was threatened by the lord chancellor, because, at his commandment, not knowing his highness's pleasure, he refused to rack her; which he, for compassion, could not find in his heart to do, and therefore humbly craved his highness's pardon. Which when the king had understood, he seemed not very well to like of their so extreme handling of the woman, and also granted to the lieutenant his pardon, willing him to return and see to his charge.

Great expectation was in the mean season among the warders and other officers of the Tower, waiting for his return; whom when they saw come so cheerfully, declaring unto them how he had sped with the king, they were not a little joyous, and gave thanks to God there-for.

ANNE ASKEW'S ANSWER UNTO JOHN LACEL'S LETTER.

O friend, most dearly beloved in God! I marvel not a little what should move you to judge in me so slender a faith as to fear death, which is the end of all misery. In the Lord I desire you not to believe of me such wickedness. for I doubt it not, but God will perform his work in me, like as he hath begun. I understand the council is not a little displeased, that it should be reported abroad that I was racked in the Tower. They say now, that what they did there was but to fear me; whereby I perceive they are ashamed of their uncomely doings, and fear much lest the king's majesty should have information thereof; wherefore they would no man to noise it. Well! their cruelty God forgive them.

Your heart in Christ Jesu. Farewell and pray.

THE PURGATION OR ANSWER OF ANNE ASKEW, AGAINST THE FALSE SURMISES OF HER RECANTATION.

I have read the process, which is reported of them that know not the truth to be my recantation. But, as the Lord liveth, I never meant a thing less than to recant. Notwithstanding this I confess, that in my first troubles I was examined of the bishop of London about the sacrament. Yet had they no grant of my mouth but this: that I believed therein as the word of God did bind me to believe. More had they never of me. Then he made a copy, which is now in print, and required me to set thereunto my hand; but I refused it. Then my two sureties did will me in no wise to stick thereat, for it was no great matter, they said.

Then with much ado, at the last I wrote thus: 'I, Anne Askew, do believe this, if God's word do agree to the same, and the true catholic church.' Then the bishop, being in great displeasure with me because I made doubts in my writing, commanded me to prison, where I was awhile; but afterwards, by means of friends, I came out again. Here is the truth of that matter. And as concerning the thing that ye covet most to know, resort to John vi., and be ruled always thereby. Thus fare ye well quoth Anne Askew.

THE CONFESSION OF THE FAITH WHICH ANNE ASKEW MADE IN NEWGATE, BEFORE SHE SUFFERED.

I, Anne Askew, of good memory, although my merciful Father hath given me the bread of adversity and the water of trouble, yet not so much as my sins have deserved, do confess myself here a sinner before the throne of his heavenly Majesty, desiring his forgiveness and mercy. And forasmuch as I am by the law unrighteously condemned for an evil doer concerning opinions, I take the same most merciful God of mine, who hath made both heaven and earth, to record, that I hold no opinions contrary to his most holy word. And I trust in my merciful Lord, who is the giver of all grace, that he will graciously assist me against all evil opinions which are contrary to his blessed verity. For I take him to witness that I have done, and will unto my life's end utterly abhor them to the uttermost of my power.

But this is the heresy which they report me to hold: that after the priest hath spoken the words of consecration, there remaineth bread still. They both say, and also teach it for a necessary article of faith, that after those words be once spoken, there remaineth no bread, but even the self-same body that hung upon the cross on Good Friday, both flesh, blood, and bone. To this belief of theirs say I, nay. For then were our common creed false, which saith, that he sitteth on the right hand of God the Father Almighty, and from thence shall come to judge the quick and the dead. Lo, this is the heresy that I hold, and for it must suffer the death. But as touching the holy and blessed supper of the Lord, I believe it to be a most necessary remembrance of his glorious sufferings and death. Moreover, I believe as much therein as my eternal and only Redeemer Jesus Christ would, I should believe.

Finally, I believe all those Scriptures to be true, which he hath confirmed with his most precious blood. Yea, and as St. Paul saith, those Scriptures are sufficient for our learning and salvation, that Christ hath left here with us, so that I believe we need no unwritten verities to rule his church with. Therefore look, what he hath said unto me with his own mouth in his holy gospel, that have I, with God's grace, closed up in my heart and my full trust is, as David saith, that it shall be a lantern to my footsteps.

There be some do say, that I deny the eucharist or sacrament of thanksgiving; but those people do untruly report of me. For I both say and believe it, that if it were ordered like as Christ instituted it and left it, a most singular comfort it were unto us all. But as concerning your mass, as it is now used in our days,

I do say and believe it to be the most abominable idol that is in the world: for my God will not be eaten with teeth, neither yet dieth he again. And upon these words that I have now spoken, will I suffer death.

A PRAYER OF ANNE ASKEW.

O Lord! I have more enemies now, than there be hairs on my head: yet Lord, let them never overcome me with vain words, but fight thou, Lord, in my stead; for on thee cast I my care. With all the spite they can imagine, they fall upon me, who am thy poor creature. Yet, sweet Lord, let me not set by them that are against me; for in thee is my whole delight. And, Lord, I heartily desire of thee, that thou wilt of thy most merciful goodness forgive them that violence which they do, and have done, unto me. Open also thou their blind hearts, that they may hereafter do that thing in thy sight, which is only acceptable before thee, and to set forth thy verity aright, without all vain fantasies of sinful men. So be it, O Lord, so be it!

By me, Anne Askew.

Hitherto we have entreated of this good woman: now it remaineth that we touch somewhat as concerning her end and martyrdom. After that she (being born of such stock and kindred that she might have lived in great wealth and prosperity, if she would rather have followed the world than Christ) now had been so tormented, that she could neither live long in so great distress, neither yet by her adversaries be suffered to die in secret, the day of her execution being appointed, she was brought into Smithfield in a chair, because she could not go on her feet, by means of her great torments. When she was brought unto the stake, she was tied by the middle with a chain, that held up her body. When all things were thus prepared to the fire, Dr. Shaxton, who was then appointed to preach, began his sermon. Anne Askew, hearing and answering again unto him, where he said well, confirmed the same; where he said amiss, "There," said she, "he misseth, and speaketh without the book."

The sermon being finished, the martyrs, standing there tied at three several stakes ready to their martyrdom, began their prayers. The multitude and concourse of the people was exceeding; the place where they stood being railed about to keep out the press. Upon the bench under St. Bartholomew's church sat Wriothesley, chancellor of England; the old duke of Norfolk, the old earl of Bedford, the lord mayor, with divers others. Before the fire should be set unto them, one of the bench, hearing that they had gunpowder about them, and being alarmed lest the faggots, by strength of the gunpowder, would come flying about their ears, began to be afraid: but the earl of Bedford, declaring unto him how the gunpowder was not laid under the faggots, but only about their bodies, to rid them out of their pain; which having vent, there was no danger to them of the faggots, so diminished that fear.

Then Wriothesley, lord chancellor, sent to Anne Askew letters, offering to her the king's pardon if she would recant; who, refusing once to look upon them, made this answer again, that she came not thither to deny her Lord and Master. Then were the letters likewise offered unto the others, who, in like manner, following the constancy of the woman, denied not only to receive them, but also to look upon them. Whereupon the lord mayor, commanding fire to be put unto them, cried with a loud voice, "Fiat justitia."

And thus the good Anne Askew, with these blessed martyrs, being troubled so many manner of ways, and having passed through so many torments, having now ended the long course of her agonies, being compassed in with flames of fire, as a blessed sacrifice unto God, she slept in the Lord A.D. 1546, leaving behind her a singular example of christian constancy for all men to follow.

PRINCE ANDREY MIKHAILOVICH KURBSKY (1528–83) AND TSAR IVAN IV (1530–84)

Correspondence (1564)

At the age of twenty-one, the minor Smolensk-Yaroslavl prince Andrey Mikhailovich Kurbsky was appointed groom-in-waiting to "the first tsar of Russia" Ivan IV ("the Terrible"). In 1553, as one of his military commanders and advisers in the "chosen council," Kurbsky pledged to support the Tsar's son Fyodor as heir. As a reward, in 1556 Kurbsky was created a *boyar*, which gave him an official voice in government. But his voice was too progressive, even for the relatively enlightened Ivan. When the Tsar failed to renew his appointment in 1564, Kurbsky feared for his life and deserted the Muscovite forces. He sought asylum in the camp of King Sigismund II Augustus of Poland-Lithuania, where he was commissioned by the king, and elected to become the spokesman for the *boyars'* refusal to support the Tsar's despotism. From the town of Wolmar Kurbsky wrote this first of five letters to Ivan IV. The exchange of letters between him and Ivan IV is one of the most important historical documents of sixteenth-century Russia, clearly revealing the conflict between the conservative nobles and their autocratic sovereign who was determined to Europeanize his country. Kurbsky later wrote a *History of the Grand Duke of Muscovy,* an account of Ivan's reign.

First Epistle of Prince Andrey Kurbsky, Written to the Tsar and Grand Prince of Moscow in Consequence of His Fierce Persecution

To the tsar, exalted above all by God, who appeared [formerly] most illustrious, particularly in the Orthodox Faith, but who has now, in consequence of our sins, been found to be the contrary of this. If you have understanding, may you understand this with your leprous conscience—such a conscience as cannot be found even amongst the godless peoples. And I have not let my tongue say more than this on all these matters in turn; but because of the bitterest persecution from your power, with much sorrow in my heart will I hasten to inform you of a little.

Wherefore, O tsar, have you destroyed the strong in Israel and subjected to various forms of death the *voevodas* given to you by God? And wherefore have you spilt their victorious, holy blood in the churches of God during sacerdotal ceremonies, and stained the thresholds of the churches with their blood of martyrs? And why have you conceived against your well-wishers and against those who lay down their lives for you unheard-of torments and persecutions and death, falsely accusing the Orthodox of treachery and magic and other abuses, and endeavouring with zeal to turn light into darkness and to call sweet bitter? What guilt did they commit before you, O tsar, and in what way did they, the champions of Christianity, anger you? Have they not destroyed proud king-

doms and by their heroic bravery made subject to you in all things those in whose servitude our forefathers formerly were? Was it not through the keenness of their understanding that the strong German towns were given to you by God? Thus have you remunerated us, [your] poor [servants], destroying us by whole families? Think you yourself immortal, O tsar? Or have you been enticed into unheard-of heresy, as one no longer wishing to stand before the impartial judge, Jesus, begotten of God, who will judge according to justice the universe and especially the vainglorious tormentors, and who unhesitatingly will question them "right to the hairs. . . of their sins", as the saying goes? He is my Christ who sitteth on the throne of the Cherubims at the right hand of the power of the Almighty in the highest—the judge between you and me.

What evil and persecution have I not suffered from you! What ills and misfortunes have you not brought upon me! And what iniquitous tissues of lies have you not woven against me! But I cannot now recount the various misfortunes at your hands which have beset me owing to their multitude and since I am still filled with the grief of my soul. But, to conclude, I can summarize them all [thus]: of everything have I been deprived: I have been driven from the land of God without guilt, hounded by you. I did not ask [for aught] with humble words, nor did I beseech you with tearful plaint; nor yet did I win from you any mercy through the intercession of the hierarchy. You have recompensed me with evil for good and for my love with implacable hatred. My blood, spilt like water for you, cries out against you to my Lord. God sees into hearts—in my mind have I ardently reflected and my conscience have I placed as a witness [against myself], and I have sought and pried within my thoughts, and, examining myself, I know not now—nor have I ever found—my guilt in aught before you. In front of your army have I marched—and marched again; and no dishonour have I brought upon you; but only brilliant victories, with the help of the angel of the Lord, have I won for your glory, and never have I turned the back of your regiments to the foe. But far more, I have achieved most glorious conquests to increase your renown. And this, not in one year, nor yet in two—but throughout many years have I toiled with much sweat and patience; and always have I been separated from my fatherland, and little have I seen my parents, and my wife have I not known; but always in far-distant towns have I stood in arms against your foes and I have suffered many wants and natural illnesses, of which my Lord Jesus Christ is witness. Still more, I was visited with wounds inflicted by barbarian hands in various battles and all my body is already afflicted with sores. But to you, O tsar, was all this as nought; rather do you show us your intolerable wrath and bitterest hatred, and, furthermore, burning stoves.

And I wanted to relate all my military deeds in turn which I have accomplished for your glory by the strength of my Christ, but I have not recounted them for this reason, that God knows better than man. For he is the recompenser for all these things, and not only for them, but also for a cup of cold water, and I know that you yourself are not unaware of them. And furthermore may this be known to you, O tsar; you will, I think, no longer see my face in this world until the glorious coming of my Christ. Think not that concerning these things I will remain silent before you; to my end will I incessantly cry out with tears against you to the everlasting Trinity, in which I believe; and I call to my aid the Mother of the Lord of the Cherubims, my hope and protectress, Our Lady, the Mother of God, and all the Saints, the elect of God, and my master and forefather, Prince Fedor Rostislavich, whose corpse remains imperishable, preserved throughout the ages, and emits from the grave sweet odours, sweeter than aromatics, and, by the grace of the Holy Ghost, pours forth miraculous healing streams, as you, O tsar, know well.

Deem not, O tsar, and think not upon us with your sophistic thoughts, as though we had already perished, massacred by you in our innocence and banished and driven out by you without justice; rejoice not in this, glorying, as it were, in a vain victory; those massacred by you, standing at the throne of Our Lord, ask vengeance against you; whilst we who have been banished and driven out by you without justice from the land cry out day and night to God, however much in your pride you may boast in this temporal, fleeting life, devising vessels of torture against the Christian race, yea, and abusing and trampling on the Angelic Form, with the approbation of your flatterers and comrades of the table, your quarrelsome boyars, the destroyers of your soul and body, who urge you on to aphrodisiacal deeds and, together with their children, act more [viciously] than the priests of Cronus. So much for this. And this epistle, soaked in my tears, will I order to be put into my grave with me, when I come with you before the Judgment of my God, Jesus Christ. Amen.

Written in Wolmar, the town of my master, King Augustus Sigismund, from whom I hope to receive much reward and comfort for all my sorrow, by his sovereign grace, and still more with God's help.

Epistle of the Tsar and Sovereign to all his Russian Kingdom against those that violate the oath of allegiance, against Prince Andrey Kurbsky and his comrades, concerning their treacheries

Our God, Tripersonal, who was from everlasting and is now, Father, Son and Holy Ghost, who has neither beginning nor end, in whom we live and move, and by whom tsars rule and the mighty make laws, and the conquering banner, the Holy Cross of the only-begotten Word of God—nor is this banner ever conquerable—was given by Jesus Christ, Our Lord, to the first tsar in piety, Constantine, and to all Orthodox tsars and upholders of Orthodoxy, and to the divine servants, by whose vigilance the Word of God was fulfilled everywhere. And as the words of God encircled the whole world like an eagle in flight, so a spark of piety reached even the Russian kingdom. The autocracy of this Russian kingdom of veritable Orthodoxy, by the will of God, [has its] beginning from the great tsar Vladimir, who enlightened the whole Russian land with holy baptism, and [was maintained by] the great tsar Vladimir Monomach, who received the supreme honour from the Greeks and the brave and great sovereign, Alexander Nevsky, who won a victory over the godless Germans, and the great and praiseworthy sovereign, Dimitry, who beyond the Don won a mighty victory over the godless sons of Hagar, [and autocracy was handed down] even to the avenger of evils, our grandfather, the Grand Prince Ivan, and to the acquirer of immemorially hereditary lands, our father of blessed memory, the great sovereign, Vasily—and has come down even to us, the humble sceptre-bearer of the Russian kingdom. And we praise [God] for his great mercy bestowed upon us, in that he has not hitherto allowed our right hand to become stained with the blood of our own race; for we have not seized the kingdom from anyone, but, by the grace of God and with the blessing of our forefathers and fathers, as we were born to rule, so have we grown up and ascended the throne by the bidding of God, and with the blessing of our parents have we taken what is our own, and we have not seized what belongs to others; [From the ruler] of this Orthodox true Christian autocracy, which has power over many dominions, a command [should be sent to you]; but this is our Christian and humble answer to him who was formerly boyar and adviser and voevoda of our auto-

cratic state and of the true Christian Orthodox faith, but who is now the perjurer of the holy and life-giving Cross of the Lord and the destroyer of Christianity, the servant of those enemies of Christianity who have apostatized from the worship of the divine icons and trampled on all the sacred commandments and destroyed the holy temples and befouled and trampled on the sacred vessels and images, like the Isaurian and the one who is called Putrefaction and the Armenian—to him, who has cast in his lot with all these, to Prince Andrey Mikhailovich Kurbsky, who with his treacherous ways wished to become master of Yaroslavl'; let [this] be known.

Why, O Prince, if you think that you have piety, have you cast out your very soul? What will you give in exchange for it on the day of the last judgment? Even if you gain the whole world, in the end death will in any case seize you! Why did you betray your soul for the sake of your body, if you feared death according to the lying word of your devilish friends and spies? In all places, like devils [warring] against all the world, so too are those who have consented to be your friends and servants, who have rejected us having broken the oath on the Cross [i.e. of allegiance], imitating devils, in all manner of ways casting nets everywhere [to catch] us, spying on us in every way possible in their devilish manner, watching our movements and words, imagining themselves to be unnoticeable, and fabricating from this much abuse and reproach against us; and this do they bring to you, disgracing us before all the world. For this evil you gave them much reward with our land and our treasury, falsely calling them [our] servants. And you were filled with these devilish rumours, like a serpent with deadly poison, and having raged against me and destroyed your soul, you have even embarked upon the destruction of the Church. Consider not that it is right to give offence to God, having fallen into wrath against man. It is one thing [to give offence to] a human even if he wears the purple, but it is another thing [to offend] God! Or do you think, accursed one, that you will protect yourself from this [i.e. from offending God]? By no means! If you wage war together with them, then will you also destroy churches and trample on icons and annihilate Christians; and even if you do not dare [to act] with your hands, still with your deadly poisonous thoughts will you cause much of this evil. Consider how in a battle attack the soft limbs of infants are crushed and maimed by the legs of horses! And if the attack is in winter, then is the evil wrought still worse! And this your devilish scheming—how can it not be likened to the fury of Herod, manifested by his massacre of the innocents! Do you consider this—the perpetration of such evils—to be piety? Should you accuse us of warring against Christians—namely against Germans and Lithuanians—then your accusations are groundless. [For] even if there were Christians in those lands, we would [still] wage war according to the customs of our forefathers, just as has happened many times before now; but now we know that in those lands there are no Christians except for a very few ministers of the Church and secret servants of the Lord. Furthermore, even the Lithuanian struggle began because of your treachery and malevolence and your inconsiderate carelessness.

You, however, for the sake of your body have destroyed the soul and for the sake of short-lived fame have scorned imperishable glory, and having raged against man, you have risen against God. Consider, wretch, from what heights and into what depths you have descended in body and soul! On you have come to pass the words: "from him. . . shall be taken away even that which he hath". Is this then your piety, that you have destroyed yourself because of your self-love and not for the sake of God? Those who live there [i.e. in your new fatherland] and those who have understanding can understand your evil poison, how, desiring short-lived glory and wealth, and not in order to escape from death, you have done this deed. If you are just and pious as you say, why did you fear a guiltless death, which is no death but gain? In the end you will die anyhow! If you

did fear a false death sentence against you owing to the villainous lying of your friends, the servants of Satan, then is your treacherous intention clear from the beginning up to now. Why did you despise even the apostle Paul? For he said: "Let every soul be subject unto the higher powers. For there is no power ordained that is not of God. . . . Whosoever, therefore, resisteth the power, resisteth the ordinance of God." Think on this and reflect, that he who resists power, resists God; and who resists God is called an apostate, which is the worst sin. And these words were said concerning all power, even when power is obtained by blood and strife. But consider what I said above, that I did not take my kingdom by rape; if you then resist [such] power, all the more so do you resist God. Thus, as elsewhere the Apostle Paul said (and these words have you too scorned): "Servants, be obedient to your masters, . . . not with eye-service, as men-pleasers", but to God, "and not only to the good. . . , but also to the froward", "not only for wrath, but also for the conscience sake"; for this is the will of God, "to suffer for well-doing." And if you are just and pious, why do you not permit yourself to accept suffering from me, your froward master, and [so] to inherit the crown of life?

But for the sake of temporary glory and self-love and the delights of this world, you have trampled down all your spiritual piety together with the Christian faith and law, and you have become like unto the seed falling on stone and springing up, and when the sun shone scorchingly, then were you, because of a false word, led astray and you fell away and bore no fruit. And because of the false words you have acted like [the seed] falling by the wayside; and as for faithful service to the true God, who has sown the word, and to us—all this has the foe seized from your heart and made you follow him with all your will. Likewise do all the divine writings teach, forbidding children to resist their fathers, and a servant his master, except in the cause of the Faith. And if, having learned such things from your father the devil, you assert with lying words that you ran away because of the Faith, then, "as the Lord my God liveth", "as my soul liveth", [do I declare] that not only you but all your partisans and devilish servants cannot impute this [sin] to us. But above all we hope—by the Incarnation of the Word of God and the mercy of his most pure Mother, the Interceder for Christians, and by the prayers of all the Saints—not only to answer you in this, but also [to fight] against those who have trampled on the holy icons and have rejected all the Christian divine mystery and have turned aside from God—those whom you have joined in friendship—to unmask their godlessness and to reveal righteousness and to proclaim how the Grace has shone forth. . .

Your epistle has been received and clearly understood. And since you have put adder's poison under your lips, [your epistle] was filled, according to your understanding, with honey and the honeycomb and yet is found to be bitterer than wormwood, according to the prophet who says: "their words were softer than oil, yet were they drawn swords." Are you thus accustomed, being a Christian, so to serve a Christian sovereign? And is this then the fitting honour to pay to a master given by God, that you should belch forth poison in a devilish manner? The beginning of your epistle you have written without [due] reflexion, thinking in the manner of Novatian, for of repentance [you know] nothing, but you consider that men should be above human nature, just like Novatian. As for your writing that we "appeared most illustrious in Orthodoxy", this is indeed so; as then, so now do we believe, with true belief, in the living and true God. And as for your "[being found] the contrary of this" and "understand, having a leprous conscience", behold you think Novatianist thoughts, and you do not consider the word of the Gospel which says, "Woe to the world because of offences! for it must needs be that offences come (not); but woe to that man to whom the offence cometh!" "It were better for him that a millstone were hanged about his neck, and that he were drowned in the depth of the sea." And you, blinded by your evil ways, cannot see the truth. How, thinking that you will stand at the throne of the Almighty and serve for ever with the angels, and how, having deemed yourselves worthy to slaughter the Sacrificial Lamb for the salvation of the world,—how, when you have trampled under foot all these things with your devilish advisers, could you bring so many torments on us with your evil designs? And therefore, in view of your having in devilish manner shattered piety since the days of my youth, and in view of your having seized and appropriated the power handed down to me by God from our forefathers—is this then the sign of a "leprous conscience" to hold my kingdom in my hand and not to let my servants rule? And is it contrary to reason not to wish to be possessed and ruled by my own servants? And is this "illustrious Orthodoxy"—to be ruled over and ordered about by my own servants? . . .

SANTA TERESA DE JESÚS, DE AVILA (1515–82)

The Life (1565)

The simplicity of the devout life is exemplified in the life of Saint Teresa, who, at the age of seven, ran away from home to become a martyr. She ended up as a Carmelite nun, eventually a Mother Superior, and was responsible, along with St. John of the Cross, for reforming that order, forming a branch known as the "Barefoot Carmelites" which emphasized primitive asceticism and prayerful reparation. Her career was indeed an "imitation of Christ," a perfect model of the Renaissance "fool" whose folly is the wisdom and serenity that come with innocence and single-mindedness. In addition to her *Foundations, Method for the Visitation of Convents, Spiritual Relations,* and *The Way of Perfection,* she unflaggably wrote thousands of letters—to her brother Lorenzo and sister Juana, to her spiritual charges, her prioresses, bishops, judges, aristocratic ladies and gentlemen, and King Philip II himself. She once said that the worry of her letter-writing, sometimes keeping her up till two in the morning, "is killing me." She hated writing: "I am almost stealing the time for writing, and that with great difficulty, for it hinders me from spinning and I am living in a poor house and have numerous things to do." We can be grateful that she obeyed her superiors' orders to record her autobiography, for the *Life,* one of the great classics of the Spanish language and comparable to St. Augustine's *Confessions,* offers unique psychological insight into the spiritual progress of this inspired reformer. Her attempt to guide others to perfection displays a combination of brashness, tact, candor, determination, and sanctity that remind us of her modern namesake, Mother Teresa. Perhaps the greatest mystic of the late Renaissance, Teresa was canonized a saint in 1622.

. . . Two or three days before, there had been a meeting between the Mayor and certain members of the City Council and of the Chapter, and they had all agreed that this new convent must on no account be sanctioned, that it would cause notable harm to the common weal, that the Most Holy Sacrament must be removed and that the matter must on no account be allowed to go any farther. They summoned a meeting of representatives of all the Orders—two learned men from each—to obtain their opinions. Some said nothing; others were condemnatory. Finally, they decided that the foundation must be dissolved at once. There was only one of them, a Presentado of the Order of Saint Dominic, who was not opposed to the convent, though he objected to its poverty: he said that there was no reason for dissolving it, that the question should be gone into with care, that there was plenty of time for doing so, that it was the Bishop's affair, and other things of that kind. This did a great deal of good: to judge by their fury, it was fortunate for us that they had not proceeded to dissolve the foundation on the spot. The fact was that the convent had been destined to be founded, for its foundation was the Lord's will and against that the whole body of them were powerless. . . .

A priest, who was a great servant of God and a lover of all perfection, and who had always been a great help to me, went to the capital to take the matter in hand and worked very hard at it. That saintly gentleman of whom I have made mention also did a very great deal in the matter and helped in every way he could. He suffered many trials and great persecution over this and I always found him a father in everything and find him so still. Those who helped me were inspired by the Lord with such fervour that each of them regarded the matter as if it were his own and as if his own life and reputation were at stake, when it had really nothing to do with them except in so far as they believed it to be for the Lord's service. It seemed clear, too, that His Majesty was helping the cleric I have referred to, who was another of my great helpers, and whom the Bishop sent to represent him at an important meeting which was held. Here he stood out alone against all the others and eventually pacified them by suggesting certain expedients which did a great deal to bring about an agreement. But nothing was sufficient to dissuade them from putting their whole weight, as we say, into smashing us. It was this servant of God of whom I am speaking who gave us the habit and reserved the Most Holy Sacrament for us, and as a result found himself sorely persecuted. This commotion lasted for six months, and it would take a long time to give a detailed description of the severe trials which we had to suffer.

I was astonished at all the trouble that the devil was taking to hurt a few poor women, and how everybody thought that twelve women and a prioress (for I must remind those who opposed the plan that there were to be no more) could do such harm to the place, when they were living so strictly. If there had been any harm or error in their project it would have concerned themselves alone; harm to the city there could not possibly be, and yet our opponents found so much that they fought us with a good conscience. Eventually they said they would allow the matter to go forward if the convent had an endowment. By this time I was so wearied, more by all the trouble my helpers were having than by my own, that I thought it would not be a bad idea to accept some money until the storm subsided, and then to give it up. At other times, like the wicked and imperfect woman I am, I would wonder if perhaps it was the Lord's will that we should have an endowment, as it seemed impossible for us to get anywhere without one. So in the end I agreed to this arrangement.

The discussion of it had already begun, when, on the very night before it was to be concluded, the Lord told me that I must not agree to such a thing, for, if once we had an endowment, we should never be allowed to give it up again. He said various other things as well. That same night there appeared to me the holy Fray Peter of Alcántara, who was now dead. Before his death, knowing how much opposition and persecution we were meeting with, he had written to me saying he was delighted the foundation was encountering all this opposition, for the efforts which the devil was making to prevent the establishment of the convent were a sign that the Lord would be very well served there; and he had added that I must on no account allow the place to have any revenue. He had insisted upon this in the letter two or three times, and said that, if I were firm about it, everything would turn out as I wished. Since his death I had seen him on two previous occasions and had had a vision of the great bliss that he was enjoying. So his appearance caused me no fear—indeed, it made me very happy, for he always appeared as a glorified body, full of great bliss, and it gave me the greatest joy to see him. I remember that, the first time I saw him, he told me among other things how great was his fruition, adding that the penances he had done had been a happy thing for him, since they had won him such a great reward.

As I think I have already said something about this, I will say no more here than that on this occasion he spoke to me with some severity. All he said was that I was on no account to accept any endowment and asked why I would not take his advice; he then immediately disappeared. I was astounded, and on the next day I told that gentleman what had happened, for I used to consult him about everything, as he was the person who helped us most. I told him on no account to allow the agreement about our endowment to be concluded, but to let the lawsuit continue. He was more definite about this than I and was delighted at what I said; he told me afterwards how much he had regretted having given the agreement his approval.

There then came forward another person, a zealous and devoted servant of God, who suggested that, now this point was satisfactorily settled, the matter should be put into the hands of learned men. This caused me a good deal of uneasiness, for some of my helpers agreed to that course and the unravelling of this tangle in which the devil now involved us was the most difficult task of all. Throughout everything the Lord helped me, but in this summary narrative it is impossible to give an adequate description of what happened in the two years between the beginning of the foundation and its comple-tion. The first six months and the last were the most troublesome.

When the city was finally somewhat calmed, the Dominican Father-Presentado who was helping us managed things for us very well. He had not previously been there, but the Lord brought him at a time which was very convenient for us, and His Majesty seems to have done so for that end alone, for he told me afterwards that he had had no reason for coming and had only heard of the matter by accident. He stayed with us for as long as was necessary. When he left, he managed somehow—it seemed impossible that he could have done this in so short a time—to get our Father Provincial to give me leave to go and live in the new house and to take some other nuns with me so that we might say the Office and instruct the sisters who were there. It was the happiest of days for me when we went in.

While at prayer in the church, before entering the convent, I all but went into a rapture, and saw Christ, Who seemed to be receiving me with great love, placing a crown on my head and thanking me for what I had done for His Mother. On another occasion, after Compline, when we were all praying in choir, I saw Our Lady in the greatest glory, clad in a white mantle, beneath which she seemed to be sheltering us all. From this I learned what a high degree of glory the Lord would give to the nuns in this house. . . .

BERNAL DÍAZ DEL CASTILLO (1492–1581)

HISTORIA VERDADERA DE LA CONQUISTA DE LA NUEVA ESPAÑA

The True History of the Conquest of Mexico (1568)

Here, in the voice of a conquistador, is an account of the 1519 Spanish invasion of Mexico City aimed at justifying Hernán Cortés for his destruction of Moctezuma's capital: "There never existed in the world men who by bold achievement have gained more for their Lord and King, than we brave conquerors." Díaz was the last living survivor of Cortés' expedition when he composed his *History* to respond to increasing charges of cruelty and to correct what he considered to be errors in earlier accounts. He was particularly angry at Bartolomé de las Casas' charges of genocide, proclaiming that, if the expedition had not dealt punitively with the Indians, "our lives would have been in the greatest danger, and had we been destroyed this country of New Spain would not have been so easily gained, or a second expedition attempted." Bernal's account of the dazzling Aztec capital, favorably comparable to Rome or Constantinople, was not published in his lifetime, reaching print only in 1632.

PREFACE

I BERNAL DIAZ DEL CASTILLO, regidor of this loyal city of Guatimala, and author of the following most true history, during the time I was writing the same, happened to see a work composed by Francisco Lopez de Gomara, the elegance of which made me blush for the vulgarity of my own, and throw down my pen in despair. But when I had read it, I found that the whole was a misrepresentation, and also that in his extraordinary exaggerations of the numbers of the natives, and of those who were killed in the different battles, his account was utterly unworthy of belief. We never much exceeded four hundred men, and if we had found such numbers bound hand and foot, we could not have

put them to death. But the fact was, we had enough to do to protect ourselves, for I vow to God, and say Amen thereto, that we were every day repeating our prayers, and supplicating to be delivered from the perils that surrounded us. Alaric a most brave king, and Attila a proud warrior, never killed so many of their foes as we are said by that historian to have done in New Spain. He also says we burned many cities and temples; and this he does to astonish his reader; not seeming to recollect that any of the true conquerors existed, to contradict him. He also enhances the merit of one officer at the expence of another; speaking of some as captains who were not with us.

He says that Cortes gave orders, secretly, for the destruction of the ships; whereas it was done by the common consent of all, to have the assistance of the mariners. He also depreciates Juan de Grijalva most unjustly; he being a very valiant captain. He omits the discovery of Yucatan by De Cordova, and is in an error again when he speaks of the first expedition of Garray, as if Garray had come with it. In what concerns the defeat of Narvaez, his account is conformable to the relations given; but in that of the wars of Tlascala he is as erroneous as ever. As to the war in Mexico, where we lost above eight hundred and seventy soldiers, this he treats as a matter of little importance; and he makes no mention of our losses in the subsequent siege, but speaks of it as if it had been a festival, or a marriage! but why should I waste paper and ink in the detection of his numerous errors; I will therefore proceed with my relation, for according to what the wise say, the art and beauty of historical composition is, to write the truth; and proceeding upon this rule, with such embellishment and ornament as I shall hereafter judge expedient, I will relate and bring into full light the conquest of New Spain, and the heroic services of us the true conquerors, who with our small numbers, under the adventurous and brave Captain Hernando Cortes, and with great danger and hardships, gained to his Majesty this rich country; for which service his Majesty has frequently issued his orders that we should be amply rewarded. Moreover, as a good pilot sounds, and discovers shoals and sands as he proceeds, by the lead and line, so will I, with my pen in my hand, expose misrepresentations, in my voyage through the history of Gomara, to the haven of truth; but if I were to point out every error, the chaff would outweigh the grain.

My relation will give to historians sufficient whereby to celebrate our general, Cortes, and the brave conquerors by whose hands this holy and great undertaking succeeded; for this is no history of distant nations, nor vain reveries; I relate that of which I was an eye witness, and not idle reports and hearsay: for truth is sacred. Gomara received and wrote such accounts as were intended to enhance the fame and merit of Cortes; no mention being made by him of our valiant captains and soldiers; and the whole tenor of the work shews how much he was influenced by his attachment to that family by whom he and his are patronised. He has also misled the Doctor Illescas, and Bishop Paulus Jovius.

The following history I have brought to its conclusion, in the loyal city of Guatimala, the residence of the royal court of audience, on this twenty sixth day of February, in the year of our Lord, one thousand five hundred and seventy two.

. . . At day break on the ensuing morning, after recommending ourselves to God, we sallied out with our turrets, which as well as I recollect were called burros or mantas, in other places where I have seen them, with some of our musquetry and cross-bows in front, and our cavalry occasionally charging. The enemy this day shewed themselves more determined than ever, and we were equally resolved to force our way to the great temple, although it should cost the life of every man of us; we therefore advanced with our turrets in that direction. I will not detail the desperate battle which we had with the enemy in a very strong house, nor how their arrows wounded our horses, notwithstanding their armour, and if at any time the horsemen attempted to pursue the Mexicans, the latter threw themselves into the canals, and others sallied out upon our people and massacred them with large lances.

As to setting fire to the buildings, or tearing them down, it was utterly in vain to attempt; they all stood in the water, and only communicating by draw bridges, it was too dangerous to attempt to reach them by swimming, for they showered stones from their slings, and masses of cut stone taken from the buildings, upon our heads, from the terraces of the houses. Whenever we attempted to set fire to a house, it was an entire day before it took effect, and when it did, the flames could not spread to others, as they were separated from it by the water, and also because the roofs of them were terraced.

We at length arrived at the great temple, and immediately and instantly, above four thousand Mexicans rushed up into it, without including in that number other bodies who occupied it before, and defended it against us with lances, stones, and darts. They thus prevented our ascending for some time, neither turrets, nor musquetry, nor cavalry availing, for although the latter body several times attempted to charge, the stone pavement of the courts of the temple was so smooth, that the horses could not keep their feet, and fell. From the steps of the great temple they opposed us in front, and we were attacked by such numbers on both sides, that although our guns swept off ten or fifteen of them at each discharge, and that in each attack of our infantry we killed many with our swords, their numbers were such that we could not make any effectual impression, or ascend the steps. We were then forced to abandon our turrets, which the enemy had destroyed, and with great concert, making an effort without them, we forced our way up. Here Cortes shewed himself the man that he really was. What a desperate engagement we then had! every man of us was covered with blood, and above forty dead upon the spot. It was Gods will that we should at length reach the place where we had put up the image of our Lady, but when we came there it was not to be found, and it seems that Montezuma, actuated either by fear or by devotion, had caused it to be removed. We set fire to the building, and burned a part of the temple of the gods Huitzilopochtli and Tezcatepuco. Here our Tlascalan allies served us essentially. While thus engaged, some setting the temple on fire, others fighting, above three thousand noble Mexicans with their priests were about us, and attacking us, drove us down six and even ten of the steps, while others who were in the corridores, or within side the railings and concavities of the great temple, shot such clouds of arrows at us that we could not maintain our ground, when thus attacked from every part. We therefore began our retreat, every man of us being wounded, and forty six left dead upon the spot. We were pursued with

a violence and desperation which is not in my power to describe, nor in that of any one to form an idea of who did not see it. During all this time also other bodies of the Mexicans had been continually attacking our quarters, and endeavoring to set fire to them. In this battle, we made prisoners two of the principal priests. I have often seen this engagement represented in the paintings of the natives, both of Mexico and Tlascala, and our ascent into the great temple. In these our party is represented with many dead, and all wounded. The setting fire to the temple when so many warriors were defending it in the corridores, railings, and concavities, and other bodies of them on the plain ground, and filling the courts, and on the sides, and our turrets demolished, is considered by them as a most heroic action.

With great difficulty we reached our quarters, which we found the enemy almost in possession of, as they had beaten down a part of the walls; but they desisted in a great measure from their attacks on our arrival, still throwing in upon us however showers of arrows, darts, and stones. The night was employed by us in repairing the breaches, in dressing our wounds, burying our dead, and consulting upon our future measures. No gleam of hope could be now rationally formed by us, and we were utterly sunk in despair. Those who had come with Narvaez showered maledictions upon Cortes, nor did they forget Velasquez by whom they had been induced to quit their comfortable and peaceable habitations in the island of Cuba. It was determined to try if we could not procure from the enemy a cessation of hostilities, on condition of our quitting the city; but at day break they assembled round our quarters and attacked them with greater fury than ever, nor could our fire arms repel them, although they did considerable execution.

Cortes perceiving how desperate our situation was, determined that Montezuma should address his subjects from a terrace, and desire them to desist from their attacks, with an offer from us to evacuate Mexico. He accordingly sent to the King to desire him to do so. When this was made known to Montezuma, he burst out into violent expressions of grief saying, "What does he want of me now? I neither desire to hear him, nor to live any longer, since my unhappy fate has reduced me to this situation on his account." He therefore dismissed those sent to him with a refusal, adding as it is said, that he wished not to be troubled any more with the false words and promises of Cortes. Upon this the Reverend Father Fray Bartholome and Christoval de Oli went to him, and addressed him with the most affectionate and persuasive language, to induce him to appear, to which he replied, that he did not believe that his doing so would be of any avail, that the people had already elected another sovereign, and were determined never to permit one of us to quit the city. The enemy continued their attacks, and Montezuma was at length persuaded. He accordingly came, and stood at the railing of a terraced roof, attended by many of our soldiers, and addressed the people below him, requesting, in very affectionate language, a cessation of hostilities, in order that we might quit the city. The chiefs and nobility, as soon as they perceived him coming forward, called to their troops to desist and be silent, and four of them approached, so as to be heard and spoken to by Montezuma. They then addressed him, lamenting the misfortunes of him, his children, and family, and also told him that they had raised Coadlavaca Prince of Iztapalapa to the throne, adding, that the war was drawing to a conclusion, and that they had promised to their gods never to desist but with the total destruction of the Spaniards; that they every day offered up prayers for his personal safety, and as soon as they had rescued him out of our hands, they would venerate him as before, and trusted that he would pardon them.

As they concluded their address, a shower of arrows and stones fell about the spot where Montezuma stood, from which the Spaniards, interposing their bucklers, protected the King; but expecting that while speaking to his people they would not make another attack, they unguarded him for an instant, and just then three stones and an arrow struck him in the head, arm, and leg.

The King when thus wounded refused all assistance, and we were unexpectedly informed of his death. Cortes and our captains wept for him, and he was lamented by them and all the soldiers who had known him, as if he had been their father; nor is it to be wondered at, considering how good he was. It was said that he had reigned seventeen years, and that he was the best King Mexico had ever been governed by. It was also said that he had fought and conquered in three occasions that he had been defied to the field, in the progress of subjugating different states to his dominion.

All the endeavors of our Reverend Father Fray Bartholome, could not prevail on the King to embrace our faith, when he was told that his wounds were mortal, nor could he be induced to have them attended to. After the death of Montezuma, Cortes sent two prisoners, a nobleman and a priest, to inform the new sovereign, Coadlavaca, and his chiefs, of the event, and how it had happened by the hands of his own subjects. He directed them to express our grief on the occasion, and our wish that he should be interred with the respect due to so great a monarch. Cortes farther signified to them, that he did not admit or acknowledge the right of the sovereign that they had chosen, but that the throne should be filled either by a son of the great Montezuma, or his cousin who was with us in our quarters. Also, that we desired unmolested egress from the city, on condition of our committing no more acts of hostility by fire or sword. Cortes then caused the body of the King to be borne out by six noblemen, attended by most of the priests whom we had taken prisoners, and exposed it to public view. He also desired them to obey the last injunctions of Montezuma, and to deliver his body to the Mexican chiefs. These noblemen accordingly related the circumstances of the King's death to Coadlavaca, and we could hear the exclamations of sorrow which the people expressed at the fight of his body. They now attacked us in our quarters with the greatest violence, and threatened us that within the space of two days we should pay with our lives the death of their king, and the dishonor of their gods, saying that they had chosen a sovereign whom we could not deceive, as we had done the good Montezuma.

PAOLO VERONESE (1528–88)

Trial before the Holy Tribunal (1573)

Veronese was called before the Venetian Inquisition to defend his "Feast in the House of Simon," which he'd painted for the refectory of Saints John and Paul. The issue: He was accused of willfully introducing profanity into the holy subject matter of his work. In this rare transcript, the forces of orthodoxy are aligned against the freedom of artistic vision in a conflict as old, and as contemporary, as human nature itself. In this case, the conflict was resolved when Veronese changed the name of the painting to "The Feast in the House of Levi," making it clear that it was not a depiction of the sacrosanct "Last Supper."

Venice, July 18, 1573. The minutes of the session of the Inquisition Tribunal of Saturday, the 18th of July, 1573. Today, Saturday, the 18th of the month of July, 1573, having been asked by the Holy Office to appear before the Holy Tribunal, Paolo Caliari of Verona, domiciled in the Parish Saint Samuel, being questioned about his name and surname, answered as above.

QUESTIONED ABOUT HIS PROFESSION:
ANSWER. I paint and compose figures.

QUESTION. Do you know the reason why you have been summoned?
A. No, sir.

Q. Can you imagine it?
A. I can well imagine.

Q. Say what you think the reason is.
A. According to what the Reverend Father, the

Prior of the Convent of SS. Giovanni e Paolo, whose name I do not know, told me, he had been here and Your Lordships had ordered him to have painted [in the picture] a Magdalen in place of a dog. I answered him by saying I would gladly do everything necessary for my honor and for that of my painting, but that I did not understand how a figure of Magdalen would be suitable there for many reasons which I will give at any time, provided I am given an opportunity.

Q. What picture is this of which you have spoken?
A. This is a picture of the Last Supper that Jesus Christ took with His Apostles in the house of Simon.

Q. Where is this picture?
A. In the Refectory of the Convent of SS. Giovanni e Paolo.

Q. Is it on the wall, on a panel, or on canvas?
A. On canvas.

Q. What is its height?
A. It is about seventeen feet.

Q. How wide?
A. About thirty-nine feet.

Q. At this Supper of Our Lord have you painted other figures?
A. Yes, milords.

Q. Tell us how many people and describe the gestures of each.
A. There is the owner of the inn, Simon; besides this figure I have made a steward, who, I imagined, had come there for his own pleasure to see how the things were going at the table. There are many figures there which I cannot recall, as I painted the picture some time ago.

Q. Have you painted other Suppers besides this one?
A. Yes, milords.

Q. How many of them have you painted and where are they?
A. I painted one in Verona for the reverend monks at San Nazzaro which is in their refectory. Another I painted in the refectory of the reverend fathers of San Giorgio here in Venice. . . .

Q. In this Supper which you made. . . what is the significance of the man whose nose is bleeding?
A. I intended to represent a servant whose nose was bleeding because of some accident.

Q. What is the significance of those armed men dressed as Germans, each with a halberd in his hand?
A. This requires that I say twenty words!

Q. Say them.
A. We painters take the same license the poets and the jesters take and I have represented these two halberdiers, one drinking and the other eating nearby on the stairs. They are placed here so that they might be of service because it seemed to me fitting, according to what I have been told, that the mater of the house, who was great and rich, should have such servants.

Q. And that man dressed as a buffoon with a parrot on his wrist, for what purpose did you paint him on that canvas?
A. For ornament, as is customary.

Q. Who are at the table of Our Lord?
A. The Twelve Apostles.

Q. What is St. Peter, the first one, doing?
A. Carving the lamb in order to pass it to the other end of the table.

Q. What is the Apostle next to him doing?
A. He is holding a dish in order to receive what St. Peter will give him.

Q. Tell us what the one next to this one is doing.
A. He has a toothpick and cleans his teeth.

Q. Who do you really believe was present at that Supper?
A. I believe one would find Christ with His Apostles. But if in a picture there is some space to spare I enrich it with figures according to the stories.

Q. Did any one commission you to paint Germans, buffoons, and similar things in the picture?
A. No, milords, but I received the commission to decorate the picture as I saw fit. It is large and, it seemed to me, it could hold many figures.

Q. Are not the decorations which you painters are accustomed to add to paintings or pictures supposed to be suitable and proper to the subject and the principal figures or are they for pleasure—simply what comes to your imagination without any discretion or judiciousness?
A. I paint pictures as I see fit and as well as my talent permits.

Q. Does it seem fitting at the Last Supper of the Lord to paint buffoons, drunkards, Germans, dwarfs and similar vulgarities?

A. No, milords.

Q. Why did you do it then?

A. I did it because I supposed these people were outside the room in which the supper took place.

Q. Do you not know that in Germany and in other places infected with heresy it is customary with various pictures full of scurrilousness and similar inventions to mock, vituperate, and scorn the things of the Holy Catholic Church in order to teach bad doctrines to foolish and ignorant people?

A. Yes that is wrong; but I return to what I have said, that I am obliged to follow what my superiors have done.

Q. What have your superiors done? Have they perhaps done similar things?

A. Michelangelo in Rome in the Pontifical Chapel painted Our Lord, Jesus Christ, His Mother, St. John, St. Peter, and the Heavenly Host. These are all represented in the nude—even the Virgin Mary—and in different poses with little reverence.

Q. Do you not know that in painting the Last Judgment in which no garments or similar things are presumed, it was not necessary to paint garments, and that in those figures there is nothing that is not spiritual? There are neither buffoons, dogs, weapons, or similar buffoonery. And does it seem because of this or some other example that you did right to have painted this picture in the way you did and do you want to maintain that it is good and decent?

A. Illustrious Lords, I do not want to defend it, but I thought I was doing right. I did not consider so many things and I did not intend to confuse anyone, the more so as those figures of buffoons are outside of the place in a picture where Our Lord is represented.

[After these things had been said, the judges announced that the above named Paolo would be obliged to improve and change his painting within a period of three months from the day of his admonition and that according to the opinion and decision of the Holy Tribunal all the corrections should be made at the expense of the painter and that if he did not correct the picture he would be liable to the penalties imposed by the Holy Tribunal. . . .]

LUIZ DE CAMÕES (C.1524–80)

The Lusiads (1572)

The author of the Portuguese national epic lived in torment and died in impoverished obscurity. Although his epic won him the only renown he enjoyed during his lifetime, Camões is more highly honored today for his lyric poetry. Nationalism defines the exuberant spirit of *The Lusiads*: "I sing the Lusian spirit bright and bold," and it is not "arms, and the man" of Homer's *Odyssey* and Virgil's *Aeneid* and all epics modeled upon them, but of "arms, and those matchless chiefs" that Camões sings. The primary character of his story is not the navigator-admiral Vasco da Gama (who is a cardboard figurehead) but the Portuguese nation (Lusitania) itself. The narrator insists that recent events in Portugal's exploration of the Orient are as worthy of monumentalization as the ancient exploits of Achilles and Aeneas. In a sense, *The Lusiads* marks the coming of age of the Renaissance, a point at which its most expressive spirits recognized that the magnificence of the age in which they lived was superior to that of the classical times which the early Renaissance harked back to with envy and longing.

THE FIRST BOOK

Arms, and those matchless chiefs who from
Of Western Lusitania began [the shore
To track the oceans none had sailed before,
Yet past Tapróbané's far limit ran,
And daring every danger, every war,
With courage that excelled the powers of Man,
Amid remotest nations caused to rise
Young empire which they carried to the skies;

2

So, too, good memory of those kings who went
Afar, religion and our rule to spread;
And who, through either hateful continent,
Afric or Asia, like destruction sped;
And theirs, whose valiant acts magnificent
Saved them from the dominion of the dead,
My song shall sow through the world's every
     part,
So help me this my genius and my art.

3

Of the wise Greek, no more the tale unfold,
Or the Trojan, and great voyages they made.
Of Philip's son and Trajan, leave untold
Triumphant fame in wars which they essayed.
I sing the Lusian spirit bright and bold,
That Mars and Neptune equally obeyed.
Forget all the Muse sang in ancient days,
For valor nobler yet is now to praise.

4

And you, my nymphs of Tagus, who created
Within me such a genius new and glowing,
If ever yet your stream was consecrated
In humble verses which were my bestowing,
Grant me a music great and elevated,
Give me the style magnificent and flowing,
For thus your springs, so Phoebus doth ordain,
Shall never envy Hippocrene again.

5

Give me sonorous fury vast and strong,
No country reed or any pan-pipe base,
But the loud trump, whose notes to war
    belong,
Which burn the breast and lighten in the face;
And equal to their actions make my song,
Who gave such aid to Mars, your glorious race,
That it may be sown and sung throughout the
    earth,
If but my verse possess such precious worth

6

And thou, the nobly born high guarantor
Of our old Lusitanian free estate,
And, no less certainly, fair omen for
This little Christendom that shall be great,
New terror for the lances of the Moor,
Our Century's miracle decreed by Fate,
Vouchsafed the world by God, Who all com-
    mands,
To give its better portion in God's hands;

7

O youthful branch, tender and flourishing,
Branch of a tree Christ loveth best of all,
Whatever in these western regions spring,
That men "Most Christian" or "Imperial" call,
Behold thy scutcheon doth declare the thing,

Pattern of victory that could once befall,
For as armorials Christ left to thee
The wounds that once He suffered on the Tree.

8

Strong King, whose haughty realm, in his
    career,
The new-born sun has first of all in sight,
Sees from the center of the hemisphere,
And leaves the latest when he takes his flight,
Who art, we trust, to yoke and strike with fear
The sullen horsemen of the Ishmaelite,
The Orient Turk and all the heathen train,
The water of the sacred stream who drain;

9

Descend a little from thy majesty
That I thy kindly countenance may know,
Appearing as through life thou art to be,
Till to the eternal temple thou shalt go.
And cast thine eyes kindly and royally
Upon the ground. Thou shalt discover so
Fresh proof of love of patriot acts divine,
Now sung abroad in the sweet-cadenced line.

10

Love of country, thou shalt see, not dominated
By vile reward but a deathless thing and high.
My prize must not be basely estimated,
Who still my native land would magnify.
Hark and behold their glory celebrated,
Whose lord thou art at height of sovranty,
And thou shalt judge which is the better case,
To rule the earth or govern such a race.

11

Hark! Thou shalt never see, for empty deed
Fantastical and feigned and full of lies,
Thy people praised, as with the foreign breed

Of muses that still vaunt them to the skies.
So great and true those acts that they exceed
Utterly all such fabulous fantasies,
And Rodomont and the vain Roger too,
And Roland's tale, even if that were true.

12

Instead I give you Nuno grim and dire,
Whose prowess well for King and Realm was
    shown,
With Egas and with Fuas. Homer's lyre
I covet, for the like of them alone.
For the Twelve Peers, Magriço I desire
Among the Twelve of England shall be known,
And offer likewise Gama's noble name,
Who for himself snatched all Aeneas' fame.

13

For if, in lieu of Charles the King of France
Or Caesar, equal glory you would see,
Mark well the first Afonso then, whose lance
Tarnished whatever foreign fame might be,
Or him who left his land the inheritance
Of freedom with his splendid victory,
Or the second John unconquered, or, in a word,
The fourth and fifth Afonsos, or the third.

14

Nor shall my verses let their memory wane,
Who once beyond the realms of morning went,
And by their good swords could such height
    attain
They kept your banner still armipotent:
Pacheco strong, the dread Almeidas twain,
For whom yet Tagus grieves with sad lament,
And Albuquerque stern and Castro brave,
And all who scaped dominion of the grave.

15

While them I chant, who cannot celebrate
Your worth, great King, for I am not so bold,
Take in your hand the bridle of the state,
Making matter for an epic yet untold.
They feel already the tremendous weight
(The fear whereof makes the whole world
    grow cold)
Of hosts and deeds as splendid as may be,
On Afric's coasts or on the Orient sea. . . .

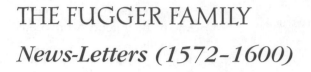

THE FUGGER FAMILY
News-Letters (1572–1600)

Student riots, a UFO over Vienna, royal bankruptcies, and the execution of Mary Stuart, Queen of Scots, are but a few of the subjects revealed by the correspondents of the House of Fugger in a remarkable "news-letter" originally published simultaneously in Latin, French, Italian, Spanish, and German. At the same time that Europe was fragmenting linguistically, from the universal Latin to the burgeoning vernacular, globalization was being achieved through economic interdependence. The tentacles of the Fugger family—of weavers, goldsmiths, mint masters, spice merchants, miners, and financiers—who had become bankers to Sigismund of Tyrol in 1487 and eventually to the emperors Maximilian I and Charles V, Henry VIII, and the papacy, reached from the counting house to the royal boudoir, from cathedral to confessional. Kings could not start wars, navigators expeditions, nor could popes be elected, without seeking financial counsel and assistance from Jakob "the Rich" Fugger, whose motto was: "I want to gain while I can." Like the Medici, Jakob used bullion to gain political power, buying countships from the Habsburgs. Defying the medieval prohibitions against charging interest, he may be called the first "capitalist." His division of the family company into cash, factories, real estate, precious stones, and merchandise established the principles of diversification still applied in the financial capitals of the world. His son Anton, who at Jakob's death in 1525 inherited over two million guilders, more than doubled his inheritance by financing mining ventures and slave-trading throughout the new world, and the wars of Charles V (whose election he financed) and Philip II. As remarkable in retrospect as they were functional in their own time, the Fugger *News-Letters* were the email by which this banking family remained in contact with political, religious, and intellectual developments that might impact upon the business of Europe.

7. DISTURBANCES CAUSED BY STUDENTS IN PARIS

From Paris, the 12th day of February 1573.

On the 5th day of February, being the first Sunday in Lent, the Queen Mother of France drove with her daughter, the Queen of Navarre, and other Princes and Attendants of the Court, about vesper time to the College of Jesuits to hear the reading of vespers. She was escorted by M. de Lorraine, M. de Bourbon and three Cardinals driving and on horseback. The students of Paris, who are wont to indulge in scuffles with the servants of the Court, had collected in bands outside the College, where they

The banker and his wife (Quentin Metsys), in the Louvre, Paris

began quarrelling and brawling with the muleteers. When the courtiers and the Princes came out of the College and were about to bestride their horses and enter their coaches, the students attacked them with rapiers and cudgels, surrounded the carriages with great turbulence, thrust their hands into the bosom of the Queen of Navarre and mockingly stroked her plumes. The Cardinal de Lorraine they pushed into the deepest hole in the deepest mud. The aged Queen they not only assaulted with unsheathed foils, but also insulted in obscene, foul and lewd terms, which it would be shameful to repeat. The reason thereof had not been imparted to me, neither what devilry drove them unto such disorderly conduct.

The King, with just cause, has been very greatly incensed thereat. . . .

28. A Christ Taken Prisoner

From Seville, the 8th day of June 1579.

Of news we have none of import to give you these days. But a curious occurrence recently took place five miles from here, in a village, St. Ginar by name. An inhabitant thereof took refuge in the church to escape his creditors. But whereas, according to custom, on the day of the Blessed Sacrament, all kinds of entertainment were to take place before the Procession of the Blessed Host, some inhabitants had erected a cart, on which they wished to hold a mystery play showing how our Lord Jesus Christ was captured by the Jews as he was kneeling on the Mount of Olives. But they stood in need of a stately and beauteous man and knowing of none more worthy or better looking, they craved of the man, who had taken refuge in the church because of his debts, that he would play the part of the Lord God in their play. He resisted for a long time as he dared not leave the church on account of those to whom he owed money, but the others gave him the assurance that they would bring the cart, on which the play was to be held, in front of the church; where he could mount and descend and need not harbour fear. Thereupon the latter consented. But when one of his creditors learnt this, he bethought himself of many ways in which he could have his debtor seized and thrust into prison. To that end he held counsel with an Alguazil, who informed him that he had a good friend who would play the part of Judas in the said performance. This man he would present with half a dozen ducats and instruct him that, when they arrived on the Market Place, and Judas gave our dear Lord the kiss, he should likewise give him a strong push, so that he might fall from the cart. Once he touched the ground he would immediately be made prisoner. This proposal pleased the creditor greatly. He thereupon gave the Alguazil some money and promised him more as soon as he had got his debtor into prison. Thus, when the procession reached the market, where the Alguazil and his minions were lying in wait, Judas at once strove to carry out his purpose, and with the Jews proceeded to approach the Lord, whom he took to the tail of the cart, where he gave him so forcible a kiss and a push, that he fell to the ground. The Alguazil captured him then and there; but as the good Lord was looking most woefully at his disciples, St. Peter, who stood next to him with his sword, took pity upon him and almost cleft the Alguazil's head in twain. Thereupon a great turmoil ensued in the whole village, so that the Justice intervened and arrested St. Peter, the Lord, and Judas with all his Jews. Thereupon the Judge proclaimed: S E N T E N T I A, Firstly, Judas to be given the birch for a scoffer of God. Secondly, the Alguazil to have himself physicked at his own cost. Thirdly, St. Peter to be set free, as a pious and faithful apostle, and the Lord likewise. The merchant to forfeit that which the Lord owes unto him and to make no further demands upon him for all eternity.

Of this, for lack of better news, have I wished to give tidings unto you. . . .

46. Marriage Plans of the Queen of England

From Paris, the 22nd day of November 1581.

Our King received tidings yesterday from England that his brother was married to the Queen on the 22nd day of the month. Some say that they have already slept together. All manner of things are said about this marriage, also that our King and his Lady Mother do not view it with displeasure. The French proverb holds good: *Jeune folle, vieille enragée.* . . .

56. Arrival of the Indian Gold Fleet

From Madrid, the 26th day of September 1583.

The fleet from Spanish India, praise be to God, arrived upon the 13th day of this month without mishap. It carries a shipment of about fif-

teen millions. It is said that they unloaded and lcft a million in Havanna, because the ships were too heavily laden. This is a pretty penny, which will give new life to commerce.

57. The Plague in Prague

From Vienna, the 15th day of October 1583.

Rumour has it that His Imperial Majesty will again shortly come here, because the plague has spread, not only in Prague itself, but also on the outskirts, so that His Majesty knows of no safe place for his Court. The aforementioned contagious disease is on the increase here also, and up to four-and-twenty persons succumb daily of the plague, wherefore amongst other measures it was ordered to close the public baths.

Concerning the Papal Calendar, practically no one takes any heed of it. Neither has His Majesty decreed that it should be observed, but he has merely announced that this should be done because, in fulfilling the Pope's injunction and request, His Majesty was but rendering a service unto him. . . .

77. Sentence of Death against Mary Stuart

On the 27th day of December 1586.

In letters from London it is written that Parliament has condemned the Queen of Scotland to be executed by the sword. But the Queen of England will not suffer this. The King of France has dispatched Monsieur de Bellièvre to the Queen of England, earnestly to beseech her to spare the life of the Queen of Scotland. How this matter will further develop is awaited with anxiety. . . .

79. EXECUTION OF MARY STUART

Exhaustive report of the way in which Queen Mary Stuart of Scotland and Douairière of France was beheaded on the 18th day of February of the new calendar, in the castle of Fotheringhay in England.

After there had been revealed to the Queen of England, Elizabeth, several plots, hatched at the instigation of the Pope and the heads of the neighbouring states, enemies of the Crown of England, the said Queen found that she had not only to fear for her throne, but also for her life. She then realized that their aim was to release the Queen Mary of Scotland from her durance and to establish her as the next heir, although she was a Catholic and had been detained in prison in England for many years. In this prison she was persecuted for a long time by the Parliament and the States of the Scottish Kingdom, in order that she might be condemned to death, for she had murdered a king, and had set fire to a house with gunpowder, because she was in love with Bothwell, a Scottish baron. Thereupon she abdicated in favour of her son James, the present King of Scotland. But when she again escaped from prison, she assembled troops, so as to rob the said son of his crown. However she was put to flight and returned again to England. In spite of these charges Queen Elizabeth yet desired to spare her life, not wishing to be her judge, on account of her being such a near blood relation.

But as the Scottish Queen now presumed to covet the Crown of England, the English Queen could not let her go free and scathless, because her life, her country and religion were imperilled. Also she did not wish to create any suspicion in the minds of the Scots. Although the Scottish Queen was kept in such lax and pleasurable confinement that she could even go hunting and enjoy all the pleasures of the chase, she, nevertheless, did not rest content

Mary Stewart, Queen of France in the Musée Conde, Chantilly

with the pastimes that were allowed to her. She tried many and various devices to become free again, namely through encompassing the death of the Queen of England. To this end she enticed many persons of the nobility, among them the Duke of Norfolk, as well as other earls and gentlemen, so that the Queen of England was to have lost her life at her Court in the previous summer. On that account the above-named lords met a miserable end. Also England was to have been attacked by foreign troops, the Scottish Queen set upon the thrones of Scotland and England, and the Romish faith established in both kingdoms. All of this the Queen of England gathered from various informants, and the Queen of Scotland was proved guilty in the presence of the nobility, the knighthood and the officials.

It was discussed in Parliament and by the States, how the person of the Queen and the religion of the country could be guarded in future against such dangers. As, however, the Scottish Queen was a close blood relation, her life was to be spared. Since also she was not in the free enjoyment of her liberty and rights, a sentence of death would make a rare and amazing departure.

Thereupon Parliament decided thus:—the life of the Scottish Queen would mean the death of the English Queen and the ruin and destruction of England and of her religion. Therefore it is admitted that she, the Scottish Queen, has to be put to death. Shortly thereafter, a conspiracy was discovered against the person of Her Majesty, wherein her ambassador and others of her retinue were involved. Thereupon, latterly, the Queen of England has resolved to abolish the cause of such evil and of the above-mentioned danger, although she agreed to the execution with but a heavy heart. She therefore dispatched several persons to carry out the sentence upon the Queen of Scotland. The officials who received this command hastened forward the execution, but this against the repeated injunction of the English Queen. Because of this, the secretary of Her Majesty, Davison, was thrown into the Tower and several others fell into disgrace.

And the execution therefore took place in this wise:

At the command of the Queen of England (through the secretary, Beale) the Earls of Shrewsbury and Kent, who were at the time in the neighbourhood of the castle of Fotheringhay, together with other gentlemen, knights and noble persons, with Sir Amias Paulet and Sir Drury, who had order to guard the Queen of Scotland, had on the previous day, namely the 17th day of February, made known to the imprisoned Queen the will of Her Majesty of England. Thereupon she made reply that she was prepared and had long awaited this. She inquired when the execution would take place. Although this was left to her own choice, she asked that it might take place at once, on the very next day, namely on the 18th day of February of the new calendar, on a Wednesday. She besought God's help thereto. At the same time as this notification there were laid before the Queen various apologies, namely that the kingdom of England and its Queen had been compelled to make such a decision.

Hence on the 18th day of February, at 7 o'clock of the morning, the aforementioned earls, knights and noblemen forgathered in the castle of Fotheringhay. Two followers were allocated to each knight, but only one to the others present, so that about eighty to a hundred persons entered the castle, beside the guard and the officials of the court.

There, in the large hall, in front of the fireplace, in which burnt a great fire, a dais had been set up, which was twelve feet wide and eight feet high. It was completely covered with black cloth, and thereon stood a chair with a cushion. As now all was ready, and the gentlemen had collected there between the hours of eight and nine, a message was sent to the imprisoned Queen that the gentlemen had come on the errand of which she had been forewarned in the afternoon of yesterday, and wished to know whether she were ready.

The messenger, however, found the door of her chamber locked and bolted. All her people were with her in the chamber. When the gentlemen heard this, they sent a messenger once more commanding him to knock at the door, should he not find it open and to deliver the former message.

But he found the door unlocked. He sent one of the Queen's servants to her in order to acquaint her with his command. The servant brought answer that the Queen was not yet ready. After half an hour, the gentlemen sent to her once more, and thereto she made answer that she would be ready in half an hour.

After this time the chief official went to the Queen. He found her on her knees with her ladies-in-waiting, praying, and told her that her time was now come. Thereupon she stood up and said that she was ready. She was led between two men of her retinue into the antechamber. There she found all her people assembled. She exhorted them all to fear God and to live in humility of spirit. She took leave of them all, kissed the women and held out her hand to the men to kiss. She begged them not to grieve on her account but to be of good cheer and to pray for her. Then she was led to the stairway. There all the gentlemen advanced from the hall towards her, and the Earl of Shrewsbury said to the sorrowing Queen: "Madame, we are here to carry out the behest of our most gracious Queen of England, which was communicated unto you yesterday." The warrant and sentence the Earl of Kent held in his hand. The Great Seal of the Crown of England was thereon. Then the Queen replied that she would as lief die as live any longer. As she turned round she perceived her most distinguished servitor, Melville, and said to him: "My faithful servant Melville, though thou art a Protestant and I a Catholic, there is nevertheless but one Christendom and I am thy Queen, born and anointed, of the lineage of Henry VII. And so I adjure thee before God that thou give this command to my son: I beg him to serve God, and the Catholic Church, and to rule and keep his country in peace and to submit (as I have done) to no other Master, although I had the right good will to unite the kingdoms of this island. I renounce this, may he do likewise, and do not let him put overmuch trust in the presumption of the world. Let him trust God and then he will be blessed by Him. Let him speak no evil of the Queen of England, and thou, Melville, art my witness that I die like a true Scotswoman, Frenchwoman and Catholic, which belief has ever been mine." These words and such like did she repeat.

Thereupon Melville made answer: "Most venerable and most august Princess, as I have been at all times your Majesty's faithful servant, so will I now with the help of God, faithfully and honestly transmit to the King, your Son, Your Majesty's words and message."

Thereupon she turned to the above-mentioned gentlemen and desired to have her priest with her on the dais, so that he might bear witness for her to the King of France and in other places, that she had died righteously and a good Catholic. To this the gentlemen made reply that it had been ordained otherwise.

She then demanded that her servants might remain with her. This was refused, in order to curb her impatience and to free her mind from certain superstitions. Nevertheless five of her servants and two tiring-women were permitted to come to her, because she complained that she was being poorly served. She promised that she would cause no hindrance, either by cries or by tears. Further she demanded for her servants and her maids liberty to depart, with good escort, and free of cost to their own countries without let or hindrance. This the gentlemen promised her. Also that they should be permitted to retain everything that the Queen of Scotland had presented to them. But she repeated once more: "I desire that this take place." Thereupon she was led by two servants of the Governor to the dais. There she seated herself upon a chair, for she could stand but with difficulty. The two earls seated themselves beside her. Then the Secretary Beale read the warrant and the sentence of execution in an over loud voice.

The gown in which the Queen was attired was of exquisite black velvet, which she had likewise worn when she appeared before the gentlemen. In her hand she held a small cross of wood or of ivory with the picture of Christ thereon, and a book. On her neck hung a golden crucifix, and from her girdle a rosary.

Near her stood a doctor of theology, Dean of Peterborough, who, at the command of the gentlemen spoke words of Christian comfort to her, exhorting her to die as a Christian with a repentant heart. She at once interrupted him and begged him to keep his peace, for she was fully prepared for death. The Dean answered that he had been commanded to speak the truth to her. But she said for the second time: "I will not listen to you, Mr. Dean. You have naught to do with me. You disturb me." Thereupon he was bidden to be silent by the gentlemen.

The Earl of Kent said to her: "Madame, I am grieved on your account to hear of this superstition from you and to see that which is in your hand." She said it was seemly that she should hold the figure of Christ in her hand thereby to think of Him. Thereupon he answered that she must have Christ in her heart, and further said that though she made demur in paying heed to the mercies vouchsafed to her by God All-Highest, they would nevertheless plead for her with God Almighty, that He would forgive her sins and receive her into His Kingdom. Thereto the Queen made reply: "Pray, then will I also pray." Then the aforesaid Doctor fell on his knees on the steps of the dais and read in an over loud voice a fervent and godly prayer for her, most suitable to such an occasion, also for the Queen of England and the welfare of the Kingdom. All those standing round repeated the prayer. But as long as it lasted the Queen was praying in Latin and fairly audibly, holding the crucifix in her hand.

When this prayer was now ended on both sides, the executioner knelt in front of the Queen. Him she forgave his deed, as also all those who lusted after her blood, or desired her death. She further forgave all and sundry and craved from God that He might also forgive her own trespasses. Thereafter she fell on her knees in ardent supplication and besought the remission of her sins. She said that she trusted to be saved through the death of Christ and His Blood and that she was ready to have her own blood spilt at His feet, wherefore she held His picture and the crucifix in her hands. Further she prayed for a happy, long and prosperous reign for the Queen of England, for the prosperity of the British Isles, for the afflicted Christian Church and the end of all misery. She also prayed for her son, the King of Scots, for his upright and honourable Government and of his conversion to the Catholic Faith. At the last she prayed that all the saints in heaven might intercede for her on this day, and that God of His great goodness might avert great plagues from this Island, forgive her her sins and receive her soul into His heavenly hand.

Thereupon she stood up and prepared herself for death. She doffed her jewels and her gown, with the help of two women. When the executioner wished to assist her, she said to him that it was not her wont to be disrobed in the presence of such a crowd, nor with the help of such handmaidens. She herself took off her robe and pushed it down as far as the waist. The bodice of the underskirt was cut low and tied together at the back. She hastened to undo this.

Thereafter she kissed her ladies, commended them to God, and because one of them was weeping too loudly, she said to her: "Have I not told you that you should not weep? Be comforted." To her she gave her hand, and bade her leave the dais. When she was thus prepared, she turned to her servitors, who were kneeling not far off, blessed them and made them all witnesses that she died a Catholic and begged them to pray for her. Afterwards she fell on her knees with great courage, did not change colour, and likewise gave no sign of fear. One of her tirewomen bound a kerchief before her eyes. As she knelt down she repeated the 70th Psalm: "*In te, Domine, speravi. . . .*" When she had said this to the end, she, full of courage, bent down with her body and laid her head on the block, exclaiming: "*In manuas tuas, Domine, commendo spiritum meum.*" Then one of the executioners held down her hands, and the other cut off her head with two strokes of the chopper. Thus ended her life.

The executioner took the head and showed it to the people, who cried: "God spare our Queen of England!"

When the executioner held up the head, it fell in disarray so that it could be seen that her hair was quite grey and had been closely cropped.

Her raiment and other belongings were by command taken from the executioner, but he was promised their equivalent in money. Everything that had been sprinkled with her blood, also the garments of the executioner and other objects, were promptly taken away and washed. The planks of the dais, the black cloth and all else were thrown into the fire, at once, so that no superstitious practices could be carried on therewith.

Her body was carried out, embalmed and made ready for burial. Where this will take place is as yet unknown. Her servants and courtiers were instructed to abide there until her remains had been honourably laid to rest. She was four-and-forty years of age, and was the most beautiful princess of her time.

She had as first spouse, Francis II, King of France, after him Henry Stuart, the son of the Earl of Lennox, her cousin, a truly handsome young man, by whom she had issue James V, King of Scotland. But after she had caused Henry Stuart to be murdered, she took in marriage the Earl of Bothwell, who was imprisoned in Denmark, lost his senses and there died.

After this execution had taken place, the portals of the castle remained shut, until Henry Talbot, son of the Earl of Shrewsbury, had been dispatched to the English Court. When, the other day, he brought the tidings to London, the citizens of this town lit bonfires on all sides and rang the bells, because they were rid of the danger in which they had lived so long. It looks as if the populace believed that a new era had begun in which they hope that all will remain at peace.

Described by Emanuel Tomascon, who was present at the happenings. . . .

113. ATTEMPT TO POISON PHILIP II

From Venice, the 6th day of April 1590.

A terrifying miracle, so they say, has occurred in Spain. One morning, as the King after praying in his oratory before a crucifix, which he held in great devotion, as was his daily custom, wished to kiss the image of Christ, the latter turned away from him. This greatly horrified and frightened the King and he once more began to pray that God might forgive him his sins. He thereupon once more tried to kiss the image of Christ, which again withdrew from him. When the King had perceived this with great concern and affliction, he sent for his Father Confessor, to whom he related this miracle. The latter then

began praying to God that He might reveal this secret unto him. When he had concluded his prayers, he told the King to send for two of his most eminent councillors and bid them kiss the crucifix. They did so and soon thereafter fell sick and died. Some aver that the crucifix was poisoned so that the King might lose his life thereby.

115. ANOTHER BURNING OF WITCHES

From Schwab-München, the 4th day of May 1590.

Last Wednesday the innkeeper's wife of Möringen and the baker's wife of Bobingen were tried here for their misdeeds in witchcraft. Mine hostess is a short, stout, seventy-year-old doxy, who had taken to her accursed witchery when eighteen years of age. This she has practised fifty-two years, and it is easy to imagine what havoc she has wrought in such a long time. As the result of fervent petitioning, her sentence has been lightened inasmuch as she was first strangled and then only burned.

The other was only seduced to this work of the Devil by Ursula Krämer, who was the first to be executed here. So far, she has not perpetrated any sore misdeeds, but so much has she owned to, that her life is forfeit. Even on her day of judgment she still thought she could vindicate herself, and even at the place of execution I myself heard her say that she was dying innocent. Most unwillingly did she submit to her fate. But in the end she was reconciled to it and prayed long to God that He might pardon her misdeeds.

This morn another woman was brought hither from Möringen. Only half a year ago she married off one of her sons to a widow, who is said to be of the same craft. Thus it is hoped that it may incriminate others here. To-morrow or next week some more are to be brought here, but no one knows from whence. There is much discussion here about the hostess of Göggingen. May the Lord grant that this be but idle talk. . . .

119. FAMINE IN PARIS

From Lyons, the 11th day of August 1590.

Although it was hoped that we should know before ending this letter how matters stand in the city of Paris, there have been no reliable tidings from that city since the 15th day of July. At this date, the Parisians still held out, but it is said that the troops of Navarre stormed the Faubourg St. Antoine on the 19th day of July. The Duc de Mayenne is reported to have received four thousand infantry and six hundred horse from the Netherlands together with a regiment of lansquenets from Lützelburg. There is great hunger in Paris; a pound of white bread costs half a crown; mutton, fore or hind part, legs or quarters for roasting, five crowns; ox or cow, one hundred and forty crowns; six sheep, one hundred crowns; a pound of horseflesh, five sous. Rumour has it that people are eating mice, cats and dogs, and also that wine is very scarce. . . .

120. FRIGHTFUL APPARITION IN THE SKY AT VIENNA

From Vienna, the 11th day of August 1590.

These days at 10 o'clock at night a most alarming wonder has manifested itself in the skies. The firmament was rent asunder and through this gap one could distinguish chariots and armies, riders with yellow, white, red and black standards, moving as though to do battle against each other. This awesome and unusual vision continued from ten at night till about two of the morning, and was witnessed with alarm and dismay by many honest and trustworthy people. The significance thereof is known but to God Almighty, Who may graciously prevent the shedding of innocent blood. . . .

157. ATTEMPTED MURDER OF HENRY IV

From Antwerp, the 2nd day of January 1595.

A letter from Paris of the 29th brings news that the King of Navarre all but perished in the palace of Madame de Lioncourt. For as he was returning the salute of one who had made obeisance to him, a youth between seventeen and eighteen years of age essayed to stick a knife into his throat. But the thrust went too high and pierced the right cheek, whereby the King has lost two of his teeth. The handle of the knife remained cleft between the teeth. How this is going to develop we shall know by the following letters.

194. PHILIP'S LACK OF MONEY

From Madrid, the 20th day of November 1598.

The new King of Spain, with his cavaliers, on the 8th of this month held his entry in most magnificent fashion into San Hieronymo, not far from here, under a canopy which was carried by twenty men, and on this occasion there was a display of much gold and silver and precious stones. Now the King is preparing to sally forth to Barcelona with his sister and his mother. This is due to take place next December. But there is great penury. And whereas the fleet is expected in January with gold and silver, His Majesty had countenanced negotiation with the purveyors of the Court for a sum of four hundred thousand ducats to be paid out at different dates in the Netherlands.

On the 7th day of November on account of the plague, which is spreading more and more, several streets in Lisbon have been barricaded and in the Palace all gates have been closed excepting one. Also in front of this palace a whole street has been walled up and so has a house in which there were many different articles of value; the people who lived in it were also driven out. But some daring youngsters assembled and carried everything away at night time. In Galicia as well death holds sway. . . .

212. THE REMARRIAGE OF HENRY IV

From Rome, the 6th day of May 1600.

It is learned that the Grand Duke of Florence has given a royal banquet in honour of the French Ambassador and of the new Queen of France, at which the Queen sat, under a canopy to which there were two steps, at the head of the table, and that M. de Selleri sat next to her. The Grand Duke and the Grand Duchess waited upon them at the table with many other noblemen and noblewomen, and the Bracciano-Orsini and two Princes of Medici. The above-named Grand Duke has given a beautifully trained horse as a present to M. de Lincourt and the latter has immediately left for France.

The Queen is so beautifully and well-proportioned a woman and is adorned as well with so many virtues and the fear of God that it is hoped that much happiness may accrue out of this marriage for the throne of France. As the Cardinal Aldobrandino will travel with the new Queen to Marseilles and after that to Avignon, in order to show all honour in the name of the Pope to the King and his affianced wife, the galleys of the Pope have already been set in readiness, and provisioned with biscuits at Naples. . . .

215. CONFERENCES OF PHILIP III OF SPAIN FOR PURPOSES OF OBTAINING CREDIT

From Rome, the 17th day of June 1600.

The gentlemen we named recently who a short time ago were resolved upon arranging a new financial transaction with the King of Spain, are now, for lack of ready money, no longer wishful to lend him these sums. For this reason they have begged the gentlemen of the Monte San Giorgio to pay the deficit required to complete the needed amount, in return for which they have offered to place in the Monte as much fine gold and silver as would be necessary as a security. This, however, was refused, and therefore His Majesty suffers from some lack of cash. Although the Spanish kingdom had declared itself prepared to advance six more millions as Assignation on the fleet which is due to arrive, and to pay the royal debt therewith, this money has not been found to be sufficient. The merchants, who are concerned in this, have offered to withhold their loan in the meantime, in order that the intended Assignation may be extended until the arrival of the fleet.

PIERRE DE RONSARD (1524–85)

QUAND VOUS SEREZ BIEN VIEILLE

When You Are Very Old (1578)

Pierre Ronsard's courtly birth displays itself in the delicacy and sensitivity of his odes, elegies, sonnets, and songs which molded the French language into an instrument of delicate precision. Although his poetry followed classical and Petrarchan models, its purity and forcefulness, drawn as well from the robustness of medieval French, earn him the titles "prince of poets" and "founder of French lyric poetry." He was also the brightest star and cofounder of the *Pléiade,* the constellation of seven writers who, following the example of the Italian humanists, resolved to elevate and purify their national language. Ronsard's first odes imitated Pindar and Horace, and his sonnets "to Cassandre" followed Catullus and Anacreon; but gracefully adapting his models to the needs of the French language, his best work, in metaphorical reach and subtlety, transcends them. Although he set out to write a Homeric epic, *La Françiade,* Ronsard did not complete it; preferring to follow the genius of his own lyrical Muse. His *Amours de Marie* and *Sonnets pour Hélène* remain among the finest love poems in the French language. "When You Are Very Old", the most famous of all his poems, from *Sonnets for Helen,* shows its Greek sources in its image of the myrtle tree associated with death, and ends with a haunting line characteristic of Renaissance intensity: "Cueillez des aujourdhuy les roses de la vie."

Charles VII (Jean Fouquet), in the Louvre, Paris

When You Are Very Old

When you are very old, one evening by candle-
    light,
Seated by the fire, spinning your memories,
You will sing my verses, and marvel:
"Ronsard celebrated me in the time of my
    beauty."
Under your breath, half asleep,
Reweaving words past,
You will not rekindle the love of
The one who once blessed your name.
The flames, dead. I, a phantom amongst the
    ashes,
Will take my repose by the myrtles' shadows;
You will be an old woman, seeking warmth by
    the hearth,
Regretting my love and your proud disdain.
Live—if you believe me now. Wait not for
    tomorrow:
Gather from today the roses of life.

SIR PHILIP SIDNEY (1554–86)

The Defence of Poetry (1579-80)

A friend of Edmund Spenser and favorite of Queen Elizabeth, Philip Sidney was the most brilliant unpublished poet of the era—also distinguished for his didactic and entertaining prose romance, *Arcadia*. With his chivalric charisma and dashing good looks, memorialized in Veronese's painting, Sidney was the embodiment of the Renaissance courtier. The battle between his gentle demeanor and the passion within made him the personification of Castiglione's *sprezzatura*. Throughout his life Sidney combined government service with the pursuit of letters, a tradition that persists in England to this day. His sequence of love sonnets *Astrophel and Stella,* the first such sequence to be written in English, shows the influence of Petrarch. He died a hero in battle and was given a splendid burial at St. Paul's Cathedral. After his death, Sidney's literary fame took hold in earnest with the publication of his poetry and prose. No better introduction to the literature of Renaissance England can be found than his *Defence of Poetry*. In response to Stephen Gosson's Puritanical *School of Abuse,* attacking the immorality and frivolity of poetry, Sidney's celebration of the priestly powers and responsibilities of the poet, whose vision brings the perspective of integrity and innocence to his society, remains a guiding influence in our century when prime ministers and presidents appoint poet laureates.

And first, truly, to all them that, professing learning, inveigh against poetry may justly be objected that they go very near to ungratefulness, to seek to deface that which, in the noblest nations and languages that are known, hath been the first lightgiver to ignorance, and first nurse, whose milk by little and little enabled them to feed afterwards of tougher knowledges. And will they now play the hedgehog that, being received into the den, drave out his host? Or rather the vipers, that with their birth kill their parents?

Let learned Greece in any of his manifold sciences be able to show me one book before Musaeus, Homer, and Hesiod, all three nothing else but poets. Nay, let any history be brought that can say any writers were there before them, if they were not men of the same skill, as Orpheus, Linus, and some other are named, who, having been the first of that country that made pens deliverers of their knowledge to the posterity, may justly challenge to be called their fathers in learning: for not only in time they had this priority (although in itself antiquity be venerable) but went before them, as causes to draw with their charming sweetness the wild untamed wits to an admiration of knowledge. So, as Amphion was said to move stones with his poetry to build Thebes, and Orpheus to be listened to by beasts—indeed stony and beastly people—so among the Romans were Livius Andronicus and Ennius. So in the Italian language the first that made it aspire to be a treasure-house of science were the poets Dante, Boccaccio, and Petrarch. So in our English were Gower and Chaucer, after whom, encouraged and delighted with their excellent fore-going, others have followed, to beautify our mother tongue, as well in the same kind as in other arts.

This did so notably show itself, that the philosophers of Greece durst not a long time appear to the world but under the masks of poets. So Thales, Empedocles, and Parmenides sang their natural philosophy in verses; so did Pythagoras and Phocylides their moral counsels; so did Tyrtaeus in war matters, and Solon in matters of policy: or rather they, being poets, did exercise their delightful vein in those points of highest knowledge, which before them lay hid to the world. For that wise Solon was directly a poet it is manifest, having written in verse the notable fable of the Atlantic Island, which was continued by Plato. And truly even Plato whosoever well considereth shall find that in the body of his work, though the inside and strength were philosophy, the skin, as it were, and beauty depended most of poetry: for all standeth upon dialogues, wherein he feigneth many honest burgesses of Athens to speak of such matters, that, if they had been set on the rack, they would never have confessed them, besides his poetical describing the circumstances of their meetings, as the well ordering of a banquet, the delicacy of a walk, with interlacing mere tales, as Gyges' ring and others, which who knoweth not to be flowers of poetry did never walk into Apollo's garden.

And even historiographers (although their lips sound of things done, and verity be written in their foreheads) have been glad to borrow both fashion and, perchance, weight of the poets. So Herodotus entitled his History by the name of the nine Muses; and both he and all the rest that followed him either stale or usurped of poetry their passionate describing of passions, the many particularities of battles, which no man could affirm; or, if that be denied me, long orations put in the mouths of great kings and captains, which it is certain they never pronounced.

So that truly neither philosopher nor historiographer could at the first have entered into the gates of popular judgements, if they had not taken a great passport of poetry, which in all nations at this day where learning flourisheth not, is plain to be seen; in all which they have some feeling of poetry.

In Turkey, besides their law-giving divines, they have no other writers but poets. In our neighbour country Ireland, where truly learning goeth very bare, yet are their poets held in a devout reverence. Even among the most barbarous and simple Indians where no writing is, yet have they their poets who make and sing songs, which they call *areytos,* both of their ancestors' deeds and praises of their gods: a sufficient probability that, if ever learning come among them, it must be by having their hard dull wits softened and sharpened with the sweet delights of poetry—for until they find a pleasure in the exercises of the mind, great promises of much knowledge will little persuade them that know not the fruits of knowledge. In Wales, the true remnant of the ancient Britons, as there are good authorities to show the long time they had poets, which they called bards, so through all the conquests of Romans, Saxons, Danes, and Normans, some of whom did seek to ruin all memory of learning from among them, yet do their poets even to this day last; so as it is not more notable in soon beginning than in long continuing.

But since the authors of most of our sciences were the Romans, and before them the Greeks, let us a little stand upon their authorities, but even so far as to see what names they have given unto this now scorned skill.

Among the Romans a poet was called *vates,*

which is as much as a diviner, foreseer, or prophet, as by his conjoined words *vaticinium* and *vaticinari* is manifest: so heavenly a title did that excellent people bestow upon this heart-ravishing knowledge. And so far were they carried into the admiration thereof, that they thought in the chanceable hitting upon any such verses great foretokens of their following fortunes were placed. Whereupon grew the word of *Sortes Virgilianae,* when by sudden opening Virgil's book they lighted upon any verse of his making, whereof the histories of the emperors' lives are full: as of Albinus, the governor of our island, who in his childhood met with this verse

Arma amens capio nec sat rationis in armis

and in his age performed it. Which, although it were a very vain and godless superstition, as also it was to think spirits were commanded by such verses—whereupon this word charms, derived of *carmina,* cometh—so yet serveth it to show the great reverence those wits were held in; and altogether not without ground, since both the oracles of Delphos and Sibylla's prophecies were wholly delivered in verses. For that same exquisite observing of number and measure in the words, and that high flying liberty of conceit proper to the poet, did seem to have some divine force in it.

And may not I presume a little further, to show the reasonableness of this word *vates,* and say that the holy David's Psalms are a divine poem? If I do, I shall not do it without the testimony of great learned men, both ancient and modern. But even the name of Psalms will speak for me, which being interpreted, is nothing but songs; then that it is fully written in metre, as all learned hebricians agree, although the rules be not yet fully found; lastly and principally, his handling his prophecy, which is merely poetical: for what else is the awaking his musical instruments, the often and free changing of persons, his notable *prosopopoeias,* when he maketh you, as it were, see God coming in His majesty, his telling of the beasts' joyfulness and hills leaping, but a heavenly poesy, wherein almost he showeth himself a passionate lover of that unspeakable and everlasting beauty to be seen by the eyes of the mind, only cleared by faith? But truly now having named him, I fear me I seem to profane that holy name, applying it to poetry, which is among us thrown down to so ridiculous an estimation. But they that with quiet judgements will look a little deeper into it, shall find the end and working of it such as, being rightly applied, deserveth not to be scourged out of the Church of God.

But now let us see how the Greeks named it, and how they deemed of it. The Greeks called him a 'poet', which name hath, as the most excellent, gone through other languages. It cometh of this word ποιεῖν, which is, to make: wherein, I know not whether by luck or wisdom, we Englishmen have met with the Greeks in calling him a maker: which name, how high and incomparable a title it is, I had rather were known by marking the scope of other sciences than by any partial allegation.

There is no art delivered to mankind that hath not the works of nature for his principal object, without which they could not consist, and on which they so depend, as they become actors and players, as it were, of what nature will have set forth. So doth the astronomer look upon the stars, and, by that he seeth, set down what order nature hath taken therein. So doth the geometrician and arithmetician in their diverse sorts of quantities. So doth the musicians in time tell you which by nature agree, which not. The natural philosopher thereon hath his name, and the moral philosopher standeth upon the natural virtues, vices, or passions of man; and follow nature (saith he) therein, and thou shalt not err. The lawyer saith what men have determined; the historian what men have done. The grammarian speaketh only of the rules of speech; and the rhetorician and logician, considering what in nature will soonest prove and persuade, thereon give artificial rules, which still are compassed within the circle of a question according to the proposed matter. The physician weigheth the nature of man's body, and the nature of things helpful or hurtful unto it. And the metaphysic, though it be in the second and abstract notions, and therefore be counted supernatural, yet doth he indeed build upon the depth of nature. Only the poet, disdaining to be tied to any such subjection, lifted up with the vigour of his own invention, doth grow in effect another nature, in making things either better than nature bringeth forth, or, quite anew, forms such as never were in nature, as the Heroes, Demigods, Cyclops, Chimeras, Furies, and such like: so as he goeth hand in hand with nature, not enclosed within the narrow warrant of her gifts, but freely ranging only within the zodiac of his own wit. Nature never set forth the earth in so rich tapestry as divers poets have done; neither with so pleasant rivers, fruitful trees, sweet-smelling flowers, nor whatsoever else may make the too much loved earth more lovely. Her world is brazen, the poets only deliver a golden.

But let those things alone, and go to man— for whom as the other things are, so it seemeth in him her uttermost cunning is employed— and know whether she have brought forth so true a lover as Theagenes, so constant a friend as Pylades, so valiant a man as Orlando, so right a prince as Xenophon's Cyrus, so excellent a man every way as Virgil's Aeneas. Neither let this be jestingly conceived, because the works of the one be essential, the other in imitation or fiction; for any understanding knoweth the skill of each artificer standeth in that *idea* or foreconceit of the work, and not in the work itself. And that the poet hath that *idea* is manifest, by delivering them forth in such excellency as he had imagined them. Which delivering forth also is not wholly imaginative, as we are wont to say by them that build castles in the air; but so far substantially it worketh, not only to make a Cyrus, which had been but a particular excellency as nature might have done, but to bestow a Cyrus upon the world to make many Cyruses, if they will learn aright why and how that maker made him.

Neither let it be deemed too saucy a comparison to balance the highest point of man's wit with the efficacy of nature; but rather give right honour to the heavenly Maker of that maker, who having made man to His own likeness, set him beyond and over all the works of that second nature: which in nothing he showeth so much as in poetry, when with the force of a divine breath he bringeth things forth surpassing her doings—with no small arguments to the credulous of that first accursed fall of Adam, since our erected wit maketh us know what perfection is, and yet our infected will keepeth us from reaching unto it. But these arguments will by few be understood, and by fewer granted. This much (I hope) will be given me, that the Greeks with some probability of reason gave him the name above all names of learning.

Now let us go to a more ordinary opening of him, that the truth may be the more palpable: and so I hope, though we get not so unmatched a praise as the etymology of his names will grant, yet his very description, which no man will deny, shall not justly be barred from a principal commendation.

Poesy therefore is an art of imitation, for so Aristotle termeth it in the word μίμησις—that is to say, a representing, counterfeiting, or figuring forth—to speak metaphorically, a speaking picture—with this end, to teach and delight....

. . . For conclusion, I say the philosopher teacheth, but he teacheth obscurely, so as the learned only can understand him, that is to say, he teacheth them that are already taught; but the poet is the food for the tenderest stomachs, the poet is indeed the right popular philosopher, whereof Aesop's tales give good proof: whose pretty allegories, stealing under the formal tales of beasts, make many, more beastly than beasts, begin to hear the sound of virtue from these dumb speakers. . . .

So that since the ever-praiseworthy Poesy is full of virtue-breeding delightfulness, and void of no gift that ought to be in the noble name of learning; since the blames laid against it are either false or feeble; since the cause why it is not esteemed in England is the fault of poet-apes, not poets; since, lastly, our tongue is most fit to honour poesy, and to be honoured by poesy; I conjure you all that have had the evil luck to read this ink-wasting toy of mine, even in the name of the nine Muses, no more to scorn the sacred mysteries of poesy; no more to laugh at the name of poets, as though they were next inheritors to fools; no more to jest at the reverent title of a rhymer; but to believe, with Aristotle, that they were the ancient treasurers of the Grecians' divinity; to believe, with Bembus, that they were first bringers-in of all civility; to believe, with Scaliger, that no philosopher's precepts can sooner make you an honest man than the reading of Virgil; to believe, with Clauserus, the translator of Cornutus, that it pleased the heavenly Deity, by Hesiod and Homer, under the veil of fables, to give us all knowledge, logic, rhetoric, philosophy natural and moral, and *quid non?;* to believe, with me, that there are many mysteries contained in poetry, which of purpose were written darkly, lest by profane wits it should be abused; to believe, with Landino, that they are so beloved of the gods that whatsoever they write proceeds of a divine fury; lastly, to believe themselves, when they tell you they will make you immortal by their verses. Thus doing, your name shall flourish in the printers' shops; thus doing, you shall be of kin to many a poetical preface; thus doing, you shall be most fair, most rich, most wise, most all, you shall dwell upon superlatives; thus doing, though you be *libertino patre natus,* you shall suddenly grow *Herculea proles,*

Si quid mea carmina possunt;

thus doing, your soul shall be placed with Dante's Beatrice, or Virgil's Anchises. But if (fie of such a but) you be born so near the dull-making cataract of Nilus that you cannot hear the planet-like music of poetry; if you have so earth-creeping a mind that it cannot lift itself up to look to the sky of poetry, or rather, by a certain rustical disdain, will become such a mome as to be a Momus of poetry; then, though I will not wish unto you the ass's ears of Midas, nor to be driven by a poet's verses, as Bubonax was, to hang himself, nor to be rhymed to death, as is said to be done in Ireland; yet thus much curse I must send you, in the behalf of all poets, that while you live, you live in love, and never get favour for lacking skill of a sonnet; and, when you die, your memory die from the earth for want of an epitaph.

MICHEL EYQUEM, SEIGNEUR DE MONTAIGNE (1533–92)

ESSAIS

On the Cannibals (1580)

Born in Perigord's Château Montaigne of an affluent family, his father Catholic, his mother Sephardic, Michel de Montaigne was raised straddling two worlds. He served as parliamentarian and judge, and was appointed mayor of Bordeaux. In the midst of France's Protestant-Catholic civil wars, he chose to pursue the lifestyle of a skeptical observer by retiring from the forum to private reflection in his library tower. His *Essays*—we owe the word "essay" to him—are an intellectual autobiography, revealing an egocentric preoccupation with his inner self whose contradictions faithfully reflect the characteristic uncertainty of his troubled times. Like Socrates, his motto was, "What do I know?" He saw his role as asking questions, not supplying answers. Yet, despite his belief that ultimate truths are inaccessible to human reason, his faith in human nature is steadfast. His ideal was universal toleration. In the pages of Roger Bacon, François-Marie Arouet Voltaire, Ralph Waldo Emerson, Anatole France, Mark Twain, and even Art Buchwald, we hear echoes of Montaigne's vividly engaging conversational manner. His essay "On the Cannibals," given here in the Renaissance English translation of John Florio, at the same time that it demonstrates Renaissance curiosity in the new world, also romanticizes the new world's inhabitants in a fashion that would become identified with the Age of Enlightenment. Jean-Jacques Rousseau's "noble savage" is foreshadowed in Montaigne's descriptions of routine activities of the native Americans, even in his attempt to justify their reputed cannibalism as being less cruel than revenge practiced by contemporary Europeans.

Montaigne (engraved portrait)

. . . I finde (as farre as I have beene informed) there is nothing in that nation, that is either barbarous or savage, unlesse men call that barbarisme which is not common to them. As indeed, we have no other ayme of truth and reason, than the example and Idea of the opinions and customes of the countrie we live in. There is ever perfect religion, perfect policie, perfect and compleat use of all things. They are even savage, as we call those fruits wilde, which nature of her selfe, and of her ordinarie progresse hath produced: whereas indeed, they are those which our selves have altered by our artificiall devices, and diverted from their common order, we should rather terme savage. In those are the true and most profitable vertues, and naturall properties most lively and vigorous, which in these we have bastardized, applying them to the pleasure of our corrupted taste. And if notwithstanding, in divers fruits of those countries that were never tilled, we shall finde, that in respect of ours they are most excellent, and as delicate unto our taste; there is no reason, art should gaine the point of honour of our great and puissant mother Nature. We have so

much by our inventions surcharged the beauties and riches of her workes, that we have altogether overchoaked her: yet where ever her puritie shineth, she makes our vaine and frivolous enterprises wonderfully ashamed. . . .

Those nations seeme therefore so barbarous unto me, because they have received very little fashion from humane wit, and are yet neere their originall naturalitie. The lawes of nature doe yet command them, which are but little bastardized by ours, and that with such puritie, as I am sometimes grieved the knowledge of it came no sooner to light, at what time there were men, that better than we could have judged of it. I am sorie, Lycurgus and Plato had it not: for me seemeth that what in those nations we see by experience, doth not only exceed all the pictures wherewith licentious Poesie hath proudly imbellished the golden age, and all her quaint inventions to faine a happy condition of man, but also the conception and desire of Philosophy. They could not imagine a genuitie so pure and simple, as we see it by experience; nor ever beleeve our societie might be maintained with so little art and humane combination. It is a nation, would I answer Plato, that hath no kinde of traffike, no knowledge of Letters, no intelligence of numbers, no name of magistrate, nor of politike superioritie; no use of service, of riches or of povertie; no contracts, no successions, no partitions, no occupation but idle; no respect of kindred, but common, no apparell but naturall, no manuring of lands, no use of wine, corne, or mettle. The very words that import lying, falshood, treason, dissimulations, covetousnes, envie, detraction, and pardon, were never heard of amongst them. How dissonant would hee finde his imaginarie common-wealth from this perfection?

Hos natura modos primùm dedit.
Nature at first uprise,
These manners did devise.

Furthermore, they live in a country of so exceeding pleasant and temperate situation, that as my testimonies have told me, it is verie rare to see a sicke body amongst them; and they have further assured me they never saw any man there, either shaking with the palsie, toothlesse, with eies dropping, or crooked and stooping through age. They are seated alongst the sea-coast, encompassed toward the land with huge and steepie mountaines, having betweene both, a hundred leagues or thereabout of open and champaine ground. They have great abundance of fish and flesh, that have no resemblance at all with ours, and eat them without any sawces, or skill of Cookerie, but plaine boiled or broiled. The first man that brought a horse thither, although he had in many other voyages conversed with them, bred so great a horror in the land, that before they could take notice of him, they slew him with arrowes. Their buildings are very long, and able to containe two or three hundred soules, covered with barkes of great trees, fastned in the ground at one end, enterlaced and joyned close together by the tops, after the manner of some of our Granges; the covering whereof hangs downe to the ground, and steadeth them as a flancke. They have a kinde of wood so hard, that ryving and cleaving the same, they make blades, swords, and gridirons to broile their meat with. Their beds are of a kinde of cotten cloth, fastned to the house-roofe, as our ship-cabbanes: everie one hath his severall cowch; for the women lie from their husbands. They rise with the Sunne, and feed for all day, as soone as they are up: and make no more meales after that. They drinke not at meat, as Suidas reporteth of some other people of the East, which dranke after meales, but drinke many times a day, and are much given to pledge carowses. Their drinke is made of a certaine root, and of the colour of our Claret wines, which lasteth but two or three daies; they drinke it warme: It hath somewhat a sharpe taste, wholsome for the stomack, nothing heady, but laxative for such as are not used unto it, yet verie pleasing to such as are accustomed unto it. In stead of bread, they use a certaine white composition, like unto Corianders confected. I have eaten some, the taste wherof is somewhat sweet and wallowish. They spend the whole day in dancing. Their young men goe a hunting after wilde beasts with bowes and arrowes. Their women busie themselves therewhil'st with warming of their drinke, which is their chiefest office. Some of their old men, in the morning before they goe to eating, preach in common to all the houshold, walking from one end of the house to the other, repeating one selfe-same sentence many times, till he have ended his turne (for their buildings are a hundred paces in length) he commends but two things unto his auditorie, First, valour against their enemies, then lovingnesse unto their wives. They never misse (for their restraint) to put men in minde of this dutie, that it is their wives which keepe their drinke luke-warme and well-seasoned. The forme of their beds, cords, swords, blades, and woodden bracelets, wherewith they cover their hand wrists, when they fight, and great Canes open at one end, by the sound of which they keepe time and cadence in their dancing, are in many places to be seene, and namely in mine owne house. They are shaven all over, much more close and cleaner than wee are, with no other Razors than of wood or stone. They beleeve their soules to be eternall, and those that have deserved well of their Gods, to be placed in that part of heaven where the Sunne riseth, and the cursed toward the West in opposition. They have certaine Prophets and Priests, which commonly abide in the mountaines, and very seldome shew themselves unto the people; but when they come downe, there is a great feast prepared, and a solemne assembly of manie towneships together (each Grange as I have described maketh a village, and they are about a French league one from another). The Prophet speakes to the people in publike, exhorting them to embrace vertue, and follow their dutie. All their morall discipline containeth but these two articles; first and undismaied resolution to warre, then an inviolable affection to their wives. Hee doth also Prognosticate of things to come, and what successe they shall hope for in their enterprises: hee either perswadeth or disswadeth them from warre; but if he chance to misse of his divination, and that it succeed otherwise than hee foretold them, if hee be taken, he is hewen in a thousand peeces, and condemned for a false Prophet. And therefore he that hath once misreckoned himselfe is never seene againe. Divination is the gift of God; the abusing whereof should be a punishable imposture. When the Divines amongst the Scythians had foretold an untruth, they were couched along upon hurdles full of heath or brushwood, drawne by oxen, and so manicled hand and foot, burned to death. Those which manage matters subject to the conduct of mans sufficiencie, are excusable, although they shew the utmost of their skill. But those that gull and conicatch us with the assurance of an extraordinarie facultie, and which is beyond our knowledge, ought to be double punished; first because they performe not the effect of their promise, then for the rashnesse of their imposture and unadvisednesse of their fraud. They warre against the nations, that lie beyond their mountaines, to which they go naked, having no other weapons than bowes, or woodden swords, sharpe at one end, as our broaches are. It is an admirable thing to see the constant resolution of their combats, which never end but by effusion of bloud and murther: for they know not what feare or rowts are. Every Victor brings home the head of the enemie he hath slaine as a Trophey of his victorie, and fastneth the same at the entrance of his dwelling place. After they have long time used and entreated their prisoners well, and with all commodities they can devise, he that is the Master of them; sommoning a great assembly of his acquaintance, tieth a corde to one of the prisoners armes, by the end whereof he holds him fast, with some distance from him, for feare he might offend him, and giveth the other arme, bound in like manner, to the dearest friend he hath, and both in the presence of all the assembly kill him with swords: which done, they roast, and then eat him in common, and send some slices of him to such of their friends as are absent. It is not as some imagine, to nourish themselves with it, (as anciently the Scithians wont to doe,) but to represent an extreme, and inexpiable revenge.

Which we prove thus; some of them perceiving the Portugales, who had confederated themselves with their adversaries, to use another kinde of death, when they tooke them prisoners; which was, to burie them up to the middle, and against the upper part of the body to shoot arrowes, and then being almost dead, to hang them up; they supposed, that these people of the other world (as they who had sowed the knowledge of many vices amongst their neighbours, and were much more cunning in all kindes of evils and mischiefe than they) undertooke not this manner of revenge without cause, and that consequently it was more smartfull, and cruell than theirs, and thereupon began to leave their old fashion to follow this. I am not sorie we note the barbarous horror of such an action, but grieved, that prying so narrowly into their faults we are so blinded in ours. I thinke there is more barbarisme in eating men alive, than to feed upon them being dead; to mangle by tortures and torments a body full of lively sense, to roast him in peeces, to make dogges and swine to gnaw and teare him in mammockes (as wee have not only read, but scene very lately, yea and in our owne memorie, not amongst ancient enemies, but our neighbours and fellow-citizens; and which is worse, under pretence of pietie and religion) than to roast and eat him after he is dead. Chrysippus and Zeno, arch-pillers of the Stoicke sect, have supposed that it was no hurt at all, in time of need, and to what end soever, to make use of our carrion bodies, and to feed upon them, as did our forefathers, who being besieged by Cæsar in the Citie of Alexia, resolved to sustaine the famine of the siege, with the bodies of old men, women, and other persons unserviceable and unfit to fight.

> *Vascones (fama est) alimentis talibus usi*
> *Produxere animas.*
> Gascoynes (as fame reports)
> Liv'd with meats of such sorts.

And Physitians feare not, in all kindes of compositions availefull to our health, to make use of it, be it for outward or inward applications: But there was never any opinion found so unnaturall and immodest, that would excuse treason, treacherie, disloyaltie, tyrannie, crueltie, and such like, which are our ordinarie faults. We may then well call them barbarous, in regard of reasons rules, but not in respect of us that exceed them in all kinde of barbarisme. Their warres are noble and generous, and have as much excuse and beautie, as this humane infirmitie may admit: they ayme at nought so much, and have no other foundation amongst them, but the meere jelousie of vertue. They contend not for the gaining of new lands; for to this day they yet enjoy that naturall ubertie and fruitfulnesse, which without labouring toyle, doth in such plenteous abundance furnish them with all necessary things, that they need not enlarge their limits. They are yet in that happy estate, as they desire no more, than what their naturall necessities direct them: whatsoever is beyond it, is to them superfluous. Those that are much about one age, doe generally enter-call one another brethren, and such as are younger, they call children, and the aged are esteemed as fathers to all the rest. These leave this full possession of goods in common, and without division to their heires, without other claime or title, but that which nature doth plainely impart unto all creatures, even as shee brings them into the world. If their neighbours chance to come over the mountaines to assaile or invade them, and that they get the victorie over them, the Victors conquest is glorie, and the advantage to be and remaine superior in valour and vertue: else have they nothing to doe with the goods and spoyles of the vanquished, and so returne into their countrie, where they neither want any necessarie thing, nor lacke this great portion, to know how to enjoy their condition happily, and are contented with what nature affoordeth them. So doe these when their turne commeth. They require no other ransome of their prisoners, but an acknowledgement and confession that they are vanquished. And in a whole age, a man shall not finde one, that doth not rather embrace death, than either by word or countenance remissely to yeeld one jot of an invincible courage. There is none seene that would not rather be slaine and devoured, than sue for life, or shew any feare: They use their prisoners with all libertie, that they may so much the more hold their lives deare and precious, and commonly entertaine them with threats of future death, with the torments they shall endure, with the preparations intended for that purpose, with mangling and slicing of their members, and with the feast that shall be kept at their charge. All which is done, to wrest some remisse, and exact some faint-yeelding speech of submission from them, or to possesse them with a desire to escape or run away; that so they may have the advantage to have danted and made them afraid, and to have forced their constancie. For certainly true victorie consisteth in that only point. . . .

TORQUATO TASSO (1544–95)

GERUSALEMME LIBERATA

Jerusalem Delivered (1575; 1581)

Many scholars consider Torquato Tasso's *Jerusalem Delivered* the greatest modern epic. Its mighty theme—the capture of Jerusalem in the First Crusade (1099), seen through the fervent lens of medieval chivalry—combines classical thought with romantic emotion in the traditional *ottava rima* verse (eight line stanzas, with rhyme scheme abababcc) so powerful, scenes so dramatic, vision so universal as to produce an impression of unity equaled only by Dante Alighieri's *Commedia* and perhaps by John Milton's *Paradise Lost*. The mission of the hero, Godfrey de Bouillon, is a sacred one—initiated by his own private visitation from the Archangel Gabriel, who is sent to Godfrey by God himself. The revelation of God's will to Godfrey allows him the unique security of exercising his own free will with the assurance of predestined success. Satan, embodied as a full-blown character, intervenes to halt the Christians' initial progress. The epic's clash of magic and reality, history and fantasy, restlessness and melancholy, lyricism and sentimentalism, eroticism and nationalism uniquely captures and celebrates the best spirit of the Middle Ages. *Jerusalem Delivered* also reflects the fading ideals of an Italian Renaissance that had overreached itself in unbridled ambition for the potential of the human spirit. Tasso had barely passed thirty when he completed his masterpiece, a tribute to the Church militant and to his era's renewed faith in Catholicism as a bastion of retrenchment against the excesses of an age of rebellion. By the time he was thirty-three, he had become so disturbed mentally that he was confined for his own protection by the d'Este family. The crown of laurel, awarded to no one since Petrarch, was bestowed on Tasso by Pope Clement VIII. He died before he could receive it; the crown was laid upon his tomb. Voltaire said of Tasso's musical verse: "It is astonishing how Tasso impresses a new character upon the soft Italian tongue, enhancing it by majesty, and informing it with strength."

CANTO I

1. I sing the pious armies and the man
    who freed the mighty Sepulchre of Christ.
    Much did his spirit and his body bear,

much did he suffer in his glorious gain.
Hell fought in vain against him, and in vain
both Libya and Asia came to war:
back to the holy flag, with God's protection,

he brought his fellow knights from their defection.

2. O Muse, who do not wear around your brow
the perishable leaf of Helicon,
but up in heaven's happy-ringing choirs
display your diadem of deathless stars,
oh, breathe celestial fire in my breast,
ennoble this my song, and pardon me
if I weave truth with fiction, and adorn
in part my words with pleasures not your own.

3. You know too well this world most eager goes
where Mount Parnassus sheds its dulcet stream,
and, if revealed in soothing verses, truth
wins and convinces those who shun it most.
Thus to a sickly child we hand a glass
its rim besprinkled with a potion sweet:
deceived, the bitter medicine he drinks,
and such deception a new vigor brings.

4. Magnanimous Alfonso, you who save
from rage of fate and to his haven bring
a wandering pilgrim swept from cliff to cliff
and nearly swallowed by the wrathful sea,
benevolently welcome these my sheets
which as a vow I consecrate to you.
The day may dawn when my foreseeing quill
will write of you what it now fails to tell.

5. Surely, if that bright day will ever dawn
when the good Christian peoples be at peace
and try to snatch with horses and with ships
from the fierce Thracian his ill-gotten prey,
you will be offered sovereignty on land
or, if you choose, high lordship on the seas.
But meanwhile, emulous of Godfrey, hear
my song, and for your own campaign pre-pare.

6. Already the sixth year was turning since
the Christians had come east for their high task;
and they had won Nicaea in a siege
and mighty Antioch with stratagem;
the latter, then, in battle was upheld
against a countless horde of Persian foes;
Tortosa, too, had fallen. In the drear
season they now awaited the new year.

7. But the sweet end of winter and of rain,
which kept all weapons idle, was not far,
when from his lofty throne the Eternal Father,
Who in the brightest part of heaven dwells,
so high above the sphere of all His stars
as is the chasm between them and hell,
looked on the earth and in an instant saw
the entire world as one small speck below.

8. All things He saw, and He in Syria then
rested His sight upon the Christian knights,
and with His scanning glance that pierces through
the innermost recesses of men's hearts,
Godfrey He saw, who from the holy Town
was longing to dislodge the impious Pagans
and, full of faith and zeal, had laid aside
empire and wealth and every mortal pride.

9. But He saw Baldwin who with restless mind
was only dreaming of his earthly glory,
and then saw Tancred who, oppressed and crushed
by vain and mortal love, disdained to live;
Bohemund, too, who only strove to give
his newly founded realm of Antioch
high principles and laws, and wished to start
the cult of the true God in peace and art.

10. He was so much in that one thought enrapt
that for no other thing he seemed to care.
God in Rinaldo saw a dauntless soul
and a brave heart impatient of repose,
with neither greed for gold or for command

but only a burning, boundless thirst for fame.
Look at him: Guelfo's words with joy he hears,
and learns the lucent feats of his forebears.

11. But as the Ruler of the world perceived
the faintest beats of those and other hearts,
from the angelic splendors to Himself
He summoned Gabriel, second of the first.
He speeds between each blessed soul and God,
faithful interpreter, glad messenger.
Heaven's decrees he carries down, and then
brings back the zealous pleas of mortal men.

12. God to His angel said: "Find Godfrey, quick,
and tell him in my name: Why all this rest?
Why not resume the holy war at once,
to liberate Jerusalem oppressed?
Let him the princes summon; let him spur
to the high cause the slow; and let him lead!
I choose him here, and they on earth will too,—
so far his peers, now his obedient crew.

13. These words He spoke to him, and Gabriel
was ready to obey the ordered things.
He grit his form invisible with air,
and then with mortal senses rounded it.
Man's aspect and man's limbs he seemed to take,
with a celestial majesty composed:
the age he feigned that turns child into lad,
and, quick, adorned with rays his golden head.

14. White wings he donned, with tips of beaming gold,
agile and indefatigably swift.
Cutting with them the winds and clouds, he flew
sublime above the earth, above the sea.
In such a guise, the messenger of God
came toward the deepest regions of the world.
First on Mount Lebanon he stopped awhile,
keeping his balance with angelic style;

15. Then to the shores of Tarsus right from there
he aimed his flight precipitously down.
Up from the eastern sky the new sun rose,
part out, and part still hidden in the sea.
Godfrey was lifting at that very hour
(as usual) his morning prayer to God
when with the sun at once, but far more bright,
the Angel came and stood before his sight.

16. He spoke these words to him: "O Godfrey, long
have you awaited the right time to fight.
Why, then, let this delay still keep you from
delivering Jerusalem oppressed?
Right now, all princes to a council call,
and urge the slow to reach their destined goal.
God chose you as their leader, and they too
must willingly submit themselves to you.

17. "God's messenger am I, and in His name
reveal His will to you. Oh, how much hope
in your bright triumph must you now possess,
and how much zeal to meet your destined foe!"
He spoke no more, but back to heaven sped
into the highest, most resplendent spheres.
Godfrey was stunned by both that speech and light,
his vision dazed, his heart astir with fright.

18. But when, reheartened, he could clearly see
who had come, who had sent, what had been said,
if once he longed, he now was all afire
to end the war God chose him to command:
not that to see himself preferred to all

could swell his breast with any breath of
pride:
but more and more his will from God's
desire,
a spark in conflagration, caught new fire.

ST. JOHN OF THE CROSS (JUAN DE YEPES Y ALVÁREZ) (1542–91)

Dark Night of the Soul (1583)

Equal to the mystical innocence of his spiritual director St. Teresa de Jesus is the *Dark Night* of the Carmelite Juan de la Cruz. The central metaphor of his *Dark Night*, probably conceived of while he was imprisoned by opponents of his reform efforts, is reminiscent of Dante Alighieri's dark woods at the opening of the *Divine Comedy*. The soul in its ascent to the divine is absolutely dependent on a spiritual director. Through experienced direction the aspiring soul will strip itself of all worldly desires and undergo a purgation of sinfulness that will prepare it for entrance into the eternal presence of its Beloved. The purged soul, moreover, acquires a powerful charisma that makes it effective in life as well as blissful in the life to come. The mystic's enraptured love for God, as St. John expresses it in his graceful lyrics and earnest prose, reminds us of the romantic love poetry of the troubadours. Total passivity in submission to God's love alone leads to salvation. Contemporary practitioners of meditation techniques recognize the balance that comes from emptying the mind in order to activate it with greater focus and energy. The process described by St. John, of submitting the soul to the dark night of purgation and humiliation, resembles nothing so much as the courtly ritual vigil of medieval knighthood.

ARGUMENT.

The stanzas to be explained are set forth at the beginning of this book, then an explanation of each severally, the stanza being placed before it. After that an explanation of each line, which is also set before the explanation. The first two stanzas explain the two spiritual purgations of the sensual and spiritual part of man, and the other six the various and admirable effects of the spiritual enlightenment and union of love with God.

Stanzas.

I.

In a dark night,
With anxious love inflamed,
O, happy lot!
Forth unobserved I went,
My house being now at rest.

II.

In darkness and in safety,
By the secret ladder, disguised,
O, happy lot!
In darkness and concealment,
My house being now at rest.

III.

In that happy night,
In secret, seen of none,
Seeing nought myself,
Without other light or guide
Save that which in my heart was burning.

IV.

That light guided me
More surely than the noonday sun
To the place where He was waiting for me,
Whom I knew well,
And where none appeared.

V.

O, guiding night;
O, night more lovely than the dawn;
O, night that hast united
The lover with His beloved,
And changed her into her love.

VI.

On my flowery bosom,
Kept whole for Him alone,
There He reposed and slept;
And I cherished Him, and the waving
Of the cedars fanned Him.

VII.

As His hair floated in the breeze
That from the turret blew,
He struck me on the neck
With His gentle hand,
And all sensation left me.

VIII.

I continued in oblivion lost,
My head was resting on my love;
Lost to all things and myself,
And, amid the lilies forgotten,
Threw all my cares away. . . .

BOOK I. OF THE NIGHT OF SENSE.

In a dark night,
With anxious love inflamed,
O, happy lot!
Forth unobserved I went,
My house being now at rest.

In the first stanza the soul sings of the way and manner of its going forth, as to its affections, from self and all created things, dying thereto by real mortification, that it may live the life of love, sweet and delicious in God. It went forth, from itself and from all things, in a dark night, by which is meant here purgative contemplation—as I shall hereinafter explain—which causes in the soul passive denial of self and of all besides. This departure, it says, it was able to accomplish in the strength and fervour which the love of the Bridegroom supplied, in the obscure contemplation for that end. The soul magnifies its own happiness in having journeyed Godwards in that night so successfully as to escape all hindrance on the part of its three enemies—the world, the devil, and the flesh—which are always found infesting this road; for the night of purgative contemplation had lulled to sleep and mortified, in the house of sensuality, all passions and desires, in their rebellious movements.

Chapter I.

Begins with the first stanza and treats of the imperfections of beginners.

1. Three states: beginners, proficients and perfect.
2. Beginners encouraged by sweetness.
3. Continuation.
4. Selfish spirituality of beginners. Work proportioned to habit.
5. Imperfections.

In a dark night. Souls begin to enter the dark night when God is drawing them out of the state of beginners, which is that of those who meditate on the spiritual road, and is leading them into that of proficients, the state of contemplatives, that, having passed through it, they may arrive at the state of the perfect, which is that of the divine union with God. That we may the better understand and explain the nature of this night through which the soul has to pass, and why God leads men into it, it may be well to touch first upon certain peculiarities of beginners, which, though treated in the briefest possible way, it is well for them to know, that they may perceive the weakness of the state they are in, take courage, and desire to be led of God into this night, where the soul is established in virtue and made strong for the inestimable delights of His love. Though I shall dwell at some length upon this point, I shall do so no longer than suffices for the immediate discussion of this dark night.

2. We are to keep in mind that a soul, when seriously converted to the service of God, is, in general, spiritually nursed and caressed, as an infant by its loving mother, who warms it in her bosom, nourishes it with her own sweet milk, feeds it with tender and delicate food, carries it in her arms, and fondles it. But as the child grows up the mother withholds her caresses, hides her breasts, and anoints them with the juice of bitter aloes; she carries the infant in her arms no longer, but makes it walk on the ground, so that, losing the habits of an infant, it may apply itself to greater and more substantial pursuits.

3. The grace of God, like a loving mother, as soon as the soul is regenerated in the new fire and fervour of His service, treats it in the same way; for it enables it, without labour on its own part, to find its spiritual milk, sweet and delicious, in all the things of God, and in devotional exercises great sweetness; God giving it the breasts of His own tender love, as to a tender babe. Such souls, therefore, delight to spend many hours, and perhaps whole nights, in prayer; their pleasures are penances, their joy is fasting, and their consolations lie in the use of the sacraments and in speaking of divine things.

4. Now spiritual men generally, speaking spiritually, are extremely weak and imperfect here, though they apply themselves to devotion, and practise it with great resolution, earnestness, and care. For being drawn to these things and to their spiritual exercises by the comfort and satisfaction they find therein, and not yet confirmed in virtue by the struggle it demands, they fall into many errors and imperfections in their spiritual life; for every man's work corresponds to the habit of perfection which he has acquired. These souls, therefore, not having had time to acquire those habits of vigour, must, of necessity, perform their acts, like children, weakly.

5. To make this more clear, and to show how weak are beginners in virtue in those good

works which they perform with so much ease and pleasure, I proceed to explain by reference to the seven capital sins, pointing out some of the imperfections into which beginners fall in the matter of each of them. This will show us plainly how like children they are in all they do, and also how great are the blessings of this dark night of which I am about to speak; seeing that it cleanses and purifies the soul from all these imperfections.

GIORDANO BRUNO OF NOLA (1548–1600)

Concerning the Cause, Principle, and One (1584)

At the idealistic end of the spectrum, the Renaissance humanists espoused a monism worthy of Aristotle. The belief that the universe is a unified reality, that can be interpreted by reference to a single principle accessible to the persistent human mind, continues to this day to propel the explorations of twentieth-century physicists like Albert Einstein and Stephen Hawking. Yet poet, playwright, and philosopher Giordano Bruno, associate of Philip Sidney and William Gilbert and irrepressible celebrator of Copernican astronomy, was truly anti-Aristotelian, in the degree to which he rejected prior authority and insisted on the unqualified abilities of human intelligence to reach conclusions based on its own perceptions and reason. He was, in the end, expelled from the Dominican order and burned at the stake by the Inquisition for heresy, because he rejected the Immaculate Conception and the doctrine of transubstantiation, and because his concept of the universal mind—what might today be called "the force"—seemed to threaten the Roman Catholic belief in the hierarchical superiority of divinity. Some say the Renaissance ended with his death. Bruno's pantheism is similar to the Hindu conception that the soul becomes one with the ultimate reality. His almost poetic love for the infinite and eternal one behind a multiplicity of worlds is apparent in the treatise that follows. His argument that simplicity is superior to multiplicity, and that we approach unity as we move away from the plurality of things, just as logic looks for the defining cause behind related data, is an extension of the "great chain of being" metaphor so important to classical, medieval, and Renaissance thought.

. . . First of all, concerning the prime active qualities of corporeal nature, who does not know that the principle of heat is indivisible and, therefore, separated from every kind of heat, because the principle must not be something of the originated? If this is so, who can object to the affirmation that the principle is not warm, nor cold, but an identity of warmth and cold? Whence does it happen, then, that one contrary is the principle of the other—and, therefore, that the transformations are circular—unless there exists a substratum, a principle, a term, and a continuation and a coincidence of one and the other? Are not the minimum warmth and the minimum cold the same throughout? Isn't the principle of movement toward the cold to be found in the limit of the maximum warmth? It is obvious, therefore, that not only do the two maximums (maxima) sometimes coincide in resistance, and the two minima (coincide) in agreement, but also the maximum and the minimum through the vicissitude of transmutation; therefore, it is not without good cause that the doctors are apprehensive of the perfect state of health; in the highest level of felicity the provident are cautious. Who does not see that the principle of generation and corruption is one? Is not the end of corruption the principle of generation? Do we not similarly say that taken, this placed; that was, this is? Certainly, if we consider well, we see that corruption is not other than a generation, and the generation is not other than a corruption; the love is a kind of hate; (finally) the hate is a kind of love; the hate of the contrary is the love of the convenient; the love of this is the hate of that. In substance and root, therefore, love and hate, friendship and conflict, is one and the same thing. From whence does the doctor seek the antidote more fittingly than from venom? What gives better treacles than the viper? In the worst poisons [are] the best medicines. Is not the same potency common to two contrary objects? Now, where do you believe this comes from, if not from that; that as one is the principle of being, so one is the principle of conceiving one and the other object; and that the contraries are about one substratum, as they are apprehended by one and the same sense? Not to speak of that—that the circular rests on the level, the concave tarries and lies on the convex, the irascible lives together with the patient, the humble is pleasing to the most arrogant, the liberal to the avaricious.

In conclusion, he who wishes to know the greatest secrets of nature should regard and contemplate the minimum and maximum of contraries and opposites. It is profound magic to know how to draw out the contrary after having found the point of union. The poor Aristotle directed his thought to this, establishing privation, to which is joined a certain disposition, as progenitor, parent, and mother of form; but he could not attain the end. He has not been able to arrive at this point because he stopped at the genus of opposition; he remained entangled in such a manner that in not descending to species from contrariety, he did not arrive, nor did he fix his eyes upon the goal; therefore, he has, with this one assertion—that contraries cannot actually harmonize in the same subject—missed the entire way.

The following dialogue ensues between the characters Polyhymnius, Theophilus, Gervasius, and Dixon.

POL. You have discoursed sublimely, rarely, and extraordinarily of the all, of the maximum, of the being, of the principle, and of the one. But I would like to see you show forth the difference of unity; because I find it written: "It is not good to be alone." Besides, I feel great anxiety because there, in my purse and money bag, but one penny is lodged.

THEO. That unity is all which is not unfolded, not under distribution and distinction of number, and does not exist in such singularity—as you would like to understand it—but is complicative and comprising.

POL. An example? Because to tell the truth, I hear, but I do not understand.

THEO. Just as the decade is a unity, but is embracing, so the hundred is not less a unity, but is more embracing; the thousand is a unity no less than the others, but is still more embracing. This that I propose to you in arithmetic, you ought to understand, in a higher and simpler sense, of all things. The highest good, the highest object of desire, the highest perfection, the highest beatitude, consists in the unity that embraces all. We take delight in colors but not in one express color, whatever that may be, but the greatest delight is in such a one that embraces all colors. We delight in sound, not in a particular one, but in an embracing one which results from the harmony of all. We delight in a sensible, but greatest delight is in that which comprehends all the sensibles; we delight in a knowable that comprises everything knowable; we delight in the apprehensible that embraces all that which can be comprehended; we delight in a being which embraces all, but greatest delight is in that one which is the all itself. As you, Polyhymnius, would be more

delighted in the unity of a gem so precious that it would be more valuable than all the gold in the world than in the multitude of thousands and thousands of such pennies as the one which you have in your pocket-book.

POL. EXCELLENT.

GERV. I am now too a learned person; because just as he who does not understand the one does not understand anything, so he who understands the one truly understands all; and he who advances more to the knowledge of the one, more nearly approaches the knowledge of all.

DIX. And so go I—if I have understood well— being tremendously enriched by the thoughts of Theophilus, faithful reporter of the Nolan philosophy.

THEO. Praised be the Gods, and extolled by all the living be the infinite, the simplest, the most unified, the highest, and the most absolute cause, principle, and the one.

RICHARD HAKLUYT (C.1552–1616)

The Principall Navigations, Voiages, and Discoveries of the English Nation (1589)

The imagination of sixteenth-century England was inflamed by popular accounts of the great voyages of discovery that had begun with Christopher Columbus and continued in an accelerating curve for the hundred years that followed. Geographer Richard Hakluyt, from his positions at Oxford and Westminster Abbey, was one of the realm's strongest proponents of exploration. His hobby of collecting interviews, eyewitness accounts, log books, and manuscript and published accounts, British and foreign, of the great voyages made him a frequent commentator in his own lifetime and an invaluable historical and anthropological resource ever since. His encyclopedic work is said to have inspired Shakespeare's *Tempest.* Hakluyt himself had never been in a boat. In this account of John Davis' first voyage in search of the Northwest Passage, the European attitude toward native Americans is all too apparent.

The first voyage of Master John Davis, undertaken in June 1585, for the discovery of the Northwest Passage. Written by John Janes, Merchant, sometimes servant to the worshipful Master William Sanderson.

The next morning being the 30 of July, there came 37 Canoas rowing by our ships, calling to us to come on shore. We not making any great haste unto them, one of them went up to the top of the rock and leapt and danced as they

Fourteenth-century Italian astrolabe, in the Jagellon Library Museum, Cracow

had done the day before, showing us a seal's skin and another thing made like a timbrel, which he did beat upon with a stick, making a noise like a small drum. Whereupon we manned our boats and came to them, they all staying in their Canoas. We came to the water side where they were; and after we had sworn by the sun, after their fashion, they did trust us. So I shook hands with one of them, and he kissed my hand, and we were very familiar with them. We were in so great credit with them upon this single acquaintance, that we could have any thing they had. We bought five Canoas of them; we bought their clothes from their backs, which were all made of seals' skins and birds' skins; their buskins, their hose, their gloves, all being commonly sewed and well dressed, so that we were fully persuaded that they have divers artificers among them. We had a pair of buskins of them full of fine wool like beaver. Their apparel for heat was made of birds' skins with their feathers on them. We saw among them leather dressed like glovers' leather, and thick thongs like white leather of a good length. We had of their darts and ores, and found in them that they would by no means displease us, but would give us whatsoever we asked of them, and would be satisfied with whatsoever we gave them. They took great care one of another; for when we had bought their boats, then two other would come and carry him away between them that had sold us his. They are very tractable people, void of craft or double dealing, and easy to be brought to any civility or good order. But we judge them to be idolaters and to worship the sun.

During the time of our abode among these islands we found reasonable quantity of wood, both fir, sprucc, and junipcr; which whether it came floating any great distance to these places where we found it, or whether it grew in some great islands near the same place by us not yet discovered, we know not; but we judge that it groweth there further into the land then we were, because the people had great store of darts and ores which they made none account of, but gave them to us for small trifles, as points and pieces of paper. We saw about this coast marvelous great abundance of seals skulling together like skulls of small fish. We found no fresh water among these islands, but only snow water, whereof we found great pools. The cliffs were all of such ore as M. Frobisher brought from Meta Incognita. We had divers shows of study or muscovy glass shining not altogether unlike to crystal. We found an herb growing upon the rocks, whose fruit was sweet, full of red juice; and the ripe ones were like corinths. We found also birch and willow growing like shrubs low to the ground. These people have great store of furs, as we judge. They made shows unto us the 30 of this present, which was the second time of our being with them, after they perceived we would have skins and furs, that they would go into the country and come again the next day with such things as they had. But this night the wind coming fair, the captain and the master would by no means detract the purpose of our discovery. And so the last of this month about four of the clock in the morning in God's name we set sail, and were all that day becalmed upon the coast.

The first of August we had a fair wind, and so proceeded towards the Northwest for our discovery.

EDMUND SPENSER (C.1552–99)

Letter to Raleigh (1590)

Spenser's letter to his patron Sir Walter Raleigh, like Dante Alighieri's letter to Can Grande della Scala, provides insight into the shaping of his unfinished epic of allegorical morality, *The Faerie Queene.* Dedicated to Queen Elizabeth, this intentionally archaic masterpiece celebrates her mythical virtues in the heroic personage of Gloriana. The energy provided by such exuberant nationalism sustained him only through six of the twelve proposed books. Each book was to exemplify a different Aristotelian virtue, with the whole intent on providing a courtly model for the ideal gentleman in service of the ideal lady. But instead of finishing the ambitious poem with a presentation of a utopia made possible by the good works of Arthur and the planned twelve Arthurian knights, Spenser followed Book 6 with "the Cantoes of Mutabilitie," published only after his death, which counter the idealism of the completed books. As deeply moving as anything this prolific poet had written, the *Cantoes* are written in a meditative vein laced with skeptical despair of ever apprehending the "blatant Beast" which will remain forever at large to wreak havoc on humanity's best laid plans and most sincere aspirations. In this movement from the adventurous optimism of the mid-sixteenth century to the ultimate doubt of the late, Spenser's work reflects its sources, especially Ludovico Ariosto's *Orlando Furioso* and Torquato Tasso's *Jerusalem Delivered*, and prefigures John Milton's *Paradise Lost* which sought to attain the apotheosis of the epic tradition Spenser had aimed at. Unlike the emblematic figures of medieval allegorical narratives like *The Romance of the Rose,* Spenser's characters are fully personified and compelling.

A Letter of the Authors expounding his whole intention in the course of this worke: which for that it giueth great light to the Reader, for the better vnderstanding is hereunto annexed.

To the Right noble, and Valorous, Sir Walter

Raleigh knight, Lo. Wardein of the Stanneryes, and her Maiesties liefetenaunt of the County of Cornewayll.

Sir knowing how doubtfully all Allegories may be construed, and this booke of mine, which I have entituled the Faery Queene, being a continued Allegory, or darke conceit, I have thought good as well for auoyding of gealous opinions and misconstructions, as also for your better light in reading therof, (being so by you commanded,) to discouer vnto you the general intention and meaning, which in the whole course thereof I haue fashioned, without expressing of any particular purposes or by-accidents therein occasioned. The generall end therefore of all the booke is to fashion a gentleman or noble person in vertuous and gentle discipline: Which for that I conceiued shoulde be most plausible and pleasing, being coloured with an historicall fiction, the which the most part of men delight to read, rather for variety of matter, then for profite of the ensample: I chose the historye of king Arthure, as most fitte for the excellency of his person, being made famous by many mens former workes, and also furthest from the danger of enuy, and suspition of present time. In which I have followed all the antique Poets historicall, first Homere, who in the Persons of Agamemnon and Vlysses hath ensampled a good gouernour and a vertuous man, the one in his Ilias, the other in his Odysseis: then Virgil, whose like intention was to doe in the person of Aeneas: after him Ariosto comprised them both in his Orlando: and lately Tasso disseuered them againe, and formed both parts in two persons, namely that part which they in Philosophy call Ethice, or vertues of a private man, coloured in his Rinaldo: The other named Politice in his Godfredo. By ensample of which excellente Poets, I labour to pourtraict in Arthure, before he was king, the image of a braue knight, perfected in the twelue private morall vertues, as Aristotle hath deuised, the which is the purpose of these first twelue bookes: which if I finde to be well accepted, I may be perhaps encouraged, to frame the other part of polliticke vertues in his person, after that hee came to be king. To some I know this Methode will seeme displeasaunt, which had rather have good discipline deliuered plainly in way of precepts, or sermoned at large, as they vse, then thus clowdily enwrapped in Allegoricall deuises. But such, me seeme, should be satisfide with the vse of these dayes, seeing all things accounted by their showes, and nothing esteemed of, that is not delightfull and pleasing to commune sence. For this cause is Xenophon preferred before Plato, for that the one in the exquisite depth of his iudgement, formed a Commune welth such as it should be, but the other in the person of Cyrus and the Persians fashioned a gouernement such as

might best be: So much more profitable and gratious is doctrine by ensample, then by rule. So have I laboured to doe in the person of Arthure: whome I conceiue after his long education by Timon, to whom he was by Merlin deliuered to be brought vp, so soone as he was borne of the Lady Igrayne, to haue seene in a dream or vision the Faery Queen, with whose excellent beauty rauished, he awaking resolued to seeke her out, and so being by Merlin armed, and by Timon throughly instructed, he went to seeke her forth in Faerye land. In that Faery Queene I meane glory in my generall intention, but in my particular I conceiue the most excellent and glorious person of our soueraine the Queene, and her kingdome in Faery land. And yet in some places els, I doe otherwise shadow her. For considering she beareth two persons, the one of a most royall Queene or Empresse, the other of a most vertuous and beautifull Lady, this latter part in some places I doe expresse in Belphœbe, fashioning her name according to your owne excellent conceipt of Cynthia, (Phœbe and Cynthia being both names of Diana.) So in the person of Prince Arthure I sette forth magnificence in particular, which vertue for that (according to Aristotle and the rest) it is the perfection of all the rest, and conteineth in it them all, therefore in the whole course I mention the deedes of Arthure applyable to that vertue, which I write of in that booke. But of the xii. other vertues, I make xii. other knights the patrones, for the more variety of the history: Of which these three bookes contayn three, The first of the knight of the Redcrosse, in whome I expresse Holynes: The seconde of Sir Guyon, in whome I setle forth Temperaunce: The third of Britomartis a Lady knight, in whome I picture Chastity. But because the beginning of the whole worke seemeth abrupte and as depending upon other antecedents, it needs that ye know the occasion of these three knights seuerall aduentures. For the Method of a Poet historical is not such, as of an Historiographer. For an Historiographer discourseth of affayres orderly as they were donne, accounting as well the times as the actions, but a Poet thrusteth into the middest, euen where it most concerneth him, and there recoursing to the thinges forepaste, and diuining of thinges to come, maketh a pleasing Analysis of all. The beginning therefore of my history, if it were to be told by an Historiographer should be the twelfth booke, which is the last, where I deuise that the Faery Queene kept her Annuall feaste xii. dayes, uppon which xii. seuerall dayes, the occasions of the xii. seuerall aduentures hapned, which being vndertaken by xii. seuerall knights, are in these xii books seuerally handled and discoursed. The first was this. In the beginning of the feast, there presented him selfe a tall clownishe younge man, who falling before the Queen of Faries desired a boone (as the manner then was) which during that feast she might not refuse: which was that hee might haue the atchieuement of any aduenture, which during that feaste should happen, that being graunted, he rested him on the floore, vnfitte through his rusticity for a better place. Soone after entred a faire Ladye in mourning weedes, riding on a white Asse, with a dwarfe behind her leading a warlike steed, that bore the Armes of a knight, and his speare in the dwarfes hand. Shee falling before the Queene of Faeries, complayned that her father and mother an ancient King and Queene, had bene by an huge dragon many years shut up in a brasen Castle, who thence suffred them not to yssew: and therefore besought the Faery Queene to assygne her some one of her knights to take on him that exployt. Presently that clownish person vpstarting, desired that aduenture: whereat the Queene much wondering, and the Lady much gainesaying, yet he earnestly importuned his desire. In the end the Lady told him that vnlesse that armour which she brought, would serue him (that is the armour of a Christian man specified by Saint Paul v. Ephes.) that he could not succeed in that enterprise, which being forthwith put vpon him with dewe furnitures thereunto, he seemed the goodliest man in al that company, and was well liked of the Lady. And eftesoones taking on him knighthood, and mounting on that straunge Courser, he went forth with her on that aduenture: where beginneth the first booke, vz.

A gentle knight was pricking on the playne. &c.

The second day ther came in a Palmer bearing an Infant with bloody hands, whose Parents he complained to haue bene slayn by an Enchaunteresse called Acrasia: and therfore craued of the Faery Queene, to appoint him some knight, to performe that aduenture, which being assigned to Sir Guyon, he presently went forth with that same Palmer: which is the beginning of the second booke and the whole subiect thereof. The third day there came in, a Groome who complained before the Faery Queene, that a vile Enchaunter called Busirane had in hand a most faire Lady called Amoretta, whom he kept in most grieuous torment, because she would not yield him the pleasure of her body. Whereupon Sir Scudamour the louer of that Lady presently tooke on him that aduenture. But being vnable to performe it by reason of the hard Enchauntments, after long sorrow, in the end met with Britomartis, who succoured him, and reskewed his loue.

But by occasion hereof, many other aduentures are intermedled, but rather as Accidents, then intendments. As the loue of Britomart, the ouerthrow of Marinell, the misery of Florimell, the vertuousnes of Belphœbe, the lasciuiousnes of Hellenora, and many the like.

Thus much Sir, I have briefly ouerronne to direct your vnderstanding to the wel-head of the History, that from thence gathering the whole intention of the conceit, ye may as in a handfull gripe al the discourse, which otherwise may happily seeme tedious and confused. So humbly crauing the continuaunce of your honorable fauour towards me, and th'eternall establishment of your happines, I humbly take leaue.

23. Ianuary. 1589.

Yours most humbly affectionate.

Ed. Spenser.

GALILEO GALILEI (1564–1642)

Treatise on the Universe (1590)

Pisan mathematician and astronomer Galileo Galilei's name is popularly synonymous with the telescope, which he perfected in 1610 to observe mountains on the moon and previously undiscovered planets; and with the Inquisition, which tried him for heresy in 1632 and forced him to recant his belief that the earth revolved around the sun. He was judged unforgivable because he not only insisted on the new order of individual observation and analysis but also completely rejected the old Scholastic reverence for authority. He dared to say that, when it comes to mathematics, humans were capable of perfection equal to God's. But his controversial career was distinguished as well by his invention of the thermometer, by his experiments with gravity from the leaning tower of Pisa, by his discovery of the parabolic trajectory of missiles, by his announcement that the stars were made of the same stuff as our "vile earth," and by his theory of inertia which extended Leonardo da Vinci's studies on the necessary laws of nature and provided the foundation upon which Sir Isaac Newton would build his laws of motion. His belief that mathematics alone provided the mind with absolute certainty foreshadows Descartes. Galileo's major work was *The Sidereal Messenger* (1610), the roots of which can be traced to his *Treatise on the Universe*, written as a young professor at the University of Pisa and heavily influenced by his Jesuit education at the College of Rome. Despite his later disparagement of Aristotle, the *Treatise* indicates that the Aristotelian method of analysis and exposition was integral to Galileo's approach.

First Question. On the Opinion of Ancient Philosophers Concerning the Universe

Although, as Plato taught, there are three universes, one ideal or intelligible, another sensible and large, and a third sensible but small, for the present the discussion here is of the large sensible universe. The latter is nothing more than the universe of things, so named originally by Pythagoras because of the ornamentation it contains or because in itself it is cleansed (*mundus*) of all dirt. Similarly Aristotle called it a "universe," for it contains everything within itself; a "whole," for it has integral parts; and a "heaven," naming it from the nobler part, or also because he sometimes takes "heaven" to mean the universe. . . .

That this universe began at a certain time and was made in time has been the opinion of practically all the naturalists of antiquity, as Aristotle testifies in the first *De caelo*, . . . and the eighth *Physics;* though Galen, in the book *De claris physicis,* asserts that Xenophon thought it existed from eternity. But while they agreed on that, they yet disagreed on the following. First, on its matter, as can be seen in the question on the opinions of philosophers near the beginning of the *Physics.* Second, on its efficient cause, for some of them were unaware of this or made no mention of it; others posited such a cause, the first of whom was Anaxagoras, who proposed a kind of mind bringing all things together, and then Empedocles, who thought of strife and love, as Aristotle attests in the eighth *Physics.* . . . Third, on the mode of its production: for, as Aristotle teaches in the place noted above, some, such as Empedocles and Anaxagoras, thought that it was generated by aggregation and desegregation; others, by condensation and rare-faction; yet others, such as Democritus and Leucippus, from a concourse of atoms and an interstitial void; and finally others made the soul, by its own motion, the principle of all movement. Fourth, on this, that some thought it was so constituted that it must cease to be after the fashion of other things and never return to being; others, that it might cease to be but still should return to being—read Simplicius on the eighth *Physics,* and Aristotle in the first *De caelo.* . . .

Concerning Plato, there is uncertainty among philosophers as to what he did think. Taurus, in the *Timaeus* of Plato, Porphyry, Proclus, Plotinus, Alcinous, and Simplicius, in the eighth *Physics,* thought that for Plato the universe was sempiternal. And if one show

Galileo presents his telescope to the Venetian senate (Luigi Sabatelli), in the Tribuna di Galileo, Museo della Scienza, Florence

them Plato's text where he teaches in so many words in the *Timaeus* that the universe was generated, they reply that "generated" has different meanings for Plato, and in that place it means that it is made up of many component parts.

Many learned men, on the other hand, hold that Plato thought the universe was made in time and from a matter that previously moved with a kind of disordered motion; also, that it is corruptible by nature, although by God's will it will never corrupt. Aristotle teaches that this was Plato's opinion in the eighth *Physics,* and elsewhere; also Alexander (as referenced by Philoponus in the solution of the sixth argument of Proclus), Theophrastus, Themistius, and practically all commentators on Aristotle; Plutarch, Cicero, Diogenes Laërtius, Apicus, Seleucus, and Pleto the Platonist; and these are followed by St. Basil in his *Hexämeron,* Justin Martyr, Clement of Alexandria, Eusebius of Caesaria, Theophilactus, St. Augustine, and all the Schoolmen.

With regard to Aristotle it is certain that he defended tenaciously that the universe had existed from all eternity and that it would never end. This he thought he had proved in the eighth *Physics* when he attempted to establish that motion is sempiternal and, in the first *De caelo,* last chapter, that everything that is generated has a corruptible existence; as opposed to this, he frequently stated that the universe would never cease to be. Add to this that if the universe was made, it was made from something and not from nothing, since for Aristotle there is no such thing as creation. Here also the authority of all philosophers and theologians citing Aristotle agree on this point.

Yet some object that Aristotle, in the first *Topics,* chapter 9, states that it is a "problem" that the universe existed from eternity. But then one may reply, first, that Aristotle said this by way of example, especially since in his time there was doubt concerning this matter. Second, it might be called a problem by Aristotle in the sense that probable arguments could be adduced for both sides; but from this it does not follow, as is apparent from the principles of the teaching he passed on, that Aristotle denied that the world existed from eternity.

The opinion of the philosophers of antiquity concerning the creation of the world, while favoring the truth in asserting that the universe had a beginning, nonetheless departs from it in two respects. First, in that it says that the universe was made of matter, and thus is refuted by this argument: if the universe was made from some kind of matter, either this was generated from another kind, or it existed from eternity; if the first, then there would be a regress to infinity in matters, and so on; if the second, either some efficient principle existed together with matter from the beginning, or not; if not, then everything was made from such matter by chance, which is absurd; if so, then such matter existed to no purpose for all eternity; therefore [the universe was not made from matter].

Second, it is opposed to the truth in that it asserts that the universe, while created in time, is not going to corrupt, or that it will corrupt in such fashion as to return to being. Therefore it can likewise be refuted, by this argument: if the universe was generated, then either it will corrupt at some time or not; if the first, then it is not incorruptible; if it does not corrupt, to the contrary, everything that is generated in time is corruptible, as is obvious from experience and by induction; therefore [the universe will corrupt]. Confirmation: because the universe is said to be generated either from corruptibles or from incorruptibles; not the second, as is obvious; if the first, then it will corrupt. You say: it will cease to be, but in such a way that it will come back into being. To the contrary: because no cause can be assigned for such a return.

The opinion of Aristotle is opposed to the truth. For his arguments and those of Proclus, Averroës, and others supporting the eternity of the world, together with the solutions, read Pererius, book 15.

Second Question. The Truth Concerning the Origin of the Universe

I say, first: there must exist some first uncreated and eternal being, on whom all others depend, and to whom all others are directed as to an ultimate end. Proof of the first part of the conclusion: because otherwise it would follow that a thing would have produced itself, or that everything would have come into existence without an agent, and either is absurd. Proof of the second part: because there must be some first efficient cause of everything; but this cannot be other than a first and uncreated being; therefore all things will depend on, and be referred to, that being. Confirmation: because the correct order requires that we proceed from inferiors to the heavens, and from the heavens to the first mover, which is this uncreated being; it requires, moreover, that there be only one universal end of all things, which cannot be other than the said being.

I say, second: this eternal and uncreated being is not only the first final cause of all things but also the efficient cause of all existence in an unqualified way. Proof of the conclusion: for a particular effect there must be a particular cause; therefore a universal effect must have a universal cause; but this universal cause must also be the first, and this is the aforementioned being; therefore [there must be a first final and efficient cause]. Second: wherever there is more and less there must also be something absolute in that order; but in the genus of being there is more or less; therefore there is also a being in the absolute sense on whom all things depend efficiently. For, since all the finite beings of the universe are also imperfect, they cannot have existence from themselves in the order of efficient causality; existence of itself can only be said of the most perfect being, which is the uncreated being that is God. It is not to be wondered that this attribute should be said of God, moreover, insofar as he himself gave natural agents the power to educe forms from the potency of matter.

I say, third: this first and uncreated being has existence through its essence, and therefore is infinite, and has infinite virtue and power. Proof of the first part of the conclusion: because what has existence of itself has an unlimited existence; but unlimited existence is infinite; therefore, since the aforesaid being has existence of itself and otherwise would not be first and uncreated, it must have infinite existence—for whatever is finite is "finished," [i.e., terminated] by something. Confirmation: because whatever lacks all potency in the order of being is infinite being; but the first being lacks all potency in the order of being, for otherwise it would not have existence of itself nor would it be first; therefore [it is infinite being]. Proof of the second part of the conclusion: because virtue and power follow on existence; therefore, infinite existence implies infinite virtue and power. From this it follows that the first being can create things from nothing: for if an agent can produce an effect from a more remote potency the more perfect it is in power, and the first being has infinite power, it is no wonder that it should produce an effect from the most remote potency, that is, from nothing.

I say, fourth: this being, first, uncreated, and infinite, operates freely and contingently *ad extra.* Proof of the conclusion: because, since it is infinite, if it were to operate *ad extra* necessarily, it would produce as much as it were able and, as a consequence, an infinite effect; but there is no such effect; therefore [it does not act necessarily]. Add to this: a necessary cause is uniquely determined; but this infinite being can produce whatever it wills. Proof: because, since it is first, it has nothing over it that can force it to do anything; and, since it is completely sufficient unto itself, it can depend on no other. Hence it happens that freedom in operating is a perfection and so is not to be denied to the first being as most perfect and as the creator of other free beings.

I say, fifth: this first being, uncreated, infinite, and free, could have created the universe *de novo,* and in fact did create it. Proof of the first part of the conclusion: because, if it could not, either it could not because from nothing nothing can be made, or because it was a necessary agent, or because it was unchanged. The first is no argument, because of the first being's infinite power, which can take away any defect; nor is the second, because of the freedom of the same being in acting; nor is the third, because relations that come to be between God and creatures are relations of reason—therefore, just as a column does not change when my position changes, though it is now on my right and now on my left, so neither does God change; he is purest act and free of all potency whatever (even though he may be called creator, etc., which previously he would not have been), and so he remains always the same. Proof of the second part of the conclusion: first, because [creation in time] cannot be demonstrated, from the authority of Holy Scripture and from the determination of the Lateran Council; second, because it would follow that infinite numbers of arts and disciplines would have come down to us, and this is contrary to history—read Aristotle, second *Metaphysics*, chapter 2; again, no one has been found among writers worthy of credence who affirms that the universe existed more than six thousand years ago.

You say: fires and floods destroyed everything. But, to the contrary: how could it be that these fires and floods were never written about? Add to this: since, according to Aristotle, what is actually infinite cannot exist, the universe could not have existed from eternity and, as a consequence, it came to exist in time; otherwise, since rational souls are immortal, they would be actually infinite in number.

I say, sixth: the universe must have been created by God in time—so that it might be shown that it depends on God and that God is in need of no other thing, and so that we might know him to be most perfect, and having infinite power, and most free in his operations; also, so that the human mind, awakened by such goodness, liberality, and power, might be more readily moved to worship God.

To anyone asking how much time has passed from the beginning of the universe, I reply: though Sixtus of Siena in his *Bibliotheca* enumerated various calculations of the years from the world's beginning, the figure we give is most probable and accepted by almost all educated men. The universe was created 5748 years ago, as is gathered from Holy Scripture: for from Adam to the flood 1656 years intervened; from the flood to the birth of Abraham, 322; from the birth of Abraham to the exodus of the Jews from Egypt, 505; from the exodus of the Jews from Egypt to the building of the temple of Solomon, 621; from the building of the temple to the captivity of Sedechia, 430; from the captivity to its dissolution by Cyrus, 70; from Cyrus, who began to reign in the 54th Olympiad, to the birth of Christ, who was born in the 191st Olympiad, 560; the years from the birth of Christ to the destruction of Jerusalem, 74; from then up to the present time, 1510. . . .

CHRISTOPHER MARLOWE (1564–93)

The Tragicall History of the Life and Death of Doctor Faustus (1592?)

Before Shakespeare eclipsed him, no one had captured the imagination of British playgoers as much as Christopher Marlowe, whose youthful *Tamburlaine* (1587)—about a shepherd boy whose vision and energy conquered the world—established him immediately as a force to be reckoned with. His brilliant blank verse set the standard for dramatic expression. Marlowe's rebellious nature and atheism drew him to superhuman characters, whose ambitions could not be bound by traditional constraints. All his plays, in one way or another, glorify the triumphant human will. But in *Faustus,* that unbridled will must pay the price for its own excesses. Dr. Faustus, in his insatiable thirst for knowledge, power, and pleasure, has made a pact with the devil himself. The devil, as he comes to collect Faustus' soul, may be seen as a metaphor for the risk the Renaissance took by abandoning the Christian universe with its rigid hierarchical structures. Marlowe's defiance of orthodoxy, and his lyrical fascination with the underdog "superman" who defines his own world at the risk of insanity, is revisited in Miguel de Cervantes' *Don Quixote* and Wolfgang von Goethe's *Faust*—as well as in Friedrich Nietzsche's philosophy, Fyodor Dostoevsky's *Crime and Punishment,* and Sylvester Stallone's *Rocky.* Legend has it that Marlowe did not die in a Deptford tavern brawl as substantiated by contemporary records, but went underground to avoid the wrath of Elizabeth—and proceeded to write the great tragedies credited to Shakespeare.

[Scene XIII.—The House of Faustus.*]*

Enter Wagner, *solus*

WAG. I think my master means to die shortly.
    He has made his will and given me his wealth:
    His house, his goods, and store of golden plate,
    Besides two thousand ducats ready coin'd.
    And yet, methinks, if that death were near,

He would not banquet and carouse and swill
    Amongst the students, as even now he doth,
    Who are at supper with such belly-cheer
    As Wagner ne'er beheld in all his life.
    See where they come! Belike the feast is ended.

Enter Faustus, *with two or three* Scholars [*and* Mephistophilis]

1 SCHOL. Master Doctor Faustus, since our con-
ference about fair ladies, which was the
beautiful'st in all the world, we have determined with ourselves that Helen of Greece
was the admirablest lady that ever lived.
Therefore, Master Doctor, if you will do us
that favour, as to let us see that peerless
dame of Greece, whom all the world
admires for majesty, we should think ourselves much beholding unto you.

FAUST. Gentlemen,
For that I know your friendship is
unfeigned,
And Faustus' custom is not to deny
The just requests of those that wish him
well,
You shall behold that peerless dame of
Greece,
No otherways for pomp and majesty
Than when Sir Paris cross'd the seas
with her,
And brought the spoils to rich Dardania.
Be silent, then, for danger is in words.

Music sounds, and Helen *passeth over the
stage*.

2 SCHOL. Too simple is my wit to tell her praise,
Whom all the world admires for majesty.

3 SCHOL. No marvel though the angry Greeks
pursu'd
With ten years' war the rape of such a
queen,
Whose heavenly beauty passeth all compare.

1 SCHOL. Since we have seen the pride of
Nature's works,
And only paragon of excellence,

Enter an Old Man
Let us depart; and for this glorious
deed
Happy and blest be Faustus evermore.

FAUSTUS. Gentlemen, farewell—the same I wish
to you.

Exeunt Scholars [*and* Wagner]

OLD MAN. Ah, Doctor Faustus, that I might pre-
vail
To guide thy steps unto the way of life,
By which sweet path thou may'st attain
the goal
That shall conduct thee to celestial rest!
[O gentle Faustus, leave this damned art,
*This magic, that will charm thy soul to
hell,*
And quite bereave thee of salvation!
*Though thou hast now offended like a
man,*
Do not persever in it like a devil:
Yet, yet, thou hast an amiable soul,
If sin by custom grow not into nature.
*Then, Faustus, will repentance come
too late,*
*Then thou art banish'd from the sight
of heaven.*
No mortal can express the pains of hell!
It may be, this my exhortation
*Seems harsh and all unpleasant: let it
not!*
For, gentle son, I speak it not in wrath,
Or envy of thee, but in tender love,
And pity of thy future misery.
*And so have hope that this my kind
rebuke,*
*Checking thy body, may amend thy
soul.]*
Break heart, drop blood, and mingle it
with tears,
Tears falling from repentant heaviness
Of thy most vild and loathsome filthi-
ness,
The stench whereof corrupts the inward
soul
With such flagitious crimes of heinous
sins
As no commiseration may expel,
But mercy, Faustus, of thy Saviour sweet,
Whose blood alone must wash away thy
guilt.

FAUST. Where art thou, Faustus? Wretch, what
hast thou done?

Damn'd art thou, Faustus, damn'd; despair and die!

Hell claims his right, and with a roaring voice 70 days "Faustus! come! thine hour is almost come!"

And Faustus now will come to do thee right.

Mephistophilis *gives him a dagger*

OLD MAN. Ah stay, good Faustus, stay thy desperate steps!
See an angel hovers o'er thy head,
And, with a vial full of precious grace,
Offers to pour the same into thy soul:
Then call for mercy, and avoid despair.

FAUST. Ah, my sweet friend, I feel
Thy words to comfort my distressed soul.
Leave me a while to ponder on my sins.

OLD MAN. I go, sweet Faustus, but with heavy cheer,
Fearing the ruin of thy hopeless soul.

[*Exit*]

FAUST. Accursed Faustus, where is mercy now?
I do repent; and yet I do despair;
Hell strives with grace for conquest in my breast:
What shall I do to shun the snares of death?

MEPH. Thou traitor, Faustus, I arrest thy soul
For disobedience to my sovereign lord;
Revolt, or I'll in piecemeal tear thy flesh.

FAUST. I do repent I e'er offended him.
Sweet Mephistophilis, entreat thy lord
To pardon my unjust presumption,
And with my blood again I will confirm
My former vow I made to Lucifer.

MEPH. Do it then quickly, with unfeigned heart,
Lest greater danger do attend thy drift.

FAUST. Torment, sweet friend, that base and crooked age,
That durst dissuade me from thy Lucifer,

With greatest torments that our hell affords.

MEPH. His faith is great, I cannot touch his soul;
But what I may afflict his body with
I will attempt, which is but little worth.

FAUST. One thing, good servant, let me crave of thee,
To glut the longing of my heart's desire,—
That I might have unto my paramour
That heavenly Helen, which I saw of late,
Whose sweet embracings may extinguish clean
These thoughts that do dissuade me from my vow,
And keep mine oath I made to Lucifer.

MEPH. Faustus, this or what else thou shalt desire
Shall be perform'd in twinkling of an eye.

Enter Helen [*again, passing over between two Cupids*]

FAUST. Was this the face that launch'd a thousand ships,
And burnt the topless towers of Ilium?
Sweet Helen, make me immortal with a kiss.

[*Kisses her*]
Her lips sucks forth my soul; see where it flies!—
Come, Helen, come, give me my soul again.

[*Kisses her*]
Here will I dwell, for Heaven be in these lips,
And all is dross that is not Helena.

Enter Old Man
I will be Paris, and for love of thee,
Instead of Troy, shall Wittenberg be sack'd;

And I will combat with weak Menelaus,
And wear thy colours on my plumed
crest;
    Yea, I will wound Achilles in the heel,
And then return to Helen for a kiss.
Oh, thou art fairer than the evening air
Clad in the beauty of a thousand stars;
Brighter art thou than flaming Jupiter
When he appear'd to hapless Semele:
More lovely than the monarch of the sky
In wanton Arethusa's azur'd arms:
And none but thou shalt be my para-
mour.

Exeunt [Faustus *and* Helen]

OLD MAN. Accursed Faustus, miserable man,
    That from thy soul exclud'st the grace of
Heaven,
    And fly'st the throne of his tribunal seat!

Enter the Devils
    Satan begins to sift me with his pride.
    As in this furnace God shall try my
faith,
    My faith, vile hell, shall triumph over
thee.
    Ambitious fiends! see how the heavens
smiles
    At your repulse, and laughs your state to
scorn!
    Hence, hell! for hence I fly unto my
God.

Exeunt

[Scene XIV.—Faustus' Chamber.]

Enter Faustus *with the* Scholars

FAUST. Ah, gentlemen!

1 SCHOL. What ails Faustus?

FAUST. Ah, my sweet chamber-fellow, had I
lived with thee, then had I lived still! but
now I die eternally. Look, comes he not,
comes he not?

2 SCHOL. What means Faustus?

3 SCHOL. Belike he is grown into some sickness
by being over solitary.

1 SCHOL. If it be so, we'll have physicians to
cure him. 'T is but a surfeit. Never fear, man.

FAUST. A surfeit of deadly sin that hath damn'd
both body and soul.

2 SCHOL. Yet, Faustus, look up to Heaven;
remember, God's mercies are infinite.

FAUST. But Faustus' offence can ne'er be pardoned. The serpent that tempted Eve may
be sav'd, but not Faustus. Ah, gentlemen,
hear me with patience, and tremble not at
my speeches! Though my heart pants and
quivers to remember that I have been a student here these thirty years, oh, would I had
never seen Wittenberg, never read book!
And what wonders I have done, all Germany
can witness, yea, all the world; for which
Faustus hath lost both Germany and the
world,—yea Heaven itself, Heaven, the seat
of God, the throne of the blessed, the kingdom of joy; and must remain in hell for ever:
hell, ah, hell, for ever! Sweet friends! what
shall become of Faustus being in hell for
ever?

3 SCHOL. Yet, Faustus, call on God.

FAUST. On God, whom Faustus hath abjur'd! On
God, whom Faustus hath blasphemed! Ah,
my God, I would weep, but the Devil draws
in my tears. Gush forth, blood, instead of
tears! Yea, life and soul! Oh, he stays my
tongue! I would lift up my hands, but see,
they hold them, they hold them!

ALL. Who, Faustus?

FAUST. Lucifer and Mephistophilis. Ah, gentlemen, I gave them my soul for my cunning!

ALL. God forbid!

FAUST. God forbade it indeed; but Faustus hath
done it. For vain pleasure of four-and-twenty
years hath Faustus lost eternal joy and felic-

ity. I writ them a bill with mine own blood: the date is expired; the time will come, and he will fetch me.

1 SCHOL. Why did not Faustus tell us of this before, that divines might have prayed for thee?

FAUST. Oft have I thought to have done so; but the Devil threat'ned to tear me in pieces if I nam'd God; to fetch both body and soul if I once gave ear to divinity: and now 't is too late. Gentlemen, away! lest you perish with me.

2 SCHOL. Oh, what shall we do to save Faustus?

FAUST. Talk not of me, but save yourselves, and depart.

3 SCHOL. God will strengthen me. I will stay with Faustus.

1 SCHOL. Tempt not God, sweet friend; but let us into the next room, and there pray for him.

FAUST. Ay, pray for me, pray for me! And what noise soever ye hear, come not unto me, for nothing can rescue me.

2 SCHOL. Pray thou, and we will pray that God may have mercy upon thee.

FAUST. Gentlemen, farewell! If I live till morning I'll visit you: if not, Faustus is gone to hell.

ALL. Faustus, farewell!

EXEUNT SCHOLARS

MEPH. *Ay, Faustus, now thou hast no hope of heaven;*
Therefore, despair; think only upon hell,
For that must be thy mansion, there to dwell.

FAUST. *O thou bewitching fiend! 't was thy temptation*
Hath robb'd me of eternal happiness.

MEPH. *I do confess it, Faustus, and rejoice.*
'T was I that, when thou wert i' the way to heaven,
Damm'd up thy passage; when thou took'st the book
To view the Scriptures, then I turn'd the leaves
And led thine eye.
What, weep'st thou? 'T is too late: despair.
Farewell.
Fools that will laugh on earth must weep in hell.

THOMAS DELONEY (1543–1600)

The Most Pleasant and Delectable Historie of John Winchcombe, otherwise called Jacke of Newberie (1596-97)

No one painted the middle class of Elizabeth's reign with greater ardor and vividness than silk-weaver Thomas Deloney. His *Gentle Craft, Thomas of*

Reading, and *Jack of Newbury* may lay claim to being among the earliest English "novels," with Thomas Nashe's *The Unfortunate Traveler.* Though episodic in structure, their romantic and realistic way of turning everyday fact into fiction with verbal facility, ready wit, and comic energy places the author's journalism at the headwaters that lead to Art Buchwald and Gary Trudeau. Deloney was an apologist for the middle class. His celebration of the lowly apprentice who rises to influence and adventure makes Deloney's heroes predecessors of Horatio Alger. Written for profit, to entertain, his working class novels are invaluable documentation of the colloquial English of Cheapside and Westminster among clothiers, cobblers, cordiers, and drapers. So popular was *Jack* that the first surviving manuscript is the eighth edition.

Against Thursday shee drest her house fine and braue, and set her selfe in her best apparell: the Taylor nothing forgetting his promise, sent to the Widow a good fat Pigge, and a Goose. The Parson being as mindfull as hee, sent to her house a couple of fat Rabbets and a Capon: and the Tanner came himselfe, and brought a good shoulder of Mutton, and halfe a dozen Chickens, beside hee brought a good gallon of Sacke, and halfe a pound of the best Sugar. The Widow receiuing this good meate, set her maide to dresse it incontinent, and when dinner time drew neere, the Table was couered, and euery other thing prouided in conuenient and comely sort.

At length the guests being come, the Widow bade them all heartily welcome. The Priest and the Tanner seeing the Taylor, mused what hee made there: the Taylor on the other side, maruelled as much at their presence. Thus looking strangely one at another, at length the Widow came out of the Kitchen, in a faire traine gowne stucke full of siluer pinnes, a fine white Cap on her head, with cuts of curious needle worke vnder the same, and an Apron before her as white as the driuen snow: then very modestly making curtsie to them all, she requested them to sit downe. But they straining courtesie the one with the other, the Widow with a smiling countenance tooke the Parson by the hand, saying, Sir, as you stand highest in the Church, so it is meete you should sit highest at the Table: and therefore I pray you sit downe there on the bench side. And Sir (said shee to the Tanner) as

age is to bee honoured before youth for their experience, so are they to sit aboue Bachelers for their grauity: and so shee set him downe on this side the Table, ouer against the Parson. Then comming to the Taylor, she said, Batcheler, though your lot bee the last, your welcome is equall with the first, and seeing your place points out it selfe, I pray you take a cushion and sit downe. And now (quoth she) to make the boord equall, and because it hath been an old saying, that three things are to small purpose, if the fourth be away: if so it may stand with your fauour, I will call in a Gossip of mine to supply this voide place.

With a good will (quoth they).

With that shee brought in an old woman with scant euer a good tooth in her head, and placed her right against the Batcheler. Then was the meate brought to the boord in due order by the Widowes seruants, her man *Iohn* being chiefest seruitor. The Widow sate downe at the Tables end, betweene the Parson and the Tanner, who in very good sort carued meate for them all, her man *Iohn* waiting on the Table.

After they had sitten awhile, and well refreshed themselues, the Widow, taking a Chrystal glasse fild with Claret Wine, drunke vnto the whole company, and bade them welcome. The Parson pledged her, and so did all the rest in due order: but still in their drinking, the cup past ouer the poore old womans Nose; insomuch that at length the old woman (in a merry vaine) spake thus vnto the company: I haue had much good meate among you, but as for the drinke I can nothing commend it.

Alas, good Gossip (quoth the Widow) I perceiue no man hath drunke to thee yet.

No truly (quoth the old woman): for Churchmen haue so much minde of yongue Rabbets, old men such ioy in young Chickens, and Batchelers in Pigs flesh take such delight, that an old Sow, a tough Henne, or a gray Cony are not accepted: and so it is seen by mee, else I should haue beene better remembred.

Well old woman (quoth the Parson) take here the legge of a Capon to stop thy mouth.

Now by *S.Anne,* I dare not (quoth she).

No, wherefore (said the Parson)?

Marry, for feare lest you should goe home with a crutch (quoth shee).

The Taylor said, then taste here a peece of a Goose.

Now God forbid (said the old woman) let Goose goe to his kinde: you haue a yongue stomacke, eate it your selfe, and much good may it doe your heart, sweet yongue man.

The old woman lackes most of her teeth (quoth the Tanner): and therefore a peece of a tender Chicke is fittest for her.

If I did lacke as many of my teeth (quoth the old woman) as you lacke points of good husbandry, I doubt I should starue before it were long.

At this the Widow laught heartily, and the men were striken into such a dumpe, that they had not a word to say.

Dinner being ended, the Widow with the rest rose from the Table, and after they had sitten a prety while merrily talking, the Widow called her man *Iohn* to bring her a bowle of fresh Ale, which he did. Then said the Widow: My masters, now for your courtesie and cost I heartily thanke you all, and in requitall of all your fauour, loue and good will, I drinke to you, giuing you free liberty when you please to depart.

At these words her sutors looked so sowerly one vpon another, as if they had beene newly champing of Crabs. Which when the Taylor heard, shaking vp himselfe in his new russet Ierkin, and setting his Hat on one side, hee began to speake thus. I trust sweet Widow

(quoth hee) you remember to what end my comming was hither to day: I haue long time beene a sutor vnto you, and this day you promised to giue mee a direct answer.

'Tis true (quoth shee) and so I haue: for your loue I giue you thankes, and when you please you may depart.

Shall I not haue you (said the Taylor)?

Alas (quoth the Widow), you come too late.

Good friend (quoth the Tanner) it is manners for yongue men to let their elders bee serued before them: to what end should I be here if the Widow should haue thee? a flat deniall is meete for a sawcy sutor: but what saiest thou to me, faire Widow (quoth the Tanner?)

Sir (said shee) because you are so sharpe set, I would wish you as soon as you can to wed.

Appoint the time your selfe (quoth the Tanner).

Euen as soone (quoth shee) as you can get a wife, and hope not after mee, for I am already promised.

Now Tanner, you may take your place with the Taylor (quoth the Parson): for indeede the Widow is for no man but my selfe.

Master Parson (quoth shee) many haue runne neer the goale, and yet haue lost the game, and I cannot helpe it though your hope be in vaine: besides, Parsons are but newly suffered to haue wiues, and for my part I will haue none of the first head.

What (quoth the Taylor) is your merriment growne to this reckoning? I neuer spent a Pig and a Goose to so bad a purpose before: I promise you, when I came in, I verily thought, that you were inuited by the Widow to make her and I sure together, and that this iolly Tanner was brought to be a witnesse to the contract, and the old woman fetcht in for the same purpose, else I would neuer haue put vp so many dry bobs at her hands.

And surely (quoth the Tanner) I knowing thee to bee a Taylor, did assuredly thinke, that thou wast appointed to come and take measure for our wedding apparell.

But now wee are all deceiued (quoth the Parson): and therefore as we came fooles, so we may depart hence like asses.

That is as you interpret the matter (said the Widow): for I euer doubting that a concluding answer would breede a iarre in the end among you euery one, I thought it better to be done at one instant, and in mine owne house, than at sundry times, and in common Tauernes: and as for the meate you sent, as it was vnrequested of mee, so had you your part thereof, and if you thinke good to take home the remainder, prepare your wallets and you shall haue it.

Nay Widow (quoth they) although wee haue lost our labours, we haue not altogether lost our manners: that which you haue, keepe; and GOD send to vs better lucke, and to you your hearts desire. And with that they departed.

The Widow being glad shee was thus rid of her guests, when her man *Iohn* with all the rest sate at supper, she sitting in a Chaire by, spake thus vnto them. Well my masters, you saw, that this day your poore Dame had her choice of husbands, if shee had listed to marry, and such as would haue loued and maintained her like a woman.

'Tis true (quoth *Iohn*) and I pray God you haue not withstood your best fortune.

Trust mee (quoth she) I know not, but if I haue, I may thank mine owne foolish fancy.

Thus it past on from *Bartholmewtide,* till it was neere Christmas, at what time the weather was so wonderfull cold, that all the running Riuers round about the Towne were frozen very thicke. The Widow being very loth any longer to lye without company, in a cold winters night made a great fire, and sent for her man *Iohn,* hauing also prepared a Chaire and a cushion, shee made him sit downe therein, and sending for a pinte of good Sacke, they both went to supper.

In the end, bed time comming on, she caused her maid in a merriment to plucke off his hose and shooes, and caused him to be laid in his masters best bed, standing in the best Chamber, hung round about with very faire curtaines. *Iohn* being thus preferred, thought himselfe a Gentleman, and lying soft, after his hard labour and a good supper, quickly fell asleepe.

About midnight, the Widow being cold on her feet, crept into her mans bed to warme them. *Iohn* feeling one lift vp the cloathes, asked who was there? O good *Iohn* it is I (quoth the Widow); the night is so extreme cold, and my Chamber walles so thin, that I am like to bee starued in my bed, wherefore rather than I would any way hazzard my health, I thought it much better to come hither and try your courtesie, to haue a little roome beside you.

Iohn being a kind yongue man, would not say her nay, and so they spent the rest of the night both together in one bed. In the morning betime she arose vp and made her selfe readie, and wild her man *Iohn* to run and fetch her a linke with all speede: for (quoth shee) I haue earnest businesse to doe this morning. Her man did so. Which done, shee made him to carry the Linke before her, vntill she came to Saint *Bartholmewes* Chappell, where Sir *Iohn* the Priest with the Clark and Sexton, stood waiting for her.

Iohn (quoth she) turne into the Chappell: for before I goe further, I will make my prayers to S. *Bartholmew,* so shall I speed the better in my businesse.

When they were come in, the Priest according to his order, came to her, and asked where the Bridegroome was?

(Quoth she) I thought he had been here before me. Sir (quoth she) I will sit downe and say ouer my Beades, and by that time hee will come.

Iohn mused at this matter, to see that his Dame should so suddenly be married, and he hearing nothing thereof before. The Widow rising from her prayers, the Priest told her that the Bridegroome was not yet come.

Is it true (quoth the Widow)? I promise you I will stay no longer for him, if hee were as good as *George a Green:* and therefore dispatch (quoth she) and marry mee to my man *Iohn.*

Why Dame (quoth he) you do but iest.

I trow, *Iohn* (quoth shee) I iest not: for so I

meane it shall bee, and stand not strangely, but remember that you did promise mee on your faith, not to hinder mee when I came to the Church to be married, but rather to set it forward: therfore set your link aside, and giue mee your hand: for none but you shall be my husband.

Iohn seeing no remedy, consented, because hee saw the matter could not otherwise bee amended; and married they were presently.

When they were come home, *Iohn* entertained his Dame with a kisse, which the other seruants seeing, thought him somewhat sawcy. The Widow caused the best cheare in the house to bee set on the Table, and to breakfast they went, causing her new husband to be set in a chaire at the tables end, with a faire napkin laid on his trencher: then shee called out the rest of her seruants, willing them to sit downe and take part of their good cheare. They wondring to see their fellow *Iohn* sit at the tables end in their old masters chaire, began heartily to smile, and openly to laugh at the matter, especially because their Dame so kindly sate by his side: which shee perceiuing, asked if that were all the manners they could shew before their master? I tell you (quoth shee) he is my husband: for this morning we were married, and therefore hence forward looke you acknowledge your duety towards him.

The folkes looked one vpon another, maruelling at this strange newes. Which when *Iohn* perceiued, he said: My masters, muse not at all: for although by Gods prouidence, and your Dames fauour, I am preferred from being your fellow to be your master, I am not thereby so much puft vp in pride, that any way I will forget my former estate: Notwithstanding, seeing I am now to hold the place of a master, it shall be wisedome in you to forget what I was, and to take mee as I am, and in doing your diligence, you shall haue no cause to repent that God made me your master.

The seruants hearing this, as also knowing his good gouernment before time, past their yeares with him in dutifull manner. . . .

BALTHAZAR AYALA (1543–1612)

DE JURE ET OFFICIIS BELLICIS ET DISCIPLINE MILITARI LIBRI III

Three Books on the Law of War and on the Duties Connected with War and on Military Discipline (1597)

Characteristic of the Renaissance, this work combines the classical Greco-Roman belief in the symmetry and basic orderliness of the universe with the vicious motivations that make wars expedient means to royal, political, or

social ends. Chief justice of Philip II's military court, Balthazar Ayala says that "there are laws of war just as much as of peace. The use of force against those who will not submit to fair demands or will not be restrained by reason is not an injustice." Using Roman and Hebrew precedent, Ayala charts an Aristotelian course along the edges of right, might, and wrong. Slavery he justifies as the State's proper punishment of "those who wage an unjust war," arguing that "slavery is a blessing to such wrong-doers, for the opportunity of further wrong-doing is taken away from them and they will behave better under restraint than as their own masters." Most importantly, the good citizen must lament the necessity of war but embrace it when the State itself is jeopardized. Then, as now, primate tribal behavior is justified by elaborate jingoism: War is good if we wage it, evil when waged by the enemy. Many of his arguments are still in use.

CHAPTER II. OF JUST WAR AND JUST CAUSES OF WAR.

1. The laws of war must be observed.
2. Two kinds of conflict.
3. The object of wars is to secure peaceful life.
4. Many ills arise even out of just wars.
5. An honorable war to be preferred to a disgraceful peace.
6. Just wars permitted alike by the Law of Nations [*jus gentium*], the Canon Law and the Divine Law.
7. The authorization of a sovereign required for a just war.
8. Among the Romans the determination of

The battle of San Egidio (Paolo Uccello), in the National Gallery, London

questions of peace and war was in the hands of the people.

9. War may sometimes be waged without the authorization of the prince.
10. The penalties of rebellion are incurred by the fact itself [*ipso jure*].
11. Just causes of war.
12. Rebellion.
13. An outrage on the prince is deemed an outrage offered to God.
14. A rebel and an enemy quite different persons.
15. Whether the laws of war apply to rebels.
16. Civil discord.
17. The law of Solon.
18. In war not always safe to keep aloof from both sides.
19. The middle course hazardous.
20. The authority of the prince must always be supported against rebels.
21. There can not be a just cause for rebellion.
22. The fatherland or State, what it is.
23. Rebellion a most heinous offense.
24. A tyrant may be killed.
25. A lawful sovereign can not be dubbed tyrant.
26. The *lex regia*.
27. The Pope may deprive a king of his crown for cause.
28. Whether a war against infidels is just, and how far.
29. The emperor is not lord of the whole world.
30. Just war waged on heretics.
31. The soldier incurs no guilt even if the cause of war be unjust.
32. A Christian soldier may take service under a pagan ruler.
33. How far obedience is due to a pagan king.
34. A war may be "just," even though the cause thereof be unjust.
35. Whether a war can be "just" on both sides.
36. Money the sinews of war.
37. Who ought to bear the expenses of a war.
38. Trajan compared the *fiscus* to the spleen.
39. The custom of the Gauls.
40. Whether private losses sustained in war ought to be made good.

[1,2] Cicero lays it down that in a well-ordered State the laws of war should be scrupulously observed. Alike in beginning a war and in carrying it on and in ending it, law has a most important position and so has good-faith. The rules of fecial law, to which we have just alluded, aim at securing this. For, as Cicero also says, there are two kinds of strife—one conducted by discussion and the other by force: the one appropriate to men and the other to beasts; and recourse must be had to the latter when the former can not be used. And this is taken to have been the meaning of the poetical conceit that Chiron, the centaur—whose upper part (so the fiction ran) was that of a man and his lower that of a horse—was the preceptor of Achilles, as if to show that a good prince ought not only to be endowed with wisdom and judgment and other mental gifts, but also to be trained to feats of strength and arms; for the use of force against those who will not submit to what is fair nor be restrained by reason is not unjust. Nevertheless, a general, like a surgeon (it was a saying of Scipio's) ought to use steel only in the last resort for effecting his cures.

[3,4] War, therefore, is justifiable when its object is to procure peaceful existence and freedom from outrage, and when begun in such a way as that peace may appear to be its sole object. That is what Martianus Cæsar was aiming at in his memorable saying: "So long as a prince can live in peace he ought not to take up arms—so many and so great are the ills which spring even from what may be styled a just war." And these ills drew from St. Augustine the following outburst:

"If I should stop to recite the massacres and the extreme effects hereof, as I might (though I can not do it as I should), the discourse would be infinite. Yea, but a wise man, say they, will wage none but just war. He will not! As if the very remembrance that himself is man ought not to procure his greater sorrow in that he has cause of just wars, and must needs wage them, which if they were not just were not for him to deal in, so that a wise man should never have war; for it is the other men's wickedness that works his cause just, that he ought to deplore whether ever it produce wars or not. Wherefore he that does but consider with compassion all those extremes of sorrow and bloodshed must needs say that this is a mystery, but he that endures them without a sorrowful emotion, or thought thereof, is far more wretched to imagine he has the bliss of a god when he has lost the natural feeling of a man."

So far St. Augustine. For there are certain lawful incidents of war (as Livy says) which each side must be ready to endure, just as it may also produce them—e.g. burning of crops, destruction of buildings, loss of men and horses as booty. These are of course a hardship to him who has to endure them, although not in every case dishonoring. Our first care, then, must be for peace, which, as Cicero says, refuses to have any truck with treachery and baseness.

[5] Further, as the same writer says, although the name of peace is musical and the thing itself both pleasant and profitable (for he can not hold dear either private hearths or public ordinances or the laws of liberty who delights in dissension and slaughter of his fellow-citizens and in public war) yet an honorable war, according to the saying of Demosthenes, is ever to be preferred to a disgraceful peace.

[6] Just wars are, indeed, enjoined by the Law of Nations (*jus gentium*), and are permitted both by the canon law and by the law of God, for God himself ordered the Jews to make war on the Amorites and other peoples. St. Augustine, accordingly, wrote: "Beware of thinking that no one who follows arms pleases God, for David, a man after God's own heart, was of the military profession and so was that centurion whose faith is commended by divine attestation, and other holy men also."

[7] Now in order that a war may be styled just, it ought in the first place to be declared and undertaken under the authority and warrant of a sovereign prince, in whose hands is the arbitrament of peace and war. For a private person has no business to begin a war, seeing that he can, and ought to, assert his right in the courts; and it is a breach of the prince's prerogative for a private person, unwarranted by law, to assert his right himself with royal hand. Nor is any one competent to initiate any variety of hostile activity without the knowledge and counsel of the prince. And he is liable under the Julian law against treason who, without the warrant of the prince, has either made war or summoned a levy or gathered an army together. And so Cato urged the recall of the army and the surrender of Cæsar to the enemy on the ground that Cæsar was campaigning in Gaul without having been authorized by the people. . . .

[9] There are occasions, however, when, e.g., pressing necessity or the absence of the prince, coupled with the hazards of delay, may justify a commencement of war even without his sanction, and this is especially so for purposes of defense, which is open to any one by the law of nature. On such occasions it will be lawful not only to ward off the wrong, but also to take vengeance for it and to drive the enemy out of his own land if we can not otherwise obtain safety from him, for one can not be said to overstep permissible precaution who does what it would be dangerous to omit. And this is shown at length by Marianus Socinus (the grandson), who holds that such a war ranks as a just war even as regards the consequences, and that the rules of war apply (consequences being deduced from their causes) and therefore that anything captured during that war belongs to the captor.

[10] And this, he says, is especially so in dealing with rebels, for every one not only may, but must, foil their attempts without waiting for the prince's command, should delay be perilous. For, one who has it in his power to ward off a wrong from a comrade, yet forbears to do so, is as much in fault as the actual perpetrator. This being so in ordinary cases, what are we to say when it is the prince who is threatened, especially seeing that these machinations against the sovereignty of the prince and the peace of the State render their authors liable, by the very fact, to the penalty of treason and to death or

captivity as enemies and, much more, to forfeiture of their property to the captor. . . .

Beside this, war may not be made save for just and necessary cause, and there should be an entire absence of the passion to do hurt and of vengeful savagery and of the lust of conquest. It was the securing of this that was the object of the rules prevailing among the Romans under their fecial law. Now he who makes war for an unjust cause not only sins, but the opinion is widely spread among men that he is nearly always beaten. . . .

[11] Now the principal just causes of war are: the defense of our own empire, of our persons, of our friends, of our allies, and of our property; for no other warrant than the law of nature is needed to justify even private persons in defending themselves. A war, therefore, as Caius Pontius, the Samnite general, used to say, is a just one for those to whom it is necessary, and recourse to arms is a duty for those who have no hope left save in arms. A war is based on a just cause, again, when it is waged in order to regain from the enemy something which he is forcibly and unjustly detaining, in the same way as the authors of a wrong or harm done with private and not public intent are handed over to punishment: we have shown above that this is provided for by the fecial law.

And so, after the death of Saul, David made war on Ishbosheth, Saul's son, who was trying to obtain the kingship in Israel which God had given to David by the mouth of the prophet Samuel. And Romulus made war on the Albans because their dictator, Cluilius, would neither restore certain captured property nor surrender the captors.

Another just cause of war is to take vengeance for some wrong which has been unjustifiably inflicted. Thus we read that King David made war on the king of the children of Ammon for his contemptuous treatment of David's messengers. And on the same ground of a wrong done, a war will be ranked as just which arises on a State's refusal to allow passage over its territory, provided such passage is innocent; by the law of human society such passage ought to be open. Accordingly, the Jews made war on the kings of the Amorites for refusing them innocent passage into the land which God had allotted to them.

PART 3

SEVENTEENTH CENTURY

WILLIAM SHAKESPEARE (1564–1616)
Hamlet (c.1600)

More than any of the great characters associated with the name of the greatest of British playwrights, Hamlet seems most characteristic of Renaissance man, as though William Shakespeare had set out to assimilate all the contradictions of this volatile and fervent age: between inner vision and external authority, traditional doctrine and individual will, reality and appearance, courage and remorse, cynicism and idealism, courtliness and pragmatism, perilous sanity and innocent madness. An eternal portrait of the endlessly agonizing intellectual still with us today ("men who are afraid to commit"), Hamlet is wary of decision and reluctant to act. In this dither, he dominates this busiest of all plays. Yet for all the ramifications this play has caused among the literary critics, the dilemma beneath the mechanism which is Hamlet's character is quite simple: He loves his mother most, believes his father most, and, with this set of predilections, is unable to distinguish between that still voice inside him and what may very well be a ghost along the balustrades. Wolfgang von Goethe saw *Hamlet* clearly as the story of a highly moral nature lacking in a hero's nerve who sinks beneath a necessary but unbearable burden. Yet the burden is only unbearable because Hamlet, ironically after an age in which fashioning the mind is the highest of all fashionings, cannot make up his mind: "The native hue of resolution. . . sicklied o'er with the pale cast of thought." Hamlet's tragedy is not that he is too rigid to adjust to changing times. It's that he can't change roles quickly enough to adapt to a script not of his own writing. In Machiavelli's terms, he can't conform his behavior with his circumstances. In like fashion Shakespeare's Othello is too trustful to see the truth before his eyes, Julius Caesar too egocentric to recognize the limits of personal power, Richard II too bound in tradition to adapt to rebellion, Lear too fixed on preconceived notions to undo the repercussions his hypothesis has caused. The Shakespearean ideal, by default, is the ever-changing perfectly sensitive chameleon, able to be all things to all men. Madness is avoided only by embracing moral relativity in an age when every moral system has been subjected to question. The irony of his great tragedies is that while the playwright must intellectually admire the Henry IVs and Falstaffs who are nothing if not changeable, his emotional sympathies, expressed in the most powerful poetry in English history, lie with those who are left behind by the new order of things. Here is Richard II's lament to his followers, as he recognizes his own failure to adapt:

No matter where; of comfort no man speak:
Let's talk of graves, of worms and epitaphs;
Make dust our paper and with rainy eyes
Write sorrow on the bosom of the earth.
Let's choose executors and talk of wills:
And yet not so, for what can we bequeath
Save our deposed bodies to the ground?
Our lands, our lives, and all are Bolingbroke's,
And nothing can we call our own but death,
And that small model of the barren earth
Which serves as paste and cover to our bones.
For God's sake, let us sit upon the ground
And tell sad stories of the death of kings:
How some have been deposed; some slain in war;
Some haunted by the ghosts they have deposed;
Some poison'd by their wives; some sleeping kill'd;
All murder'd: for within the hollow crown
That rounds the mortal temples of a king
Keeps Death his court, and there the antic sits,
Scoffing his state and grinning at his pomp,
Allowing him a breath, a little scene,
To monarchize, be fear'd and kill with looks,
Infusing him with self and vain conceit,
As if this flesh which walls about our life
Were brass impregnable, and humour'd thus
Comes at the last and with a little pin
Bores through his castle wall, and farewell king!
Cover your heads and mock not flesh and blood
With solemn reverence: throw away respect,
Tradition, form, and ceremonious duty,
For you have but mistook me all this while:
I live with bread like you, feel want,
Taste grief, need friends: subjected thus,
How can you say to me, I am a king?

For all his "divine right," Richard is doomed, just as for all his education, Hamlet is not equipped to deal with the caprice of emotions he faces in his slain father's court.

POLONIUS. I hear him coming: let's withdraw, my lord.

Exeunt King *and* Polonius

Enter Hamlet

HAMLET. To be, or not to be, that is the question;
Whether 'tis nobler in the mind to suffer

The slings and arrows of outrageous for-
tune,
Or to take arms against a sea of troubles,
And by opposing, end them. To die; to
sleep,
No more, and by a sleep to say we end
The heart-ache, and the thousand natural
shocks
That flesh is heir to; 'tis a consummation
Devoutly to be wish'd, to die, to sleep;
To sleep; perchance to dream; ay, there's
the rub;
For in that sleep of death what dreams
may come,
When we have shuffled off this mortal
coil,
Must give us pause; there's the respect
That makes calamity of so long life:
For who would bear the whips and
scorns of time,
The oppressor's wrong, the proud man's
contumely,
The pangs of despis'd love, the law's
delay,
The insolence of office, and the spurns
That patient merit of the unworthy
takes,
When he himself might his quietus make
With a bare bodkin? who would fardels
bear,
To grunt and sweat under a weary life,
But that the dread of something after
death,
The undiscover'd country, from whose
bourn
No traveller returns, puzzles the will,
And makes us rather bear those ills we
have
Than fly to others that we know not of?
Thus conscience does make cowards
{of us all,}
And thus the native hue of resolution
Is sicklied o'er with the pale cast of
thought,
And enterprises of great pitch and
moment
With this regard their currents turn awry

And lose the name of action. Soft you
now,
The fair Ophelia! Nymph, in thy orisons
Be all my sins remember'd.

OPHELIA. Good my lord,
How does your honour for this many a
day?

HAMLET. I humbly thank you, well, {well, well.}

OPHELIA. My lord, I have remembrances of yours,
That I have longed long to re-deliver;
I pray you now receive them.

HAMLET. No, not I;
I never gave you aught.

OPHELIA. My honour'd lord, you know right well
you did,
And with them words of so sweet breath
compos'd
As made these things more rich: their
perfume lost,
Take these again; for to the noble mind
Rich gifts wax poor when givers prove
unkind.
There, my lord.

HAMLET. Ha, ha! are you honest?

OPHELIA. My lord?

HAMLET. Are you fair?

OPHELIA. What means your lordship?

HAMLET. That if you be honest and fair, your
honesty should admit no discourse to your
beauty.

OPHELIA. Could beauty, my lord, have better
converse than with honesty?

HAMLET. Ay, truly; for the power of beauty will
sooner transform honesty from what it is to
a bawd than the force of honesty can translate beauty into his likeness: this was sometime a paradox, but now the time gives it
proof. I did love you once.

OPHELIA. Indeed, my lord, you made me believe
so.

HAMLET. You should not have believ'd me, for virtue cannot so inoculate our old stock but we shall relish of it: I lov'd you not.

OPHELIA. I was the more deceiv'd.

HAMLET. Get thee to a nunnery; why wouldst thou be a breeder of sinners? I am myself indifferent honest, but yet I could accuse me of such things that it were better my mother had not borne me: I am very proud, revengeful, ambitious, with more offences at my beck than I have thoughts to put them in, imagination to give them shape, or time to act them in. What should such fellows as I do crawling between earth and heaven? We are arrant knaves, believe none of us, go thy ways to a nunnery. Where's your father?

OPHELIA. At home, my lord.

HAMLET. Let the doors be shut upon him, that he may play the fool no where but in 's own house. Farewell.

OPHELIA. O, help him, you sweet heavens!

HAMLET. If thou dost marry, I'll give thee this plague for thy dowry: be thou as chaste as ice, as pure as snow, thou shalt not escape calumny. Get thee to a nunnery, farewell. Or, if thou wilt needs marry, marry a fool, for wise men know well enough what monsters you make of them. To a nunnery, go, and quickly too, farewell.

OPHELIA. Heavenly powers restore him!

HAMLET. I have heard of your paintings well enough; God hath given you one face, and you make yourselves another: you jig and amble; an you list you nickname God's creatures, and make your wantonness ignorance. Go to, I'll no more on 't, it hath made me mad. I say we will have no more marriage; those that are married already, all but one shall live, the rest shall keep as they are. To a nunnery, go.

[Exit]

OPHELIA. O, what a noble mind is here o'erthrown!
     The courtier's, soldier's, scholar's, eye, tongue, sword,
     The expectancy and rose of the fair state,
     The glass of fashion, and the mould of form,
     The observ'd of all observers, quite, quite down,
     And I of ladies most deject and wretched,
     That suck'd the honey of his music'd vows;
     Now see that noble and most sovereign reason,
     Like sweet bells jangled out of time, and harsh,
     That unmatch'd form, and stature of blown youth,
     Blasted with ecstasy: O, woe is me,
     To have seen what I have seen, see what I see! . . .

SIR WALTER RALEIGH (1552–1618)

Letter to His Wife (1603)

If one person only were to be chosen to represent England for his Renaissance qualities, Walter Raleigh would be my choice. His life reads like fiction, spanning the great chain of being from the highest offices under Queen Elizabeth, and possible sexual dalliance with her, to his execution, by order of King James I, at the behest of the Spanish for pirating their galleons. Leading expeditions back and forth across the Atlantic, he founded the Virginia colony, naming it for the "Virgin Queen" Elizabeth; he brought back potatoes and tobacco. He patronized her poet Edmund Spenser, who dedicated *The Faerie Queene* to him. Courtier, soldier, statesman, scholar, he wrote outstanding lyrics, *Travels to Virginia, The Discovery of Guiana,* and a *History of the World* (the last while awaiting death in the Tower). His "Description of Love" is Raleigh at his most exuberant:

Now what is love? I pray thee, tell.
It is that fountain and that well
Where pleasure and repentance dwell.
It is perhaps that sauncing bell
That tolls all into heaven or hell:
And this is love, as I hear tell.

Yet what is love? I pray thee say.
It is a work on holy-day;
It is December matched with May;
When lusty bloods, in fresh array,
Hear ten months after of the play:
And this is love, as I hear say.

Yet what is love? I pray thee sain.
It is sunshine mixed with rain;
It is tooth-ache, or like pain;
It is a game where none doth gain;
The lass saith no, and would full fain:
And this is love, as I hear sain.

Yet what is love? I pray thee say.
It is a yea, it is a nay,
A pretty kind of sporting fray;

It is a thing will soon away;
Then take the vantage while you may:
And this is love, as I hear say.

Yet what is love, I pray thee show.
A thing that creeps, it cannot go;
A prize that passeth to and fro;
A thing for one, a thing for mo;
And he that proves must find it so:
And this is love, sweet friend, I trow.

When James I imprisoned him at Winchester in 1603, Raleigh wrote this letter to his wife, fully expecting to die the next morning. His sentence was commuted by the King, only to be fulfilled in 1618.

Sir Walter Raleigh (engraved portrait)

Letter written by Sir Walter Ralegh to his wife

You shall now receive, dear wife, my last words in these my last lines. My love I send you, that you may keep it when I am dead; and my counsel, that you may remember it when I am no more. I would not, by my will, present you with sorrows, dear Besse. Let them go to the grave with me, and be buried in the dust. And, seeing it is not the will of God that ever I shall see you any more in this life, bear it patiently and with a heart like thy self.

First, I send you all the thanks which my heart can conceive, or my words can express, for your many travails and cares taken for me, which—though they have not taken effect as you wished—yet my debt to you is not the less; but pay it I never shall in this world.

Secondly, I beseech you, for the love you bare me living, do not hide yourself many days after my death, but by your travails seek to help your miserable fortunes, and the right of your poor child. Your mourning cannot avail me; I am but dust.

You shall understand that my land was conveyed *bona fide* to my child. The writings were drawn at midsummer twelvemonths. My honest cousin Brett can testify so much, and Dalberie, too, can remember somewhat therein. And I trust my blood will quench the malice that have thus cruelly murdered me; and that they will not seek also to kill thee and thine with extreme poverty.

To what friend to direct thee I know not, for all mine have left me in the true time of trial; and I plainly perceive that my death was determined from the first day. Most sorry I am (God knows) that, being thus surprised with death, I can leave you in no better estate. God is my witness I meant you all my office of wines, or all that I could have purchased by selling it; half my stuff, and all my jewels; but some on't for the boy. But God hath prevented all my resolutions; even that great God that ruleth all in all. If you can live free from want, care for no more; the rest is but vanity.

Love God, and begin betimes to repose yourself on Him; therein shall you find true and lasting riches, and endless comfort. For the rest, when you have travailed and wearied all your thoughts over all sorts of worldly cogitations, you shall sit down by Sorrow in the end. Teach your son also to love and fear God, while he is yet young, that the fear of God may grow up with him. And the same God will be a husband unto you, and a father unto him; a husband and a father which can not be taken from you.

Bayly oweth me two hundred pounds, and Adrian Gilbert six hundred pounds. In Jersey I have also much money owing me. Besides, the arrearages of the wines will pay my debts. And, howsoever you do, for my soul's sake, pay all poor men.

When I am gone, no doubt you shall be sought by many, for the world thinks that I was very rich; but take heed of the pretences of men and of their affections; for they last not but in honest and worthy men. And no greater misery can befall you in this life than to become a prey, and afterwards to be despised. I speak not this (God knows) to dissuade you from marriage—for it will be best for you, both in respect of the world and of God. As for me, I am no more yours, nor you mine. Death hath cut us asunder; and God hath divided me from the world, and you from me.

Remember your poor child for his father's sake, who chose you and loved you in his happiest times. Get those letters (if it be possible) which I writ to the Lords, wherein I sued for my life. God is my witness, it was for you and yours that I desired life. But it is true that I disdain myself for begging it. For know it (dear wife) that your son is the son of a true man, and one who, in his own respect, despiseth Death, and all his misshapen and ugly shapes.

I cannot write much. God he knows how hardly I steal this time, while others sleep; and it is also high time that I should separate my thoughts from the world. Beg my dead body, which living was denied thee; and either lay it at Sherbourne, if the land continue, or in Exeter church, by my father and mother. I can say no more. Time and Death call me away.

The everlasting, powerful, infinite and omnipotent God, that almighty God who is goodness itself, the true life and true light, keep thee and thine; and have mercy on me, and teach me to forgive my persecutors and accusers; and send us to meet in His glorious kingdom. My dear wife, farewell. Bless my poor boy; pray for me; and let my good God hold you both in His arms.

Written with the dying hand of sometime thy husband, but now (alas!) overthrown.

Wa. Raleigh
Yours that was; but now not my own,
W. R.

MIGUEL DE CERVANTES SAAVEDRA (1547–1621)

Don Quixote de la Mancha (1605)

Another soldier of fortune whose career began with high hopes, included bouts in prison, and ended in near poverty, Cervantes, in *Don Quixote*, created both the highest expression of the Spanish soul and the greatest flowering of the Spanish *siglo de oro*. *Don Quixote* may also claim to be the first truly modern novel, its action almost entirely based on issues surrounding its hero's sanity—and his own investigation thereof. Its underlying theme, the madness that comes from reading too much, is a haunting final comment on the Renaissance. That Cervantes' heroic knight has method in his madness is all too insufficient consolation for the uncertainties his remarkable story gives rise to in the reader's consciousness, uncertainties reflected in the comment of Quixote's twentieth-century successor, Spanish painter Salvador Dali: "The difference between myself and a madman is that *I* am not mad." Cervantes was christened in Alcalá de Henares. The next thing we know is that in 1568, at the age of twenty-one, he was enrolled at the City School of Madrid. A warrant issued for him in 1569 for wounds inflicted in a duel may have led him to enlist in the Spanish legion stationed in Italy. He fought at the battle of Lepanto under John of Austria in 1571, where his left hand was mangled. By 1580, after being captured by Moorish pirates and ransomed because of John's intercession, he was back in Madrid. He took service as a messenger for the king and, in 1588, after marrying a peasant, Catalina de Placios Slazar y Vozmediano, who caused him nothing but grief, he was appointed deputy purveyor to the Great Armada being prepared against England. In and out of jail from 1592 to 1602 for raising the hackles of the clergy whose property he confiscated and for failing to keep perfect books, his own personal renaissance occurred between the ages of fifty-eight and sixty-nine. Before that he'd failed at nearly everything he put his hand to, public or private. His poetry, pastoral romances, and plays could not compete with those of his predecessors and contemporaries. He found his mastery when he set out to write not for the intelligentsia, but, like Nashe's *The Unfortunate Traveler*, for innkeepers, page boys, students, and soldiers in that newly literate popular audience the printing press had brought into existence. His parody of chivalric romances, about a crackpot idealist whose insanity is equaled only by his sincerity, was an instant success throughout Europe with translations, pirated editions, and imitations so rampant that Cervantes himself wrote "the sequel," in *The Second Book,* for the express purpose of killing off Don Quixote to stop the rip-offs. The novel's satirical comedy is in the vein of Rabelais, yet surpasses *Gargantua and Pantagruel* because the knight errant Don Quixote and his page Sancho Panza express the aesthetic integrity of fully rounded fictional characters. Although Cervantes' knowledge of the classics was, like William Shakespeare's, less than perfect, he used that knowledge to such comic advantage, ironically couching respect as disrespect, as to eclipse entirely his more erudite contemporaries. Don Quixote's account of his descent into the cave of the Montesinos is both a magnificent tribute to the "descent into hell" theme of Homer's *Odyssey* and Virgil's *Aeneid* so seriously imitated by Dante's *Commedia,* and an uncanny, intriguing representation of the hero's enigmatic state of mind. Turning the epic tradition on its nose, *Don Quixote* explores the unconscious as a metaphor as its messianic hero's self-defined mission is to redefine the relationship between reason and intuition, magic and realism, right brain and left brain, unbridled imagination and cynical accountability. The energy of this masterpiece, which deserves to be read when you're on a tropical island with no distractions, comes directly from the storyteller's relationship to his story. The narrator's own partial disbelief has the effect of suspending the reader's disbelief more effectively than if the chronicles of the great adventurer had been presented with all due seriousness. Tasso, in *Jerusalem Delivered,* had taken seriousness to the point where it merges with insanity. Cervantes leads us with him to dance on the edge between the real and the imagined, the cock-eyed optimistic and the painfully realistic. His prologue, "to the idle reader," creates an immediate complicity between storyteller and audience at the same time that it honors the act of *storying*—whether telling or listening—as the central activity of human consciousness. André Gide, William Faulkner, Jorge Luis Borges, and Gabriel García-Márquez could not have created their masterpieces without *Don Quixote* as a reference point. The novel's visual parallel is Diego Velázquez's "The Royal Family," a painting of a painter painting himself and his observers. Cervantes has inspired works as diverse as Fyodor Dostoevsky's *The Idiot,* Mark Twain's *Tom Sawyer,* Lewis Carroll's *Alice in Wonderland,* Luigi Pirandello's *Six Characters in Search of an Author,* Ken Kesey's *One Flew Over the Cuckoo's Nest,* and William Wharton's *Birdie*; all of them present a hero who behaves like a "foolish child," but whose heroism forces us to redefine the boundary between sanity and insanity. If reading too much, which is Don Quixote's flaw, makes us "mad," it is a "consummation devoutly to be wished." The choice, to live or to read, is always in the hands not of the writers but of the person holding the book.

PART ONE

Prologue

Idling reader, you may believe me when I tell you that I should have liked this book, which is the child of my brain, to be the fairest, the sprightliest, and the cleverest that could be imagined; but I have not been able to contravene the law of nature which would have it that like begets like. And so, what was to be expected of a sterile and uncultivated wit such as that which I possess if not an offspring that was dried up, shriveled, and eccentric: a story filled with thoughts that never occurred to anyone else, of a sort that might be engendered in a prison where every annoyance has its home and every mournful sound its habitation? Peace and tranquility, the pleasures of the countryside, the serenity of the heavens, the murmur of fountains, and ease of mind can do much toward causing the most unproductive of muses to become fecund and bring forth progeny that will be the marvel and delight of mankind.

It sometimes happens that a father has an ugly son with no redeeming grace whatever, yet love will draw a veil over the parental eyes which then behold only cleverness and beauty in place of defects, and in speaking to his friends he will make those defects out to be the signs of comeliness and intellect. I, however, who am but Don Quixote's stepfather, have no desire to go with the current of custom, nor would I, dearest reader, beseech you with tears in my eyes as others do to pardon or overlook the faults you discover in this book; you are neither relative nor friend but may call your soul your own and exercise your free judgment. You are in your own house where you are master as the king is of his taxes, for you are familiar with the saying, "Under my cloak I kill the king." All of which exempts and frees you from any kind of respect or obligation; you may say of this story whatever you choose without fear of being slandered for an ill opinion any more than you will be rewarded for a good one.

I should like to bring you the tale unadulterated and unadorned, stripped of the usual prologue and the endless string of sonnets, epigrams, and eulogies such as are commonly found at the beginning of books. For I may tell you that, although I expended no little labor upon the work itself, I have found no task more difficult than the composition of this preface which you are now reading. Many times I took up my pen and many times I laid it down again, not knowing what to write. On one occasion when I was thus in suspense, paper before me, pen over my ear, elbow on the table, and chin in hand, a very clever friend of mine came in. Seeing me lost in thought, he inquired as to the reason, and I made no effort to conceal from him the fact that my mind was on the preface which I had to write for the story of Don Quixote, and that it was giving me so much trouble that I had about decided not to write any at all and to abandon entirely the idea of publishing the exploits of so noble a knight.

"How," I said to him, "can you expect me not to be concerned over what that venerable legislator, the Public, will say when it sees me, at my age, after all these years of silent slumber, coming out with a tale that is as dried as a rush, a stranger to invention, paltry in style, impoverished in content, and wholly lacking in learning and wisdom, without marginal citations or notes at the end of the book when other works of this sort, even though they be fabulous and profane, are so packed with maxims from Aristotle and Plato and the whole crowd of philosophers as to fill the reader with admiration and lead him to regard the author as a well read, learned, and eloquent individual? Not to speak of the citations from Holy Writ! You would think they were at the very least so many St. Thomases and other doctors of the Church; for they are so adroit at maintaining a solemn face that, having portrayed in one line a distracted lover, in the next they will give you a nice little Christian sermon that is a joy and a privilege to hear and read.

"All this my book will lack, for I have no citations for the margins, no notes for the end. To tell the truth, I do not even know who the authors are to whom I am indebted, and so am unable to follow the example of all the others by listing them alphabetically at the beginning, starting with Aristotle and closing with Xenophon, or, perhaps, with Zoilus or Zeuxis, notwithstanding the fact that the former was a snarling critic, the latter a painter. This work will also be found lacking in prefatory sonnets by dukes, marquises, counts, bishops, ladies, and poets of great renown; although if I were to ask two or three colleagues of mine, they would supply the deficiency by furnishing me with productions that could not be equaled by the authors of most repute in all Spain.

"In short, my friend," I went on, "I am resolved that Señor Don Quixote shall remain buried in the archives of La Mancha until Heaven shall provide him with someone to deck him out with all the ornaments that he lacks; for I find myself incapable of remedying the situation, being possessed of little learning or aptitude, and I am, moreover, extremely lazy when it comes to hunting up authors who will say for me what I am unable to say for myself. And if I am in a state of suspense and my thoughts are woolgathering, you will find a sufficient explanation in what I have just told you."

Hearing this, my friend struck his forehead with the palm of his hand and burst into a loud laugh.

"In the name of God, brother," he said, "you have just deprived me of an illusion. I have known you for a long time, and I have always taken you to be clever and prudent in all your actions; but I now perceive that you are as far from all that as Heaven from the earth. How is it that things of so little moment and so easily remedied can worry and perplex a mind as mature as yours and ordinarily so well adapted to break down and trample underfoot far greater obstacles? I give you my word, this does not come from any lack of cleverness on your part, but rather from excessive indolence and a lack of experience. Do you ask for proof of what I say? Then pay attention closely and in the blink of an eye you shall see how I am going to solve all your difficulties and supply all those things the want of which, so you tell me, is keeping you in suspense, as a result of which you hesitate to publish the history of that famous Don Quixote of yours, the light and mirror of all knight-errantry."

"Tell me, then," I replied, "how you propose to go about curing my diffidence and bringing clarity out of the chaos and confusion of my mind?"

"Take that first matter," he continued, "of the sonnets, epigrams, or eulogies, which should bear the names of grave and titled personages: you can remedy that by taking a little trouble and composing the pieces yourself, and afterward you can baptize them with any name you see fit, fathering them on Prester John of the Indies or the Emperor of Trebizond, for I have heard tell that they were famous poets; and supposing they were not and that a few pedants and bachelors of arts should go around muttering behind your back that it is not so, you should not give so much as a pair of maravedis for all their carping, since even though they make you out to be a liar, they are not going to cut off the hand that put these things on paper.

"As for marginal citations and authors in whom you may find maxims and sayings that you may put in your story, you have but to make use of those scraps of Latin that you know by heart or can look up without too much bother. Thus, when you come to treat of liberty and slavery, jot down:

Non bene pro toto libertas venditur auro.

And then in the margin you will cite Horace or whoever it was that said it. If the subject is death, come up with:

Pallida mors aequo pulsat pede pauperum tabernas Regumque turres. . . .

With these odds and ends of Latin and others of the same sort, you can cause yourself to be taken for a grammarian, although I must say that is no great honor or advantage these days.

"So far as notes at the end of the book are concerned, you may safely go about it in this manner: let us suppose that you mentioned some giant, Goliath let us say; with this one allusion which costs you little or nothing, you have a fine note which you may set down as follows: *The giant Golias or Goliath. This was a Philistine whom the shepherd David slew with a mighty cast from his slingshot in the valley of Terebinth, according to what we read in the Book of Kings,* chapter so-and-so where you find it written.

"In addition to this, by way of showing that you are a learned humanist and a cosmographer, contrive to bring into your story the name of the River Tagus, and there you are with another great little note: *The River Tagus was so called after a king of Spain; it rises in such and such a place and empties into the ocean, washing the walls of the famous city of Lisbon; it is supposed to have golden sands, etc.* If it is robbers, I will let you have the story of Cacus, which I know by heart. If it is loose women, there is the Bishop of Mondoñedo, who will lend you Lamia, Laïs, and Flora, an allusion that will do you great credit. If the subject is cruelty, Ovid will supply you with Medea; or if it is enchantresses and witches, Homer has Calypso and Vergil Circe. If it is valorous captains, Julius Caesar will lend you himself, in his *Commentaries,* and Plutarch will furnish a thousand Alexanders. . . .

"And now we come to the list of authors cited, such as other works contain but in which your own is lacking. Here again the remedy is an easy one; you have but to look up some book that has them all, from A to Z as you were saying, and transfer the entire list as it stands. What if the imposition is plain for all to see? You have little need to refer to them, and so it does not matter; and some may be so simpleminded as to believe that you have drawn upon them all in your simple unpretentious little story. If it serves no other purpose, this imposing list of authors will at least give your book an unlooked-for air of authority. What is more, no one is going to put himself to the trouble of verifying your references to see whether or not you have followed all these authors, since it will not be worth his pains to do so.

"This is especially true in view of the fact that your book stands in no need of all these things whose absence you lament; for the entire work is an attack upon the books of chivalry of which Aristotle never dreamed, of which St. Basil has nothing to say, and of which Cicero had no knowledge; nor do the fine points of truth or the observations of astrology have anything to do with its fanciful absurdities; geometrical measurements, likewise, and rhetorical argumentations serve for nothing here; you have no sermon to preach to anyone by mingling the human with the divine, a kind of motley in which no Christian intellect should be willing to clothe itself.

"All that you have to do is to make proper use of imitation in what you write, and the more perfect the imitation the better will your writing be. Inasmuch as you have no other object in view than that of overthrowing the authority and prestige which books of chivalry enjoy in the world at large and among the vulgar, there is no reason why you should go begging maxims of the philosophers, counsels of Holy Writ, fables of the poets, orations of the rhetoricians, or miracles of the saints; see to it, rather, that your style flows along smoothly, pleasingly, and sonorously, and that your words are the proper ones, meaningful and well placed, expressive of your intention in setting them down and of what you wish to say, without any intricacy or obscurity.

"Let it be your aim that, by reading your story, the melancholy may be moved to laughter and the cheerful man made merrier still; let the simple not be bored, but may the clever admire your originality; let the grave ones not despise you, but let the prudent praise you. And keep in mind, above all, your purpose, which is that of undermining the ill-founded edifice that is constituted by those books of chivalry, so abhorred by many but admired by many more; if you succeed in attaining it, you will have accomplished no little."

Listening in profound silence to what my friend had to say, I was so impressed by his reasoning that, with no thought of questioning them, I decided to make use of his arguments in composing this prologue. Here, gentle reader, you will perceive my friend's cleverness, my own good fortune in coming upon such a counselor at a time when I needed him so badly, and the profit which you yourselves are to have in finding so sincere and straight-forward an account of the famous Don Quixote de la Mancha, who is held by the inhabitants of the Campo de Montiel region to have been the most chaste lover and the most valiant knight that had been seen in those parts for many a year. I have no desire to enlarge upon the service I am rendering you in bringing you the story of so notable and honored a gentleman; I merely would have you thank me for having made you acquainted with the famous Sancho Panza, his squire, in whom, to my mind, is to be found an epitome of all the squires and their drolleries scattered here and there throughout the pages of those vain and empty books of chivalry. And with this, may God give you health, and may He be not unmindful of me as well. VALE.

Chapter I. Which treats of the station in life and the pursuits of the famous gentleman, Don Quixote de la Mancha.

In a village of La Mancha the name of which I have no desire to recall, there lived not so long ago one of those gentlemen who always have a lance in the rack, an ancient buckler, a skinny nag, and a greyhound for the chase. A stew with more beef than mutton in it, chopped meat for his evening meal, scraps for a Saturday, lentils on Friday, and a young pigeon as a special delicacy for Sunday, went to account for three-quarters of his income. The rest of it he laid out on a broadcloth greatcoat and velvet stockings for feast days, with slippers to match, while the other days of the week he cut a figure in a suit of the finest homespun. Living with him were a housekeeper in her for-

ties, a niece who was not yet twenty, and a lad of the field and market place who saddled his horse for him and wielded the pruning knife.

This gentleman of ours was close on to fifty, of a robust constitution but with little flesh on his bones and a face that was lean and gaunt. He was noted for his early rising, being very fond of the hunt. They will try to tell you that his surname was Quijada or Quesada—there is some difference of opinion among those who have written on the subject—but according to the most likely conjectures we are to understand that it was really Quejana. But all this means very little so far as our story is concerned, providing that in the telling of it we do not depart one iota from the truth.

You may know, then, that the aforesaid gentleman, on those occasions when he was at leisure, which was most of the year around, was in the habit of reading books of chivalry with such pleasure and devotion as to lead him almost wholly to forget the life of a hunter and even the administration of his estate. So great was his curiosity and infatuation in this regard that he even sold many acres of tillable land in order to be able to buy and read the books that he loved, and he would carry home with him as many of them as he could obtain.

Of all those that he thus devoured none pleased him so well as the ones that had been composed by the famous Feliciano de Silva, whose lucid prose style and involved conceits were as precious to him as pearls; especially when he came to read those tales of love and amorous challenges that are to be met with in many places, such a passage as the following, for example: "The reason of the unreason that afflicts my reason, in such a manner weakens my reason that I with reason lament me of your comeliness." And he was similarly affected when his eyes fell upon such lines as these: ". . . the high Heaven of your divinity divinely fortifies you with the stars and renders you deserving of that desert your greatness doth deserve."

The poor fellow used to lie awake nights in an effort to disentangle the meaning and make sense out of passages such as these, although

Aristotle himself would not have been able to understand them, even if he had been resurrected for that sole purpose. He was not at ease in his mind over those wounds that Don Belianís gave and received; for no matter how great the surgeons who treated him, the poor fellow must have been left with his face and his entire body covered with marks and scars. Nevertheless, he was grateful to the author for closing the book with the promise of an interminable adventure to come; many a time he was tempted to take up his pen and literally finish the tale as had been promised, and he undoubtedly would have done so, and would have succeeded at it very well, if his thoughts had not been constantly occupied with other things of greater moment.

He often talked it over with the village curate, who was a learned man, a graduate of Sigüenza, and they would hold long discussions as to who had been the better knight, Palmerin of England or Amadis of Gaul; but Master Nicholas, the barber of the same village, was in the habit of saying that no one could come up to the Knight of Phoebus, and that if anyone *could* compare with him it was Don Galaor, brother of Amadis of Gaul, for Galaor was ready for anything—he was none of your finical knights, who went around whimpering as his brother did, and in point of valor he did not lag behind him.

In short, our gentleman became so immersed in his reading that he spent whole nights from sundown to sunup and his days from dawn to dusk in poring over his books, until, finally, from so little sleeping and so much reading, his brain dried up and he went completely out of his mind. He had filled his imagination with everything that he had read, with enchantments, knightly encounters, battles, challenges, wounds, with tales of love and its torments, and all sorts of impossible things, and as a result had come to believe that all these fictitious happenings were true; they were more real to him than anything else in the world. He would remark that the Cid Ruy Díaz had been a very good knight, but there was no comparison between him and the Knight of the Flaming Sword, who with a single backward stroke had cut in half two fierce and monstrous giants. He preferred Bernardo del Carpio, who at Roncesvalles had slain Roland despite the charm the latter bore, availing himself of the stratagem which Hercules employed when he strangled Antaeus, the son of Earth, in his arms.

He had much good to say for Morgante who, though he belonged to the haughty, overbearing race of giants, was of an affable disposition and well brought up. But, above all, he cherished an admiration for Rinaldo of Montalbán, especially as he beheld him sallying forth from his castle to rob all those that crossed his path, or when he thought of him overseas stealing the image of Mohammed which, so the story has it, was all of gold. And he would have liked very well to have had his fill of kicking that traitor Galalón, a privilege for which he would have given his housekeeper with his niece thrown into the bargain.

At last, when his wits were gone beyond repair, he came to conceive the strangest idea that ever occurred to any madman in this world. It now appeared to him fitting and necessary, in order to win a greater amount of honor for himself and serve his country at the same time, to become a knight-errant and roam the world on horseback, in a suit of armor; he would go in quest of adventures, by way of putting into practice all that he had read in his books; he would right every manner of wrong, placing himself in situations of the greatest peril such as would redound to the eternal glory of his name. As a reward for his valor and the might of his arm, the poor fellow could already see himself crowned Emperor of Trebizond at the very least; and so, carried away by the strange pleasure that he found in such thoughts as these, he at once set about putting his plan into effect.

The first thing he did was to burnish up some old pieces of armor, left him by his great-grandfather, which for ages had lain in a corner, moldering and forgotten. He polished and adjusted them as best he could, and then he noticed that one very important thing was lacking: there was no closed helmet, but only a morion, or visorless headpiece, with turned up brim of the kind foot soldiers wore. His ingenuity, however, enabled him to remedy this, and he proceeded to fashion out of cardboard a kind of half-helmet, which, when attached to the morion, gave the appearance of a whole one. True, when he went to see if it was strong enough to withstand a good slashing blow, he was somewhat disappointed; for when he drew his sword and gave it a couple of thrusts, he succeeded only in undoing a whole week's labor. The ease with which he had hewed it to bits disturbed him no little, and he decided to make it over. This time he placed a few strips of iron on the inside, and then, convinced that it was strong enough, refrained from putting it to any further test; instead, he adopted it then and there as the finest helmet ever made.

After this, he went out to have a look at his nag; and although the animal had more *cuartos,* or cracks, in its hoof than there are quarters in a real, and more blemishes than Gonela's steed which *tantum pellis et ossa fuit,* it nonetheless looked to its master like a far better horse than Alexander's Bucephalus or the Babieca of the Cid. He spent all of four days in trying to think up a name for his mount; for—so he told himself—seeing that it belonged to so famous and worthy a knight, there was no reason why it should not have a name of equal renown. The kind of name he wanted was one that would at once indicate what the nag had been before it came to belong to a knight-errant and what its present status was; for it stood to reason that, when the master's worldly condition changed, his horse also ought to have a famous, high-sounding appellation, one suited to the new order of things and the new profession that it was to follow.

After he in his memory and imagination had made up, struck out, and discarded many names, now adding to and now subtracting from the list, he finally hit upon "Rocinante," a name that impressed him as being sonorous and at the same time indicative of what the steed had been when it was but a hack, whereas now it was nothing other than the first and foremost of all the hacks in the world.

Having found a name for his horse that pleased his fancy, he then desired to do as much for himself, and this required another week, and by the end of that period he had made up his mind that he was henceforth to be known as Don Quixote, which, as has been stated, has led the authors of this veracious history to assume that his real name must undoubtedly have been Quijada, and not Quesada as others would have it. But remembering that the valiant Amadis was not content to call himself that and nothing more, but added the name of his kingdom and fatherland that he might make it famous also, and thus came to take the name Amadis of Gaul, so our good knight chose to add his place of origin and become "Don Quixote de la Mancha"; for by this means, as he saw it, he was making very plain his lineage and was conferring honor upon his country by taking its name as his own.

And so, having polished up his armor and made the morion over into a closed helmet, and having given himself and his horse a name, he naturally found but one thing lacking still: he must seek out a lady of whom he could become enamored; for a knight-errant without a ladylove was like a tree without leaves or fruit, a body without a soul.

"If," he said to himself, "as a punishment for my sins or by a stroke of fortune I should come upon some giant hereabouts, a thing that very commonly happens to knights-errant, and if I should slay him in a hand-to-hand encounter or perhaps cut him in two, or, finally, if I should vanquish and subdue him, would it not be well to have someone to whom I may send him as a present, in order that he, if he is living, may come in, fall upon his knees in front of my sweet lady, and say in a humble and submissive tone of voice, 'I, lady, am the giant Caraculiambro, lord of the island Malindrania, who has been overcome in single combat by that knight who never can be praised enough, Don Quixote de la Mancha, the same who sent me to present myself before your Grace that your Highness may dispose of me as you see fit'?"

Oh, how our good knight reveled in this speech, and more than ever when he came to think of the name that he should give his lady! As the story goes, there was a very good-looking farm girl who lived near by, with whom he had once been smitten, although it is generally believed that she never knew or suspected it. Her name was Aldonza Lorenzo, and it seemed to him that she was the one upon whom he should bestow the title of mistress of his thoughts. For her he wished a name that should not be incongruous with his own and that would convey the suggestion of a princess or a great lady; and, accordingly, he resolved to call her "Dulcinea del Toboso," she being a native of that place. A musical name to his ears, out of the ordinary and significant, like the others he had chosen for himself and his appurtenances. . . .

BOOK 2

From Chapter XXII: Wherein is related the great adventure of the Cave of Montesinos in the heart of La Mancha, which the valiant Don Quixote brought to a triumphant conclusion.

With this and other pleasing talk they spent the day, and when night came found lodgings in a little village which, as the cousin informed Don Quixote, was not more than a couple of leagues from the Cave of Montesinos; and their guide took occasion to remind the knight that if he was resolved to make the descent, he would have to find ropes with which to lower himself into the depths. To this Don Quixote's answer was that even if it was as deep as Hell, he proposed to see the bottom of it; and so they bought nearly a hundred fathoms of rope, and the following day, at two o'clock in the afternoon, they reached the cave, the mouth of which is broad and spacious, but clogged with boxthorn, wild fig trees, shrubs, and brambles, so dense and tangled an undergrowth as wholly

to cover over and conceal the entrance. All three of them then dismounted, and Sancho and the cousin bound Don Quixote very stoutly with the ropes.

"Look well what you do, master," said Sancho as they were girdling him. "Don't go burying yourself alive or get yourself caught so you will hang there like a bottle that has been let down into the well to cool. If you ask me, I would say it is none of your Grace's affair to be prying into this cave, which must be worse than a dungeon."

"Keep on trying and keep still," Don Quixote admonished him. "It is just such an undertaking as this, Sancho, that is reserved for me."

The guide then addressed him. "Señor Don Quixote," he said, "I beg your Grace to view thoroughly and inspect with a hundred eyes what you find down there; who knows, maybe it will be something that I can put in my book on *Transformations.*"

"Leave the tambourine," Sancho advised him, "to the one who knows how to play it."

By this time they had finished tying Don Quixote, passing the rope over his doublet, not over his battle harness.

"It was careless of us," said the knight, "not to have provided ourselves with a cattle bell to attach to the rope at my side so that you might be able to tell from the sound of it whether I was still descending and still alive. However, there is nothing for it now. I am in God's hands and may He be my guide."

He knelt and prayed to Heaven in a low voice, imploring God to aid him and grant him success in this adventure, which impressed him as being a rare and dangerous one. Then he raised his voice:

"O lady who dost inspire my every deed and action, O most illustrious and peerless Dulcinea del Toboso! If it be possible for the prayers and entreaties of this thy fortunate lover to reach thine ears, I do beseech thee to hear them. What I ask of thee is nothing other than thy favor and protection, of which I so greatly stand in need at this moment. I am now about to sink, to hurl and plunge myself into the abyss that yawns before me here, simply in order that the world may know that there is nothing, however impossible it may seem, that I will not undertake and accomplish, provided only I have thy favor."

Having said this, he went up to the chasm and perceived that if he was to make a descent he would first have to clear an entrance by force of arm or by hacking away the underbrush; and accordingly, taking his sword, he began cutting and felling the brambles at the mouth of the cave, the noise of which caused a very great number of crows and jackdaws to fly out. There were so many of these birds and such was their velocity that they knocked Don Quixote down, and had he been as much of a believer in augury as he was a good Catholic Christian, he would have taken this as an ill omen and would have declined to bury himself in such a place as that. Finally, he arose and, seeing that no more crows or other night birds were emerging, such as the bats that flew out with the crows, he allowed himself to be lowered into the depths of the horrendous cavern, with Sancho and the cousin letting out the rope as the squire bestowed his benediction and crossed himself an endless number of times.

"May God be your guide," exclaimed Sancho, "and the Rock of France, along with the Trinity of Gaeta, O flower, cream, and skimming of knights-errant! There you go, daredevil of the earth, heart of steel, arms of brass! Once more, may God be your guide and bring you back safe, sound, and without a scratch to the light of this world which you are leaving to bury yourself in that darkness that you go to seek!"

The cousin, meanwhile, was offering up practically the same prayers. Don Quixote then went on down, calling for them to give him rope and more rope, and they let it out for him little by little. By the time they could no longer hear his voice, which came out of the cave as through a pipe, they had let him have the entire hundred fathoms, all the rope there was, and were of a mind to pull him up again. They decided, however, to wait for half an hour, and

then they once more began hauling in the line, with no effort whatever, for they could feel no weight on the other end, which led them to think that Don Quixote must have remained behind. Believing this to be the case, Sancho began weeping bitterly and started pulling with all his might in order to learn the truth of the matter; but when they had come to a little more than eighty fathoms, as it seemed to them, they once more felt a tug, which made them very happy indeed. Finally, at ten fathoms, they could see Don Quixote quite distinctly, and as he caught sight of him, Sancho cried out, "Welcome, master, we are glad to see you again. We thought you had stayed down there to found a family."

But Don Quixote said not a word in reply, and when they had him all the way up they saw that his eyes were closed and that, to all appearances, he was sound asleep. They laid him on the ground and untied him, but even this did not wake him. It was not until they had turned him over first on one side and then on the other and had given him a thorough shaking and mauling that, after a considerable length of time, he at last regained consciousness, stretching himself as if he had been roused from a profound slumber and gazing about him with a bewildered look.

"God forgive you, friends," he said, "you have taken me away from the most delightful existence mortal ever knew and the pleasantest sight human eyes ever rested upon. Now truly do I begin to understand how it is that all the pleasures of this life pass away like a shadow or a dream or wither like the flower of the field. O unfortunate Montesinos! O, sorely wounded Durandarte! O unhappy Belerma! O tearful Guadiana! And you, hapless daughters of Ruidera, who in your waters display the tears your eyes once wept!"

The cousin and Sancho listened attentively to Don Quixote's words, which appeared to have been uttered in great pain, as though drawn from his entrails. They thereupon begged him to tell them the meaning of it all and what it was he had seen in that Hell he had visited.

"Hell do you call it?" said Don Quixote. "Do not call it that, for it does not deserve the name, as you shall see."

He then asked them to give him something to eat, as he was exceedingly hungry; and so they spread the cousin's sackcloth upon the green grass and laid out what fare the saddle-bags could afford, and, sitting down together like the three good friends and companions that they were, they proceeded to make a meal of it, combining lunch and supper. When the sackcloth had been removed, Don Quixote de la Mancha spoke.

"Let no one arise," he said, "but both of you listen most attentively to what I have to say."

Chapter XXIII. Of the amazing things which the incomparable Don Quixote told of having seen in the deep Cave of Montesinos, an adventure the grandeur and impossible nature of which have caused it to be regarded as apocryphal.

It was around four in the afternoon when the subdued light and tempered rays of the sun, which was now covered over with clouds, afforded Don Quixote an opportunity to tell his two illustrious listeners, without undue heat or weariness, what it was he had seen in the Cave of Montesinos. He began in the following manner:

"At a depth corresponding to the height of twelve or fourteen men, on the right-hand side of this dungeon, there is a concave recess capable of containing a large cart with its mules. A small light filters into it through distant chinks or crevices in the surface of the earth; and I caught sight of this nook just at a time when I was feeling tired and vexed at finding myself dangling from a rope in that manner as I descended into those dark regions without any certain knowledge as to where I was going. And so I decided to enter the recess and rest a little. I called to you, asking you not to give out any more rope until I told you to do so, but you must not have heard me. Accordingly, I gathered it in as you sent it to me and, making a coil or pile of it, I seated myself upon it, meanwhile

thinking what I should have to do in order to let myself all the way down to the bottom, as I now had no one to hold me up.

"As I sat there lost in thought and deeply perplexed, suddenly and without my doing anything to bring it about a profound sleep fell upon me; and then, all unexpectedly and not knowing how it happened, I awoke and found myself in the midst of the most beautiful, pleasant, and delightful meadow that nature could create or the most fertile imagination could conceive. Opening my eyes, I rubbed them and discovered that I was not sleeping but really awake. Nevertheless, I felt my head and bosom to make sure it was I who was there and not some empty and deceptive phantom. And my sense of touch and feeling and the coherence of my thoughts were sufficient to assure me that I was the same then and there that I am here and now.

"It was at that moment that my eyes fell upon a sumptuous royal palace or castle, the walls and battlements of which appeared to be built of clear, transparent crystal. The two wings of the main gate were suddenly thrown open, and there emerged and came toward me a venerable old man clad in a hooded cloak of mulberry-colored stuff that swept the ground. Around his head and his bosom was a collegiate green satin sash, and on his head a black Milanese bonnet. His beard was snow-white and fell below his waist, and he carried no arms whatever, nothing but a rosary which he held in his hand, a string on which the beads were larger than fair-sized walnuts, every tenth one being as big as an ordinary ostrich egg. His bearing, his stride, the gravity of his demeanor, and his stately presence, each in itself and all of them together, filled me with wonder and astonishment. Upon reaching my side, the first thing he did was to give me a close embrace.

"'It is a long time,' he said, 'O valiant knight, Don Quixote de la Mancha, that we in these enchanted solitudes have been waiting for a sight of you, that you might go back and inform the world of what lies locked and concealed in the depths of this cave which you have entered, the so-called Cave of Montesinos, an exploit solely reserved for your invincible heart and stupendous courage. Come with me, most illustrious sir, and I will show you the hidden marvels of this transparent castle of which I am the governor and perpetual guardian; for I am Montesinos himself, after whom the cave is named.'

"No sooner had he informed me that he was Montesinos than I asked him if the story was true that was told in the world above, to the effect that with a small dagger he had cut out the heart of his great friend Durandarte and had borne it to the lady Belerma as his friend at the point of death had requested him to do. He replied that it was all true except the part about the dagger, for it was not a dagger, nor was it small, but a burnished poniard sharper than an awl."

"It must have been such a poniard," said Sancho at this point, "as that of Ramón de Hoces of Seville."

"I cannot say as to that," replied Don Quixote, "for Ramón de Hoces lived only yesterday and the battle of Roncesvalles, where this unfortunate affair occurred, was many years ago; and, in any case, it does not alter in any way the truth and substance of the tale."

"That is right," said the cousin. "Continue, Señor Don Quixote, for I am listening to your Grace with the greatest of pleasure."

"And mine in relating the story is no less," Don Quixote assured him. . . .

The cousin now put in a word. "I do not understand, Señor Don Quixote," he said, "how your Grace in the short time you were down there could have seen so many things and done so much talking."

"How long has it been since I went down?" asked Don Quixote.

"A little more than an hour," Sancho told him.

"That cannot be," said the knight, "for night fell and day dawned, and it was day and night three times altogether; so that, according to my count, it was three whole days that I spent in those remote regions that are hidden from our sight."

"My master," averred Sancho, "must be speaking the truth; for since all the things that happened to him came about through magic, who knows? what seemed to us an hour may have been three days and nights for him."

"That is right," said Don Quixote.

"And did your Grace eat in all that time?" the cousin inquired.

"Not a mouthful," replied Don Quixote, "nor did I feel the least bit hungry."

"Then, those that are enchanted do not eat?" the student persisted.

"They neither eat nor are they subject to the major excretions," was Don Quixote's answer, "although it is believed that their nails, beard, and hair continue to grow."

"And do they sleep by any chance?" asked Sancho.

"No, certainly not," said Don Quixote, "or, at least, during the three days I was with them, none of them shut an eye, and the same was true of me."

"The proverb, 'Tell me what company you keep and I'll tell you what you are,' fits in here," observed Sancho. "Seeing your Grace has been keeping company with the bewitched, who fast and stay awake, it is small wonder if you didn't sleep either while you were with them. But forgive me, master, if I tell you that God—I was about to say the devil—may take me if I believe a word of your Grace's story."

"How is that?" asked the cousin. "Do you mean to say that Señor Don Quixote is lying? Why, even if he wished to, he had no opportunity to imagine and invent such a lot of falsehoods."

"I do not think that my master is lying," said Sancho.

"Well, then, what do you think?" Don Quixote wanted to know.

"I think," replied Sancho, "that Merlin or those enchanters that laid a spell on the whole crew you say you saw and talked with down there have put into your noddle or your memory all this rigmarole that you've been telling us, and all that remains to be told."

"Such a thing could be," said Don Quixote, "but it is not so in this case; for I have simply told you what I saw with my own eyes and felt with my own hands. Montesinos showed me countless other marvelous things which I will relate to you in due time and at leisure in the course of our journey, for this is not the place to speak of them. But what will you say when I tell you he pointed out to me three peasant lasses who were gamboling and disporting themselves like goats in those lovely meadows; and no sooner did I see them than I recognized one of them as being the peerless Dulcinea del Toboso and the other two as the same girls who had come with her and with whom we spoke upon the El Toboso road.

"I asked Montesinos if he knew them and he replied that he did not, but that he thought they must be some highborn ladies with a spell upon them. He added that they had arrived but a few days ago, which to me was not surprising in view of the fact that many other ladies of the present time as well as of past ages were to be found there in various strange and enchanted shapes, among whom he said he recognized Queen Guinevere and her duenna Quintañona, she who poured the wine for Lancelot 'when from Britain he came.'"

As he heard his master say this, Sancho Panza thought he would lose his mind or die of laughing. Knowing as he did the truth respecting Dulcinea's supposed enchantment, since he himself had been the enchanter and the concoctor of the evidence, he now was convinced beyond a doubt that the knight was out of his senses and wholly mad.

"It was an evil hour, my dear master," he said, "a worse season, and a sad day when your Grace went down into the other world, and an unlucky moment when you met that Señor Montesinos, who has sent you back to us like this. You would have been better off if you had stayed up here, with all your wits about you as God gave them to you, speaking in proverbs and giving advice at every step of the way, in place of telling us the most foolish stories that could be imagined."

"Knowing you as I do, Sancho," said Don Quixote, "I take no account of your words."

"Nor I of your Grace's," was the reply, "even though you beat me or kill me for those I have already spoken or those that I mean to speak, unless you correct and mend your own. But tell me, seeing that we are now at peace: how or by what sign did you recognize the lady who is our mistress? Did you speak to her, and if so, what did you say and what did she answer you?"

"I recognized her," said Don Quixote, "by the fact that she wore the same clothes that she did when you first made me acquainted with her. I spoke to her, but she did not answer a word; she merely turned her back on me and fled so swiftly that a bolt from a cross-bow would not have overtaken her. I was for following her and should have done so had not Montesinos advised me not to waste my strength as it would be in vain; and, moreover, the hour had come for me to leave the cavern. He further assured me that, in the course of time, he would let me know how he and Belerma and Durandarte and all the others who were there had been disenchanted. What gave me the most pain, however, of all the things that I saw and observed, was this. Even as Montesinos was speaking, one of the damsels who accompanied the hapless Dulcinea came up to me from one side, without my having noticed her, and, her eyes brimming with tears, addressed me in a low and troubled voice.

"'My lady Dulcinea del Toboso,' she said, 'kisses your Grace's hand and implores your Grace to do her the favor of informing her how you are; and being in great want, she also begs your Grace in all earnestness to be so good as to lend her, upon this new dimity petticoat that I am wearing, half a dozen reales or whatever your Grace may have upon you, and she gives you her word that she will pay them back just as soon as she can.'

"I was astonished to receive such a message as this, and, turning to Señor Montesinos, I asked him, 'Is it possible, sir, for the highborn who have been enchanted to suffer want?' To which he made the following reply:

"'Believe me, your Grace, Señor Don Quixote de la Mancha, this thing that is called want is to be found everywhere; it extends to and reaches all persons and does not even spare the enchanted; and since the lady Dulcinea del Toboso has sent you a request for those six reales and has offered you good security, there is nothing to be done, as I see it, but to give them to her, for she must undoubtedly be hard pressed.'

"'Security I will not take,' I told him, 'nor can I give her what she asks, for I have only four reales on me.'

"With this, I handed the coins to the damsel—they were the ones that you let me have the other day to bestow as alms upon the poor that I might meet with along the road.

"'Tell your lady, my dear,' I said, 'that her sufferings weigh upon my heart, and that I only wish I were a Fugger that I might cure them. And you may inform her, further, that there can be no such thing as health for me so long as I am deprived of the pleasure of seeing her and enjoying her discreet conversation. Tell her, also, that I most earnestly beg her Grace to permit herself to be seen and addressed by her captive servant and world-weary knight, and that when she least expects it she will hear that I have taken an oath and made a vow similar to that of the Marquis of Mantua, who swore to avenge his nephew, Baldwin, that time he found him expiring in the heart of the mountains, his vow being not to eat bread off a cloth, along with other trifling stipulations which he added, until vengeance had been had. For I mean to take no rest but to roam the seven parts of the world more faithfully than did the prince Dom Pedro of Portugal until I shall have freed her from this spell.'

"'All this and more you owe my lady,' was the damsel's answer; and, taking the four reales, in place of dropping a curtsy she cut a caper, leaping more than two yards into the air."

"Holy God!" cried Sancho as Don Quixote reached this point of his story. "Can it be that there are in this world enchanters of such power that they have changed my master's good sense into such madness as this? O master, master! in God's name, think what you are doing, look to your Grace's honor, and do not go believing all this nonsense that has turned your head and left you short of wit."

"It is because you love me, Sancho, that you talk that way," said Don Quixote. "Since you are not experienced in worldly matters, everything that is a little difficult seems to you impossible; but, as I said before, I will tell you more later on of what I saw down there, and you shall hear things that will compel you to believe that what I have already told you is the truth and admits of neither question nor reply.". . .

FRANCIS BACON (1561–1626)

The Advancement of Learning (1605)

"The inquiry of truth, which is the love-making or wooing of it; the knowledge of truth, which is the presence of it; and the belief in truth, which is the enjoying of it—is the sovereign good of human nature." Themes writ large by the Italian humanists are engraved in the heart of the British Renaissance by Sir Francis Bacon, the master of prose who, like his martyred predecessor, was to become the Lord Chancellor of England (1618–21), and then to fall from grace. Philosopher, scientist, defender of the crown, Bacon, in his most famous work, *Novum Organum,* enunciated the principles of the "scientific method" which has served the human race, for better or for worse, until today. Its purpose, according to the author, was to "enlarge the bounds of reason, and to endow man's estate with new value." Bacon argued that humanity before the Greeks had followed its natural instincts and had achieved great insight into the workings of the world and our place within it. Along with Plato and Aristotle came trouble. According to Bacon, they replaced instinct with reason, turning inward for visions of order instead of outward, through scientific observation. His praise of James I, to whom *The Advancement of Learning* is dedicated, indicates a characteristically Renaissance idealism that belies the scientific method at the same time that it serves Bacon's self-promoting purposes in promulgating his favorite theories: the primacy of inductive reasoning, and experimentation with nature as the highest method of inquiry. If James had indeed been the ideal monarch Bacon addresses, his arguments would have been unnecessary because already fulfilled. *The Advancement of Learning* foreshadows the approach articulated fully in the *New Organon* (1608–1626).

The First Book of Francis Bacon; of the Proficience and Advancement of Learning, Divine and Human.

To the King.

1. There were under the law, excellent King, both daily sacrifices and freewill offerings; the one proceeding upon ordinary observance, the other upon a devout cheerfulness: in like manner there belongeth to kings from their servants both tribute of duty and presents of affection. In the former of these I hope I shall not live to be wanting, according to my most humble duty, and the good pleasure of your Majesty's employments: for the latter, I thought it more respective to make choice

of some oblation, which might rather refer to the propriety and excellency of your individual person, than to the business of your crown and state.

2. Wherefore, representing your Majesty many times unto my mind, and beholding you not with the inquisitive eye of presumption, to discover that which the Scripture telleth me is inscrutable, but with the observant eye of duty and admiration; leaving aside the other parts of your virtue and fortune, I have been touched, yea, and possessed with an extreme wonder at those your virtues and faculties, which the Philosophers call intellectual; the largeness of your capacity, the faithfulness of your memory, the swiftness of your apprehension, the penetration of your judgement, and the facility and order of your elocution: and I have often thought, that of all the persons living that I have known, your Majesty were the best instance to make a man of Plato's opinion, that all knowledge is but remembrance, and that the mind of man by nature knoweth all things, and hath but her own native and original notions (which by the strangeness and darkness of this tabernacle of the body are sequestered) again revived and restored: such a light of nature I have observed in your Majesty, and such a readiness to take flame and blaze from the least occasion presented, or the least spark of another's knowledge delivered. And as the Scripture saith of the wisest king, *That his heart was as the sands of the sea;* which though it be one of the largest bodies, yet it consisteth of the smallest and finest portions; so hath God given your Majesty a composition of understanding admirable, being able to compass and comprehend the greatest matters, and nevertheless to touch and apprehend the least; whereas it should seem an impossibility in nature, for the same instrument to make itself fit for great and small works. And for your gift of speech, I call to mind what Cornelius Tacitus saith of Augustus Cæsar: *Augusto*

profluens, et quæ principem deceret, eloquentia fuit. For if we note it well, speech that is uttered with labour and difficulty, or speech that savoureth of the affectation of art and precepts, or speech that is framed after the imitation of some pattern of eloquence, though never so excellent; all this hath somewhat servile, and holding of the subject. But your Majesty's manner of speech is indeed prince-like, flowing as from a fountain, and yet streaming and branching itself into nature's order, full of facility and felicity, imitating none, and inimitable by any. And as in your civil estate there appeareth to be an emulation and contention of your Majesty's virtue with your fortune; a virtuous disposition with a fortunate regiment; a virtuous expectation (when time was) of your greater fortune, with a prosperous possession thereof in the due time; a virtuous observation of the laws of marriage, with most blessed and happy fruit of marriage; a virtuous and most Christian desire of peace, with a fortunate inclination in your neighbour princes thereunto: so likewise in these intellectual matters, there seemeth to be no less contention between the excellency of your Majesty's gifts of nature and the universality and perfection of your learning. For I am well assured that this which I shall say is no amplification at all, but a positive and measured truth; which is, that there hath not been since Christ's time any king or temporal monarch, which hath been so learned in all literature and erudition, divine and human. For let a man seriously and diligently revolve and peruse the succession of the emperors of Rome, of which Cæsar the Dictator, who lived some years before Christ, and Marcus Antoninus were the best learned; and so descend to the emperors of Grecia, or of the West, and then to the lines of France, Spain, England, Scotland, and the rest, and he shall find this judgement is truly made. For it seemeth much in a king, if, by the compendious extractions of other men's wits and labours, he can take hold of any superficial ornaments and shows of learning; or if he countenance and prefer learning and learned men: but to drink indeed of the true fountains of learning, nay, to have such a fountain of learning in himself, in a king, and in a king born, is almost a miracle. And the more, because there is met in your Majesty a rare conjunction, as well of divine and sacred literature, as of profane and human; so as your Majesty standeth invested of that triplicity, which in great veneration was ascribed to the ancient Hermes; the power and fortune of a king, the knowledge and illumination of a priest, and the learning and universality of a philosopher. This propriety inherent and individual attribute in your Majesty deserveth to be expressed not only in the fame and admiration of the present time, nor in the history or tradition of the ages succeeding, but also in some solid work, fixed memorial, and immortal monument, bearing a character or signature both of the power of a king and the difference and perfection of such a king.

3. Therefore I did conclude with myself, that I could not make unto your Majesty a better oblation than of some treatise tending to that end, whereof the sum will consist of these two parts; the former concerning the excellency of learning and knowledge, and the excellency of the merit and true glory in the augmentation and propagation thereof: the latter, what the particular acts and works are, which have been embraced and undertaken for the advancement of learning; and again, what defects and undervalues I find in such particular acts: to the end that though I cannot positively or affirmatively advise your Majesty, or propound unto you framed particulars, yet I may excite your princely cogitations to visit the excellent treasure of your own mind, and thence to extract particulars for this purpose, agreeable to your magnanimity and wisdom.

I

1. In the entrance to the former of these, to clear the way, and as it were to make silence, to have the true testimonies concerning the dignity of learning to be better heard, without the interruption of tacit objections; I think good to deliver it from the discredits and disgraces which it hath received, all from ignorance; but ignorance severally disguised; appearing sometimes in the zeal and jealousy of divines; sometimes in the severity and arrogance of politiques; and sometimes in the errors and imperfections of learned men themselves.

2. I hear the former sort say, that knowledge is of those things which are to be accepted of with great limitation and caution: that the aspiring to overmuch knowledge was the original temptation and sin whereupon ensued the fall of man: that knowledge hath in it somewhat of the serpent, and therefore where it entereth into a man it makes him swell; *Scientia inflat:* that Salomon gives a censure, *That there is no end of making books, and that much reading is weariness of the flesh;* and again in another place, *That in spacious knowledge there is much contristation, and that he that increaseth knowledge increaseth anxiety:* that Saint Paul gives a caveat, *That we be not spoiled through vain philosophy:* that experience demonstrates how learned men have been arch-heretics, how learned times have been inclined to atheism, and how the contemplation of second causes doth derogate from our dependence upon God, who is the first cause.

3. To discover then the ignorance and error of this opinion, and the misunderstanding in the grounds thereof, it may well appear these men do not observe or consider that it was not the pure knowledge of nature and universality, a knowledge by the light whereof man did give names unto other creatures in Paradise, as they were brought before him, according unto their propri-

eties, which gave the occasion to the fall: but it was the proud knowledge of good and evil, with an intent in man to give law unto himself, and to depend no more upon God's commandments, which was the form of the temptation. Neither is it any quantity of knowledge, how great soever, that can make the mind of man to swell; for nothing can fill, much less extend the soul of man, but God and the contemplation of God; and therefore Salomon, speaking of the two principal senses of inquisition, the eye and the ear, affirmeth that *the eye is never satisfied with seeing, nor the ear with hearing;* and if there be no fulness, then is the continent greater than the content: so of knowledge itself, and the mind of man, whereto the senses are but reporters, he defineth likewise in these words, placed after that Kalendar or Ephemerides which he maketh of the diversities of times and seasons for all actions and purposes; and concludeth thus: *God hath made all things beautiful, or decent, in the true return of their seasons: Also he hath placed the world in man's heart, yet cannot man find out the work which God worketh from the beginning to the end:* declaring not obscurely, that God hath framed the mind of man as a mirror or glass, capable of the image of the universal world, and joyful to receive the impression thereof, as the eye joyeth to receive light; and not only delighted in beholding the variety of things and vicissitude of times, but raised also to find out and discern the ordinances and decrees, which throughout all those changes are infallibly observed. . . .

JOHANNES KEPLER (1571–1630)

Conversation with Galileo's "Sidereal Messenger" (1610)

In March of 1610, the imperial mathematician to Emperor Rudolph II was startled by a messenger from the emperor bearing a book from Kepler's Italian colleague Galileo Galilei. The emperor, before forming his own opinion, wanted to know what the learned Kepler thought about Galileo's announcement that he had, through telescopic observation, discovered new planets and their moons. A few weeks later, the Tuscan ambassador at the court in Prague received a second copy of Galileo's book, which had been sent care of him by the astronomer himself. The interaction between the observational genius Galileo and the German theoretical astronomer Kepler allows us to eavesdrop on the email between two of the great Nobel Prize minds of Cal Tech. Kepler had established his fame for his laws of geometrical planetary motion (the planets move around the sun in elliptical orbits), as well as for his work on optics (inventing the ray theory of light) and calculus. His response to Galileo's announcements, for all its rambling and citation of authorities, clearly though somewhat reluctantly recognizes his colleague's momentous accomplishment. Though Kepler had studied at the observatory of Tycho Brahe, he could not bring himself to completely reject the symbolism of traditional astrology. Unable to dispense with the social pleasures of "predictive astrology," Kepler remained enamored of Neoplatonic principles of inherent forms: "I . . . am playing with symbols—in such a way that I never forget that I am playing." Galileo knew only what he saw with his senses, and had caused the split between astronomy and astrology that persists to this day.

Clock in the old city (Nicolas de Kadan), in Prague

To the Noble and Most Excellent Signor

Galileo Galilei, Gentleman of Florence, Professor of Mathematics at the University of Padua,

Johannes Kepler, His Sacred Imperial Majesty's Mathematician, sends his most cordial greetings.

I

For a long time I had stayed at home to rest, thinking of nothing but you, most distinguished Galileo, and your letters. For at the latest book fair there had been released to the public my treatise entitled "Commentary on the Motions of Mars," a labor of many years. From that time on, like a general who had won glory enough through a most strenuous military campaign, I took some respite from my studies. I supposed that among others Galileo too, the most highly qualified of all, would discuss with me by mail the new kind of astronomy or celestial physics which I had published, and that he would resume our interrupted correspondence, which had begun twelve years before.

But behold, a surprise report about my Galileo is brought to Germany by the couriers around March 15th. Instead of reading a book by someone else, he has busied himself with a highly startling revelation (to say nothing about the other subjects in his little book) of four previously unknown planets, discovered by the use of the telescope with two lenses. Johann Matthäus Wackher of Wackenfels, the illustrious Councilor of His Sacred Imperial Majesty and Referendary of the Sacred Imperial Aulic Council, told me the story from his carriage in front of my house. Intense astonishment seized me as I weighed this very strange pronouncement. Our emotions were strongly aroused (because a small difference of opinion of long standing between us had unexpectedly been settled). He was so overcome with joy by the news, I with shame, both of us with laughter, that he scarcely managed to talk, and I to listen. My amazement grew when Wackher stated that men of the highest reputation, raised by their erudition, seriousness, and steadfastness far above the unreliability of ordinary people, were transmitting these messages about Galileo, while his book was still at the printer's and would be made available by the next couriers.

When I left Wackher's presence, I was influenced most by Galileo's prestige, achieved by the soundness of his judgment and the subtlety of his mind. Therefore I bethought myself how there could be any increase in the number of planets without harm to my "Cosmographic Mystery," which I published thirteen years before. In that book Euclid's five solids, to which Proclus, following Pythagoras and Plato, applies the term "cosmic," permit no more than six planets around the sun.

Yet it is apparent from the preface to that book that I too at that time was looking for additional planets around the sun, but in vain.

Then, as I pondered over this development, the following idea occurred to me and I promptly conveyed it to Wackher. The earth, which is one of the planets (according to Copernicus), has its own moon revolving around it as a special case. In the same way, Galileo has quite possibly seen four other very tiny moons running in very narrow orbits around the small bodies of Saturn, Jupiter, Mars, and Venus. But Mercury, the last of the planets around the sun, is so deeply immersed in the sun's rays that Galileo has not yet been able to discern anything similar there.

Wackher, on the other hand, maintained that these new planets undoubtedly circulate around some of the fixed stars (he had for a considerable time been making some such suggestion to me on the basis of the speculations of the Cardinal of Cusa and of Giordano Bruno). If four planets have hitherto been concealed up there, what stops us from believing that countless others will be hereafter discovered in the same region, now that this start has been made?

Therefore, either this world is itself infinite, as Melissus thought and also the Englishman William Gilbert, the founder of the science of magnetism; or, as Democritus and Leucippus taught, and among the moderns, Bruno and Bruce, who is your friend, Galileo, as well as mine, there is an infinite number of other worlds (or earths, as Bruno puts it) similar to ours.

Such was my opinion, such was his, while, our hopes aroused, we waited for Galileo's book with an extraordinary longing to read it.

I succeeded in seeing the first copy, by permission of the emperor, and in leafing through it rapidly. I behold "great and most marvelous sights proposed to philosophers and astronomers," including myself, if I am not mistaken; I behold "all lovers of true philosophy summoned to the commencement of great observations."

At once I craved to plunge into the subject, inasmuch as I was invited; and since I had written on the same topic six years before, I yearned to discuss with you, most accomplished Galileo, in a highly agreeable kind of discourse, the many undisclosed treasures of Jehovah the creator, which He reveals to us one after another. For who is permitted to remain silent at the news of such momentous developments? Who is not filled with a surging love of God, pouring itself copiously forth through tongue and pen?

My eagerness was stimulated by the orders of the Most August Emperor Rudolph, who requested my opinion about this subject. But what shall I say about Wackher? I went to see him without the book, avowing that I had read it. There was bad feeling and even a quarrel. In the end we both agreed that I was not to delay becoming as expert as possible in this field.

While I was thinking the matter over, your letter to the ambassador of the Most Illustrious Grand Duke of Tuscany arrived, full of affection for me. You did me the honor of thinking that so great a man in particular should encourage me to write; and you sent along a copy of the book and added your own admonition. With the utmost graciousness the ambassador fulfilled this function as a kindness to you, and he most generously placed me under his patronage.

By my own inclination, then, at the instance of my friends, and at your urgent request I shall undertake this task. I am moved by some hope that if you should deem this letter of mine worthy of display, it may bring you this advantage: against the obstinate critics of innovation, for whom anything unfamiliar is unbelievable, for whom anything outside the traditional boundaries of Aristotelian narrowmindedness is wicked and abominable, you may advance reinforced by one partisan.

II

I may perhaps seem rash in accepting your claims so readily with no support from my own experience. But why should I not believe a most learned mathematician, whose very style attests the soundness of his judgment? He has no intention of practicing deception in a bid for vulgar publicity, nor does he pretend to have seen what he has not seen. Because he loves the truth, he does not hesitate to oppose even the most familiar opinions, and to bear the jeers of the crowd with equanimity. Does he not make his writings public, and could he possibly hide any villainy that might be perpetrated? Shall I disparage him, a gentleman of Florence, for the things he has seen? Shall I with my poor vision disparage him with his keen sight? Shall he with his equipment of optical instruments be disparaged by me, who must use my naked eyes because I lack these aids? Shall I not have confidence in him, when he invites everybody to see the same sights, and what is of supreme importance, even offers his own instrument in order to gain support on the strength of observations?

Or would it be a trifling matter for him to mock the family of the Grand Dukes of Tuscany, and to attach the name of the Medici to figments of his imagination, while he promises real planets?

Why is it that I find part of the book verified by my own experience and also by the affirmations of others? Is there any reason why the author should have thought of misleading the world with regard to only four planets?

Three months ago the Most August Emperor raised various questions with me about the spots on the moon. He was convinced that the images of countries and continents are reflected in the moon as though in a mirror. He asserted in particular that Italy with its two adjacent islands seemed to him to be distinctly outlined. He even offered his glass for the examination of these spots on subsequent days, but this was not done. Thus at that very same time, Galileo, when you cherished the abode of Christ our Lord above the mere appellation [of a Galilean], you vied in your favorite occupation with the ruler of Christendom (actuated by the same restless spirit of inquiry into nature).

But this story of the spots in the moon is also quite ancient. It is supported by the authority of Pythagoras and Plutarch, the eminent philosopher who also, if this detail helps the cause, governed Epirus with the power of a proconsul under the Caesars. I say nothing about Mästlin and my treatise on "Optics," published six years ago; these I shall take up later on in their proper place.

Such assertions about the body of the moon are made by others on the basis of mutually self-supporting evidence. Their conclusions agree with the highly illuminating observations which you report on the same subject. Consequently I have no basis for questioning the rest of your book and the four satellites of Jupiter. I should rather wish that I now had a telescope at hand, with which I might anticipate you in discovering two satellites of Mars (as the relationship seems to me to require) and six or eight satellites of Saturn, with one each perhaps for Venus and Mercury.

For this search, so far as Mars is concerned, the most propitious time will be next October, which will show Mars in opposition to the sun and (except for the year 1608) nearest to the earth, with the error in the predicted position exceeding 3°.

III

Well then, I shall discuss with you, Galileo, things which are absolutely certain and which may be seen, I confidently hope, with my own eyes. I shall follow the plan of your book, but I shall also touch upon all the parts of philosophy which are threatened with destruction or strengthened or clarified by your "Messenger." Hence there will be no residue to worry the reader who is devoted to philosophy, either to deter him from having faith in you, or to induce him to spurn the philosophy which has hitherto prevailed.

IV

The first section of your little book deals with the construction of the telescope. Its magnifying power is so great that the object viewed shows a thousandfold increase in surface. This enlargement is possible if the diameter appears 32 times longer. But if the observer's estimate approximates an impression of the normal size, the object must then seem 32 times nearer. For the eye does not see distance, but infers it, as we learn in optics. Suppose, for example, that a man 3200 paces away is subtended by an angle 32 times greater than that which, without a telescope, subtends a second man 100 paces away. Since the eye regards it as certain that the distant man has the usual height, it will judge that he is no more than 100 paces away. A contributing factor is the sharp definition bestowed on the image by the telescope.

So powerful a telescope seems an incredible undertaking to many persons, yet it is neither impossible nor new. Nor was it recently produced by the Dutch, but many years ago it was announced by Giovanni Battista della Porta in his "Natural Magic," Book XVII, Chapter 10, "The Effects of a Crystal Lens." And as evidence that not even the combination of a concave with a convex lens is a novelty, let us quote Della Porta's words. Here is what he says:

When you put your eye behind the middle of the lens, you will see far-away things so near that you seem almost to touch them with your hand. You will recognize your friends at a considerable distance. You will see the writing in a letter, placed at the proper range, so big that you may read it clearly. If you turn the lens, so that you look at the letter sideways, you will see the characters enlarged enough to be read even at a distance of 20 paces. *Indeed, if you know how to multiply the lenses, I have no doubt that you will descry the tiniest symbol at 100 paces,* as the characters are magnified by one lens after another. People with bad eyesight should use glasses according to the condition of their vision. Anybody who learns how to fit them correctly will gain no small secret. Concave lenses enable us to see quite clearly objects at a distance; convex lenses, objects close at hand. Hence you will be able to use them to improve your vision. Through a concave lens you see distant objects small but clear; through a convex lens, nearby objects larger but blurred. *If you know how to combine both types correctly,* you will see remote as well as nearby objects larger and clear. To many of my friends, to whom distant objects used to look obscure and nearby objects blurred, I have given no small help, with the result that they saw everything to perfection.

This is what he says in Chapter 10.

Over Chapter 11 he sets a new heading. "Lenses Whereby Anyone Can See to Unimaginable Distances." But his discussion of their construction (which he also explains) is so involved that you do not know what he is talking about, whether he is still dealing with transparent lenses, as in the previous chapter, or introducing an opaque polished mirror. I myself recall one such mirror, which reflects far-away objects on a very large scale without regard to their distance. Hence it shows them close by and also magnified in proportion, as clearly as can be expected from a mirror (which is necessarily dark in color).

Preceding this passage of Della Porta's book I noticed the following complaint at the beginning of Chapter 10:

"Nobody has yet published the theory and properties of concave and convex lenses and glasses, which are so essential to human needs." Six years ago in my "Optical Part of Astronomy" I endeavored to make clear by a lucid geometrical proof what happens in simple lenses.

In my fifth chapter, where I set forth the details of the process of vision, there may be seen on page 202 a diagram in which drawings of a concave and convex lens are joined exactly as they are generally combined nowadays in the familiar tubes. Did the reading of Della Porta's "Magic" give rise to this device? Or did some Dutchman, following Della Porta's instructions, manufacture many examples of this instrument as commodities for sale, the obligation to refrain from doing so having ceased with Della Porta's death? Even if not, that diagram on page 202 of my book could itself surely have indicated the construction to an alert reader, especially if he examined my proofs in conjunction with Della Porta's text.

Nor is it beyond belief that expert sculptors of painstaking workmanship, who use glasses to inspect the details of a figure, may also have accidentally stumbled on this device, while uniting convex lenses with concave in various ways, in order to choose the combination most serviceable to the eyes.

I do not advance these suggestions for the purpose of diminishing the glory of the technical inventor, whoever he was. I am aware how great a difference there is between theoretical speculation and visual experience; between Ptolemy's discussion of the antipodes and Columbus' discovery of the New World, and likewise between the widely distributed tubes with two lenses and the apparatus with which you, Galileo, have pierced the heavens. But here I am trying to induce the skeptical to have faith in your instrument.

After I began to work on my "Optics," the Emperor questioned me quite frequently about Della Porta's aforementioned devices. I must confess that I disparaged them most vigorously, and no wonder, for he obviously mixes up the incredible with the probable. And the title of Chapter 11 ("To Extend Vision to Unimaginable Distances") seemed to involve an optical absurdity; as though vision took place by a process of emanation, and lenses sharpened the ejaculations of the eye so that they would travel farther than if no lenses were employed; or if vision takes place by a process of reception, as Della Porta acknowledges, as though in that case lenses supplied or increased the light to make things visible. Rather is it true that no lens can ever detect objects which do not of themselves impart to our eyes some degree of light as the medium through which the objects acquire visibility.

Furthermore, I believed that the air is dense and blue in color, so that the minute parts of visible things at a distance are obscured and distorted. Since this proposition is intrinsically certain, it was vain, I understood, to hope that a lens would remove this substance of the intervening air from visible things. Also with regard to the celestial essence, I surmised some such property as could prevent us, supposing that we enormously magnified the body of the moon to immense proportions, from being able to differentiate its tiny particles in their purity from the lowest celestial matter.

For these reasons, reinforced by other obstacles besides, I refrained from attempting to construct the device.

But now, most accomplished Galileo, you deserve my praise for your tireless energy. Putting aside all misgivings, you turned directly to visual experimentation. And indeed by your discoveries you caused the sun of truth to rise, you routed all the ghosts of perplexity together with their mother, the night, and by your achievement you showed what could be done.

Under your guidance I recognize that the celestial substance is incredibly tenuous. To be sure, this property is made known on page 127 of my "Optics." If the relative densities of air and water are compared with the relative densities of the aether and air, the latter ratio undoubtedly shows a much greater disparity. As a result, not even the tiniest particle of the sphere of the stars (still less of the body of the moon, which is the lowest of the heavenly bodies) escapes our eyes, when they are aided by your instrument. A single fragment of the lens interposes much more matter (or opacity) between the eye and the object viewed than does the entire vast region of the aether. For a slight indistinctness arises from the lens, but from the aether none at all. Hence we must virtually concede, it seems, that that whole immense space is a vacuum.

With eagerness, then, I await your instrument, Galileo. Yet, if fate smiles on me so that I can overcome the obstacles and attempt the mechanical construction, I shall exert myself energetically in that endeavor, pursuing alternative courses. On the one hand, I shall increase the number of lenses. They will have on either side perfectly spherical surfaces of very slight curvature. I shall place them at fixed intervals in the tube, the outer lenses being a little wider. Even so, the eye will be located within the lim-its of the area where parallel rays passing through all the lenses converge. . . . On the other hand, to enable me more easily to correct the aberration (should there be any) in a single surface, I shall design a lens shaped like a nipple, to be used by itself. One of its surfaces will be practically plane, because its curvature will amount to only ½° or 30' of a spherically convex shell. The other surface, which is directed toward the eye, will not be spherical. My intention is to avoid. . . distortion and confusion of the parts of the object under observation. . . . Instead, the second surface will take the shape of a nipple. . . . Hence it will resemble the crystalline lens of the eye, because it will be bounded by the curvature of a hyperbolic line. . . . The aim is to achieve undistorted vision, in which the images of the parts of the object under observation are enlarged proportionally. . . .

ST. FRANCIS DE SALES (1567–1622)

INTRODUCTION À LA VIE DÉVOTE

Introduction to the Devout Life (1608; 1619)

After studying at the Jesuit school in Paris, Francis de Sales received his doctorate in law at the University of Padua. Then he opted for the priesthood and, after his ordination, was sent by the Roman Catholic Duke of Savoy to convert the Calvinists of Chablais. He became bishop of Geneva, where he founded the Order of the Visitation. The "patron saint of writers and journalists," canonized in 1665, he was the first writer in French to be named a "doctor of the Church." Francis wrote sermons, letters, essays, and canonical documents, in addition to a book entitled *The Love of God.* But his most influential writing, called by one pope, "the most perfect work of its kind," was the *Introduction to the Devout Life,* a series of spiritual instructions for persons wishing to pursue a spiritual life while remaining active in the secular world.

Although Francis had been taking notes along this line for years, his inspiration for compiling them was Madame de Charmoisy, the wife of an ambassador of the Duke of Savoy, who had placed herself under Francis' spiritual direction. Can a public official, whether secular prince or prince of the church, remain devout and attendant to the simplicities of Christian charity? Francis says yes, reversing Chaucer's warning, "What, if the gold rust, will the iron do?" We can see the impact of Francis' teachings today in the Cardinal of New York's visitations to AIDS clinics, Pope John Paul's insistence on meeting the poor and underprivileged in his worldwide travels, and Jesuit-educated Jerry Brown's sojourn with Mother Teresa in Calcutta.

AUTHOR'S PREFACE

For your own satisfaction and for mine, please read this preface.

The flower girl Glycera was so skilful that by rearranging her flowers she could make so many different bouquets that the painter Pausias, try as he might, could not capture their variety in his pictures.

In the same way, the Holy Spirit arranges the spiritual teaching which he puts before us through the tongues and pens of his servants with equal variety; the doctrines remain ever the same yet the manner in which they are presented differs according to the way they are arranged.

This *Introduction* contains nothing which has not already been written; the bouquet that I offer you is made up of the same flowers, but I have arranged them differently. Nearly everyone who has written about the spiritual life has had in mind those who live apart from the world, or at least the devotion they advocate would lead to such retirement. My intention is to write for those who have to live in the world and who, according to their state, to all outward appearances have to lead an ordinary life; and who, often enough, will not think of undertaking a devout life, considering it impossible; no one, they believe, ought to aspire to the palm of Christian piety while surrounded by the affairs of the world.

I will show them that a strong and resolute person may live in the world without being tainted by it, find spiritual springs amid its salt waters and fly through the flames of temptation without burning the wings on which they soar to God. True, it is no easy task and must be undertaken with much more zeal than many have so far shown, and I hope that this work will help those who undertake it with a generous heart.

This *Introduction* is not published entirely through my own choice or wish; an upright and virtuous person who, through the grace of God, aspired to a devout life, sought my help and, seeing how well disposed she was and being in many ways under an obligation to her, I set myself to do what I could.

Having led her through the suitable and necessary spiritual exercises, I left her some written notes to which she might refer. She later showed these notes to a wise and devout religious, who urged me to publish them, as he thought that they would be of great help to others. Because I valued his friendship and respected his judgement, I readily consented.

To make the whole work more presentable, I revised the notes and reduced them to some sort of order, adding various suitable pieces of advice, but I had to do this with very little leisure and so nothing has been treated at any great length; but what I have treated I have explained clearly and simply, at least that is what I have aimed at, but I have given no thought to style, as I have too much else to do.

My words are addressed to 'Philothea', because it is a name signifying one who loves God, or at least desires to do so, and I have divided this *Introduction* into five parts.

In the first part I seek to lead Philothea from a simple desire for the devout life to a strong resolution to embrace it, making this resolution after a general confession, and following it up with Holy Communion, when she receives her Saviour, gives herself to him and enters into his love.

In the second part, I show her two great means by which she may unite herself more closely to him; the Sacraments, by which he comes to us; prayer, by which we unite our-selves to him.

In the third part, I show her how to practise the various virtues by which she will advance, concentrating on those points which she could not have discovered for herself or easily have found anywhere else.

In the fourth part, I show her some of the snares of the Enemy, how she may escape them and go forward.

In the last part, I make her go aside for a while to refresh herself, take breath and renew her strength for further progress in the devout life.

In a capricious age such as this, many will say that it is the task of religious and spiritual directors to guide individual souls on the way to devotion, that such a work requires more leisure than a bishop with a diocese as large as mine can well afford, and must prove a distraction from affairs of greater importance. I answer, however, with St Denis, that it belongs primarily to bishops to lead souls to perfection since their order is supreme among men as that of the seraphim is among the angels, so their leisure could never be more worthily employed.

The ancient bishops and fathers of the Church were no less assiduous than we are yet their epistles witness that they willingly guided individual souls who sought their aid, imitating the Apostles themselves who garnered with special care and affection certain outstanding grains of corn while harvesting the whole world; everyone knows that Timothy, Titus, Philemon, Onesimus, St Thecla and Appia were specially guided by St Paul, as St Mark and St Petronilla were by St Peter (St Petronilla, as has been proved by Baronius and Galonius, being the spiritual daughter of St Peter, not his true daughter); and St John addressed one of his epistles to a devout woman named Electa.

To guide individual souls, I will admit, is exacting; but it is consoling work like that of the labourer in the vineyard, who is happiest when he has most to do. It is a work which refreshes the heart of those who undertake it, being a source of joy. A tigress, rescuing one of her young from the huntsman, feels it no bur-den, no matter how heavy it may be; love light-ens her load and rather than hindering her it makes her swifter in her race for safety. How much more willingly then will a father take upon himself the charge of one who seeks holi-ness, carrying the burden as a mother her child upon her breast, never weary of bearing one whom she loves so much. It is true that one must have a fatherly heart for such a task and that is why the apostles called their disciples not only their children but, to show their ten-derness, their *little* children.

It is true that I write about the devout life without being devout myself, though I certainly desire to be so, and it is my desire for devotion that encourages me to write. As a wise man once said, 'To become learned it is good to study, better to have a learned master, but best of all to teach others.' St Augustine, writing to Florentina, says: 'To give disposes us to receive', so, to teach disposes us to learn.

Alexander commanded Apelles to paint the beautiful Campaspe whom he loved, and Apelles, gazing upon her while he carried out his work, found her image impressed upon his heart and became so much in love with her that Alexander, when he saw this, took pity on him and allowed him to marry her, depriving himself for the sake of Apelles of the woman he loved most; showing, as Pliny says, the greatness of his heart more clearly than had he won a mighty battle.

I am convinced that it is God's will that as a bishop I should paint upon men's hearts, not merely the ordinary virtues but above all that of devotion, which is the most pleasing in his sight, and I undertake the work most willingly, as much to fulfil my duty as to become more devout myself through imprinting this virtue on the hearts of others, and I hope that if ever God sees that I truly love devotion, he will give her to me in an eternal marriage.

The beautiful Rebecca, watering the camels of Isaac, was chosen to be his wife and she received as pledge golden earrings and bracelets; so I hope that while I am leading God's beloved sheep to the waters of devotion, he in his goodness will make my soul his own; place in my ears the golden words of his love, and on my arms the bracelets of his strength, that I may put those words into practice, for this is the essence of that true devotion which I beg God to bestow on me and upon all the children of his Church; to which Church I wish always to submit my writings, actions, words, desires. . . my every thought.

Anneçy.

The Feast of St Mary Magdalen, 1609.

1. TRUE DEVOTION

You seek devotion, Philothea, because you know, as a Christian, that this virtue is most pleasing to God.

Since slight mistakes in beginning any scheme are magnified as it progresses until they become almost irreparable, it is of prime importance that you know the exact nature of this virtue.

As there is only one true devotion while there are many imitations, unless you know how to recognize the true you may easily be deceived and waste your time in pursuit of what is merely false and superstitious.

Aurelius used to paint all the faces in his pictures in the image and likeness of the woman he loved, in the same way everyone depicts devotion according to his own liking and fancy.

One who is bent on fasting considers himself devout on this account even though his heart is full of bitterness. He fears to moisten his tongue with wine or even water, in the name of sobriety, yet does not hesitate to drink deep of his neighbour's blood by calumny and detraction.

Another thinks himself devout because he recites a great number of prayers every day, even though he follows this up by saying peevish, proud and hurtful things to those about him.

Another cheerfully opens his purse to give alms to the poor, yet will not open his heart to forgive his enemies; another will forgive his enemies yet will not pay his debts until forced to do so by the law. Such people are often considered devout though they certainly are not.

When Saul's servants were seeking David in his house, Michol dressed a statue in David's clothes and laid it on his bed so that they thought he was sick and asleep; in the same way many people clothe themselves in various externals of devotion which pass for the real thing when in fact they are no more than statues, mere phantoms of devotion.

Real living devotion, Philothea, presupposes the love of God; is in fact that very love, though it has many aspects. In so far as this love adorns the soul and makes us pleasing to God it is called grace; in so far as it empowers us to do good, it is called charity; when it is so perfect that it moves us, not merely to do good, but to do good carefully, frequently and readily, then it is called devotion.

Ostriches never fly, hens fly sometimes but clumsily and not very high, but eagles, doves and swallows soar upwards swiftly and frequently.

In the same way sinners never fly towards God but travel on the earth seeking only earthly things. Those who are good but not yet devout do fly sometimes on the wings of good deeds, but slowly and ungracefully. Those who are devout soar on high to God frequently and readily.

In fact, then, devotion is nothing else but that spiritual alertness and vivacity which enables us to co-operate with charity promptly and wholeheartedly; and as it is the work of charity to make us keep generally and universally all God's commandments, so it is the work of devotion to make us do so promptly and diligently. No one, then, who fails to keep God's commandments can be counted either good or devout, for to be good one must have charity while to be devout one must not only have charity but practise it cheerfully and with alacrity.

Since devotion is a high degree of charity it not only makes us ready, active and diligent in keeping God's commandments but also moves us to do as much good as we can vigorously and zealously, going beyond what is commanded to what is merely counselled or inspired.

A man who has recently recovered from some illness walks slowly and heavily and only as far as necessary. Similarly, a sinner who has just been healed of his iniquity walks slowly and heavily and only as far as God commands, until he attains to devotion. Then, like a man in sound health, he not only walks but runs and leaps in the way of God's commandments and beyond that in the path of heavenly counsels and inspirations.

In conclusion, then, charity is to devotion what the fire is to the flame, for charity is a spiritual fire which is called devotion when it breaks into flame, which, added to charity, makes it ready, active and diligent not only in keeping God's commandments but also in practising the heavenly counsels and inspirations. . . .

3. DEVOTION SUITABLE TO ALL

At the creation God commanded the plants to bear fruit each according to its kind and he likewise commands Christians, the living branches of the vine, to bear fruit by practising devotion according to their state in life.

The practice of devotion must differ for the gentleman and the artisan, the servant and the prince, for widow, young girl or wife. Further, it must be accommodated to their particular strength, circumstances and duties.

Is the solitary life of a Carthusian suited to a bishop? Should those who are married practise the poverty of a Capuchin? If workmen spent as much time in church as religious, if religious were exposed to the same pastoral calls as a bishop, such devotion would be ridiculous and cause intolerable disorder.

Such faults are however very common; and the world, which cannot or will not distinguish between true devotion and the indiscretions of the self-styled devout, blames and criticizes devotion itself as responsible for those disorders.

True devotion, Philothea, never causes harm, but rather perfects everything we do; a devotion which conflicts with anyone's state of life is undoubtedly false.

Aristotle tells us that the bee sucks honey from the flowers without injuring them, leaving them as whole and fresh as when it found them. Devotion goes further, not only is it unharmful to any state of life, it adorns and beautifies it.

It makes the care of a family peaceful, the love of a husband and wife more sincere, the service of one's king more faithful, and every task more pleasant and a joy.

It is not only erroneous, but a heresy, to hold that life in the army, the workshop, the court, or the home is incompatible with devotion.

True, Philothea, monastic or religious devotion cannot be practised in these callings, yet these are not the only kinds of devotion; there are many others suitable for those who live in the world and capable of leading them to perfection.

Under the old law, the lives of Abraham, Isaac, Jacob, David, Job, Tobias, Sara, Rebecca and Judith are a proof of this. Under the new law, St Joseph, Lydia and St Crispin were perfectly devout in the workshop; St Anne, St Martha, St Monica, Aquila, Priscilla in their homes; Cornelius, St Sebastian, St Maurice in the army; Constantine, Helen, St Louis, Blessed

Amadeus and St Edward in the courts. It has even happened that many have fallen away in solitude, in itself so conducive to perfection, and preserved their virtue in the midst of crowds, which are unconducive to it, as hap-pened in the case of Lot who, as St Gregory says, lost in solitude the chastity he had so well preserved in the city. No, Philothea, wherever we find ourselves we not only may, but should, seek perfection.

DON LUIS DE GÓNGORA Y ARGOTE (1561–1627)

SOLEDADES

Solitudes (c.1615)

Recognized as the greatest poet of Spain's *siglo de oro,* the Cordovan Don Luis de Góngora was also so esoteric that "gongorism" has become synony-mous with self-conscious preciosity. In his work, as ornamentation disguises passionate clarity, the Renaissance has moved into the Baroque. The deca-dence and profanity of the poet's early life as a law student is reversely reflected in the dense conceits, syntactical convolutions, and Latinate neolo-gisms of his "cult" verse, written while serving as chaplain to Philip III. Aimed at the most cultivated reader, who might delight in the obscure allusions and highly contrived versification, Góngora's work has been compared to John Lyly's Euphues both in its mannered style and its popularity among the intelli-gentsia of his time. He is important for leading the Spanish language into unexplored territory. His idealism and stylistic celebration of beauty, his cre-ation of an entire word world in the image of his punning wit, influenced Edward Blake and Paul Verlaine as well as, in the twentieth century's revival of interest in Góngora, American poets Ezra Pound and Wallace Stevens.

The First Solitude

It was the flowery season of the year
In which Europa's perjured robber strays
—Whose brow the arms of the half-moon adorn,
The sun the shining armour of his hide—

Through sapphire fields to feast on stellar corn,
When, fitter cupbearer than Ganymede
For Jupiter, the lovesick boy gave tears
(Absent, disdained and shipwrecked) to the tide
And winds, which moved by his complaining
    lays
As to a new Arion's harp gave heed.

A pitying limb from mountain pine, opposed,
The constant enemy to Notus' strife,
Became no puny dolphin on that day
To the unthinking traveller who reposed,
Trusting to miserable boards his life,
And to an Ocean's Libya his way.

   Close by a headland, crowned
With sheltering feathers and dry rushes, he,
Engulfed before, then spewed up by the sea,
(Covered with foam, with seaweed girded)
    found
   A hospitable rest,
Where built the bird of Jupiter his nest.

   And having kissed the sand,
The fragment from the shivered hull he gave
As offering to the rocks, now from the wave
   Safe, and restored to land;
   For even boulders rude
Are flattered by the marks of gratitude.

Naked the youth, that ocean which before
His raiment drank, he gave back to the shore;
And then the garments to the sun he spread,
Which, with its gentle tongue of temperate fire,
Slowly attacked, but with no fierce desire,
The least wave sipping from the smallest
   thread.

Then the horizon from the evening light
—Which made unequal and confusedly
Mountains of water, oceans of the height—
   Not well distinguishing,
   And clad the youth forlorn
In what he had redeemed from the wild sea,
He trod the twilight down 'mid many a thorn;
Rocks, which to equal hardly had availed
   A swift intrepid wing,
He—more confused than he was weary—
   scaled.

   The summit crowned at last
   ——Of the resounding sea
   And of the silent land
A rampart strong and equal arbiter—
   With safer foot he passed

   Toward where, tremblingly,
Light indistinct and of brief splendour there
The lantern of a cottage, stood displayed,
At anchor in the uncertain gulf of shade,
   Showing the port at hand.

'O rays—if not the wavering sons,' he said,
'Of Leda—then of my misfortune be
   The shining boundary.'
And—of the barbarous, envying grove in dread
Lest it an obstacle should interpose,
Lest too the winds against him should cam-
   paign
He feared; thus as a hunter swiftly goes
Across both rugged mountains and soft plain,
   Who still retains in sight
(Despite the darkness all its beauty glows;
Even compared to stars it still is bright)
   The stone, unworthily
(If apocryphal tradition does not lie)
The crown of a dark animal whose brow
Is the bright chariot of nocturnal day:
   So diligently now
   He hastened on his way,
   With equal foot he strode
   Through thickets and smooth ground,
Still seeking—though the cold mist hid the
   road—
That ruby, his magnetic pole, the blaze,
   Despite the threatening sound
Of cracking branches and of Auster's rage.

   The watchdog was his guide,
Even though it bayed to affright the wanderer;
   That which far off he deemed
A little lantern now much greater seemed:
   The holm-oak, sturdy, bare,
Huge butterfly in cinders lay untied.

The youth arrived to be saluted there
Without ambition or the pomp of words
   By leaders of the herds
   Now holding Vulcan crowned.

   'O hermitage well found
   Whatever hour it be,
Temple of Pales, Flora's granary!

No artificer new
Models designed for thee, or sketches drew,
Adjusting to the skies' concavity
An edifice sublime; for here reveal
   The woods of oak and broom
   Thy poor and modest room,
   In which, instead of steel,
   Pure Innocence can keep
   The shepherd safe and sound—
   More than his pipe, the sheep.
   O hermitage well found
   Whatever hour it be!

   'Here no ambitious care
Can dwell, hydroptic of the empty air;
   Nor Envy with her food,
   The Egyptian serpent's brood;
Nor monster with a woman's face that springs
Out of a bestial body, who persuades—
Sphinxlike—the new Narcissus of our glades
To follow echoes and desert the springs;
Nor she who wastes in shows impertinent
The gunpowder that Time so meanly lent,
   O foolish Courtesy!
At whom the honest villagers may laugh
   Over their crooked staff.
   O well found hermitage
   Whatever hour it be!

   'Nor does thy threshold know
   Of Adulation bland,
Syren of royal palaces, whose sand
   So many vessels greet;
Of a canorous dream the trophies sweet.
Nor turning now her feathered sphere around
Is Pride seen here, while Flattery gilds her feet;
And Favour falls not to the foam below
On wings of wax from false security.
   O hermitage well found
   Whatever hour it be!'

Not of those hills—which rather seemed to
   show
A savage nature than fair courtesy—

These men appeared to be,
   Who the youth entertained
With the good-will of that first age unstained
   When in the woods content
The oak-tree gave them food, the ash their tent.

Instead of linen white, their sackcloth clean
   Covered the squared pine soon;
In boxwood (which, though rebel to the wheel,
Did elegance, not ornament reveal)
Milk—which pressed out that day the Dawn
   had seen,
Whose lilies white beneath her brow of gold
   With it could not compare—
   They gave him thick and cold,
Impenetrable almost to the spoon,
Ancient Alcimedon's invention rare.

He, who for near a lustrum was the spouse
Of twice a hundred she-goats,—whose sharp
   tooth
Allowed no cluster even on the brows
Of Bacchus, how much less upon his shoot—
(Always the conqueror in jealous strife
Love crowned him then, till rival tender-born
With no long beard and hardly hard of horn,
By killing him redeemed the threatened vine)
Offering himself as dried meat to the knife,
The purple threads displayed of scarlet fine.

Then the soft skins upon the cork-bed laid
Invited him to take more gentle rest,
Than to the prince between his Holland
   sheets
Purple of Tyre or Milanese brocade.
No Sisyphus, by fuming wines oppressed,
Climbing Ambition's hillside till he greets
The summit of his ponderous vanity,
The jest of Fortune when awake, was he.
No soldiers' trumpet nor disturbing sound
Of drums was there, to break his sleep pro-
   found;
Only the watch-dog could, enraged to hear
The dry leaves' rustle on an oak-tree near. . .

TIRSO DE MOLINA (GABRIEL TÉLLEZ) (C.1583–1648)

El burlador de Sevilla

The Playboy of Seville (1616)

"Don Juan" has become synonymous with that special brand of misogynism that preys on women in the guise of loving them. He is the unrestrained Renaissance man of hedonistic sexuality, the Doctor Faustus of the bedchamber, who breaks free from the bonds of medieval morality—leaving in his wake a trail of broken hearts. What unconquered worlds are to Christopher Marlowe's Tamburlaine, the female sex is to the atheistic free-spirited Don Juan. The ultimate seducer, Don Juan expresses his contempt for the women by amassing as many of their scalps as time allows. The idea of commitment, of taking a woman seriously as an equal, never occurs to him. His primary love is not for women but for himself. An itinerant Narcissus who must act out his self-infatuation at the expense of others, Don Juan's primary weapons are his own eloquence, grace, and wit. He is Castiglione's gentle courtier run amok among the ladies of street and court, his sexual "aberration" the opposite of his contemporary Hamlet's, whose madness makes him shy even of the fair Ophelia. François Truffaut's "The Man Who Loved Women" and Robin Hardy's *The Education of Don Juan* are but two of many twentieth-century renditions of the myth of which Tirso de Molina's *Playboy of Seville* is the first surviving dramatic treatment. Scarlett O'Hara, in *Gone With the Wind,* is a reverse Don Juan, with her "I'll worry about that tomorrow." Tirso, a widely traveled monk and devoted protégé of Lope de Vega, wrote nearly four hundred works, and was recognized in his own lifetime as a notable comedian and as the greatest tragedian of the *siglo de oro.* Yet he is remembered more for this play than for any of the eighty or so others that have come down to us. Tirso did not include it in his own compilation of his works. Although in other plays he shows great skill in portraying dominant women, in *Playboy* Tirso's women are as superficial as Don Juan considers them to be.

The Judgment of Paris (Peter Paul Rubens), in the Prado, Madrid

D. JUAN In that case you won't mind if I come
too.
    There's a little love-nest I'd like to find.
    A little plot I'd like to hatch. What about
    Courting ladies at their windows from
    The terrace below?

MOTA Don't mention below.
    Below ground's where I'll find myself
quite soon.
    Believe me. I'm a sick man, doomed to
die.

D. JUAN But what is your affliction?

MOTA Hopeless love!

D. JUAN You mean she doesn't favour you at all?

MOTA She does! She loves me, thinks the world
of me.

D. JUAN Who is she?

MOTA She's my cousin, Doña Ana!
    It's only recently she's come to live
    Here in Seville.

D. JUAN Where was she?

MOTA Lived in Lisbon
    With her father. He was ambassador.

D. JUAN Good looking girl?

MOTA No, more than that. Outstanding!
    When nature fashioned Ana de Ulloa,
    It must have been amazed by its achieve-
ment.

D. JUAN No woman is as beautiful as that!
    You prove it to me! I'll have to see her!

MOTA See her and you will see the greatest
beauty
    Any king could hope to cast his eyes on.

D. JUAN Well, why not marry her if she's so
pretty?

MOTA I can't. The King has just arranged her
marriage.
    But no one knows who she's supposed
to marry.

D. JUAN And yet she loves you?

MOTA Writes me daily too!

CATAL. *[Aside]* If he says any more, it serves him
  right!
  Spain's greatest trickster's got her in his
  sights!

D. JUAN A man can have such faith in a woman's
  Love and fear still some terrible misfor-
  tunc?
  You ought to show her off, be more
  forthcoming,
  Bombard her with your letters, lead her
  up
  The garden-path and stuff the world's
  opinion.

MOTA The only reason why I'm here's to find
  Out what decision's taken on the girl.

D. JUAN Then don't waste time! Go and find
  out! I'll wait
  Here for you. Come and tell me what
  they've done!

MOTA Alright! You wait for me! I'll be back soon.

Mota and his servant exit

CATAL. Farewell then, Mister Square or Mister
  Round.

SERVANT Farewell.

D. JUAN Well since we're on our own again,
  My friend, here's what you have to do
  for me.
  Just keep an eye on Mota! Follow him
  Closely. Go after him into the palace!

*Exit Catalinón. A woman calls to Don Juan
through the bars of her window*

WOMAN You there! Who are you?

D. JUAN Did someone call me?

WOMAN You seem a good and honest gentle-
  man,
  A friend of the Marquis. Give him this
  letter!
  I beg of you, please place it in his hands!
  The only other thing I need to say,
  My friend, is a lady's life depends on it.

D. JUAN I give my word, madam. You have my
  promise.
  In me you find both friend and gentleman
  Combined.

WOMAN My thanks, sir. I appreciate
  Your kindness. Fare you well!

The woman withdraws

D. JUAN She's disappeared.
  Was that a vision, a fantastic dream
  That seemed so magical but also real?
  I swear this letter reached me as though
  it
  Were transported by the wind or air!
  I wonder if the woman is the one
  Whose beauty our friend Mota's just
  been praising
  To the skies! If so, it's a piece of luck
  I'll not despise! Not for nothing am I
  Labelled the greatest trickster of Seville.
  My very favourite pastime, my delight's
  To trick a woman, steal away her honour,
  Deprive her of her treasured reputation.
  As for this letter, now I've left the
  square,
  I'm sorry, but I'll have to open it.
  Could be there's yet another trick in this
  For me. Already it gives me good cause
  To laugh. Let's have a look. At least I
  know
  That Ana de Ulloa is the sender.
  Here, clearly written, is her signature.
  And this is what it says: 'My love, my
  father
  Has betrayed me. Secretly he's arranged
  That I be married. It's impossible
  For me to disobey. I have no say
  In it. I don't know how I'll go on living.
  I'm certain this will bring about my
  death.
  If you, as I am sure you do, esteem
  My love and know my will, I beg of you,
  In honour of our love, do what I ask.
  I'll prove to you the depth of my affec-
  tion.

Come to my door at eleven o'clock
tonight.
　　You'll find the door already open. Come
Inside and there, cousin, your love for
me
　　And all your deepest hopes will be ful-
filled.
　　My maids will need to know you by your
dress.
　　So for their benefit it's best you wear
　　A cloak—crimson would be most suit-
able.
　　My love, my fate's entirely in your hands.
　　Farewell.' Farewell to love's appropriate,
I think, given these happy circum-
stances!
　　This trick delights me even as I think
　　Of how I'll see it through! I'll have this
girl
　　With all the ingenuity with which
　　The Duchess Isabela succumbed in
Naples!

Enter Catalinón

CATAL.　Here comes the Marquis, master!

D. JUAN　Both of us
　　Have pressing business to attend to,
designed
　　To occupy us half the night!

CATAL.　Executors
　　Of some new trick!

D. JUAN　The best of all! You'll see!

CATAL.　Not me! I don't approve of it. Besides,
　　The way you're going you are bound to
get
　　Your fingers burnt, and mine. I'm telling
you,
　　The man who spends his time deceiving
others
　　Is in the end deceived and comes off
second
　　Best. Live now and pay later! On the day
　　Of reckoning!

D. JUAN　You are a boring preacher,

And you've become too forward for a
servant!

CATAL.　Wisdom and reason make a brave man,
sir!

D. JUAN　And fear makes a coward! Some men,
fool,
　　Are born to serve, not born for bravery!
　　A servant has no will to call his own!
　　Does everything he's told and bites his
tongue!
　　A servant's like a man who's playing
cards.
　　To profit from the game he has to work,
　　The more he works the more he always
wins.
　　You work and shut your mouth you'll be
a winner!

CATAL.　Wise words, master! Many's the man
who's lost
　　At cards through opening his mouth too
soon!

D. JUAN　Make sure you learn the lesson. Don't
forget
　　It. I don't want to have to teach you
more!

CATAL.　I promise, master. Seen and never heard
　　I'll be! Obedient to your every word,
　　That's me! At your side my loyalty
　　Will force an elephant or fierce tiger
　　To its knees. And as for any blabbing
preacher,
　　He'd best look out! Give me the order,
sir,
　　To shut him up, I'll do it silently,
　　To good effect, and not a word I'll speak!

D. JUAN　Be silent! The Marquis is coming back!

CATAL.　Is he the one whose mouth I have to
shut?

Enter the Marquis of Mota

D. JUAN　A message for you, Marquis, that someone's
　　Just this minute asked me to give to you.

The message was delivered through this window,
    And though the speaker wasn't visible,
    The voice was unmistakably a woman's;
    Of that there's not the slightest doubt at all.
    She asks that you at twelve o'clock tonight
    Proceed with all discretion to her door
    (She says she'll leave it open from eleven),
    Where all your fondest hopes and steadfast love
    Will have their just reward and satisfaction.
    To avoid confusion and make recognition
    By the maids more certain, ensure you wear
    A crimson cloak.

MOTA Are you quite sure?

D. JUAN As sure
    As I'm your loyal friend! The message came
    From that window, and every word was clear,
    But not the speaker.

MOTA Oh, my friend! The message
    Has given me new hope where there was none!
    What proof of friendship! You, my dear friend,
    Bear all responsibility for my
    Rebirth! How can I show my gratitude?

D. JUAN Remember, friend, I'm not your lovely cousin!
    Your obligation, as I understand
    It, is to show your love for her, not me!
    I fancy your embraces would be better
    Spent on your lover!

MOTA Oh, my pleasure's such,
    I'm quite beside myself! How can I wait!
    Oh, sun, I beg of you, quicken your pace!

D. JUAN The sun's already sinking in the west.

MOTA Let's go quickly! We must prepare ourselves
    And dress in preparation for tonight.
    I'm quite beside myself!

D. JUAN *[Aside]* That's pretty plain
    To anyone. At twelve o'clock tonight
    It's not beside himself, more out of his mind
    He'll be!

MOTA Oh, cousin dear to my soul!
    That you reward me for my loyalty!

CATAL. *[Aside]* By God, look at the way this fellow prances!
    Who'd give a farthing for his cousin's chances?

Exit the Marquis. *Enter* Don Diego

D. DIEGO Don Juan! Where are you?

CATAL. It's your old father!

D. JUAN I'm here, my lord. Command me as you wish!

D. DIEGO I wish you were a bit more sensible,
    More honest, and a better reputation!
    I can't believe your every deed's designed
    Deliberately with my death in mind!

D. JUAN Oh, father! What is it makes you so angry?

D. DIEGO Your own stupidity! Tomfoolery!
    The King's just told me he's commanded you
    Be exiled from the city, thrown right out
    On account of a certain misdemeanour
    Of yours that with good cause has angered him.
    Although you hid the truth from me, the King
    Has been informed of it here in Seville.
    A crime so serious, hideously offensive,
    That I can barely force myself to speak!
    Such terrible behavior in the palace!
    Such treachery, committed in the name

Of friendship! Traitor! May God seek of you
A punishment appropriate to your crime!
And take note now that though it seems that God
Gives you permission for the things you do,
The day of judgement's never far behind.
The one thing that is absolutely sure
Is punishment for those who take His name
In vain. There's no judge more severe than God
In matters after death!

D. JUAN Why speak of death?
Plenty of time for me to pay that debt!
In any case, who's ready for it yet?

D. DIEGO My boy, the journey's shorter than you think.

D. JUAN And what about this journey I'm to make
To save my skin and satisfy the King?
You'll tell me next that journey has no end!

D. DIEGO Until you satisfy the grave offence
Against Octavio, who is a Duke no less,
And give sufficient time for all the scandal
To die down in Naples over that affair
With Isabela, the King's command is this:
You're exiled to Lebrija where you'll pay
For all your cunning and your treachery.
The King thinks such a punishment is just.
As far as I'm concerned, it's far too light!

CATAL. *[Aside]* If only the old man knew how his son
Had fooled the fishergirl, I'm sure that trick
Would let you see him even more choleric!

D. DIEGO In that case, seeing that my good advice
And prudent admonition are quite useless,
I recommend your punishment to God!

Exit Don Diego

CATAL. Look what you've done! The old man's left in tears!

D. JUAN Don't tell me you're about to join him too,
Though tears are quite appropriate to dotage!
Come on! It's dark already! I must find
The Marquis.

CATAL. Yes. Come on! Let's go and seek
An opportunity to fool his girl!

D. JUAN And this, you'll see, will be the best trick yet!

CATAL. Please God, I pray that you watch over me
And save your servant from catastrophe!

D. JUAN True to your name, a man who runs away!

CATAL. And you, master, a locust to all women!
There ought to be a public proclamation,
A timely warning of your destination
Delivered to all virgins everywhere:
'Beware this locust and this plague embodied
In a man! Take the greatest care with him,
Or he will rob you of your treasured harvest.
This man deceives all women as he will,
He is, no less, the trickster of Seville'.

D. JUAN Congratulations! What a fine description!

ROBERT BURTON (1577–1640)

The Anatomy of Melancholy (1621)

The downward-spiralling, nostalgic mood of Edmund Spenser's *Cantoes of Mutabilitie* is formalized in Burton's *Anatomy*, intended by the author to "analyze melancholy in all its causes and manifestations" as thoroughly and scientifically as Vesalius set out to dissect human anatomy. Burton's questioning of the relationship between melancholy and madness was published, fittingly, in the year the authors of *Hamlet* and *Don Quixote* died, and five years after Ariosto's *Orlando Furioso* appeared. Seventeenth-century thought considered melancholy to be caused by an overbalance of one of the four "humours" or bodily fluids, an intuitive foreshadowing of today's biochemical discoveries. If Prozac had existed in Burton's Oxford, he would have been among the first to experiment with its personal and sociological impact. The morbid depression he describes may be as characteristic of a fading era as it is of personal imbalance. Noteworthy for its sexist, racial, and nationalistic prejudices, *The Anatomy* reflects the popular attitude at the end of the twentieth century that spiritual diseases must be spiritually cured. Like his classical predecessor Plato and the medieval Dante, Burton carries on the belief in the vital integrity of the human body. But true to the Renaissance he chooses not a living but a mechanical model: "for our body is like a clock; if one wheel be amiss, all the rest are disordered, the whole fabrick suffers. . . ." In keeping with "modern" scholarly method, Burton calls upon all previous authority in order to continue the dialogue and to transcend those who wrote on the subject before him. Foreshadowing Sigmund Freud, Burton also draws from the well of literature and myth which he analyzes psychologically for the light they may throw on his concerns. As for the author himself, he lived his work: To those who objected to his subject matter he answered that he wrote about melancholy to avoid melancholy. Choosing the pen name Democritus Junior, he emulated the life of this classical melancholic. While Democritus cured himself of depressions by walking through the marketplace of Abdera and laughing at the human comedy, Burton, according to A. H. Bullen, stationed himself at a bridge in Oxford where he listened to the bargemen cursing, "at which he would set his hands to his sides and laugh most profusely."

MEMBER 3

Subsection 1—Definition of Melancholy, Name, Difference

Having thus briefly anatomized the body and soul of man, as a preparative to the rest, I may now freely proceed to treat of my intended object to most men's capacity, and after many ambages perspicuously define what this *Melancholy* is, shew his *name* and *differences.* The *name* is imposed from the matter, and disease denominated from the material cause, as Bruel observes, Melancholia, a sort of melaina (black) chole (choler), from black Choler. And whether it be a cause or an effect, a disease, or symptom, let Donatus Altomarus and Salvianus decide, I will not contend about it. It hath several descriptions, notations, and definitions. Fracastorius, in his second book of intellect, calls those *melancholy, whom abundance of that same depraved humour of black choler hath so misaffected, that they become mad thence, and dote in most things, or in all, belonging to election, will, or other manifest operations of the understanding.* Melanelius (out of Galen, Ruffus, Aetius) describes it to be *a bad and peevish disease, which makes men degenerate into beasts:* Galen, *a privation or infection of the middle cell of the head, &c.,* defining it from the part affected, which Hercules de Saxonia approves, calling it *a depravation of the principal function:* Fuschius, Arnoldus, Guianerius, and others: *by reason of black choler,* Paulus adds. Halyabbas simply calls it a *commotion of the mind;* Aretæus, *a perpetual anguish of the soul, fastened on one thing, without an ague;* which definition of his Mercurialis taxeth: but Ælianus Montaltus defends for sufficient and good. The common sort define it to be *a kind of dotage without a fever, having for his ordinary companions fear and sadness, without any apparent occasion.* So doth Laurentius, Piso, Donatus Altomarus, Jacchinus (on Rhasis), Valesius, Fuchsius, &c., which common definition, how-

soever approved by most, Hercules de Saxonia will not allow of, nor David Crusius; he holds it insufficient, *as rather shewing what it is not, than what it is:* as omitting the specifical difference, the phantasy and brain: but I descend to particulars. The most general class is *dotage, or anguish of the mind,* saith Aretæus, *of a principal part,* Hercules de Saxonia adds, to distinguish it from cramp and palsy, and such diseases as belong to the outward sense and motion; *depraved,* to distinguish it from folly and madness (which Montaltus makes the suffocation of the mind, to separate) in which those functions are not depraved, but rather abolished; *without an ague,* is added by all, to sever it from *phrenzy,* and that *melancholy* which is in a pestilent fever. *Fear* and *Sorrow* make it differ from *madness: without a cause* is lastly inserted, to specify it from all other ordinary passions of *Fear* and *Sorrow.* We properly call that *dotage,* as Laurentius interprets it, *when some one principal faculty of the mind, as imagination, or reason, is corrupted, as all melancholy persons have.* It is without a fever, because the humour is most part cold and dry, contrary to putrefaction. *Fear & Sorrow* are the true characters, and inseparable companions, of most melancholy, not all, as Hercules de Saxonia well excepts; for to some it is most pleasant, as to such as laugh most part; some are bold again, and free from all manner of fear and grief, as hereafter shall be declared.

Subsection 2—Of the Part Affected. Affection. Parties Affected

Some difference I find amongst writers about the principal part affected in this disease, whether it be the *brain,* or *heart,* or some other member. Most are of opinion that it is the *brain:* for, being a kind of *dotage,* it cannot otherwise be but that the *brain* must be affected, a similar part, be it by *consent* or *essence,* not in his ventricles, or any obstructions in them, for then it would be an apoplexy or epilepsy, as Laurentius well observes, but in a cold dry distemperature of it in his substance, which is corrupt and becomes too cold, or too dry, or else too hot, as in mad-men, and such as are inclined to it, and this Hippocrates confirms, Galen, Arabians, and most of our new writers. Marcus de Oddis (in a consultation of his, quoted by Hildesheim), and five others there cited are of the contrary part, because fear and sorrow, which are passions, be seated in the heart. But this objection is sufficiently answered by Montaltus, who doth not deny that the heart is affected (as Melanelius proves out of Galen) by reason of his vicinity; & so is the *midriff* and many other parts. They do sympathize, & have a fellow-feeling, by the law of nature: but forasmuch as this malady is caused by precedent *imagination,* with the *appetite,* to whom spirits obey, and are subject to those principal parts, the *brain* must needs primarily be misaffected, as the seat of *reason;* and then the *heart,* as the seat of *affection.* Cappivaccius and Mercurialis have copiously discussed this question, and both conclude the subject is the inner brain, and from thence it is communicated to the *heart,* and other inferior parts, which sympathize and are much troubled, especially when it comes by consent, and is caused by reason of the *stomack,* or *myrach,* as the Arabians term it, whole body, liver, or spleen, which are seldom free, *pylorus, meseraick veins, &c.* For our body is like a clock; if one wheel be amiss, all the rest are disordered, the whole fabrick suffers: with such admirable art and harmony is a man composed, such excellent proportion, as Lodovicus Vives, in his Fable of Man, hath elegantly declared.

As many doubts almost arise about the *affection,* whether it be *imagination* or *reason* alone, or both. Hercules de Saxonia proves it out of Galen, Aetius, and Altomarus, that the sole fault is in *imagination;* Bruel is of the same mind. Montaltus confutes this tenet of theirs, and illustrates the contrary by many examples: as of him that thought himself a shell-fish, of a Nun, & of a desperate Monk that would not be persuaded but that he was damned. *Reason* was in fault as well as *imagination,* which did

not correct this error. They make away themselves oftentimes, and suppose many absurd & ridiculous things. Why doth not *reason* detect the fallacy, settle and persuade, if she be free? Avicenna therefore holds both corrupt, to whom most Arabians subscribe. The same is maintained by Aretæus, Gordonius, Guianerius, &c. To end the controversy, no man doubts of *imagination,* but that it is hurt and misaffected here. For the other I determine with Albertinus Bottonus, a Doctor of Padua, that it is first in *imagination, and afterwards in reason, if the disease be inveterate, or as it is more or less of continuance:* but by accident, as Hercules de Saxonia adds; *faith, opinion, discourse, ratiocination, are all accidentally depraved by the default of imagination.*

To the part affected, I may here add the parties, which shall be more opportunely spoken of elsewhere, now only signified. Such as have the *Moon, Saturn, Mercury,* misaffected in their genitures; such as live in over-cold or over-hot climes: such as are born of *melancholy* parents: such as offend in those six non-natural things, are black, or of an high sanguine complexion, that have little heads, that have a hot heart, moist brain, hot liver and cold stomack, have been long sick: such as are solitary by nature, great students, given to much contemplation, lead a life out of action, are most subject to *melancholy.* Of sexes both, but men more often, yet women misaffected are far more violent, and grievously troubled. Of seasons of the year, the *Autumn* is most melancholy. Of peculiar times; old age, from which natural melancholy is almost an inseparable accident; but this artificial malady is more frequent in such as are of a middle age. Some assign 40 years, Gariopontus 30; Jubertus excepts neither young nor old from this adventitious. Daniel Sennertus involves all of all sorts, out of common experience. Aetius and Aretæus ascribe into the number *not only discontented, passionate, and miserable persons, swarthy, black; but such as are most merry & pleasant, scoffers & high coloured. Generally,* saith Rhasis, *the finest wits, and most generous spir-*

its, are before other obnoxious to it. I cannot except any complexion, any condition, sex, or age, but fools and Stoicks, which, according to Synesius, are never troubled with any manner of passion, but, as Anacreon's grasshopper, free from pain and flesh and blood, almost a little god. Erasmus vindicates fools from this melancholy catalogue, because they have most part moist brains, and light hearts, *they are free from ambition, envy, shame and fear, they are neither troubled in conscience, nor macerated with cares, to which our whole life is most subject.*

Subsection 4—Of the Species or Kinds of Melancholy

When the matter is diverse and confused, how should it otherwise be, but that the species should be diverse and confused? Many new and old writers have spoken confusedly of it, confounding *melancholy and madness,* as Heurnius, Guianerius, Gordonius, Sallustius Salvianus, Jason Pratensis, Savanarola, that will have *madness* no other than *melancholy* in extent, differing (as I have said) in degrees. Some make two distinct species, as Ruffus Ephesius, an old writer, Constantinus Africanus, Aretæus, Aurelianus, Paulus Ægineta: others acknowledge a multitude of kinds, and leave them indefinite, as Aetius in his Tetrabiblos, Avicenna, Arculanus, Montanus. *If natural melancholy be adust, it maketh one kind; if blood, another; if choler, a third, differing from the first; and so many several opinions there are about the kinds, as there be men themselves.* Hercules de Saxonia sets down two kinds, *material and immaterial; one from spirits alone, the other from humours and spirits.* Savanarola will have the kinds to be infinite; one from the *myrach,* called *myrachialis* of the Arabians; another *stomachalis,* from the *stomack;* another from the *liver, heart, womb, hemrods, one beginning, another consummate.* Melancthon seconds him, *as the humour is diversely adust and mixed, so are the species diverse.* But what these men speak of species, I think ought to be understood of symptoms, and so doth Arculanus interpret himself: infinite species, that is, symptoms: and in that sense, as Jo. Gorrhæus acknowledgeth in his medicinal definitions, the species are infinite, but they may be reduced to three kinds, by reason of their seat; *head, body,* and *hypochondries.* This threefold division is approved by Hippocrates in his Book of Melancholy (if it be his, which some suspect); by Galen, by Alexander, Rhasis, Avicenna, & most of our new writers. Th. Erastus makes two kinds; one perpetual, which is *head melancholy;* the other interrupt, which comes and goes by fits, which he subdivides into the other two kinds, so that all comes to the same pass. Some again make four or five kinds, with Rodericus à Castro, and Lod. Mercatus, who in his second book will have that melancholy of nuns, widows, and more ancient maids, to be a peculiar species of melancholy differing from the rest. Some will reduce enthusiasts, exstatical and demoniacal persons, to this rank, adding *love melancholy* to the first, and *lycanthropia.* The most received division is into three kinds. The first proceeds from the sole fault of the *brain,* & is called *head melancholy:* the second sympathetically proceeds from the *whole body,* when the whole temperature is melancholy: the third ariseth from the bowels, liver, spleen, or membrane called *mesenterium,* named *hypochondriacal or windy melancholy,* which Laurentius subdivides into three parts, from those three members, *Hepatick, splenetick, meseraick. Love melancholy,* which Avicenna calls *ilishi,* & *lycanthropia,* which he calls *cucubuth,* are commonly included in head melancholy: but of this last, which Gerardus do Solo calls *amorous,* and most, *Knight melancholy,* with that of *religious melancholy, of virgins & widows, maintained by Rod.* a Castro and Mercatus, and the other kinds of *love melancholy,* I will speak apart by themselves in my third partition. The three precedent species are the subject of my present discourse, which I will anatomize, & treat of, through all their causes, symptoms, cures, together and apart; that every man that is any measure affected with this malady, may know how to examine it in himself, and apply remedies unto it.

It is a hard matter, I confess, to distinguish these three species one from the other, to express their several causes, symptoms, cures, being that they are so often confounded amongst themselves, having such affinity, that they can scarce be discerned by the most accurate Physicians, & so often intermixed with other diseases, that the best experienced have been plunged. Montanus names a patient that had this disease of melancholy & *caninus appetitus* both together: and with *vertigo;* Julius Cæsar Claudinus with stone, gout, jaundice; Trincavellius with an ague, jaundice, *caninus appetitus,* &c. Paulus Regoline, a great Doctor in his time, consulted in this case, was so confounded with a confusion of symptoms, that he knew not to what kind of melancholy to refer it. Trincavellius, Fallopius, and Francanzanus, famous Doctors in Italy, all three conferred with about one party at the same time, gave three different opinions. And, in another place, Trincavellius being demanded what he thought of a melancholy young man, to whom he was sent for, ingenuously confessed, that he was indeed melancholy, but he knew not to what kind to reduce it. In his 17th consultation, there is the like disagreement about a melancholy monk. Those symptoms, which others ascribe to misaffected parts and humours, Herc. de Saxonia attributes wholly to distempered spirits, & those immaterial, as I have said. Sometimes they cannot well discern this disease from others. In Reinerus Solenander's counsels, he and Dr. Brande both agreed, that the patient's disease was hypochondriacal melancholy. Dr. Matholdus said it was *asthma,* and nothing else. Solenander and Guarionius, lately sent for to the melancholy Duke of Cleve, with others, could not define what species it was, or agree among themselves. The species are so confounded, as in Cæsar Claudinus his 44th consultation for a Palonian Count; in his judgment *he laboured of head melancholy, and that which proceeds from the whole temperature, both at once.* I could give instance of some that have had three kinds at one and the same time, and some successively. So that I conclude of our melancholy species, as many Politicians do of their pure forms of Commonwealths, Monarchies, Aristocracies, Democracies, are most famous in contemplation, but in practice they are temperate and usually mixed, (so Polybius informeth us) as the Lacedæmonian, the Roman of old, German now, and many others. What Physicians say of distinct species in their books, it much matters not, since that in their patients' bodies they are commonly mixed. In such obscurity, therefore, variety and confused mixture of symptoms, causes, how difficult a thing it is to treat of several kinds apart; to make any certainty or distinction among so many casualties, distractions, when seldom two men shall be like affected in every respect. 'Tis hard, I confess, yet nevertheless I will adventure through the midst of these perplexities, & led by the clue or thread of the best writers, extricate myself out of a labyrinth of doubts and errors, and so proceed to the causes.

BEN JONSON (1572–1637)

To the memory of my beloved the author, Mr. William Shakespeare, and what he hath left us (1623)

Dramatists, like all human creators, must depend upon Fortune's roulette wheel for their fame or lack of it. One of the great ironies in the history of the British theater is the eclipse of so many dramatic luminaries by William Shakespeare. In any other time, Thomas Decker, Thomas Kyd, Christopher Marlowe, and John Webster might have captured and maintained the spotlight of supreme recognition and honor in their own lifetimes. All were outstanding writers, worthy of the highest aspirations of theater. Like Shakespeare, Ben Jonson, who among many in his own century was considered greater than Shakespeare, began his theatrical career as an actor. Jonson's greatest plays *Volpone, The Silent Woman, The Alchemist,* and *Every Man in his Humour,* show an unsurpassed classical precision and symmetry. Shakespeare himself acted in Jonson's *Every Man in His Humour* in 1598. Jonson, for his outstanding court masques (of which he wrote and produced thirty-three), was made Poet Laureate by James I in 1616. His best known poem is perhaps his second "Song to Celia":

> Drink to me only with thine eyes,
> And I will pledge with mine;
> Or leave a kiss but in the cup,
> And I'll not look for wine.
> The thirst that from the soul doth rise
> Doth ask a drink divine;
> But might I of Jove's nectar sup,
> I would not change for thine.
> I sent thee late a rosy wreath,
> Not so much honoring thee,
> As giving it a hope that there
> It could not withered be.
> But thou thereon didst only breathe,
> And sent'st it back to me,
> Since when it grows and smells, I swear,
> Not of itself, but thee.

That Jonson was chosen to write this verse eulogy to Shakespeare's memory, in the 1623 edition of "Mr. William Shakespeare's Comedies, Histories, and Tragedies," is tribute to his respect and popularity among the frequenters of London's literarily famous Mermaid Tavern.

To draw no envy, Shakespeare, on thy name,
  Am I thus ample to thy book and fame,
While I confess they writings to be such
  As neither man nor Muse can praise too
    much;
'Tis true, and all men's suffrage. But these ways
  Were not the paths I meant unto thy praise,
For seeliest ignorance on these may light,
  Which when it sounds at best but echoes
    right;
Or blind affection which doth ne'er advance
  The truth, but gropes and urgeth all by
    chance;
Or crafty malice might pretend this praise,
  And think to ruin where it seemed to raise.
These are as some infamous bawd or whore
  Should praise a matron; what could hurt her
    more?
But thou art proof against them, and indeed
  Above th' ill fortune of them, or the need.
I, therefore, will begin. Soul of the age!
  The applause, delight, the wonder of our
    stage!
My Shakespeare, rise; I will not lodge thee by
  Chaucer, or Spenser, or bid Beaumont lie
A little further to make thee a room;
  Thou art a monument, without a tomb,
And art alive still, while thy book doth live
  And we have wits to read and praise to give.
That I not mix thee so, my brain excuses—
  I mean with great but disproportioned
    muses,—
For if I thought my judgment were of years
  I should commit thee surely with thy peers,
And tell how far thou didst our Lyly outshine,
  Or sporting Kyd, or Marlowe's mighty line.
And though thou hadst small Latin and less
    Greek,
  From thence to honor thee I would not seek
For names, but call forth thund'ring Æschylus,
  Euripides, and Sophocles to us,

Pacuvius, Accius, him of Cordova dead,
  To life again, to hear thy buskin tread
And shake a stage; or, when thy socks were on,
  Leave thee alone for the comparison
Of all that insolent Greece or haughty Rome
  Sent forth, or since did from their ashes come.
Triumph, my Britain, thou hast one to show
  To whom all scenes of Europe homage owe.
He was not of an age, but for all time!
  And all the Muses still were in their prime,
When like Apollo he came forth to warm
  Our ears, or like a Mercury to charm!
Nature herself was proud of his designs,
  And joyed to wear the dressing of his lines
Which were so richly spun, and woven so fit,
  As since, she will vouchsafe no other wit;
The merry Greek, tart Aristophanes,
  Neat Terence, witty Plautus, now not please,
But antiquated and deserted lie
  As they were not of nature's family.
Yet must I not give nature all; thy art,
  My gentle Shakespeare, must enjoy a part;
For though the poet's matter nature be,
  His art doth give the fashion; and that he
Who casts to write a living line, must sweat,
  Such as thine are, and strike the second heat
Upon the Muses' anvil, turn the same,
  And himself with it, that he thinks to frame;
Or for the laurel he may gain a scorn,
  For a good poet's made, as well as born;
And such wert thou. Look how the father's face
  Lives in his issue; even so the race
Of Shakespeare's mind and manners brightly
    shines
  In his well-turnëd and true-filëd lines,
In each of which he seems to shake a lance,
  As brandished at the eyes of ignorance.
Sweet swan of Avon! what a sight it were
  To see thee in our waters yet appear,
And make those flights upon the banks of
    Thames

That so did take Eliza, and our James!
But stay, I see thee in the hemisphere
   Advanced, and made a constellation there!
Shine forth, thou star of poets, and with rage

Or influence chide or cheer the drooping stage;
Which since thy flight from hence, hath
   mourned like night,
And despairs day, but for thy volume's light.

FRANCISCO GÓMEZ DE QUEVEDO Y VILLEGAS (1580–1645)

SUEÑOS

Visions (1627)

The darkness of Quevedo's dreamlike meditation, regarded as the masterpiece of seventeenth-century Spanish literature, sounds the death knell for an age that experienced a revolutionary breakdown of the rigid feudal order. In this twilight of the Renaissance, the excitement of rebirth and exploration has evolved into suffocation and terror. The *siglo de oro* is tarnished by its own excesses. When all is permitted to the human mind without restriction, the results may be brilliant self-expression. But they may also be the self-destructive implosion that comes from over-extending one's ambitions and denying all discipline. Dreams turn into nightmares, as illustrated by the eighteenth-century Francisco de Goya's famous *Capricho,* "The Sleep of Reason Produces Monsters," which Quevedo inspired. A self-proclaimed stoic and biting critic of the corruption he saw all around him in the courts of Philip II and Philip III, Quevedo was constitutionally unable to practice his stoicism and was himself as decadent as the next courtier. Like the Italian Pietro Aretino and the French François Villon before him, he takes as the subject of his satirical dreams the scandals of the aristocracy, but also the machinations of greedy lawyers, the quackery of doctors, the avarice of corrupt judges, the usury of bankers, and the blackmails practiced by whores and their pimps. The gap between his ideals and his habits could not have been greater. His pervasive pessimism could not be further, on the spectrum, from Castiglione's optimistic idealism. In Quevedo's *Sueños,* a guided tour of hell that does justice to the imagination of Hieronymous Bosch, melancholy has become high anxiety; and the Renaissance, its banquet of infinite courses winding down, receives the final check.

Dead Christ (El Greco), in the Prado, Madrid

II

Of Death and Her Empire

I have made it a common remark, that mean souls generally breed sad thoughts, and in solitude, they gather in troops to assault the wretched, which is the trial wherein the coward does most betray himself; and yet I cannot, notwithstanding my utmost efforts, when I am alone, avoid those accidents and surprises in myself, which I condemn in others. I have sometimes, upon reading the grave and severe Lucretius, been seized with a surprising damp; whether from his striking counsels upon my passions, or some tacit reflection of shame upon myself, I know not. However, to render this confession of my weakness the more excusable, I will begin my discourse with somewhat out of that elegant and inimitable poet.

"Let us imagine", says he, "that a voice from Heaven should thus speak to any of us: What ails thee, O mortal man! or to what purpose is it to spend thy life in groans and complaints, under the fear of death! Where are thy past years and pleasures? Are they not vanished and lost in the flux of time, as if thou hadst put water into a sieve? Bethink thyself then of a retreat, and leave the world with the same content and satisfaction, as thou wouldst do a table genteelly furnished, and a merry company, upon a full stomach. Wretched mortal that thou art! thus to weary and torment thyself, when thou mayest live peaceably and with content".

This passage brought into my mind the words of Job, chap. xiv.; and I was carried on from one meditation to another, till at length I fell fast asleep over my book; which I ascribed rather to a favourable providence, than to my natural disposition. So soon as my soul felt herself at liberty, she entertained me with the following comedy, my fancy supplying both the stage and the actors.

In the first scene entered a troop of physicians, upon their mules, with deep housings, marching not very regularly, sometimes fast, sometimes slow, and, to say the truth, most commonly in a group. They were all wrinkled and withered about the eyes, I suppose with casting so many sour looks upon the urinals and close-stools of their patients; bearded like goats; and their faces so overgrown with hair, that their fingers could hardly find the way to their mouths: in the left hand they held the reins, and their glove, rolled up together; and in the right a cane, which they carried rather for show than correction; for they understood no other way of managing their animals but by the heels; and all along head and body went together, like a baker upon his panniers. Several of them, I observed, had huge gold rings upon their fingers, set with stones of so large a size, that they could hardly feel a patient's pulse, without minding him of his monument. There were a great many of them, with several puny licentiates at their heels, that came out graduates, by conversing rather with the mules than with the doctors. Well, said I to myself, if there requires no more than this to make a physician, it is no wonder we pay so dear for their experience.

These were followed by a vast multitude of apothecaries, laden with pestles and mortars, suppositories, spatulas, glister-pipes, and syringes, all ready charged, and as mortal as gunshot; together with several boxes, intituled, "Remedies without, but poisons within". You may observe, that when a patient comes to die, the apothecary's mortar rings the passing bell, as the priest's requiem finishes the business. An apothecary's shop is, in effect, no other than the physician's armoury, that supplies him with weapons; and, to say the truth, the instruments of the apothecary and the soldier are much of a quality; what are their boxes, but pikes; their syringes, but pistols; and their pills, but bullets? Yet, after all, considering their purgative medicines, we may properly enough call their shops Purgatory; and why not their persons, Hell; their patients, the Damned; and their masters, the Devils? . . .

After these came the surgeons laden with pincers, crane-bills, catheters, disquamatories, dilators, scissors, and saws; and with them so dreadful an outcry of cut, tear, open, saw, flay, burn, that my bones were ready to creep one into another, for fear of an operation.

Then came a set of people, whom, by their dress, I should have taken for devils in disguise, if I had not spied their chains of rotten teeth, which put me in some hope they might be tooth-drawers; and so they proved. This is one of the lewdest trades in the world; for they are good for nothing but to depopulate our mouths, and make us old before our time. Let a man but yawn, and you shall have one of these rogues examining his grinders; and there is not a sound tooth in your head, but he had rather see it at his girdle, than in the place of its nativity; nay, rather than fail, he will pick a quarrel with your gums. But that which puts me out of all patience, is to see these scoundrels ask twice as much for drawing an old tooth, as would have bought me a new one.

I now said to myself, we are now past the worst, unless the devil himself come next: and in that instant I heard the brushing of guitars, and the rattling of citterns, raking over certain allegros and sarabands. These are a kennel of barbers, thought I, or I will be hanged; and any man that had ever seen a barber's shop, might have told you as much without a conjuror, both by the music, and by the very instruments, which are as proper a part of a barber's furniture, as his comb-cases and wash-bowls. It was droll enough to see them lathering asses' heads, of all sorts and sizes, and their customers all the while winking and spluttering over their basins. Presently, after these, appeared a concert of loud and tedious talkers, that tired and deafened the company with their shrill and constant babbling. These were of various kinds; some they called swimmers, from the motion of their arms in all their discourses, which was just as if they had been paddling. Others they call apes, or mimics. These were perpetually making faces, and a thousand antic, foolish gestures, in derision and imitation of others. In the third place were sowers of dissension; and these were still rolling their eyes like a Bartlemy puppet, without so much as moving the head, and leering over their shoulders, to surprise people at unawares in their familiarities and privacies, and gather matter for calumny and detraction. Liars followed next; and these seemed to be a jolly, contented sort of people, well fed and well clothed; and having nothing else to trust to, methought it was a strange trade to live upon. I need not tell you that they always have a full audience, since their congregation consists of all the fools and impertinents.

After these came a company of meddlers; a pragmatical, insolent generation of men, that will have an oar in every boat, and are, indeed, the bane of honest conversation, and the pest of all companies. Then came the most prostitute of all, I mean flatterers, who were only devoted to their own profit. I thought this had been the last scene, because no more came upon the stage for a considerable time; and indeed I wondered that they came so late; but one of the babblers told me, unasked, that this kind of serpent, carrying his venom in his tail, it seemed reasonable, that being the most poisonous of the whole gang, they should bring up the rear.

I then began to consider what might be the meaning of this olio of people, of several conditions and humours met together; but I was presently diverted from that consideration, by the apparition of a creature, which looked as if it were of the feminine gender. It was a person of a thin and slender make, laden with crowns, garlands, sceptres, scythes, sheep-hooks, pattens, hob-nailed shoes, tiaras, straw hats, mitres, caps, embroideries, skins, silk, wool, gold, lead, diamonds, shells, pearl and pebbles. She was dressed up in all the colours of the rainbow; she had one eye shut, the other open; young on the one side, and old on the other. I thought at first she had been at a great distance, when indeed she was very near me; and when I took her to be at my chamber-door, she was at my bed's head. How to unriddle this mystery I knew not; nor was it possible for me to understand the meaning of an equipage so extravagant, and so fantastically put together. It gave me no fright, however; but, on the contrary, I could not forbear laughing; for it came just into my mind, that I had formerly seen, in Italy, a farce where the mimic, pretending to come from the infernal regions, was just thus accoutred; and never was anything more nonsensically pleasant. I held as long as I could, and at last I asked what she was? She answered, "I am Death." Death! the very word made me tremble: I beseech you, Madam, said I, with great humility and respect, whither is your honour going? No farther, said she, for now I have found you I am at my journey's end. Alas! and must I die then? said I. No, no, replied Death, but I will take thee alive along with me: for since so many of the dead have been to visit the living, it is but equal, for once, that one of the living should return a visit to the dead. Get up, then, and come along, without reluctance; for what you will not do willingly, you shall do in spite of your teeth. This put me in a cold fit; but, without more delay, up I started, and desired leave to put on my breeches. No, no, said she, no matter for clothes, no body wears them upon this road: Come away, naked as you are, and you will travel the better. So up I got, without saying any more, and followed her, in such a terror and amazement, that I was in an ill condition to take a strict account of my passage; yet I remember, upon the way, that I told her that under correction, she was no more like the Deaths I had seen, than a horse is like a cat: Our Death, I said, was represented with a scythe in her hand, and a carcass of bones, as clean as if the crows had picked it. Yes, yes, said she, turning short upon me, I know that very well; but, in the meantime, your designers and painters are but a parcel of blockheads. The bones you talk of, are the dead, or, otherwise, the miserable remainders of the living; but let me tell you, that you yourselves make your own death; and that which you call death, is but the period of your life, as the first moment of your birth is the beginning of your existence: And, actually you die living, and your bones are no more than what Death has left, and committed to the grave. If this were rightly understood, every man would find a *memento mori,* or a Death's head, in his own looking-glass; and consider every house with a family in it, but as a sepulchre filled with dead bodies; a truth which you little dream of, though within your daily view and experience. Can you imagine a Death elsewhere, and not in yourselves? Believe it, you are greatly mistaken; for you yourselves are skeletons before you know anything of the matter.

But pray, Madam, cried I, what may all these people be that keep your ladyship company? And since you are Death, as you say, what is the reason that the babblers and the slanderers are nearer your person, and more in your graces than the physicians? Why, replied she, there are more people talked to death, and despatched by babblers, than by all the pestilential diseases in the world. And then, your slanderers and meddlers kill more than your physicians;

though (to give the gentlemen of the faculty their due) they labour perpetually for the enlargement of our empire: For you must understand, that though distempered humours make a man sick, it is the physician kills him; and he expects to be well paid for it too; and it is fit that every man should live by his trade. So that, when a man is asked what such and such a one died of, he is not presently to make answer, that he died of a fever, a pleurisy, the plague, or the palsy, but that he died of the doctor. In one point, however, I must needs acquit the physician: You know that the style honourable and worshipful, which was heretofore appropriated only to persons of eminent degree and quality, is, nowadays, used by all degrees of people; nay, the very bare-foot friars, that live under vows of humility and mortification, are stung with this itch of title and vain glory. Your ordinary tradesmen, as vintners, tailors and masons, must be all dressed up, forsooth, in the worshipful; whereas, your physician does not so much court honour: Even if it should rain dignities, he would scarce be persuaded to venture the wetting; but sits down contented with the honour of disposing of your lives and money, without troubling himself about any other reputation.

The entertainment of these lectures and discourses made the way seem short and agreeable; and we were just now entering into a place, but barely illuminated, and of horror enough, if Death and I had not, by this time, been very well acquainted. Upon one side of the passage I saw three moving spectres, armed, and of human shape, and so like each other that I could not say which was which. Just opposite, on the other side, was a dreadful monster, in a fierce and obstinate combat with these. Here Death made a stop, and facing about, asked me if I knew these people? Alas! no, said I; Heaven be praised I do not; and I shall put it in my Litany, that I never may. How ignorant thou art! cried Death; these are thy old acquaintance, and thou hast hardly ever kept any other company since thou wert born. Those three are the World, the Flesh and the Devil, the capital enemies of thy soul: And they so much resemble each other, as well in quality as appearance, that effectually, whoever has one, has all. The proud and ambitious man thinks he has got the World, but it proves the Devil. The lecher and the epicure persuade themselves that they have gotten the Flesh, but that is the Devil too; and, in a word, thus it fares with all other kinds of extravagants. But what is here, said I, that appears in such various shapes, and fights against the other three? That, replied Death, is the Devil of Money, who maintains that he himself alone is equivalent to the three, and that whenever he comes, there is no need of them. Against the World, he urges from its own confession: For it passes for an oracle, that there is no world but money. He that is out of money, is out of the world. Take away a man's money, and take away his life. Money answers all things. Against the second enemy, he pleads that money is the flesh too; witness the girls and Ganymedes it procures and maintains. And against the third he urges that there is nothing to be done without money. Love does much, but money does everything: And money will make the pot to boil, though the devil piss in the fire. So that, for ought I see, said I, the Devil of Money has the better end of the staff.

After this, advancing a little farther, I beheld on the one hand Judgment, and Hell on the other, for so Death called them. Making a stop, upon the sight of Hell, to view it more narrowly. Death asked me what it was I looked at. I told her it was Hell; and I was the more intent upon it, because I thought I had seen it somewhere else before. She asked me, where? I told her that I had seen it in the corruption and avarice of wicked magistrates; in the pride and haughtiness of courtiers; in the appetites of the voluptuous; in the lewd designs of Ruin and Revenge; in the souls of oppressors; and in the vanity of princes. But he that would see it whole and entire, in one subject, must examine the hypocrite, who is a kind of religious broker, and puts out at five-and-forty per cent. the very sacraments and the ten commandments.

I am very well pleased too, said I, that I have seen Judgment, as I find it here, in its purity; for that which we call judgment in the world, is a mere mockery: If it were like this, men would live in another manner than they do. If it be expected that our judges should govern themselves and us by this Judgment, the world is in an ill case, for there is but little of it there: And to deal plainly, as matters are, I have no great inclination to go home again; for it is better being with the dead, where there is justice, than with the living, where there is none. . .

PEDRO CALDERÓN DE LA BARCA (1600–81)

LA VIDA ES SUEÑO

Life Is a Dream (1635)

One of the most popular plays of the *siglo de oro,* and to this day of the Spanish language, *Life Is a Dream* (also known as *Such Stuff as Dreams Are Made Of*) brings the Renaissance full circle. The Middle Ages had been in love with the "dream vision," stiffly allegorical at its worst, brilliantly dramatic at its best in Dante Alighieri's *Commedia.* At its height of self-definition, the Renaissance turned vision inward to explore the apparently unlimited potential of the human psyche, and outward to conquer the unknown continents of the earth and of the no longer geocentric universe. Where medieval vision was reined in by the hierarchical rigidities of feudal society ("a visionary saw what was acceptable for him to see"), Renaissance vision at its finest observed what had never been seen before. By the winding down of the Renaissance, in Spain, the excesses of vision danced on the line between sanity and insanity. Where dream and reality, in the Middle Ages, were clearly separate though interrelated, by the time of Cervantes and Calderón their clear separation had blurred. More intellectual than his predecessors Lope de Vega and Tirso de Molina, Calderón creates a theater of ideas, foreshadowing Samuel Beckett and Eugene Ionesco. Modern dream theory can trace its origins to Clotaldo's insistence that Segismund's drugged state reveals his true nature. Segismund's final decision honors the old man's wisdom, choosing his enduring dream nature over his transitory waking inclinations. The ideal is found only in the dream, its first, final, and safest refuge.

[*Skirmishes, shouts, firing, etc. After some time enter* King Basilio, Astolfo, *and* Clotaldo.]

KING. The day is lost!

AST. Do not despair—the rebels—

KING. Alas! the vanquish'd only are the rebels.

CLOTALDO. Ev'n if this battle lost us, 'tis but one
    Gain'd on their side, if you not lost in it;
    Another moment and too late: at once
    Take horse, and to the capital, my liege,
    Where in some safe and holy sanctuary
    Save Poland in your person.

AST. Be persuaded:
    You know your son: have tasted of his temper;
    At his first onset threatening unprovoked
    The crime predicted for his last and worst.
    How whetted now with such a taste of blood,
    And thus far conquest!

KING. Ay, and how he fought!
    Oh how he fought, Astolfo; ranks of men
    Falling as swathes of grass before the mower;
    I could but pause to gaze at him, although,
    Like the pale horseman of the Apocalypse,
    Each moment brought him nearer—Yet I say,
    I could but pause and gaze on him, and pray
    Poland had such a warrior for her king.

AST. The cry of triumph on the other side
    Gains ground upon us here—there's but a moment
    For you, my liege, to do, for me to speak,
    Who back must to the field, and what man may,
    Do, to retrieve the fortune of the day.
    (*Firing.*)

FIFE (*FALLING FORWARD, SHOT*).
    Oh, Lord, have mercy on me.

KING. What a shriek—
    Oh, some poor creature wounded in a cause
    Perhaps not worth the loss of one poor life!—
    So young too—and no soldier—

FIFE. A poor lad,
    Who choosing play at hide and seek with death,
    Just hid where death just came to look for him;
    For there's no place, I think, can keep him out,
    Once he's his eye upon you. All grows dark—
    You glitter finely too—Well—we are dreaming—
    But when the bullet's off—Heaven save the mark!
    So tell my mister—mastress—

[*Dies.*]

KING. Oh God! How this poor creature's ignorance
    Confounds our so-call'd wisdom! Even now
    When death has stopt his lips, the wound through which
    His soul went out, still with its bloody tongue
    Preaching how vain our struggle against fate!
    (*Voices within.*) After them! After them! This way! This way!
    The day is ours—Down with Basilio, etc.

AST. Fly, sir—

KING. And slave-like flying not out-ride
    The fate which better like a King abide!

Enter Segismund, Rosaura, Soldiers, *etc.*

SEGISMUND. Where is the King?

KING (PROSTRATING HIMSELF). Behold him,—by this late
    Anticipation of resistless fate,

Thus underneath your feet his golden
crown,
    And the white head that wears it, laying
down,
    His fond resistance hope to expiate.

SEGISMUND. Princes and warriors of Poland—
you
    That stare on this unnatural sight aghast,
    Listen to one who, Heaven-inspired to
do
    What in its secret wisdom Heaven fore-
cast,
    By that same Heaven instructed prophet-
wise
    To justify the present in the past.
    What in the sapphire volume of the
skies
    Is writ by God's own finger misleads
none,
    But him whose vain and misinstructed
eyes,
    They mock with misinterpretation,
    Or who, mistaking what he rightly read,
    Ill commentary makes, or misapplies
    Thinking to shirk or thwart it. Which has
done
    The wisdom of this venerable head;
    Who, well provided with the secret key
    To that gold alphabet, himself made me,
    Himself, I say, the savage he fore-read
    Fate somehow should be charged with;
nipp'd the growth
    Of better nature in constraint and sloth;
    That only bring to bear the seed of
wrong
    And turn'd the stream to fury whose out-
burst
    Had kept his lawful channel uncoerced,
    And fertilized the land he flow'd along.
    Then like to some unskilful duellist,
    Who having over-reach'd himself push-
ing too hard
    His foe, or but a moment off his guard—
    What odds, when Fate is one's antago-
nist!—
    Nay, more, this royal father, self-dismay'd

At having Fate against himself array'd,
    Upon himself the very sword he knew
    Should wound him, down upon his
bosom drew,
    That might well handled, well have
wrought; or, kept
    Undrawn, have harmless in the scabbard
slept.
    But Fate shall not by human force be
broke,
    Nor foil'd by human feint; the Secret
learn'd
    Against the scholar by that master turn'd
    Who to himself reserves the master-
stroke.
    Witness whereof this venerable Age,
    Thrice crown'd as Sire, and Sovereign,
and Sage,
    Down to the very dust dishonour'd by
    The very means he tempted to defy
    The irresistible. And shall not I,
    Till now the mere dumb instrument that
wrought
    The battle Fate has with my father fought,
    Now the mere mouth-piece of its vic-
tory—
    Oh, shall not I, the champion's sword
laid down,
    Be yet more shamed to wear the
teacher's gown,
    And, blushing at the part I had to play,
    Down where that honour'd head I was
to lay
    By this more just submission of my own,
    The treason Fate has forced on me
atone?

KING. Oh, Segismund, in whom I see indeed,
    Out of the ashes of my self-extinction
    A better self revive; if not beneath
    Your feet, beneath your better wisdom
bow'd,
    The Sovereignty of Poland I resign,
    With this its golden symbol; which if
thus
    Saved with its silver head inviolate,
    Shall nevermore be subject to decline;

But when the head that it alights on now
Falls honour'd by the very foe that must,
As all things mortal, lay it in the dust,
Shall star-like shift to his successor's
brow.

[*Shouts, trumpets, etc.*] God save King
Segismund!

SEG. For what remains—
As for my own, so for my people's
peace,
Astolfo's and Estrella's plighted hands
I disunite, and taking hers to mine,
His to one yet more dearly his resign.
[*Shouts, etc.*] God save Estrella, Queen of
Poland!

SEG. [TO CLOTALDO]. You
That with unflinching duty to your King,
Till countermanded by the mightier
Power,
Have held your Prince a captive in the
tower,
Henceforth as strictly guard him on the
throne
No less my people's keeper than my
own.

You stare upon me all, amazed to hear
The word of civil justice from such lips
As never yet seem'd tuned to such dis-
course.
But listen—In that same enchanted tower,
Not long ago I learn'd it from a dream
Expounded by this ancient prophet
here;
And which he told me, should it come
again,
How I should bear myself beneath it; not
As then with angry passion all on fire,
Arguing and making a distemper'd soul;
But ev'n with justice, mercy, self-control,
As if the dream I walk'd in were no
dream,
And conscience one day to account for
it.
A dream it was in which I thought
myself,

And you that hail'd me now then hail'd
me King,
In a brave palace that was all my own,
Within, and all without it, mine; until,
Drunk with excess of majesty and pride,
Methought I tower'd so high and swell'd
so wide,
That of myself I burst the glittering bub-
ble,
That my ambition had about me blown,
And all again was darkness. Such a dream
As this in which I may be walking now;
Dispensing solemn justice to you shad-
ows,
Who make believe to listen; but anon,
With all your glittering arms and
equipage,
King, princes, captains, warriors, plume
and steel,
Ay, ev'n with all your airy theatre,
May flit into the air you seem to rend
With acclamation, leaving me to wake
In the dark tower; or dreaming that I
wake
From this that waking is; or this and that
Both waking or both dreaming; such a
doubt
Confounds and clouds our mortal life
about.
And, whether wake or dreaming, this I
know,
How dream-wise human glories come
and go;
Whose momentary tenure not to break,
Walking as one who knows he soon may
wake
So fairly carry the full cup, so well
Disorder'd insolence and passion quell,
That there be nothing after to upbraid
Dreamer or doer in the part he play'd,
Whether To-morrow's dawn shall break
the spell,
Or the Last Trumpet of the eternal Day,
When Dreaming with the Night shall
pass away.
[Exeunt.]

RENÉ DESCARTES (1596–1650)

DISCOURS DE LA MÉTHODE POUR BIEN CONDUIRE SA RAISON ET DE CHERCHER LA VERITÉ DANS LES SCIENCES

Discourse Concerning Method (1637)

René Descartes' most famous statement, "I think, therefore I am" (*Cogito, ergo sum*), long before it became T-shirt fodder in our century, may be considered the ultimate expression of Renaissance philosophy at the same time that it ushers in the Age of Reason. The Greek sophist Protagoras had argued that, "Man is the measure of all things; of things that are, that they are; and of things that are not, that they are not." Descartes takes this anthropocentric theory further by arguing that the human mind itself is the only thing we can be certain exists, but that certainty is sufficient to reveal the existence of God and the entire universe. In the "fourth part" of *The Discourse,* Descartes brings his analytical and synthesizing argument to analyzing the nature of the human mind and the nature and existence of God. It is possible to doubt the nature and existence of the material world, but impossible to doubt the existence of the mind. Consequently our highest assurance is that the mind exists, thereby providing one unimpeachable certainty with which the secrets of all existence can be unlocked. *The Discourse* is the first important work of philosophy written in French. Descartes presents four rules for the pursuit of knowledge:

- To accept nothing as true unless it can be clearly proved to be true;
- To attack problems through analysis, reducing them to their parts;
- To proceed systematically from simpler to more complex statements;
- To review everything systematically before concluding one's synthesis.

The Jesuit-educated mathematician-scientist is considered the father of modern philosophy, who set the stage for the existentialist relativism of Henri Bergson, Jean-Paul Sartre, and Albert Camus.

FOURTH PART

I do not know whether I ought to share with you the first meditations I made here; for they are so metaphysical and so uncommon that perhaps they will not be to everyone's taste. And yet in order that one may judge whether the foundations I have employed are sufficiently firm, I find myself in some way constrained to speak of these first meditations. I had been aware for many years that in respect to customs it is sometimes necessary to follow opinions one knows to be very uncertain just as if they were indubitable, as has been said above; but because at that time I desired to attend only to the search for truth, I thought it necessary to do exactly the contrary, and to reject, as if absolutely false, everything in which I could imagine the least doubt, in order to see if there would not afterward remain among my beliefs something entirely indubitable. Thus because our senses sometimes deceive us, I wished to suppose there was nothing such as they make us imagine it. And because there are men who make a mistake in reasoning even regarding the most simple matters of geometry, and form paralogisms, I, judging myself subject to error as much as any other man, rejected as false all the reasons I had previously taken as demonstrations. And finally, considering that all the same thoughts we have when awake can also come to us when we are sleeping without any of them being true at that time, I resolved to suppose that all the things that had ever entered my mind were no more true than the illusions of my dreams. But immediately afterward I noticed that, while I thus wished to think that everything was false, it was necessary that I who was thinking be something. And noting that this truth, *I think, therefore I am,* was so firm and so assured that all the most extravagant suppositions of the skeptics were not capable of disturbing it, I judged that I could receive it, without scruple, as the first principle of the philosophy I was seeking.

Then, examining with attention what I was,

and seeing that I was able to suppose I had no body, and that there was no world nor any place where I might be; and seeing also that, for all of that, I was not able to suppose that I was not; but seeing, on the contrary, that, from the very fact that I was thinking of doubting the truth of other things, it followed very evidently and very certainly that I was; whereas had I only ceased to think, even if all the rest of what I had ever imagined had been true, I should have no reason to believe that I had been: from that I knew that I was a substance whose entire essence or nature is only to think, and which, in order to exist, has no need of a place nor depends upon any material thing. So that this I, that is to say, the soul by which I am what I am, is entirely distinct from the body, and is even easier to know than the body, and even if the body had never been, the soul would not fail to be everything that it is.

After that I considered in general what is required for a proposition to be true and certain; for since I came to find one which I knew to be such, I thought I must also know in what this certitude consists. And having noticed that there is nothing at all in this *I think, therefore I am* that assures me I am speaking the truth except that I see very clearly that in order to think it is necessary to exist, I judged that I could take it as a general rule that things we conceive very clearly and very distinctly are all true; but there is only some difficulty to note well the things that we conceive distinctly.

Following this, in reflecting upon the fact that I doubted, and that consequently my being was not completely perfect—since I saw clearly that it was a greater perfection to know than to doubt—I resolved to inquire whence I had learned to think of something more perfect than I was; and I recognized evidently that this ought to be from some nature that was in fact more perfect than myself. For as regards the thoughts I had of things outside me—such as of heaven, earth, light, heat, and a thousand other things—I was not very hard pressed to know whence they came; because, not noticing anything in them that seemed to render them superior to myself, I was able to believe that if they were true, they were dependent upon my nature inasmuch as it had some perfection; and if they were not true, that I derived them from nothingness, that is to say, they were in me because I had some defect. But it could not be the same as regards the idea of a more perfect being than my own; for to derive that idea from nothingness was something manifestly impossible; and because for the more perfect to be a consequence of, and dependent on, the less perfect is no less contradictory than that nothing proceed from something, I was not able to maintain that that idea derived from myself. Thus it remained that that idea had been placed in me by a nature that was truly more perfect than I was, and that had in itself all the perfections of which I could have some idea, that is to say, to explain myself in a word, who was God. To which I added that, since I knew of some perfections I did not have, I was not the only being who existed (if you please, I shall here make free use of the words of the school), but that it followed of necessity that there was another more perfect being upon which I was dependent, and from which I had acquired everything that I had. For if I had been alone and independent of every other thing, in such a way that I had had from myself all this meager amount of perfect being in which I participate, by the same reasoning I would have been able to derive from myself all the other perfections I recognized myself to lack, and thus to be myself infinite, eternal, immutable, all-knowing, all-powerful, and lastly, to have all the perfections I was able to distinguish to be in God. For according to the reasonings I used in order to know the nature of God, insofar as I was capable of knowing it, I had only to consider, in respect of all things of which I found an idea in myself, whether it was or was not a perfection to possess these things; and I was assured that none of those things that indicated some imperfection was in God, but that all the other things were in him. Thus I saw that doubt, inconstancy, sadness, and similar things could not be there, since I saw that I myself would have been very

comfortable in being rid of them. Then, besides that, I had ideas of many sensible and corporeal things: for although I supposed I was dreaming, and that all I saw or imagined was false, I was nevertheless unable to deny that these ideas were truly in my thought. But because I had already recognized very clearly in myself that the intellectual nature is distinct from the corporeal, and because I recognized that all composition testifies to dependency, and that dependency is manifestly a defect, I judged from that that it couldn't be a perfection in God to be composed of these two natures, and that, as a consequence, he was not so composed; but I judged that if there were some bodies in the world, or even some intelligences or other natures that were not all perfect, their being ought to depend upon his power in such a way that they could not subsist without him for a single moment.

After that I wished to seek out other truths. I proposed to my study the object of the geometers, which I conceived as a continuous body, or as a space indefinitely extended in length, breadth, altitude or depth, and which is divisible into different parts that could have different figures and sizes, and be moved or transported in all sorts of ways—for the geometers assume all these things in their object. I then ran through some of their most simple demonstrations. And having noticed that this great certitude that everyone attributes to the demonstrations of geometry is founded only on the fact that one conceives them evidently, following the rule I a little while ago laid down, I also noted that there was nothing at all in these demonstrations to assure me of the existence of their object. For example, I saw indeed that, in supposing a triangle, it was necessary that its three angles be equal to two right angles; but I did not on that account see anything that assured me there was any triangle in the world; whereas returning to examine the idea I had of a perfect being, I found that existence was included there in the same way as, or even still more evidently than, the equality of its three angles to two right angles is included in the idea of a triangle, or the equality of distance of all its parts from its center is included in the idea of a sphere; and therefore I concluded that it is at least as certain as any of the demonstrations of geometry could be, that God, who is this perfect being, is or exists.

But what makes many people persuade themselves there is difficulty in recognizing God, and also even in recognizing what their soul is, is that they never elevate their mind above sensible things, and they are so accustomed to consider nothing except by imagining it, which is a manner of thought specifically appropriate to thinking of material things, that everything that cannot be imagined seems to them unintelligible. This is sufficiently manifest from the fact that even the philosophers in the schools espouse as a maxim that there is nothing in the understanding that has not initially been in the senses, when nevertheless it is certain that the ideas of God and of the soul have never been in the senses. And it seems to me that those who wish to use their imagination to comprehend the ideas of God and the soul act just like those who wish to use their eyes to hear sounds or smell odors: unless there is yet this difference, that the sense of sight does not assure us any less concerning the truth of its objects than the senses of smell and hearing assure us concerning theirs; whereas neither our imagination nor our senses could ever assure us of anything unless our understanding intervened.

Finally, if there are men who are still not sufficiently persuaded of the existence of God and their soul by the reasons brought forward, I strongly wish that they may know that every other thing of which they think themselves perhaps more assured, such as the fact that they have a body, and that there are stars and an earth and similar things, is less certain. For although one has a moral assurance of these things such that one cannot doubt them without being extravagant, nevertheless unless one is to be unreasonable when it is a question of metaphysical certitude, one cannot deny there are grounds enough for not being entirely assured of them if only one attends to the fact that while sleeping one can in the same way imagine that one has another body, that one sees other stars, another earth, without any of these things existing. For on what basis does one know that the thoughts that come during dreams are false rather than the others, having seen that often they are not less vivid and expressive? And were the best minds to study this matter as much as it pleases them to do so, I do not believe they could give any reason sufficient to banish this doubt unless they presuppose the existence of God. For in the first place what I recently took as a rule—namely, that the things we conceive very clearly and very distinctly are all true—is assured only because God is or exists and is a perfect being, and because everything in us comes from him. From which it follows that our ideas or notions, being real things and things that come from God, must be true as regards everything in which they are clear and distinct. Thus if often enough we have ideas that contain falsity, this falsity can only be in those ideas that contain something confused and obscure, because insofar as they are confused and obscure, they participate in nothingness—which is to say, they are in us in a confused manner only because we are not completely perfect. And it is evident that it is not less contradictory that falsity *qua* falsity or imperfection *qua* imperfection proceed from God than that truth or perfection proceed from nothingness. But if we do not know that everything in us that is real and true comes from a perfect and infinite being, no matter how clear and distinct our ideas would be, we would have no reason that assured us that they have the perfection of being true.

But, now, after the knowledge of God and of the soul has thus rendered us certain of this rule, it is very easy to recognize that the reveries we imagine when asleep should not make us doubt at all the truth of the thoughts we have while awake. For if it happened even while sleeping that one had some very distinct idea, as if, for example, a geometer discovered some new demonstration, his sleeping would not prevent that demonstration from being true. And as for the most ordinary error of our dreams, which consists in that they represent various objects to us in the same fashion as do our external senses, it makes no difference that they provide us with an occasion to be distrustful of the truth of such ideas, because the senses can also trick us often enough when we are not sleeping: as when those who have jaundice always see the color yellow, or as when the stars or other very distant bodies seem very much smaller than they are. For finally, whether we are sleeping or waking, we should never allow ourselves to be persuaded except by the evidence of our reason. And it is to be noted that I say of our reason, and not of our imagination or senses. Consider the following cases. When we see the sun very clearly we ought not to judge on that account that it is only the size

we see it to be; and certainly we can distinctly imagine the head of a lion placed upon the body of a goat without it being necessary to conclude that there exists a Chimera in the world—in such cases reason does not tell us that what we thus see or imagine is genuine. However, reason certainly does tell us that all our ideas or notions have to have some foundation in the truth; for it would not be possible that God, who is all-perfect and all-truthful, had placed them in us without that being so. And since our reasonings are never so evident nor so complete during sleep as during waking—although our imaginations may be equally or more vivid and expressive—reason tells us also that our thoughts cannot all be true, because we are not all-perfect, and that what truth is in them should without question be discovered in those we have while awake, rather than in our dreams.

WILLIAM HARVEY (1578–1657)

De motu cordis

The Circulation of the Blood (1649)

Renaissance individualism serves the scientific method in William Harvey's standard-setting comment: "Careful observation is needed in every discipline, and sensation itself is often to be consulted. One's own experience is to be relied upon, not that of someone else." Physician to King James I and Charles I, at St. Bartholomew's Hospital he allowed students to attend his operations and experiments. Harvey was educated in medicine at Cambridge and at Padua. Under the guidance of Italian anatomist, embryologist, and surgeon Hieronymus Fabricius (author of *De venarum ostiolis,* 1603, dealing with the valves or "little flood-gates" in veins), Harvey learned to move beyond Vesalius and Aristotle's comparative anatomy and to depend entirely upon observation of and experiment with nature instead of abstract thinking. Charles I made the royal deer available to Harvey for dissection.

Not many months ago there appeared a small anatomical and pathological work written by the distinguished Riolan, and I acknowledge very gratefully the author's personal gift of a copy to myself. I certainly congratulate him on his happy choice of so outstandingly praiseworthy an object for his investigations. To demonstrate the seats of all diseases is a task demanding an altogether unusual capacity, and certainly the man who reveals those diseases which all but defy comprehension has undertaken a difficult task. Such efforts become the leading anatomist, for there is no knowledge except that which is based on pre-existing perception, and no certain and fully accepted idea which has not originated from sensation. For this reason the subject itself, and the example set by so great a man, kept demanding a corresponding activity on my own part, and determining me to indite and commit to writing in similar fashion my medical anatomy also, that is, my anatomy most closely adapted to medical use. This was not solely, as in Riolan's case, for the purpose of showing from the cadavers of healthy subjects the sites of diseases and of listing what others had thought must be the appearances of diseases in those places. But it was rather so that from many dissections of patients dying of very severe and remarkable complaints I should undertake an account of the ways and manners in which the internal parts change in site, size, constitution, figure, substance, and other appreciable variables from the natural form and appearance commonly described by all anatomists, and the various remarkable ways in which they are affected.

For just as the dissection of healthy and well-conditioned bodies is of very great help in advancing natural knowledge and correct physiology, so is the inspection of diseased and cachectic bodies of very great assistance in the understanding of pathology. The contemplation of those things which are normal is physiology, and it is the first thing to be learned by medical men. For that which is normal is right and serves as a criterion for both itself and the abnormal. By defining in its light departures from it and unnatural reactions, pathology becomes more clearly obvious for the future, and from pathology the practice and art of therapeusis, and opportunities for discovering multiple new remedies, derive. Nor would one readily believe the extent to which the inner parts are corrupted in diseases, especially those of long standing, and what horrible monstrosities are produced in those parts by diseases. And, if I may so state, one dissection and opening up of a decayed body, or of one dead from chronic disease or poisoning, is of more value to medicine than the anatomies of ten people who have been hanged.

This does not mean that I disapprove the schema advanced by the very learned and skilful anatomist, Riolan. On the contrary, I regard it as extremely praiseworthy for, in as much as it throws light on the physiological aspect, it is very useful to medicine. I thought, however, it would be no less profitable to the art of healing were I to reveal not only the sites affected but at the same time the affections of those sites, describe what I had seen in them, and put on record my findings derived from my many dissections.

The passages in Riolan's booklet, however, which appeared to refer to me only, namely, the accounts of the blood-circuit discovered by me, are the matters which need first consideration, especially by myself. For Riolan is easily the leader and doyen of all contemporary anatomists, and the judgment of so great a man upon so major a subject cannot be lightly esteemed. Rather is his approval more important than the acclaim of all other critics, his censure more deserving of respect and consideration than the opposition of all others in the field. In Book 3, Chap. 8, then, of his *Encheiridium,* he accepts my movement of the blood in animals, sides with me, and adopts my view about the blood circuit. He does not, however, do so fully and openly, for in Book 2, Chap. 21, he says that the blood contained in the portal vein does not circulate in the way that that in the vena cava does. Then in Book 3, Chap. 8, he says that there is a circulation of blood, and the circulatory vessels are presumably the aorta and vena cava. He denies, however, that their branches get a circulation. 'For', he says, 'the blood poured out into all parts of the second and third region remains in them for their nourishment and does not flow back into the larger vessels unless it is compelled thereto by the extreme dearth of blood in those vessels, or flows to them in the excitement of a frenzied rush.' And a little farther on he writes, 'so the blood in the veins is constantly ascending naturally or flowing back to the heart, while the blood in the arteries is descending or passing away from that organ. However, if the smaller veins of the arms and legs are emptied of blood, the blood in the veins can descend as the vessels are successively depleted. This I have clearly demonstrated, contrary to the belief of Harvey and of de Wale.' And, as Galen and daily experience confirm the anastomoses of veins and arteries, and there is need for a circulation of blood, 'you will see', he says, 'how such a circulation takes place without causing upset and mixing of the body's humours and destruction of traditional medicine'.

These words reveal the motives actuating this distinguished scientist so that he wished in part to acknowledge, in part to deny, a circuit of the blood; they show that the reason for his hesitant and variable opinion in the matter is his fear of destroying traditional medicine. It was not love of the truth (which he could not have missed seeing) which led him to refrain from speaking freely, but rather excessive caution lest he should offend traditional medicine, or perhaps appear to retract from the physiology he himself put forward in his *Anthropologia*. For the concept of a circuit of the blood does not destroy, but rather advances, traditional medicine. It goes against the [current] physiology of the physicians and their speculation about natural matters, and contradicts anatomical teaching about the functional anatomy of the heart and lungs and remaining viscera. That these things are so will readily be apparent from Riolan's own words of avowal, in part also from the arguments which I here subjoin. These are that the whole of the blood, wherever it is in the living body, moves and alters its position (whether it is within the larger vessels and their offshoots and divisions, or within the porosities of any region of the body's parts), and flows both to the heart and away from it continuously and uninterruptedly, and stays nowhere without loss, though I grant that in places and from time to time it moves forward relatively more rapidly or more slowly.

In the first place, then, the learned gentleman merely denies, without proving his point, that the blood contained in the offshoots of the portal vein circulates. Nor could he have made such denial had he not minimized the strength of his own evidence [to the contrary]. For in Book 3, Chap. 8, he says that if the heart takes in at each beat one drop of blood and expels it into the aorta, and if within the hour it beats two thousand times, then a large part of the blood must pass [through the organ in question in the time stated]. He must make a similar admission with respect to the mesentery. For at each heartbeat more than one drop of blood is forced in through the coeliac artery and the mesenteric arteries and driven into the mesentery and its veins. It must, therefore, get out again somewhere in like amount, or else the branches of the portal vein must in time be disrupted. And one cannot (to resolve the difficulty) regard as probable or possible an Euripus-like inflow and outflow of the mesenteric blood, through one and the same set of vessels, in useless ineffective activity. Nor is it likely that blood passes through these same vessels to discharge into the aorta, for this it cannot do against the force of the blood entering the vessel in the opposite direction. And alternation in flow is not possible where inflow is so definitely continuous, uninterrupted, and unceasing, but, just as is the case with the heart, so blood driven into the mesentery must get out elsewhither. As is obvious, for Riolan could upset all idea of a circulation by the same specious argument if he makes the like declaration with the same amount of probability in speaking about the ventricles of the heart. Namely, if he says that in the systole of the heart the blood is driven into the aorta and in its diastole flows back [into the ventricles]; and the aorta empties itself into the ventricles of the heart as the ventricles of the heart in their turn into the aorta. And so there is a circulation neither in the heart nor in the mesentery, but there is an alternate flux and reflux in ineffective effort. If, therefore, in the heart for the reason approved by Riolan there is of necessity a circulation of blood, the same force of argument holds good also in respect of the mesentery. If, however, there is no circuit of blood in the mesentery, there is similarly none in the heart. For both declarations, namely, the one about the heart and the other about the mesentery, stand or fall similarly by virtue of the same evidence with merely the words changed.

Riolan says 'the sigmoid valves prevent backflow in the heart, but there are no valves in the mesentery'. To which I reply that this too is untrue, for a valve has been found in the splenic vein and often also in other veins. Moreover, valves are not required everywhere in veins, and they are not found in the deep veins of the limbs but rather in the skin vessels. For what need is there of valves where the blood is flowing naturally down from smaller branches to larger ones, and is adequately or more than adequately prevented from flowing backwards by the pressure of the surrounding muscles, but is forced on to where a way lies open to it? Moreover, the amount of blood driven into the mesentery at each pulsation can be calculated if you compress at the wrist with a medium-tight ligature the veins emerging from the hand and going up amongst the arteries, and remember that the arteries of the mesentery are larger than those of the wrist. If you count the number of pulsations required to distend the vessels of the hand and cause the hand as a whole to swell up, then divide by that number and do a little arithmetic; you will find that at each beat, unhindered by the ligature, more

than a drop of blood goes in and is prevented from coming out again. Nay, rather, by filling up in this way [the arteries] the blood forcibly distends the whole of the hand and makes a mass of it. By analogy one can infer that the mesenteric blood inflow is as great or greater in proportion as the mesenteric arteries exceed in size those of the wrist. And, if one looks and thinks how much difficulty and effort are involved, and what compresses, ligatures, and apparatus of all sorts are needed to confine the headlong outrush of blood from a cut or tear in even the smallest arteriole, how forcibly (as if shot out by a pipe) it ejects, expels, or saturates all the means taken to deal with it, he will, I think, scarcely believe it probable that any backflow can take place without opposition of this order against so great an impulse and inflow of blood. Turning all of which over in his mind, therefore, I hardly think he will bring himself to believe that against so violent and powerful an inflow the blood from the branches of the portal vein percolates through the same channels to empty the mesentery.

Moreover, if the learned gentleman thinks that the blood does not move in a circle and change, but stagnates unaltered in the branches of the mesentery, he seems to suppose that there are two different blood supplies serving different functions and purposes, and therefore of different nature, in the portal vein and vena cava. The one needs a circulation for its own preservation, the other does not. This is not apparent, nor does he demonstrate that it is true.

Further (*Encheiridium,* Book 2, Chap. 18), he adds 'a fourth kind of vessels to the mesentery; these are styled lacteals and were discovered by Aselli'. With them added to the picture, he appears to imply that all the food extracted by the intestines is carried by these lacteals to the liver, where the blood is manufactured. In the liver the food is digested and changed into blood (as he says in Book 2, Chap. 8) and 'this blood is carried from the liver and passes across to the right ventricle of the heart. With these vessels accepted', he says (*ibid.,* Book 2, Chap.

18), 'all the difficulties, that previously arose about the distribution of chyle and blood through the same channel, cease. For the lacteal vessels carry the chyle to the liver and' are channels in their own right, and 'can be separately obstructed'. But how indeed, I ask, can that milk be transfused and cross over into the liver, and thence through the cava into the ventricle of the heart (since the learned gentleman denies that the blood contained in the very numerous branches distributed to the snub-nosed porta hepatis can cross to bring about a circulation)? May I be told how this can be shown possible, especially since blood appears more spirituous and penetrative than the chyle or milk contained in those lacteal vessels; and is so driven on by the pulsation of the arteries that it finds a way elsewhither?

The learned gentleman makes mention of a certain treatise of his about the circulation of the blood. I would that I could see it. Perhaps I would change my mind. But if the learned gentleman had preferred, I do not see but that, having granted the circular movement of the blood (in the veins, as he says in Book 3, Chap. 8, the blood goes continuously and naturally up to the heart or flows down to the heart; just as in all the arteries the blood descends or leaves the heart), with this movement—I say—granted, all the difficulties which used to arise about the distribution of the chyle and the blood through the same channels, would equally cease to exist, so that there would be no further need to search for or suppose separate vessels for the chyle. Seeing that, just as the umbilical veins absorb the nutrient juice from the fluids of the egg, and carry it off for the nourishment and increase of the chick, now existing as the embryo, so do the mesenteric veins drive the chyle from the intestines and carry it to the liver; and why do we hesitate to postulate the same function in the adult? For all the difficulties that used to arise vanish if we assume not two opposing movements, but one continuous one in the mesenteric vessels from the intestines to the liver.

I shall state elsewhere what I must feel about the lacteal veins when I deal with the milk which I have recently found in various parts of newborn animals, especially human ones. For it is found in the mesentery and all its glands, also in the thymus, and in the axillae and the breasts of infants. This milk the midwives get rid of, as they think, for the good of the offspring.

Moreover, the learned Riolan has not only decided that the blood in the mesentery lacks a circulation, but he also asserts that the same is true of the branches of the vena cava and of the arteries and of all the parts of the second and third region, so that the only circulatory vessels which he names are the vena cava and the aorta. In Book 3, Chap. 8, he gives a very weak reason, namely, 'that the blood poured out into all parts of the second and third region remains in them for their nutrition, and does not flow back into larger vessels except it is removed by force and through extreme dearth of blood in the larger vessels, or through a sudden rush flows into the circulatory vessels'.

It is indeed necessary that the portion which is to go off for nutrition should remain. For it would not nourish were it not assimilated in place of that which has been lost, and did it become adherent to the rest and fuse with it. But it is not necessary for the whole of the inflowing blood to remain there for the conversion of only so small a portion of it. For no part uses for its food as much as it contains all told in its arteries, veins, and porosities. It is also unnecessary for it to leave any nutriment behind during its flux and reflux, so in order to nourish it does not all have to remain behind. But the learned gentleman, in the very booklet in which he states this, appears almost everywhere to declare strongly the opposite, especially where he is describing the circulation in the brain and says 'in so far as the brain sends blood back through the circulation to the heart and so the heart is cooled'. In this way all the distant parts may be said to cool the heart. Whence also in fevers when the praecordia are violently consumed and burn with febrile heat, the patients remove their clothing and discard their bedding in their search for cooling for the heart. While, as the learned gentleman states in respect of the brain, the cooled and heat-tempered blood then seeks out the heart through the veins and cools it. In this way the learned gentleman seems to make it more or less obligatory for there to be a circulation from all parts as there is from the brain, a circulation which he had previously openly opposed. But he cautiously and ambiguously asserts that the blood does not return from the parts of the second and third region unless, as he says, it is removed by force and through extreme dearth in the larger vessels, or through a sudden rush flows into the larger circulatory vessels. Which is very true if these words are understood in their true sense. For by the larger vessels in which dearth causes a backflow, I think he must understand the vena cava or the circulating veins, not the arteries. For the arteries are never emptied except into veins or porosities of the parts, but are continuously being distended by the pulsation of the heart. In the vena cava and the circulatory vessels, however, into which the blood slips quickly and hastens to the heart, there would be immediate very great dearth of blood unless all parts incessantly returned the blood poured into them. Add to this that, by the force of the blood which is stretched and driven at each pulsation into all parts of the second and third region, the contained blood is forced from the porosities into the venules and from the branches into the larger vessels, and, moreover, by the movement and pressure of the surrounding parts, for from every container that is compressed and contracted the content is squeezed out. Thus by the movements of muscles and joints the pressure and constraint exerted upon the intervening venous branches push the blood from the smaller into larger vessels.

That the blood, moreover, is continuously and unceasingly driven from the arteries into the individual parts, producing an impulse without backflow, cannot be doubted. If it be admitted that at each pulsation all the arteries are simultaneously distended by the forward drive of blood, and that (as the learned gentleman himself confesses) the diastole of the arteries is produced by the systole of the heart, and that the blood, once it has emerged, never gets back into the ventricles of the heart on account of the closure of the valves; if, I say, the learned gentleman (as it appears) accepts all this, the propulsive force with which the expelled blood is emitted in the individual parts of each region will be obvious. For the inflow and drive reaches everywhere as far as the arterial pulsation extends, whence it is felt in all parts of each region. For pulsation is present everywhere, even in the tips of the fingers and under the nails, and there is no small part at all in the whole body which, suffering from an inflammation or a furuncle, does not feel keenly the lacerating movement of the arterial pulsation attempting to sunder it.

But further, that the blood goes back in the porosities of the parts is obvious in the skin of the hands and feet. For often in severe frost and cold weather we see the hands and limbs so chilled, especially in children, that to the touch they almost give the coldness of ice, and they are so benumbed and stiff as to be almost without feeling and scarcely able to move: meantime, however, they are seen to be full of blood, red or livid. These parts can in no way get warm again except through the circulation, the cold blood deprived of spirits and warmth being driven off and in its place a new, warming, and spirituous excessive heat in the lungs and the centre of the body, and looks after the expulsion of suffocating fumes, so in turn does the hot blood, sent through the arteries to the whole of the body, warm all the farthest parts, sustain them and keep them alive, and prevent them from being killed by the power of the external cold.

It would thus be unfair and surprising if individual parts of any region failed to benefit by the transmutation of the blood and the help of the circulation, as Nature appears particularly to have intended by its institution. May I thus conclude? You see how circulation of the blood avoids confusion and disturbance of the humours, both in the body as a whole and in its individual small parts, and both in the larger and in the smaller vessels, and all as is necessary and for the benefit of all parts; without which cooled and weakened parts would never be restored, or remain among the living. For it is clear enough that the protective warmth flows in through the blood flowing in from the arteries revives the parts, rewarms them, and restores their movement and sensation. For they could not be refreshed and restored by fire or external heat any more than dead limbs could unless they were revived by the inflow of internal heat. And, indeed, that is the chief use and object of the circulation, and for its sake the blood goes around on its continuous course and perpetual inflow and moves in a circle; namely, so that all parts, depending on it, may be kept by their prime innate heat in life and their vital and vegetative existence, and perform all their functions; while (as physiologists say) they are sustained and actuated by the inflow of warmth and of the spirits of life. Thus, by the help of two extremes, namely, cold and warmth, the temperature of animal bodies is kept in its medium state. For as the inspired air tempers the arteries, and that its provision constitutes the work of the circulation.

OLIVER CROMWELL (1599–1658)

On the Dissolution of Parliament (1655)

The ironic fate of the victorious underdog permeates the history of Puritan Oliver Cromwell. This Cambridge-educated brewer's son led the revolutionary republican forces in the English Civil Wars, defeated the armies of Charles I, and ordered the King's execution. Then, after conquering Scotland and Ireland, Cromwell dissolved parliament, formed a new parliament entirely under his control, and declared himself, by the grace of God, Lord Protector of the commonwealth of England. When Charles II was restored to power, he ordered Cromwell's body dug up from Westminster Abbey and hung at the Tyburn gallows. Cromwell's head remained on a stake until the end of Charles II's reign. Echoing the rolling cadences of Cicero, and foreshadowing those of Patrick Henry in his speech to the Virginia Assembly, Cromwell's oration resounds with the complexities of exploring the paradox of rebel turned governor, the paradox of all rebellion that it must replace the establishment it has overturned and become the authority it destroyed. In the vacuum, we find an awful lot of reliance upon God by the self-made demagogue. Direct appeals to divine authority shall be characteristic of demagoguery for the next two hundred years.

This government called you hither; the constitution thereof being limited so—a single person and a Parliament. And this was thought most agreeable to the general sense of the nation;—having had experience enough, by trial, of other conclusions; judging this most likely to avoid the extremes of monarchy on the one hand, and of democracy on the other;—and yet not to found *dominium in gratia* "either." And if so, then certainly to make the authority more than a mere notion, it was requisite that it should be as it is in this "frame of" government; which puts it upon a true and equal balance. It has been already submitted to the judicious, true and honest people of this nation, whether the balance be not equal? And what their judgment is, is visible—by submission to it; by acting upon it; by restraining their trustees from meddling with it. And it neither asks nor needs any better ratification? But when trustees in Parliament shall, by experience, find any evil in any parts of this "frame of" government, "a question" referred by the government itself to the consideration of the Protector and Parliament—of which evil or evils time itself will be the best discoverer:—how can it be reasonably imagined that a person or persons, coming in by election, and standing under such obligations, and so limited, and so necessitated by oath to govern for the people's good, and to make their love, under God, the best under-propping and only safe footing:—how can it, I say, be imagined that the present or succeeding Protectors will refuse to agree to alter any such thing in the government as may be found to be for the good of the people? Or to recede from anything which he might be convinced casts the balance too much to the single person? And although, for the present, the keeping up and having in his power the militia seems the hardest "condition," yet if the power of the militia should be yielded up at such a time as this, when there is as much need of it to keep this cause (now most evidently impugned by all enemies), as there was to get it "for the sake of this cause":—what would become of us all! Or if it should not be equally placed in him and the

Parliament, but yielded up at any time—it determines his power either for doing the good he ought, or hindering Parliaments from perpetuating themselves; from imposing what religion they please on the consciences of men, or what government they please upon the nation. Thereby subjecting us to dissettlement in every Parliament, and to the desperate consequences thereof. And if the nation shall happen to fall into a blessed peace, how easily and certainly will their charge be taken off, and their forces be disbanded! And then where will the danger be to have the militia thus stated? What if I should say: If there be a disproportion, or disequality as to the power, it is on the other hand!

And if this be so, wherein have you had cause to quarrel? What demonstrations have you held forth to settle me to your opinion? I would you had made me so happy as to have let me know your grounds! I have made a free and ingenuous confession of my faith to you. And I could have wished it had been in your hearts to have agreed that some friendly and cordial debates might have been toward mutual conviction. Was there none amongst you to move such a thing? No fitness to listen to it? No desire of a right understanding? If it be not folly in me to listen to town talk, such things have been proposed; and rejected, with stiffness and severity, once and again. Was it not likely to have been more advantageous to the good of this nation? I will say this to you for myself; and to that I have my conscience as a thousand witnesses, and I have my comfort and contentment in it; and I have the witness too of divers here, who I think truly would scorn to own me in a lie: That I would not have been averse to any alteration, of the good of which I might have been convinced. Although I could not have agreed to the taking it off the foundation on which it stands; namely, the acceptance and consent of the people.

I will not presage what you have been about, or doing, in all this time. Nor do I love to make conjectures. But I must tell you this: That as I undertook this government in the simplicity of my heart and as before God, and to do the part of an honest man, and to be true to the interest—which in my conscience "I think" is dear to many of you; though it is not always understood what God in His wisdom may hide from us, as to peace and settlement:—so I can say that no particular interest, either of myself, estate, honor, or family, are, or have been, prevalent with me to this undertaking. For if you had, upon the old government, offered me this one, this one thing—I speak as thus advised, and before God; as having been to this day of this opinion; and this hath been my constant judgment, well known to many who hear me speak:—if, "I say," this one thing had been inserted, this one thing, that the government should have been placed in my family hereditary, I would have rejected it. And I could have done no other according to my present conscience and light. I will tell you my reason;—though I cannot tell what God will do with me, nor with you, nor with the nation, for throwing away precious opportunities committed to us.

Now to speak a word or two to you. Of that, I must profess in the name of the same Lord, and wish there had been no cause that I should have thus spoken to you! I told you that I came with joy the first time; with some regret the second; yet now I speak with most regret of all! I look upon you as having among you many persons that I could lay down my life individually for. I could, through the grace of God, desire to lay down my life for you. So far am I from having an unkind or unchristian heart towards you in your particular capacities! I have this indeed as a work most incumbent upon me; this of speaking these things to you. I consulted what might be my duty in such a day as this; casting up all considerations. I must confess, as I told you, that I did think occasionally, this nation had suffered extremely in the respects mentioned; as also in the disappointment of their expectations of that justice which was due to them by your sitting thus long. "Sitting thus long;" and what have you brought forth? I did not nor cannot comprehend what it is. I would be loath to call it a fate; that were too paganish a word. But there hath been something in it that we had not in our expectations.

I did think also, for myself, that I am like to meet with difficulties; and that this nation will not, as it is fit it should not, be deluded with pretexts of necessity in that great business of raising of money. And were it not that I can make some dilemmas upon which to resolve some things of my conscience, judgment and actions, I should shrink at the very prospect of my encounters. Some of them are general, some are more special. Supposing this cause or this business must be carried on, it is either of God or of man. If it be of man, I would I had never touched it with a finger. If I had not had a hope fixed in me that this cause and this business was of God, I would many years ago have run from it. If it be of God, He will bear it up. If it be of man, it will tumble; as everything that hath been of man since the world began hath done. And what are all our histories, and other traditions of actions in former times, but God manifesting Himself, that He hath shaken, and tumbled down and trampled upon, everything that He had not planted? And as this is, so let the All-wise God deal with it. If this be of human structure and invention, and if it be an old plotting and contriving to bring things to this issue, and that they are not the births of Providence—then they will tumble. But if the Lord take pleasure in England, and if He will do us good—He is very able to bear us up! Let the difficulties be whatsoever they will, we shall in His strength be able to encounter with them. And I bless God I have been inured to difficulties; and I never found God failing when I trusted in Him. I can laugh and sing, in my heart, when I speak of these things to you or elsewhere. And though some may think it is a hard thing to raise money without Parliamentary authority upon this nation; yet I have another argument to the good people of this nation, if they would be safe, and yet have no better principle: Whether they prefer the having of their will though it be their destruction, rather than comply with things of necessity? That will excuse me. But I should wrong my native country to suppose this.

For I look at the people of these nations as the blessing of the Lord: and they are a people blessed by God. They have been so; and they will be so, by reason of that immortal seed which hath been, and is, among them: those regenerated ones in the land, of several judgments; who are all the flock of Christ, and lambs of Christ.

We know the Lord hath poured this nation from vessel to vessel till He poured it into your lap, when you came first together. I am confident that it came so into your hands; and was not judged by you to be from counterfeited or feigned necessity, but by Divine providence and dispensation. And this I speak with more earnestness, because I speak for God and not for men. I would have any man to come and tell of the transactions that have been, and of those periods of time wherein God hath made these revolutions; and find where he can fix a feigned necessity! I could recite particulars, if either my strength would serve me to speak, or yours to hear. If you would consider the great hand of God in His great dispensations, you would find that there is scarce a man who fell off, at any period of time when God had any work to do, who can give God or His work at this day a good word.

"It was," say some, "the cunning of the Lord Protector"—I take it to myself—"it was the craft of such a man, and his plot, that hath brought it about!" And, as they say in other countries, "There are five or six cunning men in England that have skill; they do all these things. Oh, what blasphemy is this! Because men that are without God in the world, and walk not with Him, know not what it is to pray or believe, and to receive returns from God, and to be spoken unto by the Spirit of God—who speaks without a Written Word sometimes, yet according to it! God hath spoken heretofore in divers manners. Let Him speak as He pleaseth. Hath He not given us liberty, nay, is it not our duty to go to the law and the testimony? And there we shall find that there have been impressions, in extraordinary cases, as well without the Written Word as with it. And therefore there is no difference in the thing thus asserted from truths generally received—except we will exclude the Spirit; without whose concurrence all other teachings are ineffectual. He doth speak to the hearts and consciences of men; and leadeth them to His law and testimony.

There is another necessity, which you have put upon us, and we have not sought. I appeal to God, angels and men—if I shall "now" raise money according to the article in the government, whether I am not compelled to do it! Which "government" had power to call you hither; and did;—and instead of seasonably providing for the army, you have labored to overthrow the government, and the army is now upon, free quarter! And you would never so much as let me hear a title from you concerning it. Where is the fault? Has it not been as if you had a purpose to put this extremity upon us and the nation? I hope this was not in your minds. I am not willing to judge so:—but such is the state into which we are reduced. By the designs of some in the army who are now in custody it was designed to get as many of them as possible—through discontent for want of money, the army being in a barren country, near thirty weeks behind in pay, and upon other specious pretences—to march for England out of Scotland; and, in discontent, to seize their General there [General Monk], a faithful and honest man, that so another [Colonel Overton] might head the army. And all this opportunity taken from your delays. Whether will this be a thing of feigned necessity? What could it signify, but "The army are in discontent already; and we will make them live upon stones; we will make them cast off their governors and discipline?" What can be said to this? I list not to unsaddle myself, and put the fault upon your backs. Whether it hath been for the good of England, whilst men have been talking of this thing or the other, and pretending liberty and many good words—whether it has been as it should have been? I am confident you cannot think it has. The nation will not think so. And if the worst should be made of things, I know not what the Cornish men nor the Lincolnshire men may think, or other counties; but I believe they will all think they are not safe. A temporary suspension of "caring for the greatest liberties and privileges" (if it were so, which is denied) would not have been of such damage as the not providing against free-quarter hath run the nation upon. And if it be my "liberty" to walk abroad in the fields, or to take a journey, yet it is not my wisdom to do so when my house is on fire!

I have troubled you with a long speech; and I believe it may not have the same resentment with all that it hath with some. But because that is unknown to me, I shall leave it to God;—and conclude with this: That I think myself bound, as in my duty to God, and to the people of these nations for their safety and good in every respect—I think it my duty to tell you that it is not for the profit of these nations, nor for common and public good, for you to continue here any longer. And therefore I do declare unto you, that I do dissolve this Parliament.

DIEGO RODRIGUEZ DE SILVA Y VELÁSQUEZ (1599–1660)

LAS MENINAS

The Royal Family (1656)

No image is more hauntingly retrospective of the Renaissance than Diego Velásquez's painting of the Royal Family. Here the self-reflexiveness of this remarkable age reaches both its height and its completion. The painter is in the painting, painting himself. As you stand in the Prado in Madrid in front of this masterpiece of heightened realism, surprise at the autobiographical depiction slowly gives way to confusion, then to uneasiness, then to awe. The image draws us into itself, involves us, portrays us. Who is *infanta*, the daughter of Philip IV and Queen Mariana, staring at—who is the dwarf, and the painter himself, staring at? Whoever stands at the focus of their vision must be the "fictional" subject of the painting, standing "in front of the frame"—standing exactly where we are standing! Is the painter painting us? Then we notice that, in the background of the scene on the canvas, a mirror is reflecting the place where we are standing, reflecting the subject of the fictional painter's concentration: the king and queen. They are standing, in the time of the artist, where we stand today in the time of the audience. The painting reaches out from its sixteenth-century origins into the moment of our encounter with it, whenever that moment may occur. We are the subject, we are the royal family, we ourselves are standing in the space of the subject in this paradigm of magical realism that the artist has created. And the artist clearly sees the humor and power of his creation. For to the right of the mirror, a door is open—and a second Velásquez arrives to oversee the magic, and our enchantment! As Michel Foucault, in *The Order of Things,* comments: "the function of that reflection is to draw into the interior of the picture what is intimately foreign to it: the gaze which has organized it and the gaze for which it is displayed." Although he developed his naturalistic style through his apprenticeship to the Sevillan Francisco Pacheco, Velásquez's true masters were Titian and Rubens. He was appointed court painter in 1623. Through the ages *The Royal Family,* like the Renaissance it brings to a close, reaches out to involve us in its mighty self-consciousness—which we recognize because we have inherited it.

The family of Philip IV. The Infanta Margarita, accompanied by two maids of honor, a duenna and two dwarfs, visits Velásquez in his studio (Diego Velásquez de Silva), in the Prado, Madrid

JOHN MILTON (1608–74)

Paradise Lost (1667)

If Dante Alighieri's *Commedia* was the harbinger of the Renaissance with its reliance on the potency of the author's private vision, *Paradise Lost*, like a bookend, reasserts humanity's subjectivity to the divine. Where Dante's purpose was to lead human beings from a state of misery to a state of felicity, John Milton's purpose was to "justify the ways of God to man." Vigorously pursuing this purpose his powerful heroic blank verse and sharp characterizations (especially of Adam and Satan) sweep the reader forward through the first half of the epic. By the second half, Milton's doubts about the efficacy of human action, perhaps affected by his own blindness—and his inability to reconcile the paradox of free will versus divine providence, of humanity's culpability and God's harsh justice—have turned splendor into gloom, its closing lines ultimately justifying the poem's title as a reflection of a faded era:

> They, looking back, all th' eastern side beheld
> Of Paradise, so late their happy seat,
> Waved over by that flaming brand; the gate
> With dreadful faces thronged and fiery arms.
> Some natural tears they dropped, but wiped them soon,
> The world was all before them, where to choose
> Their place of rest, and Providence their guide,
> They, hand in hand, with wandering steps and slow,
> Through Eden took their solitary way.

BOOK I THE ARGUMENT

This First Book proposes, first in brief, the whole subject—Man's disobedience, and the loss thereupon of Paradise, wherein he was placed: then touches the prime cause of his fall—the Serpent, or rather Satan in the Serpent; who, revolting from God, and drawing to his side many legions of Angels, was, by the command of God, driven out of Heaven, with all his crew, into the great Deep. Which action passed over, the Poem hastes into the midst of things; presenting Satan, with his Angels, now fallen into Hell—described here not in the centre (for heaven and earth may be supposed as yet not made, certainly not yet accursed), but in a place of utter darkness, fitliest called Chaos. Here Satan, with his Angels lying on the burning lake, thunderstruck and astonished, after a certain space recovers, as from confusion; calls up him who, next in order and dignity, lay by him: they confer of their miserable fall. Satan awakens all his legions, who lay till then in the same manner confounded. They rise: their numbers; array

Resurrection (Piero della Francesca), in the Pinacoteca Communale, Sansepolcro

of battle; their chief leaders named, according to the idols known afterwards in Canaan and the countries adjoining. To these Satan directs his speech; comforts them with hope yet of regaining Heaven; but tells them, lastly, of a new world and new kind of creature to be created, according to an ancient prophecy, or report, in Heaven—for that Angels were long before this visible creation was the opinion of many ancient Fathers. To find out the truth of this prophecy, and what to determine thereon, he refers to a full council. What his associates thence attempt. Pandemonium, the palace of Satan, rises, suddenly built out of the Deep: the infernal Peers there sit in council.

Of Man's first disobedience, and the fruit
Of that forbidden tree whose mortal taste
Brought death into the World, and all our woe,
With loss of Eden, till one greater Man
Restore us, and regain the blissful seat,
Sing, Heavenly Muse, that, on the secret top
Of Oreb, or of Sinai, didst inspire
That shepherd who first taught the chosen seed
In the beginning how the heavens and earth
Rose out of Chaos: or, if Sion hill
Delight thee more, and Siloa's brook that
　　flowed
Fast by the oracle of God, I thence
Invoke thy aid to my adventurous song,
That with no middle flight intends to soar
Above th' Aonian mount, while it pursues
Things unattempted yet in prose or rhyme.
And chiefly thou, O Spirit, that dost prefer
Before all temples th' upright heart and pure,
Instruct me, for thou know'st; thou from the
　　first
Wast present, and, with mighty wings out-
　　spread,
Dove-like sat'st brooding on the vast Abyss,
And mad'st it pregnant: what in me is dark
Illumine, what is low raise and support;
That, to the height of this great argument,
I may assert Eternal Providence,
And justify the ways of God to men.
　　Say first—for Heaven hides nothing from thy
　　　　view,
Nor the deep tract of Hell—say first what cause
Moved our grand parents, in that happy state,
Favoured of Heaven so highly, to fall off
From their Creator, and transgress his will
For one restraint, lords of the World besides.
Who first seduced them to that foul revolt?
　　Th' infernal Serpent; he it was whose guile,
Stirred up with envy and revenge, deceived
The mother of mankind, what time his pride
Had cast him out from Heaven, with all his host
Of rebel Angels, by whose aid, aspiring
To set himself in glory above his peers,
He trusted to have equalled the Most High,
If he opposed, and with ambitious aim
Against the throne and monarchy of God,
Raised impious war in Heaven and battle
　　proud,

With vain attempt. Him the Almighty Power
Hurled headlong flaming from th' ethereal sky,

With hideous ruin and combustion, down
To bottomless perdition, there to dwell
In adamantine chains and penal fire,
Who durst defy th' Omnipotent to arms.
   Nine times the space that measures day and
     night
To mortal men, he, with his horrid crew,
Lay vanquished, rolling in the fiery gulf,
Confounded, though immortal. But his doom
Reserved him to more wrath; for now the
     thought
Both of lost happiness and lasting pain
Torments him: round he throws his baleful
     eyes,
That witnessed huge affliction and dismay,
Mixed with obdurate pride and steadfast hate.
At once, as far as Angels ken, he views
The dismal situation waste and wild.
A dungeon horrible, on all sides round,
As one great furnace flamed; yet from those
     flames
No light; but rather darkness visible
Served only to discover sights of woe,
Regions of sorrow, doleful shades, where peace
And rest can never dwell, hope never comes
That comes to all, but torture without end
Still urges, and a fiery deluge, fed
With ever-burning sulphur unconsumed.
Such place Eternal Justice had prepared
For those rebellious; here their prison ordained
In utter darkness, and their portion set,
As far removed from God and light of Heaven
As from the centre thrice to th' utmost pole.
Oh how unlike the place from whence they
     fell!
There the companions of his fall, o'erwhelmed
With floods and whirlwinds of tempestuous
     fire,
He soon discerns; and, weltering by his side,
One next himself in power, and next in crime,
Long after known in Palestine, and named
Beëlzebub. To whom th' Arch-Enemy,
And thence in Heaven called Satan, with bold
     words
Breaking the horrid silence, thus began:—
   "If thou beest he—but O how fallen! how
     changed

From him who, in the happy realms of light
Clothed with transcendent brightness, didst
     outshine
Myriads, though bright!—if he whom mutual
     league,
United thoughts and counsels, equal hope
And hazard in the glorious enterprise,
Joined with me once, now misery hath joined
In equal ruin; into what pit thou seest
From what height fallen: so much the stronger
     proved
He with his thunder: and till then who knew
The force of those dire arms? Yet not for those,
Nor what the potent Victor in his rage
Can else inflict, do I repent, or change,
Though changed in outward lustre, that fixed
     mind,
And high disdain from sense of injured merit,
That with the Mightiest raised me to contend,
And to the fierce contentions brought along
Innumerable force of Spirits armed,
That durst dislike his reign, and, me preferring,
His utmost power with adverse power opposed
In dubious battle on the plains of Heaven,
And shook his throne. What though the field be
     lost?
All is not lost—the unconquerable will,
And study of revenge, immortal hate,
And courage never to submit or yield:
And what is else not to be overcome?
That glory never shall his wrath or might
Extort from me. To bow and sue for grace
With suppliant knee, and deify his power
Who, from the terror of this arm, so late
Doubted his empire—that were low indeed;
That were an ignominy and shame beneath
This downfall; since, by fate, the strength of
     Gods,
And this empyreal substance, cannot fail;

Since, through experience of this great event,
In arms not worse, in foresight much advanced,
We may with more successful hope resolve
To wage by force or guile eternal war,
Irreconcilable to our grand Foe,
Who now triúmphs, and in th' excess of joy
Sole reigning holds the tyranny of Heaven."

So spake th' apostate Angel, though in pain,
Vaunting aloud, but racked with deep despair;
And him thus answered soon his bold com-
     peer:—
     "O Prince, O Chief of many thronèd Powers
That led th' embattled Seraphim to war
Under thy conduct, and, in dreadful deeds
Fearless, endangered Heaven's perpetual King,
And put to proof his high supremacy,
Whether upheld by strength, or chance, or fate,
Too well I see and rue the dire event
That, with sad overthrow and foul defeat,
Hath lost us Heaven, and all this mighty host
In horrible destruction laid thus low,
As far as Gods and heavenly Essences
Can perish: for the mind and spirit remains
Invincible, and vigour soon returns,
Though all our glory extinct, and happy state
Here swallowed up in endless misery.
But what if he our Conqueror (whom I now
Of force believe almighty, since no less
Than such could have o'erpowered such force
     as ours)
Have left us this our spirit and strength entire,
Strongly to suffer and support our pains,
That we may so suffice his vengeful ire,
Or do him mightier service as his thralls
By right of war, whate'er his business be,
Here in the heart of Hell to work in fire,
Or do his errands in the gloomy Deep?
What can it then avail though yet we feel
Strength undiminished, or eternal being
To undergo eternal punishment?"
     Whereto with speedy words th' Arch-Fiend
          replied:—
"Fallen Cherub, to be weak is miserable,
Doing or suffering: but of this be sure—
To do aught good never will be our task,
But ever to do ill our sole delight,
As being the contrary to his high will
Whom we resist. If then his providence
Out of our evil seek to bring forth good,
Our labour must be to pervert that end,
And out of good still to find means of evil;
Which ofttimes may succeed so as perhaps
Shall grieve him, if I fail not, and disturb
His inmost counsels from their destined aim.

But see! the angry Victor hath recalled
His ministers of vengeance and pursuit
Back to the gates of Heaven: the sulphurous
     hail,
Shot after us in storm, o'erblown hath laid
The fiery surge that from the precipice
Of Heaven received us falling; and the thunder,
Winged with red lightning and impetuous rage,
Perhaps hath spent his shafts, and ceases now
To bellow through the vast and boundless
     Deep.
Let us not slip th' occasion, whether scorn
Or satiate fury yield it from our Foe.
Seest thou yon dreary plain, forlorn and wild,
The seat of desolation, void of light,
Save what the glimmering of these livid flames
Casts pale and dreadful? Thither let us tend
From off the tossing of these fiery waves;
There rest, if any rest can harbour there;
And, re-assembling our afflicted powers,
Consult how we may henceforth most offend
Our enemy, our own loss how repair,
How overcome this dire calamity,
What reinforcement we may gain from hope,
If not, what resolution from despair."

     Thus Satan, talking to his nearest mate,
With head uplift above the wave, and eyes
That sparkling blazed; his other parts besides
Prone on the flood, extended long and large,
Lay floating many a rood, in bulk as huge
As whom the fables name of monstrous size,
Titanian or Earth-born, that warred on Jove,
Briareos or Typhon, whom the den
By ancient Tarsus held, or that sea-beast
Leviathan, which God of all his works
Created hugest that swim th' ocean-stream.
Him, haply slumbering on the Norway foam,
The pilot of some small night-foundered skiff,
Deeming some island, oft, as seamen tell,
With fixed anchor in his scaly rind,
Moors by his side under the lee, while night
Invests the sea, and wishèd morn delays.
So stretched out huge in length the Arch-fiend
     lay,
Chained on the burning lake; nor ever thence
Had risen, or heaved his head, but that the will

And high permission of all-ruling Heaven
Left him at large to his own dark designs,
That with reiterated crimes he might
Heap on himself damnation, while he sought
Evil to others, and enraged might see
How all his malice served but to bring forth
Infinite goodness, grace, and mercy, shewn
On Man by him seduced, but on himself
Treble confusion, wrath, and vengeance poured.
   Forthwith upright he rears from off the
      pool
His mighty stature; on each hand the flames
Driven backward slope their pointing spires,
    and, rolled
In billows, leave i' th' midst a horrid vale.
Then with expanded wings he steers his flight
Aloft, incumbent on the dusky air,
That felt unusual weight; till on dry land
He lights—if it were land that ever burned

With solid, as the lake with liquid fire,
And such appeared in hue as when the force
Of subterranean wind transports a hill
Torn from Pelorus, or the shattered side
Of thundering Etna, whose combustible
And fuelled entrails, thence conceiving fire,
Sublimed with mineral fury, aid the winds,
And leave a singèd bottom all involved
With stench and smoke. Such resting found the
    sole
Of unblest feet. Him followed his next mate;
Both glorying to have scaped the Stygian flood
As gods, and by their own recovered strength,

Not by the sufferance of supernal Power.
  "Is this the region, this the soil, the clime,"
Said then the lost Archangel, "this the seat
That we must change for Heaven?—this mourn-
    ful gloom
For that celestial light? Be it so, since he
Who now is sovereign can dispose and bid
What shall be right: farthest from him is best,
Whom reason hath equalled, force hath made
    supreme
Above his equals. Farewell, happy fields,
Where joy for ever dwells! Hail, horrors! hail,
Infernal world! and thou, profoundest Hell,
Receive thy new possessor—one who brings
A mind not to be changed by place or time.
The mind is its own place, and in itself
Can make a Heaven of Hell, a Hell of Heaven.
What matter where, if I be still the same,
And what I should be, all but less than he
Whom thunder hath made greater? Here at least
We shall be free; th' Almighty hath not built
Here for his envy, will not drive us hence:
Here we may reign secure; and, in my choice,
To reign is worth ambition, though in Hell:
Better to reign in Hell than serve in Heaven.
But wherefore let we then our faithful friends,
Th' associates and co-partners of our loss,
Lie thus astonished on th' oblivious pool,
And call them not to share with us their part
In this unhappy mansion, or once more
With rallied arms to try what may be yet
Regained in Heaven, or what more lost in
    Hell?"...

GENERAL SOURCES AND RECOMMENDATIONS

Although sources used in preparing this anthology are too numerous to list here, the following provided invaluable ready reference and should form part of any basic library on the Renaissance:

The New Encyclopedia Britannica. 15th Edition.

Allen, D. C. *Doubt's Boundless Sea: Skepticisim and Faith in the Renaissance.* Baltimore, 1964.

Allen, J. W. *A History of Political Thought in the Sixteenth Century.* London, 1957.

Atchity, Kenneth J., and Giose Rimanelli. *Italian Literature: Roots & Branches.* New Haven, 1976.

Atkins, J. W. N. *English Literary Criticism: The Renascence.* London, 1947.

Bainton, R. H. *The Reformation of the Sixteenth Century.* Boston, 1962.

Baron, H. *The Crisis of the Early Italian Renaissance.* 2 vols. Princeton, 1955.

Black, J. R. *The Reign of Elizabeth, 1558-1603.* Oxford, 1936.

Burckhardt, Jacob. *The Civilization of the Renaissance in Italy.* Trans. S. G. C. Middlemore. New York, 1958.

Bush, D. *The Renaissance and English Humanism.* Toronto, 1939.

Buxton, J. *Elizabethan Taste.* London, 1963.

Cassirer, Ernst. *The Individual and the Cosmos in Renaissance Philosophy.* [Oxford, 1963.] New York, 1963.

Cassirer, Ernst, Paul Oskar Kristeller, and John Herman Randall, Jr. (eds.). *The Renaissance Philosophy of Man.* Chicago, 1948.

Chartier, Roger (ed.). *A History of Private Life: Passions of the Renaissance.* Cambridge, Mass., 1987-1991.

Clark, D. L. *Rhetoric and Poetry in the Renaissance.* New York, 1922.

Craig, H. *The Enchanted Glass.* New York, 1950.

Ferguson, Wallace K., Robert S. Lopez, George Sarton, Roland H. Bainton, Leicester Bradner, and Erwin Panofsky. *The Renaissance.* New York, 1940.

Ferguson, Wallace K., and Garrett Mattingly, E. Harris Harbison, Myron P. Gilmore, and Paul Oskar Kristeller. *Facets of the Renaissance (essays).* New York, 1963.

Giamatti, A. Bartlett. *The Earthly Paradise and the Renaissance Garden.* Princeton, 1966.

Gilmore, M. *The World of Humanism (1453-1517).* New York, 1952.

Greene, Thomas. *The Descent from Heaven: A Study in Epic Continuity.* New Haven, 1963.

——. "The Flexibility of the Self in Renaissance Literature." Peter Demetz, Thomas Greene, and Lowry Nelson, Jr., *The Disciplines of Criticism.* New Haven and London, 1968.

Grimm, H. J. *The Reformation Era: 1500-1600.* New York, 1952.

Hartt, Frederick. *The Renaissance in Italy and Spain.* New York, 1969.

Hall, A. R. *The Scientific Revolution, 1500-1800.* London, New York, Toronto, 1954.

Hay, Denys. *The Italian Renaissance.* London, 1961.

Haydn, H. C. *The Counter Renaissance.* New York, 1950.

Hebel, J William, Hoyt H. Hudson, et al. *Tudor Poetry and Prose.* New York, 1953.

Hollander, J. *The Untuning of the Sky.* Princeton, 1961.

Jacob, E. F. (ed). *Italian Renaissance Studies.* London, 1960.

Johnson, A. H. *Europe in the Sixteenth Century, 1494-1598.* London, 1964.

Kaiser, Walter. *Praisers of Folly.* London, 1963.

King, Margaret L., and Albert Rabil, Jr. *Her Immaculate Hand: Selected Works By and About The Women Humanists of Quattrocento Italy.* Binghamton, New York, 1983.

Kristeller, Paul O. *Studies in Renaissance Thought and Letters.* Rome, 1956.

——. *Renaissance Thought.* New York, 1961.

Legouis, Émile, and Louis Cazamian. *A History of English Literature.* London, 1924.

Levey, Michael. *High Renaissance.* Baltimore, 1975.

Lewis, C. S. *The Allegory of Love.* New York, 1958.

Lovejoy, Arthur O. *The Great Chain of Being.* [Cambridge, Mass., 1936]. New York, 1933.

Magnus, Laurie. *A Dictionary of European Literature.* London, New York, 1927.

Mattingly, G. *Renaissance Diplomacy.* Boston, 1955.

McLuhan, H. M. *The Gutenberg Galaxy.* Toronto, 1962.

Nelson, J. C. *The Renaissance Theory of Love.* New York, 1958.

O'Faolain, Julia, and Lauro Martines (eds.). *Not in God's Image: Women in History from the Greeks to the Victorians.* New York, 1973.

Panofsky, Eric. *Meaning and Form in the Visual Arts.* Garden City, New York, 1957.

——. *Renaissance and Renascences in Western Art.* Stockholm, 1960.

——. *Studies in Iconology.* New York, 1962.

Plumb, J. H. *The Horizon Book of The Renaissance.* New York, 1961.

Reese, C. *Music in the Renaissance.* New York, 1954.

Rice, E. P., Jr. *The Renaissance Idea of Wisdom.* Cambridge, Mass., 1958.

Ross, James Bruce, and Mary Martin McLaughlin (eds.). *The Portable Renaissance Reader.* New York, 1966.

Scaglioni, Aldo. *Nature and Love in the Late Middle Ages.* Berkeley, 1963.

Schevill, Ferdinand. *The Medici.* New York, 1949.

Schweitzer, Frederick M., and Harry E. Wedeck (eds.). *Dictionary of the Renaissance.* New York, 1967.

Seznec, Jean. *The Survival of the Pagan Gods.* New York, 1953.

Symonds, J. A. *The Renaissance in Italy.* 2 vols. New York, 1935.

Thorlby, Anthony. *The Penguin Companion to European Literature.* New York, 1971.

Tillyard, E. M. H. *The Elizabethan World Picture.* London, 1960.

Wightman, W. P. D. *Science and the Renaissance.* 2 vols. Aberdeen, 1962.

Wilkins, Ernest Hatch. *The History of Italian Literature.* Revised by Thomas G. Bergin. Cambridge, Mass., 1988.

Wilson, Katharina M. *Women Writers of the Renaissance and Reformation.* Athens, Ga. and London, 1987

AUTHOR INDEX

COPYRIGHT ACKNOWLEDGMENTS

Grateful acknowledgment is made for permission to reprint:

From Dante Alighieri's *The Divine Comedy*, translated by Louis Biancolli. Reprinted by permission of Pocket Books, a division of Simon & Schuster, Inc. 1966 Louis Biancolli.

From Morris Bishop's translation of *Letters from Petrarch*. 1966 by Indiana University Press. By permission of Indiana University Press.

From Giovanni Boccaccio's *The Decameron*, translated by Frances Winwar. New York, The Modern Library. 1930, The Limited Editions Club. 1955, by Random House, Inc. By courtesy of Random House, Inc.

From Giovanni Boccaccio's *Concerning Famous Women*, translated by Guido A. Guarino. 1963 by Rutgers, the State University. By permission of Rutgers University Press and Guido A. Guarino.

From *The Book of the City of Ladies* by Christine de Pizan, translated by Earl Jeffrey Richards. 1982 by Persea Books, Inc. Reprinted by permission of Persea Books, Inc.

From *The Humanism of Leonardo Bruni*, translation and introduction by Gordon Griffiths, James Hankins, and David Thompson. Medieval & Renaissance Texts & Studies, vol. 46. Binghamton, New York. 1987 Center for Medieval and Early Renaissance Studies, SUNY Binghamton. By permission of Medieval & Renaissance Texts & Studies.

From Leon Battista Alberti's *The Family in Renaissance Florence*, translation and introduction by Renee N. Watkins. University of South Carolina Press. 1969. As reprinted in Julia O'Faolain and Lauro Martines, *Not in God's Image*. New York: Harper & Row, Publishers. 1973. By permission of Renee N. Watkins.

From *Lives of the Early Medici as Told in Their Correspondence,* translated and edited by Janet Ross. Boston. The Gorham Press, 1911.

From *The Treatise of Lorenzo Valla*, translated by Christopher B. Coleman. 1922 Yale University Press. By permission of Yale University Press.

From Aeneas Silvius' *Selected Letters of Aeneas Silvius Piccolomini,* translated by Albert R. Baca. Published by San Fernando Valley State College. 1969 by Albert R. Baca, and by permission of Albert R. Baca.

From Isotta Nogarola, translated by Margaret L. King and Albert Rabil, Jr., in *Her Immaculate Hand: Selected Works by and about the Women Humanists of Quattrocento Italy*, edited by Margaret L. King and Albert Rabil, Jr. Medieval & Renaissance Texts & Studies, vol 20. Binghamton, NY. 1982 Center for Medieval and Early Renaissance Studies, SUNY Binghamton. By permission of Center for Medieval and Early Renaissance Studies, SUNY Binghamton.

From Bianca Sforza, translated by Margaret L. King and Albert Rabil, Jr., in *Her Immaculate Hand: Selected Works by and about the Women Humanists of Quattrocento Italy,* ed. Margaret L. King and Albert Rabil, Jr. Medieval & Renaissance Texts & Studies, vol 20. Binghamton, NY. 1982. Center for Medieval and Early Renaissance Studies, SUNY Binghamton. By permission of Center for Medieval and Early Renaissance Studies, SUNY Binghamton.

From *The Poems of François Villon*, "Ballade," translated by Galway Kinnell. Copyright 1965, 1977 by Galway Kinnell. Reprinted by permission of Houghton Mifflin Co. All rights reserved.

From *Sir Thomas Malory's Le Morte Darthur*, edited by R.M. Lumiansky. 1982 R. M. Lumiansky. Reprinted by permission of Scribner's, an imprint of Simon & Schuster.

From *Three Books on Life by Marsilio Ficino*, edited by Carol V. Kaske and John R. Clark. Medieval &

Renaissance Texts & Studies, vol. 57: pp. 371, 373, 375, 377. 1989 Center for Medieval and Early Renaissance Studies, SUNY Binghamton. By permission of Center for Medieval and Early Renaissance Studies.

From *The Diario of Christopher Columbus' First Voyage to America, 1492–1493,* translated by Oliver Dunn and James E. Kelley, Jr. 1989 by Oliver Dunn and James E. Kelley, Jr. Reprinted by permission of the University of Oklahoma Press.

From Girolamo Savonarola's "Advent Sermon," translated by Linda Villari, in P. Villari's *Life and Times of Girolamo Savonarola.* London: T. Fisher Unwin, 1896. A&C Publishers, Ltd. By permission of A&C Black (Publishers) Limited.

From Frater Lucas Pacioli's *Treatise on Double-Entry Book-keeping,* translated by Pietro Crivelli, F.C.R.A. London. Published 1924, by the Institute of Book-keepers, Ltd. By permission of Pietro Crivelli, and by courtesy of the Institute of Book-keepers, Ltd.

From Pietro Perugino's "Contract for the Altarpiece of St. Peter's, Perugia," in Elizabeth G. Holt (ed)., *A Documentary History of Art, Vol I.* Doubleday Anchor Books. 1947, 1957, Princeton University Press. By permission of Princeton University Press.

From Giovanni Pico della Mirandola's "On the Dignity of Man," translated by Nancy Lenkeith, from Ernst Cassirer, editor, *The Renaissance Philosophy of Man.* Chicago: University of Chicago Press. 1948 and by permission of the University of Chicago Press.

From *The Letters of Amerigo Vespucci,* translated and edited by Clements Markham. Burt Franklin, Publisher, 1894. Reprinted by, and with kind permission of, the Hakluyt Society, London.

From Hopewell Hudson's translation of Desiderius Erasmus' *The Praise of Folly.* 1941 (renewed 1969) by Princeton University Press. Reprinted by permission of Princeton University Press. Quotation from Erasmus regarding Sir Thomas More from *Johan Huizinga, Erasmus and the Age of Reformation,* New York, Harper, 1957, p.234. By permission of HarperCollins Publishers.

From *The Writings of Albrecht Dürer,* translated by William Martin Conway. 1958. By permission of The Philosophical Library, New York.

From Niccolò Machiavelli's *The Prince and the Discourses,* translated by Luigi Ricci, revised by E. R. P. Vincent, introduction by Max Lerner. New York, Modern Library. 1950. Random House, Inc. By courtesy of Random House, Inc.

From Ludovico Ariosto's *Orlando Furioso,* translated by Sir John Harrington (1591) and edited by Robert McNulty. Oxford University Press 1972. By permission of Oxford University Press.

From *Sir Thomas More, Utopia,* edited by Edward Surtz, S. J. 1964 Yale University Press. By permission of Yale University Press.

From Pietro Aretino's *The Art of the Courtesan*, translated by Samuel Putnam. Published by Pascal Covici, Publisher. 1926.

Selected excerpts from *The Bed and the Throne: The Life of Isabella d'Este* by George R. Marek. Copyright 1976 by George R. Marek. Reprinted by permission of HarperCollins Publishers, Inc.

From *Michelangelo: A Self-Portrait*, translated and edited by Dr. Robert J. Clements. 1963. Englewood Cliffs, New Jersey. Prentice-Hall, Inc.

From Vittoria Colonna's poems, translated by Joseph Gibaldi, as published in *Women Writers of the Renaissance and Reformation,* edited by Katharina M. Wilson. 1987. Athens and London: University of Georgia Press. By permission of University of Georgia Press.

From Philipp Melanchthon's *On Christian Doctrine*, translated by Clyde L. Manschreck. 1965. Oxford University Press. By permission of Oxford University Press.

From Leonardo da Vinci's *Notebooks,* vol. 1, translated by Edward MacCurdy. New York, George Braziller. First published 1939, by Reynald & Hitchcock, Inc.

From Juan Luis Vives' "A Fable About Man," translated by Elizabeth L. Forbes from Ernst Cassirer, editor, *The Renaissance Philosophy of Man.* Chicago: University of Chicago Press. 1948. By permission of the University of Chicago Press.

From *Reformation Writings of Martin Luther*, translation from the Definitive Weimar Edition by Bertram Lee Woolf. 1953. The Philosophical Library. By permission of The Philosophical Library.

From Anna Bijns' "Poems," translated by Kristiaan P. G. Aercke, as published in *Women Writers of the Renaissance and Reformation,* edited by Katharina M. Wilson. 1987. Athens and London: University of Georgia Press. By permission of University of Georgia Press.

From François Rabelais' *Gargantua and Pantagruel,* translated by Jacques Le Clerq. New York, The Modern Library, Random House, Inc. 1936 by The Limited Editions Club. Reprinted by permission of The Limited Editions Club.

⚜ ILLUSTRATION CREDITS